FOOD & WINE

MAGAZINE'S 2001 COOKBOOK

an entire year's recipes

FOOD & WINE

MAGAZINE'S 2001 COOKBOOK

an entire year's recipes

American Express Publishing Corporation
New York · FOOD & WINE BOOKS

FOOD & WINE MAGAZINE
EDITOR IN CHIEF Dana Cowin
CREATIVE DIRECTOR Stephen Scoble
EXECUTIVE FOOD EDITOR Tina Ujlaki

FOOD & WINE BOOKS
EDITOR IN CHIEF Judith Hill
ART DIRECTOR Perri DeFino
MANAGING EDITOR Miriam Harris
ASSOCIATE EDITOR Dana Speers
EDITORIAL ASSOCIATE Colleen McKinney
PRODUCTION MANAGER Stuart Handelman

SENIOR VICE PRESIDENT, CHIEF MARKETING OFFICER Mark V. Stanich
VICE PRESIDENT, BRANDED PRODUCTS Bruce Rosner
OPERATIONS MANAGER Catherine Bussey
BUSINESS MANAGER Doreen Camardi

COVER AND BACK PHOTOS Quentin Bacon (Shrimp with Citrus Mojo, p. 146)

AMERICAN EXPRESS PUBLISHING CORPORATION
©2001 American Express Publishing Corporation

ISBN 0-916103-65-X (hardcover)   ISSN 1097-1564

Published by American Express Publishing Corporation
1120 Avenue of the Americas, New York, New York 10036

Manufactured in the United States of America

contents

371

210

93

foreword

As the editors of FOOD & WINE Magazine and FOOD & WINE Books, we spend a lot of time behind our desks. But in the magazine this year, we've ventured far and wide: Besides journeying to Italy in the October wine issue, we've gone from Madagascar to the Caribbean, from France and Spain to India and Morocco. We've experienced the pleasures of Korean Bibimbop (page 306), Sardinian Seafood Stew (page 152) and Hungarian Palascinta (page 376), without ever traveling farther than down the hall to the test kitchen.

We've balanced such sensual exoticism with some downright delicious traditional American food. In addition, as the magazine does every year, we've searched to find the most promising young chefs in America—the ones who continually push the boundaries of our nation's cuisine. They have rewarded us with dishes such as Cauliflower Vichyssoise (page 82) and Black Sea Bass with Somen Noodles (page 131). And while our commitment to discovering new talent is unwavering, we have an ever greater appreciation of the recipes that come out of our own kitchen. Test Kitchen Supervisor Marcia Kiesel and Test Kitchen Associate Grace Parisi are two of the best cooks in the business. If you see either of their names at the end of a recipe, we urge you to try it. You won't be disappointed.

Dana Cowin

EDITOR IN CHIEF
FOOD & WINE MAGAZINE

Judith Hill

EDITOR IN CHIEF
FOOD & WINE BOOKS

KEY TO SYMBOLS

Some special recipes have been marked with colorful symbols so that you can easily find the dishes that fall in the categories below. Complete lists of these recipes begin on page 394.

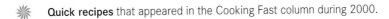 **Quick recipes** that appeared in the Cooking Fast column during 2000.

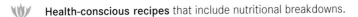 **Health-conscious recipes** that include nutritional breakdowns.

♛ **Recipes from this year's winners** of the FOOD & WINE America's Best New Chefs awards.

AND PLEASE NOTE

Our annual FOOD & WINE collections are identified by the year in which each is released, rather than by the year in which the magazine issues were published. Hence this year's book, published in January of 2001, is titled *FOOD & WINE Magazine's 2001 Cookbook* and is a compilation of the recipes from the 2000 magazines.

hors d'oeuvres

chapter 1

Tapas Bar Roasted Almonds

Smoked Olives

MAKES 1 ½ PINTS

- 1 pound mixed briny green olives, such as Picholine, Barese or Sicilian
- 1 cup extra-virgin olive oil
- 4 strips of lemon zest
- 1 bay leaf
- ½ teaspoon fennel seeds
- 2 thick 3-inch pieces of dried grapevine

1. In an 8- or 9-inch metal cake pan, combine the olives with the olive oil, lemon zest, bay leaf and fennel seeds. Set a round wire cake rack in a large cast-iron skillet. Warm the skillet over moderate heat until it is too hot to touch; add the grapevine cuttings. When they begin to smoke, set the cake pan on the rack. Cover the skillet with foil and a tight-fitting lid. Reduce the heat to low. If the smoke smells quite strong or a lot of it is coming from the side of the skillet, reduce the heat. Smoke the olives for 20 minutes, or until the oil has a nice smoky flavor.

2. Turn off the heat and allow the olives to cool gradually, with the lid on. Serve warm or at room temperature. —*Sally Schneider*

MAKE AHEAD Store the olives in their oil in a glass jar for up to 6 months.

ONE SERVING Calories 66 kcal, Total Fat 7.5 gm, Saturated Fat .9 gm

Tapas Bar Roasted Almonds

MAKES 1 POUND

Buy the biggest, freshest almonds you can find to make these toasty snacks. This recipe can easily be multiplied; do be sure, however, to spread the almonds on the baking sheet in a single layer so that they brown nicely.

- 1 pound blanched whole almonds
- 1 teaspoon extra-virgin olive oil
- 1 tablespoon fine sea salt

1. Preheat the oven to 300°. Spread the almonds on a heavy rimmed baking sheet. Drizzle with the oil, sprinkle with the salt and toss well. Roast the almonds for about 40 minutes or until lightly browned; stir them 4 times as they roast to ensure even browning.

2. When the almonds are done, turn the oven off and open the door for 30 seconds; close the door and leave the almonds in the oven until completely cool. Pack the almonds in tins, jars or wooden boxes. —*Sally Schneider*

MAKE AHEAD The almonds can be stored in an airtight tin for 3 weeks.

ONE 1-OUNCE SERVING Calories 178 kcal, Total Fat 14.8 gm, Saturated Fat 1.3 gm, Protein 6.0 gm, Carbohydrates 5.2 gm

Smoked Olives

an olive buyer's guide

Life cycle of an olive All olives start out green. As they mature, their color changes to pinkish beige then to purplish brown, and their texture softens as the oil content increases. Olives are too bitter to eat until they're cured—with brine, salt or sometimes lye. It's the curing that makes the difference between a great olive and a merely mediocre one.

Pasteurization The best olives are unpasteurized; these have a more complex, resonant flavor and a firmer texture than pasteurized varieties. (Unpasteurized green olives are noticeably crisper; unpasteurized black olives are meatier.) When olives are pasteurized, as with bottled olives, the high-temperature processing virtually cooks them, often making them mushy and their flavors one-dimensional.

Freshness Exposure to air causes olives to deteriorate quickly. To be sure the olives you get are fresh, buy bulk olives that are immersed in brine (they can last indefinitely that way), or seek out a vendor with a rapid turnover who frequently replenishes his olive display.

The color-wrinkle-taste test Look for plump olives with few bruises or wrinkles (except for naturally wrinkled olives). Green olives should be bright; drabness indicates pasteurization. If possible, taste olives before buying them. Remember that inferior olives are often pitted or assertively flavored with hot pepper, herbs or spices, and given fancy names. And ask your purveyor. A reputable one will know where his olives come from and whether they've been pasteurized.

Quick Cucumber Pickles (Kachori)

6 SERVINGS

- 3 medium Kirby cucumbers, 1 peeled
- ½ teaspoon coarse salt
- 2 teaspoons Sesame Salt (p. 272)
- 2 scallion greens, cut into 2-inch matchsticks
- 1 teaspoon coarsely ground Korean red chile (gocho karu)
- 1 garlic clove, minced
- 1 teaspoon finely grated fresh ginger
- ½ teaspoon sugar
- 2 teaspoons Asian sesame oil

1. Slice all 3 cucumbers crosswise ¼ inch thick. In a bowl, toss the slices with the salt and let stand for 1 hour. Pat dry with paper towels.
2. Add the Sesame Salt, scallions, red chile, garlic, ginger and sugar, toss and let stand for 30 minutes. Toss with the sesame oil and serve.

—Anya von Bremzen

Crudités Platter

8 SERVINGS

Americans tend to think of crudités as raw vegetables served with a dip, but they can also be drizzled with vinaigrette, as they are here.

- ½ cup extra-virgin olive oil
- ¼ cup fresh lemon juice
- Kosher salt and freshly ground pepper
- ¼ pound thin green beans
- 2 small heads Boston or Bibb lettuce, leaves separated
- 1 large head radicchio, cut lengthwise into thick wedges
- 1 fennel bulb—halved, cored and thinly sliced crosswise
- 1 pint cherry tomatoes
- 2 yellow tomatoes, thinly sliced
- ½ cup loosely packed basil leaves
- ½ pound Parmesan cheese, cut into shavings

1. Whisk together the olive oil and lemon juice; season with salt and pepper.
2. Bring a medium saucepan of lightly salted water to a boil. Add the green beans and cook until crisp-tender, about 5 minutes. Drain the beans in a colander set in the sink and refresh them under cold water; pat dry.
3. Arrange the lettuce, radicchio, fennel, green beans, tomatoes, basil and

Roasted Red Pepper Dip

Parmesan on a platter and drizzle with some of the vinaigrette. Serve the crudités immediately and pass the remaining vinaigrette separately.

—Ina Garten, Barefoot Contessa

WINE The clean, bright flavors of the fresh vegetables and herbs here need a vibrant wine with good acidity and fruit, such as the 1999 Wölffer rosé.

Roasted Red Pepper Dip

MAKES ABOUT 1½ CUPS

You can make this creamy dip more quickly by substituting ⅔ cup of drained jarred roasted red peppers or smoky jarred roasted piquillo peppers.

- 2 medium red bell peppers
- 1 tablespoon minced garlic
- 1 teaspoon extra-virgin olive oil
- 1 tablespoon balsamic vinegar
- 1 cup sour cream
- 1 tablespoon finely chopped basil
- Salt and freshly ground pepper

1. Roast the peppers over a gas flame or under the broiler until charred all over. Transfer to a bowl, cover with plastic wrap and let steam for 20 minutes. Discard the skins, cores and seeds. Pat

CLOCKWISE FROM TOP: Zucchini Saltimbocca,
Crispy Frico with Ripe Pear (p. 22),
Wild Mushroom and Tomato Panzanella (p. 55),
Pickled Vegetable Antipasto (p. 34)
and Italian Tuna Mousse (p. 16).

the peppers dry and finely chop them. **2.** In a skillet, cook the garlic in the oil over moderate heat until fragrant, about 30 seconds. Add the peppers and vinegar and cook over moderately low heat, stirring, until dry, about 12 minutes. Transfer to a bowl to cool. Stir in the sour cream and basil and season with salt and pepper. Refrigerate until chilled.

—*Thomas Gay*

SERVE WITH Plain or black pepper breadsticks and thick-cut potato chips.

MAKE AHEAD The dip can be refrigerated for up to 2 days.

Zucchini Saltimbocca

MAKES ABOUT 28 SLICES

Saltimbocca (Italian for "jump in the mouth") is traditionally prepared with veal, sage and prosciutto. This version substitutes zucchini for the veal, and is equally delicious.

- 4 medium zucchini (about 2 pounds)

Salt and freshly ground pepper

- 4 ounces thinly sliced prosciutto
- 1 small bunch of sage
- ⅓ pound Fontina cheese, thinly sliced
- 2 large eggs
- 1 cup all-purpose flour

Pure olive oil, for frying

- 2 tablespoons freshly grated Parmigiano-Reggiano cheese
- 1 tablespoon finely chopped flat-leaf parsley
- 1 lemon, cut into wedges

1. Cut each zucchini lengthwise into ¼-inch-thick slices. You should have 28 slices. Season with salt and pepper. **2.** Lay the prosciutto over half the zucchini slices. Top with 2 small sage leaves and the Fontina. Cover with the remaining zucchini slices. Cover the zucchini with paper towels and press down to extract any excess moisture. **3.** Beat the eggs in a shallow bowl. In a plate, season the flour with salt and pepper. Dip the zucchini in the egg, then dredge in the flour. Transfer to a plate.

4. In a large skillet, heat 2 tablespoons of olive oil until shimmering. Add the stuffed zucchini without crowding the pan and cook over moderately high heat until golden brown, about 2 minutes per side. Transfer to a baking sheet and keep warm in a low oven. Repeat with the remaining zucchini, adding oil to the skillet as needed. 5. Add some sage leaves to the skillet and fry until crisp. Cut the zucchini into triangles and transfer to a platter. Top with the fried sage leaves. Sprinkle with Parmigiano-Reggiano and parsley and serve with the lemon wedges.

—*Michael Chiarello*

MAKE AHEAD The recipe can be prepared through Step 2 and refrigerated for up to 4 hours.

Artichokes with Anchoïade

12 SERVINGS

Anchoïade, the garlicky Provençal dip made with anchovies, green olives and extra-virgin olive oil, is usually served with a mixed platter of raw and cooked vegetables, including artichokes.

- 1 large lemon, halved, plus 2 tablespoons fresh lemon juice
- 6 large artichokes
- 6 cups water
- 4 thyme sprigs
- 7 garlic cloves—4 halved, 3 coarsely chopped
- ½ cup plus 2 tablespoons extra-virgin olive oil
- 1 teaspoon kosher salt

Two 3-ounce jars oil-packed anchovies, drained and chopped

- ⅔ cup green olives, such as Picholine, pitted and chopped
- 2 tablespoons sherry vinegar
- ¼ cup grapeseed oil
- ½ teaspoon finely grated lemon zest

Freshly ground pepper

1. Squeeze the lemon halves into a large bowl of water. Working with one artichoke at a time, snap off the outer leaves. Using a sharp knife, cut off the top third of the artichoke. Peel the

stem, leaving it long. Cut the artichoke in half lengthwise. Using a spoon, scrape out the furry choke. Cut each half lengthwise into thirds and add to the lemon water.

2. In a large saucepan, combine the 6 cups of water with the thyme, halved garlic, 2 tablespoons of the olive oil and the salt and bring to a boil. Add the artichokes, cover and simmer over low heat until tender, about 12 minutes. Drain and transfer to a large platter to cool.

3. In a blender, puree the chopped garlic with the anchovies, olives, vinegar and lemon juice. With the machine on, slowly pour in the remaining ½ cup olive oil and the grapeseed oil to make a smooth sauce. Scrape the dip into a bowl, stir in the lemon zest and season with pepper. Serve the artichokes with the *anchoïade* at room temperature. —*Jean-Louis Palladin*

MAKE AHEAD The prepared artichokes and the *anchoïade* can be refrigerated overnight.

WINE The pronounced acidity in a good Blanc de Blancs Champagne

Artichokes with Anchoïade

stands up nicely to the acidity in the artichokes, which makes most wines taste metallic and sweet. Look for an elegant Brut, such as the 1993 Billecart-Salmon or the 1993 Deutz.

Tuna Mousse

MAKES 1 CUP

Using imported canned tuna in olive oil and pureeing it with cream cheese in addition to the usual mayonnaise turns the mousse into a rich hors d'oeuvre. This recipe can easily be doubled.

One 6-ounce can tuna packed in olive oil, drained

¼ cup mayonnaise

2 tablespoons finely chopped onion

2 tablespoons cream cheese, softened

1½ teaspoons fresh lemon juice

1 tablespoon finely chopped parsley

Salt and freshly ground pepper

1 baguette, thinly sliced and toasted, for serving

1. In a food processor, combine the tuna with the mayonnaise, onion, cream cheese and lemon juice and pulse until smooth. Add the parsley and pulse just until combined.

2. Transfer the mousse to a bowl, season with salt and pepper and refrigerate for at least 1 hour. Serve chilled, with the baguette toasts.

—*Mina Vachino*

MAKE AHEAD The mousse can be refrigerated for up to 8 hours.

WINE Try an Italian sparkling wine, such as the 1994 Bruno Giacosa Extra Brut, to balance the salty, creamy mousse.

Italian Tuna Mousse

MAKES 1 CUP

Scoop up this simple spread with *grissini* (breadsticks) or spread it on toasted slices of baguette or small triangles of toast made from almost any bread. Serve the mousse as is or garnished with asparagus or artichokes.

One 6-ounce can Italian tuna packed in olive oil, drained

2 teaspoons balsamic vinegar

2 teaspoons fresh lemon juice

1 teaspoon soy sauce

2 tablespoons unsalted butter, softened

Sea salt and freshly ground pepper

3 tablespoons heavy cream

1. In a food processor, pulse the tuna with the balsamic vinegar, lemon juice and soy sauce to blend. Add the butter and process until smooth.

2. Season with salt and pepper. Add the heavy cream and pulse to blend. Check the seasoning and add as needed. Scrape into a bowl and serve.

—*Michael Chiarello*

MAKE AHEAD The tuna mousse can be refrigerated for up to 3 days. Bring to room temperature before serving.

Deviled Ham

MAKES ABOUT 2 CUPS

Use the deviled ham as a sandwich filling, cracker topping or vegetable dip, or fold it into an egg-white omelet.

½ pound baked ham, cut into ½-inch dice

3 scallions, minced

¼ cup sour cream

2 tablespoons Creole mustard

2 medium celery ribs, peeled and cut into ¼-inch dice

1½ teaspoons minced tarragon

⅛ to ¼ teaspoon cayenne pepper

Salt and freshly ground black pepper

Hot sauce

1. In a food processor, pulse the baked ham until it's finely chopped. Add the scallions and pulse again, just long enough to blend.

2. In a medium bowl, mix the sour cream and the Creole mustard. Fold in the ham, celery, tarragon and cayenne pepper. Season to taste with salt and black pepper. Add a few dashes of hot sauce and set aside for at least 10 minutes before serving.

—*Marcia Kiesel*

ham lexicon

A true ham comes from the hind leg of a pig. Fine hams are either dry-cured (rubbed with salt) or brined (soaked in a salt solution). Ham varieties also differ from each other in how they're smoked, aged or cooked. Some of the most flavorful hams are:

Baked ham A generic term that includes a variety of hams that are cured, smoked and precooked, often with a glaze. Ready-to-eat American baked hams include honey baked, Virginia baked, Vermont corncob and apple smoked.

Black Forest ham A German ham that is also produced domestically. Traditionally, Black Forest hams were heavily brined, then dipped in beef blood and smoked to create the black coating. Today, the coating comes from smoking alone. Some brands are dry-cured rather than brined; most are sold cooked and ready to eat. The ham is sweetly nutty, with a mild smoky taste.

Country ham Any ham processed by traditional curing, smoking and aging methods. The most famous United States country-style hams come from the Southeast, such as Smithfield hams from Virginia. These hams are dry-cured, smoked slowly and aged for 6 to 18 months. Smithfield and other country hams have a wonderfully complex, salty, gamy flavor.

Prosciutto An Italian ham that is also produced in the U.S., prosciutto is dry-cured, air-dried and aged like a country ham, but it's not usually smoked. The rich, rosy, nutty flavored meat is firm but moister than that of American country hams. The most famous prosciutto comes from Parma, although the towns of Carpegna and San Daniele produce excellent hams as well.

Serrano ham A dry-cured, air-dried Spanish ham similar to prosciutto. Serrano has a chewy texture and a rich, sweet flavor. —*Lily Barberio*

Gougères

MAKES ABOUT 6 DOZEN GOUGERES

Serve these puffs warm or let them cool and fill them with herbed cream cheese.

½ cup milk

½ cup water

1 stick (4 ounces) unsalted butter, cut into pieces

1 teaspoon sugar

½ teaspoon salt

Pinch of cayenne pepper

Pinch of freshly grated nutmeg

1¼ cups all-purpose flour

5 large eggs

1¾ cups finely shredded Gruyère cheese (5 ounces)

1. Preheat the oven to 400°. Lightly butter 2 large baking sheets. In a large saucepan, combine the milk with the water, butter, sugar, salt, cayenne and nutmeg and bring to a boil. Remove the pan from the heat, add the flour and stir with a wooden spoon until a thick, smooth pastelike batter forms. Cook the batter over moderate heat for 1 minute, stirring constantly.

2. Scrape the batter into a large heat-proof bowl and add 4 of the eggs, beating them in one at a time until mixed in. Beat in 1¼ cups of the cheese.

3. Using a pastry bag fitted with a ½-inch plain round tip or 2 small spoons, pipe or spoon slightly rounded tablespoons of the batter onto the prepared baking sheets, spacing them 1 inch apart. Lightly beat the remaining egg. Brush the tops of the *gougères* with the egg wash, then sprinkle them with the remaining ½ cup of shredded cheese. Bake the *gougères* for 20 minutes, or until puffed and golden; shift the pans from front to back and top to bottom halfway through. Serve warm.

—*Jeremy Strode*

MAKE AHEAD The baked *gougères* can be cooled completely and frozen in airtight containers for up to 1 month. Reheat them in a 325° oven for 6 to 7 minutes. Do not let them get crisp.

WINE Serve the rich and salty *gougères*

Mushroom and Goat Cheese Phyllo Triangles

with a French Champagne, such as the Nonvintage Louis Roederer Premier Brut, or an Australian sparkling wine, such as the 1995 Green Point Brut or the 1992 Green Point Blanc de Blancs.

Mushroom and Goat Cheese Phyllo Triangles

MAKES 32 TRIANGLES

1 pound Portobello mushrooms

1 stick (4 ounces) unsalted butter, plus 4 tablespoons, melted

1 medium shallot, minced

½ pound white button mushrooms, stemmed, caps sliced ¼ inch thick

Salt and freshly ground pepper

2 garlic cloves, minced

¼ cup coarsely chopped flat-leaf parsley

2 teaspoons finely chopped thyme

½ cup fresh mild goat cheese (3½ ounces)

8 sheets of phyllo dough, thawed

1. Stem the Portobellos and cut the caps in half. Using a sharp paring knife, cut the black gills from the undersides of the caps. Slice the caps crosswise ¼-inch thick.

2. Melt the stick of butter in a large skillet. Add the shallot and cook over low heat until softened, about 4 minutes. Stir in all of the mushrooms and season with salt and pepper. Cook over moderate heat, stirring occasionally, until the mushrooms are tender and their liquid has evaporated, about 10 minutes. Stir in the garlic, parsley and thyme and cook for 2 more minutes, stirring. Put the mixture in a food processor and pulse to a coarse puree. Scrape the puree into a medium bowl, stir in the goat cheese and season with salt and pepper. Let cool.

3. Preheat the oven to 400°. Lay 1 sheet of the phyllo dough on a work surface; keep the rest covered with damp paper towels. Brush the phyllo sheet with melted butter and cut it lengthwise into 4 even strips. Place 1 level tablespoon of the mushroom filling in a corner of one of the strips, about ½ inch from the top. Fold the corner down to form a triangle. Continue folding the triangle onto itself, across and down, until you have a neat phyllo triangle. Set the triangle on a large rimmed baking sheet. Repeat with the remaining phyllo, melted butter and mushroom filling. Brush the triangles with melted butter and bake for about 20 minutes, or until browned and crisp. Let cool slightly before serving. —*Victor Scargle*

WINE Earthy mushrooms coupled with tangy goat cheese call for a young Pinot Noir with dark cherry fruit, such as the 1996 Logan Sleepy Hollow Vineyard.

Olive and Fennel Crostini

MAKES 4 DOZEN CROSTINI

½ pound oil-cured black olives, pitted (1¾ cups)

¼ cup fresh orange juice

3 tablespoons extra-virgin olive oil

1½ teaspoons fennel seeds

½ teaspoon finely grated orange zest

Salt

1 baguette, sliced ½ inch thick and toasted

hors d'oeuvres

Cauliflower Crostini

In a food processor, combine the olives with the orange juice, olive oil, fennel seeds and orange zest and process to a coarse paste. Scrape into a bowl and season with salt. Spread each toast with 1 teaspoon of the paste and serve.

—*Sabine Busch and Bruno Tramontana*

MAKE AHEAD The paste can be refrigerated for up to 2 days.

Cauliflower Crostini

MAKES 16 CROSTINI

The combination of cauliflower and fennel seeds makes a delicious topping for crostini.

One 2-pound head of cauliflower, broken into florets

3 tablespoons extra-virgin olive oil
1 small red onion, finely chopped
1 teaspoon fennel seeds
Salt and freshly ground pepper
Eight ⅓-inch-thick slices peasant bread (2 ounces each), cut in half
1 garlic clove, halved lengthwise
2 tablespoons finely chopped flat-leaf parsley

1. In a large nonstick skillet, bring 1 inch of lightly salted water to a boil. Add the cauliflower florets, then cover and cook over high heat until just tender, approximately 12 minutes. Using a slotted spoon, transfer the cauliflower florets to a bowl; reserve the cooking liquid.

2. Heat 1 tablespoon of the olive oil in the skillet. Add the onion and cook over moderate heat, stirring occasionally, until golden. Add the cauliflower florets, fennel seeds and a pinch of salt and pepper. Cook, stirring occasionally, until the cauliflower is very tender, approximately 8 minutes; add a few tablespoons of the cooking liquid if it begins to look dry. Use a potato masher to reduce the cauliflower to a chunky puree; season with salt and pepper.

3. Toast the bread and brush with 1 tablespoon of the olive oil. Rub the crostini with the cut sides of the garlic clove, sprinkle with salt and spoon the cauliflower puree on top. Drizzle the crostini with the remaining 1 tablespoon of olive oil, garnish with the parsley and serve.

—*Sally Schneider*

ONE SERVING Calories 223 kcal, Total Fat 7.1 gm, Saturated Fat 1.1 gm, Carbohydrates 33.2 gm

WINE A mild-flavored, soft and somewhat simple white wine, such as the 1998 Swanson Pinot Grigio from California, is an attractive and refreshing aperitif in any case. It would make a lovely partner to the cauliflower in this hors d'oeuvre.

Crostini with Lentil and Green Olive Salad

Crostini with Lentil and Green Olive Salad

MAKES 2 DOZEN CROSTINI

- ½ pound lentils, preferably from Abruzzi, rinsed and picked over
- 1 small onion
- 1 garlic clove
- 1 bay leaf
- ½ dried red chile
- ½ pound green olives, pitted and coarsely chopped
- 1 large celery rib, thinly sliced
- 1 large shallot, minced
- ¼ cup extra-virgin olive oil, plus more for drizzling
- 1½ tablespoons red wine vinegar

Salt and freshly ground pepper
- 24 small thin slices crusty country bread
- 1 small fresh red chile, very thinly sliced lengthwise

1. Preheat the oven to 400°. In a medium saucepan, generously cover the lentils with water. Add the onion, garlic, bay leaf and dried chile and bring to a simmer. Cover and cook over low heat until the lentils are tender, about 30 minutes. Drain the lentils, reserving ¼ cup of the cooking liquid; discard the bay leaf and chile.

2. In a medium bowl, mash 1 cup of the lentils with a potato masher, and then stir in the remaining lentils. Add the olives, celery, shallot, ¼ cup of olive oil and the red wine vinegar. Season the lentil salad with salt and pepper and stir in the reserved ¼ cup of cooking liquid.

3. Arrange the bread slices on a cookie sheet and bake for about 8 minutes or until thoroughly crisp.

4. Drizzle the crostini with olive oil and generously spoon the lentil salad on top. Garnish the crostini with slivers of red chile and serve.
      —*Nancy Harmon Jenkins*

MAKE AHEAD Both the lentil salad and the crostini can be made hours ahead. Wait to proceed to step 4 until shortly before serving.

Artichoke Bruschetta

MAKES 6 BRUSCHETTA

The artichokes for this bruschetta are sautéed, not steamed, and stay pleasantly crunchy when cooked.

- 1 lemon, halved
- 6 medium artichokes
- ¼ cup extra-virgin olive oil

Salt and freshly ground pepper
Six ½-inch-thick slices Italian bread
Small basil leaves, for garnish (optional)

1. Squeeze 1 lemon half into a medium bowl of cold water. Working with 1 artichoke at a time, snap off the outer leaves. Using a sharp knife, cut off the top half of the leaves and trim the base and stem. Using a melon baller or a spoon, scoop out the furry choke. Rub the artichoke bottom all over with the other lemon half and add it to the lemon water. Repeat with the remaining artichokes.

2. Drain the artichokes and pat dry, then coarsely chop them. Heat the olive oil in a large skillet. Add the artichokes, cover and cook over low heat, stirring occasionally, until tender, about 15 minutes. Season with salt and pepper.

3. Toast the bread. Top the toast with the artichokes, garnish with basil and serve.   —*Cristina and Mauro Rastelli*

MAKE AHEAD The artichokes can be prepared through Step 2 and refrigerated for up to 2 days. Reheat and season before serving.

Eggplant Bruschetta with Tomato and Basil

MAKES 16 BRUSCHETTA

Cooking eggplant slowly on the stove brings out its sweetness and intensifies its flavor.

Two 1-pound eggplants
Kosher salt
- ½ cup extra-virgin olive oil
- 4 garlic cloves, minced
- ½ teaspoon crushed red pepper
- ½ teaspoon freshly ground black pepper

- ¼ cup packed basil leaves, coarsely shredded

One 14-ounce can peeled Italian plum tomatoes, drained and finely chopped

Sixteen ½-inch slices of country bread

1. Using a vegetable peeler, remove 1 lengthwise strip of skin from opposite sides of each eggplant. Slice the eggplants crosswise ¼ inch thick. Stack several slices and cut them into ¼-inch matchsticks; repeat with the remaining eggplant.

2. Transfer the eggplant to a colander, sprinkle generously with salt and toss to coat. Let drain for at least 30 minutes. Squeeze handfuls of the eggplant to extract the bitter juices.

3. Warm ¼ cup plus 2 tablespoons of the olive oil in a large skillet over high heat. Add the eggplant and toss it quickly to coat with the oil before it's absorbed. Reduce the heat to moderate, add the garlic and crushed red pepper and season with black pepper. Cook, stirring, until the eggplant begins to soften, about 15 minutes. Add 3 tablespoons of the basil and cook until just wilted. Add half the tomatoes and cook over moderately low heat, stirring, until the liquid has evaporated, about 5 minutes. Add the remaining tomatoes and cook until thick, about

Eggplant Bruschetta with Tomato and Basil

15 minutes longer. Season with salt and keep warm.

4. Meanwhile, preheat a grill or broiler. Brush the bread on both sides with the remaining 2 tablespoons of olive oil. Grill or broil the bread until lightly charred. Spoon the eggplant on the grilled bread, top with the remaining 1 tablespoon of basil and serve immediately. —*Darryl Joannides*

MAKE AHEAD The cooked eggplant can be refrigerated for up to 3 days. Rewarm before serving.

WINE The 1998 Regaleali Bianco Tasca d'Almerita from Sicily has soft honey-lemon notes that will help tame the heat of this spicy dish.

Esca Bruschetta

MAKES 8 BRUSCHETTA

Esca, an Italian seafood restaurant in New York City, uses mackerel for the bruschetta, but tuna is fine, too.

- ¼ cup plus 2 tablespoons extra-virgin olive oil
- ¼ cup red wine vinegar
- ¼ cup finely shredded basil
- 2 small garlic cloves, minced
- 1 teaspoon crushed red pepper
- 1 teaspoon minced rosemary, plus whole sprigs for garnish

Salt and freshly ground pepper

Two 19-ounce cans cannellini beans, drained and rinsed

Two 6-ounce cans mackerel or tuna packed in olive oil, drained and broken up into large chunks

- 1 small red onion, finely chopped

Eight 1-inch-thick slices Italian peasant bread, grilled or toasted

1. In a bowl, combine the olive oil, vinegar, basil, garlic, crushed red pepper and minced rosemary. Season the dressing with salt and pepper.

2. In a large bowl, combine the beans with the mackerel and onion and toss gently. Add the dressing and toss again.

3. Mound ¼ cup of salad on each toast, garnish with rosemary sprigs and serve. —*Mario Batali*

Sardines with Garlic Bread and Tomatoes

MAKES 10 TOASTS

If you prefer, have the fishmonger clean and fillet the sardines for you.

- 5 small fresh sardines, cleaned and filleted
- 2 garlic cloves, 1 thinly sliced and 1 whole
- 4 flat-leaf parsley sprigs
- ½ cup extra-virgin olive oil, plus more for drizzling
- 3 tablespoons fresh lemon juice
- 3 large plum tomatoes—peeled, cored and finely chopped

Coarse sea salt and freshly ground pepper

Ten ½-inch-thick slices of French or Italian bread

1. Arrange the sardines, skin side down, in a shallow glass or ceramic baking dish just large enough to hold them in a single layer. Scatter the sliced garlic and parsley sprigs all over the sardines. Pour 6 tablespoons of the olive oil along with the lemon juice on the sardine fillets, cover with plastic wrap and refrigerate for at least 2 but not more than 6 hours. Drain the sardines, discarding the parsley and garlic, and pat dry. Transfer the sardines to a baking sheet.

Sardines with Garlic Bread and Tomatoes

2. In a small bowl, toss the chopped tomatoes with the remaining 2 tablespoons of olive oil. Season the tomatoes with salt and pepper.

3. Preheat the broiler. Toast the bread on both sides until golden and crisp. Rub the toast with the whole garlic clove, drizzle lightly with oil and transfer to a platter.

4. Heat the sardines under the broiler for 20 to 30 seconds, or just until slightly warm; be careful not to cook the fish. Spoon the tomatoes on the bread and top with the fish. Sprinkle with salt and pepper and serve right away. —*Julian Serrano*

MAKE AHEAD The recipe can be made through Step 1 up to 1 day ahead.

Spicy Crawfish Salad on Brioche

MAKES 16 TOASTS

You can enjoy this New Orleans dish even if you live far from the bayou: Frozen cooked crawfish tails are sold at many specialty food shops.

- 1 tablespoon unsalted butter
- ¼ cup minced light green leek
- ½ teaspoon chili powder
- 1 pound thawed crawfish tails, with their juices
- 1 small red bell pepper, finely chopped

Salt

- ¼ cup mayonnaise
- 1 small celery rib, finely chopped
- ¼ small red onion, finely chopped
- 1 tablespoon finely chopped seeded dill pickle
- 1 tablespoon fresh lemon juice
- ½ teaspoon minced garlic
- ½ teaspoon paprika
- ¼ teaspoon celery salt

Cayenne pepper

- 8 thin slices brioche loaf, crusts removed, slices halved to form triangles
- 2 tablespoons finely chopped tomato

Basil sprigs, for garnish

1. Melt the butter in a medium saucepan. Add the leek and cook over moderate heat until lightly browned, about 6 minutes. Stir in the chili powder and cook until fragrant, about 1 minute. Add the crawfish tails with their juices and the bell pepper and season with salt. Cook until the liquid evaporates, about 8 minutes. Refrigerate until chilled, about ½ hour.

2. In a medium bowl, combine the mayonnaise with the celery, red onion, pickle, lemon juice, garlic, paprika and celery salt. Stir in the crawfish and season with salt and cayenne. Cover and refrigerate for up to 1 day.

3. Toast the brioche. Top each triangle with 1 tablespoon of the salad, garnish with some of the chopped tomato and a basil sprig and serve.

—Dominique Macquet

WINE The crisp acidity and bright fruit of the 1998 Matanzas Creek Sauvignon Blanc will set off the flavors of the spicy crawfish. This wine also has enough body to marry well with the ham in the following recipe.

Smithfield Ham and Asparagus Toasts

MAKES 16 TOASTS

You'll need only the tips of the asparagus for this recipe; save the stalks for a soup, a salad or a pasta.

- 32 thin asparagus tips (2 inches in length)
- 2 tablespoons olive oil
- Salt and freshly ground pepper
- 8 thin slices brioche loaf, crusts removed, slices halved to form triangles
- 2½ tablespoons unsalted butter
- 8 thin slices Smithfield ham (¼ pound), halved crosswise
- 2½ tablespoons balsamic vinegar

1. On a grill pan, brush the asparagus tips with the olive oil and season with salt and pepper. Grill over medium high heat until tender, about 4 minutes.

2. Toast and lightly butter the brioche

triangles. Fold the ham slices in half and set on the toasts. Arrange the asparagus tips on top, drizzle with the balsamic vinegar and serve.

—Dominique Macquet

Chopped Liver with Beets and Horseradish

MAKES ABOUT 2½ CUPS

Port and Cognac have been added to this recipe, creating a cross between Jewish chopped liver and French *pâté de foies de volaille*. Note that the beet must be refrigerated overnight.

- 4 tablespoons unsalted butter
- 1 pound turkey and chicken livers, trimmed
- 2 medium onions, minced
- 2 large hard-cooked eggs, finely chopped
- 1 tablespoon Cognac
- 1 tablespoon port
- ½ tablespoon kosher salt
- ¼ teaspoon freshly ground white pepper
- 1 cup white vinegar
- 1 large beet, peeled and coarsely shredded
- Grated horseradish, preferably fresh
- 24 slices cocktail-size rye bread, toasted

1. Melt 2 tablespoons of the butter in a large skillet. Add the livers and cook over moderately high heat, stirring occasionally, until barely pink in the center, about 7 minutes. Transfer the livers to a medium bowl and let cool completely, then chop coarsely.

2. Meanwhile, melt the remaining 2 tablespoons of butter in the skillet. Add the onions and cook over moderately low heat, stirring occasionally, until browned, about 12 minutes. Let the onions cool completely.

3. Add the onions, eggs, Cognac, port, salt and white pepper to the chicken livers and stir to combine. Cover and refrigerate overnight.

4. In a medium bowl, combine the white vinegar with the shredded beet

and add horseradish to taste. Cover and refrigerate the beet overnight.

5. To serve, spread each toast with about 1 tablespoon of the chopped liver and then sprinkle with a pinch of the beet. Arrange the toasts on a platter and serve. *—Bruce and Eric Bromberg*

MAKE AHEAD The chopped liver, covered directly with plastic wrap, and the beet topping can be refrigerated separately for up to 2 days.

WINE Chicken liver pâté and a well-chilled fino sherry are made for each other. The tanginess of the sherry complements the richness of the chopped liver, and vice versa. An excellent choice would be the Lustau Light Fino Jarana.

Goat Cheese and Pepper Empanadillas

MAKES 30 EMPANADILLAS

- 3 cups all-purpose flour
- 1 tablespoon kosher salt
- 1 stick (4 ounces) cold unsalted butter, cut into small pieces
- ½ cup dry white wine
- 2 tablespoons sherry vinegar
- 1 large egg yolk mixed with 2 tablespoons water
- 5 ounces mild goat cheese, crumbled
- ¼ cup finely chopped jarred *piquillo* peppers, or roasted red peppers mixed with a few dashes of Tabasco

1. In a food processor, pulse the flour with the salt to combine. Add the butter and pulse until the mixture resembles coarse meal. Transfer the mixture to a large bowl and stir in the wine and vinegar just until a stiff dough forms. Turn the dough out onto a lightly floured work surface and shape it into two 6-inch disks; do not overwork the dough. Wrap the disks in plastic and refrigerate for at least 30 minutes or overnight.

2. Preheat the oven to 400°. Working with 1 disk at a time, roll out the dough

Smoked Trout Tostadas

Stuffed Cherry Peppers

a scant ⅛ inch thick. Using a 3½-inch biscuit cutter, stamp out 15 dough rounds from each disk. Brush each round with egg wash and top with 1 slightly rounded teaspoon of goat cheese and about ¼ teaspoon of *piquillo* pepper. Fold the dough over the filling and crimp the edges with a fork to seal them decoratively.

3. Brush the empanadillas lightly with the egg wash and arrange them on a baking sheet. Bake them for about 25 minutes, or until golden and slightly puffed. Let the empanadillas cool slightly before serving.

—*Julian Serrano*

MAKE AHEAD You can refrigerate the unbaked empanadillas overnight. Or alternatively, you can arrange the empanadillas on a baking sheet in a single layer and freeze until solid, and then transfer them to an airtight container and freeze for up to 1 month. Take care not to allow the empanadillas to thaw until you're ready to bake and serve them.

Smoked Trout Tostadas

MAKES 2 DOZEN TOSTADAS

At Enchantment Resort in Sedona, Arizona, the tortilla chips are made from scratch using blue corn flour and crushed red pepper. You will find, however, that store-bought baked tortilla chips are a fine substitute.

One 6-ounce smoked trout fillet, skinned and flaked into small pieces
2 plum tomatoes—halved, seeded and finely chopped
½ Hass avocado, finely chopped
1 tablespoon fresh lime juice
Salt and freshly ground pepper
2 dozen baked blue corn chips
1 tablespoon snipped chives

In a medium bowl, combine the trout, tomatoes, avocado and lime juice and toss gently. Season with salt and pepper. Spoon the mixture onto the corn chips and sprinkle with the chives. Serve immediately.   —*Kevin Maguire*

THREE TOSTADAS Calories 82 kcal, Total Fat 4.5 gm, Saturated Fat 0.9 gm

Crispy Frico with Ripe Pear

MAKES 32 HORS D'OEUVRES
2 cups freshly grated Parmigiano-Reggiano cheese (6 ounces)
¼ cup all-purpose flour
1 large, firm ripe pear
Excellent balsamic vinegar, for drizzling (optional)

ı. In a medium bowl, toss all of the Parmigiano-Reggiano cheese with 2 tablespoons of the flour. Heat a 10-inch nonstick skillet over moderate heat and lightly dust with flour. Sprinkle 1 tablespoon of the cheese into a 4-inch round in the skillet. Repeat to make 2 more rounds. Cook until the rounds are set and lightly browned around the edges, about 30 seconds. Turn each *frico* and cook for about 10 seconds longer, then carefully transfer it to a plate to cool. Repeat to cook the remaining *frico* in single layers, lightly dusting the pan with more flour as necessary.

2. Cut the pear into thin slices. Arrange the slices on the *frico*. Top each with a few drops of balsamic vinegar. Arrange on a platter and serve at once.

—*Michael Chiarello*

MAKE AHEAD The *frico* themselves can be kept in an airtight container for up to 1 day.

Stuffed Cherry Peppers

MAKES 2 DOZEN PEPPERS

- 24 sweet or hot cherry peppers
- 5 cups wine vinegar
- 24 anchovy fillets
- 48 capers
- 1 teaspoon fennel seeds

About 2 cups olive oil

Sliced Pecorino cheese and baguette
   toasts, for serving

1. Slice off the stems of the cherry peppers and discard. Scrape out the ribs and seeds. In a ceramic or glass bowl, cover the cherry peppers with the vinegar. Weigh down the peppers with a plate and refrigerate overnight.

2. Drain the peppers; save the vinegar for another use. Stuff each pepper with 1 anchovy fillet and 2 capers. Pack the peppers into a glass jar. Add the fennel seeds and enough olive oil to cover the peppers completely; refrigerate. Serve with Pecorino cheese and toasts.

—*Sabine Busch and Bruno Tramontana*

MAKE AHEAD The jarred peppers can be refrigerated for up to 1 week.

Zucchini Fritters with Deep-Fried Capers

6 SERVINGS

The tangy deep-fried capers and rich crème fraîche accompaniments balance these salty fritters nicely, but lemon wedges would make an easy alternative.

- 1 medium zucchini (about
     ½ pound), coarsely grated

Kosher salt

- 1 tablespoon pure olive oil
- 1 small onion, finely chopped
- ¾ cup all-purpose flour
- 2 teaspoons baking powder

Freshly ground pepper

- 3 tablespoons milk
- 1 large egg, lightly beaten

Vegetable oil, for frying

- ¼ cup drained capers
- ⅓ cup crème fraîche

1. In a colander set in the sink, toss the zucchini with 1 teaspoon of salt;

let drain for 20 minutes. Squeeze the zucchini, a handful at a time, to remove as much liquid as possible.

2. Meanwhile, heat the olive oil in a medium skillet until shimmering. Add the onion and cook over moderately high heat, stirring, until softened, about 5 minutes. Transfer to a plate to cool.

3. In a medium bowl, sift the flour with the baking powder, 1 teaspoon of salt and ¼ teaspoon of ground pepper. Add the zucchini, onion, milk and egg and stir until smooth. Let the batter rest at room temperature for 20 minutes.

4. In a medium skillet, heat ¾ inch of vegetable oil until shimmering. Pat the capers dry with paper towels. Add them to the oil and fry until crisp, about 4 minutes. Transfer the capers to paper towels to drain.

5. Scoop scant tablespoonfuls of the fritter batter into the hot oil, without crowding, and fry until crisp and golden all over, about 2 minutes per side. Drain the fritters on paper towels and sprinkle with salt. Top each fritter with a scant teaspoon of crème fraîche and a few fried capers and serve right away.

—*Alison Tolley*

**Zucchini Fritters with
Deep-Fried Capers**

Parmesan Potato Puffs

MAKES ABOUT 3 DOZEN PUFFS

The rich yet airy Parmesan-flavored potato puffs are slightly flattened before baking, making a perfect spot to hold the chopped olive and basil mixture given here. You can vary the topping using anything you like with potatoes and cheese, such as mascarpone sprinkled with dill.

- 1½ pounds Yukon Gold potatoes,
      peeled and cut into 2-inch chunks
- ¾ cup heavy cream
- ¾ cup freshly grated Parmigiano-
     Reggiano or Grana Padano
     cheese, plus more for sprinkling
     (about 2 ounces)

Parmesan Potato Puffs

3 tablespoons unsalted butter, plus
2 tablespoons melted butter

Salt and freshly ground pepper

4 large egg whites

6 ounces brine-cured black olives,
such as Gaeta, pitted and coarsely
chopped (¾ cup)

Small basil leaves, for garnish

I. Cook the potatoes in a medium saucepan of boiling salted water until tender, about 15 minutes. Drain the potatoes and return them to the pan. Set the pan over moderately high heat and shake for about 1 minute to dry out the potatoes. Mash them with a potato masher, right in the pan. Stir in the cream, the Parmigiano-Reggiano and the 3 tablespoons of butter and season generously with salt and pepper. Scrape the mashed potatoes into a large bowl and set aside to cool to room temperature.

2. Preheat the oven to 475°. In a large stainless-steel bowl, beat the egg whites with a pinch of salt until they hold soft peaks. Stir one-third of the whites into the mashed potatoes to loosen them, then fold in the remaining whites with a rubber spatula until blended.

3. Butter 2 large rimmed baking sheets. Drop rounded tablespoons of the potato mixture onto the sheets about ½ inch apart. Flatten each mound slightly to form a disk. Brush the mounds with the melted butter and sprinkle each with some grated cheese. Bake for about 10 minutes, or until lightly puffed and golden.

4. Meanwhile, in a small bowl, combine the chopped olives and the basil leaves. Top each puff with about ½ teaspoon of the olive mixture and serve.

—Marcia Kiesel

MAKE AHEAD The puffs can be prepared through Step 2 and refrigerated for up to 2 days. Or they can be baked early on the day you plan to serve them and then reheated in a 400° oven for 5 minutes.

Mini Potato Pancakes with Lemon and Cilantro

MAKES 3 DOZEN CAKES

All over India, potato pancakes are a very popular street food. The fried cakes are pushed to the edge of large, black steel griddles to keep warm.

2¼ pounds medium red
potatoes, scrubbed

8 slices firm-textured white bread

4 serrano chiles, seeded
and minced

3 tablespoons chopped
cilantro leaves

2 tablespoons fresh lemon juice

1½ teaspoons salt

Vegetable oil, for frying

Sour cream and assorted chutneys
(p. 323), for serving

I. In a large pot of water, bring the potatoes to a boil. Reduce the heat to moderate; simmer until tender, 25 to 30 minutes. Drain and cool slightly, then peel.

2. Meanwhile, preheat the oven to 250°. Place the bread directly on the rack in the oven and toast for about 15 minutes, or until pale golden. Break the bread into the bowl of a food processor and pulse until fine crumbs form.

3. In a large bowl, mash half of the potatoes until smooth. Break the remaining potatoes into rough ⅓-inch chunks and add them to the mashed potatoes. Add the chiles, cilantro, lemon juice and salt to the potatoes and mix well. Blend in 1 cup of the bread crumbs and press the potato mixture into a dense dough.

4. Line a baking sheet with wax paper. Spread the remaining bread crumbs in a pie plate. Scoop up slightly rounded tablespoons of the potato dough and pat them into ½-inch-thick cakes. Dip the cakes into the bread crumbs to coat them and set on the baking sheet. Let the potato cakes cool completely.

5. Heat ½ inch of oil in a large nonstick skillet. Fry the potato cakes in batches over moderately high heat until golden and crisp, 5 to 6 minutes. The potato cakes are fragile; don't turn them until golden. Drain and serve warm, with sour cream and assorted chutneys.

—Neela Paniz

MAKE AHEAD The potato cakes can be prepared through Step 4 and refrigerated for up to 2 days.

WINE The Nonvintage Piper Sonoma Brut and the Nonvintage Domaine Chandon Réserve Brut will balance the sweetness of the chutneys. The tartness of these wines will echo the lemony pancakes.

Roast Dates with Ham

MAKES 10 HORS D'OEUVRES

For an even simpler hors d'oeuvre, don't roast the dates.

10 small pitted California dates

5 thin slices Serrano ham
(about 1½ ounces), halved
lengthwise

I. Preheat the oven to 350°. Arrange the dates in a pie plate and bake for 10 minutes, or until heated through.

2. Wrap the ham around the dates and secure with a toothpick. Serve warm or at room temperature.

—Julian Serrano

Picadillo-Stuffed Mushrooms

MAKES 10 HORS D'OEUVRES

Picadillo—ground meat cooked with onion, garlic and tomatoes—is often used as a filling for savory pastries and tacos in Central America and the Caribbean. The version served at Las Vegas's Picasso restaurant was inspired by a dish at a Cuban restaurant in Miami. This recipe uses white mushrooms, but you could vary it by substituting creminis, which have the same cuplike shape as white mushrooms but a heartier flavor.

3 tablespoons extra-virgin olive oil

⅓ cup finely chopped onion

1 garlic clove, minced

1 medium tomato—peeled, seeded
and coarsely chopped

½ pound lean ground pork

3 tablespoons chicken stock or
canned low-sodium broth
1 tablespoon tomato paste
½ teaspoon fennel seeds, coarsely
chopped
Salt and freshly ground pepper
10 white mushrooms with
2-inch-wide caps, stems discarded

1. Heat 1 tablespoon of the oil in a large skillet. Add the onion and cook over moderately low heat, stirring, until softened, about 10 minutes. Add the garlic and cook until fragrant, about 1 minute. Add the tomato and cook, stirring occasionally, until the liquid is evaporated and the sauce is thick, 7 to 8 minutes.

2. Transfer the sauce to a bowl and wipe out the skillet. Add ½ tablespoon of the oil and heat until shimmering. Add the pork in small clumps and cook over moderately high heat until browned, 8 to 10 minutes. Add the tomato sauce along with the chicken stock, tomato paste and fennel seeds and cook over low heat until thickened, about 5 minutes. Season the *picadillo* with salt and pepper and transfer to a plate.

3. Preheat the oven to 350°. Using a melon baller or small spoon, scrape out the brown gills from the mushroom caps. Wipe out the skillet again and heat the remaining 1½ tablespoons of olive oil until shimmering. Add the mushrooms, top side down, and cook over moderately high heat until golden brown, about 2 minutes. Turn the mushrooms and cook until brown on the other side, about 2 minutes longer.

4. Transfer the mushroom caps to a medium baking dish and fill them with the *picadillo*. Bake the mushrooms for about 15 minutes, or until cooked through. Transfer the mushrooms to a platter or individual plates and serve.
—*Julian Serrano*

MAKE AHEAD The *picadillo* can be refrigerated for up to 2 days. Be sure to allow the *picadillo* to return to room temperature before filling and baking the mushrooms.

Vietnamese Summer Rolls

MAKES 16 ROLLS

4 ounces rice vermicelli
1 pound medium shrimp, shelled
Sixteen 8-inch round Asian
rice papers
1 bunch watercress, large
stems discarded
2 large carrots, finely shredded
1 red bell pepper, cored and cut
into thin strips
2 Hass avocados—peeled,
pitted and sliced lengthwise
½ inch thick
Herbed Nuoc Cham (recipe follows)

1. In a medium bowl, cover the vermicelli with cool water and let soak until pliable, about 20 minutes.

2. Meanwhile, in a saucepan of boiling water, cook the shrimp until bright pink, 1 to 2 minutes. Using a slotted spoon, transfer the shrimp to a colander. Rinse under cold water and pat dry. Halve the shrimp lengthwise; cover and refrigerate.

3. Bring the water back to a boil. Add the drained vermicelli noodles and cook, stirring, until al dente, about 1 minute. Drain and rinse until completely cool. Let the vermicelli dry in the colander for about 20 minutes, tossing occasionally.

4. Dip each rice paper in a bowl of cool water to wet it. Set the rice paper on a work surface to soften; the paper will become opaque and pliable. Pat dry. Put 4 shrimp halves, cut side up, in a line across the lower third of each rice paper. Top with 2 or 3 sprigs of watercress, a large pinch of shredded carrot, 2 strips of red pepper and some of the vermicelli noodles. Press to flatten, then top with a slice of avocado. Pull the rice paper up and over the filling and roll up tightly, folding in the sides as you go.

5. Place the roll on a large platter, seam side down, and repeat the process with the remaining ingredients. When all the summer rolls are made, cut them in half crosswise and arrange, cut side up, on the platter. Serve the summer rolls with the Herbed Nuoc Cham for dipping.
—*Marcia Kiesel*

MAKE AHEAD The summer rolls can be tightly wrapped in plastic and refrigerated for up to 1 hour.

WINE The brisk acidity and bright, tangy fruit of an Italian Pinot Grigio would play off the spicy watercress in these rolls and the citrusy lime sauce. Try the 1998 Colterenzio Alto Adige or the 1998 Ronco del Gnemiz Friuli.

HERBED NUOC CHAM

MAKES ABOUT ½ CUP

1 large garlic clove, halved
1 jalapeño, seeded and
coarsely chopped
3 tablespoons light brown sugar
2 tablespoons Vietnamese fish
sauce *(nuoc nam)*
2 tablespoons fresh lime juice
2 tablespoons water
¼ cup finely chopped cilantro
2 tablespoons finely
chopped spearmint

In a mortar or a mini processor, combine the garlic, jalapeño and light brown sugar, and pound or pulse until a paste forms. Transfer to a small bowl and stir in the remaining ingredients. —*M.K.*

MAKE AHEAD The sauce can be refrigerated for up to 1 day.

Eggplant and Mozzarella Roll-Ups

MAKES ABOUT 2 DOZEN ROLL-UPS

All-purpose flour, for dredging
3 large eggs, lightly beaten
Pure olive oil, for frying
One 1-pound eggplant, peeled
and sliced lengthwise ⅛ inch
thick with a mandoline or a
sharp stainless-steel knife
Salt and freshly ground pepper
3 ounces thinly sliced prosciutto
¼ pound fresh mozzarella, cut into
about 24 strips

Eggplant and Mozzarella Roll-Ups

1. Have ready the flour and beaten eggs, each in a shallow bowl. Heat ¼ cup of olive oil in a large skillet. One at a time, dredge the eggplant slices in the flour and then dip them into the beaten eggs, allowing the excess to drip off.

2. Fry 2 coated eggplant slices at a time in the olive oil over moderate heat until golden brown, about 2 minutes per side. Transfer the slices to paper towels to drain. Add more olive oil to the skillet as needed and adjust the heat if the eggplant is browning too quickly.

3. Preheat the oven to 400°. Lay the eggplant slices on a work surface and lightly season on both sides with salt and pepper. Cover with the prosciutto, trimming the prosciutto to fit and using

the trimmings to cover any uncovered eggplant. Cut each eggplant slice in half crosswise. Set 1 strip of mozzarella at 1 end of each eggplant slice, roll up neatly and secure with a toothpick.

4. Transfer the eggplant rolls to a baking sheet and bake for about 10 minutes, or until the cheese is melted and the eggplant is tender and piping hot. Remove the toothpicks and cut the rolls crosswise into 1-inch lengths. Serve the roll-ups hot or warm.

—*Silvana Daniello*

MAKE AHEAD The roll-ups can be prepared through Step 2 and refrigerated overnight. Bring to room temperature before baking.

WINE 1998 Villa Matilde Falerno del Massico Bianco.

Bell Pepper and Goat Cheese Rolls

MAKES 2 DOZEN HORS D'OEUVRES

- ¼ cup pine nuts
- 6 small red bell peppers
- 6 small yellow bell peppers
- 11 ounces soft goat cheese, at room temperature
- ⅓ cup extra-virgin olive oil
- ¼ cup fresh orange juice

Zest of 1 small orange, cut into fine julienne

Salt and freshly ground pepper

- ¼ cup currants or raisins

1. Preheat the oven to 400°. Put the pine nuts in a pie plate and toast for about 3 minutes, or until golden brown. Let cool. Put the red and yellow bell peppers on a large rimmed baking sheet and roast for 25 minutes, or until browned all over. Cover the peppers with foil and let steam for 10 minutes.

2. Remove the skins, stems and seeds from the peppers and halve them lengthwise. Spread 1 tablespoon of goat cheese on each pepper half and roll it up. Arrange the red and yellow bell pepper roll-ups on a large platter.

3. In a small bowl, combine the olive oil with the orange juice and orange zest and season with salt and pepper. Pour the dressing over the bell pepper and goat cheese rolls. Sprinkle with the pine nuts and currants and serve.

—*Sabine Busch and Bruno Tramontana*

MAKE AHEAD The bell pepper and goat cheese roll-ups can be refrigerated for up to 1 day.

WINE The strong flavors of the nuts, currants and oranges require a wine with as much character. An excellent choice would be the 1999 Le Calcinaie Vernaccia di San Gimignano Vigna ai Sassi, which is an unusually rich Vernaccia with a brilliant and nervous disposition. It's angular and vibrant, yet smooth in the finish, with a bittersweet almond touch.

Quail Eggs with Celery Salt

MAKES 3 DOZEN HORS D'OEUVRES

Eggs have long been a part of spring rituals. Quail eggs are a perfect English starter, often served with the shells half peeled, ready to dip into celery salt.

3 dozen quail eggs
Celery salt

Bring a large pot of water to a boil over moderately high heat. Place the quail eggs in a wire basket or strainer and lower them into the boiling water. Cook for 5 minutes, then cool under running water and pat dry. Serve them in the shell or peeled, with a bowl of celery salt alongside for dipping.

—*Tamasin Day-Lewis*

Grape Leaves with Quinoa, Shrimp and Beets

MAKES 2 DOZEN HORS D'OEUVRES

One 1-pound jar of grape leaves in brine, drained and rinsed
½ cup quinoa, rinsed
1 cup water
Salt
½ pound medium shrimp, shelled and deveined
1 small beet
1 tablespoon salt-packed capers
½ teaspoon cumin seeds
3 tablespoons coarsely chopped flat-leaf parsley
2 tablespoons fresh lemon juice
2 tablespoons extra-virgin olive oil
1 large garlic clove, minced
¾ teaspoon finely grated lemon zest
Freshly ground pepper

1. Cut off the grape-leaf stems and any tough center ribs, keeping the leaves intact. Select the 24 largest leaves. If necessary, fit 2 smaller leaves together to make 1 large one.

2. In a small saucepan, cover the quinoa with the water and bring to a boil. Add a pinch of salt, cover and cook over low heat for 12 minutes. Remove from the heat and let stand, covered, for 5 minutes. Fluff the quinoa.

3. In a saucepan of boiling salted water, simmer the shrimp until just cooked through, about 1 minute. With a slotted spoon, transfer them to a plate to cool, and then cut the shrimp in half lengthwise. Add the beet to the shrimp water and simmer until tender, about 20 minutes; add more water if necessary to keep it covered. Drain the beet and let cool, then peel and cut it into ¼-inch dice.

4. Put the capers in a bowl, cover with water and soak for 3 minutes, then drain and rinse. Coarsely chop the capers.

5. In a small skillet, toast the cumin seeds over moderately high heat until fragrant, about 30 seconds. Transfer the seeds to a work surface to cool and then finely chop them. Put the cumin seeds in a bowl and stir in the capers, parsley, lemon juice, oil, garlic and lemon zest.

6. In a large bowl, combine the quinoa, shrimp and beet. Add the dressing, season with salt and pepper and mix well.

7. Spread 6 grape leaves on a work surface. Place a rounded tablespoon of the quinoa filling near the stem end of each leaf. Fold the bottom of the leaves up and over the filling, then roll them up, pressing firmly and folding in the sides. Transfer the rolls to a large platter, seam side down. Repeat with the remaining grape leaves and filling. Refrigerate the rolls, but let them return to room temperature before serving.

—*Marcia Kiesel*

MAKE AHEAD The stuffed grape leaves can be refrigerated overnight.

Deviled Eggs with Shrimp and Radishes

MAKES 2 DOZEN HORS D'OEUVRES

The shrimp add a briny sweetness to the egg filling. If you can find fresh small Maine shrimp, use them whole.

12 large eggs
1 tablespoon pure olive oil
⅔ pound medium shrimp, shelled and deveined
Salt and freshly ground pepper
½ cup mayonnaise
¼ cup finely diced red radishes (about 4 large)
2 tablespoons minced parsley
2 teaspoons capers, chopped
1 medium shallot, minced
1 garlic clove, minced

1. Put the eggs in a large saucepan and cover with cold water. Bring to a boil over moderate heat, then simmer over low heat for 10 minutes and drain. Transfer the eggs to a large bowl of ice water to chill thoroughly before peeling. Cut the eggs in half lengthwise. Put the yolks in a bowl and mash lightly with a fork. Arrange the whites on a serving platter.

2. Heat the olive oil in a large skillet. Add the shrimp, season them with salt and pepper and cook over moderately high heat, stirring, until opaque, about 3 minutes. Transfer the shrimp to a work surface, let cool enough to handle and cut 12 of them in half lengthwise. Cut the remaining shrimp into ⅓-inch dice.

3. Add the diced shrimp to the egg yolks. Add the mayonnaise, radishes, parsley, capers, shallot and garlic, season with salt and pepper and stir to blend.

4. Mound a rounded tablespoon of the filling in each egg-white half and top with a shrimp half. Serve at room temperature or chilled.

—*Jean-Louis Palladin*

MAKE AHEAD The eggs can be prepared through Step 3 and refrigerated, covered, overnight. Stuff the whites just before serving.

WINE The crispness and pleasing citrusy notes of an Alsace Riesling will play up both the sweetness of the shrimp and the tartness of the mayonnaise and capers in the dressing. Try the 1998 Lucien Albrecht Riesling d'Alsace or the 1997 Domaine Zind Humbrecht Riesling Alsace Herrenweg Turkheim.

Grilled Shrimp with Cocoa-Nib
Romesco Sauce

Rock Shrimp Cakes

Grilled Shrimp with Cocoa-Nib Romesco Sauce

MAKES 3 DOZEN SHRIMP

Red peppers, tomatoes, almonds and garlic form the base of *romesco,* a classic Spanish sauce from Catalonia. Here it's embellished with hazelnuts, *masa harina* and cocoa nibs, small pieces of husked roasted cocoa beans. They have all the earthy flavor of eating chocolate without the sweetness. Cocoa nibs are available from specialty food stores and via mail-order from Scharffen Berger (800-930-4528) or Chocolates El Rey (800-357-3999).

> 2 tablespoons tequila
> 2 teaspoons sugar
> 3 dozen large shrimp (about 2 pounds), shelled and deveined
> ¼ cup almonds
> ¼ cup hazelnuts
> 1 red bell pepper
> ¼ cup cocoa nibs or grated unsweetened chocolate
> 1 medium tomato—halved, seeded and coarsely chopped
> 2 garlic cloves, minced
> 1 tablespoon sherry vinegar
> 2 teaspoons *masa harina* or fine cornmeal
> 2 teaspoons fresh lemon juice
> 1 teaspoon kosher salt
> ½ teaspoon crushed red pepper
> ¼ cup extra-virgin olive oil

1. In a large shallow glass or ceramic dish, stir the tequila with the sugar. Add the shrimp and toss to coat. Cover and refrigerate for at least 30 minutes.

2. Preheat the oven to 400°. Put the almonds and hazelnuts in separate pie plates and roast for 8 minutes, or until fragrant. Transfer the hot hazelnuts to a kitchen towel and rub together to remove the skins. Let cool, then coarsely chop the hazelnuts and almonds.

3. Roast the pepper over a gas flame or under the broiler, turning, until charred all over. Put the pepper in a bowl, cover with plastic wrap and steam for 5 minutes. Peel the pepper and discard the seeds. Strain any accumulated juices into a bowl. Coarsely chop the pepper and put it in the bowl.

4. In a food processor, combine the almonds, hazelnuts, roasted pepper, cocoa nibs, tomato, garlic, vinegar, *masa harina,* lemon juice, salt and crushed red pepper. Process to a fine paste. With the machine on, slowly add the olive oil to form a thick sauce. Scrape the *romesco* sauce into a bowl and season with salt.

5. Light a grill. Season the shrimp with salt and grill over a hot fire for about 2 minutes per side, or until just cooked through. Serve the shrimp hot, with the *romesco* sauce alongside for dipping.

—*Elizabeth Falkner*

MAKE AHEAD The marinated shrimp and the *romesco* sauce can be refrigerated overnight. Bring the sauce to room temperature before serving.

BEER Cold beer is a perfect foil for the nutty *romesco* sauce. Try Anchor Steam Pale Ale or Mendocino Brewing Company Peregrine Pale Ale.

Rock Shrimp Cakes

MAKES 2 DOZEN HORS D'OEUVRES

At Mélisse in Santa Monica, California, *kataifi*—finely shredded wheat common in many Greek pastries—is used in place of bread crumbs to make the seafood cakes extra crisp. This appetizer is wonderful with lemony whipped cream, but you can also serve it with simple lemon wedges.

> ½ pound rock shrimp or shelled and deveined medium shrimp, finely chopped
> ½ teaspoon finely grated orange zest
> ½ teaspoon finely grated lime zest
> 1½ teaspoons finely grated lemon zest
> Salt and freshly ground pepper
> ¼ cup all-purpose flour, for dusting
> 2 large eggs, lightly beaten
> 2 cups finely chopped *kataifi*
> ½ cup heavy cream
> 1 tablespoon fresh lemon juice
> 1 tablespoon minced chives
> Vegetable oil, for frying

1. In a bowl, mix the shrimp with the orange zest, lime zest and ½ teaspoon of the lemon zest. Stir in 1½ teaspoons salt and ¼ teaspoon pepper. Cover and chill about 30 minutes.

2. Put the flour, eggs and *kataifi* in separate bowls. Divide the shrimp mixture in half. Using lightly oiled hands, shape each half into twelve ⅓-inch-thick

Salt Cod Fritters, with Sautéed Plantains Gloria (p. 292).

cakes. Dip each cake in the flour and shake off the excess. Dip the cakes in the egg, then coat with *kataifi*. Put on a plate and refrigerate until ready to fry.

3. In a medium bowl, whip the cream until firm. Stir in the lemon juice, chives and the remaining 1 teaspoon of lemon zest. Season with salt and pepper.

4. Preheat the oven to 300°. In a large skillet, heat ¼ inch of vegetable oil until shimmering. Add 6 to 8 shrimp cakes and fry over moderately high heat until browned and crisp, about 2 minutes per side; lower the heat to moderate if the oil gets too hot. Transfer the cakes to a baking sheet and keep warm in the oven. Fry the rest of the cakes; add oil to the skillet as needed.

5. Put the cakes on a warm platter and top each with a bit of the whipped cream. Serve hot or warm. —*Josiah Citrin*

MAKE AHEAD The shrimp cakes can be made through Step 2 and refrigerated for up to 2 days.

Salt Cod Fritters

MAKES ABOUT 2 DOZEN FRITTERS
These addictive fritters are called *acras de morue* in Guadeloupe. Served at many local restaurants and bistros, the fritters are often accompanied by a fiery red-pepper sauce for dipping. When shopping for salt cod, be sure to get the thickest pieces you can find.

½ pound center-cut salt cod fillet
1½ cups all-purpose flour
1½ teaspoons baking powder
½ teaspoon salt
Cold water
½ cup minced onion
3 tablespoons chopped chives
2 teaspoons minced garlic
1½ teaspoons minced jalapeño
Canola oil, for frying
Hot Sauce, for serving (p. 319)

1. Soak the salt cod for 6 to 8 hours in several changes of cold water. Drain and rinse well. In a medium saucepan, cover the salt cod with cold water and bring to a boil over high heat. Reduce the heat to low, cover and simmer until tender, about 5 minutes. Drain the salt cod and transfer to a plate to cool slightly. Discard any bones or pieces of skin and coarsely chop the fish.

2. In a bowl, whisk the flour with the baking powder, salt and 1¼ cups cold water until a smooth, thick batter forms. Stir in the chopped salt cod, the onion, chives, garlic and jalapeño until blended.

3. In a large deep skillet, heat 2 inches of oil until shimmering. Scoop heaping tablespoons of the batter into the hot oil (being careful not to crowd them together) and fry over moderately high heat, turning once, until golden brown, 5 to 6 minutes. Transfer the fritters to a wire rack to drain; keep warm in a low oven. Add more oil to the pan if necessary and repeat with the remaining batter. Serve the fritters with the Hot Sauce.

—*Jacques Pépin*

BEER A satisfying contrast to these crisp fish fritters and the fiery-hot dipping sauce that accompanies them would be a bright lager beer from the Caribbean or Mexico. Try Red Stripe or Dos Equis Special Lager.

Pan-Fried Tuna Croquettes

MAKES ABOUT 10 CROQUETTES
⅓ cup finely chopped carrot
⅓ cup finely chopped celery root
4 tablespoons unsalted butter
¼ cup minced onion
2 cups all-purpose flour
1½ cups milk, warmed
One 6-ounce can solid white tuna packed in water, well drained
1½ teaspoons salt
½ teaspoon freshly ground white pepper
5 large eggs, lightly beaten
2 cups fine dried bread crumbs
Vegetable oil, for frying

Pan-Fried Tuna Croquettes

1. Bring a small pot of salted water to a boil. Add the chopped carrot and celery root and cook over high heat until just tender, 4 to 5 minutes. Drain and let cool under running water; drain again. Transfer the vegetables to a plate lined with paper towels and pat dry.

2. Melt the butter in a large saucepan. Add the onion and cook over moderate heat until softened, about 5 minutes. Add ²/₃ cup of the flour and cook, stirring, for 1 minute. Transfer the paste to a large heatproof bowl and slowly whisk in the milk to form a smooth slurry. Return the mixture to the saucepan and cook over moderate heat, stirring, until bubbling and very thick, about 6 minutes. Add the tuna to the white sauce along with the carrots, celery root, salt and pepper. Scrape the croquette mixture into a lightly oiled medium bowl and refrigerate until chilled and firm, at least 4 hours, or preferably overnight.

3. Spread the remaining 1¹/₃ cups of flour in a shallow bowl or pie plate. Put the eggs and bread crumbs in 2 shallow bowls or pie plates. Using 2 spoons, shape slightly rounded tablespoons of the croquette mixture into oval patties and drop them, 3 or 4 at a time, into the flour. Turn the croquettes to gently coat them with flour, then dip them in the eggs and coat with bread crumbs. Return the croquettes to the eggs and then the bread crumbs to give them a light second coating. Transfer the finished croquettes to a baking sheet lined with wax paper and continue shaping and coating the remaining croquettes. Loosely cover with wax paper and refrigerate until chilled, at least 30 minutes.

4. Heat 1 inch of vegetable oil in a large deep skillet until shimmering. Working in batches, cook the croquettes over moderately high heat, until golden and crisp, turning frequently, about 2 minutes; lower the heat if they brown too quickly. Using a slotted spoon, transfer the croquettes to paper towels to drain. Serve the tuna croquettes warm or at room temperature.

—*Julian Serrano*

MAKE AHEAD The tuna croquettes can be prepared through Step 3 and refrigerated overnight.

Arancini with Peas and Mozzarella

MAKES 18 RICE BALLS

FOOD & WINE test kitchen associate Grace Parisi's Calabrian grandmother always used plain white rice to make her incredible *arancini* (rice balls), but Grace prefers to cook with plump Arborio because it makes the insides creamier.

- 5 cups chicken stock or canned low-sodium broth
- 2 tablespoons unsalted butter
- ¼ cup minced shallots
- 1½ cups Arborio rice (10½ ounces)
- ½ cup freshly grated Parmesan cheese (2 ounces)

Kosher salt and freshly ground pepper

- 2 tablespoons finely chopped parsley
- 4 large eggs
- ½ cup all-purpose flour
- 1 cup fine dry bread crumbs
- 1½ ounces mozzarella, cut into eighteen ½-inch dice
- 18 fresh or frozen peas

Vegetable oil, for frying

1. Bring the chicken stock to a simmer in a medium saucepan; keep warm.

2. Melt the butter in a medium saucepan. Add the shallots and cook over moderate heat, stirring occasionally, until softened, about 3 minutes. Add the rice and cook, stirring, for 4 minutes.

3. Add 1 cup of the stock to the pan and cook, stirring gently, until all the stock is absorbed. Add the remaining stock, ½ cup at a time, and cook, stirring gently, until the rice is al dente, about 25 minutes. Stir in the Parmesan, 2 teaspoons of salt and ¼ teaspoon of pepper.

4. Transfer the risotto to a heatproof bowl and let cool for 10 minutes. Stir in the parsley and 1 egg. Press a piece of plastic wrap directly onto the rice and refrigerate the risotto for at least 4 hours or, preferably, overnight.

5. Line a baking sheet with wax paper. In a shallow bowl, beat the remaining 3 eggs. Put the flour and bread crumbs on separate plates. Season the bread crumbs with salt. Using moistened hands, form ¼-cup portions of the rice into 2-inch balls. Tuck a piece of mozzarella and a pea in the center of each rice ball and seal any holes. Set the balls on the baking sheet.

6. Dredge the rice balls in the flour, tapping off any excess. Working with 1 at a time, dip each ball in the egg, then coat with bread crumbs, rolling and pressing it into a compact ball.

7. Heat ½ inch of vegetable oil in a large cast-iron skillet. When the oil is very hot, add all of the rice balls and cook over moderate heat, turning, until golden and crisp all over, about 8 minutes. Drain the balls on paper towels, then transfer to a large platter. Sprinkle the *arancini* lightly with salt and serve.

—*Grace Parisi*

Haroset

MAKES 30 HORS D'OEUVRES

The Seder plate displays ceremonial foods used in telling the Passover story. Everyone's favorite is *haroset,* a fruit-and-nut mixture symbolizing the mortar that the ancient Hebrews used to build the cities of the pharaohs. *Haroset* is traditionally sandwiched between matzos, which represent bricks. In this Sephardic-inspired recipe, raisins, dates and dried cherries replace the fresh apples familiar to most American Jews.

- 1 **cup walnuts (4 ounces)**
- ¼ **cup sliced almonds**
- ½ **cup raisins**
- ½ **cup pitted Medjool dates, coarsely chopped**
- ¼ **cup unsweetened purple grape juice or kosher Concord grape wine**
- 2 **tablespoons dried tart cherries or cranberries**
- 2 **tablespoons fresh lemon juice**
- ⅛ **teaspoon cinnamon**
- 30 **dried apricot halves (½ pound)**

1. Preheat the oven to 350°. Spread the walnuts and almonds in separate pie pans and toast them, shaking the pans occasionally, about 6 minutes for the almonds and 10 for the walnuts, or until lightly browned; let cool.

2. In a bowl, combine the raisins, dates, grape juice, dried cherries, lemon juice and cinnamon and let macerate for at least 15 minutes.

3. Coarsely chop the walnuts in a food processor. Add the macerated fruit and its liquid and pulse until coarsely chopped or until a coarse puree forms. Transfer to a bowl and refrigerate for at least 1 hour or for up to 5 hours.

4. Bring a small saucepan of water to a boil. Remove from the heat. Add the apricots and let soften for 15 minutes. Drain them and pat them dry.

5. Form heaping teaspoons of the fruit mixture into balls. Set a ball on each softened apricot, garnish with some of the sliced almonds and serve.

—*Jayne Cohen*

MAKE AHEAD The *haroset* can be assembled up to 1 hour ahead and stored at room temperature.

Haroset

first courses
chapter 2

Warm Feta with Sautéed Greens

Warm Feta with Sautéed Greens

4 SERVINGS ❋

Serve these peppery greens and feta as an appetizer or as an accompaniment to roast lamb or chicken. It's surprising how much the cheese mellows in flavor when it's warmed.

- ½ pound feta cheese, sliced ¾ inch thick
- ¼ cup extra-virgin olive oil
- 2 teaspoons oregano leaves
- ¼ to ½ teaspoon crushed red pepper
- ¼ teaspoon finely grated lemon zest
- 2 garlic cloves, thinly sliced
- 2 pounds cooking greens, such as kale, Swiss chard or beet greens, stemmed and coarsely chopped

Salt and freshly ground pepper

Assorted olives and crusty bread, for serving

1. Preheat the oven to 375°. Cut the feta into large triangles and arrange them in a single layer in a baking dish. In a small bowl, combine 2 tablespoons of the olive oil with the oregano, crushed red pepper, lemon zest and half of the garlic slices. Spread the marinade all over the feta cheese and let stand for at least 5 minutes or up to an hour.

2. In a large deep skillet, heat the remaining 2 tablespoons of olive oil until shimmering. Add the remaining garlic and cook over moderate heat, stirring, until pale golden, 1 to 2 minutes. Add the greens, a handful at a time, and cook, stirring, until tender, about 4 minutes. Pour off any liquid, season with salt and pepper and keep warm.

3. Bake the feta for about 5 minutes, or until heated through. Spoon the greens onto 4 plates and add the feta, olives and bread. Drizzle any feta juices over the bread and serve immediately.

—*Annie Wayte and Anna Kovel*

WINE Tart, herbal Sauvignon Blanc is almost a mandatory match here. Consider the 1998 Flora Springs or the 1998 Cakebread, both from California.

Pickled Vegetable Antipasto

MAKES 12 CUPS

This antipasto must chill overnight before serving, so plan accordingly.

- ¾ cup tomato sauce
- ½ cup ketchup
- ⅓ cup fresh lemon juice
- ¼ cup extra-virgin olive oil
- ¼ cup tarragon or white wine vinegar
- 1 tablespoon Worcestershire sauce
- 1 tablespoon bottled horseradish
- 1 tablespoon light brown sugar
- 1 garlic clove, minced

Pinch of cayenne pepper

Kosher salt

One 2-pound head of cauliflower, cut into florets

- 4 medium carrots, sliced on the diagonal ⅓ inch thick
- 4 celery ribs, sliced on the diagonal ½ inch thick
- ½ cup white wine vinegar
- 1 pound small button mushrooms, stems trimmed
- ½ cup drained *pepperoncini* peppers

Three 6-ounce cans Italian tuna packed in oil, drained

- 6 caper-filled anchovies
- ½ cup canned California black olives, pitted and drained
- ½ cup pimiento-stuffed Spanish olives, drained
- 3 small kosher dill pickles, cut into thin spears
- ½ cup pickled onions, drained

One 6½-ounce jar marinated artichoke hearts, drained

1. In a large saucepan, combine ½ cup of water with the tomato sauce, ketchup, lemon juice, olive oil, tarragon vinegar, Worcestershire sauce, horseradish, brown sugar and garlic. Add the cayenne pepper and season with salt. Bring to a boil over high heat, then simmer for 20 minutes. Transfer the marinade to a large bowl to cool.

2. In a large saucepan of boiling salted water, cook the cauliflower until barely tender, about 2 minutes. Using a slotted spoon, transfer the cauliflower to a baking sheet to cool. Return the water to a boil. Add the carrots and celery, blanch for 2 minutes and transfer to the baking sheet to cool. Add the wine vinegar to the saucepan and return to a boil. Add the mushrooms, simmer for 1 minute and drain well; transfer to the other vegetables and let cool.

3. Add the vegetables to the marinade, then add the remaining ingredients. Toss gently but thoroughly, cover and refrigerate overnight.

—*Michael Chiarello*

MAKE AHEAD The recipe can be refrigerated for up to 2 weeks.

WINE Try the 1999 Long Vineyards Pinot Grigio and the 1998 Staglin Stagliano Sangiovese, both from Napa Valley.

Herbed Goat Cheese with Potatoes and Grilled Bacon

6 SERVINGS

- 12 small white or red potatoes (about 1¼ pounds)
- ½ pound soft goat cheese, at room temperature
- 2 tablespoons minced chives, plus whole chives for garnish
- 3 garlic cloves, minced

2 teaspoons grappa or marc

2 teaspoons extra-virgin olive oil,
plus more for drizzling

Salt and freshly ground pepper

Six ¼-inch-thick slices meaty bacon
(about 6 ounces)

Six ½-inch-thick slices coarse
peasant bread

1. Steam the potatoes until tender, about 25 minutes. Keep warm. Meanwhile, in a bowl, use a wooden spoon to beat the goat cheese until fluffy. Add the minced chives, garlic, grappa and 2 teaspoons of olive oil. Season with salt and pepper.

2. In a skillet, cook the bacon over moderate heat until slightly crisp, about 3 minutes per side. Drain on paper towels.

3. Toast the bread. Spread the flavored cheese on the toast, drizzle with olive oil and top with a few whole chives. Arrange a cheese toast, a slice of bacon and 2 warm potatoes on each plate and serve. —*Corinne Chapoutier*

MAKE AHEAD The flavored cheese can be refrigerated overnight.

WINE The smoky 1997 Crozes-Hermitage Rouge Les Meysonniers is a great partner for the bacon. Or try the 1997 Châteauneuf-du-Pape Rouge La Bernardine; its thyme and rosemary aromas go beautifully with the olive oil and the herbed cheese.

Swiss Chard and Spinach Pie

8 SERVINGS

This pie is a variation on Greek spanakopita. In the past several years, dishes like these have made the leap from diners to white-tablecloth restaurants.

3 pounds spinach—stemmed,
washed and dried

½ pound Swiss chard, leaves left
whole, stems and ribs trimmed
and finely chopped

¼ cup extra-virgin olive oil

5 large scallions, thinly sliced

½ pound French feta cheese,
coarsely crumbled

½ cup whole-milk cottage cheese

¼ cup finely chopped
flat-leaf parsley

2 tablespoons finely chopped dill

1 tablespoon fresh lemon juice

Pinch of freshly grated nutmeg

Salt and freshly ground pepper

2 large eggs, beaten

⅓ cup clarified butter (see Note)

16 sheets of phyllo dough, thawed
overnight in the refrigerator
if frozen

1. Set a large saucepan over moderately high heat. Add large handfuls of the spinach, tossing constantly with tongs until the leaves are partially wilted before adding the next handful. Drain the spinach and let cool, then squeeze out as much liquid as possible. Coarsely chop the spinach and transfer to a large bowl. Return the saucepan to moderately high heat and repeat with the chard leaves, squeezing them dry.

2. Wipe out the saucepan. Add 2 tablespoons of the olive oil and heat until shimmering. Add the Swiss chard stems and ribs and cook over moderately high heat until crisp-tender, about 4 minutes. Add the scallions and sauté until tender, about 2 minutes. Add the scallions and Swiss chard stems and ribs to the bowl and stir in the feta, cottage cheese, parsley, dill, lemon juice and nutmeg. Season with salt and pepper and stir in the eggs.

3. Preheat the oven to 350°. In a small bowl, mix the clarified butter with the remaining 2 tablespoons of olive oil. Lightly grease a 9-by-13-inch glass or ceramic baking dish. Spread 1 sheet of phyllo dough on a work surface and brush with the butter mixture. Cover with a second sheet of phyllo and brush again. Continue until you have a stack of 8 buttered phyllo sheets. Repeat to form a second stack of 8 buttered phyllo sheets. Line the baking dish with a phyllo stack. Spread the spinach filling evenly on top. Cover with the second phyllo stack; trim the top layer of phyllo flush with that of the bottom layer.

Roll the phyllo edges inward to form a border. Using a sharp knife, lightly score the top stack of phyllo to divide the pie into 8 even servings. Brush any remaining butter over the top.

4. Bake the pie in the bottom of the oven for 1½ hours, or until the phyllo is golden and crisp. Let stand for at least 10 minutes before serving.

—*Grace Parisi*

NOTE Clarifying butter separates the fat from the milk solids, which can scorch at higher temperatures. To make ⅓ cup of clarified butter, melt 1 stick (4 ounces) of unsalted butter in a small saucepan over moderately low heat. Let stand for 5 minutes, then skim off the foam. Pour the clear yellow liquid into a container and discard the milky residue. Clarified butter can be kept refrigerated or frozen for 2 months.

MAKE AHEAD The recipe can be prepared through Step 3 and refrigerated overnight.

WINE A round-textured Sauvignon Blanc will complement the pie filling's

**Herbed Goat Cheese with
Potatoes and Grilled Bacon**

first courses

creamy texture. Try the 1998 Murphy-Goode Fumé Blanc Reserve from California or the 1999 Simunye from South Africa.

Bacon Quiche

MAKES ONE 9-INCH TART

1½ tablespoonsextra-virgin olive oil

1 pound shallots or yellow onions, thinly sliced (4 cups)

6 slices of bacon, cut crosswise into ½-inch strips

½ recipe Pâte Brisée (recipe follows)

1½ ounces Gorgonzola cheese, in small pieces (¼ cup)

4 large eggs, lightly beaten

½ cup heavy cream

½ cup milk

1 teaspoon kosher salt

⅛ teaspoon freshly ground pepper

Pinch of freshly grated nutmeg

I. Heat the oil in a large heavy skillet. Add the shallots and cook over moderately high heat for 2 minutes. Place a sheet of crumpled, lightly moistened parchment paper on the shallots and cook over moderately low heat, stirring occasionally, until golden brown, 30 to 35 minutes. Transfer the shallots to a plate to cool.

2. Add the bacon to the skillet and cook until lightly browned. Drain the bacon on paper towels; add it to the shallots.

3. Preheat the oven to 375°. On a lightly floured surface, roll out the Pâte Brisée to a ¼-inch-thick round. Ease it into a 9-inch fluted tart pan with a removable bottom; trim off any extra. Prick the bottom with a fork, cover and refrigerate for at least 30 minutes.

4. Line the shell with foil and fill with pie weights or dried beans. Bake for 15 minutes, or until the edge is pale gold. Remove the weights and foil. Bake the shell for 8 to 10 minutes longer, or until golden and dry.

5. Set the tart pan on a baking sheet. Spread the shallots and bacon in the shell and top with the Gorgonzola. In a bowl, whisk the eggs with the cream,

milk, salt, pepper and nutmeg. Pour the custard into the shell and bake for 35 minutes, or until the quiche is golden and set in the center. Let cool slightly before removing the side of the pan. Serve warm or at room temperature.

—Sarah Lambert

MAKE AHEAD The quiche can be refrigerated overnight. Reheat in a 325° oven for about 20 minutes.

WINE Salty-sweet flavors suggest a bright, fruity California Pinot Noir with earthy notes, such as the 1997 Morgan.

PATE BRISEE

MAKES ENOUGH DOUGH FOR SIX 4-INCH DOUBLE-CRUSTED POTPIES OR TWO 9-INCH TART SHELLS

Pâte Brisée is a buttery all-purpose French dough that can be used many ways. The recipe below works in Mitchel London's Chicken Potpies (p. 166) and Sarah Lambert's Bacon Quiche, but it can also be used to make empanadas, cookies, cheese wafers and old-fashioned double-crusted, deep-dish and lattice-topped pies.

2 cups all-purpose flour

¾ teaspoon salt

1 stick plus 2 tablespoons (5 ounces) cold unsalted butter, cut into tablespoons

1 large egg yolk

¼ cup ice water

I. In a food processor, pulse the flour with the salt. Add the butter and pulse until the mixture resembles coarse meal. In a small bowl, whisk the egg yolk with the water. With the machine on, slowly add the egg mixture and process until the dough just comes together.

2. Turn the dough out onto a work surface and gather it together. Gently knead the dough 3 times, then form it into an 8-inch log or 2 disks. Wrap the dough in plastic and refrigerate for at least 1 hour or overnight.

—FOOD & WINE Test Kitchen

MAKE AHEAD The dough can be frozen for up to 1 month.

Sweet Onion Tart with Bacon

MAKES ONE 11-INCH TART

Walla Walla onions are large, sweet and juicy. In this tart, they are cooked very slowly over low heat to bring out their flavor. Any sweet onion, such as Vidalia or Maui, would make an acceptable substitute.

PASTRY

2 sticks (½ pound) frozen unsalted butter

1⅔ cups all-purpose flour

1 tablespoon plus 1 teaspoon sugar

½ teaspoon salt

⅔ cup heavy cream

FILLING

½ pound thickly sliced bacon

3 large sweet onions, such as Walla Walla, thinly sliced

Salt and freshly ground black pepper

7 large eggs

1 cup heavy cream

½ cup shredded Gruyère cheese (2 ounces)

1½ tablespoons freshly grated Parmesan cheese

1 teaspoon minced rosemary

¼ teaspoon cayenne pepper

Pinch of freshly grated nutmeg

I. MAKE THE PASTRY: Working over a medium bowl, grate the butter on the large holes of a box grater; freeze. In another bowl, combine the flour, sugar and salt. Using a pastry blender or 2 knives, cut in the butter until the mixture resembles coarse meal. Add the cream and mix with a fork until a dough forms. Turn the dough out onto a lightly floured work surface and pat into a disk. Wrap in plastic and refrigerate until chilled, at least 1 hour.

2. MAKE THE FILLING: In a large skillet, cook the bacon over moderate heat, turning, until crisp, about 6 minutes. Drain on paper towels and cut into 1-inch pieces. Pour off all but 3 tablespoons of the fat. Add the onions to the skillet and cook over low heat, stirring occasionally, until very tender and caramelized, about 1 hour. Season

Sweet Onion Tart with Bacon

with salt and pepper. Let cool.

3. Preheat the oven to 425°. On a lightly floured surface, roll out the dough to a 15-inch round. Fold the dough in half and transfer it to an 11-inch fluted tart pan with a removable bottom. Unfold the dough and press it into the pan. Trim the overhang. Freeze the tart shell until firm, about 10 minutes.

4. Line the tart shell with foil and fill with pie weights or dried beans. Bake for about 30 minutes, or until the pastry starts to dry. Remove the foil and weights and bake for about 3 minutes longer, or until golden brown. Transfer the tart shell to a rack to cool.

5. Turn the oven down to 375°. In a bowl, whisk the eggs with the cream. Stir in the bacon, onions, Gruyère, Parmesan, rosemary, cayenne and nutmeg. Season with ½ teaspoon salt and ¼ teaspoon pepper. Pour the filling into the tart shell and bake for 25 minutes, or until the custard is set. Transfer to a rack to cool slightly. Unmold and serve.   —*Jamie Guerin*

WINE A full-bodied Sémillon makes a fine contrast to the sweet onion and rich pastry. Try L'Ecole Nº 41's 1999 Barrel Fermented Sémillon.

Corn Crespelle with Mascarpone and Capers

6 SERVINGS

These Italian crêpes combine sweet corn, creamy mascarpone, crisp scallions and salty capers. Salt-packed capers, available at specialty food shops and Italian markets, are ideal for this recipe because they keep their flavor better than the ones stored in vinegar. Capers from Pantelleria in the Lipari Islands are particularly delicious. Brined capers that have been rinsed can be substituted.

  1 cup corn kernels (from 2 ears)
  2 large eggs
  ½ cup all-purpose flour
  ½ teaspoon salt
  1 cup milk
  2 tablespoons melted unsalted butter, plus more for frying
1½ cups mascarpone cheese, at room temperature (½ pound)
  7 medium scallions, thinly sliced
  ¼ cup salt-packed capers— soaked in cold water for 5 minutes, drained and coarsely chopped

1. In a food processor, pulse the corn kernels until they become a coarse puree. In a medium bowl, beat the eggs to mix the whites and yolks thoroughly. Stir in the corn puree, flour and salt, then whisk in the milk. Stir in the 2 tablespoons of melted butter, cover with plastic wrap and refrigerate the corn batter for at least 1 hour or overnight.

2. Preheat the oven to 300°. Let the batter return to room temperature, and then whisk it gently. Heat an 8-inch crêpe pan or nonstick skillet. Remove from the heat. Dip a paper towel into about 2 tablespoons of melted butter and rub the bottom and side of the pan generously with the butter.

3. Set the pan over moderately high heat. Pour in 3 tablespoons of the batter and quickly tilt the pan to distribute it evenly; pour any excess batter back into the bowl. Cook until browned on the bottom, about 1 minute. Turn the crespella and cook the second side for about 10 seconds, then slide it out onto a baking sheet. Repeat with the remaining batter to make 12 crespelle, overlapping them slightly on the baking sheet. Just before serving, cover the crespelle loosely with foil and rewarm them in the oven for about 3 minutes.

4. Spread the paler side of each crespella with 2 tablespoons of the mascarpone. Top with 1 tablespoon of scallions and roll up or fold into quarters. Set 2 crespelle on each plate, sprinkle with 1 teaspoon of the capers and some of the remaining scallions and serve at once.

—*Marcia Kiesel*

WINE The delicate flavors and buttery-creamy texture of the mascarpone and the sweetness of the corn-based crespelle call for a round and rich-flavored sparkling wine with a mouth-filling texture as well as enough acidity to stand up to the pungent capers. The Nonvintage Bellavista Franciacorta Brut fills the bill admirably.

Myron's Crab Cocktail

MAKES ABOUT 3 CUPS

- 1 cup ketchup
- ¼ cup drained prepared horseradish
- 1 teaspoon Worcestershire sauce

Dash of Tabasco

- 1 tablespoon fresh lemon juice
- 1 pound back-fin crabmeat, picked over
- ¾ pound cream cheese, softened
- 2 tablespoons sour cream
- 2 tablespoons snipped chives
- 1 pound jumbo lump crabmeat, picked over

Cucumber slices, crackers or toasts, for serving

1. In a small bowl, combine the ketchup with the horseradish, Worcestershire sauce, Tabasco and lemon juice. Set the cocktail sauce aside at room temperature.
2. In a large bowl, combine the back-fin crabmeat with the cream cheese, sour cream and 1 tablespoon of the chives. Spread a ½-inch-thick layer of the crab mixture across a large platter and top with the cocktail sauce. Scatter the lump crabmeat on top and garnish with the remaining 1 tablespoon of chives. Refrigerate the crab cocktail until slightly chilled. Serve with cucumber slices, crackers or toasts.

—Bruce and Eric Bromberg

Myron's Crab Cocktail

Cilantro-Lime Shrimp with Avocado and Tomato Salsa

6 SERVINGS

These shrimp are refrigerated overnight in the marinade to absorb the flavors of the chili sauce, cilantro, pickled ginger and garlic.

- ¾ cup vegetable oil
- 5 tablespoons Thai sweet chili sauce (see Note)
- 3 tablespoons minced cilantro
- 1 tablespoon plus 1 teaspoon finely chopped pickled ginger (see Note)
- 5 garlic cloves—4 minced, 1 smashed
- 1¼ pounds large shrimp, shelled and deveined
- 2 tablespoons rice vinegar
- 1 teaspoon Dijon mustard
- 1 avocado—pitted, peeled and finely diced
- 1 large tomato—halved, seeded and finely chopped
- 2 scallions, finely chopped

Kosher salt

Cracked pepper

Lime wedges, for serving

1. In a large glass or ceramic baking dish, combine ½ cup of the oil with 3 tablespoons of the sweet chili sauce, the cilantro, 1 tablespoon of the pickled ginger and the minced garlic. Add the shrimp and toss well to coat. Cover tightly with plastic wrap and refrigerate overnight, stirring once or twice.
2. In a mini processor, combine the vinegar with the remaining 2 tablespoons of chili sauce, the remaining 1 teaspoon of pickled ginger, the mustard and the smashed garlic clove and puree until the mixture is smooth. With the machine on, add the remaining ¼ cup of oil in a thin stream and process until emulsified. Transfer to a bowl and add the avocado, tomato and scallions. Season with salt.
3. Light a grill. Scrape some of the marinade from the shrimp and grill them over high heat until opaque throughout, 3 to 4 minutes. Transfer the shrimp to a platter and season with cracked pepper. Serve with the salsa and lime wedges. —Alison Tolley

NOTE Thai sweet chili sauce is available at Asian markets. Pickled ginger can be found at Japanese markets.

Garlic Shrimp with Pickled Peppers

4 SERVINGS ❋

Guindilla peppers add a subtle heat to this Basque-inspired dish; if you can't find them, you can substitute Italian *pepperoncini* or other small, moderately hot pickled green peppers.

- 1 cup extra-virgin olive oil
- 1 pound large shrimp, shelled and deveined
- ¼ cup sliced *guindilla* peppers
- 6 garlic cloves, thinly sliced
- 2 tablespoons finely chopped flat-leaf parsley
- ¼ cup plus 2 tablespoons all-purpose flour

Salt

Crusty country bread, for serving

1. Heat the extra-virgin olive oil in a large heavy skillet until shimmering. Add the shrimp and fry over moderate heat, turning once, until bright pink, about 3 minutes.
2. While gently shaking the skillet, add the *guindilla* peppers, garlic and parsley. Sprinkle the flour over the shrimp and cook over low heat, stirring constantly, until a light sauce forms, about 3 minutes longer. Season the shrimp with salt.
3. Spoon the shrimp and sauce onto 4 small plates and serve with crusty country bread.

—Joseph Jiménez de Jiménez

WINE A light, refreshing white, such as the 1998 or 1999 Loriñon from Rioja or a Txacoli from the Basque region, will counter the spiciness of this simple dish without overpowering the flavor of the shrimp.

Shrimp Brochettes with Avocado-Cilantro Salad

10 SERVINGS

- ¼ cup fresh lemon juice
- ¼ cup extra-virgin olive oil, plus more for brushing

Coarse salt and freshly ground pepper

- 4 Hass avocados
- 1½ pounds tomatoes—peeled, seeded and diced
- 1 cup coarsely chopped cilantro
- 10 large shrimp, shelled and deveined

1. In a large bowl, whisk the lemon juice with ¼ cup of the olive oil. Season with salt and pepper. Halve and pit the avocados, and cut them into ¼-inch dice. Add to the bowl and toss with the dressing. Fold in the tomatoes and cilantro. Refrigerate the salad until chilled.

2. Light a grill or preheat a grill pan. Thread each shrimp lengthwise onto a skewer to keep it straight. Brush the shrimp skewers with olive oil and season them with salt and pepper. Grill the shrimp over moderately high heat until cooked, about 2 minutes per side.

3. Spoon the avocado salad onto 10 salad plates. Top each salad with a warm grilled shrimp and serve at once.

—Jean-Christophe Royer

Shrimp and Green Bean Salad with Marjoram

12 SERVINGS

- 2 bay leaves

Two 3-inch strips lemon zest

Fine sea salt or kosher salt

- 2¼ pounds medium shrimp, shelled and deveined
- 2¼ pounds thin green beans or haricots verts
- ¼ cup plus 1 tablespoon extra-virgin olive oil
- ¼ cup fresh lemon juice
- 2½ tablespoons chopped flat-leaf parsley
- 1½ tablespoons chopped marjoram

Freshly ground pepper

1. Bring a large pot of water to a boil. Add the bay leaves, lemon zest and 3 tablespoons of sea salt. Add the shrimp and cook until they start to curl, about 2 minutes. With a slotted spoon, transfer the shrimp to a bowl to cool. Cut the shrimp in half lengthwise and return to the bowl.

2. Bring the water back to a boil and add the green beans. Cook until tender, about 5 minutes. Drain the beans and refresh them under cold water. Discard the bay leaves and the lemon zest. Pat the beans dry and add them to the shrimp.

3. In a small bowl, whisk the olive oil with the lemon juice, parsley, marjoram, ¾ teaspoon of salt and ¼ teaspoon of pepper until the mixture is well combined. Pour the dressing over the shrimp and green beans and toss well to coat. Transfer the salad to a large platter and serve.

—Cesare Casella

MAKE AHEAD The shrimp, beans and dressing can be refrigerated, separately, overnight. Toss just before serving.

Saigon Crêpes with Shrimp, Bacon and Scallions

6 SERVINGS

- 3 strips thickly sliced bacon
- ¾ cup rice flour
- ½ teaspoon turmeric

Pinch of sugar

Salt

One 13½-ounce can unsweetened coconut milk

- 3 tablespoons vegetable oil
- ½ pound medium shrimp—shelled, deveined, halved lengthwise and cut into 1-inch lengths
- 3 large scallions, thinly sliced

Shallot Dipping Sauce (recipe follows)

1. In a medium skillet, cook the bacon over moderately high heat until crisp, about 6 minutes. Drain the bacon on paper towels, then coarsely chop it.

2. In a bowl, whisk the rice flour with the turmeric, sugar and ½ teaspoon salt. Whisk in the coconut milk until smooth.

Shrimp Brochettes with Avocado-Cilantro Salad

3. Heat ½ tablespoon of oil in an 8-inch nonstick skillet until it shimmers. Scatter one-sixth of the shrimp in the skillet, season with salt and cook over moderately high heat until pink, approximately 1 minute. Scatter one-sixth each of the scallions and the bacon in the skillet and cook for 1 minute. Ladle ⅓ cup of the batter over the shrimp, scallions and bacon, spreading it evenly. Cook until the bottom is golden and crisp, 2 to 3 minutes. Flip the crêpe and cook until golden and crisp on the second side, about 2 minutes longer. Transfer to a plate. Repeat to make 5 more crêpes. Serve the crêpes hot, with the dipping sauce on the side.

—Jeff Tunks

SHALLOT DIPPING SAUCE
MAKES ABOUT 1 CUP

- ¼ cup Vietnamese fish sauce (nuoc mam)
- ¼ cup water
- 2 tablespoons distilled white vinegar
- 2 tablespoons fresh lime juice

first courses

Saigon Crêpes with Shrimp, Bacon and Scallions

2 tablespoons sugar

4 garlic cloves, finely diced

4 serrano or Thai chiles, thinly sliced

3 small shallots, finely chopped

Combine all the ingredients in a small bowl and let stand for 30 minutes.

—*J.T.*

Seafood and Scallion Pancakes

6 SERVINGS

Korean pancakes called *jon* come in myriad varieties. After you have tried this classic version, you might enjoy experimenting with shredded leeks, fresh oysters, sautéed ground pork or chopped kimchi.

1 cup all-purpose flour

½ cup potato starch or rice flour

½ teaspoon baking powder

1 heaping teaspoon salt

1 egg, separated

1 cup plus 2 tablespoons cold fish stock, chicken broth or water

Vegetable oil, for frying

6 scallion greens, cut lengthwise into thin strips

6 ounces medium shrimp—shelled, halved lengthwise and deveined

6 ounces cleaned small squid, bodies and tentacles cut lengthwise into thin strips

1 medium red bell pepper, sliced into very thin strips

Soy Dipping Sauce (recipe follows)

1. Sift the flour, potato starch, baking powder and salt into a medium bowl. In a small bowl, whisk the egg white until frothy. Whisk the stock into the flour mixture, then whisk in the egg white until smooth. Let stand at least 1 hour.

2. Pour 1½ tablespoons of vegetable oil into an 8-inch cast-iron skillet and set over moderately high heat for 1 minute. Arrange one-sixth of the scallion greens on the bottom of the skillet in a neat layer, all facing in the same direction; cook for 30 seconds. Pour ⅓ cup of the batter over the scallions. Scatter one-sixth of the shrimp and one-sixth of the squid over the batter and top with one-sixth of the red pepper strips. Stir the egg yolk with a fork, then decoratively drizzle a little of it over the pancake and cook until the underside is golden, about 4 minutes.

3. Using 2 spatulas if necessary, carefully flip the pancake; drizzle a little oil under it if the skillet looks dry. Cook for 2 to 3 minutes longer, until golden brown on the bottom. Turn out onto a plate and repeat to make 5 more. Cut the pancakes into wedges with scissors and serve hot, with the Soy Dipping Sauce.　　—*Anya von Bremzen*

SOY DIPPING SAUCE

MAKES ABOUT ⅔ CUP

6 tablespoons soy sauce or tamari

2 tablespoons warm water

1 tablespoon plus 1 teaspoon Asian sesame oil

1 teaspoon sugar

¼ cup thinly sliced scallion greens

1 tablespoon plus 1 teaspoon toasted sesame seeds

2 serrano chiles, thinly sliced

Combine all of the ingredients in a small bowl and let stand for at least 10 minutes to allow the flavors to develop.

—*A.B.*

Pickled Shrimp and Cucumber Spears

10 SERVINGS

The shrimp and cucumbers need to marinate overnight, so be sure to plan accordingly.

5 cups water

12 large garlic cloves, thinly sliced

8 bay leaves

Eight 3-inch-long strips of lemon zest

6 to 8 small dried red chiles

3 tablespoons kosher salt

½ cup fresh lemon juice

¼ cup sugar

3 pounds medium shrimp, shelled and deveined

1½ pounds unwaxed Kirby or Japanese cucumbers, cut into ¾-inch-wide spears

1. In a large saucepan, combine the water, garlic, bay leaves, lemon zest and chiles. Cover and simmer over low heat for 10 minutes. Uncover, add the salt and let the brine cool.

2. In a small saucepan, combine the lemon juice and sugar and boil over high heat until reduced by half. Add the reduction to the pickling brine.

3. Bring a large saucepan of water to a boil. Add the shrimp and cook for just 1 minute, then drain.

4. Arrange the cucumber spears around the side of a large glass bowl. Put the shrimp in the center and cover with the brine. Place a plate directly on the shrimp and cucumbers and weigh it down with canned goods to keep the shrimp and cucumbers submerged. Cover and refrigerate overnight. Arrange the shrimp and cucumber spears on a platter and serve.

—*Marcia Kiesel*

MAKE AHEAD The shrimp and cucumbers must be refrigerated overnight and served the next day.

Scallop Brochettes with Haricots Verts Salad

8 SERVINGS

If you like, you can spear and grill these brochettes on lavender stems instead of wooden skewers. Fresh lavender is available from Indian Rock Produce (800-882-0512).

- 6 ounces thickly sliced apple-smoked bacon, cut crosswise into ¼-inch strips
- ¼ cup extra-virgin olive oil
- 5 teaspoons red wine vinegar
- Salt and freshly ground pepper
- 1 pound haricots verts
- 24 medium scallops (about 1¾ pounds)

1. Soak 16 wooden skewers in water for at least 30 minutes. Light a grill.

2. In a large skillet, cook the bacon over moderate heat, stirring, until crisp, about 15 minutes. Drain the bacon on paper towels. Transfer 1 tablespoon of the bacon fat to a medium bowl. Whisk in 2 tablespoons of the olive oil and the vinegar. Season with salt and pepper.

3. Cook the haricots verts in a saucepan of boiling salted water until crisp-tender, about 4 minutes; drain and rinse in cold water. Pat dry. Transfer the haricots verts to the vinaigrette and toss to coat.

4. In a bowl, toss the scallops with the remaining 2 tablespoons of oil. Thread 3 scallops onto 2 parallel skewers; repeat to make 8 brochettes. Season the brochettes with salt and pepper and grill over moderate heat until the scallops are medium rare, 2 to 3 minutes per side.

5. Mound the haricots verts on 8 plates. Top each salad with a brochette, sprinkle with the bacon and serve. —*Dominique Macquet*

WINE The creamy 1998 Matanzas Creek Chardonnay makes a delightful like-with-like pairing with the rich bacon vinaigrette. The wine's acidity keeps the combination refreshing.

Scallop Brochettes with Haricots Verts Salad

Scallop Seviche with Avocado Dressing

8 SERVINGS

The inspiration for this dish came from a conch seviche served at a small restaurant in Mérida, Mexico. Scallops make a good substitute here, as conch is not readily available in the States.

SCALLOP SEVICHE

- ¼ cup plus 2 tablespoons fresh lemon juice
- 3 tablespoons fresh orange juice
- 3 tablespoons fresh lime juice
- 2 teaspoons grated lime zest
- 2 teaspoons grated fresh ginger
- 2 teaspoons minced serrano chile
- 1¼ pounds large sea scallops, sliced horizontally ¼ inch thick
- 4 scallions, finely chopped
- 1 red bell pepper, finely diced
- ¼ cup finely chopped cilantro
- 3 tablespoons pure olive oil
- 1 large garlic clove, minced

AVOCADO DRESSING

- 1 avocado, finely diced

Pickled Shrimp and Cucumber Spears

Scallop Seviche with Avocado Dressing

1 small tomato—peeled, seeded and finely diced

1 tablespoon minced red onion

1 tablespoon finely chopped cilantro

1 serrano chile, seeded and minced

1 small garlic clove, minced

1½ tablespoons fresh lime juice

1½ tablespoons extra-virgin olive oil

Salt and freshly ground pepper

1. In a large glass baking dish, combine the lemon, orange and lime juices with the lime zest, ginger and chile. Add the scallops in a single layer and turn them to coat. Cover and refrigerate until the scallops turn white, about 1 hour. Add the scallions, red bell pepper, cilantro, olive oil and garlic and refrigerate for at least 1 hour or for up to 3 hours for firmer scallops.

2. In a medium bowl, combine the avocado with the tomato, red onion, cilantro, chile and garlic. Fold in the lime juice and olive oil and season with salt and pepper.

3. Using a slotted spoon, divide the scallops, scallions and red bell pepper evenly among 6 shallow soup plates. Spoon the avocado dressing next to or over the seviche and pour a little of the marinade all around.

—*Joyce Goldstein*

WINE Though beer is the obvious choice with seviche, the sweet scallops and sharp citrus flavors will find echoes in a crisp lime-scented Australian Riesling from the Clare Valley. Look for the 1998 Pikes or the 1998 Petaluma.

Asparagus with Scallops, Browned Butter and Prosciutto

4 SERVINGS

1 pound white asparagus, peeled, or green asparagus

3½ tablespoons unsalted butter

1 ounce thinly sliced prosciutto, cut into ½-inch-wide strips

1 pound sea scallops

Salt and freshly ground pepper

½ teaspoon finely grated lemon zest

2 tablespoons fresh lemon juice

¼ cup chicken stock or canned low-sodium broth

1. Cook the asparagus in a large saucepan of boiling salted water until tender, about 8 minutes. Using tongs, transfer the asparagus to a colander; leave the pan of water simmering on the stove.

2. Melt 1 tablespoon of butter in a large skillet. Add the prosciutto and cook over low heat until crisp, about 4 minutes. Transfer the prosciutto to a plate.

3. Melt 2 tablespoons of butter in the skillet. Add the scallops, season with salt and pepper and cook over moderately high heat until browned, about 2 minutes per side. Transfer to a plate.

4. Add the lemon zest to the skillet and cook over moderate heat 1 minute, until browned. Add the lemon juice and simmer for 10 seconds. Add the stock and simmer, scraping the bottom of the skillet, until reduced to a rich glaze, about 3 minutes. Swirl in the remaining ½ tablespoon of butter. Return the scallops and any juices to the skillet and heat through over low heat.

5. Return the asparagus to the simmering water to heat through. Season the sauce with salt and pepper. Using tongs, transfer the asparagus to a large platter and spoon the scallops and sauce over it. Top with the fried prosciutto and serve.

—*Marcia Kiesel*

Grilled Squid Skewers with Anchovy Butter

6 SERVINGS

1 pound small squid (bodies no longer than 4 inches), fresh or frozen

8 large anchovy fillets

4 tablespoons unsalted butter, softened

2 teaspoons fresh lemon juice

Salt and freshly ground pepper

Olive oil, for brushing

1. Soak twelve 8-inch wooden skewers in water for about 20 minutes. Cut off the squid tentacles in 1 piece. Cut the

bodies crosswise into 1-inch rings. Thread 3 or 4 pieces of squid body onto each skewer and finish with 1 or 2 tentacles.

2. In a small bowl, using a fork, mash the anchovies with the butter until blended. Stir in the lemon juice and season with salt and pepper.

3. Light a grill or preheat a grill pan until very hot. Brush the squid skewers with olive oil and season with salt and pepper. Grill over a hot fire or over high heat until lightly charred and just cooked, about 1 minute per side. Transfer the squid skewers to a warmed platter and dab them generously with the anchovy butter. Serve the skewers at once.   —*Marcia Kiesel*

WINE A sparkling wine with good acidity will balance the saltiness of the squid. Try either the Nonvintage Nino Franco Prosecco di Valdobbiadene Rustico or the full, bone-dry 1994 Gini Brut Gran Cuvée Millesimo.

Creamed Oysters and Leeks on Toast

10 SERVINGS

You can purchase shucked oysters from your local fish market. The oysters should be plump and fresh-smelling.

Ten ½-inch-thick slices of white bread
   or brioche, crust removed
4 tablespoons unsalted
   butter, softened
1½ pints shucked oysters
   (about 4 dozen), liquor
   drained and reserved
½ cup dry white wine
6 ounces thickly sliced smoked
   bacon, cut into ½-inch dice
2 large leeks, white and tender
   green parts, finely chopped
2 medium celery ribs,
   finely chopped
1 medium onion, finely chopped
2 tablespoons all-purpose flour
½ cup milk
½ cup heavy cream
1 teaspoon chopped thyme

3 tablespoons fresh lemon juice
Salt and freshly ground pepper
Tabasco sauce

I. Preheat the oven to 350°. Spread the bread with 3 tablespoons of the butter and arrange the slices, buttered side up, on a large baking sheet. Toast for about 10 minutes, or until golden brown and crispy. Cut the toasts in half diagonally.

2. In a medium saucepan, combine the reserved oyster liquor and the wine and bring to a simmer over moderately high heat. Add the oysters and simmer over low heat until their edges start to curl, about 3 minutes. With a slotted spoon, transfer the oysters to a plate; reserve the oyster-poaching liquid.

3. In a large skillet, cook the bacon over moderate heat, stirring occasionally, until crisp, about 8 minutes. Using a slotted spoon, transfer the bacon to paper towels to drain. Pour off all but 1 tablespoon of the bacon fat from the skillet and add the remaining 1 tablespoon of butter. Add the leeks, celery and onion and cook over low heat, stirring occasionally, until softened, about 10 minutes. Stir in the flour and cook for 1 minute. Slowly add the reserved oyster-poaching liquid, whisking constantly, until smooth. Simmer over low heat, whisking often, until no floury taste remains, about 3 minutes. Whisk in the milk, cream and thyme and simmer for 3 minutes longer, until thickened and creamy. Stir in the lemon juice, then season with salt, pepper and Tabasco. Fold in the oysters and cook just until warmed through, about 1 minute.

4. Arrange 2 toast halves on each of 10 plates. Spoon the creamed oysters on top, sprinkle with the bacon and serve at once.   —*Susan Spicer*

WINE The fruit flavors of an NV Blanc de Blancs Brut Champagne will point up the saltiness of the oysters and the

bacon; the acidity will cut the creamy sauce. Try the Larmandier Cramant Grand Cru or the Larmandier-Bernier Brut Premier Cru.

Steamed Mussels with Garlic

6 SERVINGS

4 tablespoons unsalted butter
1 medium onion, minced
4 garlic cloves, minced
¼ teaspoon crushed red pepper
1½ cups dry white wine
6 pounds mussels, scrubbed
   and debearded

I. Melt the butter in a large heavy saucepan. Add the onion and cook over moderate heat, stirring, until just softened, about 2 minutes. Add the garlic and crushed red pepper and cook until fragrant, about 1 minute. Add the wine and bring to a boil.

2. Add the mussels and about 1 cup of water. Cover and cook over high heat, stirring occasionally, until the mussels open, 8 to 10 minutes; discard any that

Steamed Mussels with Garlic

first courses

do not open. Spoon the mussels and broth into bowls and serve.

—*Liv Rockefeller*

WINE Muscadet is the classic partner for steamed mussels. Try the lively 1998 Sauvion Muscadet de Sèvre-et-Maine Sur Lie La Nobleraie or the more serious 1999 Château de la Ragotière.

Cherrystone Clam Seviche

4 SERVINGS

This spicy, refreshing seviche delivers a hit of briny, sweet clam flavor. The fishmonger can shuck the clams for you and pack them up in their liquor; be sure that you get the shells as well, for serving.

- 12 cherrystone clams, scrubbed
- ⅓ cup minced red onion
- 5 tablespoons fresh lime juice, plus lime wedges, for serving

Cherrystone Clam Seviche

- 2 jalapeños, seeded and minced
- 1 medium tomato, seeded and cut into ¼-inch dice
- 2 tablespoons chopped cilantro

Freshly ground pepper
Cilantro sprigs, for serving

1. Shuck the clams over a medium bowl. Scrape and clean 20 of the best half shells and refrigerate.
2. Cut the clams into ½-inch pieces and

place them in a clean bowl. Strain ¼ cup of the clam liquor over the clams. Add the onion, lime juice, jalapeños, tomato and cilantro and season with pepper. Cover and refrigerate for at least 1 hour or for up to 2 hours.
3. Nestle the clam half shells on a bed of finely crushed ice. Spoon the clam seviche and any clam liquor into the cleaned shells. Garnish with cilantro sprigs and serve with lime wedges.

—*Jasper White*

WINE A bright white with lots of fruit and no apparent oak will tame the kick of the jalapeños and the tang of lime in this seviche. Try the 1998 Campanile Pinot Grigio from Italy or, for a more elegant first course, the 1997 Château de Seuil Graves from France.

Fregola with Clams

6 SERVINGS

Fregola—also known as *fregula*—is the missing link between pasta from Italy and couscous from North Africa. It is made from semolina, like couscous, but is cooked in ample liquid, like pasta. *Fregola* is made by home cooks throughout Sardinia; it can be purchased at specialty stores in the U.S.

- ¼ cup extra-virgin olive oil
- 3 garlic cloves, finely chopped
- 3 oil-packed sun-dried tomato halves, drained and finely chopped
- ¼ cup finely chopped flat-leaf parsley, plus more for garnish
- 4 dozen small Manila clams or cockles, scrubbed and rinsed
- 1 cup dry white wine

Freshly ground black pepper
Pinch of crushed red pepper

- 4 cups light chicken stock or canned low-sodium broth

Salt

- ½ pound large *fregola* (1½ cups)

1. In a large saucepan, combine the olive oil, garlic, sun-dried tomatoes and 2 tablespoons of the parsley and cook over moderate heat until the garlic is

Fregola with Clams

softened but not browned. Add the clams, cover and cook over moderately high heat for 3 minutes, shaking the pan occasionally. Add the remaining 2 tablespoons of parsley and the wine, black pepper and crushed red pepper. Cook, stirring, until all of the clams have opened, 5 to 8 minutes total. As the clams open, transfer them to a bowl with a slotted spoon.

2. Pour the clam juices into a clean large saucepan, stopping before you reach any grit at the bottom. Add the stock, season with salt and bring to a boil. Gradually add the *fregola,* a little at a time so that the stock never stops boiling, and cook until just tender, about 10 minutes. Fold in the clams to heat through. Spoon the *fregola* into shallow bowls, garnish with parsley and serve. —*Nancy Harmon Jenkins*

WINE The simple flavors here are best set off by a refreshing white with a slightly salty edge. The 1998 Sella & Mosca Le Arenarie, a Sardinian Sauvignon Blanc, is ideal. Or try a Portuguese Vinho Verde with a slight sparkle, like the 1998 Quinta da Aveleda.

Marinated Fried Fish

6 SERVINGS

This fish is first deep-fried, then marinated and chilled. In Egypt, cooks use Mediterranean bream to make this dish, but you can substitute any firm, white fish.

Pure olive oil, for frying

2 pounds skinless monkfish or cod fillets, cut into 2-inch-long pieces

Kosher salt

All-purpose flour, for dredging

1 onion, finely chopped

¾ cup coarsely chopped cilantro

¼ cup plus 2 tablespoons extra-virgin olive oil

Juice of 1 lemon

2 garlic cloves, crushed

1 red or green chile—stemmed, seeded and finely chopped

1. In a medium saucepan, heat 1 inch of the pure olive oil to 350°. Season the fish with salt, then dredge it in the flour, turning to coat lightly. Working in batches, add the fish to the oil and fry, turning once, until golden, 4 to 5 minutes for monkfish, 3 to 4 minutes for cod. Using a slotted spoon, transfer the fish to paper towels to drain.

2. In a bowl, combine the onion with the cilantro, extra-virgin olive oil, lemon juice, garlic, chile and ½ teaspoon of salt. Arrange the fish in a single layer in a shallow glass or ceramic dish, then spoon the marinade over it and turn to coat. Let stand at room temperature for at least 1 hour. Refrigerate and serve cold. —*Claudia Roden*

Home-Cured Salmon

8 SERVINGS 🏵

1½ tablespoons kosher salt

1 tablespoon light brown sugar

1 pound center-cut salmon fillet, with skin

Flavoring Rub (recipes follow)

1. Combine the salt and sugar in a small bowl. Set the salmon fillet skin side down on a large sheet of plastic wrap. Rub the salt and sugar evenly over both sides of the fish.

2. Select one of the five Flavoring Rubs that follow and apply it as directed.

3. Wrap the salmon tightly in the plastic and put the package in a skillet. Top with another, smaller skillet and weigh it down with four 1-pound cans. Refrigerate for 36 hours, turning the package once. When this curing process is complete, wrap the cured salmon in a fresh sheet of plastic wrap and refrigerate until ready to serve.

4. To serve, use a long, narrow knife held almost parallel to the fish to cut the salmon fillet into about ⅛-inch thick slices. —*Sally Schneider*

ONE SERVING Calories 79 kcal, Total Fat 2.0 gm, Saturated Fat 0.3 gm, Protein 11.4 gm, Carbohydrates 2.1 gm

PEPPER AND FRESH HERB RUB

1 teaspoon finely grated lemon zest

½ teaspoon black peppercorns

½ teaspoon white peppercorns

6 allspice berries

¼ teaspoon coriander seeds

1 tablespoon plus 1 teaspoon Cognac or Armagnac

¼ cup finely chopped herbs, such as flat-leaf parsley, chervil and chives, in any combination

Spread the lemon zest over the skinless side of the salmon fillet. In a mortar or a spice grinder, coarsely grind the black and white peppercorns with the allspice berries and the coriander seeds. Rub the ground spices over both sides of the fish. Drizzle on the Cognac or Armagnac and roll the salmon fillet in the mixed fresh herbs to coat. —*S.S.*

GRAPPA RUB

1 teaspoon finely grated lemon zest

1 tablespoon plus 1 teaspoon grappa

1½ teaspoons coarsely ground black pepper

¾ cup coarsely chopped flat-leaf parsley

Sprinkle the lemon zest over the skinless side of the salmon. Drizzle the grappa on top. Rub the black pepper over both sides of the fish, then roll the fish in the chopped parsley to coat. —*S.S.*

AQUAVIT AND JUNIPER RUB

1 teaspoon finely grated lime zest

1 tablespoon plus 1 teaspoon aquavit

1 tablespoon crushed juniper berries

1½ teaspoons coarsely ground pepper

Sprinkle the lime zest over the skinless side of the salmon and drizzle with the aquavit. Rub the juniper and pepper all over both sides of the fish. —*S.S.*

first courses

salmon strategies

Six creative ways to serve cured salmon:

As carpaccio Arrange paper-thin slices on a plate garnished with herbs, fresh lemon juice and light sour cream.

As tea sandwiches Place thin slices on lightly buttered firm-textured white bread with thin slices of cucumber or watercress.

As Asian tea sandwiches Serve thin slices on molded, vinegared sushi rice, with chives or sesame seeds.

As a salad Layer thin slices with slices of ripe Hass avocado and watercress sprigs and dress them with fresh lime juice mixed with extra-virgin olive oil.

As a tartare Finely dice and toss with extra-virgin olive oil and chopped herbs.

As a topping Place thin slices on corn cakes, potato pancakes or buckwheat blini or on hot corn bread; top with chives and a dollop of light sour cream.

TARRAGON AND PERNOD RUB

- 1 teaspoon finely grated lemon zest
- 1 tablespoon plus 1 teaspoon Pernod or other anise liqueur
- 1 teaspoon coarsely ground black pepper
- ⅓ cup tarragon leaves

Spread the lemon zest over the skinless side of the salmon and drizzle with the Pernod. Rub the pepper over both sides of the fish, then roll the fillet in the tarragon leaves.   —*S.S.*

SOUTH OF THE BORDER TEQUILA AND CILANTRO RUB

- 1 teaspoon finely grated lime zest
- 1 tablespoon plus 1 teaspoon tequila
- 1 teaspoon coarsely ground pepper
- 1 cup cilantro leaves

Spread the lime zest over the skinless side of the salmon and drizzle with the tequila. Rub the pepper over both sides. Roll the salmon in the cilantro leaves.   —*S.S.*

Chopped Salmon with Capers

10 SERVINGS

This salmon spread can be served either in a bowl as an hors d'oeuvre or in small ramekins at the table as a first course.

- 2 cups water
- 2 cups dry white wine
- 2 pounds center-cut skinless salmon fillet
- ½ cup mayonnaise
- 1 small onion, minced
- One 3-ounce jar nonpareil capers, drained
- ½ cup chopped flat-leaf parsley
- 2 garlic cloves, minced
- 1 tablespoon fresh lemon juice
- 1 teaspoon Dijon mustard
- ½ pound thinly sliced smoked salmon, cut into thin strips

Salt and freshly ground pepper
Fennel Crackers (p. 248)

1. In a large deep skillet, bring the water and wine to a simmer. Add the salmon fillet, return the liquid to a simmer and poach the fish over low heat until cooked but slightly rare in the center, about 20 minutes. Transfer to a platter to cool. Flake the fish with a fork.

2. In a large bowl, combine the mayonnaise, onion, capers, parsley, garlic, lemon juice and mustard. Gently fold in the poached and smoked salmon and season with salt and pepper. Spoon the smoked salmon spread into 10 small ramekins or into a single serving bowl and serve with the Fennel Crackers.

—*Jamie Guerin*

MAKE AHEAD The salmon can be cooked and flaked and then refrigerated overnight, so that the whole dish can be finished several hours before serving and refrigerated.

WINE The rich salmon is a perfect showcase for a mouth-filling and robust Sémillon. An excellent choice would be L'Ecole Nº 41's 1999 Seven Hills Vineyard Estate.

Marinated Anchovies with Vegetables

8 SERVINGS

Fresh marinated anchovies can be purchased in the deli section of many Italian gourmet markets.

- 5 cups water
- 2 cups Champagne or white wine vinegar
- ½ cup sugar
- ½ cup kosher salt
- 2 medium carrots, cut into very thin matchsticks
- 2 large shallots, thinly sliced
- 1 medium fennel bulb—halved lengthwise, cored and sliced lengthwise ¼ inch thick
- One 2½-pound head of cauliflower, cut into 1-inch florets
- ½ pound thin green beans or haricots verts

Bagna Cauda Vinaigrette (recipe follows)

- 32 marinated anchovy fillets (about ½ pound)

Freshly ground pepper

1. In a large glass bowl, combine the water with the vinegar, sugar and salt; stir to dissolve the sugar and salt. Add the carrots, shallots, fennel and cauliflower, submerging them completely in the brine. Cover and refrigerate the vegetables for 24 hours.

2. In a medium saucepan of boiling water, cook the green beans until bright green and barely tender, about 3 minutes. Drain and refresh under cold running water. Pat the beans dry.

3. Drain the pickled vegetables and place in a large bowl. Add the green beans and the Bagna Cauda Vinaigrette and toss well. Arrange the vegetables on plates, top with the marinated anchovy fillets and a sprinkling of freshly ground pepper and serve.

—*Mario Batali*

MAKE AHEAD The pickled vegetables can be drained and refrigerated for up to 5 days. Toss with the green beans and vinaigrette before serving.

BAGNA CAUDA VINAIGRETTE

MAKES ABOUT ⅔ CUP

Traditional *bagna cauda* is served as a warm dip for raw vegetables. This version can be used as a cold dressing for hearty greens and vegetables.

- 6 anchovy fillets
- 2 garlic cloves, halved
- 3 tablespoons fresh lemon juice
- ¼ cup extra-virgin olive oil
- 3 tablespoons heavy cream

Salt and freshly ground pepper

In a mini food processor, combine the anchovies and garlic and puree until smooth. Add the lemon juice and oil and blend well. Pour in the cream and process until smooth. Scrape into a bowl and season with salt and pepper.

—*M.B.*

MAKE AHEAD The vinaigrette can be refrigerated for up to 1 day.

Chicken-Liver Terrine with Shallots

8 SERVINGS

Chicken livers never had it so good. The mellow flavor and silky, melting texture of this terrine make it reminiscent of foie gras.

- ¼ cup sugar
- 2 tablespoons water
- 10 medium shallots, coarsely chopped
- 5 tablespoons Cognac
- 3 sticks (¾ pound) plus 4 tablespoons unsalted butter, at cool room temperature, cut into tablespoons
- 2 pounds chicken livers, cleaned

Kosher salt and freshly ground pepper

Cornichons and toasted sourdough bread, for serving

1. In a medium saucepan, combine the sugar with the water and simmer over moderate heat, without stirring, until an amber caramel forms, approximately 8 minutes. Add the shallots and stir well, then add the Cognac. Cover and simmer over low heat, stirring occasionally, until the caramel

---

easy alternatives to asian ingredients

Southeast Asian food thrives on inventiveness. So when you're looking for substitutions for hard-to-find ingredients, be creative:

Bird chiles can be replaced with serranos, which are larger but have less heat, so replace one bird chile with one serrano.

Dried rice noodles can be replaced with soba noodles or Italian vermicelli noodles. If you cook them in advance, toss them with a little vegetable oil to avoid sticking.

Dried shrimp are often used in flavor pastes; try cooked and chopped fresh shrimp, and add salt or fish sauce to taste.

Fish sauce can be replaced with minced anchovies (rinse if they are salt-packed) or sea salt with a dash of good soy sauce, such as low-sodium Kikkoman.

Fresh herbs such as cilantro, mint, Thai basil and Vietnamese coriander are somewhat interchangeable. Also try chopped arugula, watercress or sorrel.

---

has dissolved and the shallots are soft, about 10 minutes. Spread the mixture in a large dish and refrigerate for 20 minutes.

2. In a large skillet, melt the 4 tablespoons of butter. Add the chicken livers and season them with salt and pepper. Cook over high heat until firm on both sides and deep pink in the center, about 3 minutes per side. Transfer the livers and their juices to a shallow dish and let cool to room temperature. Refrigerate the livers for 20 minutes.

3. In a food processor, combine the livers with the shallot mixture and process until pureed. With the machine running, gradually add the remaining 3 sticks of butter until thoroughly incorporated. Strain the puree through a fine sieve set over a large bowl. Season with salt and pepper.

4. Line a 4-cup terrine or loaf pan with sheets of plastic wrap, leaving a 3-inch overhang all the way around. Scrape the puree into the terrine and pull the overhanging plastic wrap over the top to cover it tightly. Refrigerate the terrine until very firm, at least overnight and for up to 5 days. Unwrap the terrine and turn it out on a platter. Serve the terrine chilled, with cornichons and sourdough toasts.

—*Jean-Louis Palladin*

Spicy Sausage Salad

6 SERVINGS

- 2 tablespoons long-grain rice
- 1 pound hot or sweet Italian sausages, or Thai sausages
- 3 tablespoons fresh lime juice
- 2 tablespoons Thai fish sauce
- 1 bird chile, minced

Freshly ground pepper

- 1 large shallot, thinly sliced crosswise and divided into rings
- ½ cup coarsely chopped cilantro
- ½ cup coarsely chopped mint

1. Light the grill or preheat the broiler. In a small skillet, toast the rice over moderately high heat, shaking the skillet, until the rice is golden brown, about 3 minutes. Transfer the rice to a plate to cool completely. Grind the rice to a fine powder in a spice mill.

2. Cook the sausages about 5 inches from the heat for about 4 minutes per side, or until browned and cooked through. Let cool, then slice the sausages crosswise ⅓ inch thick.

3. In a small bowl, combine the lime juice, fish sauce and chile. Season with pepper. In a shallow bowl, toss the sausage slices with the shallot, cilantro and mint. Pour the dressing over the salad and toss well. Just before serving, sprinkle the salad with 1 to 2 tablespoons of the roasted rice powder.

—*Naomi Duguid and Jeffrey Alford*

chapter 3

Mixed Salad with Three Vinegars

Baby Greens with Cider Vinaigrette

10 SERVINGS

This tangy salad makes a great partner to a cheese course.

- ¾ cup apple cider
- 2 tablespoons cider vinegar
- 1 small shallot, minced
- ½ teaspoon Dijon mustard
- 1 tablespoon vegetable oil

Salt and freshly ground pepper

- 10 cups loosely packed assorted baby greens, such as red oak leaf, arugula and mizuna (about 10 ounces)

1. In a small saucepan, boil the apple cider over high heat until reduced to 2 tablespoons, about 10 minutes; let cool.
2. In a large bowl, combine the reduced cider with the vinegar and shallot. Whisk in the mustard and oil and season with salt and pepper. Add the greens and toss. Divide among 10 plates and serve.
—*Jamie Guerin*

MAKE AHEAD The vinaigrette can be refrigerated for up to 1 day.

WINE A rich and buttery Chardonnay such as the 1999 Columbia Valley is ideal with the simple salad.

Mixed Salad with Three Vinegars

6 SERVINGS

The combination of three vinegars adds a distinctive note to this vinaigrette.

- 2 teaspoons Dijon mustard
- 2 teaspoons red wine vinegar
- 1 teaspoon balsamic vinegar
- 1 teaspoon raspberry vinegar
- 3 tablespoons extra-virgin olive oil

Salt and freshly ground pepper

- 2 large heads Boston lettuce, torn into bite-size pieces
- 1 large head radicchio, torn into bite-size pieces
- ½ cup Parmesan shavings (2 ounces)

1. In a salad bowl, combine the mustard with the three vinegars. Whisk in the olive oil and season with salt and pepper.

2. Add the Boston lettuce and radicchio; toss to coat. Mound the salad on plates, top with the Parmesan shavings and serve.
—*Ibu Poilâne*

Garlicky Palestinian Salad

6 SERVINGS

- 2 medium garlic cloves, smashed
- ½ teaspoon salt
- 2 tablespoons fresh lemon juice
- ¼ cup plus 2 tablespoons extra-virgin olive oil
- 1 large head of romaine lettuce, leaves torn into 2-inch pieces
- 3 medium tomatoes, cut in wedges
- 1 large European cucumber— peeled, seeded and cut into ¾-inch dice

1. In a mortar, pound the garlic with the salt to a smooth paste. Stir in the lemon juice, then gradually whisk in the oil.

2. In a large bowl, toss the romaine with the tomatoes and cucumber. Stir the lemon dressing. Pour the dressing over the salad, toss well and serve.
—*Sara Jenkins*

Balsamic Caesar Salad

8 SERVINGS ✳

For anchovy lovers, leave some of the fillets whole and use as garnish.

One 2-ounce can anchovies fillets, drained and coarsely chopped

- 3 tablespoons balsamic vinegar
- 2 tablespoons mayonnaise
- 1 tablespoon Worcestershire sauce
- 1 teaspoon minced garlic
- ½ teaspoon freshly ground pepper
- ¼ cup plus 2 tablespoons extra-virgin olive oil
- ¼ cup freshly grated Pecorino Romano cheese
- 2 heads romaine lettuce (about 1 pound each), torn into bite-size pieces
- 1 small red onion, thinly sliced
- 1 cup homemade or store-bought plain or Parmesan croutons

1. Put the anchovies, vinegar, mayonnaise, Worcestershire sauce, garlic

and pepper in a mini processor; process until finely chopped. With the machine on, add the olive oil in a steady stream. Add the cheese and pulse just until combined.

2. In a bowl, toss the lettuce, onion and croutons with half of the dressing. Add the remaining dressing, toss well and serve.
—*Christine Dimmick*

Grilled Fennel and Arugula Salad

20 SERVINGS

- 10 medium fennel bulbs (about 1 pound each), trimmed and cut into 2-inch-thick wedges

Extra-virgin olive oil

- ½ cup fresh lemon juice
- 5 garlic cloves, minced

Salt and freshly ground pepper

- 3 pounds arugula, large stems discarded
- 1½ cups lightly packed small basil leaves

1. In a steamer set over a large saucepan of simmering water, steam the fennel wedges in a single layer until they are just barely tender, about 5 minutes. Let the fennel cool to room temperature. Brush the wedges with olive oil.

2. In a medium bowl, whisk ¾ cup of olive oil with the lemon juice and

Balsamic Caesar Salad

garlic; season with salt and pepper.

3. Light a grill. Season the fennel wedges with salt and pepper and grill over a moderately low fire for about 6 minutes per side, or until lightly charred and crisp-tender. Transfer to a large platter.

4. In a large bowl, toss the arugula with the basil and ½ cup of the dressing. Mound the salad on serving platters and arrange the grilled fennel on top. Drizzle the remaining dressing over the fennel and serve. —*Martin Dodd*

MAKE AHEAD The recipe can be prepared through Step 2 up to 1 day ahead. Refrigerate the steamed fennel and dressing separately.

Goat Cheese Truffles with Peperonata

8 SERVINGS

- ½ cup extra-virgin olive oil, plus more for drizzling
- 2 red bell peppers, cut into thin strips
- 2 yellow bell peppers, cut into thin strips
- ¼ cup sherry vinegar

Salt and freshly ground pepper
- 1½ pounds arugula, large stems discarded
- 2 tablespoons fresh lemon juice
- 1 pound mild soft goat cheese, at room temperature
- 2 tablespoons fennel pollen or crushed fennel seeds (see Note)
- 2 tablespoons poppy seeds
- 2 tablespoons sweet paprika

Eight ½-inch-thick slices Italian peasant bread, grilled or toasted

1. In a skillet, heat ¼ cup of the olive oil. Add the peppers and cook over moderately high heat, stirring occasionally, until they start to brown, about 8 minutes. Add the vinegar and cook over low heat until the peppers are tender, about 10 minutes. Season with salt and pepper and transfer to a bowl.

2. Prepare a bowl of ice water. In a pot of boiling water, blanch the arugula until wilted, about 10 seconds. Transfer to the ice water to chill. Drain the arugula and gently squeeze it dry; chop coarsely.

3. In a small bowl, combine the lemon juice with the remaining ¼ cup of olive oil. Season with salt and pepper.

4. Put the goat cheese in a bowl; season with salt and pepper. Using a tablespoon, scoop up the cheese and roll it into 24 balls. Put the fennel seeds, poppy seeds and paprika in bowls. Roll 8 cheese balls in the fennel seeds, 8 in the poppy seeds and 8 in the paprika.

5. To serve, mound the arugula on 8 plates and top with the bell peppers. Place one of each kind of goat cheese truffle on top of the arugula and drizzle with olive oil. Place a slice of the bread next to the arugula and serve.

 —*Mario Batali*

NOTE Fennel pollen is available from Tavolo (800-700-7336).

Mixed Asian Salad with Macadamia Nuts

6 SERVINGS

- 2 tablespoons mayonnaise
- 1 tablespoon rice vinegar
- 1 tablespoon white wine vinegar
- 1 tablespoon soy sauce
- 2 teaspoons honey
- 1 teaspoon finely grated fresh ginger
- 1 teaspoon Asian sesame oil
- 1 large garlic clove, minced
- ½ teaspoon Sriracha chili sauce or other hot chili sauce
- ¼ cup vegetable oil

Salt and freshly ground pepper
- ½ cup macadamia nuts (3 ounces)
- 1 tablespoon sesame seeds
- ¾ pound baby Asian greens or mesclun (18 cups)

One 3-ounce package enoki mushrooms, trimmed and separated

1. In a blender, combine the mayonnaise, rice and white wine vinegars, soy sauce, honey, ginger, sesame oil, garlic and chili sauce and process to mix. With the machine on, blend in the vegetable oil in a thin stream. Scrape the dressing into a small bowl and season with salt and pepper.

2. In a medium skillet, toast the macadamia nuts over moderately low heat, shaking the skillet, until the nuts are a deep golden brown, 4 to 5 minutes. Transfer the nuts to a plate to cool. Add the sesame seeds to the skillet and toast until a deep golden brown, about 3 minutes. Transfer the sesame seeds to a plate to cool. Coarsely chop the macadamia nuts.

3. In a very large bowl, toss the baby Asian greens with the enoki mushrooms. Pour the dressing over the salad and toss well. Scatter the toasted macadamia nuts and sesame seeds all over the salad and toss briefly once more. Serve the salad at once.

 —*Jeff Tunks*

Frisée Salad with Lardons

8 SERVINGS

This traditional French salad has been on the menu at the Odéon bistro in New York City since it opened in 1980.

- ¾ pound lean slab bacon, cut into ½-inch dice
- 2 cups diced baguette (½ inch)
- 1 tablespoon white wine vinegar
- 8 large eggs

Peanut or vegetable oil
- 3 large shallots, thinly sliced

Salt and freshly ground pepper
- 2 large garlic cloves, chopped
- ¼ cup plus 2 tablespoons red wine vinegar

Two 1-pound heads frisée, leaves torn into bite-size pieces

1. In a large skillet, cook half the bacon over moderate heat until just crisp, 4 to 5 minutes. Transfer the bacon to a bowl and repeat with the remaining bacon. Pour all but 2 tablespoons of the bacon fat into a small glass measuring cup.

2. Reheat the bacon fat in the skillet. Add the diced baguette and cook over moderately high heat, stirring a few times, until crisp, about 4 minutes. Transfer the croutons to a plate to cool. Toss in the bowl with the bacon.

3. Bring a large skillet of water to a boil. Add the white wine vinegar. Break 1 of the eggs into a small cup and slide the egg into the water. Repeat with 3 more eggs. Simmer over moderate heat until the whites are firm and the yolks are soft, about 3 minutes. Using a slotted spoon, transfer the poached eggs to a large platter lined with paper towels. Repeat with the remaining eggs. Keep the poaching water at a low simmer.

4. Measure the reserved bacon fat into a large skillet. Add enough peanut oil to equal 1/3 cup. Add the shallots, season generously with salt and pepper and cook over low heat until softened, about 3 minutes. Add the garlic and cook until fragrant, about 1 minute. Whisk in the red wine vinegar and remove the dressing from the heat.

5. Return the poached eggs to the simmering water to reheat for 30 to 40 seconds. Bring the dressing back to a simmer over low heat. Add the frisée to the bacon and croutons in the bowl, add the hot dressing and toss well. Season with salt and pepper. Mound the salad in serving bowls or on plates and top each with a poached egg. Serve at once.

—*Marcia Kiesel*

MAKE AHEAD The eggs can be poached up to 2 hours ahead. Refrigerate; then allow time for them to return to room temperature before reheating. To reheat, place the eggs in a saucepan of simmering water for 30 to 40 seconds, drain, pat dry and serve.

WINE A dry but fruity red with good acidity and a slight earthiness, such as a Beaujolais-Villages, can balance the flavors in this salad. Two good choices: the 1999 Louis Jadot and the 1999 Georges Duboeuf Flower Label.

Frisée Salad with Bacon and Croutons

Frisée Salad with Bacon and Croutons

8 SERVINGS

This is an adaptation of the ubiquitous French salad of bitter greens tossed with a warm bacon dressing. Be sure to use double-smoked slab bacon here—its intense smoky flavor makes all the difference in this hearty salad.

- 1 garlic clove, halved
- ¾ pound cleaned frisée or a mixture of curly chicory and dandelion greens (about 16 packed cups)
- 6 ounces lean double-smoked slab bacon, sliced ⅓ inch thick, then cut into ⅓-inch dice
- 1 cup crustless peasant bread, cut into ⅓-inch dice
- 1 tablespoon pure olive oil
- 3 tablespoons balsamic vinegar
- 1 tablespoon water

Salt and freshly ground pepper

1. Rub the inside of a large salad bowl with the cut sides of the garlic clove and discard the garlic. Put the cleaned greens in the bowl, cover with plastic wrap and refrigerate until ready to finish the salad.

2. In a large skillet, cover the bacon and cook over low heat until browned and crisp, 6 to 8 minutes. With a slotted spoon, transfer the bacon to paper towels to drain. Pour the rendered bacon fat into a small bowl; you should have about 1 tablespoon.

3. Pour 2 teaspoons of the fat back into the skillet and when it is hot, add

Tomato, Avocado and Roasted-Corn Salad

over moderately high heat until golden brown, about 7 minutes. Transfer to the plate with the bacon.

4. Add the vinegar to the skillet and bring to a boil. Add the cream and boil for 1 minute. Pour the boiling vinaigrette over the dandelion greens. Add the mushrooms and bacon and season with salt and pepper. Toss well and serve immediately. *—Eric Ripert*

Tomato, Avocado and Roasted-Corn Salad

12 SERVINGS

    5 ears of corn, shucked
 ½ cup plus 2 tablespoons
       extra-virgin olive oil
Salt and freshly ground pepper
 ½ cup raw pumpkin seeds
    3 tablespoons fresh lime juice
    2 tablespoons sherry vinegar
    1 teaspoon sugar
 ¼ teaspoon hot sauce
 ⅛ teaspoon cinnamon
1½ pounds arugula (4 bunches),
       large stems discarded, leaves
       torn into bite-size pieces
    3 ripe avocados—peeled, pitted
       and cut into ½-inch dice
    2 large red tomatoes, cut into
       ½-inch dice
    2 large yellow tomatoes, cut into
       ½-inch dice
    2 medium cucumbers—peeled,
       seeded and cut into ¼-inch dice
    3 ounces *queso fresco* or *ricotta
       salata,* crumbled (¾ cup)

1. Preheat the oven to 500°. On a rimmed baking sheet, drizzle the corn with 2 tablespoons of the olive oil. Season the ears with salt and pepper and roast for about 25 minutes, turning a few times, until the kernels are browned; let cool. Cut the kernels from the cobs and transfer to a bowl.

2. Turn the oven down to 400°. Spread the pumpkin seeds in a pie plate and bake for about 4 minutes, or until lightly browned. Transfer to a plate to cool.

3. Put ½ cup of the corn kernels in a

the diced bread. Cook the croutons over moderate heat, tossing occasionally, until golden brown, about 4 minutes. Transfer the croutons to a plate to cool.

4. In the same skillet, heat the olive oil with the remaining 1 teaspoon of bacon fat. Add the crisp bacon, the balsamic vinegar and the water and bring to a boil. Pour half of this dressing over the greens and toss to coat thoroughly. Add the remaining dressing, croutons, salt and pepper and toss again. Mound the salad on 8 warm plates and serve at once.

—Sally Schneider

ONE SERVING Calories 96 kcal, Total Fat 6.4 gm, Saturated Fat 1.7 gm

Dandelion Salad with Bacon and Mushrooms

6 SERVINGS

    1 pound young dandelion greens or
       chicory, torn into bite-size pieces
    5 ounces sliced bacon, cut
       crosswise into ⅓-inch strips
 ½ pound mushrooms, thickly sliced
Salt and freshly ground pepper
    3 tablespoons aged sherry vinegar
 ¼ cup heavy cream

1. Put the dandelion greens in a heatproof bowl.

2. In a large skillet, cook the bacon over moderate heat until crisp. Transfer the bacon to a plate.

3. Add the mushrooms to the skillet and season with salt and pepper. Cook

Warm Mushroom Salad

blender. Add the lime juice, sherry vinegar, sugar, hot sauce and cinnamon and puree. With the machine on, add the remaining ½ cup of olive oil in a thin stream and blend until emulsified. Scrape the vinaigrette into a bowl and season with salt and pepper.

4. In a large bowl, toss the remaining corn kernels with the arugula, avocados, red and yellow tomatoes and cucumbers. Add the vinaigrette and toss well. Mound the salad on a large platter, scatter the pumpkin seeds and crumbled cheese on top and serve.

—*Elizabeth Falkner*

MAKE AHEAD The recipe can be prepared through Step 3 up to 1 day ahead. Refrigerate the roasted corn and the vinaigrette separately. Store the pumpkin seeds in an airtight container at room temperature.

Warm Mushroom Salad

6 SERVINGS

This terrific salad is made with warm mushrooms that develop great meaty flavor when cooked with soy sauce.

- 3 pounds medium white mushrooms, trimmed and quartered
- 3 tablespoons fresh lemon juice

- 2 tablespoons unsalted butter
- 2 tablespoons plus 1 teaspoon pure olive oil
- Salt and freshly ground pepper
- 1 tablespoon soy sauce
- 3 tablespoons extra-virgin olive oil
- 3 tablespoons sherry vinegar
- 2 tablespoons Marsala
- 2 teaspoons tomato paste
- 2 garlic cloves, minced
- 3 large shallots, thinly sliced
- 6 cups coarsely shredded romaine lettuce
- 2 cups coarsely shredded Boston lettuce
- ½ cup shredded Gouda cheese, aged Gouda or goat Gouda (1 ounce)

I. In a large bowl, toss the mushrooms with the lemon juice. Preheat the oven to 300°. In a large skillet, melt the butter in 2 tablespoons of the pure olive oil over moderately high heat. When the butter starts to brown, add the mushrooms and season with salt and pepper. Cover and cook until the mushrooms release their liquid, about 3 minutes. Uncover and cook, stirring occasionally, until the liquid evaporates and the mushrooms are deeply browned, about 8 minutes. Add the soy sauce and cook, stirring, for 2 minutes longer. Transfer to a rimmed baking sheet and keep warm in the oven.

2. In a small bowl, whisk the extra-virgin olive oil with the sherry vinegar, Marsala, tomato paste and minced garlic. Season with salt and pepper.

3. Add the remaining 1 teaspoon of pure olive oil to the skillet. Add the shallots, cover and cook over moderate heat until softened, about 3 minutes. Uncover and cook, stirring, until lightly browned. Stir in the sherry vinaigrette and remove from the heat.

4. In a bowl, toss the lettuces. Add the mushrooms and shallots and toss well. Arrange the salad on 6 plates, sprinkle with the cheese and serve at once.

—*Marcia Kiesel*

Wild Mushroom and Tomato Panzanella

8 SERVINGS

Panzanella is an Italian salad made with hunks of bread or croutons, tomatoes, onions, olive oil and other seasonings. Make this variation on the traditional salad with the most flavorful tomatoes you can find and any combination of wild mushrooms.

CROUTONS

- 4 tablespoons unsalted butter
- 2 tablespoons minced garlic
- 1 tablespoon thyme leaves, finely chopped
- 6 cups diced crustless day-old peasant bread (¾ inch)
- 2 tablespoons freshly grated Parmigiano-Reggiano cheese
- Kosher salt and freshly ground pepper

PANZANELLA

- ¼ cup extra-virgin olive oil
- ½ cup minced shallots
- 1 teaspoon thyme leaves, finely chopped
- ½ pound shiitake mushrooms, stemmed and quartered
- Salt and freshly ground pepper
- 1½ cups tomato sauce, preferably homemade
- 3 medium tomatoes, diced
- ¼ cup chopped basil
- 2 tablespoons minced red onion
- 1 teaspoon red wine vinegar
- 1 cup baby greens
- 1 cup cherry tomatoes, sliced lengthwise
- ¼ cup freshly grated Parmigiano-Reggiano cheese

I. MAKE THE CROUTONS: Preheat the oven to 375°. In a large skillet, melt the butter over moderate heat until lightly browned. Add the minced garlic and cook until golden and fragrant. Stir in the chopped thyme, diced bread and Parmigiano-Reggiano cheese. Season with salt and pepper. Spread the croutons on a large baking sheet and toast in the oven for about 10 minutes; stir occasionally, until crisp.

2. MAKE THE PANZANELLA: In a large skillet, heat 2 tablespoons of the olive oil over moderate heat until just smoking. Add the shallots and thyme and cook, stirring, until the shallots begin to brown, about 5 minutes. Add the shiitakes and cook until tender and golden brown around the edges, about 5 minutes. Season the shiitakes with salt and pepper.

3. In a large bowl, mix the croutons with the tomato sauce, diced tomatoes, basil, onion, vinegar, the shiitakes and the remaining 2 tablespoons of olive oil. Season with salt and pepper. Mound the panzanella on plates and garnish with the baby greens, cherry tomatoes and Parmigiano-Reggiano.

—*Michael Chiarello*

MAKE AHEAD The toasted croutons can be stored in an airtight container for up to 1 day.

Arugula Salad with Candied Walnuts

6 SERVINGS

Candied walnuts are available at specialty markets and nut shops. You can also use plain walnuts; it's best to toast them first in the oven.

- 1 tablespoon sherry vinegar
- 1 teaspoon minced shallot
- 2 tablespoons extra-virgin olive oil
- 1½ teaspoons walnut oil

Salt and freshly ground pepper

- 2 bunches arugula, trimmed
- ½ cup candied walnuts (about 3 ounces)
- 1 medium Bartlett pear—halved, cored and thinly sliced
- ½ cup crumbled Maytag blue cheese

In a large bowl, combine the vinegar and shallot. Whisk in the olive and walnut oils and season with salt and pepper. Add the arugula, walnuts and pear slices, season with salt and pepper and toss well. Scatter the blue cheese on top and serve. —*Thomas Gay*

Endive and Grapefruit Salad with Smoked Trout

Endive and Grapefruit Salad with Smoked Trout

6 SERVINGS

- 2 ruby grapefruits
- 1 tablespoon Champagne vinegar
- 1 tablespoon minced shallot
- 3 tablespoons crème fraîche
- 2 tablespoons extra-virgin olive oil

Kosher salt and freshly ground pepper

- 4 large endives (about 1½ pounds), leaves separated
- 2 Hass avocados, cut into ½-inch dice
- 1 pound smoked trout fillets, skinned and flaked into 1-inch pieces

I. Using a knife, carefully peel the grapefruits; be sure to remove all of the bitter white pith. Working over a bowl, cut in between the membranes to release the grapefruit sections into the bowl. Transfer the sections to a plate. Squeeze any extra grapefruit juice from the membranes into the bowl and stir in the vinegar and shallot, then whisk in the crème fraîche and oil. Season the grapefruit vinaigrette with salt and pepper.

2. Arrange the endives on a large platter. Top with the grapefruit sections, diced avocado and smoked trout and serve, passing the vinaigrette at the table. —*Gayle Pirie and John Clark*

WINE Best for this salad is a Sauvignon Blanc with herbal and grapefruit hints, such as the 1998 Delaire Stellenbosch from South Africa or the 1998 Babich Marlborough from New Zealand.

Mesclun Salad with Grilled Figs and Roasted Fig Vinaigrette

8 SERVINGS

Roasting the figs before pureeing them concentrates their flavor.

- 20 ripe black Mission figs, stemmed and halved lengthwise
- 2 tablespoons black currant or balsamic vinegar
- 1 tablespoon oregano leaves
- 1 tablespoon flat-leaf parsley leaves
- 1 garlic clove, smashed
- ¼ cup extra-virgin olive oil, plus more for brushing

Kosher salt and freshly ground pepper

- 1 pound mesclun salad

1. Preheat the oven to 400°. Set 8 fig halves on a baking sheet, cut side down, and roast in the oven for about 7 minutes on each side, or until slightly dry and just beginning to brown. Transfer the figs along with any liquid they have released to a plate and let cool to room temperature.

2. In a food processor, puree the roasted figs with the black currant or balsamic vinegar, oregano, parsley and garlic. With the machine on, slowly add ¼ cup of the olive oil in a thin stream and process until the dressing has thickened. Season with salt and pepper and refrigerate for at least 20 minutes.

3. Light a grill or preheat the broiler. Brush the 32 remaining fig halves with olive oil and grill or broil, turning once, until softened and a bit charred, about 2 minutes per side. Transfer the fig halves to a plate and allow them to cool to room temperature.

4. In a bowl, toss the mesclun with the vinaigrette and mound on plates. Arrange the grilled figs on top and serve. —*Darryl Joannides*

MAKE AHEAD The vinaigrette can be refrigerated for up to 3 days.

WINE The 1997 Bucci Verdicchio Classico is a lush white wine with light citrus and melon flavors that go well with luscious foods such as fresh figs or prosciutto and melon.

Grilled-Fig Salad with Prosciutto

8 SERVINGS

- 24 small fresh black figs, halved
- 2 tablespoons extra-virgin olive oil
- 1½ tablespoons balsamic vinegar
- 2 tablespoons minced rosemary

Salt and freshly ground pepper

- 1 pound arugula, large stems discarded
- 2 cups flat-leaf parsley leaves
- ¾ pound thinly sliced imported Italian prosciutto, preferably San Daniele

1. Light a grill or preheat a grill pan. Grill half the figs, cut side down, for 1 to 2 minutes, or until lightly charred.

2. In a large bowl, combine the olive oil, balsamic vinegar and rosemary. Season the dressing with salt and pepper. Add the arugula, parsley and the grilled figs and toss with the dressing.

3. Arrange the prosciutto slices on plates. Top with the arugula salad and the fresh figs and serve. —*Mario Batali*

Corsican Salad with Serrano Ham and Melon

10 SERVINGS

For this salad, a Corsican variation on the familiar prosciutto and melon, cut the melon into bite-size pieces and arrange it on a bed of dressed greens with figs, ham and toasted pine nuts.

- 3 tablespoons pine nuts
- ¾ cup extra-virgin olive oil
- ¼ cup balsamic vinegar

Salt and freshly ground pepper

- 2 large heads lettuce (such as Boston and red leaf), torn into pieces
- 1 cantaloupe, cut into 1-inch pieces
- 10 small fresh figs, quartered
- 8 ounces thinly sliced Serrano ham
- 1 cup small basil leaves
- ¼ cup chives, cut into 2-inch pieces

1. Preheat the oven to 350°. Put the pine nuts in a pie plate and toast in the oven 7 minutes, or until golden.

2. Whisk together the olive oil and the

Mesclun Salad with Grilled Figs and Roasted Fig Vinaigrette

TOP: **Radicchio Chopped Salad with Toasted Chickpeas.**

BOTTOM: **Parsley and Ham Salad with Sweet Potato Polenta.**

vinegar. Season the vinaigrette with salt and pepper.

3. Just before serving, toss the torn lettuce leaves with ⅓ cup of the vinaigrette, reserving the rest to pass with the salad. Arrange the lettuce on a large platter. Top with the cantaloupe pieces, quartered figs and ham slices. Garnish with the basil leaves, chives and toasted pine nuts.

—*Jean-Christophe Royer*

Radicchio Chopped Salad with Toasted Chickpeas

6 SERVINGS

The chickpeas are toasted in the pancetta fat, which gives them a rich flavor.

- 1 red bell pepper
- 2 tablespoons extra-virgin olive oil
- 5 ounces pancetta, sliced ¼ inch thick and cut into thin strips
- 1 cup canned chickpeas—drained, rinsed and patted dry (about 9 ounces)
- 2 tablespoons Prosecco
- 2 tablespoons white wine vinegar
- 1 large garlic clove, minced

Salt and freshly ground pepper

- 2 medium heads radicchio (¾ pound), coarsely chopped
- 2 bunches arugula (¾ pound), coarsely chopped
- 3 ounces aged provolone cheese, cut into thin shavings

1. Preheat the broiler. Roast the bell pepper under the broiler or over an open flame, turning, until charred all over. Transfer the pepper to a bowl, cover with a plate and let steam for 5 minutes. Peel, seed and core the pepper and cut it into ½-inch dice.

2. In a large skillet, heat 1 tablespoon of the olive oil. Add the pancetta and cook over low heat, stirring, until lightly browned, about 8 minutes. Using a slotted spoon, transfer the pancetta to a plate. Add half the chickpeas to the skillet and cook over moderately high heat, shaking the skillet, until the chickpeas are lightly browned and slightly crisp, 3 to 4 minutes; transfer to a plate. Repeat with the remaining chickpeas.

3. In a small bowl, combine the Prosecco with the vinegar, garlic and the remaining 1 tablespoon of olive oil. Season with salt and pepper.

4. Preheat the oven to 400°. Return the pancetta and chickpeas to the skillet and rewarm them in the oven for 3 minutes. In a large bowl, toss the radicchio with the arugula, provolone,

pancetta, chickpeas and roasted red pepper. Add the dressing, toss well and serve at once. —*Marcia Kiesel*

MAKE AHEAD The salad and Prosecco dressing can be prepared through Step 3 up to 4 hours ahead.

WINE The round, mouth-filling Pojer e Sandri Spumante Extra Brut Cuvée 1993/1994 softens the sharp flavors of the provolone and bitter greens in this salad, while its effervescence lightens the texture of the chickpeas.

Parsley and Ham Salad with Sweet Potato Polenta

4 SERVINGS

POLENTA

- 1 small sweet potato
- 2 cups chicken stock or canned low-sodium broth
- ½ cup polenta

Salt

- ¼ cup freshly grated Parmesan cheese

Freshly ground pepper

- 2 teaspoons pure olive oil

SALAD

- 2½ tablespoons fresh orange juice
- 1½ tablespoons sherry vinegar
- 1 garlic clove, minced

Salt and freshly ground pepper

- 4 cups flat-leaf parsley leaves
- ¾ cup finely slivered cooked country ham (3 ounces)
- 1 Granny Smith apple, thinly sliced
- ½ medium red onion, thinly sliced

1. MAKE THE POLENTA: Preheat the oven to 400°. Bake the sweet potato for about 20 minutes, or until barely tender. Peel and cut the sweet potato into ½-inch dice. Raise the oven temperature to 500°.

2. Bring the chicken stock to a boil in a medium saucepan. Lightly oil a shallow 8-inch bowl. Whisk the polenta and ½ teaspoon of salt into the stock and cook over low heat, stirring often, until the polenta thickens and begins to pull away from the side of the pan, about 12 minutes. Stir in the Parmesan cheese. Remove from the heat and season the polenta with salt and pepper, then gently fold in the diced sweet potato. Spoon the polenta into the prepared bowl and smooth the surface. Cover with plastic wrap and refrigerate until firm.

3. Heat 1 teaspoon of the olive oil in a large cast-iron skillet. Cut the polenta into 8 wedges and cook over moderate heat until browned on the bottom, about 3 minutes. Turn the polenta with a metal spatula, add the remaining 1 teaspoon of oil to the skillet and tilt to coat the bottom. Bake the polenta for about 8 minutes, or until crusty on the bottom.

4. MAKE THE SALAD: In a large bowl, whisk the orange juice with the sherry vinegar and garlic. Season with salt and pepper. Add the parsley, ham, apple and onion to the bowl and toss well. Arrange 2 wedges of warm polenta on each of 4 plates, mound the ham salad in the center and serve.

—Marcia Kiesel

Spanish Chopped Summer Salad

6 SERVINGS

This salad appears in endless variations around the Mediterranean. If you replace the ham and hard-cooked eggs with feta cheese and marinated sardines or anchovies, you have the Turkish version.

¼ cup red wine vinegar
2 tablespoons fresh lemon juice
3 large garlic cloves, minced
1 serrano chile, minced
¼ cup plus 2 tablespoons extra-virgin olive oil
Salt and freshly ground pepper
4 large tomatoes (about 2 pounds)—peeled, seeded and coarsely chopped
2 medium cucumbers—peeled, seeded and coarsely chopped
1 medium red onion, finely chopped
1 small red bell pepper, coarsely chopped
1 small green bell pepper, coarsely chopped
1 pound romaine hearts, coarsely chopped
½ cup coarsely chopped flat-leaf parsley
½ cup coarsely chopped mint
1 cup oil-cured black olives (about ¼ pound), halved and pitted
½ cup finely chopped baked ham or Serrano ham (¼ pound)
2 hard-cooked eggs, peeled and coarsely chopped

1. In a small bowl, combine the vinegar with the lemon juice, garlic and chile. Whisk in the olive oil and season with salt and pepper to make a dressing.

2. In a large bowl, combine the tomatoes with the cucumbers, onion, bell peppers, romaine, parsley and mint. Add the dressing, season with salt and pepper and toss gently. Transfer the salad to a large platter and scatter the olives, ham and chopped eggs on top. Serve immediately. *—Joyce Goldstein*

WINE A tangy white with bite and some oak will match the bold flavors of this salad. A traditional Spanish white, such as the 1998 Bodegas Montecillo Rioja Blanco Viña Cumbrero or the 1998 Torres Chardonnay Penedès Gran Viña Sol, is the best choice.

Grilled-Vegetable Salad with Cuban Mojo

6 SERVINGS

2 large red bell peppers
2 large green bell peppers
6 small Italian eggplants (1¾ pounds)
1 large sweet onion, unpeeled and halved lengthwise
2 medium zucchini, sliced lengthwise ½ inch thick
Cuban Mojo (recipe follows)
1 tablespoon red wine vinegar
2 tablespoons extra-virgin olive oil
One 1-pound head romaine lettuce, leaves torn
1 large bunch watercress, tough stems discarded
Salt and freshly ground pepper
Basil leaves, for garnish

1. Light a grill or preheat the broiler. Grill or broil the bell peppers for about 5 minutes per side, or until the skins are blistered and charred. Transfer the bell peppers to a medium bowl, cover with plastic wrap and let steam for 20 minutes. Peel, core and seed the peppers and cut them into 1-inch-wide strips.

2. Slice the eggplants lengthwise, keeping the slices attached at the stem. Fan the slices out by pressing down with your hands. Generously brush the eggplants, onion and zucchini with the

knives 101

Seven tips on buying and caring for knives from Thomas McGuane, owner of Thomas McGuane Fine Cutlery (406-522-9739):

1. Invest in at least three knives: a paring knife, a midsize utility knife and an 8- or 9-inch chef's knife.

2. Choose everyday knives that have synthetic handles—they're more durable than wood. Your hand should comfortably cradle the grip.

3. Look for a high-carbon stainless-steel blade, with molybdenum (to prevent pitting) and vanadium (for edge holding).

4. Examine the edge. It should be evenly ground, so that you can rock it in a pleasant, shallow motion on a cutting board.

5. Balance the knife on one finger placed just before the handle to check that the weight is evenly distributed.

6. Sharpen the blade when it's dull with a steel. Choose a steel coated with diamond dust or a ceramic one. Have the blade re-beveled four times a year.

7. Never put knives in the dishwasher.

—Kimberly Y. Masibay

Grilled-Vegetable Salad with Cuban Mojo

mojo, reserving 1 tablespoon for the dressing. Grill or broil the vegetables for 20 minutes, or until the eggplant and zucchini are tender and the onion is charred and crisp-tender. Carefully peel the onion and cut it into 1-inch slices.

3. In a large bowl, whisk the reserved 1 tablespoon of mojo with the red wine vinegar; slowly whisk in the extra-virgin olive oil until the dressing is emulsified. Add the romaine and watercress, season with salt and pepper and toss to combine. Transfer the greens to a serving platter and arrange the grilled vegetables on top. Garnish with the basil leaves and serve.

—Maricel Presilla

WINE The fresh, light, herby character of Sauvignon Blanc makes it a perfect partner to grilled-vegetable dishes, especially ones that have dressings featuring plenty of garlic, as does the Cuban Mojo. Two good examples are also excellent values: the 1998 Beaulieu Vineyard California Coastal and the 1999 St. Supéry Napa Valley.

CUBAN MOJO

MAKES 1 CUP

Mojo (pronounced mo-ho) is the Spanish name for a number of Latin sauces made with vinegar or citrus juice and garlic. It is a traditional accompaniment to the starchy root vegetables of the Caribbean.

- 12 small garlic cloves, finely chopped
- Sea salt
- ¼ cup fresh bitter-orange juice or lime juice (see Note)
- 1½ teaspoons ground cumin
- ½ cup extra-virgin olive oil
- Freshly ground pepper

In a mini food processor or blender, pulse the garlic with a generous pinch of salt until finely chopped. Blend in the bitter-orange juice and cumin and process until fine, about 30 seconds. With the machine on, slowly add the oil in a thin stream until the mojo is emulsified. Season the mojo with pepper and serve immediately. —M.P.

NOTE Bitter oranges, also called Seville oranges, are extremely tart. They are available at Latin markets.

MAKE AHEAD The mojo can be refrigerated for up to 4 days.

Sweet-and-Sour Eggplant Salad

6 SERVINGS

You can spoon this piquant eggplant salad on top of pieces of broken toasted pita so the bread absorbs the flavorful dressing.

- 1½ pounds eggplant, cut into 1-inch cubes
- Salt
- ½ cup extra-virgin olive oil
- 1 large Spanish onion, coarsely chopped
- 2 garlic cloves, chopped
- 1 pound tomatoes, peeled and coarsely chopped, or one 14-ounce can peeled plum tomatoes, coarsely chopped
- ¼ cup coarsely chopped flat-leaf parsley

- 2 tablespoons white wine vinegar
- 1 tablespoon coarsely chopped mint
- 1 tablespoon sugar
- Freshly ground pepper or a large pinch of ground chile pepper

1. Put the eggplant cubes in a colander and sprinkle with salt to draw out the water. Let stand for about 30 minutes. Pat dry with paper towels.

2. Heat the olive oil in a large casserole. Add the chopped onion and cook over moderate heat, stirring, until golden, approximately 8 minutes. Add the eggplant cubes and cook, stirring, for about 5 minutes. Add the garlic and cook until lightly browned, approximately 3 minutes. Stir in the tomatoes and their juices along with the chopped parsley, white wine vinegar, chopped mint and sugar. Season the mixture with pepper and cook over low heat, stirring occasionally, until the eggplant is soft, 20 to 30 minutes. Let the eggplant cool, then cover and refrigerate it for at least 1 hour or overnight. Serve the eggplant salad cold.

—Claudia Roden

Sweet-and-Sour Eggplant Salad

Swifty's Cobb Salad

6 SERVINGS

This salad is a hybrid between two traditional favorites: Cobb salad ingredients made into a chopped salad.

- 1 garlic clove, minced
- 1 teaspoon Dijon mustard
- 1 tablespoon mayonnaise
- 3 tablespoons red wine vinegar
- ¼ cup extra-virgin olive oil

Salt and freshly ground pepper

- 2 bunches watercress, stemmed and chopped
- 1 medium head romaine lettuce, chopped
- 1 medium head Boston lettuce, chopped
- ¾ pound diced, cooked chicken
- 8 slices crisp bacon, crumbled
- 3 hard-cooked eggs, chopped
- 2 tomatoes, diced
- 1 Hass avocado, diced
- 8 chives, chopped
- 2 ounces Roquefort cheese, crumbled

1. In a small bowl, combine the garlic, mustard, mayonnaise and red wine vinegar. Whisk in the olive oil and season with salt and pepper.

2. In a large bowl, toss together the remaining ingredients. Stir the dressing, pour the vinaigrette over the salad and toss well. Serve immediately.

—*Stephen Attoe*

Swifty's Cobb Salad

Sweet Daikon and Carrot Salad (*Mou Sangchae*)

4 TO 6 SERVINGS

- 1 small daikon (1 pound), peeled and cut into 3-inch matchsticks
- 1 medium carrot, cut into 3-inch matchsticks
- ¼ cup rice vinegar
- 1 tablespoon sugar
- 1 teaspoon Asian sesame oil

Salt

In a bowl, toss all of the ingredients and let them stand for at least 30 minutes before serving.

—*Anya von Bremzen*

Marinated Cabbage Slaw

10 SERVINGS

- 2 medium heads of green cabbage, shredded
- 1 large onion, shredded
- 1½ cups white wine vinegar
- 1 cup canola oil
- ¾ cup sugar
- ½ cup chicken stock
- 1½ tablespoons salt
- 1½ tablespoons dry mustard
- 1½ tablespoons celery seeds

1. Layer the cabbage and onion alternately in a large glass or ceramic bowl.

2. In a medium saucepan, combine the vinegar with the oil, sugar, stock, salt, dry mustard and celery seeds. Bring to a boil, then pour the mixture over the cabbage and onion. Do not mix.

3. Let the slaw marinate in the refrigerator for 6 to 8 hours or overnight. Toss before serving.—*Patrick O'Connell*

Red-and-White Spicy Slaw

8 TO 10 SERVINGS

- 1 cup milk
- 4 elephant garlic cloves, halved
- 1 jalapeño, stem removed
- ½ cup heavy cream
- ¼ cup mayonnaise
- 2 tablespoons cider vinegar
- 1 tablespoon honey

Salt and freshly ground pepper

One 1½-pound head napa cabbage, shredded

One 1½-pound head red cabbage, cored and shredded

- ½ cup thinly sliced scallions
- ½ cup shredded carrots

1. In a small saucepan, combine the milk, garlic and jalapeño and simmer over low heat for 5 minutes. Pour off the milk. Cover the garlic and jalapeño with the cream and simmer over low heat until the garlic and jalapeño are

Savoy Cabbage, Kohlrabi and Grapefruit Salad

tender, about 8 minutes. Let cool to room temperature.

2. Remove the jalapeño from the cream and scrape out the seeds. In a blender, puree the jalapeño with the garlic, cream and mayonnaise until smooth. Scrape the mixture into a bowl and whisk in the vinegar and honey. Season the dressing generously with salt and pepper.

3. Just before serving, in a very large bowl, toss the napa and red cabbages with the scallions and carrots. Add the dressing, toss to coat and serve.

—*Daniel Bruce*

MAKE AHEAD The dressing can be refrigerated for up to 1 day.

Savoy Cabbage, Kohlrabi and Grapefruit Salad

4 SERVINGS

This crisp, vibrant slaw would go well alongside any kind of baked fish drizzled with a little citrus juice.

One 1¼-pound head of Savoy cabbage, finely shredded (4 packed cups)
Kosher salt
1 red grapefruit

¼ cup grapeseed or other mild oil
2 tablespoons fresh lemon juice
Freshly ground pepper
1¾ pounds kohlrabi, peeled and coarsely grated
2 tablespoons finely shredded mint leaves, plus whole leaves for garnish

1. In a large glass or ceramic bowl, toss the shredded cabbage with 1 tablespoon of salt. Weigh down the cabbage with a heavy plate topped with canned goods and chill for 1 hour.

2. Using a sharp knife, peel the grapefruit, removing all of the bitter white pith. Working over a bowl, cut in between the membranes to release the sections. Squeeze 2 tablespoons of the juice from the membranes into a small bowl. Whisk in the oil and lemon juice and season with salt and pepper.

3. Squeeze the cabbage dry and transfer it to a large bowl. Add the kohlrabi and vinaigrette and toss well. Add the grapefruit sections and shredded mint and toss again. Mound the salad on plates, garnish with mint leaves and serve.

—*Bill Telepan*

WINE A tangy white with slightly herbal notes would harmonize well with this salad. Try a crisp Italian, such as the 1999 Villa Sparina Gavi di Gavi or the 1999 Ronco del Gelso Tocai Friulano.

Cucumber and Peanut Salad

10 TO 12 SERVINGS

This cool cucumber dish with a crisp peanut garnish can be served either alone as a refreshing relish, in place of chutney or on a bed of romaine leaves as a side-dish or first-course salad.

2 teaspoons cumin seeds
4 European cucumbers—peeled, halved lengthwise and thinly sliced crosswise
⅓ cup fresh lemon juice
2 teaspoons salt
½ cup finely chopped cilantro leaves
4 to 6 green serrano chiles, finely chopped

2 teaspoons sugar
1 cup dry-roasted peanuts, coarsely chopped
½ cup coarsely grated, peeled fresh coconut
Lettuce leaves

1. In a small skillet, toast the cumin seeds over moderately high heat until fragrant, about 3 minutes. Transfer to a plate and let cool. Grind the cumin to a coarse powder in a mortar or a spice mill.

2. In a large bowl, toss the cucumbers with the lemon juice, salt, cilantro, chiles and sugar. Set aside at room temperature for 30 minutes, stirring occasionally.

3. Just before serving, drain the excess liquid from the cucumbers and stir in half of the peanuts and coconut. Line a serving platter with lettuce leaves and mound the salad in the center. Garnish with the remaining peanuts and coconut and serve at room temperature.

—*Neela Paniz*

Crisp Celery Salad with Anchovy Vinaigrette

12 SERVINGS

16 large celery ribs—peeled, halved crosswise and sliced lengthwise into ⅛-inch strips
¼ cup plus 2 tablespoons extra-virgin olive oil
¼ cup fresh lemon juice
7 large anchovy fillets, chopped
3 large garlic cloves, quartered
1 tablespoon white wine vinegar
Salt and freshly ground pepper

1. Put the celery strips in a large bowl of ice water and refrigerate for at least 1 hour or overnight, until the celery strips are curled and very crisp.

2. In a mini processor, combine the olive oil, lemon juice, anchovies, garlic and white wine vinegar and process until smooth, about 30 seconds. Scrape the vinaigrette into a small bowl and season with salt and pepper.

3. Drain the celery and pat thoroughly

dry. Put the celery in a dry bowl and toss with the vinaigrette. Transfer to a platter and serve at once.

—*Cesare Casella*

MAKE AHEAD The recipe can be prepared through Step 2 and refrigerated overnight.

WINE A fresh, clean, smooth Italian white with some softness and body, such as a good Frascati Superiore, will complement the range of flavors and textures in the antipasti. Try the 1998 Villa Simone or a single-vineyard bottling from Fontana Candida, like the 1998 Vigneto Santa Teresa.

Roasted Pepper and Tomato Salad

6 SERVINGS

Every country in the Middle East makes a variation of this salad. This simple recipe is an Egyptian version.

- 4 red or green bell peppers
- ¼ cup extra-virgin olive oil

Salt and freshly ground pepper

- 6 large garlic cloves, unpeeled
- 3 large tomatoes, peeled and sliced ½ inch thick
- 1 tablespoon white wine vinegar or 2 tablespoons fresh lemon juice
- ½ cup chopped flat-leaf parsley or cilantro

1. Preheat the broiler. Roast the bell peppers under the broiler for about 10 minutes, or until charred all over. Transfer to a medium bowl, cover with plastic wrap and let steam for about 10 minutes. Peel the peppers and discard the stems and seeds. Cut the peppers into ½-inch-wide strips. Return the peppers to the bowl, add 1 tablespoon of the olive oil and season with salt and pepper. Let stand at room temperature.

2. Meanwhile, preheat the oven to 400°. Wrap the garlic in aluminum foil, put in a baking dish and bake for about 35 minutes, or until the cloves are soft. Let cool slightly, then peel.

3. Arrange the tomato slices in one layer on a platter and season with salt. In a small bowl, whisk the remaining 3 tablespoons of olive oil with the vinegar and season with salt and pepper. Scatter the peppers and garlic over the tomatoes. Spoon the vinaigrette over the top, sprinkle with the parsley and serve. —*Claudia Roden*

MAKE AHEAD This dish can be prepared up to 2 hours ahead.

Asparagus Salad with Herbs and Parmesan

10 SERVINGS

- 4 pounds asparagus, trimmed and cut diagonally into 3-inch lengths
- ½ cup extra-virgin olive oil
- 3 tablespoons fresh lemon juice

Coarse salt and freshly ground pepper

- ½ cup coarsely chopped chervil
- ½ cup coarsely chopped chives
- ½ cup coarsely chopped mint
- ½ cup coarsely chopped parsley
- 2 ounces Parmesan cheese, thinly shaved

Truffle oil (optional)

1. Bring 5 quarts of salted water to a boil over high heat. Cook the asparagus until just tender, 3 to 5 minutes for thin stalks and 8 to 10 minutes for thick stalks. Drain the asparagus, then chill it in a bowl of ice water. Drain the asparagus again, pat it dry and put it in a large mixing bowl.

2. In a small bowl, whisk the olive oil and lemon juice together, then season with salt and pepper. Stir in the chervil, chives, mint and parsley. Pour over the asparagus and toss lightly.

3. When ready to serve, top the salad

Asparagus Salad with Herbs and Parmesan

with the shavings of Parmesan and sprinkle with a few drops of the truffle oil, if desired. Pass additional coarse salt at the table.

—Jean-Christophe Royer

WINE The herby character of Sauvignon Blancs, such as the 1998 Chateau Souverain Alexander Valley from California or the 1998 Taltarni from Australia, will blend particularly well with this salad. If you prefer, you might opt for a sparkling wine.

Yellow Bean, Asparagus and Tomato Salad

8 SERVINGS

3 tablespoons balsamic vinegar
3 tablespoons extra-virgin olive oil
Salt and freshly ground pepper
2 tablespoons coarsely chopped fresh tarragon
1 pound medium asparagus
1 pound yellow wax beans
½ pint red pear or cherry tomatoes
½ pint yellow pear or cherry tomatoes

1. In a small bowl, whisk the balsamic vinegar with the olive oil. Season the vinaigrette with salt and pepper and add the tarragon.

2. In a large pot of boiling salted water, cook the asparagus until just tender, about 3 minutes. Using tongs, transfer the asparagus to a colander and refresh under cold water. Drain and pat dry. Cut the asparagus into 3-inch lengths.

3. Add the wax beans to the boiling water and cook them until tender, approximately 5 minutes. Drain the wax beans in the colander and refresh them under cold water. Drain and pat them dry.

4. In a bowl, toss the cooked beans and asparagus, tomatoes and dressing and serve. *—Daniel Bruce*

MAKE AHEAD The vinaigrette, asparagus and beans can be prepared through Step 3 and refrigerated overnight.

Green Bean Salad with Dried Shrimp and Peanuts

6 SERVINGS

Som tam is a highly seasoned green papaya salad sold by street vendors throughout northeast Thailand and Laos. It is made by pounding papaya with other ingredients in a large stone mortar. This version uses green beans, which are more readily available. To eat the salad in the traditional way, use cabbage wedges to scoop it up.

½ pound very fresh thin green beans, halved lengthwise and cut crosswise into 1½-inch lengths
6 cherry tomatoes, quartered
1 tablespoon dried shrimp, finely chopped
1 tablespoon unsalted roasted peanuts
1 or 2 bird chiles, minced
1 large garlic clove, halved
Salt
Sugar
¼ cup fresh lime juice
2 tablespoons Thai fish sauce (nam pla)
2 packed cups bite-size pieces of romaine lettuce
Green cabbage wedges, for serving

1. In a large mortar, working in batches, pound the beans in order to lightly smash them; transfer to a bowl. Add the tomatoes to the mortar and pound them briefly; add the tomatoes to the beans in the bowl.

2. Add the dried shrimp, peanuts, chiles, garlic, salt and sugar to the mortar and pound to a coarse paste. Stir in the lime juice and fish sauce until blended. Add the dressing to the smashed beans and tomatoes and toss thoroughly.

3. Line a platter with the lettuce and spoon the bean salad on top. Arrange the cabbage wedges around the salad and serve.

—Naomi Duguid and Jeffrey Alford

WINE This tangy salad, with its garlic, lime juice and chile, calls for an inexpensive, light-bodied, simple white, such as the 1998 Zonin Soave or the 1997 Bertani Due Uve, which is Pinot Grigio with a touch of Sauvignon Blanc.

Candy Cane Beet Salad with Orange and Fennel

4 SERVINGS

Any beet would work well in this dish, but the tangy blood orange and crunchy fennel slices are especially good with the candy cane's sweetness.

4 medium candy cane or *chioggia* beets (about 6 ounces each)
¼ cup extra-virgin olive oil
Salt and freshly ground pepper
2 oranges, preferably blood oranges
3 tablespoons fresh lemon juice
1 fennel bulb—halved, cored and thinly sliced lengthwise
1 teaspoon finely chopped flat-leaf parsley

1. Preheat the oven to 400°. In a small baking dish, pour ½ inch of water over the beets. Drizzle with 2 tablespoons of the olive oil and season with salt and pepper. Cover with foil and bake for about 1 hour, or until tender. When the beets are cool enough to handle, peel them and slice them ¼ inch thick.

2. Using a sharp knife, peel the oranges, removing all the bitter white pith. Working over a bowl, cut in between the membranes to release the orange sections. Squeeze the juice from the membranes into the bowl.

3. In a small saucepan, simmer ¼ cup of the orange juice over moderate heat until reduced to 1 tablespoon, about 5 minutes. Pour the reduced orange juice into a bowl and mix in 1 tablespoon of the lemon juice and 1 tablespoon of olive oil. Season with salt and pepper.

4. In a medium bowl, combine the remaining 2 tablespoons of lemon juice with the remaining 1 tablespoon of olive oil and season with salt and pepper.

Add the fennel and parsley and toss well to coat.

5. In another medium bowl, toss the beets with the orange juice vinaigrette. Arrange the sliced beets on plates and mound the fennel salad on top. Arrange the oranges around the beets and serve. —*Bill Telepan*

WINE The sweetness of this salad calls for the bold flavor of a full-bodied Grenache-based rosé. Consider the 1999 Charles Melton Rosé of Virginia from Australia or the 1999 Domaine Pélaquié Tavel from the Rhône Valley.

Beets and Fava Beans with Anchovy Vinaigrette

8 SERVINGS

- 6 small beets (about 1½ pounds), scrubbed
- 2 pounds fresh fava beans, shelled
- 4 large eggs
- ¼ pound sliced bacon, cut crosswise into ½-inch strips
- 7 tablespoons extra-virgin olive oil
- 1 medium onion, thinly sliced
- 1 garlic clove, thinly sliced
- 6 anchovy fillets
- 2 tablespoons white wine vinegar

Salt and freshly ground pepper

- 2 tablespoons finely chopped flat-leaf parsley

Mixed baby lettuces, for serving

I. Preheat the oven to 450°. Loosely wrap the beets in foil and roast for about 1 hour, or until tender when pierced. Let the beets cool, then peel them and cut them into wedges.

2. Bring a large saucepan of water to a boil. Add the fava beans and cook until tender, about 4 minutes. Drain the beans and cool them under running water. Peel off and discard the tough outer skins. Return the water to a boil. Gently add the eggs and boil them for 6 minutes. Using a slotted spoon, transfer the eggs to a bowl of cold water and let them cool completely. Peel the eggs.

3. In a medium skillet, cook the bacon

Beets and Fava Beans with Anchovy Vinaigrette

strips over moderately high heat until brown and crisp, about 6 minutes. Transfer the bacon to paper towels to drain. Pour off the fat from the pan.

4. Heat 1 tablespoon of the olive oil in the skillet. Add the sliced onion and garlic and cook over moderately low heat, stirring frequently, until the onion is golden, about 25 minutes. Stir in the anchovies and vinegar. Scrape the contents of the skillet into a blender or mini processor and pulse until smooth. With the machine on, add the remaining 6 tablespoons of olive oil in a thin, steady stream. Season the anchovy dressing with salt and pepper.

5. Put the greens on plates. Cut the eggs in half. Arrange the eggs, beets, fava beans and bacon on top. Drizzle half of the dressing over the salad, sprinkle with the parsley and serve. Pass the remaining dressing separately. —*Tamasin Day-Lewis*

Farro, Cherry Tomato and Arugula Salad

6 SERVINGS

The trick to cooking *farro,* a variety of wheat cultivated in Italy, is to boil it in lots of salted water, as with pasta.

- 1½ cups *farro* (¾ pound)
- ⅓ cup extra-virgin olive oil
- ¼ cup balsamic vinegar

Salt and freshly ground pepper

- ½ pound cherry tomatoes, halved
- 2 bunches of arugula (¾ pound), stemmed and torn into bite-size pieces

I. In a large saucepan of boiling salted water, cook the *farro* until al dente, about 25 minutes. Drain well. Transfer the *farro* to a bowl and let it cool to room temperature.

2. In a bowl, mix the olive oil and balsamic vinegar. Season the vinaigrette with salt and pepper. Add the cherry tomatoes, arugula and vinaigrette to

Farro, Cherry Tomato and Arugula Salad

the *farro* and toss well to coat. Season to taste with salt and pepper and serve at once.   —*Cristina and Mauro Rastelli*

MAKE AHEAD The cooked *farro* can be refrigerated overnight.

WINE The *farro* salad calls for a dry white wine with character, such as the 1998 Il Decugnano dei Barbi Orvieto Classico. It has enough fruit to stand up to the bitter arugula while also providing a pleasant contrast to the salad's earthiness.

Roasted Winter Squash, Ham and Parsley Salad

4 SERVINGS

You can use any round winter squash in this recipe, such as buttercup, acorn or kabocha.

     4 tablespoons unsalted butter
One 3-pound winter squash—halved,
        seeded and cut into 12 wedges
Salt and freshly ground pepper
     1 tablespoon pure maple syrup
     1 teaspoon ground coriander
  ½ cup hazelnuts (2 ounces)
     2 tablespoons hazelnut oil
     1 tablespoon sherry vinegar
     2 packed cups flat-leaf parsley
 2½ ounces baked ham, cut into
        ½-inch dice (½ cup)

1. Preheat the oven to 475°. Melt the butter on a large rimmed baking sheet in the oven. Toss the squash in the butter until coated, then lay the wedges on their sides and roast for about 15 minutes, or until browned; turn to the other side and roast for another 15 minutes.

2. Turn the squash wedges skin side down and season them with salt and pepper. Drizzle the wedges with the maple syrup and sprinkle them with the coriander. Roast the squash again for about 2 minutes, or until bubbling. Remove from the oven, cover the baking sheet loosely with foil and let the squash cool slightly.

3. Reduce the oven temperature to 375°. Toast the hazelnuts in a pie plate in the oven for about 10 minutes, or until they are browned. Transfer the hazelnuts to a kitchen towel and let them cool slightly, then rub the nuts in the towel to remove the skins. Coarsely chop the hazelnuts.

4. In a medium bowl, combine the hazelnut oil with the sherry vinegar. Season the vinaigrette with salt and pepper. Add the parsley, ham and toasted hazelnuts and toss well. Arrange 3 squash wedges on each plate, top the wedges with the salad and serve.

—*Bill Telepan*

WINE The rich trio of squash, hazelnuts and ham would combine well with a full-bodied white from the Rhône. Try a twist on tradition with a California wine made from Rhône grapes, such as the 1998 Alban Estate Roussanne.

Rice and Tuna Sashimi Salad

4 TO 6 SERVINGS

Hwe topbap is a Japanese-influenced variation of *bibimbop,* which is a traditional spicy Korean dish of rice and sautéed vegetables. This version was inspired by one tasted in the seaside town of Pohang, South Korea, where the waterfront is lined with restaurants specializing in raw seafood. The play of textures and temperatures in this otherwise simple dish is irresistible.

Steamed Rice (p. 307)
  ½ pound sashimi-quality
        tuna or fluke,
        cut into ½-inch dice
     2 cups coarsely shredded
        red-leaf lettuce
     1 cup shredded *shiso* leaves or
        spearmint (see Note)

Roasted Winter Squash, Ham and Parsley Salad

TOP: Warm Lentil Salad with Caramelized Onions and Walnuts.
BOTTOM: Marinated Black-Eyed Pea Salad.

1 small red onion, halved and thinly sliced lengthwise
2 tablespoons toasted sesame seeds

Korean Chili Sauce (p. 317)

Salt

Asian sesame oil, for drizzling

1. Mound the rice in a large bowl. Scatter the tuna, lettuce, *shiso,* onion and toasted sesame seeds over the rice and drizzle on some of the Korean Chili Sauce. Season with salt and toss with 2 large spoons until evenly mixed.

2. Drizzle a little sesame oil over the salad and serve immediately.

—*Anya von Bremzen*

NOTE *Shiso,* or perilla, is a fragrant Japanese herb with jagged-edged leaves. It is used as a flavoring and as a garnish in salads, sushi and cooked dishes. It has a gingery taste and a cinnamon-like aroma. *Shiso* is available at Asian markets from summer through fall.

Warm Lentil Salad with Caramelized Onions and Walnuts

4 SERVINGS

If you are lucky enough to be in a place where you can forage for wild greens, such as young dandelions, watercress and lamb's lettuce, you can use them as a bed for the lentils. The lentils are delicious served with thin slices of aged goat cheese.

4 cups cold water
2 cups French green lentils (about ¾ pound)
5 thyme sprigs
1 bay leaf

Coarse salt

½ cup slivered dry-cured smoky ham, such as Westphalian ham or *speck* (2 ounces), plus 2 tablespoons ham fat (¾ ounce)
2 medium onions, thinly sliced
½ cup coarsely chopped toasted walnuts (see Note)
3 tablespoons reduced balsamic vinegar (see Note)

Freshly ground pepper

1. In a medium saucepan, combine the water, lentils, thyme sprigs, bay leaf and 1 teaspoon of salt. Bring to a simmer over moderately high heat. Reduce the heat to low, cover and cook until the lentils are just tender and still very moist, about 30 minutes. Cover and set aside.

2. In a medium skillet, cook the ham fat over low heat until it is rendered and any cracklings are golden, about 4 minutes. Add the onions, cover and cook over low heat until softened, about 4 minutes. Uncover and cook, stirring, until the onions are deeply caramelized, about 10 minutes. Remove from the heat.

3. Remove the thyme sprigs and bay leaf from the lentils. Fold in the caramelized onions, toasted walnuts, ham and reduced balsamic vinegar. Season the lentils with salt and pepper, and serve. —*Sally Schneider*

NOTE To toast the walnuts, spread them in a skillet and cook over moderate heat, stirring, until fragrant and lightly browned, about 4 minutes. To make the reduced balsamic vinegar, pour ⅓ cup of balsamic vinegar into a small saucepan and cook over high heat until reduced to 3 tablespoons, about 5 minutes.

ONE SERVING Calories 482 kcal, Total Fat 15 gm, Saturated Fat 2 gm

WINE The deep, earthy flavors of the warm lentils have an affinity for Cabernet Sauvignon and Merlot. Try the 1997 Napa Ridge Cabernet Sauvignon Oak Barrel Central Coast or the 1997 Hedges Cabernet-Merlot from Washington State.

Marinated Black-Eyed Pea Salad

8 SERVINGS

Serve this salad at room temperature as a first course with slices of smoked ham and cheese and crusty bread.

2½ cups dried black-eyed peas (1 pound), soaked overnight and drained
¼ cup plus 2 tablespoons extra-virgin olive oil
¼ cup fresh lemon juice
2 teaspoons minced garlic
1 large onion, finely chopped

Salt and freshly ground pepper

¼ cup finely chopped flat-leaf parsley

I. In a large saucepan, cover the black-eyed peas with 2 inches of water. Bring to a boil, cover partially and cook over moderately low heat until tender, about 20 minutes. Drain and let cool slightly.

2. In a large bowl, whisk the olive oil with the lemon juice and garlic. Add the peas and onion and season with salt and pepper, then toss to coat. Refrigerate for at least 4 hours to let the flavors blend. Bring the salad to room temperature, stir in the parsley and serve. —*Emeril Lagasse*

MAKE AHEAD The salad can be refrigerated for up to 3 days. Add the parsley just before serving.

WINE A fresh, fruity Portuguese white, such as a Vinho Verde with mineral notes, is a bright contrast to the earthy salad. Try the 1999 Provam Alvarinho Portal do Fidalgo. Or go for an Albariño from Spain's Rías Baixas region, such as the 1999 Morgadío.

Herbed Mixed Bean Salad with Peppers

10 SERVINGS

This recipe celebrates the food of Toulouse, France. During the summer, hearty local bean dishes, such as cassoulet, give way to lighter recipes, like this salad.

1½ cups dried speckled beans (¾ pound), such as *borlotti*, soaked overnight

½ cup dried black beans (4 ounces), soaked separately overnight

2 quarts chicken stock or canned low-sodium chicken broth

Salt

2½ pounds fava beans, shelled (about 1¼ cups)

½ cup extra-virgin olive oil

2 red bell peppers, cut into ¼-inch dice

1 green bell pepper, cut into ¼-inch dice

1 yellow bell pepper, cut into ¼-inch dice

1 medium onion, minced

½ cup coarsely chopped cilantro

¼ cup coarsely chopped chervil

¼ cup coarsely chopped tarragon

4 teaspoons red wine vinegar

1 teaspoon Dijon mustard

Freshly ground black pepper

I. Drain the beans that have been soaking overnight. In a medium saucepan, bring 5 cups of chicken stock, 2½ cups of water and the speckled beans to a simmer over moderate heat. In another saucepan, bring the remaining 3 cups of stock, 1 cup of water and the black beans to a simmer over moderate heat. Cook both kinds of beans, separately, until tender, adding water when needed to keep the level of the liquid ½ inch above the beans. The speckled beans will take approximately 2½ hours and the black beans about 1 hour. Season the beans with salt. Drain the beans and put them in a large bowl.

2. While the dried beans are cooking, blanch the shelled fava beans in boiling salted water for 1 minute. Lift them from the boiling water with a slotted spoon, chill them in ice water and drain. Pinch the favas out of their skins. Return them to the boiling water and cook until just tender, about 4 minutes. Drain the favas and add them to the beans in the bowl.

3. In a medium skillet, heat 2 tablespoons of the olive oil. Add the bell peppers and cook over moderate heat until they begin to soften, 3 to 4 minutes. Add the peppers to the beans in the bowl.

4. Add the minced onion, cilantro, chervil and tarragon to the beans. Whisk the remaining 6 tablespoons of olive oil with the red wine vinegar and mustard; season the vinaigrette with salt and pepper. Toss the bean salad with the dressing and refrigerate until chilled. Check the seasoning before serving and adjust to taste as needed. —*Jean-Christophe Royer*

Tuscan Cranberry Bean and Shrimp Salad

4 SERVINGS

This main-course salad combines some classic Italian ingredients, including pancetta, garlic, rosemary and fruity olive oil. It's traditionally made with dried cannellini beans, so this version, made with fresh cranberry beans, takes less time.

1½ pounds fresh cranberry beans, shelled

2 thyme sprigs

1 small rosemary sprig

2 tablespoons finely chopped flat-leaf parsley, stems reserved

1 bay leaf

2 garlic cloves—1 crushed, 1 minced

Kosher salt

Water

¼ cup extra-virgin olive oil

2 ounces pancetta, finely chopped

1 pound medium shrimp, shelled and deveined

3 tablespoons fresh lemon juice

Freshly ground pepper

Herbed Mixed Bean Salad with Peppers

1. In a medium saucepan, combine the beans with the thyme, rosemary, parsley stems, bay leaf, crushed garlic and 1 teaspoon of salt. Cover with water and bring to a boil. Reduce the heat to moderate, cover partially and cook until the beans are tender, 15 to 20 minutes. Drain the beans and discard the herb stems, bay leaf and garlic clove. **2.** Heat 3 tablespoons of the oil in a large skillet. Add the pancetta and cook over moderately high heat, stirring, until lightly browned, about 4 minutes. Add the shrimp and minced garlic and cook, tossing, until the shrimp turn pink, about 2 minutes. Add the lemon juice, season with salt and pepper and cook for 1 minute. Add the beans and cook, tossing, for 1 minute. Stir in the parsley and the remaining 1 tablespoon of olive oil. Season with salt and pepper and transfer to a bowl. Serve warm or at room temperature.   —*Grace Parisi*

WINE A Tuscan white, such as Vernaccia di San Gimignano, is a crisp contrast to the rich beans. Try the 1998 San Quirico or 1997 Teruzzi & Puthod.

Fennel-and-Endive Slaw with Crab

Tangy Shrimp Salad
8 SERVINGS

The diced cucumbers and tomatoes in this wonderfully refreshing salad become watery if left for too long in the vinaigrette, so add them just before serving.

- 1½ **pounds medium shrimp, shelled and deveined**
- 3 **tablespoons fresh lime or lemon juice**
- 1 **garlic clove, minced**
- ¼ **cup extra-virgin olive oil**
- 1¼ **pounds Kirby cucumbers, peeled and cut into ½-inch dice**
- 1 **pound tomatoes, seeded and cut into ½-inch dice**
- ¼ **cup coarsely chopped flat-leaf parsley**

Salt and freshly ground pepper
- 1 **head red leaf lettuce, separated into leaves**

1. Bring a large saucepan of salted water to a boil. Stir in the shrimp and cook them until they are opaque throughout and curled, approximately 1 minute. Drain the shrimp and rinse under cold water. Pat dry and spread on a platter to cool. **2.** In a large bowl, combine the lime juice with the garlic. Whisk in the olive oil. Add the shrimp, cucumbers, tomatoes and parsley, season with salt and pepper and toss to coat. Line a platter with lettuce leaves, mound the shrimp salad on top and serve.

—*Corinne Trang*

MAKE AHEAD The cooked shrimp can be refrigerated overnight.

Fennel-and-Endive Slaw with Crab
12 SERVINGS

- 1 **tablespoon fennel seeds**
- 3 **tablespoons grapeseed oil**
- 4 **medium fennel bulbs, quartered and cored**
- 1½ **cups fresh grapefruit juice**
- 1 **cup fresh orange juice**
- ¼ **cup fresh lime juice**
- ¼ **cup plus 1 teaspoon fresh lemon juice**
- 2 **tablespoons extra-virgin olive oil**

Salt and freshly ground pepper
- 6 **Belgian endives, cored and thinly sliced crosswise**
- 1½ **pounds crabmeat, picked over (see Note)**
- 2 **tablespoons small flat-leaf parsley leaves**

1. In a small skillet, toast the fennel seeds over moderate heat until fragrant, about 40 seconds. Transfer to a mortar to cool, then pound to a coarse powder. In a small bowl, cover the ground fennel with 2 tablespoons of the grapeseed oil and let stand at least 30 minutes. Strain the fennel oil. **2.** Thinly slice the fennel on a mandoline. Spread the fennel in a large, wide baking dish in an even layer. Pour the grapefruit, orange and lime juices plus ¼ cup of the lemon juice over the fennel and refrigerate for 1½ hours. **3.** Drain the citrus juices into a medium saucepan and boil over high heat until reduced to ½ cup, about 20 minutes. Pour the juice into a bowl set in ice water and chill thoroughly. Transfer the juice to a blender and, with the machine on, slowly add the olive oil and the remaining 1 tablespoon of grapeseed oil until emulsified. Pour the dressing into a bowl, add the remaining 1 teaspoon of lemon juice and season with salt and pepper. **4.** In a very large bowl, toss the fennel with the endives. Add the crab and dressing and toss very gently. Season with salt and pepper and arrange the salad in a large serving bowl or on a platter. Drizzle the fennel oil all over the slaw, garnish with the parsley leaves and serve.   —*Jean-Louis Palladin*

NOTE You can use lump crabmeat, sweet claw meat from Maine crabs or king crab meat, which is the most expensive but also the most delicious.

MAKE AHEAD The fennel oil can be refrigerated for up to 2 days.

Lydon's Mussel and Herb Salad with Croutons

4 SERVINGS

½ cup bottled clam juice

3 bay leaves

2 pounds small mussels, scrubbed and debearded

2 tablespoons extra-virgin olive oil

1 tablespoon melted unsalted butter

Four 1-inch-thick slices crusty sourdough bread

1 garlic clove, split lengthwise

2 tablespoons mayonnaise

1 tablespoon fresh lemon juice

½ teaspoon Aleppo pepper or other mild red chile flakes

Salt

1 pint red cherry or grape tomatoes

¼ cup coarsely chopped flat-leaf parsley

2 tablespoons minced chives

2 tablespoons small tarragon leaves

2 cups cleaned mâche (lamb's lettuce)

½ cup baby spinach leaves

½ cup small watercress sprigs

1. Preheat the oven to 400°. In a large skillet, bring the clam juice to a boil with the bay leaves. Add the mussels, cover and cook over high heat until they open, about 2 minutes; discard any that remain closed. Shell the mussels and place in a bowl. Strain the cooking liquid over them and let cool.

2. In a small bowl, mix the olive oil and butter and brush on both sides of the bread. Toast on a baking sheet in the oven for about 10 minutes, or until golden brown and crisp. Rub the warm toast on both sides with the cut garlic clove. Cut the toast into 1-inch dice.

3. In a small bowl, whisk the mayonnaise with 2 tablespoons of the mussel cooking liquid. Add the lemon juice, Aleppo pepper and a pinch of salt.

4. Lift the mussels from the liquid with a slotted spoon and transfer them to a medium bowl. Add the tomatoes, parsley, chives and tarragon and toss. Add the croutons, mâche, spinach, watercress and the dressing and toss again. Mound the salad on 4 plates and serve. —*Amanda Lydon*

Lydon's Mussel and Herb Salad with Croutons

Smoked Tuna and Guacamole Salad

4 SERVINGS

This recipe was inspired by a dish that chef James Palmer cooks at the Strawberry Hill resort in Jamaica.

DRESSING

3 tablespoons chopped cilantro

1 small garlic clove, minced

2 tablespoons fresh lemon juice

1 tablespoon extra-virgin olive oil

Salt and freshly ground pepper

SALAD

½ teaspoon curry powder

1 large ripe avocado (¾ pound)— halved, pitted and peeled

2 scallions, minced

2 tablespoons fresh lemon juice

1 small garlic clove, minced

3 or 4 dashes hot pepper sauce

Salt and freshly ground pepper

6 cups bite-size pieces of Boston lettuce

2 cups stemmed watercress

1 Granny Smith apple—halved, cored and thinly sliced

6 ounces thinly sliced smoked tuna (see Note)

1. MAKE THE DRESSING: In a small bowl, combine the cilantro and garlic.

Using a fork, blend in the lemon juice, then the olive oil. Season with salt and pepper.

2. MAKE THE SALAD: In a small skillet, toast the curry powder over low heat until fragrant, about 30 seconds. Scrape the powder into a medium bowl. Add the avocado and mash it to a puree. Add the scallions, lemon juice and garlic and continue mashing until light and very smooth. Season with hot sauce, salt and pepper.

3. In a large bowl, combine the lettuce with the watercress and apple slices. Add the dressing and toss well. Arrange the salad on 4 plates. Using 2 spoons, shape 16 mounds of guacamole and set 4 in the center of each salad. Arrange the smoked tuna slices around the guacamole and serve.

—*Marcia Kiesel*

NOTE Smoked tuna is available at specialty food shops and many supermarkets, and from Ducktrap River Fish Farm (800-828-3825).

ONE SERVING Calories 231 kcal, Total Fat 14 gm, Saturated Fat 2 gm
WINE The smoky flavors here suggest a spicy white like Gewurztraminer. Try the 1997 Hugel Jubilée from Alsace.

Smoked Trout Salad with Creamy Walnut Vinaigrette

4 SERVINGS

- ½ cup walnuts (2 ounces)
- ½ large egg yolk (see Note)
- 1 tablespoon sherry vinegar
- ½ cup walnut oil
- 2 tablespoons heavy cream
- Salt and freshly ground pepper
- 1 large Cortland or Mutsu apple—halved, cored and thinly sliced on a mandoline
- 1 small celery root (14 ounces)—quartered, peeled and very thinly sliced on a mandoline
- 2 whole smoked trout (1 pound each), skinned and boned
- 1 tablespoon minced chives

1. Preheat the oven to 400°. Toast the walnuts in a pie plate for about 6 minutes. Let cool and coarsely chop.

2. In a small bowl, whisk the egg yolk with the vinegar. Slowly drizzle in the walnut oil, whisking until the vinaigrette begins to thicken. Slowly whisk in the remaining walnut oil until incorporated. Whisk in the cream and season with salt and pepper. Stir in the walnuts.

3. In a large bowl, combine the apple with the celery root. Add ½ cup of the vinaigrette and toss well. Transfer the salad to a platter or plates. Arrange the smoked trout fillets on top and spoon some more of the dressing on the trout. Sprinkle with the chives and serve. —*Bill Telepan*

NOTE One more tablespoon of heavy cream can be added to the walnut vinaigrette in place of the egg yolk.

WINE Grüner Veltliner from Austria, which is slightly smoky and peppery, is the perfect match for the smoked trout. Look for the 1999 Loimer Langenloiser from the Wachau region or the 1999 Wieninger Herrenholz from Vienna.

Citrus and Mesclun Salad with Marinated Trout

8 SERVINGS

For an especially colorful dish, use pink salmon trout.

- 1½ pounds trout fillets
- ½ cup plus 1½ tablespoons fresh lemon juice
- 2 teaspoons sugar
- 6 juniper berries, crushed
- 1 teaspoon whole black peppercorns, plus ¼ teaspoon crushed black pepper
- Salt
- 2 oranges
- 2 limes
- 1 pink grapefruit
- 1 white grapefruit
- ¼ cup extra-virgin olive oil
- 1 teaspoon Dijon mustard
- ½ pound mesclun
- 1 celery rib, thinly sliced
- 1 tablespoon coarsely chopped fennel fronds (optional)

1. On a work surface, using a thin sharp knife, cut the trout fillets crosswise with the knife held almost flat against the fish to make very thin slices; leave the intact skin behind. Arrange the slices in a large glass baking dish, slightly overlapping them if necessary.

2. In a small bowl, combine ½ cup of lemon juice with the sugar, juniper berries, whole peppercorns and 2 teaspoons of salt. Pour the marinade over the trout. Cover with plastic wrap and refrigerate for 2 hours.

3. Using a sharp knife, peel the oranges, limes and grapefruits, removing all of the bitter white pith. Working over a bowl to catch the juice, cut between the membranes to release the sections. Transfer the sections to a large plate and squeeze the membranes over the bowl to release the juice. Discard the membranes.

4. In a small bowl, whisk the olive oil with the remaining 1½ tablespoons of lemon juice, the mustard and reserved citrus juice. Season with salt and the crushed pepper. Toss the mesclun with some of the dressing and mound on plates. Remove the sliced trout from the marinade, scraping off the seasoning, and arrange on the salads. Garnish with the citrus sections, celery and fennel fronds. Drizzle with the remaining citrus dressing and serve right away. —*Mina Vachino*

MAKE AHEAD The marinated trout can be prepared through Step 2 up to 8 hours in advance. Pour off the marinade after 2 hours so the fish does not continue to cure.

Citrus and
Mesclun Salad
with Marinated
Trout

soups

chapter 4

Fresh Herb Soup

Gingered Broth with Shiitakes and Watercress

4 SERVINGS ✳

For the most vivid color and flavor, add the watercress to the chicken broth just before serving.

- 4 cups chicken stock or canned low-sodium broth
- One 1-inch piece of fresh ginger— peeled, sliced into coins and lightly smashed—plus 1½ teaspoons minced ginger
- 2 tablespoons canola oil
- ¾ pound shiitake mushrooms, stems discarded, caps thinly sliced
- 1 garlic clove, minced

Salt and freshly ground pepper

- 1 bunch watercress (6 ounces), stems discarded and leaves reserved

I. In a large saucepan, combine the stock with the smashed ginger and bring to a boil. Cover and simmer over low heat for 15 minutes. Strain out the smashed ginger pieces.

2. Meanwhile, heat the canola oil in a large nonstick skillet until shimmering. Add the shiitake mushrooms and cook over moderately high heat, stirring occasionally, until the shiitakes are tender and just beginning to brown, about 8 minutes. Add the minced ginger and garlic and cook until fragrant, about 1 minute. Season with salt and pepper. Stir in the shiitake mushrooms and watercress into the soup. Ladle into shallow bowls and serve.

—Judith Barrett

MAKE AHEAD The soup can be refrigerated for up to 1 day. Do not add the watercress until just before you serve the soup.

WINE A snappy, lime-fruity Australian Riesling would be a lovely partner to the earthy shiitakes and a nice contrast to the peppery watercress in this soup. Two good examples: the 1999 Frankland Estate and the 1999 Wolf Blass Gold Label.

Fresh Herb Soup

6 SERVINGS

Crème fraîche goes into the bowl *before* ladling in the soup, so that the cream spreads throughout.

- 2 tablespoons unsalted butter
- 2 large shallots, minced
- 2 small red potatoes, peeled and halved (6 ounces)
- 2 medium carrots, cut crosswise into 2-inch lengths
- 1½ quarts Basic Chicken Stock (p. 98) or canned low-sodium broth
- 2 cups flat-leaf parsley leaves
- 1 cup basil leaves
- ½ cup cilantro leaves
- 2 tablespoons tarragon leaves
- 1 tablespoon fresh lemon juice

Salt and freshly ground pepper

Crème fraîche, for serving

I. Melt the butter in a large saucepan. Add the shallots and cook over low heat until softened, about 5 minutes. Add the potatoes, carrots and chicken stock and bring to a boil. Cover and simmer over low heat until the vegetables are tender, about 10 minutes.

2. Add the parsley, basil, cilantro and tarragon to the soup. Working in batches, puree the soup in a blender. Return the soup to the saucepan, add the lemon juice and season to taste with salt and pepper. Spoon a dollop of crème fraîche into 6 bowls. Ladle the soup on top and serve immediately.

—Ibu Poilâne

MAKE AHEAD The soup can be prepared through Step 1 and refrigerated overnight. Reheat the soup before proceeding.

Farm-Stand Fresh Tomato Soup

6 SERVINGS

Make this vivid uncooked soup instead of the usual tomato salad. Buy the tomatoes a few days in advance and let them ripen on the counter.

- 5 pounds ripe heirloom tomatoes, halved crosswise and seeded
- 2½ to 3 teaspoons sherry vinegar
- Salt and freshly ground pepper
- Sugar
- 30 small red and yellow cherry, grape or pear tomatoes (½ pound), quartered lengthwise
- 3 tablespoons finely chopped basil or cilantro
- 2 tablespoons snipped chives
- 2 tablespoons fruity extra-virgin olive oil

1. Set a box grater in a wide bowl. Hold the rounded side of a tomato half in the palm of your hand and rub the cut side against the large holes of the grater until all that remains is the skin. Discard the skin. Repeat with the remaining tomato halves. Stir in the vinegar and season with salt, pepper and a pinch of sugar. Cover and chill.

2. In a small bowl, toss the cherry tomatoes with salt and a pinch of sugar. Stir the soup well and ladle it into 6 chilled shallow bowls. Mound the cherry tomatoes in the center of each bowl and sprinkle the basil and chives on top. Drizzle each serving with 1 teaspoon of the olive oil and serve right away.

—Sally Schneider

MAKE AHEAD The soup can be prepared through Step 1 early in the day.

ONE SERVING Calories 121 kcal, Total Fat 5.8 gm, Saturated Fat 0.8 gm, Carbohydrates 17.8 gm

WINE The clean flavors and powerful acidity of a brisk Sauvignon Blanc mirror the acidity of the fresh tomatoes and vinegar in the soup. Two refreshing options are the 1998 Fleur du Cap from South Africa and the 1998 Chateau Souverain Alexander Valley from California.

Golden Tomato Gazpacho

6 SERVINGS

Gazpacho started as a peasant dish based on leftover bread, but after Spanish explorers returned from the New World with tomatoes and peppers, the soup evolved into the summery version we know today.

- 1 large European cucumber, peeled and coarsely chopped
- ¼ cup white wine vinegar
- 1 small onion, coarsely chopped
- 4 garlic cloves—3 minced, 1 whole
- 2 pounds yellow tomatoes— peeled, seeded and coarsely chopped
- 2 small yellow bell peppers—cored, seeded and coarsely chopped
- ¼ cup plus 2 tablespoons extra-virgin olive oil, plus more for brushing
- 2 jalapeños, seeded and finely chopped (optional)
- Salt and freshly ground white pepper
- Hot sauce (optional)
- Three 1-inch-thick slices country bread, crusts removed

1. Put the cucumber in a blender or food processor, add the vinegar and pulse until finely chopped but not pureed. Transfer to a large bowl or pitcher. Add the onion, minced garlic, two-thirds of the tomatoes and half the yellow peppers to the blender and puree until smooth. Add this mixture to the cucumber. Finely chop the remaining tomatoes and yellow bell peppers by hand and stir them into the gazpacho. Whisk in the olive oil and jalapeños and season with salt, white pepper and hot sauce. Refrigerate the gazpacho until cold, at least 3 hours.

2. Preheat the broiler. Brush the bread on both sides with olive oil. Toast, turning once. Rub with the whole garlic clove and cut into ½-inch dice. Serve the cold soup in shallow bowls, garnished with the hot croutons. *—Joyce Goldstein*

MAKE AHEAD The gazpacho can be refrigerated for up to 2 days.

Roasted-Tomato Soup with Herbed Croutons

6 SERVINGS

SOUP

- 2 pounds medium plum tomatoes, halved lengthwise
- 2 tablespoons extra-virgin olive oil, plus more for brushing
- Salt and freshly ground pepper
- 1 large onion, finely chopped
- ¼ pound smoked ham, cut into matchsticks
- 5 cups Basic Chicken Stock (p. 98) or canned low-sodium broth

HERBED CROUTONS

- 2 tablespoons unsalted butter
- 2 tablespoons extra-virgin olive oil
- 1 tablespoon minced garlic
- 1 tablespoon minced herbs, such as parsley, rosemary and thyme
- 3 cups sourdough bread in 1-inch cubes
- Salt and freshly ground pepper

1. Preheat the oven to 250°. Arrange the tomatoes on a large rimmed baking sheet, cut side down. Brush with olive oil and season with salt and pepper. Bake for about 1½ hours, or until the skins shrivel. Let the tomatoes cool slightly, then peel and seed them over the baking sheet and transfer them to a bowl. Scrape the seeds, skins and any juices from the baking sheet into a fine sieve set over the bowl and press to extract as much juice as possible.

2. Heat the 2 tablespoons of olive oil in a large saucepan. Add the onion and cook over moderately low heat, stirring occasionally, until softened, about 10 minutes. Stir in the ham, roasted tomatoes and their juices and the stock and bring to a boil. Reduce the heat and simmer the soup for 45 minutes.

3. Preheat the oven to 325°. In a medium skillet, melt the butter in the olive oil. Add the garlic and cook over low heat, stirring, until fragrant, about 2 minutes. Stir in the minced herbs and cook for 30 seconds. Scrape the mixture into a

medium bowl, add the bread cubes and a generous pinch of salt and pepper and toss thoroughly. Spread the bread cubes on a large rimmed baking sheet in a single layer and bake for 20 minutes, stirring occasionally, until golden.

4. Coarsely mash the tomatoes in the soup and season with salt and pepper. Put the croutons in shallow bowls, ladle the soup on top and serve piping hot.

—*Leslie Mackie*

MAKE AHEAD The soup can be refrigerated and the croutons can be stored in an airtight container for up to 2 days.

WINE Try a spicy Zinfandel, like the 1997 Rodney Strong Northern Sonoma Old Vines, or go with a sharp and, earthy white, such as the 1997 Corvo from Sicily.

Spicy Tomato Soup

6 SERVINGS

1¾ pounds ripe tomatoes
2 tablespoons vegetable oil
1 teaspoon mustard seeds
1 medium onion, finely chopped
1 teaspoon ground cumin
½ teaspoon ground coriander
¼ teaspoon turmeric
2 dried red chiles
¼ cup red lentils, rinsed
6 cups water

Kosher salt

ı. Peel and mince the tomatoes. Heat the oil in a medium saucepan. Add the mustard seeds, cover and cook over high heat until the seeds begin to pop. Reduce the heat to moderately low. When the popping stops, add the onion and cook, uncovered, stirring until softened, about 5 minutes. Add all the spices and cook, stirring, until fragrant, about 1 minute.

2. Stir in the lentils, tomatoes and water; season with salt and bring to a boil. Simmer over moderately low heat until the lentils have fallen apart, about 45 minutes. Ladle the hot soup into bowls and serve. —*Jane Sigal*

Spicy Tomato Soup

Spicy Yellow Bell Pepper Soup

4 SERVINGS ✳

1 tablespoon canola oil
1 large onion, chopped
4 large yellow bell peppers, cut up
2 jalapeños, seeded and chopped
4 cups Basic Chicken Stock (p. 98) or canned low-sodium broth
1 large Yukon Gold potato (½ pound), peeled and cut into small pieces

Salt

Cayenne pepper

2 tablespoons sherry vinegar
2 tablespoons chopped cilantro leaves

ı. In a large saucepan, heat the canola oil until just shimmering. Add the chopped onion, yellow bell peppers and jalapeños and cook over moderately low heat, stirring occasionally, until the vegetables begin to soften, about 6 minutes. Add the chicken stock, potato and a pinch each of salt and cayenne pepper and bring to a boil. Cover partially and simmer over moderately low heat until the vegetables are tender, about 25 minutes.

2. Working in batches, puree the soup in a blender or food processor until smooth. (Alternatively, use an immersion blender to puree the soup.) Return the soup to the saucepan and reheat gently. Stir in the sherry vinegar and season with salt. Ladle the soup into shallow bowls, top with the chopped cilantro and serve.

—Judith Barrett

MAKE AHEAD The soup can be refrigerated for up to 2 days. Top with the cilantro just before serving

WINE The bite of jalapeños and cilantro in this soup suggests a light, high-acid Sauvignon Blanc. Look for the 1998 Buena Vista or the 1998 Voss.

Wild Mushroom Soup with Asiago Toasts

10 SERVINGS

You can make a less luxurious version of this soup by using all white—rather than a mixture of white and wild—mushrooms. Since the mushrooms are pureed, the substitution will be less noticeable than you might think.

- 6 tablespoons unsalted butter
- 1 pound white mushrooms, thinly sliced
- 1 medium Vidalia onion, chopped
- 2 shallots, minced
- 1¼ pounds mixed wild mushrooms, trimmed and thickly sliced
- 2 tablespoons Cognac
- 2½ quarts Basic Chicken Stock (p. 98) or canned low-sodium broth
- 10 thyme sprigs
- 2 bay leaves
- ¾ cup heavy cream

Salt and freshly ground pepper

- 1 cup freshly grated Asiago cheese (4 ounces)
- ¼ cup cream cheese (2 ounces)

- 1 large egg yolk
- 1 baguette, sliced ¼ inch thick and toasted
- ¼ cup snipped chives

1. Melt 2 tablespoons of the butter in a large heavy saucepan. Add the white mushrooms and cook over high heat, stirring occasionally, until golden, approximately 8 minutes. Transfer to a plate.

2. Melt the remaining 4 tablespoons of butter in the saucepan. Add the chopped Vidalia onion and the minced shallots and cook over moderate heat until softened. Add the wild mushrooms and cook, stirring occasionally, until tender, about 20 minutes. Add the Cognac and cook until it has evaporated. Stir in the stock, thyme sprigs, bay leaves and cooked white mushrooms and bring to a simmer. Reduce the heat to moderately low and cook for 45 minutes. Using a slotted spoon, scoop out the thyme sprigs and bay leaves; discard.

3. Working in batches, puree the soup in a blender until smooth. Return the soup to the saucepan, stir in the cream and season with salt and pepper.

4. In a mini food processor, combine the grated Asiago, the cream cheese and the egg yolk and pulse until smooth. Spread this Asiago cream on the baguette toasts and put them on a rimmed baking sheet.

5. Preheat the broiler. Broil the toasts, about 8 inches from the heat if possible, for about 2 minutes, or until golden and bubbling.

6. Ladle the soup into shallow bowls and float the Asiago toasts on the surface. Sprinkle the snipped chives on top and serve the soup immediately.

—Grace Parisi

MAKE AHEAD The soup can be prepared through Step 3 and refrigerated for up to 2 days. The toasts and Asiago cream can also be made ahead, but spread the cream on the toasts and broil them shortly before serving.

Asparagus Soup with Roasted Shallots and Morels

8 SERVINGS

If you'd like to garnish the soup with asparagus tips, set aside 16 two-inch tips before cutting up the stalks. Blanch or sauté the tips separately.

- 1 small onion, coarsely chopped
- 1 teaspoon finely chopped garlic
- 2½ tablespoons canola oil
- 2 pounds asparagus, cut into 1-inch lengths
- 6 cups Basic Chicken Stock (p. 98) or canned low-sodium broth
- ½ cup dried morel or porcini mushrooms (about ½ ounce)
- 2 cups hot water
- 2 large shallots, thinly sliced

Salt and freshly ground pepper

1. In a large saucepan, combine the onion, garlic and 2 tablespoons of the oil and cook over moderately high heat, stirring, until softened, about 5 minutes. Add the asparagus and cook for 5 minutes, stirring. Add the chicken stock and bring to a boil. Reduce the heat to moderately low and cook until the asparagus is very tender, about 30 minutes.

2. Preheat the oven to 350°. In a bowl, soak the morels in the hot water until softened, about 20 minutes. Swirl to dislodge any grit; drain and chop.

3. In a pie plate, lightly toss the morels, shallots, the remaining ½ tablespoon of oil and a pinch each of salt and pepper. Bake for about 15 minutes, or until the shallots are softened and lightly browned.

4. Working in batches, puree the soup in a blender. Return the soup to the saucepan and season with salt and pepper. Ladle into soup plates, garnish with the mushroom mixture and serve.

—Kevin Maguire

MAKE AHEAD The soup and morel garnish can be refrigerated separately overnight. Rewarm before serving.

ONE SERVING Calories 100 kcal, Total Fat 5.6 gm, Saturated Fat 0.9 gm

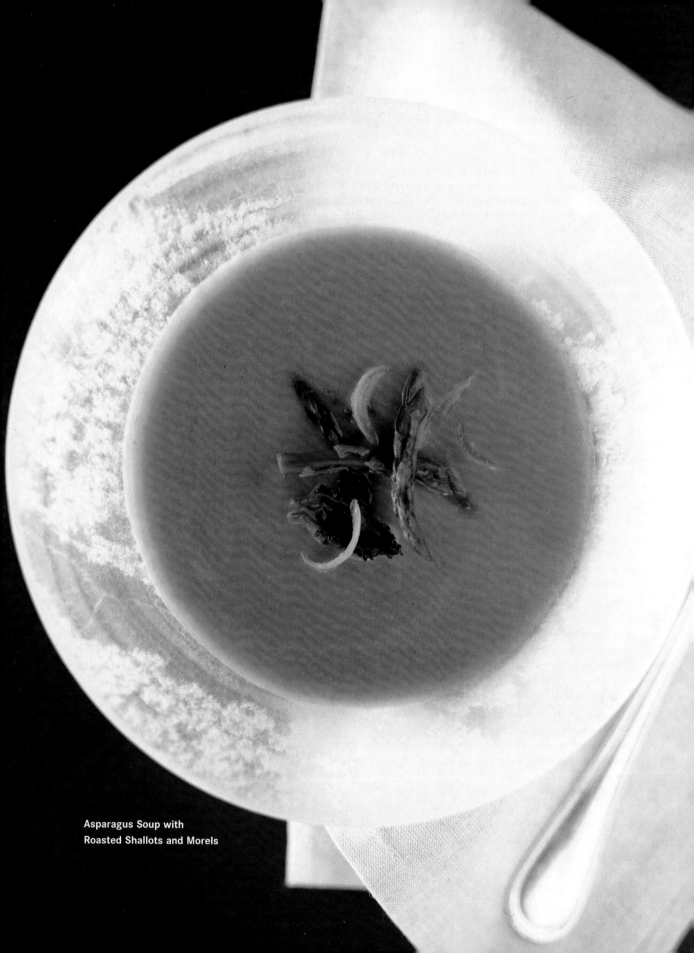

Asparagus Soup with
Roasted Shallots and Morels

Creamy Cucumber Velouté

haute soup

Seven tips for making simple soups look sophisticated:

1. Shave fresh Parmesan cheese with a vegetable peeler and use it as a garnish.

2. Drizzle a flavorful oil—Tuscan green olive oil, walnut oil—onto pureed soups.

3. Sprinkle with balsamic or aged wine vinegar from a cruet you pass at the table.

4. Add citrus zest (finely grated lemon or lime) to vegetable soups.

5. Pass fleur de sel and cracked pink peppercorns in small dishes with the soup.

6. Use shot glasses to serve soup as a passed hors d'oeuvre or present creamy soup in a demitasse cup as an elegant first course.

7. Offer black olive tapenade as a way to boost the flavor of a mild soup.

Leviton's Cauliflower Vichyssoise

Creamy Cucumber Velouté

4 SERVINGS

At Mélisse, in Santa Monica, California, a tiny bit of this cool cucumber velouté is served to customers as an *amuse-gueule* (savory tidbit) before the meal. The soup can also be served as a first course.

  1 pound European cucumbers, cut into ½-inch pieces
  ¾ cup plain whole milk yogurt
  ¼ cup water
  1 tablespoon fresh lemon juice
Pinch of curry powder
Pinch of cayenne pepper
  2 teaspoons crème fraîche or sour cream
Salt and freshly ground white pepper
  ¼ cup heavy cream
  16 small mint leaves

1. In a blender, combine the cucumbers, yogurt, water, lemon juice, curry powder and cayenne and puree until very smooth. Blend in the crème fraîche. Strain the soup through a fine sieve, pressing down on the solids to extract as much liquid as possible. Season the velouté with salt and white pepper and refrigerate until chilled.

2. In a medium bowl, gently whip the heavy cream. Season with salt and white pepper and chill. Just before serving, stir the velouté and pour it into 8 small glasses or demitasse cups. Garnish each serving with a heaping teaspoon of the whipped cream and 2 mint leaves.—*Josiah Citrin*

MAKE AHEAD The velouté can be refrigerated overnight.

WINE A bold Champagne will balance the richness of the soup. Try the 1990 Veuve Clicquot La Grande Dame or the 1996 Iron Horse Wedding Cuvée.

Leviton's Cauliflower Vichyssoise

4 SERVINGS

  2 tablespoons unsalted butter
  2 large leeks, white and tender green parts, thinly sliced
One 2-pound cauliflower, cut into large florets
  6 cups water
  ⅓ cup crème fraîche
Salt and freshly ground white pepper
  2 tablespoons finely diced peeled cucumber
  2 tablespoons minced chives
  1 tablespoon minced shallot
  1 tablespoon rice vinegar
  1 tablespoon extra-virgin olive oil
  4 Wellfleet oysters, shucked, liquor reserved
Osetra caviar (optional)

1. Melt the butter in a large saucepan. Add the leeks and cook over low heat until tender, about 8 minutes. Add the cauliflower and water and bring to a boil. Simmer over low heat until the cauliflower is soft, about 35 minutes. Add the crème fraîche, bring back to a simmer and remove from the heat.

2. Puree the soup in a blender in several batches until very smooth. Season with salt and pepper and chill thoroughly.

3. Just before serving, combine the cucumber, chives, shallot, vinegar and olive oil in a small bowl. Ladle the cold soup into 4 shallow bowls and spoon an oyster and some of its liquor into the center of each. Spoon the cucumber mixture around the oysters, top with a dollop of osetra caviar and serve.

—*Michael Leviton*

Curried Butternut Squash and Cauliflower Soup

12 SERVINGS

Chewy flat bread is a perfect accompaniment for this thick velvety soup.

  3 medium butternut squash (about 5 pounds)—halved, peeled and seeded
  2 tablespoons unsalted butter
  1 large onion, coarsely chopped
  1 tablespoon curry powder
Salt and freshly ground pepper
  2 tablespoons honey
  1 teaspoon cinnamon
One 2-pound head of cauliflower, cut into 1-inch florets
  3 quarts Vegetable Stock (p. 98)
  1 cup heavy cream
Roasted Garlic Flat Breads (p. 248) and crème fraîche, for serving

1. Cut 4 of the butternut squash halves into approximately 1-inch chunks; cut the remaining 2 squash halves into ¼-inch dice.

2. Melt the butter in a large heavy saucepan. Add the chopped onion. Cover the saucepan with a piece of crumpled wax paper and cook over moderately low heat until the onion is softened, about 10 minutes. Remove the wax paper. Add the curry powder and season with salt and pepper. Continue to cook, stirring, until fragrant, about 1 minute. Raise the heat to high, add the honey and the cinnamon and bring to a boil. Stir in the large chunks of squash and the cauliflower florets until coated with the spices. Add the Vegetable Stock and bring to a simmer. Cook over moderately low heat until the vegetables are very tender, about 40 minutes.

3. Working in batches, puree the soup in a blender until smooth. Return the soup to the saucepan. Add the heavy cream, cover partially and simmer over moderately low heat for 10 minutes, stirring occasionally. Season the curried squash soup with salt and pepper to taste.

4. Meanwhile, in a steamer basket set over boiling water, steam the finely diced squash until just tender, about 8 minutes. Lightly season the diced squash with salt.

5. Ladle the soup into shallow bowls. Garnish each bowl of soup with a sprinkling of diced squash and a dollop of crème fraîche and serve hot.

—*Bruce and Eric Bromberg*

MAKE AHEAD The soup can be prepared through Step 3 and refrigerated for up to 2 days. The steamed squash can be refrigerated overnight.

WINE A full, rich, intense Chardonnay with notes of vanilla, ripe pear and citrus, such as the 1997 Hanzell Sonoma Valley, will blend wonderfully with the light curry flavor and creamy texture of the soup.

Curried Butternut Squash and Cauliflower Soup

Spicy Cheddar Mashed Potato Soup

4 SERVINGS

What a great way to use leftover mashed potatoes, and this satisfyingly rich soup couldn't be simpler. If you don't have any turkey stock, chicken stock is just fine.

- 4 cups mashed potatoes
- 1½ cups heavy cream
- 3¾ cups turkey stock
- Salt and freshly ground pepper
- Cayenne pepper
- ¾ cup shredded Cheddar cheese (3 ounces)
- 1 thinly sliced scallion

1. In a large saucepan, stir the mashed potatoes with the heavy cream over moderate heat until well combined. Heat, stirring frequently, until warmed through.

2. Whisk in the stock. Season with salt, pepper and cayenne and bring to a simmer. Ladle the soup into bowls, garnish with the Cheddar and scallion and serve. —*Jimmy Bradley*

WINE This creamy soup is best accompanied by a richly textured white that has some crispness and a note of spice. A vibrant Pinot Blanc from Alsace, such as the 1999 Dopff au Moulin or the 1998 Albert Seltz Reserve, is perfect.

Artichoke Soup with Herbed Matzo Balls

10 SERVINGS

Artichokes and herbs create a chicken soup for spring. If you prefer, use fresh artichoke hearts rather than frozen.

SOUP

- 3 tablespoons light olive oil
- 4 medium leeks, white and pale green parts, halved lengthwise and thinly sliced crosswise
- 3 tablespoons chopped shallots

Salt and freshly ground pepper

Two 8-ounce packages frozen artichoke hearts—thawed, patted dry and cut into 1-inch pieces

- 2 garlic cloves, chopped
- 8 cups Basic Chicken Stock (p. 98) or canned low-sodium broth
- 3 tablespoons fresh lemon juice
- 3 tablespoons chopped flat-leaf parsley, plus more for garnish
- 3 tablespoons coarsely chopped dill, plus more for garnish
- 2 tablespoons coarsely chopped mint, plus more for garnish
- 2 teaspoons finely grated lemon zest

MATZO BALLS

- 4 large eggs, separated

Salt

- 3 tablespoons finely chopped dill
- 2 tablespoons minced chives
- 1 tablespoon finely grated onion
- ¼ teaspoon freshly ground pepper
- 1 cup matzo meal

I. MAKE THE SOUP: Heat the olive oil in a large pot. Add the leeks and shallots, season with salt and pepper and cook over moderate heat until softened but not browned, about 7 minutes. Add the artichokes and garlic and cook over moderately high heat until the garlic is fragrant, about 3 minutes.

2. Add 1 cup of the stock and 2 tablespoons of lemon juice, cover the pot and cook over low heat for 10 minutes. Uncover and boil until the liquid is nearly evaporated. Add the remaining 7 cups of stock, cover and simmer over low heat until the vegetables are tender, about 20 minutes. Let cool a bit.

3. In a food processor or blender, puree half of the soup with the chopped parsley, dill, mint and lemon zest until fairly smooth. Return the puree to the soup and stir.

4. MAKE THE MATZO BALLS: Beat the egg whites with a pinch of salt until stiff. In another bowl, mix the yolks with the dill, chives, onion, pepper and 1 tablespoon of salt. Fold the whites into the yolk mixture until just combined. Sprinkle with the matzo meal and gently fold it in until completely blended. Let the dough rest for 10 to 15 minutes.

5. Bring a large wide saucepan of water to a boil and add salt. Using wet hands, lightly form the matzo ball dough into 20 walnut-size balls and set on a platter. Slide the matzo balls into the water without crowding the pan, in 2 batches if necessary. Tightly cover the pan and boil for 25 minutes without lifting the lid. Using a skimmer or slotted spoon, transfer the matzo balls to a platter and cover.

6. Reheat the soup gently and add the remaining 1 tablespoon of lemon juice. Season with salt and pepper. Ladle the soup into shallow bowls and add 2 matzo balls to each. Garnish with parsley, dill and mint and serve. —*Jayne Cohen*

MAKE AHEAD The artichoke soup can be prepared through Step 3 and refrigerated for up to 1 day.

WINE The soup's artichokes and herbs pair well with a Sauvignon Blanc–based wine, such as the kosher 1997 Alphonse Mellot Sancerre from the Loire Valley.

Corn and Tomato Bisque

4 SERVINGS

- 1 large jalapeño
- 1 tablespoon sherry vinegar
- ½ teaspoon sugar
- 2 tablespoons unsalted butter
- ½ Vidalia onion, finely chopped (about 1 cup)
- 3 cups frozen corn kernels or 1 pound fresh corn kernels
- 1 large garlic clove, minced
- 4 cups Basic Chicken Stock (p. 98) or canned low-sodium broth

Salt and freshly ground pepper

- 2 tablespoons crème fraîche
- 8 frozen plum tomato halves, coarsely chopped, or 4 fresh plum tomatoes—peeled, halved lengthwise, seeded and coarsely chopped
- 1 scallion, thinly sliced
- 1 tablespoon finely chopped cilantro, plus more for garnish

I. Roast the jalapeño on a skewer directly over a gas flame or in a pan under the broiler, turning, until charred all over. Transfer the jalapeño to a bowl, cover with plastic wrap and let steam for 10 minutes. Peel, core, seed and finely chop the jalapeño. In a small bowl, combine the jalapeño with the vinegar and sugar and stir until the sugar dissolves.

2. Melt the butter in a large heavy saucepan. Add the onion and cook over moderately high heat, stirring, until lightly browned, 6 to 7 minutes. Add the corn and garlic and cook, stirring,

Corn and Tomato Bisque

until the corn is lightly browned, about 5 minutes. Add the stock and simmer until the corn is tender, about 15 minutes. Season with salt and pepper.

3. Using a slotted spoon, transfer 1½ cups of the corn to a blender, add the crème fraîche and ½ cup of the cooking liquid and puree until smooth, approximately 2 minutes. Return the puree to the soup.

4. Add the tomatoes, scallion and 1 tablespoon of cilantro to the soup and cook until heated through. Ladle the soup into 4 shallow bowls; garnish with cilantro, the jalapeño and a drizzle of the chile vinegar. Serve hot. —*Grace Parisi*

MAKE AHEAD The soup can be prepared through Step 3 and refrigerated for up to 2 days. Reheat before proceeding.

WINE Try a light, creamy-textured Chardonnay, such as the 1998 Argyle Willamette Valley from Oregon or the 1998 Waterbrook from Washington State.

Market Noodle Soup

6 SERVINGS

1½ pounds dried rice noodles

10 cups Basic Chicken Stock (p. 98) or canned low-sodium broth

1 pound skinless, boneless chicken, cut into 1-inch chunks

Salt

Thai fish sauce *(nam pla)*

¼ cup rice vinegar

¼ cup soy sauce

2 cups pea shoots or stemmed watercress

1½ cups shredded napa cabbage

1 cup mung bean sprouts

Lime wedges

½ cup chopped unsalted peanuts

½ cup cilantro leaves

½ cup sliced scallions

Asian chili sauce

Asian sesame oil

Freshly ground white pepper

1. Put the rice noodles in a large bowl and cover with warm water. Set aside

Market Noodle Soup

and soak the noodles until pliable, about 20 minutes; drain and reserve.

2. In a large saucepan, bring the chicken stock to a boil. Reduce the heat to low, add the chicken and simmer until just cooked through, about 5 minutes. Transfer the chicken to a bowl. Season the stock with salt and fish sauce. Cover the saucepan and keep the stock at a bare simmer over low heat.

3. In a small bowl, combine the rice vinegar and soy sauce. Arrange the pea shoots, cabbage and bean sprouts on a platter. Put the lime wedges, peanuts, cilantro and scallions in small bowls. Arrange all of the condiments and toppings on the table along with the chili sauce, sesame oil and white pepper.

4. Bring a large saucepan of water to a boil; have ready a strainer or colander that will fit inside the pan. Return the chicken to the stock. For each serving, put one-sixth of the noodles in the strainer and dip it into the boiling water; swirl until the noodles are al dente, about 40 seconds. Lift the strainer and shake to drain the noodles; transfer them to a soup bowl. Ladle some of the stock and chicken over the noodles; repeat for the remaining 5 servings. Let your guests garnish and season their soup as they wish.

—*Naomi Duguid and Jeffrey Alford*

WINE A fruity, low-alcohol Chenin Blanc, like the 1998 Covey Run or the 1998 Hogue, both from Washington State, will balance the strong flavors of the fish and chili sauces.

Root Vegetable Soup

potato is tender, about 25 minutes.

2. Remove the soup from the heat and let stand for 10 minutes, then remove the bay leaf. Puree the soup in batches in a blender and return it to the saucepan. Season the soup with the lemon juice and salt and pepper.

3. MAKE THE PEAR RELISH: In a medium bowl, toss the pears with the lemon juice. Fold in the parsley, allspice and nutmeg. Chill the relish.

4. MAKE THE PLANTAIN CHIPS: Peel the plantain and thinly slice it on the diagonal. In a large skillet, heat ¼ inch of oil until shimmering. Add half of the plantain slices and fry over moderate heat until golden brown and crisp, about 2 minutes per side. Drain on paper towels while you fry the rest. Season with salt just before serving.

5. Reheat the soup. Ladle into shallow bowls and garnish with the cold pear relish. Serve with plantain chips.

—*Marcia Kiesel*

MAKE AHEAD The soup can be refrigerated for up to 3 days and the pear relish for 1 day. The plantains can be fried early in the day; reheat them in the oven.

Root Vegetable Soup

6 SERVINGS

You can add cooked dried beans, ham, chicken, lamb or smoked duck to this soup to make it even more substantial.

- 6 cups water
- 3 tablespoons extra-virgin olive oil
- 2 teaspoons salt
- 3 large carrots, finely diced
- 3 medium leeks, white and tender green parts, thinly sliced
- 2 medium Yukon Gold potatoes, peeled and cut into ¼-inch dice
- 2 medium parsnips, peeled and cut into ¼-inch dice
- 2 medium turnips, peeled and cut into ¼-inch dice
- 1 medium onion, finely chopped
- ½ pound celery root, peeled and cut into ¼-inch dice

Jamaican Carrot Soup

10 SERVINGS

SOUP

- 5 tablespoons unsalted butter
- 2 pounds carrots, thickly sliced
- 1 large onion, thinly sliced

Salt and freshly ground pepper

- 4 large scallions, thinly sliced
- ¼ to ½ Scotch bonnet chile, seeded and thinly sliced
- 1 teaspoon soy sauce
- 1 teaspoon chopped thyme
- ½ teaspoon minced ginger
- ¼ teaspoon ground cumin
- ⅛ teaspoon ground allspice
- ⅛ teaspoon freshly grated nutmeg
- 6 cups Basic Chicken Stock (p. 98) or canned low-sodium broth
- 1 small red potato, peeled and thickly sliced
- 1 bay leaf
- 1 tablespoon freshly squeezed lemon juice

PEAR RELISH

- 4 firm, ripe Bartlett pears—peeled, cored and cut into ½-inch dice
- 4 teaspoons fresh lemon juice
- ¼ cup chopped flat-leaf parsley
- ¼ teaspoon ground allspice
- ⅛ teaspoon freshly grated nutmeg

PLANTAIN CHIPS

- 1 large ripe plantain

Vegetable oil, for frying

Salt

I. MAKE THE SOUP: Melt the butter in a large heavy saucepan. Add the carrots and onion and season with salt and pepper. Cook over moderately low heat, stirring occasionally, until the vegetables are softened and golden, about 30 minutes. Add the scallions, Scotch bonnet, soy sauce, thyme, ginger, cumin, allspice and nutmeg and stir until fragrant, about 4 minutes. Add the stock, potato and bay leaf and bring to a boil. Cover and simmer over low heat until the

1 small fennel bulb, cored and cut
   into ¼-inch dice
2 garlic cloves, smashed
Freshly ground pepper

1. In a large saucepan, bring the water with 1 tablespoon of the oil and the salt to a boil. Add the vegetables, cover partially and cook over moderately low heat for about 40 minutes or until they're tender.

2. Season the soup with pepper and transfer to a tureen. Drizzle the remaining olive oil on top, sprinkle with more pepper and serve immediately.

—*Sally Schneider*

ONE SERVING Calories 216 kcal, Total Fat 7.7 gm, Saturated Fat 1.1 gm

Roasted Root Vegetable Soup

4 SERVINGS ❄

You can adjust the amount of each vegetable to suit your taste or even substitute other root vegetables, but keep the total quantity the same.

1 large beet (½ pound)—peeled, halved and sliced ⅓ inch thick
1 medium turnip (½ pound)—peeled, halved and sliced ⅓ inch thick
1 medium parsnip (½ pound)—peeled and sliced on the diagonal ⅓ inch thick
1 medium onion, thickly sliced
2 tablespoons extra-virgin olive oil
4 cups Basic Chicken Stock (p. 98) or canned low-sodium broth
Salt and freshly ground pepper
Crème fraîche or sour cream, for serving
Fresh dill sprigs, for serving

1. Preheat the oven to 500°. On a large rimmed baking sheet, toss the beet, turnip, parsnip and onion with the olive oil and spread in a single layer. Roast the vegetables for about 20 minutes, stirring once or twice, until tender and golden brown around the edges.

2. Transfer the vegetables to a large saucepan. Add the stock; cover and bring to a boil. Simmer over low heat until the vegetables are tender, about 10 minutes.

3. Working in batches, puree the soup in a blender or food processor until smooth. (Alternatively, use an immersion blender to puree the soup.) Return the soup to the saucepan and reheat gently. Season with salt and pepper. Ladle the soup into deep bowls. Top each with a dollop of crème fraîche and a dill sprig and serve at once.

—*Judith Barrett*

MAKE AHEAD The soup can be refrigerated for up to 3 days.

WINE The sweet and bitter flavors of the roasted vegetables here call for a creamy Graves-style Sauvignon Blanc–Sémillon blend. Try the 1998 Carmenet Reserve or the 1998 Benziger Tribute.

Roasted Root Vegetable Soup

German Lentil Soup

MAKES 4 QUARTS

This soup is from an upcoming book to be published by HarperCollins.

2 tablespoons pure olive oil
1½ pounds shoulder lamb chops
1 pound russet potatoes
4 garlic cloves, coarsely chopped
2 red bell peppers, diced
2 carrots, diced
1 large onion, coarsely chopped
1 celery rib, diced
One 28-ounce can crushed tomatoes
1 pound brown lentils, rinsed
10 cups Basic Chicken Stock (p. 98) or canned low-sodium broth
1 bunch flat-leaf parsley, stems discarded and leaves chopped
Kosher salt and freshly ground pepper

German Lentil Soup

1. Heat the oil in a large enameled cast-iron casserole. Add the lamb chops and cook over moderately high heat until browned, about 4 minutes per side. Transfer the chops to a plate.

2. Peel and dice the potatoes. Add them, the garlic, peppers, carrots, onion and celery to the casserole and cook over moderate heat, stirring, for 5 minutes. Reserve 2 tablespoons parsley; add the rest, the lamb chops, tomatoes, lentils and stock and bring to a boil. Add 1 tablespoon salt and a few grindings of pepper. Cover and simmer over low heat until lentils are tender, about 1 hour. Remove the lamb chops and discard the bones. Cut the meat into large pieces and return to the soup. Season with salt and pepper; sprinkle with reserved parsley. —*Lydie Marshall*

MAKE AHEAD The soup can be refrigerated for up to 3 days.

WINE A rustic, earthy red with good fruit will harmonize with the earthiness of the lentils. Two bargains to look for: the 1996 Château Cascadais from Corbières and the 1998 Barton & Guestier Côtes-du-Rhône Tradition.

St. John's Club Bean and Kale Soup

8 SERVINGS

This soup was inspired by a version served by Ines de Costa at the St. John's Club, a restaurant and lounge in Fall River, Massachusetts. Note that the dried beans must soak overnight.

- 2 tablespoons pure olive oil
- 1 pound chorizo, sliced ¼ inch thick
- 1 large Spanish onion, coarsely chopped
- 8 garlic cloves, minced
- ¼ cup finely chopped flat-leaf parsley
- 2 quarts Basic Chicken Stock (p. 98) or canned low-sodium broth
- 2 quarts water
- ½ cup dried red beans (¼ pound), soaked overnight and drained

½ cup dried navy beans (¼ pound), soaked overnight and drained

2 bay leaves

¼ teaspoon dried thyme

¼ teaspoon crushed red pepper

2 large baking potatoes, peeled and cut into ¾-inch chunks

1 pound kale, tough stems and ribs removed, leaves coarsely chopped

Salt and freshly ground pepper

Crusty Portuguese bread, for serving

1. Heat the olive oil in a stockpot. Add the chorizo and onion and cook over high heat, stirring, until the onion is softened, about 3 minutes. Add the garlic and parsley and cook, stirring, for 2 minutes. Add the chicken stock, water, red and navy beans, bay leaves, thyme and crushed red pepper and bring to a boil. Cook over moderate heat until the beans are tender, about 1¼ hours.

2. Add the potatoes and kale to the stockpot, season with salt and pepper and cook over moderate heat, stirring occasionally, until the potatoes are tender, about 30 minutes. Remove the bay leaves. Serve the soup in deep bowls with plenty of crusty bread.

—Emeril Lagasse

MAKE AHEAD The soup can be refrigerated for up to 3 days.

WINE A juicy, inexpensive red with fresh berry and pepper flavors is best with this soup. Try the bargain 1998 Caves Alianca Trás-Os-Montes Terra Boa or the 1995 Luis Pato Bairrada Quinta do Ribeirinho from Portugal.

Chickpea and Spinach Soup

8 SERVINGS

The dried chickpeas need to soak overnight, so plan accordingly.

1½ cups dried chickpeas (¾ pound), soaked overnight and drained

¼ cup extra-virgin olive oil, plus more for drizzling

1 large Spanish onion, coarsely chopped

1 tablespoon finely chopped garlic

2 bay leaves

½ teaspoon crushed red pepper

2 quarts water

1½ pounds spinach, stemmed and coarsely chopped

Salt

1. In a large saucepan, cover the chickpeas with 3 inches of water and bring to a boil. Cover partially and cook over moderately low heat until the chickpeas are tender, about 1 hour; drain.

2. Wipe out the saucepan used to cook the chickpeas and add ¼ cup of the olive oil. Add the chopped onion to the saucepan and cook over moderate heat, stirring occasionally, until lightly browned, about 8 minutes. Add the chopped garlic, bay leaves and crushed red pepper and cook for 2 minutes. Add the water and bring to a boil. Add the chickpeas and cook over moderate heat until very tender, about 10 minutes. Add the spinach and cook until wilted, about 2 minutes. Remove the bay leaves.

3. In a blender, puree the soup in batches until smooth. Season with salt. Ladle into soup plates, drizzle with olive oil and serve. —Emeril Lagasse

MAKE AHEAD The soup can be refrigerated for up to 3 days. When reheating it, thin with water if necessary.

Three-Bean Minestra

6 SERVINGS

Minestra is Italian for a soup that includes a light broth, tiny pasta and a few vegetables, whereas *minestrone* ("big soup") is made with a generous quantity of vegetables.

¼ cup plus 1 tablespoon extra-virgin olive oil

1 onion, finely chopped

2 large garlic cloves, minced

One 28-ounce can peeled Italian tomatoes—drained, seeded and finely chopped

4 cups Basic Chicken Stock (p. 98) or canned low-sodium broth

2 cups water

1 cup frozen shelled cranberry beans or 1 pound fresh cranberry beans, shelled

Salt and freshly ground pepper

4 cups frozen string beans or 1 pound fresh string beans, cut into 2-inch lengths (4 cups)

2 cups frozen flat green beans or ½ pound fresh flat green beans, cut into 2-inch lengths (2 cups)

1 cup dried small tubular pasta, such as *ditali* (¼ pound)

3 tablespoons finely chopped flat-leaf parsley

1 tablespoon red wine vinegar

½ cup freshly grated Parmesan cheese, plus more for serving

1. Heat 2 tablespoons of the olive oil in a large saucepan. Add the onion and garlic and cook over moderate heat, stirring frequently, until lightly browned, about 5 minutes. Add the tomatoes, stock, water and cranberry beans and bring to a boil. Cover partially and cook over moderately low heat until the cranberry beans are tender, about 15 minutes. Season with salt and pepper. Add the string beans and flat beans, cover partially and cook over moderate heat until tender, 10 to 12 minutes.

2. Meanwhile, bring a medium saucepan of salted water to a boil. Add the pasta and cook, stirring, until al dente. Drain the pasta and add it to the beans along with the parsley, red wine vinegar, ½ cup of Parmesan and the remaining 3 tablespoons of olive oil. Season the soup with salt and pepper to taste. Serve the *minestra* in deep bowls and pass extra Parmesan at the table.

—Grace Parisi

MAKE AHEAD The *minestra* can be prepared through Step 1 and refrigerated for up to 2 days.

WINE Look for a Chianti with some spice and good acidity to stand up to the tomatoes and vinegar in the soup. Two choices: the 1997 Castellare di Castellina Chianti Classico or the 1997 Badia a Coltibuono Chianti Classico.

Two-Bean Minestrone with Pancetta and Parmesan

8 SERVINGS

Note that the dried chickpeas and beans need to soak overnight.

- ½ cup dried chickpeas (about 4 ounces), soaked overnight and drained
- 1 quart water
- ½ cup dried *borlotti* or pinto beans (about 3 ounces), soaked overnight and drained
- 2 tablespoons extra-virgin olive oil
- 5 ounces pancetta, finely chopped
- 1 large onion, coarsely chopped
- 1 medium leek, white and tender green parts, coarsely chopped
- 4 large garlic cloves, minced
- 2 large celery ribs, finely chopped
- 2 medium carrots, finely chopped
- 8 cups Basic Chicken Stock (p. 98) or canned low-sodium broth
- 4 thyme sprigs
- 2 bay leaves
- 2 large sage sprigs
- One 3-ounce piece of Parmesan rind
- ½ pound Savoy cabbage, coarsely chopped (4 cups)
- ½ pound kale, large stems discarded, leaves finely chopped (5 cups)
- 1½ cups canned peeled Italian tomatoes, coarsely chopped, juices reserved
- ½ pound green beans, cut into 1-inch lengths

Salt and freshly ground pepper

Hot sauce, for serving (optional)

1. In a medium saucepan, cover the chickpeas with the water and bring to a boil. Reduce the heat to low, cover and simmer for 30 minutes. Add the *borlotti* beans, cover and continue to simmer until tender, about 1 hour.

Remove from the heat and set aside.

2. Meanwhile, heat the olive oil in a large enameled cast-iron casserole. Add the pancetta and cook over low heat until golden, about 5 minutes. Add the onion, leek, garlic, celery and carrots and cook, stirring, for 3 minutes. Add the stock, thyme, bay leaves, sage and Parmesan rind and simmer for 5 minutes. Add the cabbage, kale, tomatoes and their juices and the cooked beans and their liquid. Cover and simmer for 45 minutes. Add the green beans, cover and continue to simmer for 1 hour.

3. Just before serving, discard the thyme sprigs, bay leaves, sage and Parmesan rind. Season with salt and pepper and remove from the heat. Serve in bowls. Pass the hot sauce.

—*Marcia Kiesel*

SERVE WITH Lightly buttered toasts rubbed with garlic and sprinkled with Parmesan. Put a toast in each soup bowl and ladle the hot soup on top.

MAKE AHEAD The minestrone can be refrigerated for up to 4 days.

WINE Try a full-flavored Sangiovese from Montalcino, such as the 1998 Altesino Rosso di Montalcino or the 1998 Argiano Rosso di Montalcino.

Bean Soup with Winter Squash

8 SERVINGS

The dried beans must soak overnight.

- 1 pound dried *emergo, borlotti* or pinto beans, picked over and rinsed
- 3 quarts plus 1 cup water
- ½ cup chopped canned Italian tomatoes
- 2 garlic cloves, crushed
- ¼ cup chopped celery leaves

Large pinch of dried oregano

- ½ cup extra-virgin olive oil

Salt

- 1 medium onion, finely chopped

One 2-pound butternut squash, peeled and cut into 1-inch chunks

Crushed red pepper

Two-Bean Minestrone with Pancetta and Parmesan

1. In a large bowl, cover the dried beans with 2 inches of water and let them soak overnight. Drain and rinse the beans, then transfer them to a medium enameled cast-iron casserole. Add 3 quarts of the water and bring to a simmer over moderate heat, skimming as necessary to remove the foam that rises to the surface. Cook the beans over low heat until almost tender, about 1 hour. Add the tomatoes, garlic, celery leaves, oregano and ¼ cup of the olive oil. Season with salt. Continue cooking until the beans are very tender, about 1½ hours longer.

2. Meanwhile, in a large skillet, heat the remaining ¼ cup of olive oil. Add the onion and cook over low heat until softened but not browned, about 8 minutes. Add the squash and the remaining 1 cup of water, cover and simmer over low heat until the squash is just tender, about 10 minutes.

3. When the beans are done, stir in the squash. Season with salt and crushed red pepper and simmer for 5 minutes. Serve in shallow soup bowls.

—*Silvana Daniello*

MAKE AHEAD The soup can be refrigerated for up to 3 days.

Farro, Bean and Chickpea Soup

Farro, Bean and Chickpea Soup

6 TO 8 SERVINGS

This thick and hearty rustic bean soup from Liguria is made with ancient ingredients that have only recently reappeared in Italian kitchens. It's traditionally made with *cicerchie,* a cross between fava beans and chickpeas, but chickpeas are a fine substitute. Note that three of the ingredients must soak overnight.

- ¼ cup extra-virgin olive oil, plus more for drizzling
- 2 large garlic cloves—1 crushed and 1 minced
- 1 large onion, halved and thinly sliced
- ¾ cup *farro* or wheat berries (4 ounces), soaked overnight
- 1½ cups dried chickpeas or *cicerchie* (½ pound), soaked overnight
- 1 dried red chile
- 1½ cups dried *borlotti* or cranberry beans (½ pound), soaked overnight and drained

Salt and freshly ground pepper
Freshly grated Pecorino Romano cheese, for serving

1. In a large saucepan, heat the ¼ cup of olive oil. Add the crushed garlic and the onion and cook over moderately low heat until softened, approximately 5 minutes. Drain the *farro* and chickpeas; add them to the saucepan along with the chile and cover generously with water. Bring to a simmer, cover and cook over low heat, skimming occasionally, until the chickpeas are almost tender, approximately 1½ hours. Uncover and continue simmering until completely tender, about 20 minutes longer. Remove the chickpeas from the heat.

2. Meanwhile, drain the *borlotti* beans. In a medium saucepan, generously cover the beans with water and bring to a simmer. Cover and cook until tender, about 2 hours. Transfer 2 cups of the cooked beans to a bowl and mash to a coarse puree. Return the mashed beans to the saucepan.

3. Drain the chickpeas and *farro* and return them to the large saucepan; discard the chile. Add the *borlotti* beans with their liquid and the minced garlic to the saucepan and bring to a simmer. Season with salt

and pepper and stir well. Serve the soup hot in bowls. Pass the olive oil for drizzling and the cheese for sprinkling at the table.

—*Nancy Harmon Jenkins*

WINE The rustic flavors of this hearty soup are brightened with a kick of chile. Look for a red with zesty fruit to provide an attractive contrast. Try the 1996 Valpolicella Classico Allegrini or a Chianti Classico, such as the 1995 Castello di Gabbiano Riserva.

Lobster Broth with Porcini

10 SERVINGS

You can save a step by substituting cooked lobsters for the live ones called for in this recipe.

Two live or cooked 1½-pound lobsters

- 3 tablespoons pure olive oil
- 4 large shallots, thinly sliced
- 2 thyme sprigs
- 2 tablespoons tomato paste
- 2 tablespoons Cognac or brandy
- 4 cups water

Salt

- 1 cup dried porcini mushrooms (1 ounce)
- 8 cups Rich Chicken Stock (recipe follows)

Freshly ground white pepper

- ¼ cup chervil or parsley leaves, for garnish

Extra-virgin olive oil, for garnish (optional)

I. If using live lobsters, bring a large pot of water to a boil. Plunge the lobsters in head first and cook over high heat until the lobsters are red almost all over, about 5 minutes. The water may just have returned to a boil at this point. Using tongs, transfer the lobsters to a large bowl and let cool.

2. When the lobsters are cool enough to handle, separate the heads from the bodies. Using kitchen shears, snip the underside of the tail shells down the center and remove the lobster tail meat in 1 piece. Remove the dark intestinal vein in the tail, then slice the meat ¼

inch thick. Twist off the claws, crack them with a mallet and remove the meat. Cut the meat from each claw into 3 pieces. Cover and refrigerate the lobster meat if not making the recipe straight through. Reserve the lobster shells, including the heads.

3. Rinse the insides of the lobster shells, then break them up into very small pieces. In a large saucepan, heat the pure olive oil. Add the lobster shells and cook over moderately high heat, stirring often, until the shells start to brown, about 5 minutes. Add the shallots and thyme sprigs and cook, stirring, until the shallots start to brown, about 3 minutes. Reduce the heat to moderate and add the tomato paste. Cook, stirring, until the tomato paste starts to stick to the bottom of the pan, about 3 minutes. Add the Cognac and simmer, scraping up the browned bits from the bottom. Add the water and a pinch of salt and bring to a simmer. Cook the lobster stock over low heat until it has reduced to 2 cups, about 20 minutes.

4. Skim the lobster oil from the surface and discard. Line a fine strainer with 4 layers of dampened cheesecloth and slowly strain the lobster stock through it into a clean large saucepan.

5. Put the dried porcini mushrooms in a heatproof bowl. Bring 2 cups of chicken stock to a simmer and pour over the porcini; let the mushrooms soften for 20 minutes. Rub the porcini to loosen any grit, then lift them out. Reserve the porcini for another use. Let the soaking liquid stand for 5 minutes so the grit falls to the bottom, then pour the liquid into the pan with the lobster stock, leaving behind any grit. Add the remaining 6 cups of chicken stock to the saucepan.

6. Bring the broth to a bare simmer. Season with salt and white pepper and keep warm partially covered over very low heat.

7. If needed, bring the lobster meat to

room temperature; season lightly with salt. Spoon the lobster into 10 warmed shallow soup plates. Ladle the broth over the lobster meat and garnish with a few chervil leaves. Drizzle with extra-virgin olive oil and serve.

—*Jeremy Strode*

MAKE AHEAD The recipe can be prepared through Step 5 up to 1 day ahead. Refrigerate the broth, lobster meat and lobster oil separately.

WINE A fresh, aromatic Australian Riesling with lime nuances is an elegant contrast to the mild soup. Try the 1998 Grosset Polish Hill or the 1999 Wolf Blass Gold Label.

RICH CHICKEN STOCK

MAKES ABOUT 12 CUPS

- 6 pounds chicken wings
- 4 quarts cold water
- 8 parsley sprigs
- 3 scallions, halved crosswise
- 1½ tablespoons kosher salt

I. In a large saucepan, cover the chicken wings with the cold water and bring to a simmer over moderate heat, skimming as necessary. Add the parsley, scallions and salt and simmer for 2 hours, skimming occasionally.

2. Line a colander with 4 layers of dampened cheesecloth. Set the colander over a heatproof bowl and pour in the stock. Let cool to room temperature, then refrigerate for up to 1 week or freeze for up to 1 month. Skim off the fat before using. —*J.S.*

Silky Fennel Soup with Crabmeat

4 SERVINGS ❋

Adding sweet crabmeat to this soup makes for a sophisticated first course, but you can serve it without the shellfish and still have a lovely dish.

- 1 tablespoon extra-virgin olive oil
- 2 fennel bulbs (2 pounds)—halved lengthwise, cored and cut into ½-inch pieces, fronds reserved
- 1 medium onion, coarsely chopped

4 cups chicken stock or canned
low-sodium broth

1 medium Yukon Gold potato,
peeled and cut into ½-inch pieces

Salt and freshly ground pepper

½ pound fresh crabmeat,
picked over

1. Heat the oil in a large saucepan until shimmering. Add the fennel pieces and onion, cover and cook over moderate heat, stirring occasionally, until crisp-tender, about 7 minutes. Add the chicken stock and potato, cover and bring to a boil. Simmer over moderately low heat until the vegetables are tender, about 10 minutes.

2. Working in batches, puree the soup in a blender or food processor until smooth. Return the soup to the saucepan and reheat gently. Season with salt and pepper. Ladle the soup into shallow bowls and mound the crab on top. Garnish with fennel fronds and serve. —*Judith Barrett*

MAKE AHEAD The soup can be refrigerated for 2 days. Wait to add the crab and the fennel fronds until just before serving.

WINE The silky texture and anise flavor of this soup go best with a dry and delicate white wine, such as an Italian Gavi. Try the 1997 Coppo La Rocca or the 1998 Banfi Cellars Principessa Gavia.

White Corn and Clam Chowder
8 SERVINGS

2 tablespoons plus 1 teaspoon
pure olive oil

2 strips of bacon, finely chopped

1 large onion, coarsely chopped

1 cup dry white wine

1½ cups heavy cream

3 pounds littleneck clams,
scrubbed

1 cup corn kernels (from 2 ears)

1 medium leek, white and tender
green parts, coarsely chopped

1 small celery rib, finely chopped

2 parsley sprigs

2 thyme sprigs

1 teaspoon ground coriander

1 tablespoon all-purpose flour

2 cups bottled clam juice

¾ pound Yukon Gold potatoes,
peeled and cut into ¼-inch dice

1 cup milk

Salt and freshly ground pepper

½ cup yellow bell pepper, cut
into ¼-inch dice

½ cup finely shredded basil

1. Heat 1 teaspoon of the olive oil in a medium saucepan. Add the bacon and cook over moderately low heat until the fat is rendered, about 4 minutes. Add the onion and cook, stirring occasionally, until softened, about 7 minutes. Add ½ cup of the wine and boil over moderately high heat until evaporated, about 7 minutes. Add 1 cup of the heavy cream and bring to a boil. Add the clams, cover and cook until they begin to open, approximately 2 minutes; as the clams open, transfer them to a shallow dish. Remove the saucepan from the heat.

2. Remove the clams from their shells and put them in a small bowl. Strain the cream mixture over the clams.

3. In a large saucepan, heat the remaining 2 tablespoons of olive oil. Add the corn, leek, celery, parsley, thyme and coriander. Cover and cook over low heat, stirring occasionally, until the vegetables soften, about 10 minutes. Add the remaining ½ cup of wine and simmer over moderately high heat until evaporated, about 4 minutes. Add the flour and cook, stirring, for 1 minute. Gradually stir in the clam juice and bring to a boil over moderately high heat, stirring constantly. Reduce the heat to low, cover and simmer for 5 minutes. Transfer the soup to a blender and puree. Strain the puree through a coarse sieve and return it to the large saucepan.

4. In a medium saucepan, cover the potatoes with water and bring to a boil; boil until just tender, about 5 minutes. Drain the potatoes and add them to the soup along with the milk and the

remaining ½ cup of heavy cream.

5. Bring the soup to a gentle simmer over low heat. Stir in the reserved clams in cream; keep stirring until warmed through. Season the soup with salt and pepper and ladle it into warmed bowls. Garnish each soup with a sprinkling of yellow bell pepper and basil and serve right away. —*Victor Scargle*

MAKE AHEAD The corn and clam chowder can be prepared through Step 3 and refrigerated for up to 1 day.

WINE This elegant chowder with its hint of basil needs the contrast of a concentrated, mouth-filling Chardonnay. Try the 1997 Cuvée Cynthia.

Panhandle Clam Chowder
8 SERVINGS

3½ cups water

5 dozen cherrystone clams,
scrubbed and rinsed

4 tablespoons unsalted butter

¼ cup all-purpose flour

2 to 3 slices of bacon, cut into
½-inch pieces

2 carrots, coarsely chopped

½ cup coarsely chopped onion

2 small celery ribs, coarsely
chopped

2 medium red-skinned potatoes,
cut into ½-inch dice

1½ cups heavy cream or half-and-half

1½ cups milk

1 teaspoon freshly ground pepper

¼ teaspoon dried thyme

1. Bring 2 cups of the water to a boil in a large soup pot. Add half of the clams, cover and cook just until they open, 5 to 8 minutes; remove the clams to a platter as they open. Return the water to a boil and repeat with the remaining clams. Strain the clam broth through 4 layers of dampened cheesecloth to remove any sand or grit; reserve 4 cups of the broth. Remove the clams from the shells and coarsely chop them.

2. In a skillet, melt the butter until foamy. Add the flour and cook over moderately low heat, stirring often, until

the roux is lightly golden, approximately 15 minutes.

3. Wipe out the soup pot. Add the bacon and cook over moderate heat, stirring occasionally, until slightly brown and crisp, about 6 minutes. Pour off all but 1 tablespoon of the bacon fat. Add the carrots, onion and celery and cook, stirring occasionally, until softened, about 12 minutes. Add the potatoes, raise the heat to moderate and cook, stirring, until crisp-tender, about 5 minutes.

4. Add the remaining 1½ cups of water to the pot along with the reserved clam broth, the light cream, the milk, pepper and thyme. Simmer over low heat until the potatoes are just tender, about 5 minutes. Thoroughly stir in the roux and cook over moderately low heat, stirring frequently, until thickened, about 10 minutes. Add the clams and cook until heated through, about 3 minutes. Ladle the clam chowder into soup bowls and serve piping hot.

—*Susan and Cassie Gary*

MAKE AHEAD The chowder can be refrigerated overnight and rewarmed over moderately low heat.

WINE To match the rich soup, go with a rich, oaky California Chardonnay, such as the 1998 Edna Valley Paragon or the 1996 Sanford.

Smoky Seafood Chowder

6 SERVINGS

Smoked scallops or smoked oysters are a wonderful substitute for the smoked mussels called for in this recipe.

One 1½-pound lobster
- 6 tablespoons unsalted butter
- 2 tablespoons finely diced lean salt pork
- 2 medium onions, coarsely chopped
- 1 pound red potatoes, peeled and cut into ½-inch dice
- 2 cups bottled clam juice

- 1 cup water
- 1 bay leaf
- 1 quart light cream
- Two 1-pound halibut or haddock fillets, without skin
- 6 ounces smoked mussels, drained and patted dry
- 6 ounces smoked shrimp, drained and patted dry
- ½ teaspoon sweet paprika
- Salt and freshly ground pepper
- 3 tablespoons chopped flat-leaf parsley, for garnish

1. In a medium pot of boiling salted water, cook the lobster until bright red all over, about 9 minutes. Transfer the lobster to a plate and let cool slightly. Twist the tail and claws from the body and crack the claws. Remove the meat from the tail in 1 piece. Make a slit down the center of the tail meat and remove the intestinal vein. Remove the meat from the claws. Cut the lobster meat into 1-inch pieces. Cover and refrigerate.

2. Melt the butter in a large saucepan. Add the salt pork and cook over moderate heat, stirring, for 1 minute. Stir in the onions and cook until softened, about 7 minutes. Add the potatoes, clam juice, water and bay leaf and bring to a simmer. Cook over moderate heat until the potatoes are just tender, about 12 minutes. Add the cream and return the chowder to a simmer. Add the fish fillets and simmer gently until they break apart and are cooked through, about 10 minutes.

3. Remove the soup from the heat and stir in the mussels, shrimp and lobster meat. Cook over low heat until the shellfish is just heated through. Add the paprika and season with salt and pepper. Ladle the chowder into mugs or bowls, garnish with the parsley and serve. —*Kristie Trabant Scott*

MAKE AHEAD The chowder can be made ahead and refrigerated for up to 1 day. Rewarm gently over moderately low heat.

Bluefish Chowder

6 SERVINGS

If you want to make a lighter version of this chowder, use light cream or half-and-half rather than the heavy cream, or omit the cream altogether and add a little bit more stock, about a cup or even less. For the best flavor, let the finished chowder stand for 1 hour and reheat gently before serving. This recipe is from *50 Chowders,* published by Scribner.

- 4 ounces meaty slab bacon, cut into ⅓-inch dice
- 4 tablespoons unsalted butter
- 3 garlic cloves, minced
- 2 medium celery ribs, cut into ⅓-inch dice
- 1 large onion, coarsely chopped
- 1 large jalapeño, seeded and minced
- 1 quart Rich Fish Stock (recipe follows)
- 3 large ears of corn, kernels cut off
- 1½ pounds Yukon Gold potatoes, peeled and sliced ⅓-inch thick
- 1 pound plum tomatoes—peeled, seeded and cut into ½-inch dice
- Salt and freshly ground pepper
- 2 pounds skinned bluefish fillets, dark flesh discarded, fish cut into 2-inch chunks
- 1½ cups heavy cream
- ¼ cup coarsely chopped basil

1. In a large enameled cast-iron casserole, cook the bacon over low heat until crisp, about 6 minutes. Pour off all but 1 tablespoon of the bacon fat.

2. Add the butter and garlic to the casserole and cook over low heat until the garlic is fragrant, about 30 seconds. Add the celery, onion and jalapeño and cook, stirring occasionally, until the onion is softened but not browned, about 8 minutes. Add the Rich Fish Stock, corn and potatoes and bring to a boil over moderately high heat. Boil until the potatoes begin to soften, about 10 minutes. Mash a few of the potato slices against the side of the casserole

Panhandle Clam Chowder

Bluefish Chowder

to thicken the soup. Add the tomatoes and season with salt and pepper.

3. Add the bluefish and cook over low heat for 5 minutes. Remove from the heat and let stand for 10 minutes. Gently stir in the cream and basil and serve.

—Jasper White

MAKE AHEAD The recipe can be prepared through Step 2 and refrigerated overnight. Bring the chowder to a simmer before proceeding.

WINE Select a creamy-textured Chardonnay, such as the 1998 Glen Carlou or the 1998 Rosemount Estate Orange Vineyard, both of which are from Australia.

RICH FISH STOCK
MAKES ABOUT 2 QUARTS
This stock is rich in flavor, not in fat.

- 2 tablespoons unsalted butter
- 4 medium celery ribs, thinly sliced crosswise
- 2 medium onions, thinly sliced crosswise
- 2 medium carrots, thinly sliced crosswise
- 2 bay leaves
- 6 to 8 thyme sprigs
- ¼ cup coarsely chopped flat-leaf parsley
- 2 tablespoons whole black peppercorns
- 4 pounds nonoily fish bones, heads and trimmings, rinsed well
- ¼ cup dry white wine
- 6 cups very hot tap water

Sea salt

1. Melt the butter in a large saucepan. Add the celery, onions, carrots, bay leaves, thyme, parsley and peppercorns to the saucepan and cook over moderate heat, stirring occasionally, until the vegetables are softened, about 8 minutes. Stir in the fish bones, heads and trimmings and the wine. Cover and cook, stirring once, until the bones turn completely white, about 15 minutes.

2. Add the hot water, stir gently and bring to a simmer over high heat. Reduce the heat to low and simmer gently for 10 minutes. Remove from the heat, stir once and let stand for 10 minutes. Strain the stock through a fine sieve. Season lightly with salt and let cool, then refrigerate. *—J.W.*

MAKE AHEAD The stock can be refrigerated for up to 1 week or frozen in an airtight container for 1 month.

Garlicky White Bean Soup with Chicken and Chard
4 SERVINGS ✺

- 2 tablespoons extra-virgin olive oil
- 1 large onion, finely chopped
- 1½ tablespoons minced garlic

Crushed red pepper

- 4 cups Basic Chicken Stock (p. 98) or canned low-sodium broth
- 1 pound Swiss chard, stems and tough ribs removed, leaves coarsely chopped

One 19-ounce can white beans, such as cannellini or Great Northern, drained and rinsed

- ½ pound boneless, skinless chicken breast, sliced crosswise ⅓ inch thick

Salt and freshly ground pepper

1. Heat the oil in a large saucepan until shimmering. Add the chopped onion, 1 tablespoon of the minced garlic and a pinch of crushed red pepper. Cook over moderately high heat, stirring frequently, until the onion is softened, about 6 minutes. Add the stock, Swiss chard and beans and bring to a boil. Reduce the heat to moderately low and simmer until the chard is tender and the soup is slightly thickened, about 15 minutes.

2. Add the chicken and the remaining ½ tablespoon of garlic and simmer gently over moderately low heat until the chicken is just cooked through, about 5 minutes. Season with salt and pepper. Ladle the soup into bowls and serve.

—*Judith Barrett*

MAKE AHEAD The soup can be refrigerated for up to 1 day.

WINE A refreshing Spanish white, such as the 1998 Cune Monopole Blanco Seco Rioja or the 1998 Torres Viña Sol, will echo the slightly bitter Swiss chard.

Chicken Albóndigas Soup

4 SERVINGS

If you use canned broth, simmer it first with a few chicken wings and some chopped onion, carrot and celery to boost the flavor.

- 1 tablespoon pure olive oil
- ¼ cup minced onion
- 1 tablespoon minced poblano plus ½ poblano chile, seeded and thinly sliced
- 1 tablespoon minced red bell pepper
- 1 tablespoon minced garlic
- 1 teaspoon ground cumin
- ½ teaspoon ground coriander
- ½ pound ground chicken
- ¼ cup cooked rice
- 1 large egg white, lightly beaten
- 2 tablespoons minced cilantro, plus leaves for garnish
- 2 canned chipotle chiles in adobo, seeded and minced
- Kosher salt and freshly ground pepper
- 4 cups Basic Chicken Stock (p. 98) or canned low-sodium broth
- ½ cup corn kernels

- ½ cup finely diced, seeded plum tomato
- Lime wedges, for serving
- Tortilla chips, for serving

1. Heat the olive oil in a medium skillet. Add the onion, minced poblano, red bell pepper and garlic and cook over moderate heat until softened, about 4 minutes. Add ½ teaspoon of the cumin and the coriander and cook until fragrant, about 1 minute. Scrape the mixture into a medium bowl and let cool.

2. Add the chicken to the bowl, along with the rice, egg white, minced cilantro, chipotles, ¾ teaspoon salt and ¼ teaspoon pepper. Mix with your hands until thoroughly combined. Roll tablespoons of the meat into balls and set on a large plate.

3. In a large saucepan, combine the chicken stock with the corn, tomato, sliced poblano and the remaining ½ teaspoon of cumin and bring to a simmer. Season with salt and pepper and cook over moderate heat until the

vegetables soften, about 5 minutes. Add the meatballs and cook over low heat until firm and cooked through, about 5 minutes. Ladle the soup into large shallow bowls and garnish with the cilantro leaves. Serve with the lime wedges and tortilla chips.

—*Roger Hayot*

Garlicky White Bean Soup with Chicken and Chard

Chicken Albóndigas Soup

Basic Chicken Stock

MAKES 2 QUARTS

Either save chicken carcasses in the freezer until you have enough to make stock or buy inexpensive parts like backs and wings.

- 6 pounds chicken carcasses, backs, legs or wings
- 3 large celery ribs, cut into 2-inch lengths
- 2 large carrots, cut into 2-inch lengths
- 2 unpeeled medium onions, quartered
- 3 quarts water

I. Combine all of the ingredients in a stockpot and bring to a boil over high heat. Reduce the heat and simmer for 20 minutes, skimming frequently. Cover partially, leaving only a small opening, and simmer over low heat for 2½ hours.

2. Strain the stock into a large bowl, pressing on the solids. Wipe out the stockpot, return the stock to it and boil until reduced to 2 quarts. Let cool slightly and refrigerate. Remove the solidified fat from the stock before using.   —FOOD & WINE Test Kitchen

MAKE AHEAD The stock can be refrigerated for up to 1 week or frozen for up to 1 month.

Vegetable Stock

MAKES 3 QUARTS

- 16 cups water
- 3 carrots, thinly sliced
- 3 celery ribs, thinly sliced
- 2 parsnips, thinly sliced
- 2 bay leaves
- 2 medium onions, quartered
- 1 tablespoon black peppercorns

Combine the ingredients in a stockpot and bring to a boil. Reduce the heat to moderately low and simmer until reduced to 3 quarts, about 1½ hours. Strain.   —Bruce and Eric Bromberg

MAKE AHEAD The vegetable stock can be refrigerated for up to 1 week or frozen for up to 1 month.

Enriched Chicken Stock

MAKES 5 CUPS

Actually doubly enriched, this stock recipe calls for canned broth instead of water and also adds beef to give a deep flavor.

- 2 tablespoons pure olive oil
- 1 pound chicken wings
- 1 pound lean beef brisket, cut into 1-inch cubes

Salt and freshly ground pepper
- 3 medium carrots, cut into ½-inch pieces
- 1 large onion, coarsely chopped
- 1 small celery root (10 ounces), peeled and cut into ½-inch dice
- 1 large tomato, cored and quartered
- 6 cups canned low-sodium chicken broth

I. Heat the oil in a large saucepan. Add the chicken wings and the brisket and cook over moderately high heat, turning, until they're browned all over, approximately 10 minutes. Season with salt and pepper and add the carrots, the chopped onion, diced celery root and the tomato. Cook over moderate heat, stirring occasionally, until the vegetables are barely softened, about 10 minutes.

2. Add the broth to the pan and bring it to a boil. Partially cover the pan and cook over moderately low heat for 30 minutes. Strain the stock and reserve the meat and vegetables for another use. Refrigerate the stock until the fat on the surface is fairly firm. Remove the fat from the surface before using the stock or freezing it.

—Lydie Marshall

MAKE AHEAD Like any stock, this one can be refrigerated for up to a week or can be frozen for up to 1 month. Or, if you're keeping it in the refrigerator, simply bring it to a boil at the end of a week, return it to the refrigerator and it will be good for another week. You can go on in this way forever if you like.

Gingered Turkey Noodle Soup

4 SERVINGS

- 2 quarts Rich Turkey Stock (recipe follows)
- One 2-inch piece of ginger, peeled and sliced ¼ inch thick
- 1 dried red chile

Salt and freshly ground pepper
- 5 ounces bean threads
- 6 medium dried shiitakes
- 2 cups boiling water
- ¾ pound spinach, large stems discarded
- 1 medium carrot, shredded
- 4 cups diced cooked turkey meat

Szechwan pepper (see Note) or black pepper
- ⅓ cup thinly sliced scallions

I. In a large saucepan, bring the stock to a boil. Using the side of a heavy knife, smash the ginger and chile and add them to the stock. Cover and simmer for 30 minutes. Discard the ginger and chile and season the soup lightly with salt and pepper. Cover and keep hot.

2. In separate heatproof bowls, cover the bean threads and shiitake mushrooms with the boiling water and set aside until softened, about 10 minutes. Drain the shiitakes; cut off and discard the stems and cut the caps into thin slices. Drain the bean threads.

3. In a medium saucepan of boiling water, blanch the spinach for 15 seconds. Using a slotted spoon, transfer it to a colander. Add the carrot to the boiling water; cook for 10 seconds. Add the carrot to the colander. Squeeze the spinach dry and coarsely chop it.

4. Put the turkey in bowls and season with salt and Szechwan pepper. Add the bean threads, shiitakes, spinach, carrot and scallions, pour the hot stock on top and serve.   —Barbara Tropp

NOTE Szechwan pepper can be found at Chinese markets.

WINE Accent this soup with a spicy Alsace Gewurztraminer, like the 1998 Domaines Schlumberger or the 1998 Bruno Hunold.

RICH TURKEY STOCK
MAKES ABOUT 3 QUARTS

- 8 pounds turkey parts, such as wings, thighs and drumsticks
- 14 cups water
- Reserved turkey neck and giblets (except the liver)
- 1 large onion, thickly sliced
- 1 large carrot, thickly sliced
- 1 large celery rib, thickly sliced
- 2 garlic cloves, sliced
- 1 teaspoon kosher salt
- Freshly ground pepper

1. Preheat the oven to 400°. In a large roasting pan, roast the turkey parts for about 1 hour, turning occasionally, until well browned; transfer to a large pot.

2. Set the roasting pan over 2 burners. Add 3 cups of the water and boil over moderately high heat, scraping up any browned bits from the bottom of the pan. Add the liquid to the pot.

3. Add the neck and giblets to the pot along with the onion, carrot, celery, garlic, salt, several pinches of pepper and the remaining 11 cups of water. Bring to a boil. Reduce the heat to moderately low, cover partially and simmer the stock for about 2½ hours. Strain the stock and skim the fat before using.

—*FOOD & WINE Test Kitchen*

MAKE AHEAD The turkey stock can be refrigerated for up to 1 week or frozen for up to 1 month.

Gingered Turkey Noodle Soup

eggs
chapter 5

Soft Scrambled Eggs with Herbs and Shaved Truffles

2 SERVINGS

- 1 tablespoon unsalted butter
- 6 large eggs, beaten

Salt and freshly ground pepper

- 1 tablespoon snipped chives
- 1 tablespoon finely chopped flat-leaf parsley
- 1 small fresh truffle

Buttered brioche toast, for serving

Melt the butter in a large nonstick skillet. Add the eggs and season with salt and pepper. Cook over moderate heat, stirring gently with a wooden spoon, until the eggs are creamy, with large, soft curds, about 4 minutes. Stir in the chives and parsley and spoon the scrambled eggs onto warmed plates. Thinly shave the truffle all over the scrambled eggs and serve right away with the buttered brioche toast.

—Grace Parisi

Tortilla Scramble with Salsa

4 SERVINGS

The toasted tortilla chips add a rich corn flavor to the Tortilla Scramble and stay crisp in the creamy, cheesy scrambled eggs.

- 1 cup broken tortilla chips (pieces about 2 inches)
- 10 large eggs
- 2 tablespoons heavy cream

Salt and freshly ground pepper

- 2 tablespoons unsalted butter
- ½ cup Fontina cheese, cut into ½-inch dice (2½ ounces)

Fourth-of-July Firecracker Salsa (p. 319) or Grilled Tomatillo and Purple Basil Salsa (p. 321)

1. Preheat the oven to 400°. Spread the tortilla chips on a baking sheet and toast in the oven for 4 minutes, or until nicely browned. Let cool.

2. In a large bowl, lightly beat the eggs. Add the cream to the bowl. Season with salt and pepper and beat again.

3. Melt the butter in a medium nonstick skillet. When the foam subsides, add the eggs and cook over moderately low heat, using a spatula to lift the cooked edges and tilting the skillet so the uncooked eggs seep underneath. When the eggs are almost set, add the tortilla chips and stir a few times. Add the cheese and stir once or twice, then remove the skillet from the heat. Serve the eggs at once, with the salsa on the side.

—Marcia Kiesel

Huevos Rancheros

6 SERVINGS

- 1 ancho chile, stemmed and seeded
- 1 cup boiling water
- 2 tablespoons pure olive oil, plus more for oiling the skillet
- 4 large garlic cloves, unpeeled
- 3 jalapeños
- 1 medium sweet onion, halved
- 1 pound plum tomatoes

Salt

- 1 dozen large eggs
- ¼ cup plus 2 tablespoons crumbled *queso blanco* or *ricotta salata*
- ¼ cup coarsely chopped cilantro

1. In a large cast-iron skillet, toast the ancho chile over moderate heat for 1 minute per side. Transfer to a heatproof bowl and add the boiling water. Cover with a plate and let stand for 20 minutes. Remove the ancho and finely chop it; reserve the soaking liquid.

2. Lightly oil the skillet. Lightly char the garlic, jalapeños and onion over low

Huevos Rancheros

heat, about 8 minutes; transfer to a plate. Lightly oil the skillet again and char the tomatoes over moderately high heat, about 4 minutes; transfer to a plate and let cool. Peel and finely chop the garlic. Peel, stem and seed the jalapeños. Coarsely chop the jalapeños and onion. Peel and coarsely chop the tomatoes.

3. In a medium saucepan, heat the 2 tablespoons of olive oil. Add the garlic, jalapeños and onion and cook over moderately low heat for 5 minutes. Add the tomatoes, ancho and reserved soaking liquid and simmer over low heat for 10 minutes. Season with salt.

4. Lightly oil the skillet and fry the eggs, sunny-side up, over low heat for 3 to 4 minutes. Spoon ½ cup of the tomato sauce onto each plate and top with 2 eggs. Sprinkle the eggs with the crumbled cheese and cilantro and serve with warmed corn tortillas.   *—Marcia Kiesel*

Crispbread with Tomato Sauce and Fried Eggs

4 SERVINGS

This quintessential Sardinian comfort food, *pane frattàu,* is made with the thin, crisp Sardinian flatbread called *pane carasau,* which is available at specialty food shops and Italian markets. The bread is moistened and then layered with tomato sauce to create a lasagna-like dish that's topped with fried eggs—perfect for a late-night supper. If you can't find *pane carasau,* use very thin lavash and soak it briefly in the stock.

  3 tablespoons extra-virgin olive oil, plus more for frying the eggs
  1 medium onion, coarsely chopped
One 28-ounce can plus one 14-ounce can Italian plum tomatoes, drained and chopped, liquid reserved
Salt and freshly ground pepper
  ½ teaspoon sugar (optional)
Pinch of crushed red pepper
  ⅓ cup slivered fresh basil

One ½-pound package *pane carasau*
  2 cups meat, chicken or vegetable stock or canned broth
About 1½ cups freshly grated aged Pecorino or Parmesan cheese
  8 eggs

1. Heat the 3 tablespoons of olive oil in a large saucepan. Add the onion and cook over moderately low heat until softened and golden, about 15 minutes. Add the tomatoes and cook over moderate heat, stirring frequently, until the sauce thickens, about 35 minutes; if the sauce begins to stick to the pan, stir in some of the reserved tomato liquid. Season the sauce with salt and pepper; if it is tangy, stir in the sugar. Add the crushed red pepper and the basil and remove from the heat.

2. Preheat the oven to 200°. You will need 12 pieces of the *pane carasau,* either the packaged triangles or 7-inch squares. Heat the stock in a medium skillet. Put 4 dinner plates in the oven to warm.

3. Using tongs, dip a piece of the *pane carasau* in the hot stock, turning it once, until it begins to soften. Transfer to a warm plate. Spread a layer of tomato sauce over the bread and sprinkle with 1 tablespoon of the grated cheese. Repeat this layering 2 more times. Assemble the remaining 3 stacks on the warmed plates in the same way and keep warm in the oven.

4. Heat a thin film of olive oil in a large nonstick skillet. Crack in as many of the eggs as will fit comfortably and fry, over easy or sunny-side up; repeat with the remaining eggs. Set 2 fried eggs on each stack and sprinkle with grated cheese. Serve the *pane frattàu* immediately, passing more cheese at the table.   *—Nancy Harmon Jenkins*

MAKE AHEAD The tomato sauce can be refrigerated for up to 5 days.

WINE Eggs are notoriously difficult to match with wine, but the red pepper in this dish suggests a wine with good acidity and some spiciness of its own.

Consider a fresh Sauvignon Blanc, like the 1998 Mark West Russian River Valley, or a soft, light red, such as the 1996 Zenato Valpolicella Classico Superiore.

Chorizo and Potatoes with Spinach and Soft-Boiled Eggs

4 SERVINGS ✳

This warm, satisfying one-dish meal is often on the bar menu served at the communal table at Nicole's, the Manhattan store and restaurant owned by clothing designer Nicole Farhi.

  8 medium new potatoes (about 1½ pounds), quartered
  4 large eggs
  2 tablespoons pure olive oil
  1 pound chorizo, sliced diagonally ½ inch thick
  4 ounces baby spinach (6 cups)
Salt and freshly ground pepper

1. Steam the potatoes over boiling water until tender, about 10 minutes. Transfer to a plate and pat dry.

2. Meanwhile, bring a saucepan of water to a boil. Add the eggs and boil for 5 minutes. Immediately transfer the eggs to a bowl of cold water and peel.

3. In a large skillet, heat the olive oil until shimmering. Add the chorizo and cook over moderate heat, turning, until browned, 6 to 7 minutes. Using a slotted spoon, transfer the chorizo to a plate.

4. Add the potatoes to the skillet and cook over moderate heat, stirring, until golden and crisp, approximately 8 to 10 minutes. Return the chorizo to the skillet and gently fold in the spinach. Season with salt and pepper and divide the chorizo mixture among 4 plates. Set an egg on top of each. Cut into the yolks and serve.

—Annie Wayte and Anna Kovel

WINE This spicy dish is best set off by a soft red Côtes-du-Rhône. Try the 1998 Jean-Luc Colombo Les Abeilles or the 1998 André Brunel Cuvée Sommelongue.

Pancetta-Wrapped Radicchio with Baked Eggs

6 SERVINGS

Baked eggs are lovely and easy to make, but you can also use poached or scrambled eggs with results that are just as delicious.

- 3 large heads of radicchio (about 1½ pounds), each cut into 6 wedges
- 2 teaspoons extra-virgin olive oil, plus more for drizzling
- Kosher salt and freshly ground pepper
- ½ pound thinly sliced pancetta (about 18 slices)
- 2 tablespoons unsalted butter, cut into 6 pieces
- 6 large eggs
- 1 cup flat-leaf parsley leaves
- 2 teaspoons fresh lemon juice

1. Preheat the oven to 350°. Drizzle the radicchio wedges with olive oil and lightly season with salt and pepper. Wrap a slice of pancetta securely around each radicchio wedge and arrange on a large baking sheet. Bake for about 30 minutes, turning once, until the pancetta is crisp and the radicchio is tender.

2. Meanwhile, put a piece of the butter in each of six ½-cup ramekins. Set the ramekins on a rimmed baking sheet and heat them in the oven until the butter melts. Carefully break 1 egg into each ramekin and season with salt and pepper. Bake for about 12 minutes, or until the whites are just set and the yolks are still runny.

3. In a medium bowl, toss the parsley with the 2 teaspoons of olive oil and the lemon juice; season with salt and pepper. Spoon the parsley salad onto 6 plates and top with the baked pancetta-wrapped radicchio. Run a knife around each egg, carefully slide them onto the plates and serve.

—*Gayle Pirie and John Clark*

MAKE AHEAD The radicchio can be wrapped in the pancetta and refrigerated for up to 1 day.

Tricolor Easter Omelet

8 SERVINGS

- 1 pound plum tomatoes—peeled, seeded and chopped
- 1 teaspoon chopped thyme leaves
- 1 pound spinach
- 1 clove garlic
- 9 large eggs
- ½ cup heavy cream
- ½ cup grated Parmesan
- ½ cup grated Gruyère
- Salt and freshly ground pepper

1. In a medium pan, sauté the tomatoes and the thyme for 10 minutes; drain. In a separate pan, sauté the spinach and the garlic for about 5 minutes; chop and drain.

2. In a medium bowl, mix the tomatoes with 3 of the eggs and 2 tablespoons of the cream. In a separate bowl, mix the spinach with 3 of the eggs and 3 tablespoons of the cream. In a third bowl, mix the remaining eggs with the remaining cream, the Parmesan, and the Gruyère. Season to taste with salt and pepper.

3. Set a buttered, 8½-by-4-inch glass loaf pan in a water bath of boiling water. Add the tomato mixture to the pan and bake at 300° for 25 minutes, until set. Top with the cheese mixture and continue baking for 25 minutes, until set. Repeat with the spinach mixture. Let cool, unmold, slice and serve.

—*Tamasin Day-Lewis*

Spanish Omelet

6 SERVINGS

- ⅓ cup canola oil
- 2 Idaho potatoes (1 pound), peeled and cut into 1-inch dice
- 1 small onion, coarsely chopped
- Salt and freshly ground pepper
- 14 large eggs
- 2 tablespoons coarsely chopped parsley

1. Preheat the oven to 500°. Warm ¼ cup of the oil in a 12-inch nonstick oven-proof skillet over moderately high heat. Add the potatoes, cover and cook over

Spanish Omelet

easy omelets

Seven great ideas for fast, delicious omelet fillings:

1. Season mascarpone with salt and pepper. Fold in finely chopped fresh chervil, parsley, chives and tarragon.

2. Cook sliced scallions in butter until softened, then stir in cider vinegar and cook until dry. Season with salt and pepper.

3. Mix chopped smoked salmon with crème fraîche and fold in salmon roe.

4. Toss shredded Gruyère cheese with minced shallots or red onion.

5. Sauté diced country ham with chopped crisp apples.

6. Steam or boil asparagus and cut it into small pieces. Toss with freshly grated Parmesan or Pecorino cheese.

7. Chop fresh mint leaves and combine with soft goat cheese. Season with salt and pepper.

—*Gayle Pirie and John Clark*

low heat until browned on the bottom and tender, about 15 minutes. Add the onion, season with salt and pepper and cook, stirring, until the onion is softened but not browned, about 3 minutes.

2. Increase the heat to moderate and drizzle the remaining 1 tablespoon of oil around the edge of the skillet. In a large bowl, whisk the eggs with a large pinch of salt and a small pinch of pepper. Pour the eggs into the skillet. As the eggs cook, use a spatula to draw them into the center, allowing the runny egg to fill the bottom of the skillet. Continue cooking and drawing the cooked egg into the center until the eggs are almost set, about 4 minutes.

3. Transfer the skillet to the oven and bake the omelet for 5 minutes, or until just firm and lightly browned on top. Slide the omelet onto a cutting board and let cool to room temperature. Sprinkle the parsley over the omelet, cut into 6 wedges and serve.

—Eric Ripert

MAKE AHEAD The omelet can be refrigerated for up to 1 day. Serve it chilled or at room temperature.

Bread Omelet with Tomato and Cheese

2 SERVINGS

Richard Olney's bread omelet from *Simple French Food* (Macmillan) inspired this rich and satisfying version.

One 2-ounce piece of crustless white or peasant bread, sliced ½ inch thick
½ cup heavy cream
¼ cup thick tomato sauce, preferably fresh (see Note)
1 tablespoon chopped basil
⅓ cup freshly grated Parmesan cheese, plus more for sprinkling
2 large eggs, lightly beaten
Salt and freshly ground pepper
1 tablespoon unsalted butter

1. Preheat the broiler. In a medium bowl, soak the bread in the cream until softened, about 10 minutes. Mash the bread to a paste with a fork. Mix in the tomato sauce, basil, Parmesan and eggs and season lightly with salt and pepper.

2. Melt the butter in a medium nonstick ovenproof skillet. Add the egg mixture and spread with a spatula to form a 9-inch round; smooth the top. Sprinkle with Parmesan cheese. Cook the omelet over moderately high heat until browned on the bottom, about 3 minutes, then broil the omelet for about 2 minutes, or until firm. Slide the omelet onto a plate, cut into wedges and serve.

—Michael London

NOTE You can substitute 2 tablespoons of pesto or chopped fresh herbs for the tomato sauce and basil.

WINE A big, fat Chardonnay will echo the cream, butter and cheese in this simple recipe. Choose a ripe, creamy example, such as the bargain 1998 Beaucanon Napa Valley Reserve or the 1998 Buehler Russian River Valley Reserve.

Zucchini-Thyme Frittata

4 SERVINGS

For this simple recipe, it's important that the zucchini be both fresh and small—no bigger than 5 inches long and 1 inch in diameter.

6 large eggs
1 teaspoon cold water
¾ teaspoon salt
¼ teaspoon freshly ground pepper
¼ cup freshly grated Parmesan cheese
5 tablespoons pure olive oil
6 small zucchini (1½ pounds), cut into ¼-inch slices
1 garlic clove, minced
2 teaspoons chopped fresh thyme

1. In a bowl, whisk the eggs, water, salt and pepper. Stir in the cheese.

2. In a medium nonstick skillet, heat 3 tablespoons of the olive oil. Add the zucchini; cook over moderately low heat until just softened, 5 minutes. Add the garlic and cook, stirring, for 2 minutes. Let cool, then stir into the egg mixture.

3. Preheat the broiler. In the skillet, heat the remaining 2 tablespoons of oil over moderate heat. Add the egg mixture, cover, reduce the heat to low and cook until firm, about 5 minutes. Uncover and broil for 2 minutes, or until golden brown.

4. Slide the frittata onto a serving plate and sprinkle with the thyme. Serve at room temperature.

—Paul Gervais

My Mother's Cheese Soufflé

4 SERVINGS

This soufflé doesn't rise nearly as high as the more traditional version because the egg whites are not beaten separately and folded into the base.

2 tablespoons unsalted butter
3 tablespoons all-purpose flour
1¼ cups cold whole milk
¼ teaspoon salt
⅛ teaspoon freshly ground pepper
⅛ teaspoon freshly grated nutmeg
1½ cups shredded Gruyère cheese (4 ounces)
3 large eggs, lightly beaten
3 tablespoons finely chopped flat-leaf parsley

1. Preheat the oven to 400°. Lightly grease a 4-cup oval gratin dish. In a medium saucepan, melt the butter over moderate heat. Add the flour and cook until it begins to sizzle, then whisk in the milk and bring to a boil, whisking constantly. Season the sauce with the salt, pepper and nutmeg and remove from the heat. Let cool slightly, then stir in the cheese, eggs and parsley.

2. Pour the soufflé mixture into the prepared gratin dish; smooth the surface. Bake for 30 to 35 minutes, until the soufflé is puffed and browned. Let cool for 10 minutes before serving.

—Jacques Pépin

MAKE AHEAD The unbaked soufflé can be refrigerated for 1 day; bring to room temperature before baking.

Cheese Grits Soufflé

10 SERVINGS

The sublime texture of this airy yet slightly chewy cheese soufflé comes from stone-ground grits, which are available at health-food stores and at Hoppin' John's (www.hoppinjohns.com; 800-828-4412).

- 5 cups water
- 1 cup milk
- 3 tablespoons unsalted butter
- 1½ teaspoons kosher salt
- 1½ cups stone-ground grits (½ pound)
- 1½ cups shredded sharp Cheddar cheese (5 ounces)
- 5 large eggs, separated

1. In a large saucepan, combine the water, milk, butter and salt and bring to a boil. Slowly whisk in the stone-ground grits and simmer over low heat, stirring frequently with a wooden spoon, until the grits are very thick, approximately 1 hour.

2. Transfer the cooked grits to a large bowl and stir in the cheese. Let cool slightly, then add the egg yolks, 1 at a time, stirring the grits well with a wooden spoon after each addition.

3. Preheat the oven to 400°. Butter a 2½-quart glass or ceramic soufflé dish. In a large bowl, beat the egg whites until they hold firm peaks. Stir one-third

Spinach, Ham and Parmesan Soufflé

of the beaten egg whites into the grits to loosen them, then fold in the remaining egg whites. Scrape the grits into the prepared soufflé dish and smooth the surface. Bake the soufflé for 30 minutes, or until it is puffed and golden brown and the center is moist but not runny. Serve at once. —Susan Spicer

Spinach, Ham and Parmesan Soufflé

4 SERVINGS

Although you can use a standard soufflé dish here, a gratin dish provides a larger surface area, making for a shallower and crustier soufflé.

- 6 ounces fresh spinach, thick stems discarded (4 packed cups)
- ½ cup fine fresh bread crumbs
- ½ cup freshly grated Parmesan cheese
- 2 tablespoons unsalted butter
- 3 tablespoons all-purpose flour
- 1½ cups whole milk
- ¼ teaspoon salt
- ¼ teaspoon freshly ground pepper
- 3 large egg yolks
- ¼ pound thickly sliced lean ham, cut into 2-by-¼-inch strips
- 5 large egg whites

1. Preheat the oven to 375°. Butter a 1½-inch-deep 6-cup gratin dish. In a medium skillet, cook the spinach over moderately high heat, tossing it with tongs until wilted. Transfer the spinach to a colander and let cool. Squeeze the spinach completely dry and coarsely chop it.

2. In a small bowl, toss the bread crumbs with 3 tablespoons of the Parmesan. Sprinkle half of the bread crumbs into the prepared gratin dish and shake to coat it evenly; pour out any excess.

3. In a small saucepan, melt the butter over moderate heat. Whisk in the flour and cook for 30 seconds. Slowly whisk in the milk until smooth and bring to a boil, whisking constantly. Season with the salt and pepper and simmer over low heat, whisking, until no floury taste remains, about 3 minutes. Transfer the mixture to a bowl and whisk in the egg yolks, spinach, ham and the remaining 5 tablespoons of Parmesan cheese.

4. In a large stainless-steel bowl, beat the egg whites until stiff. Fold one-third of the whites into the soufflé base to lighten it, then fold in the remaining whites. Scrape the mixture into the prepared baking dish; sprinkle the remaining bread crumbs on top. Bake for 20 to 25 minutes, or until the soufflé is puffed and golden brown. Serve at once.

—Jacques Pépin

WINE Contrast the smoky and salty flavors in this savory soufflé with a fresh and fruity but rich and creamy Pinot Blanc from Alsace, such as the 1998 Kuentz-Bas Cuvée Tradition; or try the 1997 Hugel Cuvée Les Amours.

pasta
chapter 6

Penne with Lemon and Herb Salad

6 SERVINGS

This simple dish is so satisfying that nonvegetarians don't even miss the meat, but you can also dress it up by adding shrimp (see Variation, below).

1 pound penne rigate or fusilli
2 cups coarsely chopped arugula
¾ cup flat-leaf parsley leaves
¾ cup torn basil leaves
½ cup mint leaves
4 scallions, thinly sliced
2 tablespoons extra-virgin olive oil
3 garlic cloves, minced
3 tablespoons unsalted butter
2 tablespoons fresh lemon juice
2 teaspoons finely grated lemon zest
Salt and freshly ground pepper

1. Cook the penne in a large pot of boiling salted water until al dente. Meanwhile, in a large bowl, toss the arugula with the parsley, basil, mint and scallions. Heat the olive oil in a small skillet. Add the garlic and cook over low heat until fragrant, about 1 minute.

2. Reserve ¼ cup of the pasta cooking water. Drain the penne and add it to the bowl. Add the ¼ cup pasta water to the skillet and bring to a simmer. Remove from the heat, add the butter and let melt. Stir in the lemon juice and zest, then pour over the penne. Season with salt and pepper and toss well. Serve at once. *—Joanne Weir*

VARIATION Use a large skillet to cook the garlic. Add 1 pound of large shelled shrimp, season with salt and pepper and cook, tossing, for about 2 minutes. Add the pasta cooking water and simmer until the shrimp are done, about 1 minute. Proceed with the recipe.

WINE The clean, citrusy-mineral flavors and brisk acidity of an Italian Pinot Grigio will complement the lemony herb butter. Try the 1998 Conti Formentini Collio or the 1998 Elena Walch Castel Ringberg Alto Adige.

Strangozzi alla Spoletina

6 SERVINGS

Strangozzi is the Spoleto region's traditional long and irregularly hand-cut pasta. *Strangozzi* means "strangled priests," and the pasta clearly dates from Spoleto's rebellion against papal dominion in the 14th century.

PASTA DOUGH

3 ⅔ cups all-purpose flour
2 teaspoons salt
5 large eggs, beaten

TOMATO SAUCE

3 tablespoons extra-virgin olive oil
2 large garlic cloves, minced
¼ to ½ teaspoon crushed red pepper
One 35-ounce can Italian plum tomatoes, tomatoes crushed, juices reserved
Salt and freshly ground black pepper
½ cup finely chopped parsley

1. MAKE THE PASTA DOUGH: Combine the flour and salt in a food processor and pulse to mix. With the machine on, add the eggs and process until moist crumbs form. Turn the dough out onto a lightly floured work surface and knead until firm and smooth. Shape it into a disk, wrap in plastic and let rest at room temperature for 1 hour.

2. MAKE THE TOMATO SAUCE: Heat the olive oil in a medium saucepan. Add the garlic and crushed red pepper and cook over low heat until the garlic is golden, about 1 minute. Add the tomatoes and their juices and simmer over moderately low heat, stirring occasionally, until thickened, about 30 minutes. Season with salt and a generous amount of black pepper.

3. Cut the dough into quarters and then work with one piece at a time, keeping the rest covered. Set a hand-cranked pasta machine at the widest setting and roll the pasta through for the first time. Then continue rolling it through, adjusting the machine each time until you have rolled it through at the

Strangozzi alla Spoletina

next-to-the-thinnest setting. Halfway through, when the sheet of dough becomes too long to work with easily, cut it in half crosswise and continue rolling. Cut the pasta sheets to 10 to 12 inches long and drape them over drying racks or the back of a wooden chair. Repeat with the remaining pasta dough. Let the sheets dry slightly before cutting them.

4. Beginning with a short end, loosely roll each pasta sheet into a log. Cut the logs crosswise into ¼-inch strands. Unfold the strands and arrange them loosely on a large rimmed baking sheet.

5. Bring a large pot of salted water to a boil. Add the pasta and cook, stirring, until just tender, about 4 minutes. Drain well and return the pasta to the pot. Add the sauce and toss well. Transfer the pasta to 6 warmed plates, garnish with the parsley and serve at once.

—*Cristina and Mauro Rastelli*

WINE Select a wine that will smooth the acidity of the tomatoes in the sauce for the *strangozzi*. An excellent choice would be the 1997 Antinori Cervaro della Sala, a medium-bodied blend of Chardonnay and Grechetto with light oak flavors.

Strozzapreti with Tomato-Pancetta Sauce

6 TO 8 SERVINGS

It's hard to cook this pasta to the perfect al dente stage; some parts will be quite soft by the time the rest is done.

- ¼ cup extra-virgin olive oil
- 2 ounces pancetta, finely chopped
- 1 medium onion, halved and thinly sliced
- 2 garlic cloves, crushed
- ½ cup minced flat-leaf parsley
- 2 tablespoons finely chopped mint
- 2 tablespoons minced celery leaves
- 1 dried red chile, crumbled

One 28-ounce can imported tomatoes, preferably from San Marzano

Salt and freshly ground pepper
- 1 pound dried *strozzapreti*

Freshly grated Grana Padana or Parmigiano-Reggiano cheese

1. Heat the oil in a large saucepan. Add the pancetta and cook over moderately high heat until it begins to brown, about 3 minutes. Add the onion and garlic and cook, stirring, until the onion softens, about 4 minutes. Add the parsley, mint, celery leaves and red chile and cook, stirring, for 2 minutes. Add the tomatoes and their liquid and simmer over moderately high heat, crushing the tomatoes with a wooden spoon, until the sauce is thick, about 25 minutes. Season with salt and pepper.

2. Cook the pasta in a large pot of boiling salted water, stirring, until slightly underdone. Drain the pasta lightly, then add it to the sauce and cook for about 1½ minutes longer, until just al dente. Transfer the *strozzapreti* to a warmed bowl and pass the cheese separately.

—*Nancy Harmon Jenkins*

WINE A straightforward red with good acidity harmonizes with this simple sauce. Try the 1997 Grasso Barbera d'Alba or the 1997 Michele Chiarolo Barbera d'Asti, both from Piedmont.

Rigatoni with Tomato Sauce and Pepato

4 SERVINGS

Pepato is a soft Pecorino cheese studded with black peppercorns.

- ¼ cup plus 1 tablespoon extra-virgin olive oil
- 2 tablespoons plus 1 teaspoon minced garlic

One 28-ounce can peeled Italian plum tomatoes, with their juices
- ¼ teaspoon dried basil
- ¼ teaspoon dried oregano

Pinch of kosher salt
- ¾ teaspoon crushed red pepper
- 1 pound rigatoni
- ½ teaspoon freshly ground black pepper
- 10 sage leaves, coarsely chopped
- 6 ounces Pepato cheese, cut into ¼-inch dice

1. Heat ¼ cup of the olive oil in a large saucepan. Add 2 tablespoons of the minced garlic and cook over moderate heat, stirring constantly, until golden, about 3 minutes. Add the plum tomatoes and crush them with the back of a spoon. Add the dried basil and oregano, the salt and ¼ teaspoon of the crushed red pepper and cook over moderately low heat, stirring occasionally, until thick, about 45 minutes.

2. Cook the rigatoni in a large pot of boiling salted water until al dente; drain. Transfer to a large warmed serving bowl.

3. Heat the remaining 1 tablespoon of olive oil in a large saucepan. Add the black pepper and the remaining 1 teaspoon minced garlic and ½ teaspoon crushed red pepper. Cook over moderate heat until the garlic is light golden, about 3 minutes. Add the tomato sauce and the sage and cook until heated through. Add the Pepato and cook over low heat until the cheese just begins to melt, about 1 minute. Immediately pour the sauce over the pasta and toss well. Serve right away.

—*Darryl Joannides*

MAKE AHEAD The tomato sauce can be prepared through Step 1 and refrigerated for up to 1 day.

WINE With its flavors of inky blackberry jam and currants combined with a hint of spice, the 1997 Vino Noceto Sangiovese is a perfect match for this peppery pasta dish.

Bucatini all'Amatriciana

12 SERVINGS

This dish originated in a hill town outside Rome called Amatrice. Authentic *bucatini all'amatriciana* is made with tomatoes, Pecorino and *guanciale,* a type of pork fat. Here pancetta is substituted for the *guanciale*.

Two 35-ounce cans peeled Italian plum tomatoes
- ¼ cup plus 2 tablespoons extra-virgin olive oil

Bucatini all'Amatriciana

1 large onion, finely chopped

2 small dried red chiles, stemmed and coarsely chopped

6 ounces pancetta, sliced ¼ inch thick and cut into thin strips

Salt

2½ pounds bucatini or perciatelli

½ cup plus 2 tablespoons freshly grated Pecorino cheese, plus more for passing

1. Working over a bowl, crush the tomatoes with your hands; reserve the juices.

2. Heat the olive oil in a large skillet. Add the onion and chiles and cook over low heat until the onion is softened, about 10 minutes. Add the pancetta and cook, stirring occasionally, until the pancetta is lightly colored, about 10 minutes. Add the crushed tomatoes and their juices and simmer over moderately low heat, stirring often, until the sauce is thick, about 40 minutes. Season with salt.

3. In a large pot of boiling salted water, cook the bucatini, stirring occasionally, until al dente. Drain the pasta and return it to the pot. Add the sauce and the Pecorino and toss well. Transfer the pasta to two large serving bowls and serve hot. Pass additional Pecorino at the table. *—Cesare Casella*

WINE The ripe fruit of a medium-bodied white, like the 1998 Greco di Tufo from Mastroberardino, will point up the tomato flavors and the saltiness of the sautéed pancetta.

Fusilli with Sun-Dried Tomatoes

4 SERVINGS

This satisfying dish is based on one from a popular Greenwich Village, New York, restaurant called Cucina Stagionale.

1 tablespoon vegetable oil

2 garlic cloves, minced

⅓ cup sun-dried-tomato paste (see Note)

1 tablespoon capers, preferably salt-packed, rinsed and chopped

¼ cup dry white wine

½ cup heavy cream

½ cup crumbled Gorgonzola cheese, preferably aged (3 ounces)

1 pound fusilli

¼ cup plus 2 tablespoons freshly grated Parmigiano-Reggiano cheese, plus more for serving

1 tablespoon finely chopped flat-leaf parsley

1. Heat the vegetable oil in a large deep skillet. Add the garlic and cook over moderately high heat until golden, about 2 minutes. Stir in the sun-dried-tomato paste and capers, add the wine and cook for 1 minute. Stir in the cream and Gorgonzola and cook just until the cheese melts, about 2 minutes.

2. Meanwhile, cook the fusilli in a pot of boiling salted water until al dente. Drain the pasta, reserving about ¼ cup of the water. Add the pasta to the sauce in the skillet and toss to coat; add some of the pasta cooking water to thin the sauce if it seems too thick. Stir in the grated cheese and the parsley. Mound the pasta on plates and serve with the extra grated cheese. *—Darryl Joannides*

NOTE Sun-dried-tomato paste is available at specialty food shops and Italian markets. It's often sold in tubes and lasts forever, just like anchovy paste. To make your own, drain 1 cup of oil-packed sun-dried tomatoes, saving the oil. Put the oil in a measuring cup and add enough extra-virgin olive oil to measure ¼ cup. In a food processor, pulse the tomatoes with 3 garlic cloves until finely chopped. With the machine on, slowly pour in the ¼ cup oil and process the mixture to a paste. You can refrigerate the homemade sun-dried-tomato paste for up to 1 month. Makes 1 cup.

WINE The 1996 Allegrini Valpolicella La Grola, a single-vineyard bottling, has bright cherry and berry flavors that help cut through the richness of the Gorgonzola and heavy cream in this pasta dish.

Rigatoni with Red Peppers

6 SERVINGS

Cooking the rigatoni twice—first in boiling water and then in the red pepper stewing liquid—infuses it with sweet and rich pepper flavor.

¾ pound rigatoni

2 tablespoons unsalted butter

2 tablespoons extra-virgin olive oil

4 large garlic cloves, lightly smashed

3 large red bell peppers—cored, seeded and cut into 2-inch pieces

⅔ cup warm water

Salt

¾ cup coarsely chopped basil

Freshly ground black pepper

Freshly grated Parmesan cheese

1. Bring a large pot of salted water to a boil. Add the rigatoni and cook, stirring often, until barely al dente, about 10 minutes. Drain the pasta, reserving 1¼ cups of the cooking water.

2. Meanwhile, in a large enameled cast-iron casserole, melt the butter in the oil. Add the garlic and peppers, cover and cook over moderately high heat until fragrant, about 2 minutes.

Rigatoni with Red Peppers

1 large garlic clove, minced

Pinch of saffron threads

½ pound linguine

¼ pound Manchego or young
Pecorino cheese, shaved
with a vegetable peeler

½ cup sliced almonds, toasted
until golden

Freshly ground pepper

1. In a blender, puree the parsley with the mint, olive oil, tarragon, thyme and lemon juice. Scrape the oil into a bowl.
2. Melt the butter in a large skillet. Add the garlic and saffron and cook over low heat until fragrant, about 1 minute.
3. Cook the linguine in boiling salted water until al dente. Set the skillet with the garlic over moderately high heat and add ½ cup of the pasta cooking water. Drain the pasta, add it to the skillet and toss well. Transfer the pasta to warmed shallow bowls. Top with the cheese shavings, toasted almonds and herb oil. Sprinkle the linguine with pepper and serve at once. —*Marcia Kiesel*
MAKE AHEAD The herb oil can be refrigerated for up to 1 day. Return it to room temperature before serving.

Pasta with Roasted Cremini and Gorgonzola

4 SERVINGS

¾ pound *gemelli* or fusilli

1¼ pounds cremini mushrooms, trimmed, quartered if large

¼ cup plus 2 tablespoons extra-virgin olive oil

Salt and freshly ground pepper

2 large red onions, thinly sliced

4 ounces Gorgonzola cheese, crumbled

3 tablespoons pine nuts

2 tablespoons snipped chives

1. Preheat the oven to 500°. In a pot of boiling salted water, cook the pasta until al dente. Drain, reserving ¼ cup of the pasta water. Transfer the pasta to a large bowl, cover with foil and keep warm.
2. Meanwhile, on a rimmed baking

Add the warm water and a pinch of salt, cover and simmer over low heat until the peppers are tender, about 10 minutes.
3. Add the rigatoni and the reserved pasta cooking water to the peppers. Cover and cook over moderately low heat, stirring a few times, until the rigatoni is al dente and the sauce has thickened slightly, about 5 minutes longer. Discard the garlic. Stir in the basil and season with salt and pepper. Transfer to a large bowl and serve at once, passing the Parmesan cheese at the table.
—*Marcia Kiesel*

Saffron Linguine with Herb Oil and Shaved Manchego Cheese

2 SERVINGS

Sharp cheeses such as Manchego and Pecorino stand up to lusty Syrah. Fresh herbs and toasted almonds add complexity and texture to the pairing.

½ cup chopped flat-leaf parsley

¼ cup chopped mint

¼ cup extra-virgin olive oil

1 teaspoon chopped tarragon

½ teaspoon chopped thyme

1 teaspoon fresh lemon juice

2 tablespoons unsalted butter

menu

eggplant bruschetta with tomato and basil (p. 19) | 1998 REGALEALI BIANCO TASCA D'ALMERITA
mesclun salad with grilled figs and roasted fig vinaigrette (p. 57) | 1997 BUCCI VERDICCHIO CLASSICO
pennette with wild mushrooms | 1995 PIO CESARE BARBERA D'ALBA
fusilli with sun-dried tomatoes (p. 112) | 1996 ALLEGRINI VALPOLICELLA LA GROLA
rigatoni with tomato sauce and pepato (p. 111) | 1997 VINO NOCETO SANGIOVESE
gingered berry crumble (p. 365) | blackberry gelato (p. 373) | 1997 LA STOPPA VIGNA DEL VOLTA

sheet, toss the mushrooms with ¼ cup of the oil. Season with salt and pepper and spread in a single layer.

3. On another baking sheet, toss the onions with the remaining 2 tablespoons of oil; season with salt and pepper and spread in one layer. Roast the mushrooms on the top rack and the onions in the middle of the oven for about 15 minutes, stirring after 10 minutes, or until the mushrooms are just tender.

4. Sprinkle the cheese over the mushrooms and the pine nuts over the onions and roast for 2 to 3 minutes, or until the cheese is melted and the pine nuts are toasted. Add the mushrooms and onions to the pasta along with the chives and toss well. If the pasta is dry, add a little of the reserved cooking water. Season with salt and pepper and serve.   —*Melissa Clark*

WINE Try a fruity, earthy California Barbera, such as the 1996 Louis M. Martini, or a Pinot Noir, such as the 1998 Coldstream Hills from Australia.

Pennette with Wild Mushrooms
4 SERVINGS

- 1½ teaspoons fennel seeds
- 3 tablespoons unsalted butter
- ¼ cup plus 1 tablespoon extra-virgin olive oil
- 3 garlic cloves, minced
- 1 pound mixed wild mushrooms— such as shiitake, oyster, Portobello, chanterelle, chicken-of-the-woods, and lobster— stemmed as needed and thickly sliced
- 1 tablespoon finely chopped rosemary
- 1 teaspoon freshly ground pepper
- 1 pound pennette or penne rigate
- 6 ounces arugula, large stems removed, leaves coarsely chopped
- ¼ cup freshly grated Pecorino Romano cheese, plus more for serving

1. In a small skillet, toast the fennel seeds over moderate heat until just golden brown and fragrant, about 2 minutes. Transfer the fennel seeds to a plate so that they stop browning in the hot pan.

2. In a large deep skillet, melt the butter in ¼ cup of the olive oil. Add the garlic and cook over moderate heat until golden. Add the mushrooms, fennel seeds, rosemary and the black pepper and cook, stirring occasionally, until the mushrooms are tender, about 15 minutes.

3. Meanwhile, cook the pennette in a large pot of boiling salted water until al dente; drain. Add the pasta to the mushrooms along with the arugula, ¼ cup of grated Pecorino and the 1 remaining tablespoon of olive oil. Mound on plates and serve with the extra Pecorino.   —*Darryl Joannides*

WINE The 1995 Pio Cesare Barbera d'Alba has dark berry fruit flavors and massive concentrations of smoke, which bring out the distinctive flavors of the mushrooms in this dish.

Virginia Fettuccine Alfredo
10 SERVINGS

The Virginia in the title refers to the Virginia ham that flavors this recipe. You can substitute any country ham or ½ pound of smoked ham.

- 2 pounds dried fettuccine
- 3 cups heavy cream
- ¼ pound country ham, thinly sliced and cut into thin strips

Pinch of freshly grated nutmeg

- 4 tablespoons unsalted butter
- 1 tablespoon olive oil
- 6 pounds Swiss chard, stems reserved for another use, leaves cut into 1-inch strips
- 4 large garlic cloves, minced
- 2 large shallots, minced

Salt and freshly ground pepper

- 1 cup freshly grated Parmesan cheese (3 ounces)
- 3 tablespoons snipped chives

1. Cook the fettuccine in a large stockpot of boiling salted water until al dente.

2. Meanwhile, in a medium saucepan, bring the cream to a boil. Simmer over

Virginia Fettuccine Alfredo

low heat for 5 minutes, stirring often. Add the country ham, stirring to separate the strips; add the nutmeg.

3. In a large saucepan, melt the butter in the olive oil over moderately high heat. Add the Swiss chard leaves by the handful and cook, stirring occasionally, until wilted, about 5 minutes. Add the garlic and shallots and cook for 2 minutes. Season with salt and pepper.

4. Drain the fettuccine and return it to the pot. Add the ham, cream, Swiss chard and Parmesan cheese and toss to mix. Season with salt and pepper and transfer to a large warmed bowl. Sprinkle with the chives and serve at once. —*Patrick O'Connell*

WINE A mostly dry, floral and spicy wine, such as the 1996 Hugel Personnelle Reserve Gewurztraminer, would provide contrast to this rich dish.

Macaroni and Three Cheeses

8 TO 10 SERVINGS

This dish is on the menu for Michael Jordan's The Steak House N.Y.C. in Manhattan because Jordan loved his mother's cheesy baked macaroni, and because he thinks it's the ideal accompaniment to steak—at least for athletes who can burn off unlimited calories.

- 1 **pound elbow macaroni**
- 1 **tablespoon vegetable oil**
- 1 **large onion, finely chopped**
- 5 **cups milk**
- 1 **stick (4 ounces) unsalted butter**
- ¾ **cup all-purpose flour**
- 3 **tablespoons Dijon mustard**
- 1 **teaspoon Worcestershire sauce**
- 2 **teaspoons kosher salt**
- ½ **teaspoon freshly ground pepper**
- 4 **cups shredded white Cheddar cheese (about 1 pound)**
- ⅔ **cup Gorgonzola (about 4 ounces), at room temperature**
- 1½ **cups freshly grated Parmesan cheese (about 6 ounces)**
- ¾ **cup fine plain bread crumbs, preferably homemade**

1. In a large pot of boiling salted water, cook the macaroni until barely al dente, about 6 minutes. Drain the macaroni and return it to the pot.

2. Heat the oil in a large saucepan. Add the onion and cook over moderately high heat until softened, approximately 5 minutes. Add the milk and bring to a simmer.

3. Meanwhile, preheat the oven to 350°. Melt 6 tablespoons of the butter in another large saucepan. Add the flour and cook over moderate heat, stirring constantly, until lightly golden, about 5 minutes; then remove the pan from the heat.

4. Gradually whisk the simmering milk into the flour and butter until the milk is fully incorporated and the mixture is smooth. Bring the sauce to a simmer and cook over low heat, still whisking, until thick and bubbling, about 7 minutes. Boil for 1 minute. Stir in the mustard, Worcestershire sauce, salt and pepper. Add the Cheddar, Gorgonzola and ¾ cup of the Parmesan and cook over low heat, stirring, just until melted. Fold in the macaroni until coated with sauce. Spread the macaroni in a 3-quart baking dish.

5. Melt the remaining 2 tablespoons of butter in a medium skillet. Add the bread crumbs and cook over low heat, stirring constantly, until coated. Transfer to a bowl and stir in the remaining ¾ cup of Parmesan. Sprinkle the crumbs over the macaroni and bake for about 25 minutes, or until lightly golden and bubbling.

6. Preheat the broiler. Brown the macaroni and cheese under the broiler for 10 to 15 seconds; don't scorch the crumbs. Let the macaroni and cheese stand for 15 minutes before serving. —*David Walzog*

WINE A full-bodied, satisfying California Merlot, such as the 1997 Shafer or the 1997 St. Supéry Dollarhide Ranch, pairs well with this equally rich and satisfying dish.

Mushroom and Tomato Lasagna

8 SERVINGS

- 10 **plum tomatoes, halved lengthwise**
- ¼ **cup chopped flat-leaf parsley**
- 7 **garlic cloves, minced**

Salt and freshly ground pepper

- ½ **cup pure olive oil, plus more for the noodles**
- 1¼ **pounds wild mushrooms, thinly sliced**
- 3 **medium leeks, white and tender green parts, coarsely chopped**
- 1 **stick (4 ounces) unsalted butter**
- ⅔ **cup all-purpose flour**
- 1 **quart milk, at room temperature**

Pinch of freshly grated nutmeg

- 1 **pound dry lasagna noodles**
- ½ **pound mild goat cheese, at room temperature**
- ⅔ **cup fresh whole-milk ricotta (6 ounces)**
- 2 **tablespoons chopped basil**
- 1 **large egg, beaten**
- 1¼ **cups shredded mozzarella (4 ounces)**

1. Preheat the oven to 250°. On a large rimmed baking sheet, toss the tomatoes with the parsley and 1 teaspoon of the minced garlic. Season with salt and pepper. Arrange the tomatoes skin side down on the sheet and bake for 1½ to 2 hours, or until wrinkled and slightly dry. Let the tomatoes cool, then coarsely chop them.

2. Meanwhile, in a large skillet, heat 2 tablespoons of the olive oil. Add one-third of the mushrooms and cook over moderately high heat until golden, about 3 minutes. Stir in one-third of the remaining minced garlic, season with salt and pepper and cook for 2 minutes longer. Transfer the cooked mushrooms to a plate. Repeat twice with the remaining mushrooms and garlic, adding 2 tablespoons of oil for each batch.

3. In a medium skillet, heat the remaining 2 tablespoons of olive oil. Add the leeks and cook over moderately low heat until softened and golden, about 15 minutes. Add the leeks to the tomatoes and season with salt and pepper.

4. Melt the butter in a medium saucepan. Whisk in the flour and cook over moderately high heat for 3 minutes, whisking constantly. Slowly whisk in the milk and bring to a simmer over moderately low heat, whisking frequently. Continue to cook the sauce until thickened and no floury taste remains, about 5 minutes. Remove the white sauce from the heat and season with salt, pepper and the nutmeg.

5. Preheat the oven to 375°. In a large pot of boiling salted water, cook the lasagna noodles until al dente, 8 to 10 minutes. Drain and rinse the noodles, then toss them with a little olive oil.

6. In a bowl, combine the goat cheese with the ricotta and basil. Season with salt and pepper and stir in the egg.

7. Spread half of the white sauce in the bottom of a 9-by-13-inch glass baking dish and top with a layer of lasagna noodles. Sprinkle the noodles with half of the mushrooms and dollop half of the goat cheese mixture on top. Cover with another layer of noodles and spread with half of the remaining white sauce. Spread the tomato and leek mixture over the sauce, cover with a third layer of lasagna noodles and dollop the remaining goat cheese mixture on top. Cover with a final layer of lasagna noodles. Spread the remaining white sauce over the noodles and top with the remaining mushrooms.

8. Sprinkle the mozzarella over the lasagna and bake for 50 minutes to 1 hour, or until golden brown on top and bubbling. Let the lasagna stand for 10 to 15 minutes before serving.

—Joanne Chang

MAKE AHEAD The lasagna can be refrigerated overnight. Bring to room temperature, cover with foil and reheat in a 350° oven for about 20 minutes.

WINE Earthy mushrooms and tangy goat cheese are particularly friendly to tart Sauvignon Blanc. Both the 1998 Dry Creek and the 1998 Markham are excellent bargains.

Three Cheese Manicotti
8 SERVINGS ✹

These tender manicotti shells are actually crêpes, and can be stuffed with a variety of fillings, including creamy chicken or a hearty Bolognese sauce.

- **2 cups ricotta cheese (15 ounces),** preferably fresh
- **1 cup shredded mozzarella** (about 6 ounces)
- **⅔ cup coarsely chopped basil**
- Salt
- **½ teaspoon freshly ground pepper**
- **1 cup all-purpose flour**
- **1 cup water**
- **4 large eggs, lightly beaten**
- Unsalted butter
- **3 cups tomato sauce,** preferably homemade
- **2 tablespoons freshly grated** Parmesan cheese

1. In a large bowl, combine the ricotta with the mozzarella, basil, 1 teaspoon of salt and the pepper.

2. In a blender, process the flour, water, eggs and ½ teaspoon of salt until smooth. Transfer to a bowl.

3. Heat an 8-inch crêpe or omelet pan over moderately high heat. Lightly butter the pan and add 2 tablespoons of the batter; working quickly, swirl the pan to coat it evenly. Cook until the top of the crêpe is dry and the bottom is lightly golden, about 1 minute. Flip the crêpe

Mushroom and Tomato Lasagna

and cook until the bottom is lightly golden, about 20 seconds longer. Transfer the crêpe to a large plate and repeat with the remaining batter to make a total of 16 crêpes.

4. Preheat the oven to 375°. Coat the bottom of a 3-quart baking dish with 1 cup of the tomato sauce. Arrange the crêpes on a work surface. Spoon 3 tablespoons of the ricotta filling in a line down the center of each crêpe. Loosely roll up the crêpes and arrange them, seam side up, side by side in the baking dish. Pour the remaining 2 cups of tomato sauce over the manicotti and sprinkle with the Parmesan cheese. Bake for 15 to 20 minutes, or until the tomato sauce is bubbling and the manicotti are heated through. Serve the manicotti piping hot.

—*Christine Dimmick*

MAKE AHEAD The unbaked crêpes can be refrigerated overnight. Allow up to 15 minutes longer for baking.

WINE Tart Chianti Classico was made for dishes with ricotta, mozzarella and tangy tomato sauce. Among a wealth of choices, consider the 1996 Antinori or the 1995 Il Palazzino.

Penne with Braised Greens, Turkey and Rosemary

4 SERVINGS

This quick and delicious recipe is a great way to use up leftover turkey and cooked greens of any kind.

- 1 **pound penne rigate**
- ¼ **cup extra-virgin olive oil**
- 2 **garlic cloves, thinly sliced**
- 1½ **teaspoons rosemary leaves**
- 1 **cup diced dark meat turkey**
- 2 **cups drained braised greens**

Salt and freshly ground pepper

Shavings of Pecorino Romano cheese, for serving

1. Cook the penne rigate in a large saucepan of boiling salted water until al dente.

2. Meanwhile, in a large skillet, combine the olive oil with the garlic and rosemary and cook over moderate heat until the garlic is lightly browned, about 2 minutes. Stir in the turkey, then add the greens and bring to a simmer. Season the turkey mixture with salt and pepper.

3. Drain the pasta and transfer it to a warmed bowl. Add the braised greens and turkey and toss well. Serve the penne hot, with the shaved cheese on the side. —*Reed Hearon*

WINE The braised greens in this pasta point to a crisp, herby Sauvignon Blanc, such as the 1999 Sterling North Coast or the 1999 Preston Dry Creek Valley, to balance their bite.

Spaghetti with Clam Sauce

4 SERVINGS

- 1 **pound spaghetti**
- ½ **cup extra-virgin olive oil**
- 3 **large garlic cloves, minced**
- ¼ to ½ **teaspoon crushed red pepper**
- 2 **pounds Manila clams or cockles, scrubbed**
- ½ **cup dry white wine**
- 1 **cup bottled clam juice**
- 2 **tablespoons minced flat-leaf parsley**

1. In a large pot of boiling salted water, cook the spaghetti until barely al dente, 7 to 8 minutes. Drain well and return to the pot. Cover with a kitchen towel and keep warm.

2. Meanwhile, in a large deep skillet, combine the oil with the garlic and red pepper and cook over moderate heat until the garlic is lightly golden, about 5 minutes. Add the clams, cover and cook over high heat, stirring occasionally, until the clams open, 5 to 8 minutes. As they open, transfer them to a bowl with a slotted spoon.

3. Add the wine to the skillet and cook over high heat until reduced to 2 tablespoons, about 5 minutes. Add the clam juice, parsley and spaghetti and cook, tossing, until the pasta is al dente and most of the broth has been absorbed, 3 to 4 minutes. Transfer the pasta to a large deep platter, top with the clams and serve immediately.

—*Agostino Sciandri*

WINE The touch of heat in the clam sauce suggests a dry, zesty Pinot Grigio for balance. The 1998 Peter Zemmer or the 1998 Lungarotti will make a good pairing.

Penne with Braised Greens, Turkey and Rosemary

Spaghetti with Clam Sauce

on the bottom rack of the oven and bake for about 1 hour, or until tender. Meanwhile, set the butternut squash, cut side down, on a lightly oiled baking pan. Cover with foil and bake on the upper rack of the oven for about 50 minutes, or until tender. Let the squash cool slightly, then peel and cut into 1-inch dice.

2. Split the potatoes, scoop out the flesh and pass it through a ricer or coarse sieve into a large bowl. Stir in the egg yolk and ½ teaspoon salt. Add the flour, ¼ cup at a time, stirring to form a crumbly dough. Turn the dough out onto a lightly floured work surface and knead until smooth. Wrap in plastic and let rest at room temperature for 30 minutes.

3. Line a large rimmed baking sheet with wax paper and dust the paper lightly with flour. Divide the dough into quarters. Working with 1 piece at a time and keeping the rest loosely wrapped in plastic, roll each piece into a ½-inch-thick rope. Using a lightly floured knife, cut the rope into ½-inch lengths. Spread the gnocchi out on the wax paper and toss to coat with flour. Roll and cut the remaining gnocchi dough and let stand uncovered at room temperature.

4. In a large skillet, melt 1 tablespoon of the butter in the oil. Add the mushrooms, season with salt and pepper and cook over high heat until tender, about 7 minutes. Transfer to a plate. Add the remaining 5 tablespoons of butter to the skillet and cook the butter over high heat until golden, 2 to 3 minutes. Add the lemon juice and sage and cook for 30 seconds longer. Add the squash and cook, stirring, just until coated with the butter. Add the mushrooms, season with salt and pepper and keep warm.

5. Meanwhile, bring a large pot of salted water to a boil. Add the gnocchi and cook, stirring once or twice, until they rise to the surface and the water

returns to a boil, about 1 minute. Drain the gnocchi and add them to the squash. Stir to coat with the butter. Transfer to a large deep platter and serve immediately. —*Thomas Gay*

MAKE AHEAD The recipe can be prepared through Step 4 and refrigerated overnight. Rewarm the squash before serving.

Gnocchi in Broth with Phyllo

4 SERVINGS

PHYLLO CRUST

1 tablespoon chopped flat-leaf parsley

1 tablespoon chopped chives

½ tablespoon chopped cilantro

4 sheets of phyllo dough

2 tablespoons unsalted butter, melted

¼ cup freshly grated Parmesan cheese

½ cup fresh bread crumbs

PARMESAN BROTH

2 tablespoons pure olive oil

1 small Idaho potato, peeled and cut into 2-inch chunks

1 small onion, chopped

1 quart Basic Chicken Stock (p. 98) or canned low-sodium broth

One 3-ounce Parmesan rind (see Note)

Potato Gnocchi (recipe follows)

¼ pound flat-leaf spinach, large stems removed

I. MAKE THE PHYLLO CRUST: In a small bowl, combine the parsley, chives and cilantro. Lay 1 sheet of phyllo on a baking sheet. Brush lightly with melted butter and sprinkle with one-third of the herbs. Repeat this layering 2 more times. Top with the last sheet of phyllo and brush with melted butter. Sprinkle with the grated Parmesan and the bread crumbs. Refrigerate or freeze until firm.

2. MAKE THE PARMESAN BROTH: Heat the olive oil in a medium saucepan. Add the potato and onion and cook over moderately high heat,

stirring occasionally, until lightly browned. Add the Basic Chicken Stock and scrape up any browned bits from the bottom of the pan. Add the Parmesan rind and simmer until the stock has reduced by half, about 15 minutes.

3. Preheat the oven to 500°. Strain the broth, discard the solids and return the broth to the saucepan. Bring to a simmer. Put 40 Potato Gnocchi in a 2-quart soufflé dish and set it on a cookie sheet. Cover the gnocchi with the spinach leaves and ladle the broth on top.

4. Center the chilled phyllo over the soufflé dish and bake for 12 to 15 minutes, or until the phyllo crust is golden brown, crisp and draped over the sides of the dish. Break the phyllo crust into several large pieces. Ladle the gnocchi and broth into soup plates and serve the phyllo crust on the side.

—*François Payard*

NOTE Parmesan rinds can be stored in the freezer for up to 3 months and used to flavor soups, stocks and stews.

MAKE AHEAD The recipe can be prepared through Step 2 and refrigerated overnight.

WINE Rich, nutty Parmesan marries well with a medium-bodied, fruity Chianti Classico from the splendid 1997 vintage. Two great choices are the Badia a Coltibuono and the Vistarenni.

POTATO GNOCCHI

MAKES ABOUT 8 DOZEN GNOCCHI

3 Idaho potatoes (1½ pounds)

Kosher salt

1 large egg

1 large egg yolk

1 teaspoon chopped parsley

¼ teaspoon sherry vinegar

1½ cups all-purpose flour

1 teaspoon table salt

¼ teaspoon freshly ground pepper

Pinch of freshly grated nutmeg

Extra-virgin olive oil

I. Preheat the oven to 400°. Sprinkle each of the potatoes with a pinch of kosher salt and wrap them individually in foil. Bake for 1 hour, or until tender. Let the potatoes cool slightly, and then halve lengthwise. Scoop out the potato flesh and press it through a ricer or a fine sieve into a large bowl. Let cool slightly.

2. In a small bowl, beat the egg with the egg yolk, chopped parsley and sherry vinegar. In a medium bowl, mix the flour with the table salt, pepper and nutmeg. Add the egg mixture to the warm potatoes and mix with your hands until just blended. Gently incorporate the flour mixture. Shape the dough into a ball, cover with a towel and let stand for 10 minutes.

3. Bring a large pot of salted water to a boil. Divide the potato dough into 6 pieces and roll each piece into a rope ½-inch thick. Cut the ropes into approximately 1-inch lengths.

4. Fill a large bowl with ice water. Add one-third of the gnocchi to the boiling water and cook until they rise to the surface, about 1 minute. Using a slotted spoon, transfer the gnocchi to the ice water to cool, then drain and transfer them to a bowl. Toss with a bit of olive oil. Spread the gnocchi on a baking sheet lined with plastic wrap. Repeat with the remaining 2 batches of gnocchi. —F.P.

NOTE This recipe makes more than the 40 gnocchi needed for the broth, leaving plenty left over to enjoy another day with a simple tomato sauce.

MAKE AHEAD The cooked gnocchi can be refrigerated for 1 day or frozen for 2 weeks in a sturdy plastic bag.

Baked Semolina Gnocchi with Sage

6 SERVINGS

This easy and decadent version of gnocchi was inspired by Elizabeth David's Gnocchi à la Romaine, from *French Country Cooking* (Penguin Classics).

- 1 stick plus 1 tablespoon unsalted butter
- 2 tablespoons chopped fresh sage
- 6 cups milk
- 1½ cups semolina flour (10 ounces)
- 2 eggs, lightly beaten
- 1½ tablespoons kosher salt
- 1 cup plus 3 tablespoons freshly grated Parmesan cheese (4½ ounces)

Freshly ground pepper

1. In a small skillet, melt the stick of butter over moderate heat. Add the chopped fresh sage and leave the butter on the heat just until fragrant, about 30 seconds. Set aside.

2. In a large saucepan, bring the milk to a simmer. Slowly add the semolina flour in a thin stream, whisking constantly. Cook over moderate heat, stirring with a wooden spoon, until very thick, about 3 minutes. Reduce the heat to low, beat in the eggs and cook for 2 minutes longer, stirring constantly. Remove from the heat and stir in the salt, the sage butter and 1 cup of the Parmesan cheese. Continue stirring until the dough is smooth and glossy. Pour the dough into a 9-by-13-inch baking dish and refrigerate until cool and firm to the touch.

3. Preheat the oven to 400°. Cut the dough into 12 squares, then cut the squares in half on the diagonal to form 24 triangles. Using a spatula, transfer the triangles to a large buttered baking dish. Sprinkle with the remaining 3 tablespoons of cheese and dot with the remaining 1 tablespoon of butter.

4. Bake for about 25 minutes, or until golden. Preheat the broiler and broil 8 inches from the heat for 2 minutes, or until golden brown. Let stand for 10 minutes. Sprinkle with pepper and serve. —Gayle Pirie and John Clark

MAKE AHEAD The recipe can be prepared through Step 3 and refrigerated for up to 1 day.

WINE Go for a smooth white with herbal overtones, ideally an inexpensive, soft and buttery Italian Chardonnay, such as the 1997 Corte Giara.

Ratatouille Couscous with Saffron

8 SERVINGS

- 1 medium eggplant
- 2 medium zucchini
- 1 medium yellow squash
- ½ cup plus 2 tablespoons olive oil
- 2 garlic cloves, minced

Salt and freshly ground pepper

- 1 medium onion, coarsely chopped

Large pinch of saffron threads

- 6 oil-packed sun-dried tomatoes, coarsely chopped
- 2⅔ cups Basic Chicken Stock (p. 98) or canned low-sodium broth
- 2 cups couscous (12 ounces)
- ¼ cup coarsely chopped basil

1. Preheat the oven to 475°. Quarter the eggplant, zucchini and yellow squash lengthwise, then trim off the central portion with the seeds. Cut the vegetables into ½-inch dice. In a large bowl, toss the vegetables with ½ cup of the olive oil and the garlic. Season with salt and pepper. Spread the vegetables on 2 rimmed baking sheets and roast for 25 to 30 minutes, stirring twice, until tender.

2. Heat the remaining 2 tablespoons of olive oil in a large saucepan. Add the onion and saffron and cook over moderate heat, stirring, until softened, about 7 minutes. Add the sun-dried tomatoes and cook for 2 minutes longer. Stir in the stock and bring to a boil; simmer for 3 minutes. Season with 1½ teaspoons of salt and ¼ teaspoon of pepper. Stir in the couscous, cover and remove from the heat. Let stand for 5 minutes. Stir in the vegetables and basil and serve. —Dominique Macquet

fish shellfish
chapter 7

Smoked Trout

6 SERVINGS

This trout is cooked slowly with indirect heat and develops a smoky flavor when wood chips are added to the fire.

Six ¾-pound trout, cleaned
Salt and freshly ground pepper
1 cup hardwood chips,
soaked in water for 30
minutes and drained
3 lemons, halved

I. Light a charcoal grill or heat 1 burner on a gas grill to moderately high. Season the trout both inside and out with salt and pepper. When the coals are very hot, rake them to one side. Sprinkle half of the wood chips over the coals. Or, for a gas grill, add the chips to a heavy-duty foil pan and set it directly on the burner. Oil the grill on the opposite side from the heat source.

2. Set the trout, backbone toward the heat, on the oiled grill. Cover and grill the trout for 15 minutes. Carefully turn the trout and sprinkle the remaining wood chips over the coals or add them to the foil pan. Cover and cook until the trout are opaque throughout, about 15 minutes more. Serve with the lemon halves.

—*Eric Ripert*

WINE Pair the fish with the smoky 1997 Château Carbonnieux Blanc, a Sauvignon Blanc–Sémillon blend.

Peanut-Crusted Fish with Swiss Chard

4 SERVINGS

½ cup plus 3 tablespoons
vegetable oil
4 garlic cloves, minced
⅓ cup toasted sunflower or
pumpkin seeds
2 pounds Swiss chard, stems
removed, leaves chopped
½ teaspoon Tabasco, plus more
for serving
Salt and freshly ground pepper
1 large tomato, coarsely chopped
1 cup peanuts (5 ounces)
1 tablespoon cornmeal
Four 5-ounce trout fillets
1 large egg white, lightly beaten
Lemon wedges, for serving

I. In a large deep skillet, heat 3 tablespoons of the vegetable oil. Add the minced garlic and toasted sunflower seeds and cook over moderate heat, stirring frequently, until both are golden, about 2 minutes. Add the chard leaves, a handful at a time, and cook each handful until just wilted before adding more. Continue cooking the chard over moderate heat until tender, about 5 minutes. Add the ½ teaspoon of Tabasco and season with salt and pepper. Add the chopped tomato to the chard and remove from the heat; keep warm.

2. In a food processor, pulse the peanuts and cornmeal until finely ground. Spread the peanut mixture on a plate. Lightly brush the trout fillets with the egg white; season with salt. Dip the trout in the peanut mixture, pressing lightly to help the coating adhere.

3. In a large skillet, heat the remaining ½ cup of oil until shimmering. Add the trout fillets and fry over moderately high heat, turning once, until golden and crisp, about 3 minutes per side.

4. Mound the chard on a large platter or on individual plates. Top with the fish and serve with Tabasco and lemon wedges. —*Jacques Pépin*

WINE A crisp South African Sauvignon Blanc, such as the 1998 Mulderbosch Stellenbosch or the 1998 Buitenverwachting Constantia, will go well with the robust chard and the mild fish.

Peanut-Crusted Fish with Swiss Chard

Cod with Corncob Broth and Gingered Eggplant

4 SERVINGS

This elegant dish is composed of three simple parts. You can prepare the eggplant and the corncob broth in advance and assemble the dish at the last minute.

2 tablespoons plus 2 teaspoons clarified butter (see Note)

½ cup water

1 large eggplant (1½ pounds), peeled and cut into ½-inch dice

2 teaspoons grated fresh ginger

4 kaffir lime leaves, torn in half, or four 1-inch strips of lime zest

4 teaspoons sherry vinegar

Salt and freshly ground pepper

Four 6-ounce skinless cod fillets, about ¾ inch thick

Corncob Broth (recipe follows)

1. In a large nonstick skillet, combine 2 teaspoons of the clarified butter with the water and bring to a boil. Add the eggplant and cook over high heat, tossing frequently, until just softened, about 3 minutes. Add 2 more teaspoons of the butter and cook, tossing, until the eggplant is tender and golden, about 5 minutes. Put the eggplant in a bowl.

2. Add the ginger, lime leaves and 1 teaspoon of clarified butter to the skillet and cook for 30 seconds. Return the eggplant to the skillet and cook for 1 minute. Discard the lime leaves. Stir in the vinegar and season with salt and pepper. Keep the eggplant warm.

3. Preheat the oven to 500°. Heat the remaining 1 tablespoon of clarified butter in a large nonstick ovenproof skillet. Season the cod fillets with salt and pepper and cook over high heat until golden on the bottom, about 2 minutes. Transfer the skillet to the oven and roast the cod for about 6 minutes, or until just cooked through.

4. Mound the eggplant in soup plates. Set the cod fillets on the eggplant and spoon the Corncob Broth around them. Serve at once.   —*Sally Schneider*

NOTE Clarifying separates the butterfat from the milk solids, which can scorch at higher temperatures. To make clarified butter, melt unsalted butter in a small saucepan over moderately low heat. Let stand for 5 minutes, then skim off the foam. Pour the clear yellow butter into a container and discard the milky residue. Clarified butter can be refrigerated or frozen for 2 months.

MAKE AHEAD The eggplant can be prepared up to 4 hours ahead.

ONE SERVING Calories 280 kcal, Total Fat 10 gm, Saturated Fat 6 gm

WINE A fresh, dry Chenin Blanc, with its edge of melon and citrus, harmonizes with the sweetness of the broth yet has enough body to stand up to the cod. Look for the 1999 Dry Creek Clarksburg Dry Chenin Blanc or the 1998 Chappellet.

CORNCOB BROTH

MAKES 2 CUPS

Corncobs give this broth its fragrant essence of sweet corn. Use the kernels in corn bread, salads or soups.

6 ears of corn, kernels cut off and reserved for another use, cobs broken in half

1 tablespoon plus 1 teaspoon clarified butter (see Note, above)

1 small shallot, quartered

1 bay leaf

1 thyme sprig

6 cups Basic Chicken Stock (p. 98) or canned low sodium broth

Salt and freshly ground white pepper

1. Preheat the oven to 400°. Set the corncobs in a roasting pan and brush with the clarified butter. Roast the corncobs for about 1 hour, turning occasionally, until they are browned and fragrant.

2. Transfer the corncobs to a large saucepan. Add the shallot, bay leaf, thyme and chicken stock and bring to a boil over moderately high heat. Reduce the heat to low, cover partially

Cod with Corncob Broth and Gingered Eggplant

and cook until reduced to 2 cups, about 2 hours. Strain the broth through a colander lined with cheesecloth and chill until the fat has solidified on the surface. Spoon off the fat. Reheat the broth and season with salt and white pepper before serving.   —*S.S.*

MAKE AHEAD The broth can be refrigerated for up to 3 days.

ONE SERVING Calories 20 kcal, Total Fat 0.6 gm, Saturated Fat 0.3 gm

Sautéed Cod with Rich Ketchup Sauce

4 SERVINGS

Ketchup is the key ingredient in the complex-tasting sauce for this sublime cod and vegetable dish.

1 stick plus 2 tablespoons (5 ounces) unsalted butter

¼ cup ketchup

¼ cup soy sauce

¼ cup red wine vinegar

½ teaspoon Tabasco

¼ cup plus 1 tablespoon extra-virgin olive oil

½ cup finely chopped onion

1 garlic clove, minced

1 red bell pepper, finely diced

2 celery ribs, finely diced

Spicy Cod, Clam and Tofu Casserole

1 serrano chile, seeded
and minced

1 plum tomato—peeled, seeded
and finely chopped

6 large green olives, pitted and
coarsely chopped

6 Calamata olives, pitted and
coarsely chopped

1 tablespoon nonpareil capers

Pinch of saffron threads

2 teaspoons shredded basil

1 teaspoon thyme leaves

Four 6-ounce skinless, boneless cod
steaks, about 1 inch thick

Salt and freshly ground pepper

1. In a medium saucepan, combine the butter with the ketchup, soy sauce, red wine vinegar and Tabasco and bring to a boil over moderate heat. Remove from the heat.

2. Heat 3 tablespoons of the olive oil in a large skillet. Add the onion and garlic and cook over moderately low heat until translucent, 5 to 6 minutes. Add the red bell pepper, celery and serrano chile and cook until crisp-tender, about 5 minutes. Transfer the sautéed vegetables to a bowl and add the tomato, olives, capers, saffron, basil and thyme.

3. In a large nonstick skillet, heat the remaining 2 tablespoons of oil until shimmering. Season the cod with salt and pepper and add the steaks to the skillet. Cook over moderately high heat, turning once, until golden and crisp and the flesh flakes easily, about 12 minutes.

4. Rewarm the ketchup sauce and pour about 2 tablespoons in the center of each of 4 large dinner plates. Set the cod steaks on the sauce and spoon the vegetables on top. Serve immediately, passing any additional sauce alongside.

—*Jean-Georges Vongerichten*

MAKE AHEAD The recipe can be prepared through Step 2 and refrigerated overnight. Let the vegetables return to room temperature before serving.

Spicy Cod, Clam and Tofu Casserole

6 SERVINGS

Brick-colored, soupy casseroles flavored with sweet-spicy chili paste *(kochujang)* are the backbone of the Korean diet. For this seafood version *(Maeun Tang),* Koreans would use a light beef broth or the water left over from soaking rice. A mixture of water and clam juice is substituted here.

1 tablespoon plus 1 teaspoon
Asian sesame oil

1½ tablespoons Korean sweet-spicy
chili paste *(kochujang)*

1 medium zucchini, halved
lengthwise and sliced crosswise
½ inch thick

One 4-inch piece of daikon—peeled,
halved lengthwise and sliced
crosswise ½ inch thick

6 scallions, white parts only

1 tablespoon minced garlic

1 tablespoon Sesame Salt
(p. 272)

4 cups water

2 cups clam juice

2 pounds cod steaks—cut 1½
inches thick, skin and bones
removed, bones reserved

18 small clams, such as Manila
clams, littlenecks or cockles

1 to 2 teaspoons coarsely
ground Korean red chile
(gocho karu)

½ pound soft tofu, cut into
1½-inch dice

Steamed Rice, for serving (p. 307)

1. Heat 1 tablespoon of the sesame oil in a medium enameled cast-iron casserole. Add the chili paste and stir over low heat for 30 seconds. Add the zucchini, daikon, scallions, garlic and Sesame Salt and stir until aromatic and the vegetables just begin to soften, about 2 minutes. Add the water and clam juice and bring to a boil.

2. Meanwhile, cut the cod into 1½-inch chunks. Wrap the reserved bones in cheesecloth. When the soup boils, reduce the heat to low and add the bones; simmer for 10 minutes. Remove and discard the bones.

3. Increase the heat to moderate and add the cod steaks. Cover and simmer until the fish is almost cooked through, about 2 minutes. Add the clams, cover and cook until they open, about 3 minutes.

4. Meanwhile, heat the remaining 1 teaspoon of sesame oil in a small skillet. Add the ground red chile and cook until fragrant, about 30 seconds. Stir the chile oil into the casserole, add the tofu and simmer for 2 minutes. Ladle into wide bowls and serve with rice.

—*Anya von Bremzen*

Oven-Roasted Whole Fish

4 SERVINGS

A large cast-iron griddle will hold a whole fish nicely and allow the dried fennel stalks to burn evenly, resulting in a wonderful woodsy aroma. For a dramatic ending, flambé the roasted fish: Set the fish and griddle on the stove, add 1 tablespoon of Pernod and carefully ignite it with a long match. Serve as soon as the flames subside.

Oven-Roasted Whole Fish

⅓ cup whole bay leaves

12 dried fennel stalks (see Note)

1 whole 3-pound sea bass or red snapper—cleaned, rinsed and patted dry

Salt and freshly ground pepper

Extra-virgin olive oil

Lemon wedges, for serving

1. Preheat the oven to 500°. On a large rimmed baking sheet, spread the bay leaves and 6 of the fennel stalks in an even layer. Bake them until they are well browned, approximately 3 minutes for the bay leaves and 6 minutes for the fennel stalks.

2. Make 3 crosswise slashes down to the bone on each side of the fish. Season the fish inside and out with salt and pepper and coat it generously all over with olive oil. Put 2 bay leaves in each slash and put the rest of the bay leaves in the cavity, along with the baked fennel stalks. Using a bamboo skewer, close the fish.

3. Set an oiled cast-iron griddle or very sturdy baking sheet on 2 burners over moderate heat. Put the remaining 6 fennel stalks on the griddle and cook them until they are browned, approximately 5 minutes. Set the fish on the fennel stalks, transfer the griddle to the oven and roast for about 18 minutes, or until the fish is just cooked through; the flesh should flake easily when lightly pressed. Transfer the fish to a platter along with any juices from the griddle and season with salt and pepper. Using 2 forks, lift the fish off the bones and arrange on plates. Pass the olive oil and lemon wedges at the table.

—*Marcia Kiesel*

NOTE Dried fennel stalks, which add a subtle anise flavor to the fish, are available at specialty food stores.

WINE Dishes with a smoky character pair well with full-bodied whites, like the fragrant 1998 Alderbrook Viognier. The 1997 Matanzas Creek Chardonnay also adds a matching note with its own smoky flavor.

Grilled Fish with Sauce au Chien

Grilled Fish with Sauce au Chien

8 SERVINGS

Sauce au chien, an exotic vinaigrette made with herbs, chiles and lime juice, is a lively, pungent and spicy complement to all kinds of grilled foods.

¼ cup plus 2 tablespoons extra-virgin olive oil

¼ cup plus 2 tablespoons coarsely chopped flat-leaf parsley

1 small onion, minced

2 garlic cloves, minced

1 tablespoon minced chives

½ teaspoon finely chopped thyme

½ teaspoon minced, seeded habanero chile

3 tablespoons fresh lime juice

Salt and freshly ground pepper

Eight 1-pound fish, such as red snapper, porgy or sea bass—cleaned, rinsed and patted dry

1 cup all-purpose flour

Vegetable oil

Steamed rice, for serving (p. 307)

1. In a small bowl, combine the olive oil with the parsley, onion, garlic, chives, thyme and chile. Whisk in the lime juice and season with salt and pepper.

2. Light a grill. Coat each fish lightly with flour, tapping off the excess. Oil the rack and grill the fish over a moderately hot fire until cooked through, about 5 minutes per side. Alternatively, heat ½ inch of vegetable oil in each of 2 large skillets and fry the fish over high heat until golden and crisp, about 5 minutes per side; drain on paper towels. Sprinkle the fish with salt and carefully transfer them to a large platter or dinner plates. Drizzle the sauce over the fish and serve right away, with rice.

—*Corinne Trang*

MAKE AHEAD The *sauce au chien* can be refrigerated for 3 days.

WINE The strong, spicy *sauce au chien* calls for a bright Australian Riesling with vibrant lime flavors, such as the 1999 Wolf Blass South Australia Gold Label or the 1999 Penfolds Eden Valley Reserve.

Grilled Sea Bass with Lemon-Mint Dressing

8 SERVINGS

10 dried chiles de Arbol or dried red Chinese chiles, stemmed and broken into pieces

2 tablespoons coarsely cracked black peppercorns

⅓ cup ground coriander

1 tablespoon ground allspice

1 tablespoon ground cinnamon

2 teaspoons salt

1 teaspoon achiote paste (optional)

Eight 6-ounce skinless sea bass fillets, about 1 inch thick

Lemon-Mint Dressing (recipe follows)

Habanero and Fruit Salsa (p. 321)

I. In a skillet, toast the chiles and peppercorns over moderately high heat, stirring, until fragrant and slightly darkened, about 3 minutes. Add the coriander, allspice, cinnamon and salt and cook, stirring, just until fragrant, about 30 seconds. Transfer to a plate to cool, then grind to a powder in a mortar or spice grinder with the achiote paste.

2. Light a grill or preheat the broiler. Rub a scant ½ teaspoon of the spice mixture all over each fillet; tap off any excess. Grill or broil the fish for about 10 minutes, or until just cooked through; turn and rotate the fillets frequently. Transfer the fish to a platter and drizzle with the Lemon-Mint Dressing. Garnish with the Habanero and Fruit Salsa and serve. —*Kevin Maguire*

NOTE This recipe makes a bit more spice rub than you are likely to use up on the sea bass fillets. Keep the extra in a jar and use it for fish, shrimp or chicken.

MAKE AHEAD The spice mixture can be stored in an airtight container at room temperature for up to 1 month.

ONE SERVING Calories 254 kcal, Total Fat 12.7 gm, Saturated Fat 2.2 gm

WINE To match the smoke and mellow the heat of this dish, serve a barrel-fermented Sauvignon-Sémillon blend, such as the 1996 Quivira Reserve or the 1997 Carmenet Reserve.

LEMON-MINT DRESSING

MAKES ½ CUP

2 tablespoons snipped chives

1 tablespoon mint leaves

1 tablespoon minced onion

½ teaspoon finely grated lemon zest

1 tablespoon fresh lemon juice

1 tablespoon sherry vinegar

⅓ cup extra-virgin olive oil

Salt and freshly ground pepper

In a blender, finely chop the chives, mint, onion and lemon zest. Add the lemon juice and vinegar and blend until all of the ingredients have been incorporated. With the machine on, add the olive oil in a thin stream until emulsified. Season the dressing with salt and pepper. —*K.M.*

MAKE AHEAD The vinaigrette can be refrigerated for up to 1 day.

ONE TABLESPOON Calories 81 kcal, Total Fat 9.2 gm, Saturated Fat 1.3 gm

Yagihashi's Black Sea Bass with Somen and Vegetables

4 SERVINGS

BROTH

1 quart water

3 stalks fresh lemongrass, thinly sliced crosswise

One 8-by-2-inch piece of *kombu* (seaweed)

1 small onion, thinly sliced

¼ cup thinly sliced, peeled fresh ginger

½ medium jalapeño

2 tablespoons mirin

2 tablespoons sake

2 tablespoons soy sauce

Salt and freshly ground pepper

SOMEN AND VEGETABLES

6 ounces somen noodles

1 tablespoon vegetable oil

1 cup thinly sliced shiitake mushroom caps

1 cup snow peas, sliced lengthwise ½ inch thick

1 cup finely shredded napa cabbage

1 cup mung-bean sprouts

½ cup daikon radish matchsticks

½ cup thinly sliced red onion

½ cup thinly sliced carrot

Salt and freshly ground pepper

1 teaspoon Asian sesame oil

1 teaspoon soy sauce

SEA BASS

Four 6-ounce black sea bass fillets, with skin

Salt and freshly ground pepper

2 tablespoons vegetable oil

2 tablespoons minced chives

1 teaspoon chopped basil

1 teaspoon chopped cilantro

1 teaspoon toasted black sesame seeds

I. MAKE THE BROTH: Combine all the ingredients in a medium saucepan

Yagihashi's Black Sea Bass with Somen and Vegetables

and bring to a simmer. Cook over low heat for 10 minutes. Strain the broth and return it to the saucepan. Boil over high heat until reduced to 2 cups, about 15 minutes. Season with salt and pepper and remove from the heat.

2. PREPARE THE SOMEN AND VEGETABLES: In a saucepan of boiling water, cook the somen until tender but still slightly chewy, about 3 minutes. Drain and rinse under cold water; drain again.

3. Heat the oil in a wok. Add the shiitakes, snow peas, cabbage, bean sprouts, daikon, onion and carrot and season lightly with salt and pepper. Stir-fry over high heat until crisp-tender, about 3 minutes. Add the sesame oil and soy sauce; remove from the heat.

4. PREPARE THE SEA BASS: Season the fillets with salt and pepper. Heat the oil in a large skillet until shimmering. Add the fish, skin side down, and cook over moderately high heat until the skin is crisp, about 4 minutes. Turn the fillets and cook until just opaque throughout, about 2 minutes longer.

5. Bring the broth to a boil. Stir-fry the vegetables over high heat to rewarm them. Put the noodles in 4 shallow soup bowls and pour the boiling broth over them. Spoon the vegetables over the noodles and top with the fish, skin side up. Sprinkle with the chives, basil, cilantro and sesame seeds and serve.

—*Takashi Yagihashi*

Grilled Halibut with Tomato and Caper Sauce

8 SERVINGS

The sauce can be made ahead and the fish grilled at the last minute. It's also good served at room temperature.

- ⅓ cup extra-virgin olive oil, plus more for brushing
- 2 cups finely chopped onions
- 2 cups chopped fennel
- 2 garlic cloves, minced

Two 28-ounce cans Italian plum tomatoes, drained

Kosher salt and freshly ground pepper

- ¼ cup dry white wine
- ¼ cup chicken stock or canned low-sodium broth
- ¼ cup capers, drained and coarsely chopped
- 1 cup coarsely chopped basil, plus small leaves for garnish
- 2 tablespoons unsalted butter
- 8 skinless halibut fillets (6 to 7 ounces each), about 1 inch thick

1. In a large deep skillet, heat ⅓ cup of olive oil. Add the chopped onions and fennel and cook over moderately low heat, stirring occasionally, until softened, approximately 10 minutes. Add the garlic and cook until fragrant, about 1 minute.

2. Add the tomatoes to the skillet and break them up with a fork. Season with salt and pepper and cook over low heat until most of the liquid has evaporated, 15 to 20 minutes. Add the wine, stock and capers and cook over low heat for 10 minutes. Stir the chopped basil and the butter into the sauce.

3. Light a grill. Brush the halibut fillets with olive oil and season generously with salt and pepper. Grill over high heat until just cooked through, about 4 minutes per side. Spoon the sauce onto a large deep platter, set the fillets

Roasted Halibut with Fresh Herb Sauce

Menu

crudités platter (p. 13)
tabbouleh with roasted chicken (p. 313)

1999 WOLFFER ROSE

---

grilled halibut with tomato and caper sauce
sautéed asparagus with sugar snap peas (p. 279)
sautéed fresh corn (p. 289)

1997 WOLFFER RESERVE CHARDONNAY

---

wölffer emmentaler

1995 WOLFFER ESTATE SELECTION MERLOT

---

country cake with strawberries and whipped cream (p. 335)

1996 WOLFFERBRUT SPARKLING WINE

on the sauce and garnish with basil leaves. Serve hot or at room temperature. —*Ina Garten, Barefoot Contessa*

MAKE AHEAD The sauce can be refrigerated for up to 2 days. Reheat gently before serving.

WINE The smoky flavor of the grilled fish would pair best with a fruity wine with some oak, such as the 1997 Wölffer Reserve Chardonnay.

Roasted Halibut with Fresh Herb Sauce

6 SERVINGS

- 1 cup coarse fresh bread crumbs
- ½ cup plus 1 tablespoon extra-virgin olive oil
- 2 teaspoons minced garlic
- 1 tablespoon dry white wine
- ¼ cup finely chopped flat-leaf parsley
- ¼ cup finely chopped arugula leaves
- 1 tablespoon finely chopped marjoram

Grilled Halibut with Tomato and Caper Sauce

1 tablespoon finely
chopped oregano

2 teaspoons red wine vinegar

Kosher salt and freshly ground pepper

Six 6-ounce skinless halibut
or cod fillets

1. Preheat the oven to 400°. In a medium bowl, toss the bread crumbs with 1 tablespoon of the olive oil, 1 teaspoon of the minced garlic and the wine. Spread the crumbs on a pie plate and toast for 8 minutes, or until lightly browned.

2. Meanwhile, in a bowl, combine the ½ cup of oil with the parsley, arugula, marjoram, oregano, vinegar and the remaining 1 teaspoon of garlic. Season the herb sauce with salt and pepper.

3. Lightly oil a large baking dish. Arrange the halibut fillets in the dish, season with salt and pepper and roast for 8 minutes. Sprinkle the fish with the toasted bread crumbs and bake for about 8 minutes longer, or until the fish is cooked through. Transfer the fish to plates, drizzle with the herb sauce and serve right away.

—*Gayle Pirie and John Clark*

MAKE AHEAD The sauce can be refrigerated for several hours.

WINE Match this simple, mild fish with a light, fresh and fruity white like the fragrant 1998 Antinori Galestro or the 1998 Anselmi Soave San Vincenzo.

Roasted Halibut with Fennel and Croutons

4 SERVINGS ✳

2 large fennel bulbs—halved, cored and thinly sliced—plus 2 tablespoons chopped feathery green tops

3 tablespoons extra-virgin olive oil

3 anchovy fillets, minced

1 teaspoon fennel seeds

Salt and freshly ground pepper

1 cup cubed (½ inch) crustless Italian bread

Four ½-pound skinless halibut or cod fillets, about 1 inch thick

1. Preheat the oven to 500°. In a 9-by-13-inch baking dish, toss the sliced fennel with 2 tablespoons of the oil, the anchovies and fennel seeds. Season with salt and pepper and spread the fennel in an even layer. Roast for about 15 minutes, stirring after 10, or until the fennel is tender and just beginning to brown.

2. In a small bowl, toss the bread cubes with the remaining 1 tablespoon of oil and season with salt and pepper. Set the halibut on the fennel and season with salt and pepper. Sprinkle the bread cubes over the fish and roast for about 8 minutes longer, or until the fish is cooked through and the croutons are golden and crisp. Sprinkle with the chopped fennel tops and serve.

—*Melissa Clark*

WINE The fragrant, sweet-licorice character of the fennel, intensified by the high heat, suggests a full-flavored Chardonnay with toasty oak nuances: the 1997 Gundlach Bundschu Sangiacomo or the 1997 St. Francis Reserve.

Baked Turbot with Herbed Hollandaise

8 SERVINGS

Baked whole turbot makes a truly spectacular dish. The firm, white flesh is a delicacy worth honoring with a serious sauce.

2½ sticks (10 ounces) unsalted butter, 4 tablespoons softened

20 flat-leaf parsley sprigs, plus 2 tablespoons finely chopped parsley leaves

10 tarragon sprigs, plus 1 tablespoon finely chopped tarragon leaves

2 whole turbot (4½ pounds each)—cleaned, rinsed and patted dry

Sea salt and freshly ground pepper

¾ cup dry white wine

4 large egg yolks

¼ cup water

2 tablespoons fresh lemon juice

1. Preheat the oven to 400°. Lightly grease 2 large rimmed baking sheets with some of the softened butter. Evenly divide the parsley and tarragon sprigs into 2 bundles and stuff 1 bundle into the cavity of each fish. Set the turbot on the baking sheets, dark-skinned side up, and season generously with sea salt and pepper. Dot with the remaining softened butter.

2. Pour half of the wine onto each baking sheet and loosely cover the fish with lightly greased foil. Bake on the middle and bottom racks of the oven for 50 minutes, or until a knife inserted in the thickest part comes out easily. Halfway through cooking, shift the baking sheets from top to bottom and from front to back and baste the fish with the pan juices. Remove the fish from the oven and let stand, covered, until serving time.

3. Meanwhile, make the sauce. In a small saucepan, melt the 2 sticks of butter. Skim the foam from the surface and let the butter cool slightly.

4. In a medium stainless steel bowl, whisk the egg yolks with the water until frothy. Set the bowl over but not in a saucepan of barely simmering water and whisk the egg yolks constantly until they have thickened slightly, about 4 minutes. Remove the bowl from the pan of water and whisk in the melted butter in a very thin stream; leave any milky solids behind. Continue whisking until the sauce is quite thick. Whisk in the lemon juice and the chopped parsley and tarragon; season the sauce with sea salt and pepper. Keep the hollandaise sauce warm by setting the bowl in a pan of warm water.

5. Remove the dark skin from one of the fish. Run a thin metal spatula along the central bone to separate the fillets. With the spatula, lift up the fillets and transfer them to a large warmed platter. Carefully lift up the bones and discard. Scrape the 2 remaining fillets clean and, using the spatula, lift the

menu

quail eggs with celery salt (p. 27) | beets and fava beans with anchovy vinaigrette (p. 65)
baked turbot with herbed hollandaise | new potatoes with thyme and saffron (p. 298)
braised fennel with olives and cardamom (p. 279) | 1996 WILLIAM FEVRE LES PREUSES CHABLIS
rhubarb and elderflower jelly (p. 364)

Baked Turbot with
Herbed Hollandaise,
with New Potatoes
with Thyme and
Saffron and Braised
Fennel with Olives
and Cardamom.

fillets off the bottom skin and transfer them to the platter. Repeat with the second fish so that you have 8 fillets all together. Transfer the fillets to individual plates, spoon some of the sauce on top and serve. Pass the remaining hollandaise sauce at the table.

—Tamasin Day-Lewis

WINE A complementary partner to the rich sauce would be an equally rich but dry white, like the 1996 William Fèvre Les Preuses Chablis or the 1996 Louis Latour Chassagne-Montrachet.

three ways to dress up pan-seared salmon fillets

Make lemon-herb butter:
In a small bowl, blend 6 tablespoons softened, unsalted butter with 2 tablespoons minced basil, 1 minced garlic clove, 1 tablespoon minced shallot and ½ teaspoon finely grated lemon zest. Season with salt and pepper. Spread the butter over the salmon. Or shape the butter into a log, wrap in plastic and freeze for up to 2 weeks.

Make curried chutney sauce:
In a small bowl, combine ½ cup chicken stock with 3 tablespoons rice vinegar, 3 tablespoons mango chutney and ½ teaspoon curry powder. Cook the salmon, pour the stock mixture into one of the skillets and boil until slightly reduced, about 3 minutes. Remove from heat and swirl in 1½ tablespoons butter. Season with salt and pepper, pour over the salmon and serve.

Make orange-Pernod sauce:
In a small bowl, mix ½ cup fresh orange juice with 2 tablespoons Pernod and 1 teaspoon finely grated orange zest. Cook the salmon. Pour the juice mixture into one of the skillets and boil until slightly reduced, about 1 minute. Remove from heat and swirl in 2 tablespoons butter. Season with salt and pepper, pour over the salmon and serve.

Pan-Seared Salmon Fillets
6 SERVINGS

Six 6-ounce center-cut salmon
   fillets with skin
2 tablespoons pure olive oil
Salt and freshly ground pepper
Lemon wedges, for serving

1. Set 2 large heavy skillets over moderate heat for 3 to 4 minutes. Put the salmon fillets on a platter and coat with the olive oil. Season the fillets with salt and pepper.

2. Add 3 fillets to each skillet, flesh side down. Cook over high heat until deeply browned, about 3 minutes. Turn the fillets and cook until the skin is deeply browned and crisp, about 5 minutes longer. Transfer the fillets to plates and serve with lemon wedges.

—Pam Anderson

Mustard Seed–Crusted Salmon
10 SERVINGS

The mustard seeds make a deliciously earthy and crunchy topping for the rich salmon.

One 4-pound salmon fillet,
   in 1 piece, with skin
Salt and freshly ground pepper
1 medium onion, thinly sliced
½ cup coarsely chopped dill
¼ cup olive oil
½ cup yellow mustard seeds

1. Preheat the broiler. Lay the salmon fillet, skin side down, on a baking sheet and season it with salt and pepper. In a medium bowl, toss the sliced onion with the chopped dill and olive oil. Spread the onion mixture on the salmon and season again with salt and pepper. Transfer the baking sheet to the lower third of the oven and broil the salmon fillet for 5 minutes, rotating the baking sheet after 2½ minutes. Remove the salmon fillet from the oven; leave the broiler on.

2. Coat the top of the salmon fillet with the mustard seeds, patting the seeds to help them adhere. Return the salmon to the oven and broil, rotating the baking sheet, for about 5 minutes, or until the fillet is just cooked through. Serve the salmon at once.

—Patrick O'Connell

WINE The richness of the broiled salmon and the earthiness of the mustard seeds are best matched by a full-bodied, crisp white with some tropical-fruit flavors, such as the 1998 Voss Sauvignon Blanc.

Mustard Seed–Crusted Salmon

Grilled Salmon with Dilled Mustard Glaze

Grilled Salmon with Dilled Mustard Glaze

4 SERVINGS

- 1 tablespoon yellow mustard seeds
- ¼ cup mayonnaise
- ¼ cup whole-grain mustard
- 1 tablespoon finely chopped dill
- 1½ teaspoons fresh lime juice
- 1½ teaspoons dark brown sugar
- Freshly ground pepper
- Vegetable oil, for the grill
- One 2-pound salmon fillet, with skin
- 1 tablespoon olive oil
- Salt

I. In a dry skillet, toast the mustard seeds over moderate heat until they darken and begin to pop, about 2 minutes. Transfer to a plate. In a bowl, whisk the mayonnaise with the mustard, dill, lime juice and brown sugar. Season with pepper.

2. Light a gas grill. Lightly brush the grate with oil. Run your fingers over the salmon fillet, feeling for bones; use sturdy tweezers to remove any you find.

3. Brush the skin side of the salmon with the olive oil and season the fillet generously with salt and pepper. Set it on the grill, skin side down, and spread the mustard glaze over the fish. Sprinkle with the toasted mustard seeds. Close the grill and cook the salmon over moderate heat until the glaze becomes golden and the fish is nearly opaque, about 25 minutes. If the skin begins to char, reduce the heat to low and move the fish to a cooler part of the grill. Transfer the salmon to a platter and serve hot or at room temperature.

—*Steven Raichlen*

WINE The lightly caramelized sweet mustard glaze and rich, smoky flavors here will find echoes in an oak-aged Chardonnay. Try the 1997 Chateau St. Jean Robert Young Vineyard or the 1997 Sequoia Grove Carneros.

Grilled Salmon with Indonesian Ketchup Sauce

4 SERVINGS

- ½ cup ketchup
- 2 tablespoons *kecep manis* or double soy sauce (see Note)
- 2 tablespoons red wine vinegar
- 2 tablespoons honey mustard
- 2 teaspoons curry powder
- 2 teaspoons ground cumin
- 1 teaspoon Tabasco
- ½ teaspoon salt
- Four 6-ounce skinless salmon fillets
- ¼ cup coarsely chopped cilantro

I. In a small bowl, combine the ketchup, *kecep manis,* vinegar, mustard, curry powder, cumin, Tabasco and salt. Refrigerate for at least 1 hour.

2. Light a grill or heat a grill pan. Grill the salmon over a medium-hot fire for about 6 minutes per side, or until browned and crisp on the outside but still slightly rare inside. Stir the cilantro into the ketchup sauce and generously brush about half of the sauce on the cooked salmon. Heat the remaining sauce just until bubbling. Transfer the salmon to plates and serve; pass the remaining sauce alongside or refrigerate for another use. —*Gray Kunz*

NOTE *Kecep manis,* a thick, sweet Indonesian soy sauce, is available at Asian markets.

MAKE AHEAD The prepared sauce can be refrigerated for up to 1 week. Add the cilantro before using.

Miso-Glazed Salmon

8 SERVINGS

- ¼ cup red miso paste (see Note)
- 1 tablespoon canola oil
- 1 tablespoon Asian sesame oil
- 1 tablespoon honey
- 1 tablespoon rice vinegar
- 1 tablespoon soy sauce
- Eight 5-ounce skinless salmon fillets
- 1 tablespoon sesame seeds
- 2 large scallions, thinly sliced

I. In a small bowl, whisk the miso with the oils, honey, vinegar and soy. In a large shallow dish, pour the marinade over the salmon and turn to coat. Cover with plastic wrap and chill for at least 30 minutes or for up to 1 hour.

2. Light a grill and lightly brush it with oil. Lift the fillets from the glaze and sprinkle both sides with the sesame seeds. Grill over a moderately hot fire for about 3 minutes per side, or until lightly charred and just cooked through. Transfer to a platter, sprinkle with the scallions and serve. —*Daniel Bruce*

NOTE Red miso paste is available at Asian groceries and health-food stores.

Miso-Glazed Salmon, with Yellow Bean, Asparagus and Tomato Salad (p. 64).

Hot-Mustard Salmon with Miso-Glazed Asparagus

4 SERVINGS

A fishmonger can bone the salmon steaks, or you can use 1½ pounds of fillet sliced into ½-inch-thick scallops.

- 2 tablespoons Dijon mustard
- 2 teaspoons honey
- 1 teaspoon Sriracha chili sauce or other hot red chile sauce
- 2 pounds salmon steaks, cut ½ inch thick—skinned, boned and divided into "chops"
- 1½ pounds thin asparagus, trimmed
- 1 teaspoon pure olive oil

Salt and freshly ground pepper

- 1 tablespoon light miso paste
- 1 tablespoon fresh lime juice

1. In a small bowl, combine the mustard with the honey and hot sauce. Spread the mixture on both sides of the salmon chops, arrange them in a single layer on a large dish and refrigerate for at least 10 minutes and up to 30 minutes.

2. Preheat the oven to 500°. On a large rimmed baking sheet, drizzle the asparagus with the olive oil and roll to coat. Season with salt and pepper; roast for 4 minutes or until just tender.

3. In a small bowl, combine the miso paste with the lime juice. Remove the baking sheet from the oven and brush the asparagus generously with the paste. Return to the oven and roast for 3 minutes, or until tender and glazed. Keep warm.

4. Preheat the broiler. Using a spatula, scrape most of the marinade off the salmon; arrange in a layer on a rimmed baking sheet. Broil on 1 side only for 3 minutes, or until well browned; rotate the sheet for even cooking. Transfer the salmon and asparagus to plates and serve at once. —*Marcia Kiesel*

ONE SERVING Calories 380 kcal, Total Fat 20 gm, Saturated Fat 4 gm

WINE Try a full-flavored California Chardonnay, such as the 1997 Iron Horse Cuvée Joy.

Salmon with Rhubarb and Roasted Beet Sauce

10 SERVINGS

This recipe offers a new take on the sweet-and-sour fish dishes of Jewish cooking, such as pickled herring.

- 4 small beets, scrubbed
- 1 pound rhubarb, stalks only, tough strings peeled, stalks cut into ½-inch pieces
- ¼ cup plus 2 tablespoons light brown sugar
- 2 tablespoons light olive oil
- 3 medium onions, coarsely chopped

Salt and freshly ground pepper

- 3 tablespoons balsamic or cider vinegar
- 3 tablespoons fresh orange juice
- 2 teaspoons finely grated fresh ginger
- 2 teaspoons finely grated orange zest
- ½ cup water

Lettuce or cabbage leaves, for steaming

- 2½ pounds center-cut salmon fillet, with skin

Thin slices of blood or navel oranges, for garnish (optional)

1. Preheat the oven to 425°. Wrap the beets individually in foil and roast for 1 hour, or until tender. Unwrap and let cool slightly. Peel and trim the beets, then cut them into ½-inch dice.

2. Meanwhile, in a large bowl, toss the rhubarb with 3 tablespoons of the brown sugar. Let the mixture stand for 30 minutes, stirring occasionally.

3. Heat the olive oil in a large skillet. Add the onions, season with salt and pepper and cook over moderate heat, stirring, until slightly softened, about 5 minutes. Cover and cook over low heat until very tender, about 30 minutes.

4. Add the vinegar, orange juice, ginger and the remaining 3 tablespoons of brown sugar and boil, stirring, until the liquid has evaporated and the onions are a rich caramel color, about

Hot-Mustard Salmon with Miso-Glazed Asparagus

8 minutes. Add the orange zest and the rhubarb with its liquid, cover and cook over moderate heat, stirring occasionally, until the rhubarb is tender, 8 to 10 minutes. Add the beets and simmer for 2 minutes. In a food processor, puree one-third of the sauce with the water. Stir the puree into the remaining sauce. Season with salt and pepper.

5. Line a steamer rack with lettuce leaves. Season the salmon with salt and pepper and set it on the lettuce. Cover and steam until the fish is just opaque throughout, about 12 minutes.

6. Transfer the salmon, skin side up, to paper towels to drain. Discard the skin, then carefully transfer the fish to a serving platter. Spoon some of the sauce around the fish and garnish with the orange slices. Serve warm or at room temperature. Pass the remaining sauce at the table. —*Jayne Cohen*

MAKE AHEAD The sauce and fish can be refrigerated separately for 2 days.

WINE Always a good match for salmon, the fruit in a Pinot Noir also complements the sweetness of the sauce. Try a kosher bottle like the 1997 Gan Eden from the Napa Valley.

Curto's Grilled Salmon with Bacon and Potato Hash

4 SERVINGS 👑

GARLICKY VINAIGRETTE

- 1 tablespoon Dijon mustard
- ½ small shallot, finely chopped
- 1 small garlic clove, minced
- 1 tablespoon bottled clam juice
- 2 tablespoons Champagne vinegar
- ½ tablespoon red wine vinegar
- ¼ cup extra-virgin olive oil

Salt and freshly ground pepper

CHIVE OIL

- ½ cup chopped chives
- ¼ cup canola oil

Salt

HASH AND SALMON

- 1 pound unpeeled small white new potatoes, sliced ¼ inch thick
- ¾ pound thin asparagus
- ½ pound sliced applewood-smoked bacon
- 1 tablespoon extra-virgin olive oil
- ¾ cup chicken stock
- ¾ cup bottled clam juice
- 4 tablespoons unsalted butter
- ¼ cup snipped chives
- ¼ cup finely chopped fresh dill

Salt and freshly ground pepper
Four 6-ounce skinless center-cut salmon fillets

I. MAKE THE GARLICKY VINAI-GRETTE: In a blender, combine the mustard, shallot, garlic, clam juice and vinegars and mix until smooth. With the machine on, add the oil in a thin stream and process until emulsified. Season with salt and pepper.

2. MAKE THE CHIVE OIL: Puree the chives with the canola oil in a blender until smooth. Season with salt.

3. MAKE THE HASH AND SALMON: Bring 2 medium saucepans of salted water to a boil. In one, cook the potatoes until just tender, about 10 minutes. Drain and cool in a bowl of ice water; drain again and pat dry. In the other, cook the asparagus until crisp-tender, about 3 minutes. Drain and cool under running water, then pat dry. Cut

the asparagus into ½-inch lengths.

4. In a large deep skillet, fry the bacon in 1 teaspoon of the olive oil over high heat until crisp, about 5 minutes. Drain the bacon on paper towels and coarsely chop it. Pour off the fat and wipe out the skillet.

5. Heat the remaining 2 teaspoons olive oil in the skillet. Add the potatoes and bacon and cook over moderately high heat, stirring, until the potatoes are just beginning to brown in spots, about 6 minutes. Add ½ cup each of the chicken stock and clam juice and cook, stirring gently, until most of the liquid is absorbed, about 6 minutes. Stir in the asparagus, butter, chives, dill and the remaining ¼ cup each of chicken stock and clam juice. Cook until most of the liquid is absorbed, about 5 minutes. Season with salt and pepper and keep warm.

6. Heat a cast-iron grill pan or skillet. Season the salmon with salt and pepper and grill over high heat until

browned on the bottom, about 3 minutes. Turn the salmon and cook until golden and crusty, about 2 minutes longer. Spoon the potato hash onto 4 plates and top with the salmon. Drizzle the garlicky vinaigrette and chive oil all around and serve immediately.

—*Andrea Curto*

Grilled Tuna with Coriander Seeds and Cilantro

6 SERVINGS

This simple dish uses both the leaves and seeds of the coriander plant. Try to save the juices from the roasted peppers; they add a lot of flavor.

- ½ cup coarsely chopped cilantro, plus sprigs for garnish
- 2 tablespoons coriander seeds, crushed
- 2 tablespoons dry white wine
- 3 tablespoons extra-virgin olive oil

Two 1-pound tuna steaks, about 1½ inches thick

Curto's Grilled Salmon with Bacon and Potato Hash

3 red bell peppers

Salt and freshly ground pepper

Soy sauce, for serving

1. In a large shallow glass or ceramic dish, combine the chopped cilantro with the coriander seeds, wine and 2 tablespoons of the olive oil. Add the tuna steaks and turn to coat. Refrigerate for at least 1 hour or overnight.

2. Preheat the broiler. Put the bell peppers in a baking pan and broil until charred all over. Transfer the peppers to a bowl, cover with plastic wrap and let steam for 10 minutes. Working over the bowl, peel, core and seed the peppers, then quarter them lengthwise. Return the peppers and their juices to the bowl, add the remaining 1 tablespoon of olive oil and season with salt and pepper.

3. Light a grill or preheat a grill pan. Remove the tuna from the dish and scrape off most of the marinade. Season the tuna with salt and pepper and grill over a hot fire or over high heat until charred on both sides and rare inside, about 3 minutes per side.

4. Slice the tuna across the grain and arrange on 6 plates. Serve 2 pieces of roasted pepper per person. Sprinkle a few drops of soy sauce over each serving and garnish with cilantro sprigs.

—*Corinne Chapoutier*

WINE A chilled, light-bodied red, like the 1998 Belleruche from the southern Rhône Valley, will have just enough weight to go with the meaty tuna.

Tuna with Tomatoes and Black Olives

4 SERVINGS

The bitter-and-sweet tuna dish at Secondo Borghero's restaurant, Al Tonno di Corsa, in Carloforte, Italy, inspired this recipe.

One 35-ounce can Italian plum
  tomatoes, drained and chopped

⅓ cup red wine vinegar

2 bay leaves

¼ cup coarsely chopped pitted
  black olives, such as Gaeta

Grilled Tuna with Coriander Seeds and Cilantro

Four 6-ounce tuna steaks, about
  1 inch thick

Salt and freshly ground pepper

2 tablespoons extra-virgin olive oil

¾ cup dry red wine

1. In a medium saucepan, combine the chopped tomatoes, red wine vinegar and bay leaves and bring the mixture to a boil. Reduce the heat to moderate and simmer, stirring, until the sauce is thick, about 35 minutes. Stir in the black olives and remove the sauce from the heat.

2. Season the tuna steaks with salt and pepper. In a large skillet, heat the olive oil until shimmering. Add the tuna and cook over moderately high heat until well browned, about 4 minutes per side.

Transfer the tuna to a plate. Add the wine to the skillet and boil until reduced by one-third, about 4 minutes. Add the tomato sauce, cover and simmer until thickened, about 15 minutes.

3. Return the tuna steaks to the skillet, cover loosely and simmer for 5 minutes. Discard the bay leaves and season the sauce with salt and pepper. Set the tuna steaks on plates and spoon the sauce on top. Serve hot or at room temperature.　　—*Nancy Harmon Jenkins*

WINE The slight bitterness in this dish suggests an assertive dry red or a white. Look for the 1996 Argiolas Costera Cannonau di Sardegna, a red from Sardinia, or, if you prefer a white, the 1998 Feudi San Gregorio Greco di Tufo.

menu

mushroom and goat cheese phyllo triangles (p. 17) | 1996 LOGAN SLEEPY HOLLOW PINOT NOIR
white corn and clam chowder (p. 93) | 1997 CUVEE CYNTHIA CHARDONNAY
lobster and heirloom tomato salad (p. 151) | 1996 DIAMOND T ESTATE CHARDONNAY
glazed grilled tuna with sweet bell pepper ragout | 1997 SLEEPY HOLLOW VINEYARD CHARDONNAY
cinnamon financiers with figs poached in port (p. 334) | 1995 CASE PINOT NOIR

Glazed Grilled Tuna with Sweet Bell Pepper Ragout

8 SERVINGS

- 1 cup unsweetened pineapple juice
- 2 tablespoons honey
- 1 red bell pepper
- 1 yellow bell pepper
- 1 medium red tomato, cut into ½-inch dice
- 1 medium yellow tomato, cut into ½-inch dice
- ½ cup julienned oil-packed sun-dried tomatoes, drained

Salt and freshly ground pepper
Eight 5-ounce tuna steaks, about 1 inch thick

- 1 tablespoon cold unsalted butter
- ¼ cup oregano leaves

1. In a small saucepan, combine the pineapple juice and honey and bring to a boil. Simmer over moderately low heat until reduced to ½ cup, about 25 minutes. Let cool.

2. Roast the red and yellow peppers directly over a gas flame or under the broiler, turning, until charred all over. Transfer to a bowl, cover and let steam for 10 minutes. Peel the peppers and discard the stems and seeds.

3. Cut the peppers into ½-inch dice and put them in a large skillet. Add the reserved pepper juices and the red and yellow tomatoes and boil over moderately high heat for 2 minutes. Add the sun-dried tomatoes, season with salt and pepper and remove from the heat.

4. Light a grill or preheat a grill pan. Season the steaks with salt and pepper; grill over a hot fire or over high heat for 2 to 3 minutes per side, brushing frequently with the pineapple and honey glaze. The tuna should be charred on the outside and medium rare within.

5. Bring the pepper ragout to a simmer. Remove from the heat and swirl in the butter until blended. Set a tuna steak on each plate and spoon the pepper ragout alongside. Garnish with the oregano and serve at once. *—Victor Scargle*

MAKE AHEAD The pineapple and honey glaze and bell pepper ragout can be prepared through Step 3 and refrigerated for up to 1 day.

WINE The grilled tuna needs a full-bodied white with toasty oak undertones. The 1997 Sleepy Hollow Vineyard Chardonnay is an ideal match.

Grilled Tuna with Artichokes and Aioli

4 SERVINGS ✳

- 2 garlic cloves, mashed

Kosher salt

- 1 tablespoon fresh lemon juice, plus lemon wedges, for serving
- ½ cup mayonnaise, preferably homemade
- ¼ cup plus 3 tablespoons extra-virgin olive oil
- 2 pounds baby artichokes (about 16), stems trimmed to 1 inch, top thirds cut off and discarded

Freshly ground pepper

- 2 tablespoons chopped flat-leaf parsley

Four 6-ounce tuna steaks, about ¾ inch thick

1. In a small bowl, combine the garlic with ¾ teaspoon of salt; mash to a paste with the back of a small spoon. Stir in the lemon juice and mayonnaise until smooth. Gradually whisk in ¼ cup of the olive oil in a thin stream until the aioli is emulsified. Refrigerate the aioli until serving.

2. Bring a large saucepan of salted water to a boil. Add the artichokes, cover with a lid slightly smaller than the saucepan to keep the artichokes submerged and cook until the bottoms are tender, about 15 minutes. Drain the artichokes and spread them out on a large plate to cool slightly. Pull off the tough outer leaves and cut each artichoke in half. Pat dry.

3. In a large skillet, heat 2 tablespoons of the olive oil until shimmering. Add

Glazed Grilled Tuna with Sweet Bell Pepper Ragout

the artichokes and cook over high heat, stirring occasionally, until golden and crisp, 4 to 5 minutes. Season with salt and pepper and sprinkle with the chopped parsley. Transfer the artichokes to a platter and keep warm.

4. Heat a cast-iron grill pan or large skillet. Rub the tuna with the remaining 1 tablespoon of olive oil and season with salt and pepper. Grill the tuna over high heat, turning once, until browned and the meat is medium rare, about 3 minutes total. Transfer the tuna to the platter and serve immediately with the aioli and lemon wedges.

—*Annie Wayte and Anna Kovel*

WINE Rare grilled tuna is meaty enough to serve with a light Pinot Noir—try the 1997 Morgan Reserve or the 1997 Sanford Barrel Select.

Hawaiian Grilled Tuna with Maui-Onion Slaw

4 SERVINGS

Dishes such as this seared sushi-quality tuna seasoned with teriyaki and served over a crisp, sweet Maui-onion slaw have made Roy Yamaguchi one of Hawaii's most celebrated chefs.

- ½ cup plus ½ teaspoon soy sauce
- ¼ cup sake
- ¼ cup sugar
- 4 scallions, thinly sliced
- 2 garlic cloves, minced
- Four 6-ounce sushi-quality tuna steaks, about 1 inch thick
- Vegetable oil
- 1 tablespoon fresh lime juice
- 1 tablespoon mirin (see Note) or sweet sherry
- Salt and freshly ground pepper
- 2 carrots, cut into thin matchsticks
- 1 European cucumber—peeled, seeded and cut into thin matchsticks
- 1 package (2 ounces) radish sprouts
- ½ Maui or other sweet onion, sliced paper thin

I. In a glass baking dish, combine ½

cup of the soy sauce with the sake, sugar, scallions and garlic; stir to dissolve the sugar. Add the tuna steaks and turn to coat. Marinate in the refrigerator, turning occasionally, for 1 hour.

2. Light a grill. Lightly brush the grate with vegetable oil. Remove the tuna from the marinade and pat dry. Brush the tuna with 1 tablespoon of vegetable oil and grill over high heat until lightly browned, about 2 to 3 minutes per side for medium rare. Transfer the tuna to a plate, cover loosely with foil and keep warm.

3. In a medium bowl, whisk 1 tablespoon of vegetable oil and ½ teaspoon of soy sauce with the lime juice and mirin. Season with salt and pepper. Add the carrots, cucumber, radish sprouts and onion and toss to combine. Mound the slaw on 4 dinner plates. Thickly slice the tuna and arrange it over the slaw. Pour any accumulated juices over the tuna and serve. —*Steven Raichlen*

NOTE You can substitute yellowfin or bigeye tuna, as long as it's fresh. Mirin is a sweet rice wine available at Asian grocery stores and many supermarkets.

MAKE AHEAD The marinade can be refrigerated in an airtight container for up to 2 days.

WINE A citrusy off-dry Riesling will blend with the tart salad and the sweet tuna. Consider the 1999 Hogue Cellars Johannisberg Riesling from Washington State or the 1999 Jekel Vineyards Monterey Riesling from California.

Fresh Tuna and Mussel Paella

8 SERVINGS

If the rice starts sticking to the bottom of the paella pan during cooking, set the pan on a flat griddle or on a flame tamer over the burner.

- 1 red bell pepper
- Fine sea salt
- 1 pound tuna steak, cut into 1½-inch cubes
- 1 large ancho chile
- 1 cup boiling water
- ⅓ cup dry white wine

- 1 pound mussels, scrubbed and debearded
- Freshly ground pepper
- ¼ cup plus 1 tablespoon olive oil
- 2 tablespoons coarsely chopped garlic
- 1¼ cups canned diced tomatoes
- 2 teaspoons Spanish smoked *pimentón* or sweet paprika
- 2 pinches of saffron threads
- 6 to 8 cups fish stock, or two 8-ounce packages frozen fish fumet diluted with 4 cups water (see Note)
- One 9-ounce package frozen artichoke hearts, cut into 1-inch pieces
- 8 scallions, cut into 1½-inch lengths
- 2 cups short- to medium-grain rice, preferably Calasparra
- 2 tablespoons chopped flat-leaf parsley
- Lemon wedges, for serving

I. Preheat the broiler. Roast the red bell pepper under the broiler, turning, until charred. Transfer the pepper to a small bowl, cover with plastic wrap and let steam for 5 minutes. Peel the pepper, discarding the core, ribs and seeds; cut it into 1-inch pieces.

2. Salt the tuna cubes and let stand for 30 minutes; pat dry with paper towels. In a heatproof bowl, cover the ancho chile with the boiling water and let stand until softened, about 20 minutes; drain. Discard the stem and seeds and coarsely chop the chile.

3. Bring the wine to a boil in a medium saucepan. Add the mussels, cover and cook over high heat until they begin to open, about 3 minutes. Using a slotted spoon, transfer the mussels to a bowl. Discard the empty shell from each mussel. Season the mussels with pepper and cover with foil; reserve the cooking liquid.

4. Heat 2 tablespoons of the olive oil in a large skillet. Add the chopped chile and the garlic. Cook over moderately high heat until the garlic is golden, about 2 minutes. Add the tomatoes, *pimentón,* saffron and 1 teaspoon of salt and cook over moderate heat for 5 minutes, stirring. Transfer to a food processor and puree to a coarse paste.

5. In a medium saucepan, bring the stock to a boil, then cover, reduce the heat and keep at a simmer. In an 18-inch paella pan or a very large skillet, heat the remaining 3 tablespoons of olive oil. Add the tuna cubes and cook over moderately high heat until browned, about 3 minutes. Transfer to a plate and cover. Add the artichokes and scallions to the pan and cook over moderately high heat for 1 minute. Add the ancho-tomato paste and cook, stirring, for 1 minute. Add 4 cups of the stock, the reserved mussel cooking liquid and ½ teaspoon of salt and bring to a boil.

6. Scatter the rice evenly into the pan and stir. Reduce the heat to moderate and cook for 7 minutes. Reduce the heat to low and continue cooking until the liquid has evaporated, about 10 minutes. Add another 2 to 4 cups of simmering stock and cook, shaking the pan and rotating it for even cooking, until the liquid has evaporated, about 10 minutes. Just before the rice is done, during the last 10 minutes of cooking, gently press the roasted red pepper, the mussels and tuna in with the back of a spoon. Continue cooking, shaking the pan, until the rice is just tender but still a bit moist.

7. Remove the pan from the heat and cover with a towel or paper towels and a foil tent. Let the paella rest for about 10 minutes. Uncover, sprinkle with the parsley and serve with lemon wedges.

—Paula Wolfert

NOTE Fish fumet is available from specialty food stores.

WINE A pleasantly sharp, acidic white, such as the New Zealand 1998 Brancott Sauvignon Blanc, will accent this slightly spicy and briny dish particularly well.

Fresh Tuna and Mussel Paella

paella imperatives for the serious cook

You can be as creative as you want with your paella as long as you have quality ingredients and the right equipment. Here's what you need:

Spanish rice Calasparra *bomba,* preferred by many Spanish cooks, is not available in the United States. Try plain Calasparra, a short- to medium-grain Spanish rice. Like *bomba,* it can soak up a maximum amount of flavorful liquid, becoming plump without turning mushy. Good paellas can also be made with other short- to medium-grain rices from Spain, California and Italy. Note that while one cup of dry Calasparra rice requires more than three cups of cooking liquid, a cup of any other short- to medium-grain rice requires only two cups of liquid.

Pimentón de La Vera A trick for imbuing kitchen-cooked paella with an outdoors wood-smoke flavor is to use *pimentón de La Vera,* paprika from Spain's western region of Extremadura. The smoky, brick-red paprika has a warm, rounded flavor. *Pimentón* is produced by drying and smoking mature red peppers over oak fires, then stone-grinding them to a uniquely smooth, almost talclike powder.

Paella pan A good, dry paella is ideally cooked in a proper paella pan—a two-handled, wide, shallow, flat-bottomed pan with sloping sides. This type of pan allows liquid to evaporate quickly while the rice cooks uncovered over low heat. As an alternative, you can choose a very wide and shallow skillet. *—Paula Wolfert* These and other paella necessities are available from The Spanish Table (206-682-2827; tablespan@aol.com).

menu

artichokes with anchoïade (p. 15)

chicken-liver terrine with shallots (p. 47) | 1993 BILLECART-SALMON BLANC DE BLANCS

deviled eggs with shrimp and radishes (p. 27) | fennel-and-endive slaw with crab (p. 70)

1998 LUCIEN ALBRECHT RIESLING D'ALSACE

tuna basquaise | 1995 DOMAINE MARCEL DEISS BURLENBERG

summer berry clafoutis (p. 371)

Tuna Basquaise

12 SERVINGS

- ⅓ cup plus ¼ cup extra-virgin olive oil
- 1 large onion plus 1 small onion, finely chopped
- ¼ pound prosciutto, sliced ¼ inch thick and cut into ½-inch dice
- 3 large shallots, finely chopped
- 6 thyme sprigs
- 4 large garlic cloves, minced
- 3 bay leaves
- 3 large red bell peppers, cut into ½-inch dice
- 2 medium yellow bell peppers, cut into ½-inch dice
- 1 medium eggplant, peeled and cut into ½-inch dice
- 2 pounds zucchini, cut into ½-inch dice
- 1 cup dry white wine
- 4 medium tomatoes—peeled, seeded and coarsely chopped
- 1½ cups V-8 juice
- ½ tablespoon tomato paste

Salt and freshly ground pepper

Four 1¾-inch-thick tuna steaks (about 1¼ pounds each)

1. Heat ⅓ cup of the olive oil in a large enameled cast-iron casserole. Add the onions, prosciutto, shallots, thyme, garlic and bay leaves and cook over moderately low heat, stirring, until the onions begin to soften, about 5 minutes. Reduce the heat to low and cook until softened, about 12 minutes.

2. Add the bell peppers and cook until softened, about 5 minutes. Add the eggplant and cook until softened, about 5 minutes. Add the zucchini and cook, stirring often, until softened, about 10 minutes. Add the wine and simmer over moderately high heat for 5 minutes. Add the tomatoes and simmer for 5 minutes longer, then add the V-8 juice and tomato paste. Simmer over moderate heat until thickened, about 15 minutes. Discard the thyme and bay leaves and season the sauce with salt and pepper.

3. Preheat the oven to 425°. Heat 2 large ovenproof skillets. Season the tuna steaks with salt and pepper. Add 2 tablespoons of the olive oil to each skillet. When the oil shimmers, add 2 tuna steaks to each skillet and cook over high heat until deeply browned on the bottom, about 4 minutes. Turn the steaks over and transfer the skillets to the oven. Roast for about 8 minutes, or until the tuna is pink inside. Transfer the tuna steaks to a carving board.

4. Ladle the Basquaise sauce onto 2 large platters. Slice the tuna across the grain ½ inch thick. Arrange the tuna on the sauce, pour the pan juices over the tuna and serve the dish very warm but not steaming hot.

—Jean-Louis Palladin

MAKE AHEAD The vegetable Basquaise can be refrigerated for up to 1 day. Reheat before serving.

WINE The best red wine match with meaty, slightly oily tuna is a light-bodied Pinot Noir. One from Alsace, such as the 1995 Domaine Marcel Deiss Burlenberg or the 1998 Hugel, would be ideal.

Pan-Grilled Shrimp on "Killed" Salad

6 SERVINGS

Fresh greens wilt slightly under the hot shrimp. You might find this recipe prepared with crawfish instead of shrimp in a Southern tearoom or lunch parlor. For a more refined dish, you can shell the shrimp before marinating.

- 5 tablespoons unsalted butter, melted
- 2 tablespoons sweet paprika
- 1 tablespoon unsulphured molasses
- 1 teaspoon dry mustard
- 1 teaspoon lemon pepper
- 1 teaspoon onion powder
- ½ teaspoon cayenne pepper
- ½ teaspoon ground cumin

Coarse salt

- 2 pounds large shrimp, butterflied through the back and deveined
- ¼ cup white wine vinegar
- ¼ cup dry white wine
- 2 tablespoons honey
- 2 tablespoons yellow mustard
- 2 tablespoons minced parsley
- 1 tablespoon minced garlic
- 1 tablespoon finely chopped anchovy fillets
- ⅓ cup extra-virgin olive oil, plus more for pan-grilling
- ½ pound sliced bacon
- 6 cups mixed greens, such as watercress and green leaf lettuce, torn into bite-size pieces
- 2 carrots, coarsely shredded

Freshly ground black pepper

Tuna Basquaise

I. In a medium bowl, combine the butter, paprika, molasses, dry mustard, lemon pepper, onion powder, cayenne, cumin and 1 teaspoon of salt. Lay the shrimp, shell side down, on a baking sheet and brush with the paste. If necessary, separate layers of shrimp with wax paper. Cover and refrigerate for at least 1 hour.

2. In a blender, combine the white wine vinegar, wine, honey, yellow mustard, parsley, garlic and anchovies and puree. With the machine on, add ⅓ cup of olive oil in a thin stream and blend until emulsified. Transfer the dressing to a jar.

3. In a large skillet, cook the bacon over moderately high heat until it is browned and crisp, about 6 minutes; drain on paper towels. Crumble the cooked bacon into a large bowl. Add the greens, shredded carrots and 2 tablespoons of the dressing, season with black pepper and toss to coat. Arrange the salad on 6 large, individual plates.

4. Heat a cast-iron grill pan or a large skillet and coat lightly with olive oil. Add the shrimp in batches and cook over high heat, occasionally drizzling the shrimp with some of the dressing and turning them once, until they are bright pink and blackened in spots, approximately 5 minutes. Arrange the

shrimp on the salads and serve immediately. Pass the remaining dressing at the table. —*Michael Lomonaco*

MAKE AHEAD The recipe can be prepared through Step 2 and refrigerated overnight.

WINE The tanginess of the pan-grilled shrimp salad requires a wine of matching acidity. Look for the 1997 Trimbach Pinot Blanc from Alsace or try the 1997 Alain Graillot Crozes-Hermitage Blanc.

Shrimp with Lemon Bread Crumbs and Potato-Caper Salad

4 SERVINGS

SHRIMP

20 medium shrimp, shelled and deveined

¼ cup coarsely chopped flat-leaf parsley

3 tablespoons extra-virgin olive oil

2 garlic cloves, thinly sliced

1 tablespoon black peppercorns, coarsely crushed

1 tablespoon coriander seeds, coarsely crushed

1 lemon, thinly sliced

¼ cup pure olive oil

Salt

POTATO SALAD

1 pound medium red potatoes, scrubbed

Salt

1 tablespoon fresh lemon juice

1 teaspoon red wine vinegar

1 teaspoon Dijon mustard

¼ cup extra-virgin olive oil

1 tablespoon capers, preferably packed in salt, rinsed

1 garlic clove, minced

1 anchovy fillet

1 shallot, minced

1 tablespoon chopped parsley

LEMON BREAD CRUMBS

2 tablespoons toasted coarse sourdough bread crumbs

1 tablespoon fresh lemon juice

1 teaspoon finely grated lemon zest

2 teaspoons minced parsley

I. MARINATE THE SHRIMP: Thread 5 shrimp onto each of four 10-inch skewers. In a small bowl, combine the parsley with the extra-virgin olive oil, garlic, peppercorns and coriander. Using half the lemon slices, make a layer in the center of a large shallow baking dish. Pour half of the peppercorn marinade on the lemon slices and set the shrimp skewers on top. Cover with the remaining lemon slices and pour the remaining marinade on top. Cover and refrigerate for 4 to 6 hours.

2. MAKE THE POTATO SALAD: In a medium saucepan, cover the potatoes with cold water and bring to a boil. Lightly salt the water and cook the potatoes until tender, about 7 minutes. Remove the pan from the heat and let the potatoes cool in the water. Drain and slice ¼ inch thick.

3. In a bowl, combine the lemon juice with the red wine vinegar and Dijon mustard; whisk in the olive oil. Chop and mash the capers with the minced garlic and anchovy fillet and add to the dressing along with the minced shallot and chopped parsley. Pour the dressing over the sliced potatoes and toss to coat thoroughly.

4. MAKE THE LEMON BREAD CRUMBS: In a small bowl, lightly toss the bread crumbs with the lemon juice, lemon zest and minced parsley.

5. Heat the pure olive oil in a large skillet. Scrape most of the marinade seasonings off the shrimp and season them with salt. Add the shrimp skewers to the skillet and cook over high heat until lightly browned, about 2 minutes per side. Remove the shrimp from the skewers and arrange on plates. Sprinkle with the lemon bread crumbs and serve with the potato salad. —*Bill Telepan*

WINE Capers and lemon are a natural match with a Mediterranean classic, the Assyrtiko grape from the island of Santorini. Try the 1999 Thalassitis from Gaia Wines or the 1999 Boutari Kallisti.

Shrimp with Citrus Mojo

4 SERVINGS

Mojo is the ubiquitous Cuban condiment that's sprinkled on meats and poultry. It also often serves as a marinade, a flavoring during cooking and an at-the-table seasoning. A Scotch bonnet chile makes this version extra spicy.

MOJO

- 1 teaspoon whole allspice berries
- ¾ teaspoon cumin seeds
- ¼ cup minced onion
- 2 garlic cloves, minced
- ½ to 1 whole Scotch bonnet or habanero chile, seeded and minced
- ½ teaspoon finely grated orange zest, with no white pith
- ½ cup fresh orange juice
- ¼ cup plus 2 tablespoons extra-virgin olive oil
- 3 tablespoons fresh lime juice
- 2 tablespoons sherry vinegar
- 1 teaspoon kosher salt
- ½ teaspoon freshly ground pepper
- ¼ teaspoon saffron threads, crumbled

SHRIMP

- 1 pound Yukon Gold potatoes, peeled and cut into 1-inch dice
- 2 cups fresh or frozen corn kernels
- 2 tablespoons vegetable oil
- 1½ pounds medium shrimp, shelled and deveined
- ¼ cup cilantro leaves, plus 2 tablespoons chopped

Salt and freshly ground pepper

1. MAKE THE MOJO: In a small skillet, toast the allspice berries and the cumin seeds over moderate heat until they're fragrant, about 1 minute. Transfer the spices to a plate to cool, and then grind in a spice grinder or mortar. In a small bowl, combine the ground spices with the onion, garlic, chile, orange zest, orange juice, olive oil, lime juice, sherry vinegar, salt, pepper and crumbled saffron threads and set aside for 1 hour.

2. MAKE THE SHRIMP: In a large saucepan of boiling salted water, cook the diced potatoes until they are just tender, about 5 minutes. Using a slotted spoon, transfer the cooked potatoes to a bowl. Add the corn kernels to the boiling water and cook them until just tender, about 3 minutes. Then drain the corn kernels and add them to the potatoes.

3. Wipe out the saucepan with a paper towel, add the vegetable oil to the pan and heat until shimmering. Add ½ cup of the *mojo* and simmer over moderate heat for 1 minute. Add the shrimp and cook, turning them once, until they are loosely curled, about 1 minute. Transfer the cooked shrimp to a plate.

4. Add another ¼ cup of the *mojo* to the saucepan and bring to a simmer over moderate heat. Add the diced potatoes and corn kernels and cook just until heated through. Stir in the chopped cilantro and season with salt and pepper. Transfer the potatoes and corn to a platter and arrange the shrimp on top. Garnish the platter with the cilantro leaves and serve, passing the extra *mojo* at the table.

—*Marcia Kiesel*

MAKE AHEAD The *mojo* can be made 1 day in advance and refrigerated overnight.

WINE A light, acidic Italian Pinot Grigio will help to tame the heat of the pepper and will also echo the bright taste of citrus from the orange and lime juice in the *mojo* sauce. Try the 1998 Zemmer or the 1998 Campanile.

Shrimp with Citrus Mojo

Punjabi Shrimp

4 SERVINGS

This spicy, richly flavored dish is inspired by the tomato-based sauces of northern India. For a vegetarian version, substitute eggplant or tofu for the shrimp.

- 1 pound medium shrimp, shelled and deveined

Salt

- 3 tablespoons vegetable oil
- ⅛ teaspoon turmeric
- 2 teaspoons ground cumin
- 2 teaspoons ground coriander
- 4 fresh curry leaves (see Note)
- 1 small onion, thinly sliced
- 1 teaspoon finely grated fresh ginger
- ½ jalapeño, seeded and minced
- 1 garlic clove, minced
- 2 medium tomatoes, coarsely chopped
- 1 tablespoon tomato paste
- 1 tablespoon coarsely chopped cilantro

Punjabi Shrimp

1. Season the shrimp with salt. In a large skillet, heat 2 tablespoons of the oil until shimmering. Add the shrimp and cook over moderately high heat until golden brown, approximately 1 minute per side. Transfer the shrimp to a plate.

2. Add the remaining 1 tablespoon of oil to the skillet and reduce the heat to moderate. Add the turmeric, cumin and coriander and cook, stirring frequently, until fragrant, about 1 minute. Stir in the curry leaves and cook for 30 seconds longer. Add the onion, ginger, jalapeño and garlic and cook until the onion softens, approximately 5 minutes; if the mixture seems dry, add up to ¼ cup of water to prevent sticking. Add the chopped tomatoes and tomato paste and cook until the sauce thickens, about 3 minutes.

3. Return the shrimp to the skillet and cook, stirring, until they are opaque throughout, approximately 2 minutes. Season with salt. Transfer the shrimp to a bowl, sprinkle with the cilantro and serve right away.

—*Gary MacGurn and Patty Gentry*

NOTE Fresh curry leaves are available at Indian and Southeast Asian markets.

MAKE AHEAD The shrimp can be refrigerated overnight.

Bruschetta with Lima Bean Salad and Lemon Shrimp

4 SERVINGS

Bruschetta are often served as an hors d'oeuvre, but these are so generously topped that they're ample enough to serve for a light lunch.

One 10-ounce package frozen baby lima beans

- ⅓ cup finely chopped mint
- ⅓ cup finely chopped parsley
- 2 tablespoons white wine vinegar
- 3 tablespoons extra-virgin olive oil

Salt and freshly ground pepper

Eight ½-inch-thick slices sourdough bread cut from a round loaf

- 1 garlic clove
- 4 tablespoons unsalted butter, softened
- 1 teaspoon finely grated lemon zest
- 8 jumbo shrimp—shelled, halved lengthwise and deveined

1. Cook the beans in a medium saucepan of boiling water until tender, about 8 minutes; drain. Transfer to a bowl and let cool slightly. Stir in the mint, parsley, vinegar and 2 tablespoons of the oil. Season with salt and pepper.

2. Toast the bread. Rub the slices with the garlic clove and drizzle with the remaining 1 tablespoon of olive oil.

3. Preheat the broiler. In a small bowl, mash the butter with the lemon zest and season with salt and pepper. Spread the butter all over the shrimp and set them in a broiling pan. Broil for

Grilled Soft-Shell Crabs with Tartar Sauce

4   rolls, split

12   cleaned soft-shell crabs

Salt and freshly ground pepper

1. MAKE THE TARTAR SAUCE: Combine all of the ingredients in a bowl.

2. MAKE THE CRAB SANDWICHES: Light a grill. Brush the grate with oil. Melt the butter in a saucepan. Add the garlic, shallots and seafood seasoning and cook over high heat until fragrant, about 2 minutes; don't let the garlic brown.

3. Grill the rolls until golden; move the rolls to a cooler part of the grill. Brush the crabs generously with the aromatic butter and season with salt and pepper. Grill the crabs over high heat, turning occasionally, until bright red, crisp and charred in spots, about 4 minutes. Spread the tartar sauce on the rolls, top with the crabs and serve.

—*Steven Raichlen*

WINE Viognier would complement the sweetness of the crab and the creaminess of the tartar sauce. Two great bottles are the 1998 McCrea Cellars from Washington State and the 1998 Arrowood from California.

Lobster and Heirloom Tomato Salad

8 SERVINGS

You can save time if you use lobsters that have already been steamed.

Four 1¼-pound lobsters

½   cup extra-virgin olive oil

1   cup lightly packed basil leaves

4   shallots, thinly sliced

1   teaspoon cracked black peppercorns

1   large plum tomato, cored and coarsely chopped

1   tablespoon balsamic vinegar

1   tablespoon red wine vinegar

Salt

1   head Boston lettuce, torn into bite-size pieces

1   small head radicchio, torn into bite-size pieces

1   cup tightly packed mâche or mesclun

2   medium red heirloom tomatoes, cored and cut into 8 wedges

2   medium yellow heirloom tomatoes, cored and cut into 8 wedges

1. Bring a large pot of water to a boil. Plunge the lobsters in headfirst and cook until bright red all over, about 10 minutes. Using tongs, transfer the lobsters to a large bowl. When cool, twist off the claws and crack them all over. Remove the claw and knuckle meat and cut into 1-inch pieces. Twist off the lobster tails. With a large, heavy knife, cut them in half lengthwise down the center. Pull out and discard the black intestinal veins. Loosen the tail meat but leave it in the shell. Cover all the lobster meat with plastic wrap and refrigerate.

2. In a small saucepan, combine the olive oil, basil, shallots and peppercorns and bring to a boil. Cover and simmer over low heat for 5 minutes, and then strain the oil into a small bowl.

3. In a mini processor, puree the plum tomato. Strain the puree into the olive oil. Stir in the vinegars and season the dressing with salt.

4. In a large bowl, toss the lettuce, radicchio and mâche with the lobster claw and knuckle meat. Add all but 2 tablespoons of the dressing and toss well. Mound the salad on plates and arrange the tomato wedges alongside. Top each salad with a halved lobster tail, cut side up. Brush the tail meat with the reserved dressing and serve at once.   —*Victor Scargle*

MAKE AHEAD The lobsters and the tomato dressing can be prepared through Step 3 and refrigerated for up to 1 day.

WINE The 1996 Diamond T Estate Chardonnay is a rich, complex wine that has the backbone and depth to complement the luxurious lobster as well as the acidity and structure to offset the vinaigrette and tomatoes.

Lobster and Heirloom Tomato Salad

Lobster and Rice Noodle Salad

4 SERVINGS ✳

½   pound medium-width rice noodles

2   teaspoons sugar

1   garlic clove, crushed

½   teaspoon crushed red pepper

¼   cup Asian fish sauce

¼   cup water

3   tablespoons fresh lime juice plus 1 lime, cut into wedges

½   tablespoon distilled white vinegar

4   cooked lobsters (1¼ pounds each)

1   seedless European cucumber, cut into 2-inch matchsticks (2 cups)

½   cup cilantro leaves

¼   cup basil leaves, shredded

1. Soak the rice noodles in a bowl of warm water until pliable, about 30 minutes.

2. Meanwhile, in a mortar, pound the sugar with the garlic and crushed red pepper to a fine paste. Stir in the fish sauce, water, lime juice and vinegar.

3. Using kitchen shears, snip the underside of the lobster tails down the center and remove the meat in 1 piece. Cut the tail meat in half lengthwise and remove the black intestinal veins.

seven seafood tips

1. Choose clams with shells that are steely gray, not chalky white, which is a sign of age. If the clam is open, pinch the shells together. If they don't stay closed, discard the clam. Never use clams with cracked shells.

2. Buy lobsters that are lively and that have hard, dark shells, and ignore the myth that small lobsters are sweeter than large ones.

3. Select fresh, firm whole fish with red gills, clear eyes and smooth, unblemished skin with a bright sheen.

4. Buy fillets that are moist, with shiny, almost translucent flesh. They should be firm and have a clean sea smell. Never buy fish that is sitting in water.

5. Keep fresh fish and shellfish refrigerated at all times. The coolest part of most refrigerators is at the back of the bottom shelf, where the temperature should be 38° or lower.

6. Cut fish with a very sharp knife; the fragile flesh can tear easily.

7. Make stock using the well-rinsed heads, bones and trimmings of haddock, cod, flounder, sole, bass or halibut.

Crack the claws with a mallet and remove the meat, then chop it into ½-inch pieces.

4. Drain the rice noodles and cook them in a large pot of boiling water until al dente, about 2 minutes, then drain. Return the noodles to the pot and add cold water to cover. Drain again and transfer the noodles to a large bowl.

5. Add the lobster claw meat, cucumber, cilantro and basil to the noodles. Add the dressing and toss well. Mound the noodles on 4 large plates and top each with 2 lobster tail halves. Garnish with lime wedges and serve.

—Donna Hay

WINE A fruity Australian Semillon, such as the 1997 Lenswood, or a light Chardonnay, such as the 1997 Hill of Content, will harmonize with the lobster.

Sardinian Seafood Stew

8 SERVINGS

This stew, called *cassola,* is said to be Catalan in origin, but it is similar to stews from all over the Mediterranean. What makes it Sardinian is the use of native fish, such as gurnard, sea robin, eel, skate, and bream as well as tiny squid, octopus, baby clams and small crabs. This recipe—a version of the stew that's served at La Ghinghetta restaurant in the little fishing port of Portoscuso—is made with seafood widely available in the U.S. If you have any fish bones or clam, shrimp or lobster shells after cleaning the seafood for the stew, add them to the fish stock.

FISH STOCK

1½ tablespoons olive oil
2½ pounds nonoily fish heads and bones, well rinsed
2 medium leeks, white and tender green parts, thinly sliced
1 shallot, thinly sliced
1 celery rib, thinly sliced
3 fresh thyme sprigs
2 parsley sprigs
½ cup dry white wine
6 cups water
1 medium tomato, chopped
1 bay leaf
Salt

STEW

2 dozen littleneck clams or cockles, scrubbed and rinsed
Two 1½-pound live or cooked lobsters
1 medium onion, coarsely chopped
½ cup extra-virgin olive oil, plus more for brushing
6 garlic cloves, coarsely chopped
3 pounds plum tomatoes—peeled, seeded and finely chopped
½ cup dry white wine
Salt and freshly ground black pepper
Large pinch of crushed red pepper
1 pound monkfish fillet, dark portions trimmed off, fish cut into 6 pieces
2 pounds medium shrimp, shelled and deveined

1 pound cleaned small squid, bodies cut into ½-inch-thick rings, tentacles left whole
⅓ cup chopped flat-leaf parsley, plus more for garnish
8 slices of toasted country bread, drizzled liberally with extra-virgin olive oil, for serving

I. MAKE THE FISH STOCK: Heat the olive oil in a small stockpot. Add the fish heads and bones, leeks, shallot, celery, thyme and parsley and cook over moderate heat, stirring occasionally, until the fish bones turn white and the vegetables are fragrant, about 4 minutes.

2. Add the wine and cook for 1 minute. Add the water, chopped tomato, bay leaf and a large pinch of salt; bring the stock to a simmer over moderately high heat. Skim any foam that rises to the surface and reduce the heat to low. Simmer the stock for 20 minutes, skimming often.

3. Slowly pour the stock into a fine strainer set over a saucepan, leaving out any solids at the bottom of the pot. You should have 4 cups; if not, simmer the strained stock until it has reduced to 4 cups.

4. MAKE THE STEW: In a medium saucepan, bring 1 inch of water to a boil. Add the clams, cover and cook over high heat until they open, about 3 minutes; using tongs, transfer any opened clams to a bowl. Cover and continue cooking until all of the clams have opened. Reserve the cooking liquid in the saucepan.

5. If using live lobsters, bring a large pot of water to a rolling boil. Add the lobsters, cover and cook for 12 minutes. Drain the lobsters and let them cool slightly. Twist off the lobster tails and remove the claws. Crack the claws and remove the meat. Using kitchen shears, cut down 1 side of each tail and remove the meat from the shell in 1 piece. Make a thin cut down the center of the outside of each lobster tail and remove the black intestinal vein. Cut the lobster tails crosswise into thick medallions.

6. In a large enameled cast-iron casserole, cook the chopped onion in the ½ cup of olive oil over moderately low heat until translucent. Add the chopped garlic and cook for 2 minutes longer. Add the plum tomatoes and cook over moderate heat for 20 minutes, stirring occasionally. Stir in the white wine and bring to a boil; simmer for 2 minutes. Pour in the fish stock. Add the reserved clam cooking liquid, taking care to stop pouring before you reach the grit at the bottom. Bring the stew to a boil, then reduce the heat and simmer for 15 minutes. Season the stew with salt and black pepper and add the crushed red pepper.

7. Add the monkfish to the casserole and gently stir it into the sauce. Cover and simmer the stew for 3 minutes, then add the shrimp and squid. Cover and cook until the squid is just tender, 2 to 3 minutes. Add the reserved clams and lobster meat and cook the stew just until heated through. Stir in the chopped parsley.

8. Put a piece of toast in the bottom of each soup plate and ladle the fish stew on top, making sure that each serving includes some of each variety of seafood. Sprinkle with parsley and serve immediately.

—*Nancy Harmon Jenkins*

MAKE AHEAD The recipe can be prepared through Step 6 and refrigerated overnight; chill the seafood and stock separately.

WINE Vermentino di Sardegna, a Sardinian white wine, has refreshing citrus notes that add contrast to the flavors of the fish. Try the zingy, crisp 1998 Sella & Mosca La Cala or the more complex 1998 Argiolas. A richer, riper alternative: the 1998 Umani Ronchi Verdicchio dei Castelli di Jesi Classico Superiore Casal di Serra.

Mussel Stew Topped with Basil Soufflé

6 SERVINGS

This unusual dish is prepared in the style of the famous lobster soufflé (a lobster sauce with a soufflé mixture on top) at the Hotel Plaza Athénée in Paris. In this version, mussels are steamed in wine and finished with onions, scallions and cream. The mussels are then removed from their shells, placed in individual ramekins and baked beneath a basil and Parmesan cheese–flavored soufflé.

MUSSEL STEW

1 cup white wine
3 pounds mussels, scrubbed and debearded
1 tablespoon unsalted butter
⅓ cup finely chopped onion
⅓ cup thinly sliced scallions
1 garlic clove, minced
½ cup heavy cream
1 tablespoon potato starch dissolved in 2 tablespoons water
Salt and freshly ground pepper

BASIL SOUFFLE

2 tablespoons unsalted butter
3 tablespoons all-purpose flour
Salt and freshly ground pepper
3 large egg yolks
6 large egg whites
⅓ cup plus 2 tablespoons freshly grated Parmesan cheese
1 cup coarsely shredded basil

1. MAKE THE MUSSEL STEW: Butter six 1½-cup ramekins. Bring the white wine to a boil in a large saucepan. Add the mussels, cover the saucepan and cook over high heat, shaking the pan occasionally, until the mussels open, about 3 minutes. Drain the mussels in a colander set over a bowl; reserve the broth. You should have about 2 cups of the mussel broth. If not, add enough water to make 2 cups. Remove the mussels from the shells. Pat the mussels dry and evenly distribute them among the prepared ramekins.

2. Melt the unsalted butter in a medium saucepan. Add the chopped onion and cook over moderate heat until softened, approximately 5 minutes. Add the sliced scallions, minced garlic, heavy cream and ¾ cup of the reserved mussel broth and bring the mixture to a boil. Stir in the dissolved potato starch and bring back to a boil, stirring well. Season the sauce with salt and pepper and pour it over the mussels in the ramekins.

3. MAKE THE BASIL SOUFFLE: Preheat the oven to 400°. Melt the unsalted butter in a medium saucepan. Stir in the flour and cook over moderate heat for 30 seconds. Gradually whisk in the remaining 1¼ cups of reserved mussel stock until smooth and bring the mixture to a boil, whisking constantly. Season the mussel sauce with salt and pepper, then whisk in the egg yolks and bring the soufflé base almost to a boil. Transfer the soufflé base to a large bowl.

4. In a large stainless-steel bowl, beat the egg whites until they hold firm peaks. Fold one-third of the egg whites into the soufflé base, then fold in the remaining egg whites along with ⅓ cup of the Parmesan cheese and the shredded basil. Spoon the soufflé mixture over the mussels in the ramekins and sprinkle with the remaining 2 tablespoons of Parmesan cheese.

5. Set the ramekins in a roasting pan; pour enough cold water into the pan to reach halfway up the sides of the ramekins. Bake the soufflés for approximately 30 minutes, or until they are puffed and golden brown. Serve the soufflés immediately. —*Jacques Pépin*

WINE A clean, somewhat assertive white with a rich, full-bodied texture will stand up to the briny flavors in the mussel stew. An excellent choice would be an Italian Greco di Tufo, such as the 1999 Mastroberardino or the 1999 Feudi di San Gregorio.

Stovetop Clambake

Mussels in Coconut-Curry Broth

4 SERVINGS

2½ teaspoons vegetable oil
½ cup minced shallots
1 tablespoon plus 1 teaspoon minced fresh ginger
1 small fresh chile, seeded and minced
1 tablespoon curry powder
½ cup dry white wine
1 cup bottled clam juice
One 2-inch strip of lime zest plus lime wedges, for serving
¾ cup unsweetened coconut milk
4 pounds small mussels, scrubbed and debearded
Salt and freshly ground pepper
½ cup chopped cilantro

1. In a large heavy saucepan, heat the vegetable oil. Add the shallots, ginger and chile, cover and cook over low heat, stirring a few times, until the shallots are soft but not browned, about 5 minutes. Add the curry powder and cook, stirring, until fragrant, about 2 minutes. Add the white wine and cook over moderately high heat until almost evaporated, about 4 minutes. Add the clam juice and lime zest and cook until the broth is reduced by half, about 4 minutes. Add the coconut milk and simmer the broth until it reduces slightly, about 5 minutes.

2. Add the mussels to the pan. Cover and cook, shaking the pan a few times, until the mussels open, about 4 minutes. Scoop the mussels into 4 large bowls. Season the broth with salt and pepper, stir in the cilantro and spoon the broth over the mussels. Serve the lime wedges on the side.

—Sally Schneider

ONE SERVING Calories 247 kcal, Total Fat 15.1 gm, Saturated Fat 9 gm
WINE To balance the heat and cut through the creaminess of this dish, try a round, rich, tart California Sauvignon Blanc–Sémillon blend, such as the 1998 Ojai or the 1997 DeLorimier Spectrum.

Stovetop Clambake

4 SERVINGS

4 cups basil
2 cups parsley
¼ cup oregano
2 tablespoons thyme
⅓ cup extra-virgin olive oil
1 quart water
3 pounds rockweed seaweed, rinsed
Four 1½-pound lobsters
12 small red potatoes, scrubbed
4 ears corn, in the husk
20 pearl onions
16 littleneck clams, scrubbed
24 mussels, scrubbed
24 steamer clams, scrubbed
2 sticks salted butter, cut into ¼-inch slices, plus melted butter, for serving
12 jumbo shrimp in their shells, deveined

1. Combine the basil, parsley, oregano and thyme in a food processor and pulse just until the herbs are coarsely chopped. Add the olive oil and process until a coarse paste forms.

2. In a 5-gallon stockpot, combine the water and two-thirds of the rockweed. Put the lobsters in the stockpot and cover them with the remaining rockweed. Atop the lobsters and rockweed, layer the red potatoes, ears of corn, pearl onions, littleneck clams, mussels and steamer clams. Top with the butter slices. Add the jumbo shrimp to the stockpot and spoon the herb paste over them.

3. Cover the stockpot, let the water come to a boil and steam the clambake over moderately high heat for 15 minutes. Check the jumbo shrimp, and if they are cooked, transfer them to a bowl. Put the lid back on the stockpot and cook for 5 to 8 minutes longer, or until the steamer clams are open and cooked through. Serve the stovetop clambake at once with generous quantities of melted butter.

—Jean Mackenzie

Wok-Charred Squid Salad with Baby Spinach and Cashews

6 SERVINGS

Baby spinach offers a cool, smooth contrast to the heat of the chili sauce, the tang of the lime juice and the crispness of the toasted cashews.

¾ pound baby spinach or *tatsoi* (4 packed cups)
2 Belgian endives, separated into spears
1½ pounds cleaned small squid, bodies sliced crosswise into ⅓-inch rings
3 tablespoons chopped mint
3 tablespoons chopped cilantro
¼ cup coarsely chopped, toasted unsalted cashews
2 tablespoons Sriracha chili sauce or other hot chili sauce
Salt
Vegetable oil, for stir-frying
3 tablespoons fresh lime juice
Lime wedges, for serving

1. Arrange the baby spinach and endive spears in 6 individual salad bowls.

2. In a medium bowl, toss the squid with the mint, cilantro, toasted cashews and chili sauce and season with salt.

3. Heat a wok or skillet until hot. Add 1 tablespoon of oil and, when it begins to smoke, add one-third of the squid. Stir-fry over high heat for 10 seconds. Deglaze the skillet with 1 tablespoon of the lime juice and spoon the squid into 2 of the bowls. Repeat 2 more times with the remaining squid. Serve the salad right away, with the lime wedges.

—Jeff Tunks

chicken other birds
chapter 8

Steamed Lime-and-Pepper Chicken with Glazed Asparagus

4 SERVINGS ✳

- 2 limes, sliced paper thin, plus 2 tablespoons fresh lime juice
- 4 skinless, boneless chicken breast halves

Salt and freshly ground pepper

- 4 tablespoons unsalted butter
- 1 tablespoon balsamic vinegar
- 2 teaspoons light brown sugar
- 1 pound medium asparagus, cut into 3-inch lengths
- ¼ cup water

1. Line a large steamer basket with the lime slices. Add the chicken breasts in a single layer and season them with salt and pepper. Steam the breasts until they are opaque throughout, about 15 minutes.

2. Meanwhile, in a large skillet, melt the butter. Add the balsamic vinegar and light brown sugar and stir until the sugar is dissolved. Add the asparagus and water to the skillet and cook over moderately high heat, stirring, until the asparagus is crisp-tender, approximately 5 minutes. Season with salt and pepper.

3. Transfer the glazed asparagus to plates. Spoon any glaze left in the pan on top of the chicken breasts. Thickly slice the chicken breasts crosswise, arrange on the asparagus and serve.

—*Donna Hay*

WINE Marry the tart and sweet flavors of the lime-steamed chicken and the balsamic–brown sugar glaze with the crisp, fruity 1998 Coriole Semillon–Sauvignon Blanc from Australia or the 1998 Cloudy Bay Marlborough Sauvignon Blanc from New Zealand.

Grilled Maple-Chile Chicken

8 SERVINGS

The sweet-spicy marinade intensifies the chicken's grilled flavor. For a deep maple flavor, choose a dark amber syrup.

- 1 medium onion, halved lengthwise and thinly sliced

Kosher salt

- ½ cup pure maple syrup
- 2 tablespoons Chinese chili paste with garlic
- 8 large skinless, boneless chicken breast halves (about 4 pounds), pounded ⅓-inch thick

1. In a large shallow dish, toss the onion with 1¼ tablespoons kosher salt. Let stand until the onion releases most of its liquid, about 15 minutes, then stir in the maple syrup and chili paste. Add the chicken breasts and turn to coat. Cover and chill for 30 to 60 minutes.

2. Light a grill. Remove the chicken from the marinade, brushing off most of the onion. Grill over a moderately hot fire for about 4 minutes per side, or until lightly charred and cooked through. Transfer to a platter and serve hot.

—*Daniel Bruce*

Glazed Chicken with Jicama Salsa

8 SERVINGS ⚜

- 2 tablespoons achiote paste
- 1 tablespoon minced garlic
- 1 tablespoon minced fresh ginger
- ½ cup ketchup
- ½ cup honey
- ½ cup fresh orange juice
- 2 tablespoons chopped cilantro

Eight 6-ounce skinless, boneless chicken breast halves

- 1 large yellow plantain
- 2 tablespoons canola oil

Salt and freshly ground pepper

- ½ cup Basic Chicken Stock (p. 98) or canned low-sodium broth

Jicama Salsa (recipe follows)

1. In a large glass or ceramic baking dish, mash the achiote paste with the garlic and ginger. Stir in the ketchup, honey, orange juice and cilantro. Set aside ½ cup. Add the chicken to the remaining marinade, turning to coat. Cover and chill for 1 to 4 hours.

2. Meanwhile, cut the tips off of the plantain. Make a cut just through the skin, then peel. Using a mandoline, thinly slice the plantain lengthwise.

3. In a large nonstick skillet, heat the oil until shimmering. Working in batches, fry the plantain strips over moderately high heat until golden and crisp, 3 to 4 minutes. Using tongs, transfer the plantain strips to paper towels; let as much oil as possible drip back into the skillet. Sprinkle the plantain strips with salt.

4. Light a grill or preheat the broiler. Remove the chicken from the marinade and season with salt and pepper. Grill or broil for about 10 minutes, turning, until browned and just cooked through. Transfer to a platter and cover with foil. In a small saucepan, stir the chicken stock into the reserved ½ cup marinade and boil over high heat until slightly reduced, about 5 minutes.

5. Set the chicken on plates and spoon the Jicama Salsa alongside. Garnish with the plantain and serve with the sauce.

—*Kevin Maguire*

MAKE AHEAD The marinade can be refrigerated for up to 4 days.

ONE SERVING Calories 349 kcal, Total Fat 4.1 gm, Saturated Fat 0.7 gm ➤

menu 1998 SHAFER RED SHOULDER RANCH CHARDONNAY | 1998 GUIGAL COTE ROTIE

yellow bean, asparagus and tomato salad (p. 64) | grilled maple-chile chicken

pork burgers with sage (p. 207) | miso-glazed salmon (p. 137) | chive and honey corn bread (p. 252)

grilled corn with tomato barbecue sauce (p. 289) | red-and-white spicy slaw (p. 61)

chocolate cake with cashews, berries and whipped cream (p. 342)

Grilled Maple-Chile
Chicken, with Chive
and Honey Corn
Bread (p. 252).

**Glazed Chicken with
Jicama Salsa**

WINE A fruity, dry to off-dry Riesling will contrast the sweetness and the smoky flavors of the Glazed Chicken with Jicama Salsa. Consider a lime-accented Australian wine, such as the 1998 Crabtree Watervale, or the 1998 Bonny Doon Pacific Rim Riesling from California.

JICAMA SALSA

MAKES ABOUT 2 CUPS

1   small jicama (about 1 pound), peeled and finely diced
1½ tablespoons fresh lime juice
2   tablespoons finely chopped mint
1   tablespoon finely chopped cilantro
¼   teaspoon salt
Pinch of cayenne pepper

In a medium bowl, combine all of the ingredients. —*K.M.*

ONE-QUARTER CUP Calories 21 kcal, Total Fat 0.05 gm, Saturated Fat 0 gm

Marinated Chicken Breasts with Salsa Verde

Marinated Chicken Breasts with Salsa Verde

20 SERVINGS

Pounding chicken breasts tenderizes them by breaking down the fibers in the meat, and it also shortens the cooking time by making the breasts thinner. Use a meat pounder, if you have one, to flatten the chicken or improvise with the flat side of a heavy cleaver, a French rolling pin or even a wine bottle. Or, of course, you can have the butcher do the work for you.

1½ cups coarsely chopped parsley
1   cup coarsely chopped basil
1   cup coarsely chopped spearmint
One 4-ounce jar anchovies, drained and chopped
One 3-ounce jar capers, drained
¼   cup tarragon leaves
10 garlic cloves, coarsely chopped
1½ cups extra-virgin olive oil
Salt and freshly ground pepper
20 skinless, boneless chicken breast halves, pounded ⅓ inch thick

1. In a food processor, combine the parsley, basil, spearmint, anchovies, capers, tarragon and garlic; pulse until the ingredients are finely chopped. With the machine on, slowly pour in the olive oil until blended. Transfer the salsa verde to a bowl and season with salt and pepper.

2. Put the chicken breasts in a large roasting pan and coat them completely with 1 cup of the salsa verde. Cover and refrigerate the chicken for 2 hours. Refrigerate the remaining salsa verde.

3. Light a grill. Season the chicken breasts lightly with salt and generously with pepper. Grill the breasts over a moderately hot fire for about 3 minutes per side, until lightly charred and just cooked through. Serve the chicken with the remaining salsa verde on the side.

—*Martin Dodd*

MAKE AHEAD The salsa verde can be made ahead and refrigerated for up to 3 days. Bring to room temperature before serving.

menu caribbean rum zing (p. 392) | zucchini fritters with deep-fried capers (p. 23) | cilantro-lime shrimp with avocado and tomato salsa (p. 38) | cumin-garlic chicken and beet kebabs | grilled corn with creole butter (p. 289) | sweet potatoes and snow peas with crème fraîche (p. 306) | 1998 BENZIGER FUME BLANC SONOMA COUNTY | coconut-fried mango with cinnamon rum sauce (p. 369)

Cumin-Garlic Chicken and Beet Kebabs

6 SERVINGS

For the best flavor, the chicken needs to be marinated overnight, so plan accordingly.

- ¼ cup cumin seeds
- ½ cup vegetable oil, plus more for brushing
- 6 garlic cloves, smashed
- ¼ cup grainy mustard
- ¼ cup honey
- 2 pounds skinless, boneless chicken breasts, cut into 1½-inch cubes
- 5 medium beets, peeled and cut into 1½-inch wedges

Kosher salt and freshly ground pepper

1. In a small skillet, toast the cumin seeds over moderately low heat, stirring, until fragrant, 2 to 3 minutes. Transfer the cumin to a mini processor and let cool. Add ¼ cup plus 3 tablespoons of the oil, the garlic, mustard and honey and process until blended. Scrape the marinade into a resealable plastic bag, add the cubed chicken and refrigerate overnight.

2. Preheat the oven to 400°. In a baking dish, toss the beets with the remaining 1 tablespoon of oil; season with salt and pepper. Cover with foil and bake for 35 minutes, or until tender. Let cool.

3. Light a grill. Thread alternating chicken cubes and beet wedges onto bamboo skewers. Brush lightly with oil and season with salt and pepper. Grill the kebabs over moderately high heat for about 10 to 12 minutes, turning and brushing occasionally, until the chicken is cooked. —*Alison Tolley*

Chicken Paillard with Tomato and Goat Cheese Salad

4 SERVINGS ✳

- 1 cup yellow cherry tomatoes, halved
- 1 cup red grape tomatoes, halved (see Note)
- Sea salt
- 2 ounces mild goat cheese, crumbled

Tomato-Braised Chicken Breasts with Green Olives

- 3 tablespoons extra-virgin olive oil
- Freshly ground pepper
- 4 skinless, boneless chicken breast halves, pounded ⅓ inch thick

1. Put the tomatoes in a colander set over a bowl. Add ¼ teaspoon of salt, toss well and let stand for 15 minutes to release the juices. Remove the tomatoes and whisk half the goat cheese into the tomato juices until smooth. Whisk in 2 tablespoons of the oil and season with pepper. Fold in the tomatoes and the remaining goat cheese.

2. Light a grill or heat a grill pan. Brush the chicken with the remaining 1 tablespoon of oil and season with salt and pepper. Grill over a hot fire or high heat, until golden on the bottom and almost cooked through, about 5 minutes. Turn the chicken and grill for 2 minutes longer, or until cooked through. Transfer to dinner plates, spoon the tomato and goat cheese salad on top and serve. —*Grace Parisi*

N O T E Grape tomatoes are small, oval tomatoes with a very high sugar content. Cherry tomatoes can be substituted but will add much less sweetness.

Tomato-Braised Chicken Breasts with Green Olives

6 SERVINGS ✳

- 6 red and yellow tomatoes (about 3 pounds), cored and halved crosswise
- ¼ cup extra-virgin olive oil
- 12 medium garlic cloves, thickly sliced
- 12 small green olives, pitted and halved
- 1 large jalapeño, seeded and thinly sliced
- Kosher salt
- ½ cup dry white wine
- 6 skinless, boneless chicken breast halves (about 2⅓ pounds)
- 6 thyme sprigs, plus more for garnish
- Freshly ground pepper
- 2 cups water
- 1½ cups couscous (about 1 box)
- Lemon wedges, for serving

1. Preheat the oven to 400°. Set a fine sieve over a bowl and, using your fingers, remove the seeds from the tomatoes, working over the sieve. Gently press the seeds against the sieve to extract the juice. Set aside the tomatoes and juice and discard the seeds.

2. Coat the bottom of a 9-by-13-inch glass or ceramic baking dish with 1 tablespoon of the olive oil. Scatter the garlic, olives and jalapeño over the bottom. Season the cut sides of the tomatoes with salt and place in the dish, cut sides down. Pour the white wine over the tomatoes along with the reserved tomato juice and arrange the chicken on top. Drizzle with 1 tablespoon of olive oil. Top each breast half with a thyme sprig and season with salt and pepper.

3. Cover the baking dish with foil and bake the chicken for about 50 minutes, or until it is cooked through and the tomatoes have released most of their juices. Transfer the chicken to a large plate, cover and keep warm. Let the tomatoes cool for about 2 minutes and carefully pull off their skins with your

Coconut Curry Chicken

fingers. Add the tomatoes to the chicken and cover loosely to keep warm. Discard the thyme sprigs.

4. In a medium saucepan, bring the water to a boil with ¼ teaspoon salt and the remaining 2 tablespoons of olive oil. Add the couscous, cover and remove from the heat. Let stand until the water is completely absorbed, about 5 minutes. Fluff the couscous with a fork and spoon it into shallow soup bowls. Top the couscous with the braised chicken and tomatoes, spooning the juices all over. Garnish with thyme sprigs and serve with lemon wedges.

—*Charles Dale*

MAKE AHEAD The tomato-braised chicken can be prepared through Step 2 and refrigerated for up to 1 day.

WINE Try a vibrant, fruity Sangiovese: the 1996 Venezia Nuovo Mundo North Coast Sangiovese from California or the 1995 Melini Chianti Classico La Selvanella Riserva from Italy.

Coconut Curry Chicken

4 SERVINGS ✳

This south Indian–style curry is equally delicious with lamb, beef or tofu.

- ¼ cup whole unsalted cashews
- 1 pound skinless, boneless chicken breasts, cut into 1-inch pieces

Salt

- ¼ cup vegetable oil
- ¼ teaspoon black mustard seeds
- ¼ teaspoon cumin seeds
- ¼ teaspoon ground coriander
- 1 tablespoon curry powder
- 1 medium onion, thinly sliced
- 1 teaspoon finely grated fresh ginger
- 1 garlic clove, minced

One 14-ounce can unsweetened coconut milk

- ¼ cup frozen peas
- 2 tablespoons chopped cilantro

1. Preheat the oven to 350°. Spread the cashews in a pie plate and bake for 5 minutes, or until fragrant and lightly toasted. Transfer to a plate to cool.

2. Lightly season the chicken with salt. In a large deep skillet, heat 3 tablespoons of the oil until smoking. Add the chicken and cook over moderately high heat until golden brown, about 1½ minutes per side. Transfer the chicken to a plate; reduce the heat under the skillet to moderate.

3. Add the remaining 1 tablespoon of oil to the skillet and heat until smoking. Add the mustard seeds and cook for about 1 minute, or until they stop popping. Add the cumin seeds, coriander and curry powder and cook, stirring occasionally, until fragrant, about 1 minute. Add the onion, ginger and garlic and cook until the onion softens, about 10 minutes; if the mixture seems dry, add up to ¼ cup of water to prevent sticking.

4. Stir in the coconut milk and bring to a boil. Reduce the heat to low. Return the chicken to the skillet and simmer until cooked through, about 5 minutes. Stir in the peas and cook for 1 minute. Transfer the curry to a bowl, sprinkle with the cilantro and serve.

—*Gary MacGurn and Patty Gentry*

MAKE AHEAD The curry can be refrigerated for 2 days.

Chicken Salad with Melon, Feta and Greens

6 SERVINGS

- ½ cup large walnut pieces (about 2 ounces)
- ¼ cup fresh lemon juice
- ¼ cup coarsely chopped mint, plus ⅓ cup small mint leaves
- ⅔ cup pure olive oil
- 2 tablespoons red wine vinegar
- ½ teaspoon sugar

Salt and freshly ground pepper

- 2 tablespoons vegetable oil
- 6 skinless, boneless chicken breast halves (6 to 8 ounces each), pounded ½ inch thick
- 1 ripe cantaloupe (2 pounds)— peeled, thinly sliced and slices cut crosswise into thirds

- ¾ pound feta cheese, coarsely crumbled
- 3 bunches watercress (about 6 ounces each), tough stems discarded

1. Preheat the oven to 350°. Spread the walnuts in a pie plate and toast for 8 minutes, or until golden and fragrant. Let cool, then coarsely chop.

2. In a small saucepan, combine the lemon juice with the chopped mint and cook over high heat just until the mint is wilted, about 1 minute. Remove from the heat and let steep for 10 minutes. Strain the lemon juice into a small bowl and discard the mint. Whisk the olive oil, vinegar and sugar into the lemon juice and season with salt and pepper.

3. Heat 1 tablespoon of the vegetable oil in each of 2 large skillets. Season the pounded chicken breast halves with salt and pepper, add 3 to each skillet and cook them over moderately high heat until they are golden and just cooked through, about 3 minutes per side. Transfer the chicken to a cutting board and let cool. Thinly slice the chicken across the grain and transfer it to a large bowl.

4. Add the cantaloupe, feta and half the mint leaves to the chicken. Whisk the vinaigrette, add half to the chicken and toss gently. Put the watercress in another large bowl, add the remaining mint leaves and vinaigrette and toss gently to coat. Season with salt and pepper. Arrange the watercress on 6 plates or a large platter. Top with the chicken salad and serve immediately.

—*Joyce Goldstein*

MAKE AHEAD The salad can be prepared through Step 3 up to 4 hours ahead. Refrigerate the chicken.

WINE A soft, round Chardonnay with good fruit and not too much oak will provide a nice contrast to the salty feta and harmonize with the sweet flavors of the cantaloupe. Try the 1998 Edna Valley or the 1997 Hess Collection Napa Valley.

Spicy Chicken Salad with Papaya

Spicy Chicken Salad with Papaya

6 SERVINGS

Note that the chicken for this salad is cooked on the bone; it's more flavorful that way. Marinating the chicken overnight in the refrigerator makes it even tastier.

1½ cups peanut or canola oil
5 teaspoons crushed red pepper
6 quarter-size slices of peeled fresh ginger, smashed, plus 2 tablespoons grated ginger
3 garlic cloves, smashed
Zest from 1 orange, removed in strips
1 tablespoon plus 1 teaspoon Asian sesame oil
2 teaspoons five-spice powder
⅓ cup fresh lemon juice
6 chicken breast halves on the bone (10 to 12 ounces each), skinned
1 tablespoon minced shallot
1 tablespoon light brown sugar
Salt and freshly ground pepper
1 large red papaya (about 2 pounds)—peeled, seeded, sliced and chilled
¾ pound mixed peppery greens, such as watercress, arugula and mizuma, tough stems removed and discarded
½ cup torn mint leaves
⅓ cup torn Thai or Italian basil leaves

I. In a small skillet, combine 1 cup of the peanut oil with 4 teaspoons of the crushed red pepper and cook over moderate heat, swirling the skillet until the pepper is sizzling, about 2 minutes. Pour the seasoned oil into a large glass baking dish and add the smashed ginger and garlic and the strips of orange zest. Let the mixture cool slightly and then add the sesame oil, the five-spice powder and 1 tablespoon plus 1 teaspoon of the lemon juice. Put the chicken breasts in the baking dish and turn them to coat. Cover and refrigerate overnight.

2. In a small bowl, combine the remaining ¼ cup of lemon juice with the grated ginger, minced shallot, the light brown sugar and the remaining 1 teaspoon of crushed red pepper. Whisk in the remaining ½ cup of peanut oil until the mixture has emulsified. Season the vinaigrette with salt and pepper to taste.

3. Preheat the broiler and position a rack about 8 inches from the heat, if possible. Drain the chicken breasts, scraping off most of the marinade but leaving on some of the crushed red pepper, and transfer the breasts to a baking sheet. Broil the chicken for about 35 minutes, turning frequently, until golden and cooked through. Transfer the breasts to a platter and let them rest until they're cool enough to handle. With your fingers, pull the chicken apart into large pieces and put them in a large bowl. Pour any accumulated cooking juices into a small bowl and spoon off the fat.

4. Add half the vinaigrette and the reserved juices to the chicken, toss well and refrigerate until chilled, about 30 minutes. Fold the papaya into the chicken salad and season with salt and pepper.

5. In another large bowl, toss the greens with the mint, basil and remaining vinaigrette. Season with salt and pepper and transfer to plates or a large platter. Mound the chicken and papaya salad on top of the greens and serve immediately.   —*Joyce Goldstein*

MAKE AHEAD The chicken salad can be prepared through Step 3 and refrigerated for up to 1 day.

BEER OR WINE This dish is a contrast of hot but subtle spices and smooth tropical fruit flavor. Cool the heat of the spices and echo the exotic papaya with a fruit-driven New Zealand Sauvignon Blanc, such as the 1999 Coopers Creek Marlborough. Alternatively, consider a beer, such as Samuel Adams Summer Ale.

Roasted Chicken with Rice and Peas

4 SERVINGS

3 tablespoons pure olive oil
2 tablespoons minced garlic
½ habanero chile, seeded and minced
1 teaspoon dried oregano
1 teaspoon dried thyme
Kosher salt and freshly ground pepper
2 whole chicken breasts on the bone, split
1 large onion, finely chopped
1 small red bell pepper, finely chopped
1 bay leaf
½ cup diced smoked ham
2 tablespoons tomato paste
½ cup dry white wine
4 cups Basic Chicken Stock (p. 98) or canned low-sodium broth
2 cups long-grain white rice (about 14 ounces)
1 cup drained canned pigeon peas *(gandules)* from one 14-ounce can, rinsed
2 tablespoons fresh lime juice

I. In a small bowl, combine 2 tablespoons of the olive oil with 1 tablespoon of the garlic, the habanero, oregano, thyme and a generous pinch each of kosher salt and pepper. Spread the seasoning paste all over the chicken. Set the chicken on a plate, cover with plastic wrap and refrigerate for up to 4 hours. Let return to room temperature before proceeding.

2. Preheat the oven to 450°. Arrange the chicken breasts in a flameproof roasting pan and roast for about 20 minutes, or until just cooked through; the skin should still be pale.

3. Preheat the broiler. Turn the chicken skin side down and broil 8 inches from the heat for about 5 minutes, or until golden; rotate the pan occasionally. Turn the chicken over and broil for 6 to 7 minutes longer, or until the skin is golden and crisp; rotate the pan occasionally. Transfer to a platter, cover loosely with foil and keep warm. Reserve the roasting pan.

4. Meanwhile, heat the remaining 1 tablespoon of olive oil in a large saucepan. Add the onion, bell pepper, bay leaf and the remaining 1 tablespoon of garlic and cook over moderate heat until softened, about 6 minutes. Add the ham and cook, stirring, until lightly browned, about 4 minutes. Stir in the tomato paste and cook until beginning to brown, 3 to 4 minutes.

5. Add the wine to the saucepan and cook until nearly evaporated, about 3 to 4 minutes. Add the chicken stock and 1½ teaspoons kosher salt and bring to a boil over high heat. Stir in the rice and pigeon peas and return to a boil. Cover and cook over low heat until all of the liquid has been absorbed and the rice is tender, approximately 20 minutes.

6. Set the roasting pan over moderately high heat and add the lime juice, stirring to scrape up any browned bits. Add any accumulated juices from the chicken, then pour the pan sauce into a bowl, cover and keep warm.

7. Fluff the rice with a fork and serve it alongside the breasts. Pour the pan sauce over the chicken.

—*La Boca del Conga Room,*
West Hollywood

WINE A fragrant, light white will unite the flavors of the earthy rice and peas and the tangy chicken. Consider a dry Chenin Blanc from California, such as the 1998 Pine Ridge, or a Vouvray from France, such as the 1998 Domaine Peu de la Moriette.

Chicken Potpies

Chicken Potpies

6 SERVINGS

- 2 quarts Basic Chicken Stock (p. 98)
- 1 bay leaf
- ½ tablespoon black peppercorns
- 6 flat-leaf parsley sprigs, plus 1 teaspoon finely chopped leaves
- 6 fresh thyme sprigs, plus ½ teaspoon finely chopped leaves
- 2 whole chicken breasts on the bone (2½ pounds total)
- 2 carrots, cut into ½-inch dice
- 2 celery ribs, cut into ½-inch dice
- 16 pearl onions, peeled (see Note)
- 5 tablespoons unsalted butter
- 4 ounces small white button mushrooms
- ¼ cup all-purpose flour
- ½ teaspoon chopped rosemary
- ½ cup frozen baby peas

Salt and freshly ground pepper

Pâte Brisée in an 8-inch log (p. 36)

- 1 egg, lightly beaten

1. In a large saucepan, combine the Basic Chicken Stock, bay leaf, peppercorns and the parsley and thyme sprigs and bring to a boil. Add the chicken breasts and simmer until just cooked through, about 20 minutes. Transfer the chicken to a plate.

2. Strain the stock, return it to the saucepan and bring to a boil. Add the carrots, celery and pearl onions and cook over moderately high heat until the vegetables are tender, about 10 minutes. Using a slotted spoon, transfer the vegetables to a large plate. Continue to boil the stock until reduced to 3 cups, about 30 minutes.

3. Meanwhile, melt 1 tablespoon of the butter in a medium skillet. Add the mushrooms and cook over moderately high heat, stirring occasionally, until tender and browned, about 7 minutes. Add the mushrooms to the vegetables on the plate. Remove the breast meat from the bones and pull into 1-inch pieces; discard the skin and bones.

4. Melt the remaining 4 tablespoons of butter in a medium saucepan. Add the flour and cook over moderate heat, stirring constantly until the roux turns light brown, 4 to 5 minutes. Gradually whisk in the reduced stock and simmer, whisking frequently, until the sauce thickens, 7 to 8 minutes. Remove from the heat and stir in the cooked chicken and vegetables, the chopped parsley, thyme and rosemary and the peas. Season the filling generously with salt and pepper.

5. Cut the log of Pâte Brisée into a 5-inch and a 3-inch piece. Cut the 3-inch piece into six ½-inch slices. On a lightly floured work surface, roll out each slice of dough ¼ inch thick; stamp out a neat round from each using a 4-inch biscuit cutter. Fit the rounds into six 4-by-2-inch ramekins. Prick the dough several times with a fork and refrigerate until chilled.

6. Cut the 5-inch piece of dough into 6 even slices. Roll out each slice ¼ inch thick; using a 6-inch plate as a template, cut out a neat round from each piece of dough. Transfer the rounds to baking sheets lined with wax paper and refrigerate until firm.

7. Preheat the oven to 400°. Set the dough-lined ramekins on a baking sheet and bake for 15 minutes, or until the pastry is golden brown. Let the pastry cool slightly, then spoon the chicken and vegetable filling into the ramekins.

8. Moisten the ramekin rims and cover with the larger rounds, lightly pressing the dough against the ramekins to seal. Brush with the beaten egg and score the tops with shallow parallel marks. Bake the potpies for about 30 minutes, or until the tops are golden brown and the filling is piping hot.

—*Mitchel London*

NOTE To peel pearl onions, trim the roots slightly and blanch the onions in boiling water for 30 seconds. Let cool slightly, then slip off the skins.

MAKE AHEAD The filling and dough rounds can be prepared up to 1 day ahead and refrigerated. Rewarm the filling before assembling the potpies.

WINE The buttery crust and creamy filling with fresh herbs pair well with a classic California Chardonnay, such as the 1998 Edna Valley or the 1998 Philippe-Lorraine California Barrel Cuvée.

Braised Chicken with Wine and Oranges

4 SERVINGS

The tangy oranges in this recipe blend with the sweet Muscatel wine to create a Spanish sweet-and-sour chicken.

½ cup pure olive oil
4 chicken breast halves, on the bone (about ½ pound each)
Salt and freshly ground pepper
5 small red new potatoes, thinly sliced
12 pearl onions, peeled (see Note)
8 baby carrots
1 garlic clove, minced
1 teaspoon thyme leaves
½ cup fresh orange juice
½ cup Muscatel wine or sweet sherry
½ cup canned low-sodium chicken broth
1 navel orange, peeled and cut into chunks

1. In a large deep skillet, heat the olive oil until shimmering. Season the chicken breasts with salt and pepper and add them to the skillet, skin side down. Top the chicken with the potatoes, onions and carrots and season with salt and pepper. Cover and cook over moderate heat until the chicken is lightly browned on the bottom, 1 to 2 minutes.

2. Turn the chicken skin side up. Add the garlic, thyme leaves and orange juice and bring to a boil. Add the wine and cook over moderate heat until the liquid reduces slightly, about 7 minutes; push the vegetables under the liquid from time to time. Add the chicken broth and cook over moderately low heat until the chicken is cooked through, the vegetables are tender and the sauce is reduced by about half, 10 to 12 minutes. Add the orange chunks and cook just until warmed through, about 1 minute.

3. Transfer the chicken to plates. Spoon the vegetables and sauce on top and serve. —*Joseph Jiménez de Jiménez*

NOTE To peel pearl onions, trim the roots slightly and blanch the onions in boiling water for 30 seconds. Let cool slightly, then slip off the skins.

WINE The sweetness of the Muscatel in this dish needs to be balanced by a wine made with a blend of grapes. Guelbenzu's 1997 Cabernet-Merlot-Tempranillo blend is a great choice.

Smothered Chicken

6 SERVINGS

All-purpose flour, for dredging
Three ½-pound chicken breast halves on the bone, halved crosswise
3 whole chicken legs, cut into drumsticks and thighs
4 tablespoons unsalted butter
1 tablespoon vegetable oil
Salt and freshly ground pepper
3 large Vidalia onions (2 pounds), thinly sliced (see Note)
½ pound white mushrooms, stems trimmed, thickly sliced
1 garlic clove, minced
½ cup Basic Chicken Stock (p. 98) or canned low-sodium broth
1 bay leaf
2 tablespoons chopped parsley

1. Put some flour in a paper bag, add the chicken pieces and shake well to coat them; shake off the excess flour. In a large cast-iron skillet, melt the butter in the oil. Add half the chicken at a time and season with salt and pepper. Brown over moderate heat for 4 to 5 minutes per side; transfer the chicken to a large plate.

2. Add the onions and mushrooms to

the skillet and cook over moderately low heat for 10 minutes. Add the garlic and cook for 3 to 4 minutes. Add the chicken and cover with the onions. Add the stock and bay leaf, season with salt and pepper and bring to a boil. Cover and simmer over low heat until the chicken is cooked, about 35 minutes; discard the bay leaf. Transfer to a large platter. Sprinkle with parsley and serve.

—James Villas

NOTE If you can't get Vidalia onions, substitute Walla Walla, Spanish or sweet yellow onions.

VARIATION When the chicken is cooked, stir in 2 tablespoons of coarsely chopped basil and 2 cups of shelled peas. Cover the skillet and cook until the peas are done, about 7 minutes.

WINE The sweet, earthy caramelized onions in this dish will find echoes in an intense Pinot Noir. Look for the 1998 Edna Valley from California or the 1998 Adelsheim from Oregon.

Moroccan-Style Lemon Chicken with Spiced Carrots

4 SERVINGS

Slice half of the lemon as thinly as possible so that it's ultra tender after cooking and can be eaten with the roasted chicken and carrot ribbons.

- 1 lemon, halved
- 6 large carrots, cut lengthwise into ribbons with a sturdy vegetable peeler
- ¼ cup extra-virgin olive oil
- ½ teaspoon coriander seeds, crushed
- ¼ teaspoon cumin seeds

Pinch of cayenne pepper

Salt

- 8 skinless, boneless chicken thighs, fat trimmed

Freshly ground pepper

- 2 tablespoons chopped cilantro

1. Preheat the oven to 500°. Slice half of the lemon crosswise as thinly as possible; discard any seeds. Squeeze

1½ teaspoons of juice from the remaining lemon half.

2. In a 9-by-13-inch baking dish, toss the carrots with 3 tablespoons of the oil, the coriander and cumin seeds, the cayenne and lemon juice. Season with salt. Spread the carrots in an even layer and roast for about 7 minutes, stirring after 4, or until just tender.

3. Brush the chicken thighs with the remaining 1 tablespoon of oil and set them on the carrots. Season with salt and pepper and top with the lemon slices. Roast the chicken for about 15 minutes, or until the juices run clear.

4. Transfer the chicken to a serving platter. Toss the carrots with the cilantro, add to the platter and serve.

—Melissa Clark

WINE The spicy-sweet notes of many North African dishes are well matched by a light, off-dry wine, like the citrusy 1996 Weingut Kurt Darting Kabinett Riesling, or, alternatively, a refreshing fruity rosé, such as the 1998 Bonny Doon Vin Gris de Cigare.

Grilled Chicken with Sweet-and-Sour Sauce

4 SERVINGS

At Chanterelle in New York City, this sweet ginger-and-ketchup-spiked sauce is used for everything from dipping Vidalia onion fritters to glazing crisp chicken thighs.

- 2 tablespoons vegetable oil
- 1 garlic clove, minced
- ¾ teaspoon grated fresh ginger
- 2 cups Basic Chicken Stock (p. 98) or canned low-sodium broth
- 2 tablespoons rice vinegar
- 2 tablespoons ketchup
- 1 tablespoon plus 1 teaspoon sugar
- 1 tablespoon soy sauce
- ¾ teaspoon Asian chili paste
- 1 teaspoon cornstarch dissolved in 1 tablespoon cold water
- 2 pounds skinless, boneless chicken thighs

Salt and freshly ground pepper

1. Heat the oil in a medium saucepan. Add the garlic and ginger and cook over moderately high heat until fragrant, about 1 minute. Add the chicken stock, vinegar, ketchup, sugar, soy sauce and chili paste and cook over moderately low heat until reduced to ¾ cup, about 20 minutes. Stir the cornstarch mixture, add it to the sauce and cook until thickened, about 1 minute. Remove from the heat, cover and keep warm.

2. Preheat the broiler; set the rack 8 inches from the heat. Arrange the chicken on a broiling pan, season with salt and pepper and broil for about 20 minutes, turning occasionally, until just cooked through. Brush the chicken thighs with the sweet-and-sour sauce and broil them for about 20 minutes longer—turning the chicken once, occasionally shifting the pan and brushing on additional sauce—until the chicken is golden and caramelized all over. Serve hot. *—David Waltuck*

MAKE AHEAD The prepared sauce can be refrigerated for up to 1 week.

Sweet and Spicy Barbecued Chicken

4 SERVINGS

The marinade on this chicken *(Dak Gui)* is also delicious on pork, and as a glaze for grilled fish steaks or for whole fish. For this dish, each person at the table wraps his bundle of chicken and seasonings in lettuce leaves.

MARINADE

- 2 tablespoons Korean sweet-spicy chili paste *(kochujang)*
- ¼ cups Korean rice wine or mirin
- 1 tablespoon soy sauce
- 1 tablespoon minced garlic
- 1 tablespoon Sesame Salt (p. 272)
- 1½ tablespoons Asian sesame oil
- 2 scallions, thinly sliced
- 1 tablespoon finely grated fresh ginger
- 2 teaspoons freshly ground pepper

Sweet and Spicy Barbecued Chicken

Chicken Baklava with Spices and Dried Fruit

10 SERVINGS

Traditional baklava is a dessert made with layers of buttery phyllo and nuts, flavored with spices and sweetened with a honey and lemon syrup. For this variation, the ideas for baklava and *bastila,* a Moroccan pigeon pie, combine in a savory and sweet filling: chicken and fresh and dried fruit. At Restaurant Christophe, in Amsterdam, this baklava is served as a side dish with pigeon roasted in a crust of Moroccan spices.

    1 tablespoon olive oil
    1 teaspoon cinnamon
    1 teaspoon ground coriander
    1 teaspoon ground cumin
    1 teaspoon ground ginger
    6 boneless, skinless chicken thighs
       (1¼ to 1½ pounds total)
    1 banana
    1 large crisp apple, such
       as Fuji or Gala
    1 large firm pear, such
       as Bosc or Bartlett
    1 tablespoon fresh lemon juice
 1½ sticks (6 ounces) unsalted butter
   ⅓ cup pine nuts
 2½ cups Basic Chicken Stock (p. 98)
       or canned low-sodium broth
Salt
    1 cup finely chopped mixed dried
       fruit, such as apricots, dates
       and figs (4 ounces)
   ½ cup chopped mint
Freshly ground pepper
    1 package phyllo dough, thawed
       if frozen (1 pound)

1. In a small bowl, combine the olive oil with the cinnamon, coriander, cumin and ginger. Put the chicken thighs in a shallow dish and rub the spice mixture into them on both sides. Cover well and marinate the chicken in the refrigerator for 1 hour.

2. Preheat the oven to 350°. Cut the banana, apple and pear into ¼-inch dice and toss with the lemon juice. In

CHICKEN AND ACCOMPANIMENTS

    8 skinless, boneless chicken thighs,
       pounded until flattened slightly
Coarse salt
Scallion Salad for Barbecues (p. 230)
Red-leaf lettuce leaves
Sesame Salt (p. 272)
Thinly sliced garlic
Korean Chili Sauce (p. 318)

1. MAKE THE MARINADE: Whisk the marinade ingredients together in a large bowl.

2. PREPARE THE CHICKEN AND ACCOMPANIMENTS: Rub the chicken with coarse salt, add it to the marinade and turn to coat. Cover and refrigerate for at least 2 hours or overnight.
3. Light a grill. Grill the chicken thighs over a moderately hot fire, turning once, until cooked through, about 4 minutes per side. Transfer the chicken to a platter. Serve with the scallion salad and all of the other accompaniments.

—*Anya von Bremzen*

Chicken Masala, with Green Beans with Onions and
Tomatoes (p. 277) and Basmati Rice with Peas (p. 307).

a medium skillet, melt 4 tablespoons of the butter over moderate heat. Add the fruit dice to the pan and cook, stirring, until just tender, approximately 10 minutes. Transfer to a large bowl and let cool.

3. Spread the pine nuts in a pie plate and toast them in the oven for about 7 minutes, or until just golden brown. Let them cool.

4. In a medium saucepan, bring the chicken stock to a boil over moderate heat. Season the stock with salt, add the chicken thighs and reduce the heat. Simmer the chicken until it's cooked through, about 10 minutes. Remove the thighs from the stock and let them cool enough to handle easily. Then cut them into ¼-inch dice. Add the chicken to the sautéed fresh fruit along with the pine nuts, the mixed dried fruit and the chopped mint. Season with salt and pepper.

5. Increase the oven temperature to 375°. Melt the remaining 1 stick of butter. Brush 1 sheet of the phyllo with some of the melted butter; keep the rest of the phyllo covered with a damp towel. Cut the buttered phyllo sheet lengthwise into 3 equal strips. Place 1 tablespoon of filling an inch from the top of a strip. Fold the phyllo strip like a flag: Fold 1 corner of the phyllo over the filling to enclose it and form a triangle. Then fold the filled corner down to form a triangle again; continue folding the triangle across and down until all of the phyllo strip is used. Set the triangle on a baking sheet and cover with a damp cloth. Continue in the same way with the remaining phyllo dough, butter and filling.

6. Brush the tops of all the triangles with butter and bake for about 15 minutes, or until golden brown.

—Jean-Christophe Royer

MAKE AHEAD The phyllo triangles can be assembled, covered with plastic wrap and refrigerated for up to 1 day before baking.

Chicken Masala

10 TO 12 SERVINGS

This simple chicken dish is ideal for feeding a crowd because it reheats well. If you prefer to use all white meat, reduce the cooking time slightly to prevent overcooking.

- **8** large garlic cloves, coarsely chopped
- **One** 2-inch piece of fresh ginger, peeled and coarsely chopped
- **¼** cup water
- **One can** (28 ounces) Italian peeled tomatoes, drained and seeded
- **¼** cup plus 2 tablespoons vegetable oil
- **1** large Spanish onion, minced
- **1½** tablespoons ground coriander
- **1½** teaspoons ground cumin
- **1** teaspoon garam masala
- **¾** teaspoon cayenne pepper
- **½** teaspoon turmeric
- **4½** pounds skinless, boneless chicken thighs, cut into 1½-inch pieces
- **2** teaspoons salt
- **½** cup coarsely chopped cilantro

1. In a blender, puree the garlic and ginger with the water until smooth. Transfer the puree to a bowl. Put the tomatoes in the blender and puree until smooth.

2. Heat ¼ cup of the vegetable oil in a large enameled cast-iron casserole. Add the minced onion to the casserole and cook over high heat, stirring frequently, until softened and golden, approximately 10 minutes. Add the garlic and ginger puree and cook, stirring, until fragrant and lightly golden, about 2 to 3 minutes. Add the remaining 2 tablespoons of vegetable oil along with the coriander, cumin, garam masala, cayenne pepper and turmeric and cook, stirring constantly, until the spices are lightly toasted, about 1 minute. Add the tomatoes and cook over high heat, stirring frequently, until thick, about 7 minutes.

3. Add the chicken and stir to coat each piece evenly. Season with salt. Reduce the heat to moderately low, cover partially and cook, stirring frequently, until the chicken is opaque and firm to the touch, about 30 minutes. Just before serving, stir in the cilantro.—Neela Paniz

MAKE AHEAD The cooked chicken and sauce can be refrigerated for up to 2 days. Rewarm over low heat and stir in the cilantro just before serving.

WINE A fruity but dry rosé made from Rhône or Sangiovese grapes, like the 1998 Swanson Rosato or the 1998 Bonny Doon Vin Gris de Cigare, has enough acidity to stand up to the tomatoes and pair with the spices.

the indian pantry

Asafoetida is an unpleasant-smelling tree resin that gives food an oniony aroma. It's sold in lump and powder forms and used in tiny amounts.

Besan, a chickpea flour, is used in batters and doughs, and to thicken vegetable curries.

Black salt has a subtle smoky flavor. Its pink crystals turn black only when wet.

Curry leaves come from the kari plant. Available fresh, dried or powdered, they add pungency and sweetness to many vegetable dishes.

Dalia are small chickpeas that have been husked, split and roasted. They're used to thicken chutneys.

Garam masala is an aromatic blend of cinnamon, black pepper, nutmeg and other ground spices. To preserve its fragrance, add it at the end of cooking.

Jaggery is a solid, dark molasses made from palm tree sap or sugar-cane juice. It imparts a caramel flavor to chutneys and other dishes.

Nigella seeds—tiny, black and tear-shaped—give a sweet, nutty flavor to chutneys. They can also be sprinkled over vegetables and doughs.

Tamarind pulp, compressed tamarind fruit, adds tartness to curries and chutneys. It must be soaked and strained before use.

—Lily Barberio

menu

gougères (p. 17) | NONVINTAGE LOUIS ROEDERER PREMIER BRUT CHAMPAGNE

lobster broth with porcini (p. 92) | 1998 GROSSET POLISH HILL RIESLING

poached chicken with tarragon | potato pancakes (p. 300) | 1996 LEEWIN CHARDONNAY

warm apple charlottes (p. 367) | 1998 MOUNT HORROCKS CORDON CUT LATE HARVEST RIESLING

Provençal Chicken Stew

4 SERVINGS ✳

- ¼ cup extra-virgin olive oil
- 8 chicken thighs (about 2½ pounds), skinned

Sea salt and freshly ground pepper

- 1 pound baby Yukon Gold or red potatoes, scrubbed and halved
- 2 to 3 teaspoons fennel pollen
- 2 pounds tomatoes—peeled, seeded and coarsely chopped
- ½ cup water

1. Heat 1 tablespoon of the olive oil in a large nonstick skillet until shimmering. Season the chicken thighs with salt and pepper and cook them over moderately high heat until browned on both sides, about 12 minutes in all. Transfer to a plate.

2. Heat the remaining 3 tablespoons of the olive oil in an enameled cast-iron casserole until shimmering. Add the halved baby potatoes and cook over moderately high heat until golden, approximately 10 minutes. Stir in the fennel pollen and cook until fragrant, about 30 seconds. Add the chopped tomatoes and the water, season with salt and pepper and bring the mixture to a boil.

3. Return the chicken to the casserole, cover partially and reduce the heat to moderately low. Simmer the stew until the chicken is just cooked through, approximately 20 minutes.

—*Grace Parisi*

MAKE AHEAD The chicken stew can be refrigerated overnight. Bring it to room temperature, heat gently and serve immediately so that the chicken doesn't overcook.

Poached Chicken with Tarragon

10 SERVINGS

- 5 whole boned chicken legs
- 1 stick (4 ounces) unsalted butter, 2 tablespoons melted

Salt and freshly ground white pepper

Chicken Mousse (recipe follows)

- ½ pound thin green beans, cut into 2-inch lengths
- 30 baby carrots
- 3 small leeks, white and tender green parts, halved lengthwise and cut into 1-inch lengths
- ¾ pound shallots, thinly sliced
- 3 garlic cloves, thinly sliced
- 2 tablespoons tarragon vinegar
- 2 cups dry white wine
- 10 cups Rich Chicken Stock (recipe follows)
- 2 cups heavy cream
- 5 chicken breast halves on the bone
- 1 cup frozen baby peas
- 1 tablespoon chopped tarragon (optional)

1. Bone the chicken legs: Set each leg, meaty side down, on a work surface. Using a sharp knife, make 1 slit from the thighbone down to the end of the drumstick. Scrape the meat from the bones; remove the bones, keeping the skin and meat intact. Using a pair of sturdy tweezers, pull out the white tendons from the drumstick.

2. Spread each boned leg between 2 sheets of plastic wrap and pound to a ½-inch thickness. Cut five 9-inch squares of foil. Lightly brush the foil with the melted butter. Discard the plastic wrap and set each chicken leg in the center of a foil square, skin side down. Sprinkle with salt and white pepper.

3. Pipe a 1-inch stripe of Chicken Mousse down the center of each chicken leg; fold the meat around the mousse and roll the chicken up in the foil. Twist the ends to form a tight log. Refrigerate for at least 1 hour or overnight.

4. Bring a large pot of salted water to a boil. Have a large bowl of ice water near the stove. Cook the beans in the boiling water until crisp-tender, about 4 minutes. Using a slotted spoon, transfer the beans to the ice water. Return the water to a boil and blanch the carrots for 6 minutes; add the carrots to the beans. Repeat with the leeks, blanching them for 2 minutes before refreshing them. Drain the vegetables.

5. Melt 4 tablespoons of the butter in a large saucepan. Add the shallots and garlic and cook over moderately low heat, stirring, until softened but not browned, about 8 minutes. Add the vinegar and cook over moderately high heat until evaporated. Add the wine and cook, stirring occasionally, until reduced to about ½ cup, about 15 minutes. Add 2 cups of the Rich Chicken Stock and boil gently until reduced to ¾ cup, about 20 minutes. Add the cream and boil until the sauce has reduced to 2 cups, about 15 minutes. Strain the sauce through a fine sieve, pressing hard on the solids. Return the sauce to the pan and season with salt and white pepper. Whisk in the remaining 2 tablespoons of butter.

6. Steam the stuffed chicken legs over high heat for 25 minutes, or until an

Poached Chicken with Tarragon

In a food processor, pulse the chicken until finely chopped. Add the egg white and pulse until blended. With the machine on, add the cream in a steady stream and puree until smooth. Scrape the mousse into a bowl and stir in the parsley, chives, tarragon and white pepper. Transfer the mousse to a resealable plastic bag and refrigerate until chilled, about 1 hour. To use, snip off a corner of the bag.   —*J.S.*

RICH CHICKEN STOCK
MAKES ABOUT 12 CUPS

- 6 pounds chicken wings
- 4 quarts cold water
- 8 parsley sprigs
- 3 scallions, halved crosswise
- 1½ tablespoons kosher salt

1. In a large saucepan, cover the chicken wings with the cold water and bring to a simmer over moderate heat, skimming as foam rises to the surface. Add the parsley, scallions and salt and simmer for 2 hours, skimming occasionally.

2. Line a colander with 4 layers of dampened cheesecloth. Set the colander over a heatproof bowl and pour in the stock. Let cool to room temperature, then refrigerate for up to 3 days or freeze for up to 1 month. Skim off the fat before using.   —*J.S.*

Mrs. Cribbs's Chicken and Dumplings
6 SERVINGS

- 3 pounds chicken legs
- 5 carrots—2 cut into large chunks, 3 sliced on the diagonal
- 2 celery ribs—1 cut into large chunks, 1 sliced on the diagonal
- 2 medium onions, coarsely chopped
- 6 cups water
- 2¼ cups all-purpose flour

Salt and freshly ground pepper

1. In a large saucepan, combine the chicken legs with the large chunks of carrot and celery, half of the chopped

instant-read thermometer inserted in the center of a leg registers 175°. Transfer the legs to a cutting board and let stand for 10 minutes.

7. In a large saucepan, bring the remaining 8 cups of Rich Chicken Stock to a boil. Add the chicken breasts and simmer gently over moderately low heat until cooked, 15 to 18 minutes. Unwrap the chicken legs and cut each in half crosswise. Remove the breast meat from the bones in 1 piece and cut in half. Rewarm the blanched vegetables and the peas in the stock.

8. Reheat the sauce over low heat. Arrange a piece of breast and stuffed leg on each plate. Using a slotted spoon, transfer the vegetables to the plates. Reserve the stock for another use. Using an immersion blender or electric mixer, whir the sauce until frothy. Spoon some sauce over the chicken and vegetables, sprinkle with the tarragon and serve. Pass the remaining sauce separately.   —*Jeremy Strode*

MAKE AHEAD The recipe can be prepared through Step 6 up to 1 day ahead. Resteam the legs until warmed through before proceeding.

WINE Try an Australian Chardonnay, such as the 1996 Leeuwin or the 1997 Lindemans Padthaway.

CHICKEN MOUSSE
MAKES 2 CUPS

- ½ pound skinless, boneless chicken breasts, cut into 1-inch pieces and chilled
- 1 large egg white
- ¾ cup heavy cream
- 1 tablespoon minced flat-leaf parsley
- 1 tablespoon snipped chives
- 1 teaspoon finely chopped tarragon

Pinch of freshly ground white pepper

Mrs. Cribbs's Chicken and Dumplings, with Mrs. Harris's Crackling Corn Bread (p. 252).

onions and the water. Simmer over moderate heat until the chicken legs are cooked through, about 15 minutes. Transfer the chicken to a plate. Let cool slightly, then remove the meat from the bones and let cool. Strain the chicken broth and discard the vegetables.

2. In a medium bowl, combine the flour with 1 cup of the chicken broth, adding a little of the fat from the broth; stir to form a stiff dough. Turn the dough out onto a lightly floured board and knead until smooth. Wrap the dumpling dough in plastic wrap and let rest at room temperature for 30 minutes.

3. Cut the dough into quarters. Working with 1 piece at a time, roll out the dough a scant ¼ inch thick on a very lightly floured work surface. Cut the dough into 3-inch-wide strips and transfer to a sheet of wax paper. Working on the paper, cut each strip crosswise into 1-inch-thick dumplings and put

on a baking sheet; do not separate the dumplings from the paper or from one another. Repeat with the remaining dough, stacking each layer on the baking sheet. Freeze until solid, at least 4 hours and preferably overnight.

4. In a large enameled cast-iron casserole, combine the sliced carrots and celery and the remaining chopped onion with 4 cups of the broth and bring to a boil. Season well with salt and pepper and cook until the vegetables are just tender, about 10 minutes. Add the cooked chicken and return to a boil.

5. Separate the frozen dumplings and add them to the simmering broth a few at a time, submerging them in the broth. Bring the broth to a simmer and cook until the dumplings are tender, about 15 minutes; tuck the dumplings into the broth occasionally. Spoon the chicken and dumplings into bowls and serve. —*Helen Cribbs*

MAKE AHEAD The recipe can be prepared through Step 3 up to 3 days ahead. Refrigerate the broth and the chicken; keep the dumplings frozen.

BEER OR WINE A good microbrew ale would showcase this rustic dish. So would a simple California Pinot Noir, such as the 1997 Echelon Vineyards or the 1997 Barefoot Cellars Reserve.

Pepper and Salt Chicken Wings

4 SERVINGS

Black and white pepper have an intense, delicious heat that, in tandem with coarse salt, makes a crisp, spicy coating for chicken wings.

  1 **tablespoon black peppercorns**
  ½ **tablespoon white peppercorns**
  ¼ **cup kosher salt**
  3 **pounds chicken wings, separated at the joints**
Peeled 3-inch celery sticks, for serving
Lemon Cream (recipe follows)

Preheat the oven to 450°. Coarsely crush the black and white peppercorns in a mortar or use a heavy-bottomed

skillet; stir in the salt. Put the chicken wings on a large baking sheet and toss with the pepper and salt. Roast on the top rack of the oven for 1 hour. Serve with celery sticks and the Lemon Cream. —*Marcia Kiesel*

WINE Tame the fiery flavors here with an Italian Pinot Grigio or an inexpensive sparkling wine. Try the bright, tangy 1998 Manlio Collavini Pinot Grigio Canlungo or the Nonvintage Mumm Cuvée Napa.

LEMON CREAM
MAKES ABOUT ⅓ CUP

  ⅓ **cup sour cream**
  2 **tablespoons fresh lemon juice**
  ½ **teaspoon finely grated lemon zest**
  1 **teaspoon Tabasco**
Salt and freshly ground pepper
  2 **large scallions, thinly sliced**

In a small bowl, mix the sour cream with the lemon juice, lemon zest and Tabasco; season with salt and pepper. Fold in the scallions and serve. —*M.K.*

MAKE AHEAD The Lemon Cream can be refrigerated overnight. Add the scallions just before serving.

Tomato-Glazed Chicken Wings

4 SERVINGS ✻

These baked Buffalo-style chicken wings have a good deal less fat than the traditional fried kind. If you want spicier wings, add a few drops of hot sauce to the tomato sauce.

  4 **pounds chicken wings, tips discarded, wings cut in half at the joint**
  ¼ **cup plus 1 tablespoon extra-virgin olive oil**
Sea salt and freshly ground pepper
  1 **pound plum tomatoes, halved lengthwise**
  2 **ounces mild goat cheese**

1. Preheat the oven to 425°. In a large bowl, toss the chicken wings with 2 tablespoons of the oil and a generous pinch each of salt and pepper. Arrange the chicken wings in a single layer on a large nonstick baking sheet and bake for about 40 minutes, or until golden and crusty. Carefully pour off the fat from the baking sheet.

2. Meanwhile, arrange the tomatoes, cut side up, in a large baking dish and drizzle evenly with 1 tablespoon of the oil. Season the tomatoes with salt and pepper and roast for 20 minutes, or until softened and lightly browned on the bottom. Transfer the tomatoes and their juices to a blender or food processor and pulse several times until smooth. Add the goat cheese and the remaining 2 tablespoons of oil and process until smooth. Season the sauce with salt and pepper.

3. Preheat the broiler. Transfer the chicken wings to a large bowl and toss with half the tomato sauce. Spread the wings in a single layer on the baking sheet and broil for 5 minutes, rotating the pan as necessary, until evenly browned and crisp. Transfer the hot chicken wings to a serving platter. Pour the remaining tomato sauce into a bowl and pass at the table for dipping.
—*Grace Parisi*

MAKE AHEAD The recipe can be prepared through Step 2 and refrigerated overnight. Rewarm the chicken wings in the oven before broiling.

Hattie's Fried Chicken

4 SERVINGS

One 3½-pound chicken—cut into
    8 pieces, rinsed and patted dry
1 tablespoon freshly ground pepper
½ tablespoon kosher salt
1 teaspoon garlic powder
1 cup all-purpose flour
1 cup vegetable oil, for frying

I. Put the chicken in a large baking dish and sprinkle with the pepper, salt and garlic powder. Refrigerate for 1 hour.

2. Put the flour in a large, sturdy plastic bag. Add the chicken, a few pieces at a time, and shake to coat; shake off any excess flour.

3. In a large cast-iron skillet, heat the oil until shimmering. Add the chicken pieces and fry over moderate heat, turning, until golden and cooked through, about 30 minutes. Lower the heat if the chicken gets too dark.
—*Hattie's, Saratoga Springs, New York*

WINE This highly seasoned chicken will showcase the flavors of a smooth, rich, fruity Chardonnay, such as the 1998 Acacia Carneros or the 1998 Chalone.

Fried Chicken with Tomato Gravy

4 SERVINGS

Watershed, in Decatur, Georgia, is a restaurant and wine bar owned by Emily Saliers of the Indigo Girls. This crispy chicken is one of her favorites.

½ cup kosher salt
2 quarts cold water
One 3½-pound chicken,
    cut into 8 pieces
3 cups buttermilk
1½ cups all-purpose flour
¼ cup cornstarch
2 tablespoons potato starch
    (optional)
Fine sea salt and freshly
    ground pepper
1 pound lard or solid vegetable
    shortening, for frying
1 stick (4 ounces) unsalted butter
4 ounces sliced bacon or unsliced
    country ham
½ cup finely chopped onion
1 garlic clove, minced
4 cups drained canned diced
    tomatoes (from three
    14-ounce cans)
2 teaspoons dried thyme
2 cups heavy cream
1½ cups milk
The Best Biscuits (p. 250)

I. In a large bowl, dissolve the kosher salt in the cold water. Add the chicken pieces, cover and refrigerate for 4 hours. Pour off the salt water, rinse the chicken and drain it well. Put the

chicken in a bowl, add the buttermilk and turn the pieces to coat thoroughly. Cover the chicken with plastic wrap and refrigerate it for 4 hours.

2. Put the flour, cornstarch, potato starch, 1½ teaspoons sea salt and ½ teaspoon pepper in a large, sturdy plastic bag and shake to combine. Set aside ½ cup of the flour mixture for the gravy. Lift the chicken from the buttermilk, wiping off any excess liquid. Arrange the pieces on a wire rack and let dry for 5 minutes. Add the chicken to the bag, a few pieces at a time, and shake to coat. Shake off any excess seasoned flour and return the chicken to the rack.

3. Meanwhile, in a large cast-iron skillet, melt the lard and butter. Add the bacon and cook over moderate heat until crisp, 5 to 6 minutes; reserve the bacon for another use. Add the chicken, in batches if necessary, and cook over moderate heat, turning, until golden, crisp and cooked through, about 30 minutes. Lower the heat if necessary. Transfer to a wire rack to drain.

4. Transfer ¼ cup of the chicken cooking fat to a large saucepan and add the onion and garlic. Cook over moderate heat, stirring occasionally, until golden, 5 to 6 minutes. Add the reserved ½ cup of seasoned flour and cook, whisking, for 2 minutes. Add the tomatoes and thyme and stir constantly until blended. Whisk in the cream and milk until the sauce is smooth. Season with sea salt and pepper and cook over moderate heat, stirring occasionally, until thickened, about 10 minutes.

5. Transfer the fried chicken to a platter. Pour the tomato gravy into a gravy boat and serve with the chicken and serve with The Best Biscuits on the side.
—*Scott Peacock*

MAKE AHEAD The chicken can marinate overnight in the buttermilk.

BEER Fried chicken and biscuits call for a good beer, such as Sam Adams or Anchor Steam.

Grilled Chicken Martinique Style

Thyme-and-Chile-Marinated Chicken and Feta

Grilled Chicken Martinique Style

8 SERVINGS

The chicken needs to marinate for four hours, so plan accordingly.

- 3 large garlic cloves, coarsely chopped
- 2 shallots, coarsely chopped
- 2 tablespoons curry powder
- 1 tablespoon thyme leaves
- 1 teaspoon freshly grated nutmeg

Finely grated zest of 1 lime

- ½ teaspoon cayenne pepper
- ¼ cup canola oil
- 3 tablespoons fresh lime juice

Salt and freshly ground pepper

- 7 pounds chicken parts

Lime wedges, for serving

1. In a mini food processor, pulse the garlic with the shallots until finely chopped. Add the curry, thyme, nutmeg, lime zest and cayenne and pulse until blended. Add the oil and process to a smooth paste. Transfer the paste to a bowl, whisk in the lime juice and season with salt and pepper.

2. Using a skewer, poke several holes in the skin of each piece of chicken. Rub the curry paste all over the chicken and spread the pieces out on 2 large rimmed baking sheets. Refrigerate for 4 to 6 hours. Let stand at room temperature for 30 minutes before grilling.

3. Light the grill. Cook the chicken over a moderately hot fire, turning occasionally, for about 35 minutes, or until browned and cooked through. Serve with lime wedges. —*Corinne Trang*

BEER The smoky grilled flavors in this chicken dish make beer a perfect match. Pick a light lager style from the Caribbean, such as Red Stripe from Jamaica or Carib from Trinidad.

Thyme-and-Chile-Marinated Chicken and Feta

4 SERVINGS ❋

Buy the feta cheese in one large chunk so you can cut eight slices thick enough to broil without crumbling.

- ½ cup plus 2 tablespoons extra-virgin olive oil
- 2 tablespoons chopped thyme
- 2 tablespoons light brown sugar
- 2 to 3 hot red chiles, seeded and finely chopped

Freshly ground pepper

One 3½- to 4-pound chicken, cut into 8 pieces

- ½ pound feta, cut into ⅓-inch slices
- 2 teaspoons white wine vinegar
- 1 large bunch arugula (6 ounces), large stems discarded

Salt

1. Preheat the broiler. In a large bowl, combine ½ cup of the olive oil with the thyme, brown sugar, chiles and a generous pinch of pepper. Reserve one-third of the marinade in a small bowl. Add the chicken pieces to the remaining marinade and turn to coat. Transfer the chicken to a broiling pan; broil 8 inches from the heat for about 35 minutes, turning once, or until cooked through.

2. Set the feta on a small baking sheet and brush with the reserved marinade. Broil, turning once, for about 2 minutes, or until sizzling and golden.

3. In a large bowl, whisk the remaining 2 tablespoons of olive oil with the vinegar. Add the arugula, season with salt and pepper and toss well. Arrange the salad, chicken and feta on 4 plates and serve. —*Donna Hay*

WINE A fruity wine with good acidity is essential to counterbalance the spicy-sweet glaze on the chicken. Try one of Australia's lime-scented Rieslings, like the 1998 Pikes Clare Valley or the 1998 Leeuwin Margaret River.

Coq au Vin

8 SERVINGS

- 2 cups full-bodied red wine, such as Côtes-du-Rhône or Zinfandel
- 1 tablespoon tomato paste
- 2 tablespoons extra-virgin olive oil

Two 3½-pound chickens, each cut into 8 pieces

Salt and freshly ground pepper

- 3 tablespoons all-purpose flour
- 3 cups Enriched Chicken Stock (p. 98)
- 1 bouquet garni, made with 5 parsley sprigs, 1 large thyme sprig and 1 bay leaf, tied in cheesecloth
- ⅓ pound slab bacon, cut into ¼-inch dice
- ½ pound small white mushrooms, quartered

1. In a large skillet, bring the wine to a boil over high heat. Remove the pan

Coq au Vin

from the heat and, using a long match, ignite the wine. When the flames subside, whisk in the tomato paste.

2. Heat 1 tablespoon of the olive oil in another large skillet. Season the chicken pieces with salt and pepper. Add half of the chicken to the skillet and cook over moderately high heat until lightly browned all over, about 12 minutes; transfer to a large enameled cast-iron casserole. Repeat with the remaining 1 tablespoon of olive oil and the rest of the chicken pieces.

3. Pour off all but 3 tablespoons of the fat in the skillet and whisk in the flour; cook over moderate heat, whisking occasionally, until chestnut colored, about 4 minutes. Add the chicken stock and wine and bring to a boil, whisking constantly.

4. Pour the liquid over the chicken in the casserole. Tuck in the bouquet garni and bring to a simmer. Cover and cook over low heat until the chicken is cooked through, about 25 minutes for the breasts and 35 minutes for the drumsticks, thighs and wings. Transfer the chicken to a large platter as it is done; cover loosely with foil and keep warm.

5. Set the casserole half on and half off the heat and bring the sauce to a boil. Skim the fat from the side that isn't boiling and continue to boil until the sauce is reduced to about 2 cups and is slightly thickened, approximately 15 minutes. Season with salt and pepper and keep warm.

6. Meanwhile, in the skillet, cook the bacon dice over moderate heat until crisp, 6 to 7 minutes. Using a slotted spoon, transfer the bacon to a paper towel–lined plate. Pour the fat into a glass measuring cup and wipe out the skillet. Add 1 tablespoon of the bacon fat to the skillet along with the mushrooms and cook over moderately high heat, stirring frequently, until softened and golden, about 7 minutes. Scatter the bacon and the mushrooms over

the chicken and serve immediately, passing the sauce separately.

—*Lydie Marshall*

MAKE AHEAD The recipe can be prepared through Step 5. In this case, put the chicken in the sauce and refrigerate overnight. Reheat the chicken and sauce gently so that the chicken pieces don't overcook.

WINE A hearty red with good fruit will echo the chicken's winey flavor. Look for the 1998 Château Mont-Redon Côtes-du-Rhône or the 1998 Rosenblum Harris Kratka Vineyard Zinfandel.

Chicken and Peanut Stew

4 TO 6 SERVINGS

This hearty stew was created with ingredients found at the Livingstone Farmers' Market in Zambia. Peanuts are a southern African staple and figure prominently in local dishes.

- ½ cup cornmeal
- Salt and freshly ground pepper
- One 3½-pound chicken—cut into 8 pieces, rinsed and patted dry
- ¼ cup vegetable oil
- 2 small onions, coarsely chopped
- 1 jalapeño—stemmed, seeded and minced
- 1 cup water
- ½ cup white wine vinegar
- ½ cup raw peanuts (2½ ounces)
- 8 unpeeled garlic cloves
- 1 large sweet potato, peeled and cut into 1½-inch chunks
- 1½ pounds long thin eggplants, sliced crosswise 1½ inches thick
- 2 small yellow squash, sliced crosswise 1½ inches thick
- 1 bunch scallions, cut into 2-inch lengths

I. In a sturdy plastic bag, combine the cornmeal with salt and pepper. Add the chicken in batches and shake to coat.

2. In a large heavy casserole, heat the oil until shimmering. Add the chicken and fry over moderately high heat, turning once, until well-browned, about 12 minutes; if the chicken seems to be

Chicken and Peanut Stew

browning too quickly, reduce the heat. Transfer the chicken to a large platter.

3. Pour off all but 2 tablespoons of the fat in the casserole. Add the onions and jalapeño and cook over low heat until just softened, about 3 minutes. Add the water, vinegar, peanuts and garlic, season with salt and pepper and bring to a simmer. Return the chicken to the casserole, cover and simmer over low heat until tender and cooked through, about 45 minutes. Transfer the chicken to a platter.

4. Add the sweet potato, eggplants and yellow squash to the casserole. Cover and cook over low heat until the vegetables are very tender, about 1 hour. Return the chicken to the casserole, add the scallions and simmer until the scallions are tender and the chicken is hot, 10 to 15 minutes. Season with salt and pepper and serve. —*Jacques Pépin*

MAKE AHEAD The stew can be refrigerated overnight.

WINE This dish pairs well with a medium-bodied, bright-flavored red wine, such as a South African Pinotage. A good possibility would be the 1997 Kanonkop or the 1996 Saxenburg.

Thai Green Curry Chicken

4 TO 6 SERVINGS

This luscious Thai chicken curry is served at actress Cameron Diaz's Miami restaurant, Bambú. The green curry paste calls for 15 ingredients; but you can substitute good-quality packaged curry paste, which is available in the ethnic section of most supermarkets.

- 1 stalk fresh lemongrass
- One 3½- to 4-pound chicken, cut into 8 pieces
- Salt and freshly ground pepper
- 1 tablespoon vegetable oil
- 4 cups unsweetened coconut milk (from 3 cans)
- 2 tablespoons Thai green curry paste
- 2 kaffir lime leaves or 1 teaspoon freshly grated lime zest
- ½ cup Basic Chicken Stock (p. 98) or canned low-sodium broth
- 2 tablespoons fish sauce (nam pla)
- 1 poblano chile, seeded and minced
- 2 tablespoons finely chopped basil, preferably Thai
- 2 tablespoons finely chopped cilantro
- Steamed jasmine rice, for serving

1. Peel the tough outer leaves from the lemongrass and discard the top two-thirds. Mince the tender white bulb.

2. Season the chicken with salt and pepper. Heat the oil in a large enameled cast-iron casserole. Add the chicken, in batches if necessary, and cook over moderate heat, turning occasionally, until golden all over, about 10 minutes. Transfer the chicken to a platter.

3. Add the coconut milk to the casserole and bring to a boil, scraping up any browned bits from the bottom of the pan. Cook over moderately high heat until reduced to 3 cups, about 15 minutes. Stir in the curry paste and simmer over moderate heat for 5 minutes. Return the chicken to the casserole along with any accumulated juices. Add the lemongrass, lime leaves, stock and fish sauce, cover partially and simmer over low heat until the meat is just cooked through, about 30 minutes.

4. Add the poblano, basil and cilantro to the chicken, cover partially and cook over low heat for 10 minutes longer. Serve right away with jasmine rice.

—*Rob Boone*

MAKE AHEAD The chicken can be prepared through Step 3 and refrigerated overnight.

WINE This aromatic dish points to an off-dry white. Try a German Riesling Kabinett, like the 1998 Prüm Erben Wehlener Sonnenuhr or the 1998 Egon Müller Scharzhofberger.

Summer Jambalaya with Chicken and Spicy Sausage

6 SERVINGS ✳

If you want to lower the heat level in this recipe, substitute sweet sausage for the *andouille* and skip the poblano.

- 3 tablespoons pure olive oil
- One 4-pound chicken, cut into 8 pieces
- Salt and freshly ground pepper
- ½ pound *andouille* sausage or spicy kielbasa, sliced ½-inch thick
- 1 Vidalia or other sweet onion, finely chopped
- 1 poblano chile or jalapeño, seeded and finely chopped
- 1 medium celery rib, chopped
- ¾ cup fresh corn kernels
- 1 teaspoon paprika
- ¼ pound chanterelles or oyster mushrooms, stemmed and thickly sliced
- ½ teaspoon dried oregano, crumbled
- 1½ cups medium-grain rice, such as Arborio
- 3 cups Basic Chicken Stock (p. 98) or canned low-sodium broth
- Hot sauce, for serving

1. In a large enameled cast-iron casserole, heat the olive oil until shimmering. Season the chicken pieces with salt and pepper and cook over moderately high heat, in batches if necessary, until nicely browned, about 6 minutes per side. Lower the heat to moderate when cooking the second batch if the skin is getting too dark. Transfer the chicken to a platter and set aside.

2. Add the sausage to the casserole and cook until lightly browned on both sides, 3 to 4 minutes. Add the sausage to the platter with the chicken.

3. Increase the heat to high and add the onion, poblano chile, celery and corn to the casserole. Cook the vegetables, stirring frequently, until softened, about 5 minutes. Add the paprika, chanterelles and oregano and cook until the mushrooms are just softened, about 3 minutes. Add the rice and cook, stirring constantly, until well coated and just beginning to brown, about 2 minutes.

4. Nestle the chicken and sausage in the rice and gently stir in the chicken stock, incorporating the ingredients on the bottom of the casserole. Bring to a boil over moderately high heat and season with salt and pepper. Cover and cook over moderately low heat until

Summer Jambalaya with Chicken and Spicy Sausage

the stock is completely absorbed, the rice is tender and the chicken is cooked through, about 30 minutes. Spoon the rice onto a platter, top with the chicken pieces, vegetables and mushrooms and serve with hot sauce.

—*Katy Sparks*

MAKE AHEAD The jambalaya can be cooked and then refrigerated overnight. Sprinkle with 3 tablespoons of water, cover and reheat in a 325° oven.

WINE Look for a red with intense berry fruit, peppery notes and lively acidity. Consider a Zinfandel, such as the 1997 Nalle Dry Creek Valley or the Rosenblum Cellars Vintner's Nonvintage Cuvée XIV.

Ragout of Chicken with Potatoes and Chorizo

10 SERVINGS

Buying whole chickens and cutting them up at home isn't just economical; it also yields trimmings that make the sauce extra flavorful.

Two 3½-pound chickens—necks, gizzards and hearts reserved
1 carrot, coarsely chopped
1 shallot, halved
4 cups water
10 medium fingerling potatoes (about 1 pound)
¾ cup plus 2 tablespoons pure olive oil
1 pound white mushrooms, trimmed and cleaned
1 pound medium yellow squash, cut into ½-inch chunks
Salt and freshly ground pepper
½ pound chorizo
1 cup all-purpose flour
3 red bell peppers, cut into 1-inch chunks
1 large onion, coarsely chopped
2 large garlic cloves, minced
2 large tomatoes—peeled, seeded and coarsely chopped
½ cup dry white wine
2 bay leaves
1 thyme sprig

I. Using sturdy kitchen shears, cut along both sides of the backbones of both chickens. Remove the backbones and cut each one into 3 pieces. Cut off the chicken wing tips, then cut each chicken into 8 pieces.

2. Put the backbones and wing tips in a large saucepan along with the reserved necks, gizzards and hearts. Add the carrot, shallot and water, cover and bring to a simmer over moderately low heat. Cook until the water is reduced to 3 cups, approximately 1 hour. Strain the broth, pressing hard on the solids to extract as much liquid as possible.

3. Meanwhile, bring a medium saucepan of salted water to a boil. Add the potatoes and cook until just tender, about 25 minutes. Drain the potatoes and let cool slightly, then peel them. Cut the potatoes in half if they seem large.

4. Heat 2 tablespoons of the olive oil in a large skillet until shimmering. Add the potatoes and cook over moderately high heat, stirring occasionally, until golden all over, about 5 minutes. Transfer the potatoes to a large plate. Add 2 more tablespoons of the olive oil to the skillet and heat until shimmering. Add the mushrooms and yellow squash chunks, season with salt and pepper and cook over high heat, stirring occasionally, until golden and just tender, about 5 minutes. Add the vegetables to the potatoes on the plate.

5. Pierce the chorizo with a fork and add it to the skillet. Cook the sausage over moderately high heat, turning, until browned all over, about 8 to 10 minutes. Drain on paper towels and cut it into thick slices.

6. Season the chicken pieces with salt and pepper. Spread the flour on a plate. Add the chicken, a few pieces at a time, and coat with the flour, shaking off any excess. Heat ¼ cup of the olive oil in a large skillet until shimmering. Add half the chicken pieces to the skillet and

Ragout of Chicken with Potatoes and Chorizo

menu

grilled tuna with coriander seeds and cilantro (p. 139) | 1998 BELLERUCHE ROUGE

herbed goat cheese with potatoes and grilled bacon (p. 34)

1997 CROZES-HERMITAGE ROUGE LES MEYSONNIERS

roast chicken with garlic and cumin | summer vegetable gratin (p. 282)

1997 HERMITAGE BLANC CHANTE-ALOUETTE

banyuls-marinated steaks with pearl onions (p. 219)

1997 HERMITAGE ROUGE LA SIZERANNE | valrhona chocolate mousse (p. 379)

cook over moderately high heat until crisp and golden all over, about 8 minutes; transfer to a large platter. Repeat the process with another ¼ cup of olive oil and the remaining chicken.

7. Heat the remaining 2 tablespoons of olive oil in a large enameled cast-iron casserole. Add the red bell peppers, onion and garlic and cook over moderately low heat, stirring often, until softened, about 10 minutes. Raise the heat to moderately high and add the tomatoes, white wine, bay leaves and thyme sprig. Simmer the mixture until the liquid is nearly evaporated, about 5 minutes. Add the browned chicken pieces along with the reserved 3 cups of broth and bring back to a simmer. Cover partially and cook over low heat until the chicken is tender when pierced with a fork, about 45 minutes.

8. Add the cooked chorizo to the casserole and cook for 5 minutes. Stir in the cooked potatoes, mushrooms and squash and cook over moderate heat until warmed through, about 5 minutes. Transfer the ragout to a platter and serve. *—Julian Serrano*

MAKE AHEAD The chicken ragout can be refrigerated overnight. Rewarm the ragout gently before serving.

WINE The simple flavors of this hearty chicken ragout point toward a subtle Burgundy-style red wine. Try the 1994 Marqués de Cáceres Rioja or the 1996 Condado de Haza Ribera del Duero Crianza; both are from Spain.

Lemon and Garlic Roast Chicken

SERVES 4

 2 garlic cloves
Kosher salt
 1 lemon, halved and juiced, halves reserved
 1 teaspoon minced rosemary
 1 teaspoon sweet paprika
 ¾ teaspoon ground cumin
 ¼ teaspoon hot paprika
Freshly ground pepper
 ¼ cup extra-virgin olive oil
One 3-pound chicken
 2 tablespoons unsalted butter, softened

I. Preheat the oven to 350°. On a work surface, mince the garlic with 1 teaspoon of kosher salt. Transfer the garlic to a small bowl and whisk in the lemon juice, rosemary, sweet paprika, cumin, hot paprika and ½ teaspoon pepper. Whisk in the olive oil.

2. Using your fingers, gently loosen the skin from the chicken breasts, thighs and drumsticks; try not to tear the skin. Season the cavity of the chicken with salt and pepper and put the chicken in a roasting pan. Using a small spoon, pour all but 1 tablespoon of the seasoning mixture under the skin of the chicken, rubbing it into the breasts, thighs and drumsticks. Rub the butter under the skin of the breast meat. Rub the remaining 1 tablespoon of the seasoned oil all over the chicken; season it with salt. Put the reserved lemon halves in the cavity of the chicken

and tie the legs together with twine.

3. Roast the chicken for about 1½ hours, or until the juices from the cavity run clear and the chicken is browned and crisp. Let the chicken rest in the roasting pan for 15 minutes.

4. Tilt the chicken to drain the juices from the cavity into the pan; transfer the chicken to a carving board. Pour the pan juices into a bowl and skim the fat from the surface. Strain the juices into a small saucepan and keep warm over low heat. Carve the chicken and serve with the pan juices.

—Marcia Kiesel

WINE The rich fruitiness of a good cru Beaujolais would provide a bright contrast to the chicken's crispy skin. Try the 1999 Georges Duboeuf Morgon or the 1997 Olivier Ravier Domaine de la Pierre Bleue Côte de Brouilly.

Roast Chicken with Garlic and Cumin

4 SERVINGS

Whole heads of garlic are roasted along with the chicken in this recipe, then chopped and added to the pan juices to make a light but rich-tasting sauce.

One 3½-pound chicken
 2 large heads of garlic, top third cut off
 2 tablespoons extra-virgin olive oil
Salt and freshly ground pepper
 ½ teaspoon cumin seeds
 ½ cup plus ⅓ cup dry white wine
 ½ cup water

1. Preheat the oven to 350°. Put the chicken in a small roasting pan. Tuck the garlic heads, cut side up, into the spaces around the chicken. Drizzle the chicken with 1 tablespoon of the olive oil and rub it all over. Drizzle the garlic heads with the remaining 1 tablespoon of olive oil. Season the garlic and chicken with salt and pepper. Turn the garlic heads so they're cut side down. Sprinkle the chicken with the cumin seeds. Pour ½ cup of the wine around the chicken.

2. Transfer the pan to the oven and roast the chicken for 20 minutes; baste well. Roast for 25 minutes more, then add the water to the pan. Baste the chicken again and roast for 30 minutes longer. Using a slotted spoon, transfer the garlic heads to a plate. Continue roasting the chicken for about 20 minutes more, or until the juices run clear. Transfer the chicken to a warmed platter and cover loosely with foil.

3. Pour the pan juices into a glass measuring cup and skim off the fat. Strain the juices into a small saucepan. Set the roasting pan on 2 burners over moderate heat. Add the remaining ⅓ cup of wine to the roasting pan and simmer, scraping up the browned bits from the bottom, until the wine reduces to ¼ cup, about 3 minutes. Add these juices to the saucepan and simmer over low heat until very flavorful, about 3 minutes.

4. Meanwhile, break off 18 large roasted garlic cloves and set aside. Squeeze the remaining garlic from the heads and discard the skins. Finely chop the garlic and add it to the pan juices. Season with salt and pepper and pour into a warmed gravy boat. Carve the chicken and serve with the reserved whole garlic cloves and the pan juices.

—*Corinne Chapoutier*

WINE The buttery texture and toasted aromas of the 1997 Hermitage Blanc Chante-Alouette will complement the roasted garlic and cumin in the dish.

Big Bob's Smoked Chicken with White BBQ Sauce
6 SERVINGS

White barbecue sauce is served throughout northern Alabama. It sounds weird. It *is* weird. But one taste of the chicken at Big Bob Gibson Bar-B-Q in Decatur—smoked to the color of mahogany, then tossed with a creamy, peppery white sauce—will make you a believer. Don McLemore, the third-generation owner of Big Bob's, says his grandfather came up with the recipe in 1925, using vinegar, mayonnaise and black pepper. It makes great sandwiches on toasted white bread with fried green tomatoes.

- 2 **cups hickory wood chips**
- 2 **teaspoons coarse salt**
- 1½ **teaspoons freshly ground pepper**
- 1½ **teaspoons light brown sugar**
- 1½ **teaspoons paprika**
- 1 **teaspoon garlic powder**
- 1 **teaspoon onion powder**

Two 4-pound chickens, rinsed and patted dry

White BBQ Sauce (recipe follows)

1. Soak the hickory chips in cold water for 1 hour. In a small bowl, combine the salt and pepper with the light brown sugar, paprika and garlic and onion powders.

2. Light a grill; if using gas, light the front and rear or outside burners. If using charcoal, rake the lit coals into two piles on opposite sides of the grill. Lightly brush the grate with vegetable oil. Place a foil drip pan in the center of the grill.

3. Drain the hickory chips and scatter them on the hot coals. If using gas, place the chips in a 12-inch square of aluminum foil; fold the foil into a 6-inch square package and poke 12 holes in the top. Place the package near the gas flame. Let the chips heat until smoking.

4. Sprinkle 2 teaspoons of the seasoning mixture made in Step 1 into the cavity of each chicken. Sprinkle the rest on the skin, and rub it in thoroughly. Set the chickens on the grill, breast up, away from the heat. Cover and grill over moderate heat for 1¼ to 1½ hours, or until the skin is golden and crisp and the juices run clear when a thigh is pierced. (If using charcoal, replenish the coals after about 1 hour.) Transfer the chickens to a platter and let rest for 10 minutes before carving. Serve hot or at room temperature, with White BBQ Sauce on the side.

—*Steven Raichlen*

WINE The smoky, spicy and slightly sweet flavors in this simple dish are a perfect foil for a fresh, fruity, inexpensive rosé, such as the 1998 Réserve St. Martin Rosé de Syrah.

WHITE BBQ SAUCE
MAKES ABOUT 1½ CUPS

- 1 **cup mayonnaise**
- 2 to 4 **tablespoons cider vinegar**
- 2 **tablespoons freshly grated or prepared horseradish**
- 2 **tablespoons water**
- 1 **teaspoon coarse salt**
- ½ **teaspoon freshly ground black pepper**
- ¼ **teaspoon cayenne pepper**

Combine all of the ingredients in a bowl and whisk until well combined and smooth. —*S.R.*

MAKE AHEAD The sauce can be refrigerated in an airtight container for up to 1 week.

Roasted Poussins with Four-Spice Dust and Garlic Sauce
4 SERVINGS

- 1 **teaspoon sesame seeds**
- ½ **teaspoon cumin seeds**
- ½ **teaspoon nigella (see Note) or black mustard seeds**
- ½ **teaspoon yellow mustard seeds**

Kosher salt

- 3 **small heads of garlic, outer skin removed, heads halved crosswise**
- 4½ **tablespoons unsalted butter, softened**

Big Bob's Smoked Chicken with White BBQ Sauce
in a sandwich with fried green tomatoes.

Freshly ground pepper

Four 1-pound poussins, legs tied

¾ cup fresh orange juice

1. In a small skillet, toast the sesame, cumin, nigella and yellow mustard seeds over low heat until fragrant. Transfer the seeds to a mortar and let cool. Add ½ teaspoon of salt and grind to a coarse powder.

2. Preheat the oven to 300°. Put the garlic in a glass baking dish, cut sides up. Dot the halved heads with 1½ tablespoons of the butter and season with salt and pepper. Cover tightly with foil and bake for about 1 hour, or until the garlic is very soft. Set aside the 4 nicest garlic halves. Squeeze the rest of the cloves into a coarse strainer set over a bowl and press the garlic through with a spatula.

3. Increase the oven temperature to 400°. Set the poussins in a shallow roasting pan, breasts up. Rub the poussins with the remaining 3 tablespoons of butter and season with salt and pepper. Roast in the upper third of the oven for 1 hour, or until golden brown; baste occasionally. Toward the end of cooking, tilt the birds to allow the juices to run into the roasting pan.

4. Put the poussins on a warmed platter. Scrape the pan juices into a small saucepan and skim off the fat. Set the roasting pan over 2 burners on moderate heat. When the pan starts smoking, add the orange juice and pan juices and simmer, scraping up the browned bits from the bottom. Strain the sauce into the small saucepan and simmer for 1 minute. Stir in the garlic puree and season with salt and pepper.

5. Set the birds on warmed plates and sprinkle generously with the spice dust. Garnish each plate with a reserved roasted garlic half and serve. Pass the garlic sauce at the table.—*Marcia Kiesel*

NOTE Tiny black nigella seeds have a slightly oniony flavor and are available at specialty shops and Indian groceries.

Poussin with Summer Succotash

4 SERVINGS

One large poussin is perfect for two people. Have your butcher halve the poussins and cut out the backbones for you.

2 medium ears of corn, kernels cut off (1½ cups)

4 ounces *haricots verts* or thin green beans, halved crosswise

1 pound fava beans, shelled

2 tablespoons clarified butter

Two 1¼-pound poussins, split in half, backbones removed

Salt and freshly ground black pepper

1 medium tomato, seeded and coarsely chopped

1 tablespoon coarsely chopped cilantro leaves

⅛ teaspoon cayenne pepper

1. Preheat the oven to 500°. Bring a large saucepan of salted water to a boil. Put the corn kernels in a strainer, set the strainer in the saucepan and cook the corn until crisp-tender, about 3 minutes. Transfer the corn to a bowl of ice water to cool. Drain and pat dry. Add the *haricots verts* to the strainer and set in the saucepan; cook until crisp-tender, about 3 minutes. Cool under running water, drain and pat dry. Add the fava beans and boil until bright green, about 1 minute. Cool under running water, then drain and pat dry. Peel off the tough skins.

2. Melt 1 tablespoon of the clarified butter in a large ovenproof skillet. Season the poussins with salt and black pepper and cook over high heat, skin side down, until golden, about 5 minutes. Turn the poussins and transfer

Poussin with Summer Succotash

the skillet to the oven for about 15 minutes, or until the juices run clear when the thighs are pierced with a knife.

3. Meanwhile, melt the remaining 1 tablespoon of butter in a medium skillet. Add the corn and cook over moderate heat, stirring frequently, until golden, about 5 minutes. Add the fava beans and *haricots verts* and cook until just warmed through; remove from the heat. Add the tomato and cilantro and season with the cayenne and salt. Cover and keep warm.

4. Cut each poussin half into a breast-wing piece and a leg-thigh piece. Spoon the succotash onto plates, top with the poussins and serve immediately.

—*Sally Schneider*

MAKE AHEAD The succotash can be made up to 1 day ahead. Rewarm over low heat; add the tomato, cilantro and seasonings just before serving.

ONE SERVING Calories 413 kcal, Total Fat 20.4 gm, Saturated Fat 7.7 gm

WINE A lush Chardonnay with good fruit and not too much oak would best pull together the vegetables in the succotash. Try the 1998 Merryvale or the 1998 Estancia Reserve Monterey.

Capon Salad

Capon Salad

6 SERVINGS

The recipe is excellent with capon, but high-quality free-range chickens or even store-bought rotisserie-roasted chickens can substitute. Leftover turkey is another possibility.

- 5 quarts cold water
- 1 bottle dry white wine
- 1 head of garlic
- 1 large carrot, halved crosswise
- 1 celery rib, halved crosswise
- 1 bunch of flat-leaf parsley
- 1 medium red onion, halved
- 1 thyme sprig
- One 8-pound capon or 2 halved 4-pound free-range chickens
- ½ cup pine nuts (2½ ounces)
- 1 bunch scallions, thinly sliced on the diagonal (1 cup)
- ½ cup golden raisins, soaked in sweet wine, such as Vin Santo, and drained
- ¼ cup snipped chives
- 2 tablespoons chopped tarragon
- ⅓ cup best-quality extra-virgin olive oil, preferably from Tuscany
- 2½ tablespoons red wine vinegar
- Salt and freshly ground pepper

I. In a stockpot, combine the water, wine, garlic, carrot, celery, parsley, onion and thyme and bring to a boil. Reduce the heat to moderately low, add the capon, breast side up, and return to a gentle boil. Simmer the capon until just cooked through but still moist, about 45 minutes. Carefully remove the capon from the pot and let cool slightly, then refrigerate until chilled, about 1 hour. Strain the broth and store it in the refrigerator or freezer for another use.

2. Preheat the oven to 350°. Spread the pine nuts in a small baking dish and bake for about 3 minutes, shaking the pan occasionally, or until lightly toasted. Let cool. Using your fingers, pull the capon meat into 2-inch pieces; discard the skin and bones. In a large bowl, toss the shredded capon with the pine nuts, scallions, raisins, chives and tarragon. Add the olive oil and vinegar, season with salt and pepper and toss the ingredients to combine. Mound the capon salad on plates and serve.

—*Sara Jenkins*

MAKE AHEAD The capon can be cooked up to 2 days in advance. Allow it to cool enough to handle, pull the meat into pieces, wrap well and refrigerate. Bring the capon to room temperature before serving.

WINE An Italian Pinot Noir that is rich with fruit but has an austere ending is the ideal choice for this rustic salad topped off with an assertive olive oil. Look for the 1995 Rocche dei Manzoni di Valentino Pinot Nero.

Guinea Hens with Lemon and Rosemary, with Winter Squash Risotto (p. 310).

Guinea Hens with Lemon and Rosemary

12 SERVINGS

Guinea hen is rich and flavorful and has a somewhat dense texture. Chicken would make a fine substitute in this recipe.

Three 3½-pound guinea hens
¼ cup pure olive oil
Salt and freshly ground pepper
1¾ cups dry white wine
5 lemons
⅓ cup finely chopped rosemary
5 large garlic cloves, halved

1. Rub the hens with 2 tablespoons of the olive oil and season them with salt and pepper. In a large skillet, heat the remaining 2 tablespoons of olive oil. Add the hens 1 at a time and brown them over moderately high heat, about 4 minutes per side. Transfer the hens to a large roasting pan and let cool slightly. Pour off the fat from the skillet. Add ½ cup of the wine to the skillet and boil over high heat for 2 minutes, using a wooden spatula to scrape up the brown bits from the bottom.
2. Preheat the oven to 400°. Using a citrus zester, zest 3 of the lemons.

Alternatively, remove the zest from 3 of the lemons using a vegetable peeler, then cut the zest into fine julienne. Thinly slice the remaining 2 lemons.
3. Rub the hens with the rosemary. Put 2 garlic-clove halves and one-third of the lemon slices in each of the hen cavities. Tie the legs together and fold the wing tips underneath. Scatter the lemon zest over the hens. Pour the reduced wine into the roasting pan and add the remaining garlic cloves. Roast the guinea hens for about 1 hour, basting after 15 minutes with ¼ cup of wine. Baste the hens 2 more times, until an instant-read thermometer inserted in an inner thigh registers 160°. Transfer the guinea hens to a carving board, cover loosely with foil and let rest for 10 minutes.
4. Pour the pan juices into a glass measuring cup and skim off the fat. Set the roasting pan over 2 burners. Add the remaining ½ cup of wine and boil over high heat, scraping up the brown bits, until almost evaporated. Pour in the reserved pan juices and simmer the sauce for 2 minutes. Strain the sauce into a warmed gravy boat and

season with salt and pepper. Carve the hens and serve with the pan sauce.

—Sabine Busch and Bruno Tramontana

WINE This elegant dish requires a flavorful, full-bodied, mature wine. Both the 1995 Pertimali Brunello di Montalcino and the 1996 Ambra Riserva Elzana Carmignano have the necessary age and size.

Roasted Guinea Hen Mediterranean Style

4 SERVINGS

Guinea hens are like deeply flavored chickens. (You can substitute chicken.) You will need a roasting pan large enough to hold the guinea hen and vegetables without crowding. You can use an oven broiling pan. The black pan helps the hen and vegetables brown, but the pan can burn easily, so baste often.

2 small zucchini (6 ounces each), cut into ¼-inch dice
½ cup extra-virgin olive oil, plus more for rubbing
1 tablespoon minced mixed tarragon, chives and thyme
Salt
3 medium tomatoes, cored and coarsely chopped
1 small Asian eggplant (6 ounces), cut into ¼-inch dice
One 3-pound guinea hen
Freshly ground pepper
1 mint sprig
2 rosemary sprigs
2 medium onions, coarsely chopped
1 red bell pepper, coarsely chopped
1 garlic clove, coarsely chopped
1 cup water
½ cup Enriched Chicken Stock (p. 98)

1. Preheat the oven to 425°. In a bowl, toss the zucchini with 2 tablespoons of the olive oil and 1 teaspoon of the minced herbs; season with salt. In another bowl, toss the tomatoes and eggplant with 2 tablespoons of the

olive oil and 1 teaspoon of the minced herbs. Season the tomatoes and eggplant with salt.

2. Cut off the first 2 wing joints from the guinea hen and reserve. Season the hen inside with salt and pepper. Put the mint sprig in the cavity and tie the legs together. Rub the hen all over with olive oil and tuck 1 rosemary sprig under each thigh. Set the hen in a large roasting pan and scatter the wings, onions, red bell pepper and garlic around it. Drizzle the vegetables with 2 tablespoons of the olive oil, season with salt and pepper and pour the water into the pan.

3. Roast the hen for 20 minutes. Add the zucchini to the pan and roast for 15 minutes. Add the tomatoes and eggplant along with the remaining 2 tablespoons of olive oil and season with salt; stir to mix. Add the Enriched Chicken Stock and baste the hen. Return the hen to the oven and roast for 20 minutes longer, or until the vegetables are tender and the hen juices run clear when a thigh is pierced. Transfer the hen to a carving board and cover loosely with foil.

4. Set a coarse sieve over a small saucepan and carefully pour in the roasting pan juices, keeping the vegetables in the pan. Eat the wing pieces or discard. Stir the remaining 1 teaspoon of minced herbs into the vegetables. Cover the saucepan with foil and keep warm. Skim the fat from the pan juices. Boil the pan juices over high heat until reduced to ½ cup, about 5 minutes. Season with salt and pepper. Carve the guinea hen and serve with the vegetables. Pass the pan juices at the table.

—Lydie Marshall

WINE A soft, round red from the southern Rhône will work with the gamey flavor of the guinea hen. Consider either the 1996 Domaine de la Roquette or the 1996 Bosquet des Papes.

Roasted Guinea Hen Mediterranean Style

Duck Breasts in Muscat and Orange Juice

4 SERVINGS

- 1 cup Muscat de Beaumes-de-Venise or ruby port
- 1 cup fresh orange juice
- 2 tablespoons soy sauce
- 1 tablespoon fresh lime juice
- ¼ cup extra-virgin olive oil

Four 6-ounce boneless duck breasts, fat trimmed to ⅛ inch thick and scored (see Note)

- 1½ cups Enriched Chicken Stock (p. 98)

Salt and freshly ground pepper

1. In a large baking dish, mix the Muscat de Beaumes-de-Venise with the orange juice, soy sauce, lime juice and olive oil. Add the duck breasts and marinate for 4 hours or overnight in the refrigerator.
2. Remove the duck breasts from the marinade and pat dry with paper towels. Pour the marinade into a medium saucepan and add the Enriched Chicken Stock. Boil over moderately high heat until reduced to ⅓ cup and syrupy, about 35 minutes.
3. Heat a large nonstick skillet. Add the duck breasts skin side down and season with salt and pepper. Cook the breasts over moderate heat until the skin is very crisp, about 5 minutes. Turn the breasts, cover and cook until the meat is rare, about 3 minutes. Transfer the breasts to a carving board, cover loosely with foil and let stand for 5 minutes. Slice the duck crosswise ¼ inch thick and arrange on plates. Pass the sauce at the table.

—*Lydie Marshall*

NOTE Boneless duck breasts are available from D'Artagnan (800-327-8246 or www.dartagnan.com.)

WINE A medium-bodied red wine with intense fruit and a smooth texture will pull together the strong flavors in this dish. Try the 1998 Delas Crozes-Hermitage Cuvée Tour d'Albon from the Rhône.

Grilled Duck Breasts and Endives with Rosemary-Juniper Oil

6 SERVINGS

In this recipe, the endives are grilled first over a relatively low fire, so if you're grilling over charcoal, keep a chimney starter filled with hot coals for raising the temperature to moderately hot for the duck.

- ½ cup extra-virgin olive oil, plus more for brushing
- 1 tablespoon minced rosemary
- 1 tablespoon crushed juniper berries
- 6 Belgian endives, quartered lengthwise

Salt and freshly ground pepper

Six ½-pound boneless duck breasts, with skin

1. In a small saucepan, combine the ½ cup olive oil with the rosemary and juniper berries. Simmer over low heat for 2 minutes. Remove from heat, cover the saucepan and let the mixture stand for at least 20 minutes.
2. Light a grill. Brush the endives with olive oil and season with salt and pepper. Grill over a low fire, turning, for about 20 minutes, or until the endives are almost tender. Transfer the endives to a platter and cover loosely with foil.
3. Season the duck breasts with salt and pepper and grill, skin side down, over a moderately hot fire for 4 minutes. Turn the duck breasts and grill for 3 minutes longer for medium rare. Transfer the duck to a carving board to rest for about 5 minutes. Slice the duck breasts crosswise ½ inch thick and arrange the slices on a large warmed platter. Return the endives to the grill briefly to reheat, then add to the platter. Drizzle the duck with the rosemary-juniper oil and serve.

—*Cristina and Mauro Rastelli*

WINE An assertive, mouth-filling red will harmonize with the rich, smoky duck. Try the 1996 Caprai Sagrantino di Montefalco.

Duck Breasts in Muscat and Orange Juice

Pan-Roasted Duck Breasts with Onions and Crisp Pancetta

4 SERVINGS ✳

This roasted duck is one of the most popular and well-reviewed dishes at Nicole's restaurant in New York City. Some say the roasted onion-ring garnish alone is worth the price of the dish, and in fact the onions would go nicely with other things as well—ham, for instance, or steak.

- 2 red onions, sliced ½ inch thick
- ¼ cup extra-virgin olive oil
- 2 thyme sprigs
- 8 sage leaves

Four 6-ounce Pekin duck breasts

Kosher salt and freshly ground pepper

- ½ pound thinly sliced pancetta
- 1 garlic clove, minced
- ½ cup chicken or duck demiglace (see Note)
- 2 tablespoons sherry vinegar
- 3 tablespoons walnut oil
- 4 ounces sturdy baby greens, such as red mustard leaves and frisée

1. Preheat the oven to 450°. In a large bowl, separate the onion slices into rings and toss them with 2 tablespoons of the olive oil, the thyme sprigs and the sage leaves. On a large rimmed baking sheet, spread the onion rings out and roast them for about 20 minutes, tossing once, until tender and golden.

Pan-Roasted Duck Breasts with Onions and Crisp Pancetta

Leave the oven on at the same temperature to roast the duck.

2. Meanwhile, score the skin on the duck breasts in a crosshatch pattern, cutting through the fat beneath the skin but not into the meat; season the duck with salt and pepper. Heat a large ovenproof skillet. Put the duck breasts in the skillet, skin side down, and cook over moderate heat until the skin is golden brown, about 7 minutes. Turn the duck and roast in the oven for about 6 minutes for medium rare. Transfer the duck to a cutting board and allow to rest for 5 minutes.

3. Add the pancetta to the skillet and cook over moderate heat until browned and crisp, about 5 minutes; drain on paper towels. Pour off all but 2 tablespoons of the fat from the skillet. Add the garlic to the skillet and cook over high heat until fragrant but not browned, about 1 minute. Add the

demiglace and vinegar and bring to a boil, scraping up any browned bits. Remove the skillet from the heat; whisk in the walnut oil and the remaining 2 tablespoons of olive oil. Season with salt and pepper.

4. Arrange the baby greens and roasted onions on 4 large plates and drizzle with some of the dressing. Thinly slice the duck breasts crosswise and arrange over the salads. Drizzle the remaining dressing on top, garnish with the pancetta and serve.

—*Annie Wayte and Anna Kovel*

NOTE Demiglace is available at specialty food stores and by mail-order from D'Artagnan (800-327-8246 or www.dartagnan.com).

WINE This robust dish calls for a full-blown Cabernet Sauvignon, such as the 1995 Cape Mentelle from Australia or the 1996 St. Francis Reserve from California.

Crisp Slow-Roasted Duck

8 SERVINGS

By the time the ducks are done (about six hours), at least four cups of delicious fat—ideal for sautéing potatoes—will have been rendered. Strain the duck fat into a glass jar and store it in the refrigerator or the freezer; it will last indefinitely.

Two 5 ½-pound Long Island ducks, wing tips removed
Sea salt and freshly ground pepper
6 garlic cloves, chopped
2 medium bunches of thyme

1. Preheat the oven to 300°. Rinse the ducks in cold water and pat dry. Cut the fat from the neck and cavity areas and discard; cut off the wing tips. Season the cavities generously with salt and pepper. Stuff the ducks with the garlic and the thyme. Holding a paring knife angled almost parallel to the ducks, pierce the skin all over in dozens of places without cutting into the flesh.

2. Set the ducks, breast up, on a rack in a large shallow roasting pan. Roast for 1 hour. Remove the rack with the ducks and carefully drain the fat from the roasting pan. Turn the ducks breast down on the rack, and return to the roasting pan; pierce the skins again. Roast for 3 more hours, draining the fat from the pan and turning the ducks every hour.

3. After 4 hours, turn the oven up to 350°. Generously season the ducks with salt and pepper and continue roasting for about 1 hour longer, until the skin is very crisp. Remove the ducks from the oven and let them rest for about 20 minutes. Carve the ducks with a sharp knife, arrange the pieces on a warmed platter and serve.

—*Sally Schneider*

ONE SERVING Calories 396 kcal, Total Fat 26.4 gm, Saturated Fat 8.4 gm

WINE A great German Riesling, such as the 1998 Schloss Johannisberg Riesling Spätlese, has the acidity to cut the richness of the duck.

Perfect Roast Turkey

10 TO 12 SERVINGS

Note that you'll need to brine this turkey for 10 to 12 hours before roasting it. Brining is well worth doing: It will make your holiday bird exceptionally juicy, as well as seasoning it throughout.

1½ cups kosher salt

1 cup sugar

One 12- to 14-pound turkey—neck, wing tips and giblets reserved, cavity fat removed

2 medium onions, coarsely chopped

1 carrot, coarsely chopped

1 celery rib, coarsely chopped

3 tablespoons unsalted butter, melted

Thanksgiving Menu

potato-apple latkes (p. 302)

myron's crab cocktail (p. 38)

chopped liver with beets and horseradish (p. 21)

LUSTAU LIGHT FINO SHERRY JARANA

———

roasted garlic flat breads (p. 248)

curried butternut squash and cauliflower soup (p. 82)

———

spice-rubbed turkey

rye bread stuffing with sausage, apples and bacon (p. 254)

collard greens with fennel and orange butter (p. 273)

tangerine cranberry sauce (p. 327)

sweet potato soufflé with molasses sauce (p. 304)

1998 ROBERT SINSKEY CARNEROS PINOT NOIR

———

apple tart with bananas and cranberries (p. 351)

pumpkin meringue pie (p. 354)

grandma martha's chocolate roll (p. 341)

MOUNT GAY EXTRA OLD RUM

---

1. In a large stockpot or plastic tub, mix 1½ gallons of water with the salt and sugar; stir to dissolve the salt and sugar. Add the turkey to the brine, breast side down, and refrigerate for 10 to 12 hours. Don't worry if a small portion of the turkey is not submerged in the brine.

2. Remove the turkey from the brine, rinse it in cold water and pat dry with paper towels. Discard the brine.

3. Preheat the oven to 400°. Place half of the onions, carrot and celery in the turkey cavity. Using a long piece of kitchen string, tie the turkey legs together, and then bring the string around the turkey and tie the wings at the breast so they'll stay close to the body. Scatter the remaining onions, carrot and celery in a large roasting pan. Oil a V-shaped rack and set it in the pan. Transfer the turkey to the rack, breast side up. Brush the turkey with the melted butter. Pour 1 cup of water into the pan and roast the turkey for 45 minutes.

4. Baste the turkey with the pan juices and add 1 more cup of water to the pan. Roast the turkey for about 1 hour and 45 minutes longer, basting it with the pan juices every 30 minutes or so and adding another ½ cup of water to the roasting pan whenever the vegetables begin to brown. (To ensure juicy breast meat, rotate the turkey a quarter turn each time you baste it.) The turkey is done when an instant-read thermometer inserted in an inner thigh registers 170°. Transfer the turkey to a carving board, cover loosely with foil and let rest for 20 to 30 minutes before carving. Reserve the juices in the roasting pan for making the gravy.

—Pam Anderson

MAKE AHEAD You can prepare the turkey through Step 2 and refrigerate it for another 8 hours, but do not leave it in the brine for longer than 12 hours.

Spice-Rubbed Turkey

12 SERVINGS

This recipe's simple, salt-based rub produces a turkey with crisp, golden-brown skin and incredibly moist and tender breast meat.

¼ cup kosher salt

2 tablespoons crumbled dried sage leaves

2 tablespoons coarsely cracked black pepper

2 tablespoons sweet paprika

1 tablespoon sugar

One 18- to 20-pound turkey, rinsed and patted dry

5 cups of Rye Bread Stuffing with Sausage, Apples and Bacon (p. 254)

6 tablespoons unsalted butter, 2 tablespoons melted

2 small onions, coarsely chopped

2 celery ribs, coarsely chopped

2 carrots, coarsely chopped

3 cups water

¼ cup all-purpose flour

1 quart Rich Turkey Stock (p. 99), chicken stock or canned low-sodium broth

Salt and freshly ground pepper

1. In a small bowl, combine the kosher salt with the sage, black pepper, paprika and sugar. Set the turkey in a large roasting pan and rub it with the spice mixture inside and out; refrigerate for at least 12 hours or for up to 24 hours. Return the turkey to room temperature before roasting.

2. Preheat the oven to 475°. Stuff the turkey body cavity and the skin flap at the top of the breast with the Rye Bread Stuffing, packing it loosely. Brush the turkey all over with the melted butter and roast for about 30 minutes, or until the skin is golden brown.

3. Scatter the onions, celery and carrots around the turkey, add the water to the pan and cover the breast loosely with foil. Lower the oven temperature to 325° and roast the turkey for

thanksgiving menu game plan

1 WEEK AHEAD
MAKE APPLESAUCE
MAKE AND FREEZE PASTRY DOUGH
MAKE CRANBERRY SAUCE
MAKE AND FREEZE SAUSAGE
MAKE AND FREEZE TURKEY STOCK
 AND VEGETABLE STOCK

3 DAYS AHEAD
ASSEMBLE RYE BREAD STUFFING
MAKE AND FREEZE FLAT BREADS

2 DAYS AHEAD
MAKE CHOPPED LIVER AND BEET AND
 HORSERADISH TOPPING
MAKE SOUP
MAKE MOLASSES SAUCE
MAKE COLLARD GREENS

1 DAY AHEAD
MAKE CRAB COCKTAIL
MAKE SWEET POTATO SOUFFLE BASE
RUB THE TURKEY WITH SPICE
 MIXTURE AND REFRIGERATE
MAKE APPLE TART
BAKE PUMPKIN PIES
MAKE CHOCOLATE ROLL
STEAM SQUASH FOR SOUP GARNISH

THANKSGIVING DAY
MAKE POTATO LATKES
ROAST TURKEY AND MAKE GRAVY
BAKE STUFFING
FINISH AND BAKE SWEET
 POTATO SOUFFLE
REHEAT COLLARD GREENS
REWARM FLAT BREADS
REHEAT APPLE TART
TOP PUMPKIN PIES WITH MERINGUE
 AND BROIL

CLOCKWISE FROM TOP: **Spice-Rubbed Turkey, Rye Bread Stuffing with Sausage, Apples and Bacon (p. 254), Collard Greens with Fennel and Orange Butter (p. 273), Tangerine Cranberry Sauce (p. 326) and Sweet Potato Soufflé with Molasses Sauce (p. 304).**

seven tips for perfect turkey

1. Choose a small, fresh turkey in the 14-pound-and-under category. Large turkeys take longer to cook, so the outer meat is likely to overcook before the interior meat is done. If you're feeding more than 12 people, buy two small turkeys rather than one big one.

2. Brine the turkey in a bath of salt-and-sugar-water. Salt is absorbed into the meat, making it juicy and deeply seasoned. Sugar rounds out the salty flavor and helps brown the turkey.

3. Do brine a frozen turkey; it will greatly improve the flavor. Do not brine kosher turkeys, which are already salted, or self-basting turkeys, which have been injected with salt.

4. Save refrigerator space by storing your brining turkey in a cool garage or basement or outside with a weighted lid. If you live in a warm climate, dissolve the salt and sugar in a small amount of lukewarm water in an ice chest and add ice water to cover the turkey.

5. Cook the dressing in an ovenproof dish, not inside the turkey. A stuffed bird takes longer to cook through than an unstuffed one. The longer the turkey sits in a hot oven, the more it overcooks and dries out.

6. When carving the turkey, remove both wings first. Separate each wing from the body at the joint. Remove each leg and set aside. Remove each breast half from the bone in one piece, then thinly slice each half crosswise. Cut each leg at the joint, then carve the meat from the thigh and drumstick.

7. If you're serving two small turkeys, cook the first one early in the day. Carve it, arrange it on an ovenproof platter and cover it with foil. Meanwhile, roast the second turkey. Just before serving, set the platter in a 350° oven. Use the whole bird for show and pass the carved turkey. Carve the second bird once everyone's had a first serving.

about 3 1/2 hours longer, or until an instant-read thermometer inserted in the thickest part of a thigh registers 165°; remove the foil for the last 15 minutes of roasting. Transfer the turkey to a carving board, cover loosely with foil and let rest for at least 30 minutes.

4. Pour the pan juices into a medium saucepan and skim the fat from the surface. Set the roasting pan over 2 burners and cook the vegetables over moderately high heat, stirring frequently, until golden, about 5 minutes. Add the remaining 4 tablespoons of butter and the flour and cook, stirring frequently, until the vegetables are coated with the flour mixture and lightly browned, about 2 minutes. Stir in half of the Rich Turkey Stock and cook, scraping up any browned bits from the bottom of the pan, until the gravy thickens a bit.

5. Strain the gravy into the pan juices in the saucepan, pressing on the vegetables; discard the vegetables. Add the remaining turkey stock to the gravy and cook over moderate heat until thickened and reduced to 4 cups, about 25 minutes. Season with salt and pepper and transfer to a large gravy boat. Carve the turkey, arrange on a platter and serve with the stuffing and gravy.

—Bruce and Eric Bromberg

WINE Choose an intense, fruity-earthy Pinot Noir from California, such as the 1998 Robert Sinskey Carneros Napa Valley. It has acidity, sweet-tart fruit and spice to accent the turkey.

Grilled Turkey

10 TO 12 SERVINGS

If you need to cook two turkeys and have just one small oven, a grill offers another cooking site. This grilled bird tastes oven-roasted. Note that brining the bird takes 10 to 12 hours.

- 1½ cups kosher salt
- 1 cup sugar
- One 12- to 14-pound turkey—neck, wing tips and giblets reserved, cavity fat removed
- 2 medium onions, coarsely chopped
- 1 carrot, coarsely chopped
- 1 celery rib, coarsely chopped
- 3 tablespoons unsalted butter, melted

1. In a large stockpot or plastic tub, mix 1½ gallons of water with the salt and sugar; stir to dissolve the salt and sugar. Add the turkey to the brine, breast side down, and refrigerate for 10 to 12 hours. Don't worry if a small portion of the turkey is not submerged in the brine.

2. Remove the turkey from the brine, rinse it in cold water and pat dry with paper towels. Discard the brine.

3. Light a charcoal grill using 5 pounds of charcoal briquettes. Rake the hot coals into 2 piles on opposite sides of the grill and replace the grill rack. Alternatively, turn the front and back burners of a gas grill to high and preheat to 400°; leave the center burner off. Turn the burners down to medium (350°) just before grilling the turkey.

4. Meanwhile, place half of the onions, carrot and celery in the turkey cavity. Using kitchen string, tie the turkey legs together, then bring the string around the turkey and tie the wings at the breast. Scatter the remaining onions, carrot and celery in a large, sturdy, disposable roasting pan. Brush the turkey with the melted butter and set it in the roasting pan, breast side down. Pour 2 cups of water into the pan.

5. Set the turkey on the grill. Cover and

cook with the vents open for 1 hour; do not open the grill. (If using a charcoal grill, heat another 1½ pounds of charcoal in a chimney starter after 45 minutes; then remove the pan and rack from the grill and stir the coals; add half of the new coals to each pile and replace the rack and pan.) Turn the turkey breast side up and baste with the pan juices. Continue to grill, covered, for about 1½ hours longer; the turkey is done when an instant-read thermometer inserted in an inner thigh registers 170°.

6. Transfer the turkey to a carving board, cover loosely with foil and let rest for 20 to 30 minutes. Reserve the pan juices for making the gravy.

—Pam Anderson

Turkey Shepherd's Pie with Two-Potato Topping

4 SERVINGS

This recipe makes a large pie, but you can also prepare the dish in individual 1½-cup ramekins. Check them for doneness after 20 minutes.

- 3 tablespoons unsalted butter, 1 tablespoon melted
- 1 medium onion, finely chopped
- 1 medium celery rib, finely chopped
- 1 medium carrot, finely chopped
- 4 cups diced turkey meat
- 1 cup turkey gravy
- 1 tablespoon chopped flat-leaf parsley
- 2 teaspoons finely chopped sage
- Salt and freshly ground pepper
- 2 cups mashed potatoes
- 1 cup mashed sweet potatoes
- 2 tablespoons minced chives
- 1 large egg, beaten

1. Melt 2 tablespoons of the butter in a large skillet. Add the onion, celery and carrot and cook over low heat until softened, about 12 minutes. Add the turkey and cook, stirring, until heated through. Add the gravy and cook until bubbling. Remove from the heat, stir in the parsley and sage and season with

salt and pepper. Transfer the filling to a 9-by-12-inch baking dish and let cool.

2. Preheat the oven to 400°. In a bowl, blend the mashed white and sweet potatoes with the chives. Season the mashed potatoes with salt and pepper and beat in the egg. Spread the potatoes over the filling and brush the top with the melted butter. Bake in the upper third of the oven for about 30 minutes, or until the topping is lightly browned and the filling is bubbling. Let the pie stand for about 10 minutes before serving. *—Jimmy Bradley*

WINE A smooth, generous Chardonnay will echo the texture of the creamy gravy and the soft mashed potato topping in this comforting baked pie. Look for an inexpensive, fruity wine, such as the 1999 Rosemount or the 1999 Lindemans Bin 65, both from southeastern Australia.

Grilled Quail with Chicories and Almonds

2 SERVINGS

The shallot marinade is good with any game bird or poultry. You can also substitute your favorite nuts and nut oil for the almonds and almond oil.

- ½ cup dry white wine
- ⅓ cup olive oil
- 2 shallots, coarsely chopped
- 2 garlic cloves, coarsely chopped
- 4 partially boned quail
- ¼ cup, plus 1 tablespoon almond oil
- 2 tablespoons sherry vinegar
- 1 teaspoon Dijon mustard
- Salt and freshly ground pepper
- ½ cup whole blanched almonds
- ¼ pound mixed chicories, such as frisée, radicchio and Belgian endive, torn into bite-size pieces (4 cups)
- 1 ripe but firm pear—peeled, cored and cut into ½-inch dice

1. In a shallow baking dish, mix the wine with the olive oil, shallots and garlic. Add the quail, turn to coat and let marinate at room temperature for 1 hour.

Turkey Shepherd's Pie with Two-Potato Topping

2. In a small bowl, combine ¼ cup of the almond oil with the vinegar and mustard. Season with salt and pepper.

3. In a small skillet, heat the remaining 1 tablespoon of almond oil. Add the almonds and cook over moderate heat until browned on both sides, about 3 minutes per side. Put on a plate to cool.

4. Light a grill or preheat a grill pan. Remove the quail from the marinade and scrape off most of the shallots and garlic. Season the quail with salt and pepper and grill, breast side down, over a hot fire or high heat until nicely charred, about 3 minutes. Turn and grill until the breast is pink throughout, about 1½ minutes more. Transfer the quail to a plate.

5. In a medium bowl, toss the chicories with the almonds and pear. Add half of the vinaigrette and toss well. Mound the salad on plates, set a quail on top and drizzle with the remaining vinaigrette. *—Bill Telepan*

WINE A young, dry rosé, such as the 1999 Wölffer Rosé from Long Island, will complement all the ingredients in this salad.

pork veal
chapter 9

Pork Chops with Mustard and Canadian Bacon

red chiles

Dried chiles, like dried herbs, have a more concentrated and complex flavor than fresh ones. When buying dried chiles, look for brilliantly or deeply colored peppers that are intact (broken chiles quickly lose their aromatic oils), free of spotting and somewhat pliable (they should feel like slightly stiff fruit leather). If kept in an airtight container in a cool, dark place, dried chiles should retain their flavor for as long as six months. Generally, they should be roasted in a skillet or in the oven, then chopped or used whole.

Pork Chops with Mustard and Canadian Bacon

4 SERVINGS

Cooking the chops *en papillote* makes them amazingly moist and tender.

Four ½-inch-thick rib pork chops (2 pounds)

Kosher salt and freshly ground pepper

2 tablespoons plus 2 teaspoons Dijon mustard

½ teaspoon thyme leaves, plus 4 tiny sprigs for garnish

4 slices Canadian bacon (2½ ounces)

1. Preheat the oven to 400°. Set each pork chop on a square of foil large enough to wrap it in. Season the pork chops with salt and pepper, then spread 1 side of each with ½ tablespoon of the mustard and sprinkle with a pinch of thyme. Cover each chop with a slice of Canadian bacon and top with ½ teaspoon of mustard and a thyme sprig.

2. Wrap the pork chops in the foil, crimping the foil to seal tightly. Set the parcels on a baking sheet. Bake for 20 minutes; the pork will still be slightly pink in the center. Remove the baking sheet from the oven and let the pork chops stand for 5 minutes. Discard the foil and serve the pork chops with their juices. —*Josette Batteault*

WINE The mustard glaze and smoky bacon call for a light, fruity red or an aromatic, full-bodied white. Great choices include a Beaujolais, such as the 1996 Olivier Ravier La Madone Fleurie, and a Viognier, such as the 1998 Domaine Canterelles Vin de Pays du Gard.

Pineapple and Red Chile–Glazed Baby Back Ribs

4 SERVINGS

Using small whole dried red chiles rather than crushed red pepper is important because whole chiles retain their biting flavor. Garlic is also critical: When added to pineapple, it creates a lovely balance between savory and sweet. This sauce can be used to glaze grilled pork chops, chicken and shrimp.

1 cup finely diced ripe pineapple

4 garlic cloves, minced

2 dried red chiles, seeded and finely chopped

1 teaspoon minced fresh ginger

Two 1½-pound racks of pork baby back ribs

Salt and freshly ground pepper

1. Preheat the oven to 400°. In a small bowl, combine the pineapple, garlic, chiles and ginger. Set the racks in a small roasting pan, meaty side up, and season generously with salt and pepper. Spoon half of the pineapple mixture over each rack of ribs, spreading it evenly. Pour ½ cup of water into the pan, cover tightly with foil and roast for 30 minutes. Remove the pan from the oven and raise the temperature to 500°.

2. Uncover the ribs and baste them with the pan juices. Roast them on the top rack of the oven for 15 minutes, rotating the pan and basting every 5 minutes with the pan juices, until nicely glazed on top. Let the ribs rest for 10 minutes, then cut down between them and serve. —*Marcia Kiesel*

WINE Only Zinfandel has the fruit and spice to stand up to the sweetness and heat in this dish. Look for the 1997 Dry Creek Vineyard Heritage Clone or the 1997 Kenwood Jack London.

Goodell's Roasted Pork Belly with Asparagus, Morels and Peas

4 SERVINGS 👑

ROASTED PORK BELLY

2 tablespoons extra-virgin olive oil
1 pound meaty fresh pork belly with skin, cut into 4 pieces
Salt and freshly ground pepper
1 large carrot, cut into ½-inch dice
1 leek, white and tender green parts, thinly sliced
1 small onion, thinly sliced
1 celery rib, thinly sliced
2 cups veal demiglace
2 cups water
4 thyme sprigs
3 flat-leaf parsley sprigs
2 bay leaves
¼ teaspoon whole black peppercorns

VEGETABLE GARNISHES

2 cups Basic Chicken Stock (p. 98) or canned low-sodium broth
1 pound asparagus, trimmed to 4-inch tips
12 medium dried morels (1½ ounces)
3 tablespoons plus 1 teaspoon extra-virgin olive oil
3 large shallots, finely chopped

1 cup heavy cream
Salt and freshly ground pepper
1 slice bacon
⅓ cup frozen baby peas
2 teaspoons unsalted butter

I. PREPARE THE PORK BELLY: Preheat the oven to 275°. Heat the oil in a medium enameled cast-iron casserole. Season the pork belly with salt and pepper and cook over moderate heat until golden brown all over, about 15 minutes. Transfer to a plate. Add the carrot, leek, onion and celery to the casserole and cook, stirring until lightly browned, about 5 minutes.

2. Return the pork to the casserole. Add the demiglace, water, thyme, parsley, bay leaves and peppercorns and bring to a simmer. Cover and bake for about 4 hours, or until the meat is fork-tender and the juices are reduced to 1 cup. Transfer the pork to a plate and refrigerate until cool, about 1 hour.

Strain the pan juices and skim off the fat. Boil until reduced to ½ cup, about 10 minutes. Cover and refrigerate.

3. PREPARE THE VEGETABLE GARNISHES: Bring 1½ cups of the chicken stock to a boil. Add the asparagus and cook until crisp-tender, about 3 minutes. Using a slotted spoon, transfer the asparagus to a bowl of ice water to cool; drain and pat dry.

4. Remove the stock from the heat, add the morels and let soften for 30 minutes. Remove the morels and rinse under cold water; pat thoroughly dry. Strain the stock through a coffee filter.

5. Heat 1 tablespoon of the olive oil in a medium saucepan. Add two-thirds of the chopped shallots and cook over moderately high heat until softened, about 2 minutes. Add the morels, reduce the heat to moderate and cook for 5 minutes, stirring frequently. Add the strained stock and simmer until

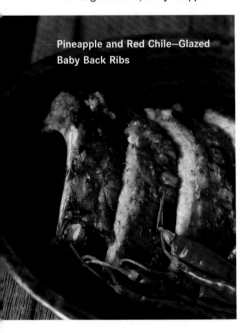

Pineapple and Red Chile—Glazed Baby Back Ribs

Goodell's Roasted Pork Belly with Asparagus, Morels and Peas

nearly evaporated, about 8 minutes. Add the cream and simmer over moderately low heat until reduced by half, about 20 minutes. Season with salt and pepper and keep warm.

6. In a small saucepan, cook the bacon in the 1 teaspoon olive oil over moderate heat until crisp and golden, about 6 minutes. Remove the bacon and reserve it for later use. Add the remaining chopped shallots to the pan and cook until translucent, about 2 minutes. Add half the peas and stir until coated with the fat. Add the remaining ½ cup chicken stock and cook over moderately high heat until the liquid is reduced by two-thirds, 8 to 10 minutes. Transfer the mixture to a blender, add the remaining peas (saving a few for garnish if you like) and puree until very smooth. Strain the sauce through a fine sieve. Return it to the saucepan and bring just to a boil. Whisk in the butter and season with salt and pepper.

7. Preheat the oven to 275°. Heat 1 tablespoon of the olive oil in a medium ovenproof nonstick skillet. Add the pork belly, skin side down, and cook until lightly browned, about 1 minute. Roast the pork belly in the oven for about 20 minutes, or until almost all the fat is rendered and the skin is crisp.

8. Meanwhile, rewarm the pork pan juices. Heat the remaining 1 tablespoon of olive oil in a medium skillet. Add the asparagus and cook over high heat until warmed through, about 2 minutes. Season with salt and pepper.

9. Place a piece of pork belly in the center of 4 large warmed plates and spoon the pan juices around the meat. Spoon the creamed morels to one side and the pea sauce on the other side. Garnish with the asparagus and serve.
—*Tim Goodell*

MAKE AHEAD The recipe can be made a day ahead through Step 6. Wrap the components separately and refrigerate. Reheat the morels and the pea sauce gently; do not let them boil.

Ted's Fiery Barbecued Pork Tenderloin
6 SERVINGS

Concentrated cane syrup tempers the chile's heat and binds the ingredients of the marinade.

⅓ cup bourbon
⅓ cup water
1 tablespoon sherry vinegar
1 tablespoon minced fresh ginger
1 habanero chile, seeded and minced (see Note)
1 teaspoon minced garlic
Two ¾-pound pork tenderloins
¼ cup cane syrup or unsulphured molasses
¼ cup ketchup
1 tablespoon vegetable oil, plus more for brushing
Salt and freshly ground pepper

1. In a shallow bowl, combine the bourbon, water, vinegar, ginger, chile and garlic. Add the pork and turn to coat. Marinate at room temperature for 1 hour, turning a few times.

2. Preheat the oven to 450°. Remove the pork from the marinade; brush off any excess and pat dry. In a small saucepan, boil the marinade over high heat until reduced by one-third, 7 to 8 minutes. Add the cane syrup and ketchup and cook over moderate heat until thickened, about 5 minutes.

3. Heat the 1 tablespoon of oil in an ovenproof skillet. Brush the tenderloins lightly with oil and season them with salt and pepper. Sear the pork in the skillet over high heat, turning occasionally until browned, 3 to 4 minutes. Pour the barbecue sauce over the pork and transfer the skillet to the oven. Roast for about 12 minutes, or until cooked through, turning the meat in the sauce. Transfer the pork to a work surface, cover with foil and let stand for at least 5 minutes. Thickly slice the meat across the grain and serve with any remaining sauce.   —*Ted Lee*

NOTE If you can find a *datil* pepper, use it in place of the habanero. Roast it

in the red

Ketchup has reclaimed its position as America's best-selling condiment, an honor temporarily ceded to salsa. Some revealing facts about this ubiquitous sauce:

• Average rate at which ketchup travels as it leaves the bottle: 25 miles per hour
• Technique preferred by women when using ketchup: dipping
• Technique preferred by men when using ketchup: covering up
• Former U.S. president who covered up his cottage cheese with ketchup: Richard Nixon
• Former U.S. president who declared ketchup to be a vegetable: Ronald Reagan
• Approximate number of tomatoes to make a 14-ounce bottle: 25
• Percentage of American homes with ketchup in the kitchen: 97
• Sweet spot to tap on the Heinz bottle to release the ketchup faster: the "57" on the neck
• Average bottles of ketchup each American consumes in a year: 3
• Number of calories and grams of fat in a tablespoon of ketchup: 15 calories, 0 grams fat
• Origin of the word "ketchup": Chinese (Amoy dialect) *ketsiap*—pickled fish sauce
• U.S. region that consumes the most ketchup: the South
• Year that Heinz introduced its bottled ketchup: 1876   —*Lisa Lee*

over a flame, then peel it, discard the seeds and finely chop it.

MAKE AHEAD The barbecued pork can be refrigerated and sliced the next day for sandwiches.

WINE A simple, round, fruity West Coast Chardonnay will set off the sweet and caramelized flavors in this dish. Try the 1997 Meridian from California or the 1997 Columbia Crest from Washington State.

Barbecued Pork Loin

4 TO 6 SERVINGS

The sauce in this recipe tastes wonderful on duck breasts or chicken, too.

¾ cup ketchup
⅓ cup soy sauce
¼ cup honey
3 tablespoons red wine vinegar
2 tablespoons Dijon mustard
1 teaspoon vegetable oil
One 2-pound pork loin, tied
Salt and freshly ground pepper

1. In a small bowl, stir the ketchup with the soy sauce, honey, vinegar and mustard until combined.

2. Preheat the oven to 375°. In a large ovenproof skillet, heat the oil until shimmering. Season the pork loin with salt and pepper and sear it in the skillet over moderately high heat until browned all over, about 6 minutes. Transfer the skillet to the oven and roast the pork for 30 minutes. Slather the pork with some of the barbecue sauce and roast 10 to 15 minutes longer, or until an instant-read thermometer inserted in the center of the roast registers 140°. Transfer the pork loin to a cutting board and let rest for 10 minutes.

3. Add the remaining sauce to the skillet and cook over moderately high heat, scraping up any browned bits, until the sauce is slightly caramelized, 5 to 6 minutes. Thinly slice the pork and serve the warm barbecue sauce alongside. —*Christian Delouvrier*

MAKE AHEAD The sauce can be refrigerated for up to 1 week.

Passion Fruit and Ginger Glazed Pork Tenderloin

6 SERVINGS ✻

Two 1-pound pork tenderloins
Salt and freshly ground pepper
Passion Fruit and Ginger Sauce
   (recipe follows)

1. Light a grill or preheat the broiler. Season the pork with salt and pepper and brush it with the Passion Fruit and Ginger Sauce. Grill or broil the pork for about 15 minutes, turning it and basting it with the sauce several times, until the meat is browned on the outside and just cooked through.

2. Transfer the tenderloin to a cutting board and let it stand for 10 minutes. Carve the pork into thick slices and pass the remaining sauce at the table.
—*Maricel Presilla*

WINE The exotic fruitiness, hints of ginger and mild sweetness of a medium-bodied Gewürztraminer make it a good match for the hot spices and sweetness of the sauce. Choose an example that has enough body to stand up to the smoky flavor of the pork, such as the 1997 Rudolf Muller QbA Pfalz from Germany or the 1997 Murphy-Goode from California.

PASSION FRUIT AND GINGER SAUCE

MAKES ¾ CUP

Intensely perfumed, and with a hint of guava and jasmine, passion fruit juice is a signature ingredient of the American tropics. Its lush flavor is lovely in sauces for pork and grilled or pan-seared fish, shrimp and scallops.

1 cup passion fruit juice (see Note) or unsweetened pineapple juice
3 tablespoons sugar
3 large garlic cloves, smashed
1½ teaspoons finely grated fresh ginger
½ habanero chile or 1 whole jalapeño, seeded and coarsely chopped
1½ tablespoons snipped fresh chives

Barbecued Pork Loin

1½ tablespoons minced
red bell pepper

1½ tablespoons cider vinegar

Pinch of ground cumin

Salt and freshly ground pepper

1. In a small saucepan, combine the passion fruit or pineapple juice with the sugar and bring to a boil over high heat. Reduce the heat to moderate and simmer until the juice is reduced by half and thickened slightly, approximately 15 minutes.

2. Transfer the juice to a blender or food processor and let cool slightly. Add the garlic, ginger and habanero chile and blend until smooth, about 30 seconds. Transfer the sauce to a medium bowl and stir in the chives, red bell pepper, vinegar and cumin. Season the passion fruit sauce with salt and pepper and let cool completely. —*M.P.*

NOTE Passion fruit juice is available in the freezer section of most Latin markets.

MAKE AHEAD The sauce can be refrigerated for up to 3 days.

Roast Pork with Fennel

6 TO 8 SERVINGS

Currently fashionable fennel pollen is used in this recipe, but you can substitute chopped fennel seeds.

4 bay leaves, minced

3 garlic cloves, finely chopped

1 tablespoon wild fennel pollen (see Note) or 1½ tablespoons finely chopped fennel seeds

1 teaspoon finely chopped rosemary

1 tablespoon sea salt

½ teaspoon freshly ground pepper

1 cup plus 2 tablespoons dry white wine

One 4-pound center-cut boneless pork loin roast, preferably with the rind attached

1. Preheat the oven to 450°. In a small bowl, combine the bay leaves with the garlic, fennel pollen and rosemary. Stir in the salt, pepper and 2 tablespoons of the wine. Rub the marinade

over the pork and tie the roast at 1-inch intervals with kitchen string.

2. Set the roast on a rack in a medium roasting pan and cook for 30 minutes, basting with the remaining wine every 15 minutes. Reduce the oven temperature to 350° and roast for another 30 minutes, basting periodically. Turn the oven down to 300° and roast for 1 hour longer, or until an instant-read thermometer inserted in the thickest part of the meat registers 145°. Transfer the roast to a cutting board and let stand for 20 minutes. Remove and discard the strings.

3. Pour the juices from the roasting pan into a small saucepan and skim off as much of the fat as possible. Rewarm the pan juices and season with salt and pepper. Thinly slice the pork and arrange on a platter or plates. Drizzle with the pan juices and serve.

—*Nancy Harmon Jenkins*

NOTE Fennel pollen is available from Tavolo (800-700-7336).

WINE Pork can often be matched with a red or a white, but the rosemary and fennel rub on this succulent roast suggests a flavorful, full-bodied white. Both Mastroberardino's 1997 Fiano di Avellino Radici and its 1997 Greco di Tufo have the requisite richness.

Tuscan Pork Roast with Herbed Salt

8 SERVINGS, WITH LEFTOVERS

This is a wonderful dish for a dinner party. Remove the rib bones in one piece and use them as a rack on which to roast the loin, which will add flavor to both the meat and the pan juices. The butcher can bone the rack, but be sure to ask for the bones and scraps.

One 7-pound pork loin, boned and trimmed of visible fat, bones reserved in 1 piece

Tuscan Herbed Salt (recipe follows)

Four 10-inch-long sturdy rosemary branches

Coarse salt

4 ounces thinly sliced meaty pancetta

1 teaspoon extra-virgin olive oil

2 cups dry white wine

Freshly ground pepper

1. Pat the pork loin thoroughly dry. Using a long-handled wooden spoon, pierce a hole through the center of the loin. Using your fingers and the wooden spoon handle, stuff 3 tablespoons of the Tuscan Herbed Salt into the hole in the roast. Insert 1 of the rosemary sprigs in each end. Mix the remaining 1 tablespoon of Tuscan Herbed Salt with 1½ teaspoons of coarse salt and rub it all over the roast.

2. Cover the pork roast with the pancetta and top with the remaining rosemary sprigs. Tie the roast at 1-inch intervals to give it a neat shape. Transfer to a platter, cover with plastic wrap and refrigerate for at least 2 hours or for up to 24 hours. Bring to room temperature before cooking.

3. Preheat the oven to 450°. Set the rack of rib bones in a large roasting pan. Unwrap the pork roast, pat it dry and rub it with the olive oil. Place the roast on the rack and roast for 15 minutes. Remove the pan from the oven, turn the pork roast over and baste it with a few tablespoons of the wine. Return the roast to the oven, reduce the temperature to 350° and cook for about 1½ hours, turning the roast and basting it with wine every 20 minutes; reserve ½ cup of wine for the sauce. The roast is done when an instant-read thermometer inserted in the center registers 145°.

4. Transfer the roast and rack to a platter and pour the pan juices into a glass measuring cup. Skim off as much of the fat that rises to the surface as possible. Set the roasting pan over 2 burners on moderate heat; when it starts to sizzle, add the reserved ½ cup of wine and cook for 2 minutes, scraping up the drippings from the bottom of the pan. Pour the pan juices into the measuring cup and let the fat rise to the surface. Skim off the fat again and season the sauce with salt and pepper. Remove the strings and carve the roast into thin slices. Serve the pork roast with the pan sauce. —*Sally Schneider*

ONE 5-OUNCE SERVING Calories 323 kcal, Total Fat 15.0 gm, Saturated Fat 5.1 gm, Carbohydrates 0.8 gm

WINE The spicy, salty rub on the roasted pork suggests an assertive, fruity red with acidity. Look for the 1998 Flora Springs Napa Valley Sangiovese or the 1995 Tiefenbrunner Merlot from Italy.

TUSCAN HERBED SALT

MAKES ¼ CUP

You can use this herbed salt to season all kinds of roasts, from pork to veal to guinea hen. It's also good on simply cooked vegetables, like green beans and potatoes. You can vary the herbs, using thyme and oregano, for instance, instead of sage and rosemary. This recipe can be doubled or tripled.

- 1 garlic clove
- 1 tablespoon sea salt
- 30 sage leaves

Leaves from 2 sprigs of rosemary

Chop the garlic clove with the sea salt. Chop the sage and rosemary together, then chop them with the sea salt. Use the herbed salt right away, or let it dry and store it in an airtight jar for 1 month. —*S.S.*

Pot-Roasted Pork Loin in Red Wine

6 SERVINGS

One 3-pound pork loin roast, tied
Salt and freshly ground pepper

- 3 tablespoons extra-virgin olive oil
- 2 ounces thinly sliced lean salt pork or pancetta, cut into thin strips
- 2 medium onions, thinly sliced
- 4 garlic cloves, crushed
- 2 large carrots, thinly sliced
- 1 large celery rib, thinly sliced
- 2 cups dry red wine

- 2 large bay leaves, minced
- 1 tablespoon minced sage leaves
- 1 tablespoon minced thyme leaves

1. Preheat the oven to 350°. Season the pork roast lightly with salt and generously with pepper, rubbing the seasonings into the meat. In an enameled cast-iron casserole just large enough to hold the roast, heat the oil until shimmering. Add the roast and cook over moderate heat until well browned all over. Transfer the roast to a large plate.

2. Add the salt pork to the casserole and cook over low heat until softened but not browned. Add the sliced onions, crushed garlic, and the carrots and celery and cook the vegetables over moderate heat, stirring occasionally, until they are very tender, about 20 minutes. Add the wine, the bay leaves, sage and thyme and bring to a boil. Remove from the heat.

3. Carefully set the roast, fat side up, in the casserole. Cover the casserole and cook in the oven for 30 minutes. Turn the roast, and if there is very little liquid left in the pan, add ½ cup of water or more to keep the vegetables moistened. Cook for about 20 minutes longer, or until an instant-read thermometer inserted in the center of the roast registers 150°.

4. Transfer the roast to a carving board, cut and discard the strings and cover the pork loosely with aluminum foil. If the pan juices are thin, boil them over high heat until thickened. Season with salt and pepper. Slice the roast and serve with the vegetables.

—*Nancy Harmon Jenkins*

WINE This richly flavored dish is best matched by an equally rich red with deep flavors and some tannin or oak. Two excellent Sardinian examples are the 1992 Sella & Mosca Marchese di Villamarina, made from 100 percent Cabernet, and the 1997 Argiolas Kore, made from a blend of several red grapes.

Pork and Clam Cataplana

8 SERVINGS

This dish relies on a lot of good Portuguese olive oil; with the wine, it creates a delicious sauce to soak up with crusty Portuguese bread. This recipe originated in the southern Algarve region, where cooks use a special copper pan called a *cataplana*. If you don't have one, use a deep skillet with a tight lid.

- 6 large garlic cloves, smashed
- 1 tablespoon plus 1 teaspoon sweet paprika
- 2½ teaspoons crushed red pepper

Sea salt

- ¾ cup pure olive oil
- 2 pounds boneless pork loin, cut into ½-inch dice
- ¾ cup extra-virgin olive oil
- 1 medium onion, finely chopped
- 2 cups dry white wine
- 3 pounds Manila clams or cockles, scrubbed and rinsed
- ¼ cup finely chopped flat-leaf parsley

1. In a mini food processor, combine the garlic with the paprika, crushed red pepper and 2 teaspoons of salt and pulse until finely chopped. Add ¼ cup of the pure olive oil and process to a paste. Add the remaining ½ cup of pure olive oil and process until smooth. Transfer the marinade to a large bowl, add the pork and toss to coat. Cover and refrigerate for at least 8 hours or overnight, stirring occasionally.

2. Heat the extra-virgin olive oil in a large deep skillet. Add the pork and its marinade and cook over high heat, stirring occasionally, until the meat loses its pink color, 3 to 4 minutes. Using a slotted spoon, transfer the pork to a large bowl, leaving the oil in the skillet. Add the onion to the skillet and cook over high heat, stirring, until softened, about 5 minutes. Add the wine and boil until slightly reduced, about 10 minutes.

3. Add the clams to the skillet, cover

Pork and Clam Cataplana

and cook just until they begin to open, 3 to 4 minutes. Return the pork to the skillet, along with any juices, and cook until the clams are open and the meat is just cooked through, about 2 minutes longer. Sprinkle with the parsley and serve in deep bowls.

—*Emeril Lagasse*

WINE The spices and clams in this pork dish suggest a smooth, well-rounded white with intensity but little oak. Try a Portuguese Chardonnay, such as the 1997 Quinta de Pancas Estremadura or the 1998 Quinta de Cidro.

Braised Pork with Shallots and Potatoes

4 SERVINGS

You'll find the richly flavored rib end of a whole loin of pork at most supermarkets. It will have six small rib bones plus a flat blade bone, which you will have to carve around, but the delicious meat makes the effort worthwhile.

2 tablespoons pure olive oil
One 4½- to 5-pound pork rib end
   roast, chine bone removed
Salt and freshly ground pepper
12 large shallots, peeled, root ends
    lightly trimmed but left intact
 1 rosemary sprig
12 medium red potatoes (2 to 3
    ounces each), peeled and halved
Horseradish or mustard, for serving

1. In a large enameled cast-iron casserole, heat the olive oil it is until almost smoking. Season the pork with salt and pepper and put it in the hot oil, meaty side down. Brown the pork over moderate heat on the 3 meaty sides, about 4 minutes per side. Turn the pork so the rib bones are on the bottom. Add the shallots, rosemary and ½ cup of water. Cover and cook over low heat, turning the shallots occasionally, until the shallots are tender; start checking after 30 minutes.

2. Meanwhile, put the potatoes in a medium saucepan and cover with water. Add a large pinch of salt and bring to a boil. Boil over moderately high heat until almost tender, about 8 minutes. Drain.

3. When the shallots are tender, transfer them to a serving bowl. Add ¼ cup of water to the casserole and continue to braise the pork for 1 hour longer, or until an instant-read thermometer inserted in the center registers 145°. Transfer the pork to a carving board, cover loosely with foil, and let rest while you make the sauce.

4. Pour the pan juices into a glass measuring cup and discard the rosemary. Skim off the fat from the juices and reserve in a bowl. Add 3 tablespoons of the reserved fat to the casserole and heat. Add the shallots, season with salt and pepper and cook over moderate heat until lightly browned, about 3 minutes; return to the bowl and cover.

5. Add 1 more tablespoon of the reserved fat to the casserole. Add the potatoes, cut side down, and season with salt and pepper. Add 2 tablespoons of water, cover and cook until the potatoes are tender and browned on the bottom, about 8 minutes. Using a metal spatula, scrape the potatoes from the casserole and add them to the shallots.

6. Add ¼ cup of water to the casserole and boil over high heat, scraping up the browned bits on the bottom with a wooden spoon. Add the pan juices and bring to a boil. Strain into a sauceboat and season with salt and pepper. Carve the roast and serve with the potatoes and shallots. Pass the pan juices and condiments at the table.

—*Lydie Marshall*

WINE The intense flavors of the pork and the rosemary-scented sauce call for a rich red. Choose a thick-textured, spicy Rhône wine with good fruit, such as the 1998 Domaine des Amouriers Vacqueyras or the 1998 Domaine Le Sang des Cailloux Vacqueyras.

Roast Leg of Pork with Fresh Herbs and Fennel Seeds

12 SERVINGS, WITH LEFTOVERS

This behemoth of a cut makes a spectacular holiday roast that won't break anyone's budget. To make carving easier, be sure to ask the butcher to remove the aitch bone (hip bone) and the main leg bone, leaving the shank bone intact. The pork is best when seasoned and refrigerated overnight before roasting, so be sure to plan accordingly.

- 3 tablespoons kosher salt
- 2 tablespoons fennel seeds
- 2 tablespoons chopped basil
- 2 tablespoons chopped thyme
- 2 tablespoons chopped garlic
- 2 tablespoons coarsely ground pepper
- 1 tablespoon chopped sage
- 1 tablespoon chopped rosemary
- 2 teaspoons ground coriander
- One 18- to 20-pound whole leg of pork with skin, partially boned, fat trimmed to ⅓ inch

1. In a mini food processor, combine the salt, fennel seeds, basil, thyme, garlic, pepper, sage, rosemary and coriander. Process to a paste. Spread one-third of the herb paste in the pocket where the hip and leg bones were. Using cotton twine, tie the roast in 5 places to give it a neat shape. With a sharp knife, make 3 dozen slits through the skin and fat all over the top of the roast. Rub the remaining herb paste all over the surface of the roast and into the slits. Refrigerate the roast overnight. Remove the meat from the refrigerator 2 hours before roasting.

2. Preheat the oven to 450°. Put the meat on a rack set in a large roasting pan and roast in the lower third of the oven for 20 minutes. Turn the pan around. Reduce the oven temperature to 325° and roast the meat for 3½ hours longer, turning the pan again after 1½ hours. Turn the pan one last time and roast the meat for 15 minutes more, or until an instant-read thermometer inserted in the thickest part registers 145°. If the skin isn't crisp, turn the heat up to 400° for the last 15 minutes. Remove from the oven, cover loosely with foil and let rest for 30 to 45 minutes; the final temperature will be 150° to 155°. Carve the roast and serve with the degreased pan juices.

—*Bruce Aidells*

WINE A dry, aromatic, spicy-fruity Gewürztraminer will accent the salty, garlicky flavors of the pork. Try either the 1997 Fetzer Mendocino County Dry Reserve from California or the 1998 Domaine Lucien Albrecht from Alsace.

Standing Pork Roast with Fresh Herbs

10 SERVINGS

Ask your butcher to remove the chine bone from the roast so you can easily slice the meat into chops for serving.

- 3 tablespoons extra-virgin olive oil
- 2 tablespoons minced garlic
- 2 tablespoons minced sage
- 2 bay leaves, minced
- Kosher salt and coarsely ground pepper
- Two 6-pound bone-in pork loin roasts, chine bones removed, loins trimmed of excess fat
- ¼ cup all-purpose flour
- 2 cups dry white wine
- 3 cups Basic Chicken Stock (p. 98) or canned low-sodium broth

1. Preheat the oven to 450°. In a bowl, combine the olive oil, garlic, sage, bay leaves and 1 tablespoon each of kosher salt and pepper. Make 8 small deep incisions in the top of each pork roast. Stuff the incisions with garlic paste and spread the remaining paste all over the roasts. Season with salt.

2. Heat a large roasting pan in the oven until it is very hot, about 10 minutes. Set the pork roasts in the hot pan, fat side up. Roast the pork for 15 minutes. Turn the oven down to 350° and continue to roast for about 1 hour and 15 minutes longer, rotating the pan twice; the roasts are done when an instant-read thermometer inserted in the thickest part of the meat registers 150°. Transfer the roasts to a carving board and cover loosely with foil.

3. Pour the pan juices into a glass measuring cup. Spoon 2 tablespoons of the fat back into the roasting pan. Spoon off the remaining fat from the pan juices and discard. Set the roasting pan over 2 burners on low heat. Whisk in the flour until a paste forms. Slowly add the wine and cook the sauce over moderate heat until thickened, scraping up any browned bits, about 4 minutes. Whisk in the stock

Menu
creamed oysters and leeks on toast (p. 43)

LARMANDIER CRAMANT GRAND CRU BLANC DE BLANCS BRUT NONVINTAGE CHAMPAGNE

---

standing pork roast with fresh herbs
spiced pear relish (p. 326)
cheese grits soufflé (p. 106)
corn bread stuffing with shrimp and andouille (p. 253)
wild and dirty rice (p. 311)
smoky greens (p. 272)

1997 J.-A. FERRET POUILLY-FUISSE

---

semolina soufflé cake with pistachio crème anglaise and tart cherry–pinot noir syrup (p. 332)
sweet-potato pie with praline sauce (p. 356)

1996 DOMAINE DU CLOS NAUDIN PHILIPPE FOREAU VOUVRAY DEMI SEC

is available at most supermarkets.

MAKE AHEAD The tamales can be prepared through Step 4 and frozen for up to 1 month in a sturdy plastic bag.

BEER These tamales are best suited to a full-flavored beer. Try the Brooklyn Brown Ale from Brooklyn Brewery or the Red Ale from Abita Brewery in Louisiana.

ESPRESSO BARBECUE SAUCE

MAKES ABOUT 2 CUPS

Espresso adds a jolt of rich taste to this unusual barbecue sauce, which works well with pork, beef and poultry, complementing and rounding out the flavor of the meat.

- 1 large onion, finely chopped
- 2 large garlic cloves, minced
- ¾ cup packed dark brown sugar
- 1 cup red wine vinegar
- 1 cup ketchup
- 1 cup brewed espresso
- 3 tablespoons molasses
- 2 tablespoons dry mustard mixed with 1 tablespoon water
- ¼ cup ancho chile powder
- 2 tablespoons Worcestershire sauce
- 2 tablespoons ground cumin

Pulled-Pork Tamales

- 1 teaspoon coarse salt
- 1 teaspoon freshly ground pepper

I. Combine all the ingredients in a medium saucepan and simmer them over moderately low heat, stirring occasionally, until the sauce has reduced by about half, approximately 45 minutes. Let cool completely, strain, then puree in a blender until smooth.

2. Serve the sauce right away or cover and refrigerate until ready to use.

—M.L.

MAKE AHEAD The Espresso Barbecue Sauce can be refrigerated in a jar for up to 3 months.

Pork Colombo

8 SERVINGS

Colombo is a spice blend named for the capital of Sri Lanka. It was introduced to the Caribbean by Indian and Sri Lankan laborers. Because *colombo* is not available in the United States, a mixture of curry powder, ginger and garlic is substituted in this recipe.

- 3 pounds boneless pork shoulder, cut into 1-inch pieces
- 2 tablespoons fresh lime juice

Sea salt and freshly ground pepper

- ¼ cup vegetable oil
- 2 onions, finely chopped
- 2 large garlic cloves, minced

One 1-by-2-inch piece fresh ginger, peeled and minced

- 1 tablespoon curry powder
- 1 teaspoon dark brown sugar
- 2 tablespoons finely chopped flat-leaf parsley
- 1 tablespoon snipped chives
- 1 teaspoon thyme leaves
- ½ habanero chile, seeded and minced
- 1½ cups water
- 1½ pounds large Yukon Gold potatoes, peeled and cut into 1-inch pieces
- 1½ pounds carrots, cut into 1-inch lengths

White rice, for serving

I. Put the pieces of pork shoulder in a large bowl, season them with salt and pepper and the lime juice and toss. Let the mixture stand for 30 minutes at room temperature.

2. Drain the pork and pat the pieces dry with paper towels. Heat 2 tablespoons of the vegetable oil in a large enameled cast-iron casserole. Add one-third of the pork and cook over moderate heat until browned all over, about 10 minutes. Using a slotted spoon, transfer the cooked pork to a large plate. Brown the remaining pork in 2 batches, adding each to the plate as it's done.

3. Add the remaining 2 tablespoons of oil to the casserole along with the onions, garlic and ginger and cook over moderately low heat, stirring frequently, until softened, about 8 minutes. Stir in the curry powder and brown sugar and cook for 1 minute. Add the parsley, chives, thyme and chile and cook just until fragrant, 1 to 2 minutes.

4. Return the pork, along with any accumulated juices, to the casserole, and stir until evenly coated with the seasonings. Add the water and bring to a simmer. Cover and cook the pork over low heat for 15 minutes. Add the potatoes and carrots, season with salt and pepper and cook until the meat and vegetables are tender, about 1 hour. Serve the pork hot in large bowls. Pass the white rice separately.

—Corinne Trang

MAKE AHEAD The Pork Colombo can be finished completely up to 2 days ahead. Cover and refrigerate. Once the stew has been thoroughly reheated for serving, leftovers can be kept for another two days.

WINE A fruity, off-dry Riesling will cool the hot spices in this dish and complement the sweet ingredients, too. Choose a citrusy Washington State bottling, such as the 1999 Hogue Cellars Johannisberg Riesling Columbia Valley or the 1999 Washington Hills White Riesling Columbia Valley.

Sausages in Red Wine Sauce

4 SERVINGS

- 2 tablespoons olive oil
- 3 large shallots, thinly sliced
- 2¼ cups full-bodied red wine
- ½ cup Basic Chicken Stock (p. 98) or canned low-sodium broth
- 1½ pounds assorted French- and German-style sausages
- 2 cups water
- 5 tablespoons cold unsalted butter, cut into tablespoons

Salt and freshly ground pepper
Potato Gratin (p. 299)

1. Heat 1 tablespoon of the olive oil in a medium saucepan. Add the shallots and cook until softened, 3 to 5 minutes. Add the wine and boil until reduced by half, about 10 minutes. Add the chicken stock and boil until reduced by one-third.

2. Meanwhile, in a medium enameled cast-iron casserole, heat the remaining 1 tablespoon of olive oil. Add the assorted sausages and cook over moderately high heat until browned, about 3 minutes per side. Add the water and bring it to a boil. Reduce the heat to low, cover and simmer until the sausages are cooked through, about 20 minutes.

3. Bring the wine sauce to a boil. Remove from the heat and whisk in the butter, 1 piece at a time. Season with salt and pepper. Cut the sausages into 2-inch pieces and arrange an assortment on each plate. Top with the sauce and serve with the Potato Gratin.

—*Marcia Kiesel*

Pork Burgers with Sage

8 SERVINGS

Use ground pork butt for juicier, more flavorful burgers, ground pork loin for leaner ones.

- ½ cup dry Marsala
- 1 tablespoon kosher salt
- 2½ pounds ground pork
- 3 tablespoons minced fresh sage
- 1 teaspoon freshly ground pepper

Pork Burgers with Sage

- ½ teaspoon *pimentón* (see Note)

Pure olive oil, for brushing

- 8 hamburger buns

1. In a small saucepan, combine the Marsala and salt and bring to a boil. Simmer over moderate heat until reduced by one-third, about 4 minutes. Let cool to room temperature.

2. In a large bowl, gently mix the pork with the Marsala, sage, pepper and *pimentón* until evenly seasoned. Shape the meat into 8 thick burgers.

3. Light the grill. Lightly brush the burgers on both sides with olive oil and grill over a moderately hot fire for about 6 minutes per side, or until nicely browned outside and barely pink inside. Serve hot, on the hamburger buns.

—*Daniel Bruce*

NOTE *Pimentón*, a smoked Spanish paprika, is available at many specialty markets.

Asian Meatballs

MAKES 12 MEATBALLS

Serve these meatballs with either chicken stock flavored with ginger and scallions or Chinese egg noodles and sautéed Asian vegetables, such as bok choy.

- 1 tablespoon vegetable oil
- 3 tablespoons thinly sliced scallions
- 3 tablespoons minced shallots
- 1½ teaspoons minced garlic
- 1 teaspoon finely grated, peeled fresh ginger
- 1 pound ground pork
- 1 large egg white, lightly beaten
- 1 tablespoon plus 2 teaspoons *kecep manis* (see Note) or sweet soy sauce
- 1 tablespoon minced cilantro
- 1 tablespoon minced basil
- 1 tablespoon minced mint

¾ teaspoon chile-garlic paste
½ teaspoon kosher salt
⅛ teaspoon freshly ground
    white pepper

1. Preheat the oven to 400°. Line a baking sheet with wax paper. Heat the oil in a medium skillet. Add the scallions, shallots, garlic and ginger and cook over moderate heat, stirring, until softened, about 4 minutes. Scrape the mixture into a medium bowl and let cool.
2. Add the ground pork to the bowl, along with the egg white, *kecep manis,* cilantro, basil, mint, chile-garlic paste, salt and white pepper and mix with your hands until thoroughly combined. Divide the mixture into 12 equal portions and roll into balls.
3. Transfer the meatballs to the prepared baking sheet and bake in the oven for 15 to 17 minutes, or until browned; Serve immediately.

—*Roger Hayot*

NOTE *Kecep manis,* Indonesian soy sauce, is available at Asian groceries.

Herbed Meat Loaf with Mushroom Gravy
8 SERVINGS
½ ounce dried porcini mushrooms
    (¾ cup)
1½ cups boiling water
3 tablespoons unsalted butter
1 large onion, finely chopped
5 large garlic cloves, minced
1 tablespoon finely
    chopped rosemary
1 tablespoon finely chopped
    thyme leaves
1 teaspoon finely chopped
    sage leaves
Six 1-inch-thick slices of Italian bread,
    crusts removed
1 pound ground beef
1 pound ground veal
1 pound ground pork
2 ounces Black Forest ham,
    finely chopped (½ cup)
3 large eggs, lightly beaten
Kosher salt

Freshly ground black pepper
1 tablespoon mayonnaise
1½ teaspoons Dijon mustard
Pinch of cayenne pepper
½ pound shiitake mushrooms,
    stemmed, caps thinly sliced
1 shallot, minced
1 cup Basic Chicken Stock (p. 98)
    or canned low-sodium broth
½ cup dry white wine
1 tablespoon all-purpose flour
    mixed with 2 tablespoons water

1. In a large glass measuring cup, soak the porcini in the boiling water until softened, about 20 minutes. Drain the porcini, reserving the soaking liquid. Rinse them briefly, pat dry and finely chop. Let the porcini soaking liquid settle, then pour it into a medium bowl, leaving the grit behind.
2. Preheat the oven to 350°. In a medium skillet, melt 2 tablespoons of the butter. Add the onion and cook over moderately high heat, stirring, until translucent, about 5 minutes. Add the garlic, chopped porcini and 2 tablespoons of the reserved porcini soaking liquid and cook over moderately low heat for about 5 minutes. Stir in the rosemary, thyme and sage and scrape the mixture into a large bowl; let cool.
3. Soak the bread in the remaining porcini liquid until evenly moistened, then squeeze dry and tear into small pieces. Reserve the porcini liquid for the gravy. Add the soaked bread to the large bowl, along with the ground beef, veal and pork and the ham and eggs. Season with 1 tablespoon of kosher salt and 1 teaspoon of black pepper. Knead the mixture with your hands until combined. Transfer the meat to a large enameled cast-iron baking dish or a small flameproof roasting pan and pat it firmly into a 10-by-6-inch oval loaf.
4. Mix the mayonnaise with the mustard and cayenne and brush over the meat loaf. Bake for 1½ hours, or until browned and firm. Using 2 large spatulas, transfer to a cutting board, cover

loosely with foil and keep warm. Set aside the baking dish.
5. Meanwhile, melt the remaining 1 tablespoon of butter in a medium skillet. Add the shiitake mushrooms and cook over moderate heat, stirring frequently, until softened, about 5 minutes. Add the shallot and cook until translucent, about 3 minutes. Add the chicken stock and porcini soaking liquid and simmer over moderate heat until reduced by half, 8 to 10 minutes.
6. Place the meat-loaf baking dish over moderately high heat and stir occasionally until the drippings start to brown, about 3 minutes. Add the wine and cook, scraping up any browned bits, until reduced by half, about 3 to 4 minutes. Strain the contents of the baking dish into the skillet, whisk in the flour mixture and boil until thickened, about 2 minutes. Season the gravy with salt and pepper. Cut the meat loaf into thick slices and pass the mushroom gravy at the table. —*Grace Parisi*
MAKE AHEAD The meat loaf and gravy can be kept refrigerated separately for up to 2 days.
WINE An intense, peppery and full-bodied Petite Syrah would pair well with this earthy, herb-filled meat loaf. Look for the 1997 Foppiano Petite Syrah from California or the 1996 Stags' Leap Winery Petite Syrah.

Fall River Boiled Dinner
8 SERVINGS
Any type of sausage can be substituted for the *linguiça,* a long, dry Portuguese sausage made with coarsely chopped pork, garlic and paprika.
4 whole chicken legs (about
    2½ pounds)
1 pound boneless beef chuck roast
1 pound boneless pork shoulder
½ pound *linguiça* or kielbasa
½ pound chorizo (about 4 links)
¼ pound meaty slab bacon
    in 1 piece
6 garlic cloves

menu

baked tomatoes stuffed with herbed rice (p. 284) | shrimp and green bean salad with marjoram (p. 39)

crisp celery salad with anchovy vinaigrette (p. 62) | 1998 VILLA SIMONE FRASCATI SUPERIORE

bucatini all'amatriciana (p. 111) | 1998 MASTROBERARDINO GRECO DI TUFO

saltimbocca di vitello | baked cabbage with cumin and pancetta (p. 273)

1995 COLLE PICCHIONI VIGNA DEL VASSALLO

almond-grappa cookies (p. 360) | whole-milk ricotta tart (p. 344) | CARAVELLA LIMONCELLO

Saltimbocca di Vitello

4 bay leaves

2 quarts water

Salt and freshly ground pepper

4 medium turnips, peeled and quartered

3 medium carrots, cut into 1-inch pieces

1 pound medium new potatoes, quartered

1 small green cabbage (about 1¾ pounds), cut into 8 wedges

¼ cup finely chopped flat-leaf parsley

White rice, for serving

1. In a large soup pot, combine the chicken, beef, pork, *linguiça*, chorizo, bacon, garlic and bay leaves; cover with the water. Season with salt and pepper and bring to a boil. Cover partially and cook over low heat until all of the meats are tender, about 1 hour and 15 minutes for the chicken, sausages and bacon and 1 hour and 45 minutes for the beef and pork. As the various meats are done, transfer them to a large platter and cover loosely with foil.

2. When all the meats have cooked, bring the liquid to a boil and add the turnips, carrots, potatoes and cabbage. Cover and cook over moderately low heat until the vegetables are tender, about 30 minutes. Stir in the parsley and season with salt and pepper.

3. Meanwhile, slice the beef and pork across the grain ½ inch thick and the sausages 1 inch thick. Cut the chicken legs into thighs and drumsticks. Arrange the meats on a large deep platter and cover loosely with foil. Pat the bacon dry and finely dice it. In a small skillet, fry the bacon over moderately high heat until crisp, about 5 minutes. Drain the bacon on paper towels.

4. Using a slotted spoon, transfer the vegetables to the platter; discard the bay leaves. Ladle some of the hot broth over the meat and vegetables and sprinkle with the bacon. Serve hot with rice.
—*Emeril Lagasse*

MAKE AHEAD The recipe can be prepared through Step 1 and refrigerated for up to 3 days. Reheat the meats in the broth before proceeding.

WINE The hearty flavors of the various meats in this dish suggest a medium-bodied red with bright fruit and a touch of tannin. Look for the 1997 Sogrape Aragones Alentejo Herdade do Peso or a Portuguese Cabernet, such as the 1995 J.P. Vinhos Terras do Sado Quinta do Bacalhôa.

Saltimbocca di Vitello

12 SERVINGS

Literally translated, *saltimbocca* means "jump in the mouth," a clear indication of just how good this classic dish tastes.

Twelve 2-ounce slices veal scaloppine, pounded very thin

24 sage leaves

12 thin slices prosciutto (about ½ ounce each)

All-purpose flour, for dredging

Salt and freshly ground pepper

¼ cup extra-virgin olive oil

4 tablespoons unsalted butter

¾ cup dry white wine

1. Lay the scaloppine on a work surface and top each slice with 2 sage leaves and a slice of prosciutto. Weave 2 toothpicks through each scaloppine

to secure the sage leaves and prosciutto.

2. In a large shallow dish, season the
flour with salt and pepper. In each of 2
large skillets, heat 2 tablespoons of
olive oil and 2 tablespoons of butter.
Dredge 6 of the scaloppine in the flour
and put 3 in each skillet. Cook over
moderately high heat until nicely
browned, about 1 minute per side.
Transfer the scaloppine to a large platter and cover loosely with foil. Repeat
with the remaining olive oil, butter and
6 scaloppine.

3. Add half the wine to each skillet and
stir to scrape up any browned bits from
the bottom. Pour the contents of 1 skillet into the other and boil the wine over
moderately high heat until slightly
reduced, about 1 minute. Remove the
toothpicks from the scaloppine, spoon
the sauce on top and serve at once.

—*Cesare Casella*

MAKE AHEAD The scaloppine can be
prepared through Step 1 and refrigerated overnight.

WINE Pair the saltimbocca with a red
that has plenty of flavor. Look for the
1995 Colle Picchioni Vigna del Vassallo from Paola di Mauro, a rich blend of
Merlot, Cabernet Sauvignon and Cabernet Franc.

Milanese Veal Cutlets

6 SERVINGS

- 2 tomatoes, coarsely chopped
- 3 tablespoons extra-virgin olive oil

Salt and freshly ground pepper

- 2 pounds boneless veal loin, sliced
  crosswise ½ inch thick
- 4 large eggs, lightly beaten
- 1½ cups crushed plain breadsticks or
  fine dry bread crumbs, preferably
  homemade

About ½ cup pure olive oil

- 2 heads Bibb or Boston lettuce,
  torn into bite-size pieces (6 cups)
- ¼ cup shredded basil leaves

Lemon wedges, for serving

1. In a large bowl, toss the tomatoes

with the extra-virgin olive oil and season
with salt and pepper.

2. Pound the veal ⅜ inch thick. Put the
eggs and bread crumbs in 2 separate
shallow bowls. Dip the veal cutlets in
the egg and then in the bread crumbs.

3. In each of 2 large skillets, heat ¼
cup of the pure olive oil until shimmering. Add the veal cutlets to the skillets
without crowding the pans and cook
over moderately high heat, turning
once, until golden and crisp, about 5
minutes. Transfer to a platter and keep
warm. Fry the remaining veal, adding
more oil to the skillet as necessary.
Lightly season the meat with salt.

4. Add the lettuce and basil to the
tomatoes and toss well; season with
salt and pepper. Transfer the salad to a
platter leaving most of the liquid behind.
Arrange the cutlets on the salad and
serve immediately with lemon wedges.

—*RL, Chicago*

WINE Go for a light but tart Piedmon-
tese red—the 1997 Franco Martinetti
Barbera Bric de Banditi or the 1996
Luigi Coppo Barbera d'Asti Pomorosso.

Veal Chops with Green Peppercorn Sauce

4 SERVINGS

Calvados is a refreshing change from
the brandy that is usually added to
green peppercorn sauces.

Four 12-ounce veal rib chops
  on the bone

Salt and freshly ground pepper

- 2 tablespoons unsalted butter
- 1 tablespoon olive oil
- 1 tablespoon plus 1 teaspoon green
  peppercorns in brine, drained
- 2 tablespoons Calvados
- ¼ cup Basic Chicken Stock (p. 98)
  or canned low-sodium broth
- ½ cup heavy cream

1. Preheat the oven to 450°. Season
the veal chops on both sides with salt
and pepper. In a large ovenproof skillet, melt 1 tablespoon of the butter in
the olive oil. When the foam subsides,

add 2 of the veal chops and cook over
moderate heat until nicely browned,
about 4 minutes per side. Transfer the
chops to a plate. Add the remaining 1
tablespoon of butter to the skillet and
brown the remaining 2 veal chops;
remove from the heat.

2. Return the veal chops from the
plate to the skillet, along with any
accumulated juices. Roast the chops
in the oven for 5 minutes, or until just
rosy in the center. Put on a warmed
platter and cover loosely with foil.

3. Set the skillet over moderately high
heat. Add the green peppercorns and
the Calvados. Carefully ignite the Calvados with a long match. When the
flames die down, add the chicken
stock and boil for 1 minute. Add the
cream and simmer until the sauce
thickens, about 3 minutes. Season the
sauce lightly with salt and pepper and
pour it over the veal chops. Serve
immediately.   —*Marcia Kiesel*

WINE A full-bodied California Chardonnay with hints of oak, such as the
1997 Morgan Reserve, will echo the
richness of the sauce.

Cizma's Grilled Veal Chop with Tasso, Foie Gras and Sorrel

4 SERVINGS ♔

An intense Pinot Noir syrup garnishes
the chops, adding a tart note that is a
perfect foil to the rich sauce. Use only
a few drops per serving.

- 2½ cups Pinot Noir
- 6 ounces fresh duck foie gras, veins
  removed, liver cut into ½-inch
  dice and chilled
- 2 teaspoons Cognac

Salt and freshly ground pepper

- 2 tablespoons unsalted butter
- 1 Rome or Granny Smith apple,
  cut into ½-inch dice
- 4 ounces tasso ham, cut into
  ½-inch dice
- 1 tablespoon minced garlic
- 1 tablespoon minced shallot
- 1 cup veal demiglace

Cizma's Grilled Veal Chop with Tasso, Foie Gras and Sorrel

Four 1½-inch-thick veal rib chops, rib
    bones frenched (1 pound each)
2 tablespoons canola oil
1 teaspoon minced flat-leaf parsley
1 teaspoon minced thyme
1½ cups (packed) stemmed small
    sorrel leaves or torn larger leaves
    (2 ounces)

1. In a small saucepan, boil 2 cups of the Pinot Noir over moderately high heat until reduced to 2 tablespoons, about 15 minutes. Scrape the syrup into a small bowl and reserve.

2. Put the foie gras in a shallow bowl and pour the Cognac over it. Season with salt and pepper and refrigerate for at least 30 minutes or overnight.

3. Melt the butter In a large skillet. Add the apple and cook over moderate heat, without stirring, until golden, about 4 minutes. Stir and cook for 1 minute longer. Add the tasso, garlic and shallot and cook, stirring, until the garlic starts to brown, about 3 minutes. Add the remaining ½ cup of Pinot Noir and boil until syrupy, about 3 minutes. Add the veal demiglace and simmer for 3 minutes longer. Remove from the heat.

4. Light a grill or preheat a grill pan. Brush the veal on both sides with the oil and season with salt and pepper. Grill over moderately hot fire or heat until lightly charred on the outside and pink in the center, about 4 minutes per side. Sprinkle with the parsley and thyme and transfer to a platter. Cover the platter loosely and keep warm.

5. Bring the sauce to a simmer over moderate heat. Add the foie gras and cook, stirring constantly, until some of it is melted but most of it retains its shape, about 3 minutes. Fold in the sorrel and cook until wilted, about 1 minute. Season the sauce with salt and pepper and remove from the heat.

6. Put the veal chops on warmed plates and spoon the sauce on top. With a teaspoon, dot each chop with a few drops of the Pinot Noir syrup and serve.

—Ted Cizma

Roasted Veal Chops with Grapes

4 SERVINGS ※

The vinegar here balances the sweetness of the grapes, which is intensified by roasting. As they cook, they break down to make a fruity sauce for the tender veal.

1 pound seedless red grapes
3 tablespoons sherry vinegar
2½ tablespoons unsalted butter,
    softened
½ teaspoon sugar
Salt and freshly ground pepper
Four 1-inch-thick veal rib chops
    (about ½ pound each)

1. Preheat the oven to 500°. On a sturdy rimmed baking sheet, toss the grapes with the vinegar, 1½ tablespoons of the butter and the sugar. Season them generously with salt and pepper and roast them for about 10 minutes, shaking the pan after 5 minutes, until the grapes are hot and the pan is sizzling.

2. Rub the veal chops with the remaining 1 tablespoon of butter and season them with salt and pepper. Push the grapes to one side of the baking sheet and set the veal chops on the sheet. Roast them for about 5 minutes, or until they're sizzling underneath. Turn the chops and roast for 5 minutes longer for medium rare meat. Transfer the veal chops to a warm platter and scrape the grapes and juices over them. Serve immediately. *—Melissa Clark*

MAKE AHEAD The grapes can be roasted up to 2 days ahead. Refrigerate them, along with all their juices. Bring to room temperature and reheat on the baking sheet for 2 minutes before proceeding to Step 2.

WINE An Italian Super-Tuscan blend, like the 1996 Tenuta del Terriccio Tassinaia, will balance the sweet-and-sour intensity of this full-flavored dish. Another good selection is a rich Syrah, such as the 1997 Jean-Luc Colombo Cornas Les Ruchets.

magnificent meats

These impressive cuts of meat are available at better supermarkets and butcher shops, but they may have to be ordered in advance.

Leg of pork If you can deal with its size (around 20 pounds), look for a leg with the skin attached to the lower two-thirds. The fat should be creamy white, the bone moist and the meat pale pink—never pale gray. Leg of pork is often available only during the holidays, even if special-ordered.

Rack of veal Make sure you're buying formula-fed veal and not "newborn calf" or "Bob veal." The meat should be pale pink to reddish pink, with white to ivory fat. Good brands are Provimi (Blue Delft brand), Plume de Veau and Dutch Valley. Range-fed veal is darker than formula-fed; the fat may be slightly yellow. The flavor is different from that of formula-fed veal, but quite good; however, since the meat can dry out, don't cook it beyond medium rare.

Roasted Rack of Veal

12 SERVINGS

The meat has to marinate overnight, so plan accordingly. Crisscrossing the two racks before roasting them makes for a dramatic presentation.

8 garlic cloves, quartered
12 sage leaves
1 tablespoon plus 1 teaspoon
    chopped thyme
1 tablespoon plus 1 teaspoon
    chopped rosemary
1 teaspoon fennel seeds
3 tablespoons extra-virgin olive oil
2 tablespoons kosher salt
2 teaspoons coarsely
    ground pepper
Two 6-bone 6- to 7-pound racks of
    veal—chine bones removed,
    fat trimmed to ¼ inch
    and ribs frenched
Truffle oil, for serving (optional)

1. In a mini food processor, combine

the garlic, sage, thyme, rosemary and fennel seeds and grind coarsely. Add the olive oil, salt and pepper and process to a paste. Rub the paste all over the racks. Set the racks in a roasting pan, cover with plastic wrap and refrigerate overnight. Remove the meat from the refrigerator 2 hours before roasting.

2. Preheat the oven to 450°. Arrange the racks back to back with the frenched bones crisscrossed and pointing upward. Roast in the lower third of the oven for 15 minutes. Reduce the temperature to 350° and continue to roast for about 1 hour and 10 minutes longer, or until an instant-read thermometer inserted in the thickest part of the meat in the center of one of the racks registers 130° for medium meat. Transfer the racks to a carving board, cover loosely with foil and let rest for 15 to 20 minutes; the final temperature will be 140° to 145°.

3. To serve, slice down between the rib bones and serve 1 chop per person. Sprinkle each chop with a few drops of truffle oil and serve. —*Bruce Aidells*

WINE The veal's subtle flavor calls for a light red or a big white with good fruit. The spicy-cherry 1998 Robert Mondavi Pinot Noir Napa Valley Reserve or the spicy-pear 1997 Kistler Chardonnay Sonoma Valley Kistler Vineyard will complement the herbal nuances of this dish.

Spring Stew of Veal and Carrots with White Asparagus

4 SERVINGS

Lightly cooked asparagus adds a fresh taste and a slightly crisp texture to a rich, slowly simmered stew.

- 1 tablespoon unsalted butter
- 1 tablespoon vegetable oil
- 2 pounds boneless veal shoulder, cut into 2-inch pieces

Salt and freshly ground pepper

Roasted Rack of Veal

- 4 large shallots, coarsely chopped
- 1 ounce sliced prosciutto, minced
- ¾ cup white wine, preferably Grüner Veltliner
- 5 cups Basic Chicken Stock (p. 98) or canned low-sodium broth
- 4 medium carrots, cut into 1-inch lengths
- 2 large thyme sprigs
- 1 pound white asparagus, peeled, or green asparagus
- ½ cup heavy cream

1. In a large enameled cast-iron casserole, melt the butter in the oil. Add half the veal, season with salt and pepper and cook over moderately high heat, turning, until browned on all sides; transfer to a plate. Repeat with the remaining meat.

2. Add the shallots and prosciutto to the casserole and cook over moderate heat, stirring, until the shallots are softened, about 3 minutes. Add the wine and cook over high heat until reduced by half, about 4 minutes. Return the veal and any accumulated juices to the casserole. Add the stock, carrots and thyme. Bring to a boil, then simmer over low heat until the veal is very tender, about 1½ hours.

3. Cook the asparagus in a saucepan of boiling salted water until tender, about 8 minutes. Drain; cut into 2-inch lengths.

4. Add the heavy cream to the casserole and simmer until slightly reduced and flavorful, about 5 minutes. Season with salt and pepper. Add the asparagus pieces, simmer 1 minute longer and serve. —*Marcia Kiesel*

MAKE AHEAD The stew can be prepared through Step 2 and refrigerated for up to 2 days. Reheat gently before continuing with the recipe.

beef lamb **game**
chapter 10

**Poached Beef Fillet with
Fines Herbes Dressing**

Poached Beef Fillet with Fines Herbes Dressing

6 SERVINGS

- 1 quart beef stock or 2 cups canned low-sodium broth mixed with 2 cups water
- 3 medium leeks, white and tender green parts, split lengthwise and tied in a bundle
- 12 large pearl onions, peeled
- 3 medium carrots, cut into 1-inch lengths on the diagonal
- 1 pound broccoli, separated into twelve 4-inch-long florets

Four 6-ounce zucchini, sliced crosswise 1 inch thick on the diagonal

- ⅓ cup finely chopped flat-leaf parsley
- 3 tablespoons finely chopped chives
- 2 tablespoons red wine vinegar
- 2 tablespoons water
- 1 tablespoon finely chopped tarragon
- ⅓ cup extra-virgin olive oil

Salt and coarsely ground pepper

Six 5-ounce beef tenderloin steaks, about 1 inch thick

1. Bring the beef stock to a boil in a large saucepan. Add the leeks, cover and simmer over low heat, turning a few times, until tender, about 5 minutes. Using a slotted spoon, transfer the leeks to a large glass baking dish and cover with foil. Repeat with the remaining vegetables, cooking the pearl onions and carrots for 12 minutes, then the broccoli for 4 minutes and the zucchini for 2 minutes. Discard the strings from the leeks and cut them crosswise into 1-inch lengths, keeping the pieces intact. Re-cover the baking dish with foil. Keep the stock covered.

2. In a small bowl, combine the parsley with the chives, vinegar, water and tarragon. Blend in the olive oil and season with salt and pepper.

3. Preheat the oven to 325°. Bring the stock back to a simmer. Add the steaks, cover and cook over low heat for 3 minutes. Turn and continue cooking until medium rare, about 3 minutes longer. Meanwhile, transfer the warm vegetables to the oven for about 3 minutes, or until warm.

4. Arrange the vegetables on the plates. Transfer the steaks to the plates and ladle a few tablespoons of the stock over them. Season generously with salt and pepper. Give the herb dressing a stir and spoon it over everything. Serve at once.—*Ibu Poilâne*

MAKE AHEAD The vinaigrette can be refrigerated for up to 3 hours.

Beef Tenderloin with Roasted Garlic Crust

10 SERVINGS

Because this tenderloin gets coated with a rub, it's best not to have your butcher tie the meat.

- 2 large heads garlic, outer skins removed
- ½ cup Dijon mustard

Two ½-inch-thick slices of peasant bread, crusts removed

- ½ cup canola oil

One 5-pound trimmed beef tenderloin, at room temperature

Salt and freshly ground pepper

- ½ cup dry red wine
- 2⅓ cups veal or beef stock
- 2 tablespoons thyme leaves
- 2 tablespoons flour mixed to a paste with 2 tablespoons unsalted butter

1. Preheat the oven to 425°. Wrap the garlic heads in a double layer of foil and bake for about 1 hour, or until soft. Lower the temperature to 350°.

2. Peel the roasted garlic. In a small bowl, mash the garlic cloves with a fork and mix in the mustard.

3. Toast the bread in the oven for 6 minutes, or until dry. Let cool, break into pieces and coarsely chop in a food processor. You should have ½ cup of crumbs. Add to the garlic and mustard mixture. Set oven at 425°.

4. Heat the oil in a large heavy roasting pan set over 2 burners on moderate heat until almost smoking. Season the tenderloin with salt and pepper. Add the tenderloin to the roasting pan and brown well on all sides, about 15 minutes total. Put on a platter to cool.

5. Pour off the fat from the roasting pan. Add the red wine to the pan and bring to a boil over moderately high heat, scraping up any browned bits from the bottom. Boil the wine until reduced by half, about 3 minutes. Add the wine to the stock and set aside.

6. Spread the garlic mixture all over the top and sides of the tenderloin. Press the thyme leaves into the garlic mixture. Transfer the tenderloin to the roasting pan and roast for 25 minutes, or until the crust is browned and an instant-read thermometer inserted in the center of the meat registers 125° for medium rare. Transfer to a cutting board and let rest for 15 minutes.

7. Set the roasting pan over 2 burners on moderately high heat. Pour in the wine and stock mixture and boil for 2 minutes, stirring with a wooden spoon.

menu
chopped salmon with capers and fennel crackers (p. 46)

1999 SEVEN HILLS VINEYARD ESTATE SEMILLON

sweet onion tart with bacon (p. 36) | 1999 BARREL FERMENTED SEMILLON

beef tenderloin with roasted garlic crust

winter vegetable pan-roast (p. 290) | 1998 WALLA WALLA VALLEY MERLOT

baby greens with cider vinaigrette (p. 51) | 1999 COLUMBIA VALLEY CHARDONNAY

double-baked chocolate cake (p. 340) | hazelnut ice cream (p. 385)

1997 PEPPER BRIDGE VINEYARD APOGEE

Beef Tenderloin with Roasted Garlic Crust, with
Winter Vegetable Pan-Roast (p. 290).

Pour the liquid into a medium saucepan and bring to a boil over moderate heat. Whisk in the flour paste until smooth and simmer, whisking frequently, until the gravy thickens, about 3 minutes. Season with salt and pepper and strain into a warmed gravy boat. Carve the roast into ⅓-inch-thick slices and pass the gravy at the table.

—*Jamie Guerin*

WINE Tenderloin demands a full-flavored red. Two terrific choices: the 1998 Seven Hills Vineyard Merlot and the 1998 Walla Walla Valley Merlot.

Bloody Mary Steaks

4 SERVINGS

- 2 cups tomato juice
- ¼ cup pepper-flavored vodka
- 2 tablespoons fresh lime juice
- 1 tablespoon plus 1 teaspoon Worcestershire sauce
- 1 tablespoon freshly grated or prepared horseradish
- 1 teaspoon hot sauce
- ½ teaspoon celery salt
- ½ teaspoon freshly ground pepper

Four 6-ounce filet mignon steaks, about 1½ inches thick

Olive oil

Salt

Tomato-Horseradish Butter, softened (recipe follows)

1. In a glass baking dish, combine the tomato juice, vodka, lime juice, Worcestershire sauce, horseradish, hot sauce, celery salt and pepper. Add the steaks and turn to coat. Cover and refrigerate for 1½ hours, turning occasionally. Remove the steaks from the refrigerator 30 minutes before grilling.
2. Light a grill. Lightly brush the grate with oil. Drain the steaks and pat dry; brush with olive oil. Season generously with salt and grill over moderately high heat, turning a few times, about 15 minutes for medium rare. Place a dollop of Tomato-Horseradish Butter on each steak and serve.

—*Steven Raichlen*

TOMATO-HORSERADISH BUTTER
MAKES ABOUT ¼ CUP

- 4 tablespoons unsalted butter, softened
- 1 sun-dried tomato packed in oil, drained and minced
- 1 garlic clove, minced
- 1½ teaspoons freshly grated or prepared horseradish
- 1 teaspoon fresh lime juice
- ¼ teaspoon freshly ground pepper
- ¼ teaspoon coarse salt

Combine all of the ingredients in a mini processor and pulse until smooth. Scrape the butter onto a 12-inch square of plastic wrap and roll it into a 2-inch cylinder; twist the ends tightly to seal. Chill the flavored butter just until firm, about 30 minutes. —*S.R.*

MAKE AHEAD The butter can be refrigerated for up to 3 days. Let soften briefly before using.

Chilean Steak Salad with Sherry Vinaigrette

6 SERVINGS ✳

Served at George's at the Cove in La Jolla, California, this main-course salad is adapted from a Chilean dish called *salpiçon,* which is usually made from leftover steak that is chopped and served cold. Grilled chicken, fish and vegetables are great substitutes.

- 1½ pounds small red new potatoes
Salt
- ½ pound green beans, cut into 1½-inch lengths

Two 1-pound strip steaks, about 1 inch thick

Freshly ground pepper

- 3 tablespoons sherry vinegar
- 1 teaspoon whole-grain mustard
- ¼ cup plus 2 tablespoons extra-virgin olive oil
- 1 head romaine lettuce (1 pound), cut crosswise into 1-inch ribbons
- 1 cup grape or cherry tomatoes
- 4 radishes, thinly sliced
- 2 carrots, coarsely grated
- 1 avocado, cut into ½-inch slices

1. In a large saucepan, cover the potatoes with lightly salted water and bring to a boil. Cook the potatoes over high heat until tender, about 20 minutes. Drain and let cool, then quarter. Meanwhile, in a medium saucepan of boiling salted water, cook the green beans until crisp-tender, 5 to 6 minutes. Transfer the beans to a colander and refresh under cold water. Drain and pat dry.
2. Preheat the broiler or light a grill. Season the strip steaks with salt and pepper and broil them about 8 inches from the heat source or grill directly over the fire for 10 to 12 minutes for medium-rare meat. Allow the steaks to rest for about 5 minutes, then slice crosswise ¼ inch thick and refrigerate until chilled.
3. In a glass jar, combine the sherry vinegar, the whole-grain mustard and the olive oil. Cover the jar tightly with a lid and shake until the vinaigrette is emulsified.
4. In a large bowl, toss the new potatoes and the green beans with the lettuce, the tomatoes, the radishes and the carrots. Pour two-thirds of the vinaigrette over the vegetables, season with salt and pepper and toss to coat. Add the remaining vinaigrette and the avocado, toss gently and mound the salad on plates. Arrange the cold steak over the salad and serve. —*Trey Foshee*

MAKE AHEAD You can prepare the potatoes, the green beans, the steak and the vinaigrette a day ahead of time. Refrigerate them separately and bring them back to room temperature before serving.

WINE Either a medium-bodied, peppery Syrah or a red Rhône blend with some bite will accent the smokiness in the grilled beef. Look, for instance, for the inexpensive 1998 Hermitage Road Shiraz from Australia, or try the 1997 Perrin Réserve, a French Côtes-du-Rhône.

Banyuls-Marinated Steaks with Pearl Onions

6 SERVINGS

Banyuls, a *vin doux naturel,* or fortified (sweet) wine, from Roussillon in southern France, produces a great crust on grilled rib-eye steaks, and the marinade reduces to a delicious red-wine sauce.

Six ¾-inch-thick rib-eye steaks
 (8 to 10 ounces each)
2 cups plus 2 tablespoons Banyuls or another fortified wine, such as port or Madeira
4 thyme sprigs
2 pints pearl onions
6 tablespoons unsalted butter, chilled
¾ cup water
1 tablespoon sugar
Salt and freshly ground pepper
2 tablespoons extra-virgin olive oil

1. Put the steaks in a large shallow glass or ceramic baking dish in a single layer. Pour in 2 cups of the Banyuls, add the thyme sprigs and turn the steaks to coat. Cover the baking dish and refrigerate for 3 hours.

2. Bring a medium saucepan of water to a boil. Add the pearl onions and cook for 2 minutes to loosen the skins. Drain the onions and peel them.

3. Melt 2 tablespoons of the butter in a large skillet. Add the pearl onions, water and sugar, cover and cook over low heat until the onions are tender and most of the water has evaporated, about 30 minutes. Season the onions with salt and pepper, add the remaining 2 tablespoons of Banyuls and cook over moderate heat, shaking the skillet, until the pearl onions are caramelized and coated with a syrupy sauce, about 3 minutes. Remove the skillet from the heat.

4. Light a grill or preheat a grill pan. Pour the marinade, along with the thyme sprigs, into a small saucepan and boil over moderate heat until reduced to ½ cup, about 10 minutes.

Discard the thyme sprigs. Remove the saucepan from the heat and whisk in the remaining 4 tablespoons of butter, 1 tablespoon at a time, until the sauce is thick and smooth. Whisk in the olive oil and season with salt and pepper.

5. Season the steaks with salt and pepper. Grill the steaks over a moderately hot fire or moderately high heat until deeply charred and rare in the center, about 4 minutes per side. Put the steaks on a large warmed platter.

6. Reheat the pearl onions. Rewarm the wine sauce over low heat, whisking constantly. Pour the sauce into a warmed gravy boat. Arrange the steaks and pearl onions on dinner plates and serve. Pass the sauce at the table. —*Corinne Chapoutier*

MAKE AHEAD The cooked pearl onions can be refrigerated overnight. Reheat gently, adding a splash of wine to keep them saucy.

WINE The velvety and supple tannins in the 1997 Hermitage Rouge La Sizeranne will accentuate the meat's tenderness.

Miami Cuban-Style Steak with Mojo

6 SERVINGS

½ cup fresh lime juice
⅓ cup water
¼ cup fresh orange juice
1½ teaspoons salt
½ teaspoon oregano
½ teaspoon freshly ground pepper
½ cup olive oil
8 large garlic cloves, thinly sliced crosswise
1 teaspoon ground cumin
6 thin sirloin steaks (8 ounces each)
3 tablespoons chopped cilantro
Vegetable oil, for the grill
2 sweet onions, sliced ¼ inch thick

1. Combine the lime juice, water, orange juice, salt, oregano and pepper in a bowl.

2. Heat the olive oil in a deep

saucepan over moderate heat. Add the garlic and cumin and cook until the garlic is fragrant and golden, about 2 minutes. Very carefully add the juice mixture and bring to a boil. Remove from the heat and let the *mojo* cool to room temperature.

3. Arrange the steaks in a large glass baking dish. Add the cilantro to the *mojo* and pour half of it over the steaks; turn several times to coat evenly. Cover and marinate in the refrigerator for 1 to 2 hours. Reserve the remaining *mojo.*

4. Light a grill. Lightly brush the grate with oil. Remove the steaks from the marinade and pat dry. Brush the onion slices with some of the reserved *mojo.* Grill the onion slices over the cooler part of the grill, until lightly charred and tender, about 4 minutes per side. Grill the steaks over high heat until medium rare, 2 minutes per side. Transfer the steaks and onions to a platter; spoon the remaining *mojo* on top and serve. —*Steven Raichlen*

Pastrami-Cured Steak

4 SERVINGS

As with most recipes for curing, this one requires that the steak stand overnight for the flavors of the rich, peppery rub to permeate the meat; plan accordingly.

1 tablespoon coriander seeds
1 tablespoon yellow mustard seeds
1 tablespoon black peppercorns
½ teaspoon whole fenugreek seeds
10 garlic cloves, minced
2 tablespoons kosher salt
2 tablespoons light brown sugar
2 teaspoons minced fresh ginger
One 2-pound sirloin steak, about 1¼ inches thick
1 tablespoon vegetable oil

1. In a medium skillet, toast the coriander and mustard seeds, peppercorns and fenugreek over moderate heat until fragrant, about 1 minute. Transfer to a work surface to cool. Using the side of a chef's knife, coarsely crush the spices. Put the crushed spices in a bowl and add the garlic, kosher salt, brown sugar and ginger. Rub the mixture onto both sides of the steak and put the meat in a sturdy plastic bag. Chill for at least 18 and up to 24 hours.

2. Scrape the seasoning mixture from the steak. Set a large cast-iron skillet over moderate heat for 3 minutes. Raise the heat to moderately high, add the oil and heat until almost smoking. Add the steak and cook until well browned on the bottom, about 4 minutes. Lower the heat to moderate, turn the steak and cook until browned on the other side, about 4 more minutes for medium rare. Transfer the steak to a cutting board and let rest for 5 minutes. Thinly slice the meat across the grain and serve.   —*Marcia Kiesel*

MAKE AHEAD The cooked steak can be refrigerated overnight.

WINE A young California Zinfandel with lots of spice and fruit would pair best with this cured steak. Try the 1997 Geyser Peak Winemaker's Selection or the 1996 St. Francis Reserve Pagani Vineyard.

Grilled Skirt Steak with Hot Chilean Salsa

Grilled Skirt Steak with Hot Chilean Salsa

6 SERVINGS ✳

 2 pounds skirt steak, trimmed
Kosher salt
Hot Chilean Salsa (recipe follows)

Light a grill or preheat a broiler. Season the steak with salt and brush with half the salsa. Grill or broil the steak 4 to 5 minutes per side, or until medium rare. Let stand for 5 minutes, then thinly slice the steak across the grain and serve with the remaining salsa.

—*Maricel Presilla*

WINE Choose a rich, spicy red with good acidity to partner the succulent steak. An Australian Shiraz, such as the 1998 Rosemount Estate Shiraz Diamond Label or the 1996 D'Arenberg d'Arry's Original, would be ideal.

HOT CHILEAN SALSA

MAKES 2 CUPS

A fine complement to soups, stews and grilled meats, this salsa also makes a great quick marinade for chicken, pork or grilled vegetables.

 1 medium onion, coarsely chopped
 ¼ cup coarsely chopped cilantro
 3 medium plum tomatoes—peeled, seeded and coarsely chopped
 ½ cup olive oil
 ¼ cup red wine vinegar
 1½ teaspoons *pimentón* (Spanish paprika), optional
 ½ teaspoon cayenne pepper
Kosher salt

In a food processor, pulse the onion with the cilantro until finely chopped. Add the tomatoes and pulse until finely chopped. Add the oil, vinegar, *pimentón* and cayenne and pulse just

until blended. Transfer the salsa to a bowl and season with salt.   —*M.P.*

MAKE AHEAD The salsa can be refrigerated for up to 2 days.

Flank Steak with Garlic and Ginger

10 SERVINGS

 ½ cup soy sauce
 ½ cup olive oil
 1 head of garlic, coarsely chopped
 ¼ cup coarsely chopped, peeled fresh ginger
 2 tablespoons coarsely chopped thyme
 2 teaspoons hot sauce
 1 bay leaf
Two 2-pound flank steaks
Salt and freshly ground pepper
Stewed Tomatoes with Ginger (p. 283)

ɪ. In a large glass or ceramic baking pan, combine the soy sauce with the olive oil, garlic, ginger, thyme, hot sauce and bay leaf. Add the flank steaks and turn them in the marinade to coat, then cover the baking pan and refrigerate the steaks for at least 2 hours or overnight.

2. Preheat the broiler. Transfer the steaks to a plate. Discard the marinade from the baking pan; scrape the marinade off the steaks. Season them with salt and pepper. Set the steaks on a baking sheet and broil about 6 inches from the heat for 4 to 5 minutes per side for medium rare. Let the steaks rest at room temperature for 5 to 10 minutes. Thinly slice the steaks and serve with Stewed Tomatoes with Ginger. —*Patrick O'Connell*

WINE The red currant and spice flavors of the 1997 Dom du Pesquier Gigondas from the southern Rhône echo both the ginger and the tomato; the gamy Syrah grapes in this wine make it big enough to stand up to the grilled meat.

Beef Satay with Chinese Spices and Cucumber Relish

4 TO 6 SERVINGS

This delectable version of satay is a house specialty at Wild Ginger, in Seattle.

1½ pounds flank steak
¼ cup mirin
¼ cup soy sauce
¼ cup Asian sesame oil
2 tablespoons honey
2 garlic cloves, finely chopped
2 quarter-size slices fresh ginger, finely chopped
2 scallions, white part only, chopped
½ teaspoon Chinese five-spice powder
½ teaspoon freshly ground pepper
Vegetable oil, for the grill
Cucumber Relish (p. 326)
Peanut Dipping Sauce (p. 318)

ɪ. Cut the flank steak across the grain into ¼-inch-thick slices. Thread the meat onto 8-inch bamboo skewers and arrange the skewers side by side on a large platter.

2. Combine the mirin, soy, sesame oil, honey, garlic, ginger, scallions, five-spice powder and pepper in a small bowl. Pour the marinade over the skewers and turn to coat. Let the beef marinate at room temperature for 30 minutes or refrigerate for up to 1 hour.

3. Light a grill. Place the grate 6 to 8 inches from the heat source. Lightly brush the grate with oil. Arrange the skewers on the grate and grill over high heat, turning once, until sizzling and nicely browned all over, 6 to 7 minutes. Transfer the skewers to a large platter and serve hot with Cucumber Relish and Peanut Dipping Sauce. —*Steven Raichlen*

MAKE AHEAD The marinade can be refrigerated for up to 3 days.

Spiced Flank Steak with Creamy Corn Sauce

4 SERVINGS

Hanger steak has a lovely rich flavor; flank steak is a leaner choice. The meat is marinated for at least 6 hours, so plan accordingly.

¼ cup low-sodium soy sauce
2 tablespoons Asian sesame oil
2 garlic cloves, minced
1 tablespoon grated fresh ginger
Zest of 1 lemon
1 Thai or serrano chile, thinly sliced
2 star anise pods, finely crushed
1 pound flank steak
½ teaspoon unsalted butter
ɪ medium ear of corn, kernels cut off
Creamy Corn Sauce (recipe follows)

ɪ. In a small bowl, combine the soy sauce with the sesame oil, garlic, ginger, lemon zest, chile and star anise. Pour the marinade into a large resealable plastic bag. Add the flank steak,

Flank Steak with Garlic and Ginger, with Stewed Tomatoes with Ginger (p. 283).

six tips for getting the most out of fresh corn

1. Look for just-picked ears with bright green husks and freshly cut stems, and remember that fresh local corn is always best. You can find heirloom varieties at farmers' markets. Of the more common varieties, Silver Queen, which is slightly less sweet, is ideal for the Creamy Corn Sauce recipe (at right). For succotash, try bicolored varieties for their visual appeal. For an all-purpose corn, opt for the candylike super-sweet hybrids.

2. Test all corn varieties for freshness by popping a kernel with a fingernail. It should explode with milky juice.

3. Try eating very fresh corn raw, straight off the cob or in salads and other cold dishes.

4. Cook corn as soon after it's picked as possible. As corn sits, its sugars convert to starch and the corn loses flavor and tenderness. If you need to refrigerate it for a day or two, wrap the ears in a dish towel to keep them moist.

5. Never salt the cooking water; this toughens the skin. You can, however, add a pinch of sugar to the pot to enhance the corn's natural sweetness.

6. Cut kernels from the cob by standing the ears, tips up, in a wide bowl (to catch the kernels) and cutting straight down the cob, all around the ear, with a serrated knife.

seal the bag and refrigerate the meat for 6 to 12 hours, turning once.

2. Light a grill or heat a cast-iron grill pan. Remove the meat from the marinade and rinse under cold water. Pat dry. Grill the flank steak over high heat, turning once, until browned and crusty, 10 to 12 minutes for medium-rare meat. Transfer the steak to a cutting board and let stand for 10 minutes.

3. Meanwhile, melt the butter in a small skillet. Add the corn kernels and cook over moderately high heat,

stirring frequently, until tender and lightly caramelized, about 5 minutes.

4. Thinly slice the steak across the grain and arrange the slices on warmed plates. Drizzle with the Creamy Corn Sauce and garnish with the sautéed corn kernels. Serve immediately. —*Sally Schneider*

ONE SERVING Calories 316 kcal, Total Fat 14.5 gm, Saturated Fat 6.4 gm

CREAMY CORN SAUCE
MAKES ABOUT ¾ CUP

- ¼ cup water
- 2 teaspoons unsalted butter
- 2 small shallots, finely chopped
- 1 garlic clove, thinly sliced
- 1 thyme sprig
- 1 large ear of corn, kernels cut off
- ¾ cup defatted canned low-sodium chicken broth
- Salt and freshly ground white pepper
- 1 tablespoon crème fraîche or heavy cream

1. In a small saucepan, combine the water, butter, shallots and garlic and bring to a simmer. Cook over moderate heat, stirring occasionally, until the shallots are translucent, about 3 minutes. Add the thyme and cook for 2 minutes. Add the corn and ½ cup of the broth, cover and cook over moderately low heat until tender, about 7 minutes.

2. Discard the thyme sprig. Transfer the contents of the saucepan to a blender and add the remaining ¼ cup of broth; blend until smooth, about 2 minutes. Strain the sauce into a clean saucepan and season with salt and white pepper; keep warm. Whisk in the crème fraîche or heavy cream just before serving. —*S.S.*

MAKE AHEAD The corn sauce can be refrigerated overnight and re-warmed over low heat. Whisk in the crème fraîche or heavy cream just before serving.

ONE SERVING Calories 77 kcal, Total Fat 3.8 gm, Saturated Fat 2.2 gm

Rolled Flank Steak with Prosciutto and Basil
6 SERVINGS

Serve this dish on its own or accompany it with chimichurri sauce: In a food processor, pulse ¾ cup of chopped flat-leaf parsley with ½ cup of chopped cilantro, 3 tablespoons of red wine vinegar and 2 quartered garlic cloves. Add ⅔ cup of extra-virgin olive oil; process to blend well. Season with salt, pepper and hot sauce.

- 1 cup coarse dry bread crumbs
- ½ cup chopped flat-leaf parsley
- ½ cup shredded Italian Fontina cheese (3 ounces)
- ¼ cup green olives, pitted and chopped (1½ ounces)
- ¼ cup freshly grated Parmesan cheese (¾ ounce)
- 3 tablespoons olive oil
- 1 tablespoon plus 2 teaspoons finely chopped thyme
- One 2-pound flank steak
- 5 ounces prosciutto, thinly sliced
- 1 cup basil leaves
- 2 teaspoons kosher salt
- 2 teaspoons minced garlic
- 1 teaspoon freshly ground pepper

1. Light a hot fire in a grill or preheat the oven to 350°. In a large bowl, combine the bread crumbs with the parsley, Fontina, olives, Parmesan, 2 tablespoons of olive oil and 1 tablespoon of thyme.

2. Lay the steak on a work surface with a short edge facing you. Press one hand flat on the meat to steady it. Using a long, sharp knife, make a horizontal cut in a long side of the steak to within ½ inch of the opposite edge. Open the flank steak like a book.

3. Cover the cut side of the steak with the prosciutto slices, then top with a layer of basil leaves. Spread the bread crumb mixture on top. Starting with the side facing you, tightly roll up the steak around the filling. Using kitchen string, tie the roll in 4 or 5 places.

4. In a small bowl, combine the

remaining 1 tablespoon of olive oil and 2 teaspoons of thyme with the salt, garlic and pepper. Rub this mixture all over the rolled steak.

5. Bank the coals to one side of the grill or turn off one side of the grill. Grill the steak over high heat until browned all over, 8 to 10 minutes; turn it 4 times as it cooks. Move it away from the direct heat and grill for 15 to 20 minutes, or until an instant-read thermometer registers 120° to 125° for medium rare. Alternatively, heat a large ovenproof skillet. Add the rolled steak and cook over moderately high heat until browned all over, 8 to 10 minutes. Move the skillet to the oven and roast the steak for 20 to 30 minutes, or until an instant-read thermometer registers 120° to 125° for medium rare. Transfer the rolled steak to a carving board, cover loosely with foil and let rest for 10 minutes. Discard the strings and slice the steak crosswise ½ inch thick. Serve.—*Bruce Aidells*

MAKE AHEAD The rolled flank steak can be refrigerated overnight. Bring to room temperature before grilling.

WINE A young, concentrated Cabernet Sauvignon will stand up to the grilled beef. The creamy cheese and bread crumb filling will tame the wine's tannin. Look for the 1997 Casa Lapostolle Cuvée Alexandre Rapel Valley from Chile or the 1996 Rodney Strong Alexander's Crown Vineyard from California.

Grilled Flank Steak with Kumquat and Red Onion Salad

6 SERVINGS

For a crisp, caramelized crust, leave the Kumquat, Green Peppercorn and Garlic Paste on the steak during grilling. If you prefer the steak itself to be charred, scrape off the paste before grilling.

2 pounds flank steak
Kumquat, Green Peppercorn and Garlic Paste (recipe follows)

Rolled Flank Steak with Prosciutto and Basil

2 tablespoons extra-virgin olive oil
2 teaspoons fresh orange juice
Salt and freshly ground pepper
1 large bunch arugula (6 ounces), large stems discarded
1 cup fresh kumquats (5 ounces), thinly sliced and seeded
½ cup thinly sliced red onion (½ small onion)
½ cup cilantro leaves

1. Set the flank steak in a large shallow glass or ceramic baking dish. Add the Kumquat, Green Peppercorn and Garlic Paste and rub it all over both sides of the flank steak. Cover the baking dish with plastic wrap and refrigerate the steak for at least 2 hours or overnight. Let the flank steak return to room temperature before grilling.

2. Light a grill or preheat the broiler and position the shelf 8 inches from the heat. Scrape the paste off the steak, if desired, then grill or broil it, turning once, until browned, about 12 minutes for medium rare. If the steak is cooked with the paste on, some of it may fall off when the steak is turned. Let the flank steak rest for 10 minutes.

3. In a large bowl, combine the olive oil with the orange juice. Season with salt and pepper and then whisk until the salt dissolves. Add the arugula, kumquats and red onion and toss well, then transfer the salad to dinner plates.

4. Using a sharp knife, thinly slice the flank steak on the diagonal across the grain. Arrange the slices on the salads. Garnish with the cilantro leaves and serve immediately. —*Janet Rosener*

MAKE AHEAD The cooked steak

Kumquat, Green Peppercorn and Garlic Paste

can be refrigerated overnight. Bring to room temperature before serving.

WINE Go with a powerful Australian Shiraz: Two good choices are the 1998 Rosemount Estate and the 1997 Penfolds Koonunga Hill Shiraz-Cabernet.

KUMQUAT, GREEN PEPPERCORN AND GARLIC PASTE

MAKES ABOUT ¾ CUP

This flavorful paste can be used to marinate fish, poultry, pork or beef.

- ½ cup (2½ ounces) coarsely chopped fresh kumquats (see Note)
- 2 tablespoons balsamic vinegar
- 2 tablespoons soy sauce
- 1 tablespoon light brown sugar
- ½ tablespoon honey
- 1 tablespoon green peppercorns in brine, drained and coarsely crushed
- ½ tablespoon black peppercorns, cracked
- 1 tablespoon minced garlic
- ¾ teaspoon coarse sea salt
- 2 tablespoons finely chopped scallions
- 2 tablespoons chopped cilantro
- ½ tablespoon extra-virgin olive oil

1. In a mini food processor, pulse the kumquats until finely chopped; do not puree. Transfer the kumquats to a small saucepan and add the balsamic vinegar, soy sauce, light brown sugar and honey. Cook over moderate heat, stirring often, until the mixture reduces to a thick paste, 4 to 5 minutes. Transfer the paste to a bowl and let cool.

2. In the processor, pulse the green and black peppercorns with the garlic and sea salt until the peppercorns are finely chopped. Do not puree the mixture. Add the scallions and cilantro to the processor and pulse to a coarse paste. Add the peppercorn mixture to the kumquat paste and stir in the olive oil until blended. —*J.R.*

MAKE AHEAD The paste can be refrigerated in a jar with a tight-fitting lid for up to 3 days.

NOTE Look for fresh kumquats in supermarkets from November through March. Frieda's, a mail-order source for specialty produce, has fresh kumquats until June (800-421-9477). Their thin rind is edible, so you don't need to peel them before eating. (The rind is actually sweeter than the pulp.)

Sirloin Strip Roast with Roquefort Mushrooms

4 SERVINGS

- 16 large white mushrooms (about 1 pound), stemmed
- 3 tablespoons dry white wine
- 3 tablespoons olive oil
- Salt and freshly ground pepper
- ½ cup water
- 2 ounces Roquefort cheese
- 2 tablespoons heavy cream
- 2 large anchovy fillets, minced
- 1 large garlic clove, minced

Grilled Flank Steak with Kumquat and Red Onion Salad

1 teaspoon Dijon mustard

¼ cup fresh bread crumbs

One 2¼-pound sirloin strip roast

2 tablespoons balsamic vinegar

1 tablespoon soy sauce

1 tablespoon cold unsalted butter

1. Preheat the oven to 450°. In a large enameled cast-iron or stainless steel baking dish, toss the mushroom caps with the wine and 2 tablespoons of the olive oil. Season with salt and pepper. Turn the caps stemmed side down and roast for 10 minutes, or until they release their liquid. Pour the liquid into a glass measuring cup. Turn the mushrooms and roast for 10 minutes longer, or until well browned on the bottom.

2. Transfer the mushrooms to a large plate. Set the baking dish over moderately high heat; when it starts to smoke, add the water. Bring to a boil, scraping up the browned bits on the bottom, and simmer until the water reduces by half, about 3 minutes. Pour the liquid into the measuring cup.

3. Return the mushroom caps to the baking dish, stemmed side up. In a bowl, combine the Roquefort with the cream, anchovies, garlic and mustard. Stir in the bread crumbs and season with salt and pepper. Stuff each mushroom cap with a heaping teaspoon of filling.

4. Season the sirloin roast with salt and pepper. Set a large ovenproof skillet over moderately high heat for a few minutes. Add the remaining 1 tablespoon of olive oil; when it starts to smoke, add the roast, fat side down. Cook until the fat is deeply browned, about 5 minutes, then quickly sear for 1 minute on each side. Turn the roast fat side up and cook for 1 minute.

5. Roast the sirloin in the oven for about 20 minutes, or until an instant-read thermometer inserted in the thickest part registers 120° for rare. Transfer the meat to a carving board and let rest for at least 10 minutes before carving.

6. Meanwhile, preheat the broiler. Set the skillet over moderately high heat. Add the balsamic vinegar and bring to a simmer, scraping up the browned bits from the bottom of the skillet. Add the soy sauce and the reserved mushroom liquid and boil for 3 minutes.

7. Remove the skillet from the heat and swirl in the butter. Season the sauce with salt and plenty of pepper and pour it into a warmed gravy boat. Broil the mushrooms for 3 minutes, or until browned. Rotate the baking dish as necessary. Carve the roast into 4 thick slices and serve with the stuffed mushrooms. Pass the sauce at the table. —*Marcia Kiesel*

WINE Pair the sirloin strip roast with a peppery Syrah.

Standing Rib Roast of Beef

12 SERVINGS, PLUS LEFTOVERS

This roasting method is an adaptation of the classic English approach, and who can argue with the Brits when it comes to roasting a joint of beef? This roast is cooked to medium rare; it comes out of the oven at 120° and reaches 130° to 135° as it rests before carving. If you like your meat cooked to medium, roast it to 130°.

⅓ cup Dijon mustard

2 tablespoons minced garlic

1 tablespoon chopped thyme leaves

2 teaspoons coarsely ground pepper

Kosher salt

3 tablespoons extra-virgin olive oil

One 5-rib 12- to 13-pound prime rib roast, chine bone removed

1. Preheat the oven to 450°. In a small bowl, mix the mustard with the garlic, thyme, pepper and 2 teaspoons of kosher salt. Whisk in the olive oil.

2. Set the meat, bone side down, in a roasting pan and season it lightly with salt. Roast the meat in the lower third of the oven for 20 minutes.

3. Remove the meat from the oven and reduce the temperature to 350°. Brush the mustard coating all over the top and sides of the meat and roast for about 1½ hours longer, rotating the roasting pan 2 or 3 times for even browning. The meat is done when an instant-read thermometer inserted in the center of the roast at the thickest part registers 120° (for medium rare). Transfer the roast to a carving board, cover it loosely with foil and let rest for 20 to 30 minutes.

4. Set the roast on its side and run a long, sharp knife between the bones and meat; remove the bones and set them aside. Turn the roast right side up. Carve the roast ¼ to ½ inch thick and transfer the slices to warmed plates. Pour any carving juices over the meat and serve at once. Alternatively, for bone-gnawing carnivores, cut down between the rib bones and pass them on a plate. —*Bruce Aidells*

WINE A rich, deep Burgundy with strong meaty flavors and good fruit acidity is a classic accompaniment to roast beef. Two good choices: the 1997 Daniel Rion Nuits-Saint-Georges Aux Vignerondes and the 1997 Domaine Perdrix Nuits-Saint-Georges Aux Perdrix.

Holiday Beef Brisket with Onions

12 SERVINGS

Brisket is perfect for a holiday meal. Look for the leaner flat-cut or first-cut brisket with a layer of fat that's at least ⅛ inch thick. If you can't find a 6-pound piece, buy 2 smaller pieces. Like most braised dishes, this brisket is best made a day or two ahead.

Kosher salt

Freshly ground pepper

2 teaspoons chopped thyme

1 teaspoon chopped oregano

1 tablespoon sweet Hungarian paprika

One 6-pound flat-cut brisket

½ cup dried porcini mushrooms (½ ounce)

1 cup hot water

3 tablespoons pure olive oil

2 cups dry vermouth or white wine

1 cup Basic Chicken Stock (p. 98)
  or canned low-sodium broth

2 cups chopped canned
  Italian tomatoes

3 bay leaves

4 medium onions, thinly sliced

3 tablespoons chopped garlic

I. In a small bowl, combine 2 teaspoons of salt and 1 teaspoon of pepper with the thyme, oregano and paprika. Rub the seasonings all over the brisket.

2. In a medium heatproof bowl, cover the porcini with the hot water and set aside until softened, about 20 minutes. Remove the mushrooms from the soaking liquid; rinse and coarsely chop them. Reserve the soaking liquid.

3. Preheat the oven to 350°. Heat the oil in a large enameled cast-iron casserole until shimmering. Add the brisket, fat side down, and cook over moderately high heat until well browned, about 8 minutes per side. Transfer the brisket to a platter and pour off any excess fat from the casserole. Add the vermouth and chicken stock, then pour in the reserved mushroom soaking liquid, stopping before you reach the grit at the bottom. Scrape up the browned bits from the bottom of the casserole and stir in the tomatoes, porcini and bay leaves.

4. Return the brisket to the casserole, fat side up. Add the onions and garlic, scattering some of each over the meat and into the liquid, and bring to a boil. Cover and cook in the oven for 1 hour. Uncover and cook for 30 minutes. Spoon the onions on top of the brisket and cook for about 30 minutes longer to brown the onions. Push some of the onions back into the liquid, cover and braise for about 2 hours, or until the meat is fork-tender.

5. Transfer the brisket to a carving board and cover loosely with foil.

Simmer the sauce for a few minutes, then season with salt and pepper. Discard the bay leaves. Carve the brisket across the grain into ³⁄₈-inch-thick slices and arrange on a large warmed platter. Spoon the sauce and onions over the meat and serve.

—*Bruce Aidells*

MAKE AHEAD The seasoned brisket can be refrigerated overnight before cooking. If cooking the brisket ahead, let the meat cool in the sauce before refrigerating. Skim the fat from the surface and slice the brisket, then rewarm the meat in the sauce.

WINE The concentrated garlic, tomato and beef flavors in this rich dish require an equally intense red. Consider a spicy and aromatic Italian Barolo, such as the 1993 Contratto Tenuta Secolo or the 1993 Massolino Vigna Rionda.

Braised Brisket with Rosemary, Shallots and Red Wine

10 SERVINGS

Many Jews avoid eating roasted meat at the Passover meal in remembrance of the destruction of the Temple (a place where the ancient Hebrews made burnt offerings) in Jerusalem. Braised brisket is a favorite choice because it can be prepared ahead, and it remains moist in its rich gravy no matter how long the pre-dinner service runs.

14 garlic cloves—6 chopped
  and 8 whole

Fresh rosemary—2 tablespoons
  whole leaves, 3 sprigs and 1
  teaspoon minced

1 tablespoon fresh lemon juice

Salt and freshly ground pepper

One 5-pound first-cut beef brisket

2 tablespoons olive oil

¾ pound shallots, coarsely
  chopped (3 cups)

2 cups full-bodied dry red wine

3 canned plum tomatoes, seeded
  and coarsely chopped

4 thyme sprigs, plus 1 teaspoon
  leaves

3 cups beef stock or canned
  low-sodium broth

I. In a blender or mini processor, combine the chopped garlic with the 2 tablespoons of rosemary leaves, the lemon juice, 1 teaspoon of salt and ¼ teaspoon of pepper; blend to a coarse paste. Make slits all over the brisket with a paring knife and insert a little of the paste into each slit using the knife tip. Rub the remaining paste all over the meat. Put the brisket in a large resealable plastic bag and refrigerate for at least 4 hours or for up to 1 day. Bring to room temperature before cooking.

2. Preheat the oven to 275°. Scrape off the seasoning paste and pat the meat dry. Season the brisket with salt and pepper. In an enameled cast-iron casserole or Dutch oven large enough to hold the brisket snugly, heat the olive oil. Add the brisket and brown over moderately high heat, about 5 minutes per side. Transfer the brisket to a platter.

3. Pour off all but 1 tablespoon of the oil from the casserole. Add the shallots and cook over moderately high heat, stirring, until softened but not browned, 3 to 4 minutes. Add 1 cup of the wine and boil, scraping up the browned bits from the bottom of the casserole, until most of the wine has evaporated, about 6 minutes. Add the tomatoes, whole garlic cloves, rosemary and thyme sprigs, beef stock and the remaining 1 cup of wine and boil for 3 minutes.

4. Reduce the heat to low and return the brisket to the casserole, fat side up. Spoon the gravy over the meat. Cover the casserole tightly and braise the meat in the oven for 3 to 3½ hours, basting it every 30 minutes. When the meat is fork-tender, remove the casserole from the oven and let the meat cool slightly in the gravy.

Skim off the fat.

5. Transfer the brisket to a cutting board and carve it across the grain on a slight diagonal into thin slices. Remove and discard the thyme and rosemary sprigs from the gravy. Transfer half of the gravy to a food processor or blender and puree. Return it to the casserole and bring to a simmer; if it seems too thin, boil it down to thicken. Stir in the thyme leaves and minced rosemary and season with salt and pepper.

6. Return the sliced brisket to the casserole and reheat in the gravy. Arrange the meat on a platter, spoon some of the gravy on top and serve. Pass the rest of the gravy at the table.

—*Jayne Cohen*

MAKE AHEAD The brisket can be made ahead through Step 4 and then refrigerated in the gravy for up to 2 days. Discard any fat that's solidified on the surface and reheat the meat gently before proceeding with the recipe.

Beef Stew with Red Wine

8 SERVINGS

Like most long-simmered dishes, this satisfying stew tastes even better the second or third day after it is made, because the flavors have then had time to develop and meld thoroughly.

3½ **tablespoons pure olive oil**
4 **pounds boneless beef chuck, cut into 2½-inch cubes**
Salt and freshly ground pepper

2 **medium onions, coarsely chopped**
3 **cups full-bodied red wine, preferably Italian**
3 **sage leaves**
2 **whole cloves**
1 **bay leaf**

1. Heat 1 tablespoon of the olive oil in a large enameled cast-iron casserole. Add one-third of the meat and season with salt and pepper. Brown the cubes well on all sides over moderately high heat, about 5 minutes; adjust the heat if the bits on the bottom of the casserole seem to be getting too dark. Transfer the meat to a plate. Repeat 2 more times, using 1 tablespoon of olive oil and half of the remaining meat for each batch.

2. When all of the meat has been well browned, add the remaining ½ tablespoon of olive oil to the casserole. Add the chopped onions and cook, stirring, over moderate heat until they're softened but not browned, approximately 5 minutes.

3. Add ¼ cup of the wine and simmer, scraping up the browned bits from the bottom of the pot with a wooden spoon, until the wine has almost evaporated, about 2 minutes. Repeat 3 more times, adding ¼ cup of the wine each time and using a total of 1 cup of the wine.

4. Return the meat to the casserole and add the remaining 2 cups of the wine, the sage leaves, cloves and bay leaf. Cover and simmer over low heat until the meat is very tender, about 2 hours. Skim the stew and season with salt and pepper. Remove the sage leaves, cloves and bay leaf and serve the stew in shallow bowls.

—*Silvana Daniello*

MAKE AHEAD This beef stew can be refrigerated for up to 3 days, or it can be frozen for up to 2 months. Defrost and reheat gently.

WINE 1997 Villa Matilde Falerno del Massico Rosso.

Braised Brisket with Rosemary, Shallots and Red Wine, with Carrot-Fennel Confit (p. 287).

Beef Daube with Wild Mushrooms

4 SERVINGS, PLUS LEFTOVERS

In Nice the beef stew is made with lots of dried porcini mushrooms and tomato paste. It's intensely flavored, thick and satisfying.

- 1 cup dried porcini mushrooms (1 ounce)
- 1 cup boiling water, plus 2 cups at room temperature
- 3 tablespoons olive oil
- 3 pounds trimmed beef chuck, cut into 2-inch cubes

Kosher salt

- 4 medium carrots, thinly sliced
- 3 medium onions, halved and thinly sliced
- 2 tablespoons all-purpose flour
- 2 cups red wine
- ¾ cup tomato paste
- 2 bay leaves
- 1 thyme sprig or ½ teaspoon dried thyme

Freshly ground pepper

1. Preheat the oven to 325°. In a heatproof bowl, soak the dried porcini in the 1 cup of boiling water until softened, about 20 minutes. Rub the mushrooms together to loosen any grit, then remove them from the water and coarsely chop. Let the soaking liquid stand for 5 minutes to settle, then pour it into a clean bowl, leaving any grit behind.

2. Heat the olive oil in a medium enameled cast-iron casserole. Add one-third of the meat at a time, season with salt and brown well on all sides over moderate heat, about 6 minutes; transfer to a plate. Repeat with the remaining meat.

3. Add the carrots and onions and cook, stirring, until lightly browned, about 10 minutes.

4. Discard any fat in the casserole. Sprinkle the flour over the vegetables and cook until it browns lightly, about 3 minutes. Gradually stir in the wine and the 2 cups of water, scraping up the browned pan juices. Return the meat to the casserole. Add the tomato paste, bay leaves, thyme and the porcini and their soaking liquid. Bring to a boil.

5. Cover the casserole tightly and bake for 3 hours, or until the cubes of beef are extremely tender. Discard the bay leaves and the thyme sprig and skim the fat from the sauce. Season with salt and pepper and serve.

—Jane Sigal

MAKE AHEAD The daube can be refrigerated for up to 2 days.

WINE Echo the beef stew's flavors with a gutsy red. An earthy Côtes-du-Rhone, such as the 1996 E. Guigal or the 1998 Georges Duboeuf Domaine des Moulins, would be a good bet.

Short Rib Stroganoff

6 SERVINGS

- 1 tablespoon hot paprika
- 1 tablespoon sweet paprika
- 6 pounds beef short ribs, cut crosswise into 2-inch pieces

Salt and freshly ground pepper

- 3 tablespoons vegetable oil
- 2 large red onions, thinly sliced
- 8 garlic cloves, finely chopped
- ¾ teaspoon caraway seeds
- 2 tablespoons Cognac
- 3 tablespoons all-purpose flour
- 4 cups beef stock or canned broth
- ½ cup thinly sliced cornichons or sour gherkins
- ⅔ cup sour cream

1. Preheat the oven to 325°. Sprinkle 2 teaspoons each of the hot and sweet paprika on the short ribs and rub it in well. Season the meat with salt and pepper.

2. In a large enameled cast-iron casserole, heat 1½ tablespoons of the vegetable oil until shimmering. Add half of the short ribs and cook slowly over moderately low heat, turning, until browned, about 10 minutes. Transfer the short ribs to a platter and repeat with the remaining oil and ribs.

3. Add the sliced onions to the casserole and cook over low heat, stirring occasionally, until softened, about 8 minutes. Add the chopped garlic, ¼ teaspoon of the caraway seeds and the remaining 1 teaspoon each of hot and sweet paprika. Cook over low heat until fragrant, about 4 minutes. Add the Cognac and simmer for 2 minutes. Whisk in the flour and cook for 3 minutes. Increase the heat to moderately high and slowly whisk in the beef stock until smooth.

4. Return the short ribs to the casserole with any accumulated juices and bring to a simmer. Cover the casserole with wax paper and then the lid and bake the Stroganoff in the oven for approximately 2 hours, or until the meat is very tender.

5. Meanwhile, in a small skillet, toast the remaining ½ teaspoon of caraway over moderate heat until fragrant, about 30 seconds. Transfer the seeds to a plate to cool and then finely grind them in a spice grinder or mortar.

6. Return the casserole to the stove over low heat. Stir in the sliced cornichons and the toasted caraway seeds. Put the sour cream in a bowl and whisk in ½ cup of the hot cooking liquid. Stir this mixture back into the casserole and turn off the heat so the cream won't curdle. Continue stirring until well blended. Serve hot, with Hand-Cut Spaetzle (p. 121) and Caramelized Carrot Mash (p. 285).

—Marcia Kiesel

MAKE AHEAD The Stroganoff can be refrigerated overnight. Rewarm the ribs and add the sour cream just before serving.

WINE A spicy, fruity, full-bodied Rhône blend would underscore the richness of the meat but also stand up to the other sweet and sour flavors in the dish. Look for the 1997 Jean-Luc Colombo Côtes-du-Rhône Les Abeilles or the 1996 Domaine de la Roquette Châteauneuf-du-Pape.

Madeira-Braised Short Ribs

8 SERVINGS

You'll need boneless short ribs for this dish. The butcher at any market will remove the ribs for you.

- 4½ pounds boneless beef short ribs, cut into 1½-inch pieces
- Salt and freshly ground pepper
- ½ cup all-purpose flour
- ½ cup extra-virgin olive oil
- 3 bay leaves
- 4 large carrots, sliced on the diagonal
- 4 celery ribs, coarsely chopped
- 1 large Spanish onion, coarsely chopped
- 8 garlic cloves, minced
- 1 large jalapeño, quartered through the stem
- 3 tablespoons tomato paste
- 1½ cups Rainwater Madeira
- 6 cups beef stock or canned low-sodium broth
- 3 tablespoons finely chopped flat-leaf parsley
- Parslied Potatoes (p. 298)

1. Season the meat with salt and pepper and dredge it in the flour, tapping off any excess. Heat 3 tablespoons of the olive oil in a large enameled cast-iron casserole. Add half of the meat and brown well on all sides, about 10 minutes; transfer to a large plate. Add 2 more tablespoons of the oil and brown the rest of the meat. Move the meat to the plate and discard the oil.

2. Add the remaining 3 tablespoons of olive oil to the casserole and heat it. Add the bay leaves and cook until lightly browned, about 20 seconds. Add the carrots, celery and onion and cook over moderate heat, stirring frequently, until barely softened, about 7 minutes. Add the garlic and jalapeño and cook until fragrant, about 1 minute. Stir in the tomato paste and cook, stirring occasionally, until lightly browned, about 1 minute. Stir in the Madeira, scraping up the browned bits from the bottom of the casserole.

3. Add the beef stock and bring to a boil. Stir in the meat and bring to a simmer. Cover partially and cook over moderately low heat until the meat is very tender, 2½ to 3 hours. Stir occasionally. Maintain at least 1 inch of liquid in the casserole, adding water if necessary. Skim off the fat and discard the bay leaves. Sprinkle with the parsley and serve with Parslied Potatoes.

—*Emeril Lagasse*

MAKE AHEAD The short ribs can be refrigerated for up to 4 days. Add the parsley just before serving.

WINE Match these succulent short ribs with a rich, mouth-filling red. The 1994 Ramos-Pinto Douro Duas Quintas Reserve, with its dark cherry, spice and meaty notes, or the intense 1994 Niepoort Redoma Red, with its plush texture, would be ideal.

Soy-Glazed Braised Short Ribs

6 SERVINGS

Short ribs are Korea's national meat, served grilled, in long-simmered soups and in this rich dark stew.

- 4 pounds meaty beef short ribs
- ¼ cup sugar
- 3 tablespoons plus 1 teaspoon Asian sesame oil
- ¼ cup Korean rice wine or mirin
- 2 tablespoons minced garlic
- 3 scallions, thinly sliced
- 2 tablespoons Sesame Salt (p. 272)
- 1 tablespoon vegetable oil
- 2 medium carrots, cut into 1-inch lengths
- ½ pound daikon, peeled and cut into 1-inch chunks (1½ cups)
- ¾ cup cooked chestnuts (see Note)
- 1 large Asian pear—halved, cored and cut into 1-inch chunks

Madeira-Braised Short Ribs, with Parslied Potatoes (p. 298).

4 cups water

½ cup soy sauce

1 egg, beaten

Toasted sesame seeds, for garnish

I. Score the ribs on both sides with a knife. In a large bowl, mix the sugar with 3 tablespoons of the sesame oil and the rice wine, garlic, scallions and Sesame Salt. Add the short ribs and toss to coat. Cover and refrigerate for at least 2 hours or overnight.

2. Scrape the marinade off the meat and reserve. Heat the vegetable oil in a large enameled cast-iron casserole. Add half of the short ribs and cook over moderate heat until nicely browned, about 5 minutes per side; transfer to a plate. Repeat with the remaining ribs, adjusting the heat as necessary if the juices on the bottom of the casserole get too dark.

3. Add the carrots, daikon, chestnuts and pear to the casserole and cook for 3 minutes, stirring frequently. Return the ribs to the casserole. Add the water, soy and the reserved marinade and bring to a boil; skim if necessary. Cover and simmer over low heat until the ribs are tender, about 1½ hours.

4. Meanwhile, heat the remaining 1 teaspoon of sesame oil in a small non-stick skillet. Add the egg and cook over moderate heat until set, about 1 minute. Carefully turn the egg as you would a crêpe and cook until set, about 10 seconds longer. Slide the omelet onto a work surface and let cool, then roll it up and cut it crosswise into thin strips.

5. Using a slotted spoon, transfer the ribs, vegetables and Asian pear to a bowl. Simmer the sauce in the casserole over moderate heat until thickened and richly flavored, about 20 minutes. Return the ribs, vegetables and Asian pear to the sauce and simmer until warmed through. Serve the stew in large shallow bowls, garnished with the omelet strips and sesame seeds. *—Anya von Bremzen*

NOTE Unsweetened cooked chestnuts are available in vacuum-packed jars and also in cans. If using canned ones, be sure to drain them.

Barbecued Short Ribs with Suwon Rib Factory Secret Marinade

6 SERVINGS

The Korean town of Suwon, near Seoul, is a mecca for barbecued short ribs *(kalbi gui)*. It even has a special rib factory with an excellent restaurant known for its secret marinade recipe, which we managed to get.

MARINATED MEAT

½ cup soy sauce

¼ cup Korean rice wine or mirin

¼ cup pineapple juice

2 tablespoons sugar

2 tablespoons Sesame Salt (p. 272)

3 tablespoons chopped garlic

¼ cup chopped scallions

¼ cup minced onion

1 tablespoon finely grated fresh ginger

1 small Asian pear, cut into 1-inch chunks

3 tablespoons Asian sesame oil

2 teaspoons coarsely ground Korean red chile *(gocho karu)*

2 teaspoons freshly ground black pepper

4 pounds meaty flanken-style short ribs (see Note)

ACCOMPANIMENTS

1 head red-leaf lettuce, separated into leaves

Sesame Salt (p. 272)

4 large garlic cloves, thinly sliced

Scallion Salad for Barbecues (recipe follows)

Korean Chili Sauce (p. 318)

I. Combine all of the marinade ingredients in a food processor and puree; transfer the marinade to a bowl. Add the ribs and let marinate at room temperature for at least 3 hours or refrigerate overnight.

2. Light a grill or preheat the broiler. Remove the ribs from the marinade and shake off any excess. Grill or broil the ribs until cooked through, about 5 minutes per side. Serve the short ribs with the accompaniments and let diners wrap their own meat.

—Anya von Bremzen

NOTE You can get *kalbi* pre-cut at Korean markets, both on and off the bone. Flanken-style, or L.A.-cut, short ribs are sliced ½ inch thick across 3 ribs.

SCALLION SALAD FOR BARBECUES

6 SERVINGS

1 large bunch scallions, white and green parts, cut into 4-inch lengths

2 tablespoons rice vinegar

2 teaspoons sugar

1 tablespoon Asian sesame oil

½ teaspoon coarsely ground Korean red chile *(gocho karu)*

Coarse salt

Slice the scallions lengthwise into fine strips. Submerge the strips in a bowl of ice water until curled, about 1 hour. Drain well just before serving. Transfer the scallions to a bowl and toss with the remaining ingredients. *—A.B.*

Smoky Short Ribs with Zinfandel-Chile Jam

6 TO 8 SERVINGS

10 cups water

2 cups white wine vinegar

1 cup packed dark brown sugar

2 tablespoons ground cumin

1 tablespoon ground cardamom

1 teaspoon cayenne pepper

1 small onion, stuck with 4 whole cloves

Freshly ground pepper

Kosher salt

6 pounds meaty beef short ribs, trimmed of excess fat

2 cups applewood or pecan-wood chips

Soy-Glazed Braised Short Ribs

Vegetable oil for brushing

Zinfandel-Chile Jam (recipe follows)

I. In a large pot, combine the water, vinegar, brown sugar, cumin, cardamom and cayenne. Add the onion, 2 tablespoons of freshly ground pepper and 1 tablespoon of salt and bring to a boil over high heat. Reduce the heat a bit and simmer for 20 minutes. Add the short ribs and simmer over moderately low heat until the meat is just tender, about 2 hours. Let the ribs cool in the broth, then transfer them to a large platter. Discard the broth. Cover the ribs and refrigerate until the meat is firm, at least 3 hours.

2. Soak the wood chips in water for 30 minutes and drain. Light a grill and lightly oil the grate. If using charcoal, push the hot coals to the sides of the grill and put a large drip pan in the center. Scatter the wood chips over the hot coals and heat until smoking. If using gas, place a large drip pan over the flames and turn the heat to moderate. Put the wood chips in a smoker box or wrap them in a 12-inch square of foil, fold the foil into a 6-inch packet and poke 12 holes in the top. Heat the chips until smoking.

3. Lightly brush the short ribs with oil and lay them on the grill directly over the drip pan. Close the lid and grill the ribs over moderate heat for 35 minutes, turning occasionally, until sizzling and beginning to brown. Reduce the heat to low. Generously brush the ribs with the Zinfandel-Chile Jam and grill for 20 minutes, uncovered, until the meat is tender and glazed; be sure that the jam does not burn. Serve with the remaining jam.—*Michael Lomonaco*

MAKE AHEAD The Smoky Short Ribs can be prepared through Step 1 and refrigerated for up to 3 days.

WINE This dish would showcase a round, deep-flavored, spicy red wine. Two good choices are the 1997 St. Francis Old Vines Zinfandel and the 1997 Pikes Shiraz from Australia.

ZINFANDEL-CHILE JAM

MAKES 3 CUPS

Although this is called a jam, the texture is more like that of a thick sauce.

- 2 tablespoons vegetable oil
- 1 small onion, finely chopped
- ½ cup ancho chile powder
- 1 teaspoon ground cumin
- 2 garlic cloves, minced
- 1½ cups red Zinfandel wine
- 1½ cups water
- ¾ cup balsamic vinegar
- ¾ cup black currant preserves
- ½ cup packed dark brown sugar
- 2 tablespoons tomato paste

Kosher salt and freshly ground pepper

I. Heat the oil in a medium saucepan over moderate heat. Add the onion and cook, stirring occasionally, until golden, about 5 minutes. Add the chile powder, cumin and garlic and cook over low heat, stirring frequently, until lightly browned, 5 minutes. Add 1 cup of the wine and cook over moderately low heat, stirring, until the mixture is thick, 5 to 6 minutes.

2. Whisk in the water, vinegar, preserves, brown sugar, tomato paste, 2 teaspoons of salt and 1 tablespoon of pepper. Cook the sauce over moderately low heat, stirring frequently, until reduced to 3 cups, about 50 minutes.

3. Whisk in the remaining ½ cup of wine and simmer over high heat for 5 minutes. Let cool. Scrape the jam into a blender and puree until smooth. Transfer to a jar and refrigerate.—*M. L.*

MAKE AHEAD The jam can be refrigerated for up to 2 weeks.

Four-Chile Chili

8 SERVINGS

Chili first made its appearance in the early 1800s as "chili con carne." It was billed as a favorite dish in Mexico, although it originated in the American Southwest and was reportedly loathed by Mexicans. Chili rose to great popularity in the 1930s, after World War I made all-American foods stylish.

- 2 tablespoons olive oil
- 3½ pounds ground sirloin or chuck

Salt and freshly ground black pepper

- 1 large Spanish onion (1½ pounds), coarsely chopped
- 8 large garlic cloves, minced
- 3 large jalapeños, seeded and minced
- 3 tablespoons ancho chile powder
- 2½ tablespoons sweet paprika
- ¼ cup tomato paste

Two 28-ounce cans peeled Italian tomatoes, coarsely chopped and juices reserved

- 3 cups chicken or beef stock or canned low-sodium broth

Two 19-ounce cans kidney beans, drained and rinsed

- 2 chipotle chiles in adobo sauce, seeded and minced
- 1 tablespoon dried oregano

Pinch of cinnamon

Coarsely chopped cilantro, for serving

Sour cream, for serving

I. Heat the olive oil in a enameled cast-iron casserole. Add half the ground beef in large chunks and season with salt and pepper. Cook over moderately high heat until brown on the bottom, about 4 minutes. Stir and cook until most of the pink is gone, about 3 minutes; keep the meat in large chunks. Transfer to a plate and repeat with the remaining meat.

2. Pour off all but 2 tablespoons of the fat from the casserole. Add the onion, garlic and jalapeños and cook over moderately low heat, stirring often, until softened, about 6 minutes. Add the ancho chile powder and paprika and cook over low heat, stirring often, until fragrant, about 5 minutes. Add the tomato paste and cook, stirring, until the paste is glossy and starts to brown, about 5 minutes. Stir in the tomatoes and their juices, the chicken stock and the cooked beef and any accumulated juices. Bring to a simmer over moderately high heat. Reduce the heat to low and simmer for 1½ hours, stirring occasionally.

3. Add the kidney beans, chipotles and oregano and simmer for 30 minutes longer. Season with salt, pepper and a large pinch of cinnamon. Remove from the heat and let stand for at least 20 minutes. Reheat before serving.

4. Serve the chili in bowls, topped with a generous sprinkling of cilantro. Pass the sour cream at the table.

—*Marcia Kiesel*

MAKE AHEAD The chili can be refrigerated for up to 4 days and frozen for up to 2 months.

North African Meatballs

MAKES 12 MEATBALLS

- 1 tablespoon pure olive oil
- ¾ cup minced onion
- 1 tablespoon minced garlic
- ¾ teaspoon ground cumin
- ½ teaspoon ground cardamom
- ½ teaspoon ground coriander
- ¼ teaspoon ground turmeric
- ⅛ teaspoon ground ginger
- 1 pound ground beef
- 3 tablespoons minced flat-leaf parsley
- 2 tablespoons minced cilantro
- 2 tablespoons minced mint
- 2 large egg whites, lightly beaten
- 1½ teaspoons kosher salt
- 1 teaspoon *harissa* or other red chile paste
- ½ teaspoon freshly ground pepper

Vegetable oil, for sautéing

1. Heat the olive oil in a medium skillet. Add the onion and garlic and cook over moderate heat until softened, about 4 minutes. Add the cumin, cardamom, coriander, turmeric and ginger and cook until fragrant, about 1 minute. Scrape the vegetable and spice mixture into a medium bowl and let cool.

2. Add the ground beef to the bowl, along with the parsley, cilantro, mint, egg whites, salt, *harissa* and pepper and mix the ingredients with your hands until thoroughly combined. Divide the meat mixture into 12 equal portions, roll into balls and set on a large plate.

3. Heat ¼ inch of vegetable oil in a large skillet. Add the meatballs and sauté over moderate heat, turning occasionally, until evenly browned and cooked through, about 10 minutes. Drain the meatballs on paper towels, then serve.

—*Roger Hayot*

NOTE *Harissa* is a hot sauce made from red chiles and such spices as coriander and caraway. It is available in tubes, cans and jars at Middle Eastern groceries and specialty food markets.

Summer Shack Corn Dogs

MAKES 10 CORN DOGS

- ½ cup fine yellow cornmeal
- ½ cup all-purpose flour
- 2 tablespoons sugar
- 1 heaping teaspoon baking powder
- ½ teaspoon salt
- ½ teaspoon freshly ground pepper
- 1 tablespoon minced scallion
- 1 large egg, beaten
- ½ cup milk

Ten 6-inch-long hot dogs

Vegetable oil, for frying

Mustard, for serving

1. In a large bowl, combine the cornmeal, flour, sugar, baking powder, salt and pepper. Add the scallion, egg and milk and mix just until blended. Let the batter stand for 20 minutes.

2. Spear each hot dog with a sturdy 8-inch wooden skewer, leaving about 2 inches of stick protruding for a handle.

3. Preheat the oven to 300°. In a large skillet, heat ½ inch of oil until shimmering. Dip a hot dog into the batter and twirl to coat; let the excess batter drip back into the bowl. Put the hot dog in the hot oil, repeat with another hot dog and fry until the batter is crisp and golden brown, 2 to 3 minutes per side. Drain the corn dogs on a rack set over a baking sheet and keep warm in the oven. Repeat with the remaining hot dogs, frying 2 at a time. Serve with mustard.

—*Jasper White*

Ratatouille Strata with Lamb and Olives

6 TO 8 SERVINGS

A strata is a savory, layered bread pudding usually made with a few household staples: eggs, milk, bread, cheese. This vegetable-rich version is somewhat more complicated to prepare, but well worth the extra effort.

One 16-ounce loaf olive bread or sourdough bread, ends removed, cut into 1-inch cubes (about 9 cups)

- 1½ cups milk
- ¼ cup plus 2 tablespoons extra-virgin olive oil
- 2 onions, halved lengthwise and thinly sliced crosswise
- 4 large garlic cloves, minced
- 6 large plum tomatoes—peeled, seeded and coarsely chopped
- 1 cup Nyons or Calamata olives (½ pound), pitted and coarsely chopped
- ¼ cup finely chopped fresh basil

Salt and freshly ground pepper

- 1 pound ground lamb
- 2 small zucchini (1 pound), cut into 2-by-¼-inch strips
- 1 red bell pepper, cut into 2-by-¼-inch strips
- 1 yellow bell pepper, cut into 2-by-¼-inch strips
- 1 medium eggplant (about ¾ pound), peeled and cut into ½-inch dice
- 6 large eggs, lightly beaten
- 2 cups heavy cream

1. In a large bowl, toss the bread with the milk. Let soak, stirring a few times, until moistened, about 30 minutes.

2. In a large deep skillet, heat 2 tablespoons of the oil until shimmering. Add the onions and cook over moderately high heat, stirring frequently, until golden brown, about 10 minutes. Add the garlic and cook until fragrant; then add the tomatoes and cook, stirring frequently, until the sauce is thick and most of the liquid has evaporated, about 6 minutes. Stir in the olives and basil and season with salt and pepper.

3. In a large skillet, heat 1 tablespoon of the oil until shimmering. Add the ground lamb, season with salt and pepper and cook over high heat, stirring occasionally, until cooked through and lightly browned, about 8 minutes. Add the lamb to the tomato sauce.

4. Wipe out the skillet. Add 2 tablespoons of the oil and heat until shimmering. Add the zucchini and bell pepper strips and cook over high heat, stirring occasionally, until crisp-tender, about 10 minutes; stir the vegetables into the tomato sauce.

5. Wipe out the skillet again. Add the remaining 1 tablespoon of oil and heat until shimmering. Add the diced eggplant and cook over high heat, tossing frequently, until very tender and deep golden, about 8 minutes. Stir the eggplant into the tomato sauce.

6. Preheat the oven to 350°. Lightly oil a 3- to 4-quart glass or ceramic baking dish. Arrange half of the soaked olive bread in the baking dish. Spread the ratatouille evenly on top and cover with the remaining soaked olive bread.

7. In a medium bowl, mix the eggs with the cream and add a generous pinch each of salt and pepper. Pour the custard evenly over the top layer of bread and let the strata stand for at least 20 minutes.

8. Bake the strata for 1 hour and 15 minutes, or until the custard is set and the top is golden brown. Let stand for 10 minutes before serving.

—*Max London*

MAKE AHEAD The ratatouille strata can be prepared through Step 7 and refrigerated overnight. Bring to room temperature before baking.

Ratatouille Strata with Lamb and Olives

Lamb and Date Brochettes with Tabbouleh Salad

10 SERVINGS

BROCHETTES

 2 tablespoons unsalted butter
 1 medium onion, cut into
   1-inch dice
30 pitted Medjool dates (about 1¼
   pounds), halved crosswise
2¾ pounds well-trimmed boneless
   leg of lamb, cut into 1-inch cubes
 ½ cup olive oil
 1 tablespoon ground cumin
 2 teaspoons *harissa* (see Note)
Salt and freshly ground pepper

TABBOULEH

 3 cups medium-coarse
   grade bulgur (1 pound)
1½ cups fresh orange juice
   (from about 4 oranges)
 ¾ cup fresh lemon juice
   (from about 4 lemons)
 ½ cup extra-virgin olive oil

Salt and freshly ground pepper
 4 tomatoes, seeded and diced
 4 cucumbers, seeded and diced
 1 cup coarsely chopped mint

I. PREPARE THE BROCHETTES: Melt the butter in a medium saucepan. Add the onion and cook over moderate heat, stirring occasionally, until golden brown, 8 to 10 minutes. Let the onion cool.

2. For each brochette, thread 1 date half, 1 piece of onion and 1 lamb cube onto a skewer, then repeat; finish the brochette with another date half. Repeat until all of the ingredients are used up.

3. In a large glass baking dish, combine the olive oil with the cumin and *harissa*. Season the lamb brochettes with salt and pepper and add them to the dish, turning to coat them thoroughly with the marinade. Cover the brochettes with plastic wrap and refrigerate for at least 1 hour or overnight.

4. MAKE THE TABBOULEH: In a large bowl, cover the bulgur generously with warm water and let soak until tender, about 20 minutes; drain thoroughly.

5. In another large bowl, whisk the orange and lemon juices with the olive oil and season with salt and pepper. Add the bulgur, tomatoes, cucumbers and mint and toss until thoroughly combined. Cover the tabbouleh and refrigerate for at least 1 hour.

6. Light a grill or preheat a grill pan. Season the brochettes again and grill them over moderate heat for about 3 minutes per side, until the lamb is medium rare. Mound the tabbouleh on a large platter. Arrange the brochettes on top and serve.

—*Jean-Christophe Royer*

NOTE *Harissa* is a hot sauce made from red chiles and such aromatic spices as coriander and caraway. It is available in tubes, cans and jars at Middle Eastern groceries and specialty food markets.

Lamb Chops with Rosemary and Garlic

6 SERVINGS

> 3 rosemary sprigs
> 3 garlic cloves, thinly sliced
> 3 tablespoons extra-virgin olive oil
> Twelve 7-ounce lamb loin chops
> Salt and freshly ground pepper

1. In a large shallow dish, combine the rosemary, garlic and oil. Add the lamb chops and let marinate for 1 hour.

2. Preheat a grill pan. Remove the lamb chops from the marinade and scrape off some of the rosemary and garlic. Season the lamb chops with salt and pepper and grill over moderate heat until medium rare, about 4 minutes on each side. Serve at once.

—*Eric Ripert*

WINE Try a classic Bordeaux, such as the 1996 Château Louvère.

Grilled Lamb Chops with Red Wine Pan Sauce

6 SERVINGS

> 2 tablespoons extra-virgin olive oil
> 12 lamb loin chops, cut 1 inch thick and trimmed of excess fat
> Salt and freshly ground pepper
> 4 medium shallots, finely chopped
> ½ cup dry red wine
> 1 tablespoon tomato paste
> 1 cup beef demiglace (see Note)
> 2 tablespoons unsalted butter

1. In each of 2 large heavy skillets, heat 1 tablespoon of the oil until almost smoking. Season the lamb chops with salt and pepper, add them to the pans and cook over high heat, turning once, until browned and crusty, 5 to 6 minutes. Transfer the lamb to a platter, cover loosely with foil and keep warm.

2. Add half of the shallots to each skillet and cook, stirring constantly, until softened, about 2 minutes. Add ¼ cup of the wine to each pan and cook until almost completely reduced, scraping up any browned bits, about 5 minutes.

3. Scrape the shallot mixture into 1 skillet and add the tomato paste. Cook over high heat until beginning to brown, about 2 minutes. Add the demiglace and cook until reduced by half, about 8 minutes. Add the butter and swirl until it melts. Add any accumulated lamb juices and season with salt and pepper. Strain the sauce through a fine sieve into a bowl. Serve the lamb chops with the pan sauce.

—*Thomas Gay*

NOTE Beef demiglace, a reduction made from thickened stock, is available at specialty food stores and by mail order from Dean & DeLuca (800-221-7714).

WINE An intense, earthy red is a good match with the lamb chops; try the 1996 Qupé Los Olivos Cuvée Syrah-Mourvèdre from California or the 1995 Paul Jaboulet Aîné Châteauneuf-du-Pape Les Cèdres from France.

Grilled Lamb Chops with Red Wine Pan Sauce

Roasted Lamb with Dijon Mustard and Thyme

8 SERVINGS

> Four 12- to 14-ounce boneless lamb loins
> Salt and freshly ground pepper
> 2 tablespoons olive oil
> ⅓ cup red wine
> ⅓ cup water
> 2 tablespoons Dijon mustard
> ¼ cup chopped thyme leaves, plus thyme sprigs for garnish
> 1 teaspoon unsalted butter

1. Preheat the oven to 350°. Season the lamb with salt and pepper. Heat the olive oil in a large skillet. Add 2 lamb loins and brown on all sides over high heat. Remove the loins to a platter and repeat with the remaining lamb. Let cool.

2. Pour off the fat from the skillet. Add the wine and water and simmer over moderate heat for 5 minutes, scraping up the browned bits from the bottom of the pan. Strain this lamb jus into a small saucepan.

3. Brush the lamb loins with the mustard and arrange on a baking sheet. Sprinkle them with the chopped thyme

menu

spicy crawfish salad on brioche (p. 20) | smithfield ham and asparagus toasts (p. 21)

1998 MATANZAS CREEK SAUVIGNON BLANC

scallop brochettes with haricots verts salad (p. 41) | 1998 MATANZAS CREEK CHARDONNAY

roasted lamb with dijon mustard and thyme | ratatouille couscous with saffron (p. 123)

1997 MATANZAS CREEK MERLOT

golden strawberry gratins (p. 369) | 1994 MATANZAS CREEK BLANC DE BLANCS

Roasted Lamb with Dijon Mustard and Thyme

leaves and roast in the oven for 15 to 20 minutes for medium rare. Transfer the lamb to a cutting board and let rest while you complete the sauce.

4. Bring the reserved lamb jus to a simmer over moderate heat and cook until it has reduced by one-fourth, about 4 minutes. Whisk in the butter and season this sauce with salt and pepper.

5. Slice the lamb crosswise into ½-inch medallions. Drizzle the meat with the sauce, garnish with the thyme sprigs and serve immediately.

—Dominique Macquet

WINE The concentrated 1997 Matanzas Creek Merlot, with its palate-cleansing tannins, offers a bright contrast to the lamb.

Rack of Lamb with Cabernet Sauce

8 SERVINGS

Three 8-bone racks of lamb (1½ pounds each), trimmed of all fat, bones frenched (see Note)
Coarse salt and freshly ground pepper
1½ tablespoons canola oil
1 cup Cabernet Sauvignon
1 garlic clove
1 thyme sprig
1 cup Basic Chicken Stock (p. 98) or canned low-sodium broth
2 tablespoons cold unsalted butter, cut into 4 pieces

1. Preheat the oven to 425°. Season the lamb racks all over with coarse salt and pepper. Heat 1 tablespoon of the oil in a large skillet and the remaining ½ tablespoon of oil in a medium skillet; both skillets should be ovenproof. Add 2 of the lamb racks to the large skillet and 1 rack to the medium skillet, meaty side down. Cook the racks over moderately high heat until well browned, about 4 minutes. Turn the racks and brown the other side, about 3 minutes longer.

2. Transfer the skillets to the oven and roast the lamb for 15 to 20 minutes, or until an instant-read thermometer inserted in the thickest part of the meat registers 120° for rare and 125° for medium rare. Transfer the racks to a carving board and let rest for 10 minutes.

3. Meanwhile, set the medium skillet over high heat. Add ½ cup of the wine and bring to a boil, scraping up any browned bits. Pour the wine into the large skillet and add the garlic and thyme. Set the large skillet over high heat, add the remaining ½ cup of wine and boil until reduced by one-third, about 3 minutes. Add the chicken stock and boil until reduced to ½ cup, about 8 minutes. Remove the skillet from the heat and discard the garlic and thyme sprig. Whisk in the butter, 1 piece at a time. Season with salt and pepper and strain the sauce into a warmed gravy boat.

4. To serve, cut the lamb into chops and arrange 3 chops on each dinner plate. Pass the Cabernet sauce at the table along with a little coarse salt for sprinkling on the lamb. —Josiah Citrin

NOTE Have your butcher french the lamb by scraping the fat and gristle from the bones.

WINE Colgin's Cabernet is very well-suited to lamb because the bold taste of the wine needs a strong-flavored dish. If you aren't lucky enough to have a bottle of Colgin's 1995 Herb Lamb Vineyard Cabernet Sauvignon, try the 1997 Jayson Red.

Grilled Leg of Lamb with Thyme Salmoriglio

20 SERVINGS

Salmoriglio is a traditional Sicilian sauce for fish and shellfish made with oil, lemon and oregano. In this adaptation, thyme serves as a substitute for the oregano. Have your butcher

Rack of Lamb with Cabernet Sauce,
with Sautéed Chard with Brandied Currants.

menu

rock shrimp cakes (p. 28) | creamy cucumber velouté (p. 82) | 1990 VEUVE CLICQUOT LA GRANDE DAME

roasted beets with cheese-stuffed dates (p. 287)

rack of lamb with cabernet sauce | sautéed swiss chard with brandied currants (p. 272)

mashed potato-barley cakes (p. 301) | 1995 COLGIN HERB LAMB VINEYARD CABERNET SAUVIGNON

flourless chocolate-almond cakes (p. 343) | 1990 CHATEAU D'YQUEM SAUTERNES

butterfly and trim the lamb for you, and make sure to leave time for the meat to marinate overnight.

LAMB

20 garlic cloves, halved

¼ cup rosemary leaves

Coarse salt and freshly ground pepper

Two 4-pound boneless legs of lamb, butterflied and trimmed

½ cup extra-virgin olive oil

¼ cup plus 2 tablespoons fresh lemon juice

THYME SAUCE

1¼ cups extra-virgin olive oil

⅔ cup finely chopped thyme leaves

½ cup fresh lemon juice

Salt and freshly ground pepper

I. PREPARE THE LAMB: In a food processor, combine the garlic, rosemary, 1 teaspoon of salt and ½ teaspoon of pepper; process to a coarse paste. Place the lamb in a large roasting pan, coat with the garlic and rosemary paste and drizzle the leg with the olive oil and the lemon juice. Cover the pan and then refrigerate the lamb overnight.

2. MAKE THE THYME SAUCE: In a bowl, combine the olive oil, chopped thyme and lemon juice; season with salt and pepper.

3. Light a grill. Scrape most of the marinade off the lamb and discard. Grill the lamb over a moderately low fire for approximately 10 minutes per side, or until an instant-read thermometer inserted in the thickest part of the leg registers 125° for medium-rare meat.

4. Transfer the lamb to a cutting board, cover loosely with foil and let stand for 10 minutes before carving into thin slices. Spoon the thyme sauce over the lamb or pass it at the table.

—Martin Dodd

MAKE AHEAD The sauce can be made ahead and refrigerated for up to 2 days. Bring to room temperature before serving.

Roast Lamb with Rosemary and Juniper

6 SERVINGS

4 large garlic cloves, chopped

2 teaspoons finely chopped rosemary

6 juniper berries

Salt and freshly ground pepper

3 pounds leg of butterflied lamb, in one piece

1 cup dry red wine

I. Preheat the oven to 450°. In a mortar, pound the garlic with the rosemary and juniper berries to a smooth paste. Season with salt and pepper. Spread half the paste all over the inside of the lamb. Roll the lamb into a compact roast and tie it at 1½-inch intervals with butcher's twine. Using a sharp paring knife, make 16 shallow slits all over the outside of the roast. With the tip of the knife, fill each slit with the remaining garlic-juniper paste.

2. Set the lamb in a medium roasting pan and season generously with salt and pepper. Roast the meat for 30 minutes. Add the wine and, using a wooden spatula, scrape up any browned bits in the pan. Roast the lamb for about 10 minutes longer for medium-rare meat.

3. Transfer the lamb to a carving board and let stand for 15 minutes before slicing. Meanwhile, pour the cooking juices into a small saucepan. Skim off any fat from the surface and simmer over moderate heat until slightly reduced. Cut the strings and carve the lamb into thick slices. Serve with the pan juices.   *—Sara Jenkins*

MAKE AHEAD The lamb can be prepared through Step 1 and refrigerated overnight. Remove from the refrigerator 1 hour before roasting.

WINE The richness of the lamb and the aromatic juniper flavor call for a bold Super-Tuscan blend of Sangiovese and Cabernet Sauvignon. Look for the 1995 Querciabella Camartina.

best buys at the butcher shop

Some of the cheaper cuts of meat offer the most flavor, especially when they are slow-cooked. The following benefit from braising or stewing, but we also suggest additional cooking methods.

Beef Short ribs (marinate and grill), brisket (barbecue), chuck boneless top blade steaks (grill, stir-fry), chuck boneless blade roast, oxtails.

Lamb Shoulder blade chops (broil), boneless shoulder (roast), breast riblets, neck, shanks.

Olive-Stuffed Boneless Leg of Lamb

12 SERVINGS

Herb-infused crushed black olives rolled up in a butterflied leg of lamb season and tenderize the meat from within as it marinates and cooks. A butcher can butterfly and trim the lamb for you. It's tastiest when it is rolled up and refrigerated for 1 to 2 days before roasting, so try to plan accordingly.

1¼ cups Calamata or Gaeta olives (½ pound), pitted and coarsely chopped

1 small garlic clove, minced

2 teaspoons thyme leaves plus 4 thyme sprigs

1 teaspoon extra-virgin olive oil

¾ teaspoon finely chopped rosemary, plus 4 rosemary sprigs

¾ teaspoon finely grated lemon zest

One 4½-pound leg of lamb—boned, butterflied and trimmed of all visible fat

Kosher salt and freshly ground pepper

½ cup dry white wine

I. In a food processor, combine the olives with the garlic, thyme leaves, olive oil, chopped rosemary and lemon zest. Pulse until a chunky puree forms. Spread the lamb on a work surface, boned side up, and season with salt and pepper. Spread the olive paste all over the lamb and roll it tightly lengthwise into a roast. Tie the lamb with kitchen string at 1-inch intervals. Wrap tightly in plastic and refrigerate for at least 6 hours. Let return to room temperature before roasting.

2. Preheat the oven to 450°. Put the lamb on a rack set in a roasting pan and season with salt and pepper. Tuck the rosemary and thyme sprigs under the lamb and roast for 10 minutes. Reduce the oven temperature to 350° and pour the wine over the lamb. Roast for about 45 minutes, basting twice; the lamb is done when an instant-read thermometer inserted in the thickest part registers 140° for medium.

3. Transfer the lamb to a cutting board, cover loosely with foil and let rest for 10 to 15 minutes. Meanwhile, pour the pan drippings into a bowl and spoon off the fat. Discard the strings and cut the lamb into thick slices. Pour any lamb juices into the pan drippings, spoon them over the meat and serve.

—*Sally Schneider*

ONE SERVING Calories 210 kcal, Total Fat 11 gm, Saturated Fat 2.8 gm

Barbecued Leg of Lamb

4 TO 6 SERVINGS

At Owensboro, Kentucky's Moonlite Bar-B-Que Inn, mutton is slow-cooked over a smoky hickory fire in an old-fashioned pit. The basting sauce is a potent mixture of Worcestershire sauce, vinegar and lemon juice. Since mutton is hard to find, this recipe has been adapted for boneless leg of lamb.

- 2 cups hickory wood chips

Cold water, for soaking

- ¾ cup water
- ½ cup cider vinegar
- ⅓ cup Worcestershire sauce
- 1 tablespoon fresh lemon juice

Coarse salt and freshly ground pepper

Vegetable oil, for the grill

One 4-pound butterflied leg of lamb

1. Soak the hickory chips in cold water for 1 hour. In a medium saucepan, combine the ¾ cup of water, vinegar, Worcestershire sauce and lemon juice. Add 2½ tablespoons of salt and ¼ teaspoon of pepper and bring to a boil. Reduce the heat to moderate and stir just until the salt dissolves. Remove the sauce from the heat.

2. Light a grill. Lightly brush the grate with oil. Drain the hickory chips and scatter them on the hot coals. If using a gas grill, place the chips in a 12-inch square of foil; fold the foil into a 6-inch square and poke 12 holes in the top. Place the package near the flames and let heat until smoking.

3. Season the lamb with salt and pepper. Grill the lamb, boned side up, over moderate heat, covered, for 10 minutes. Generously brush the lamb with sauce and cook, covered, basting frequently, and turning the meat to avoid burning, for about 45 minutes, or until an instant-read thermometer inserted in the thickest part of the lamb registers 125° for medium rare or 140° for medium.

4. Transfer the lamb to a cutting board, cover loosely with foil and let rest for 15 minutes. Thinly slice the lamb on the diagonal; transfer to a platter. Pour any accumulated juices on top and serve.

—*Steven Raichlen*

WINE Round out the saltiness and smokiness of the lamb with an intense and spicy Australian Shiraz or Shiraz blend, such as the 1999 Rosemount Shiraz or the 1997 Wolf Blass Cabernet Sauvignon–Shiraz Red Label.

Creamy Lamb Stew

4 SERVINGS

This delicate stew is a hallmark of French home cooking.

- 6 parsley stems
- 1 thyme sprig
- 1 bay leaf
- 2 cloves
- 1 large onion, halved

- 3 pounds trimmed boneless lamb shoulder, cut into 1½-inch cubes
- 1 quart water
- 1 large carrot, quartered lengthwise and thinly sliced crosswise

Kosher salt

- 3 tablespoons unsalted butter
- ¼ cup all-purpose flour
- ½ cup heavy cream
- 1½ tablespoons fresh lemon juice

Freshly ground white pepper

1. Tie the parsley stems, thyme and bay leaf in a bundle. Stick the cloves in the onion halves. In a medium enameled cast-iron casserole, combine the lamb with the water, onion halves, carrot and herb bundle. Season lightly with salt. Cover and bring to a boil, then cook over low heat for 30 minutes, skimming occasionally.

2. Using tongs, transfer the meat to a bowl. Remove and discard the herb bundle and the whole cloves, if you can find them. Pour the contents of the casserole through a fine strainer set over a bowl and press on the vegetables. Return the broth to the casserole; discard the vegetables. Return the lamb to the casserole and bring to a simmer over low heat.

3. In a small bowl, cream the butter with the flour. Gradually whisk the butter paste into the simmering stew. Continue cooking until the lamb is very tender, about 30 minutes. Using tongs, transfer the lamb to a bowl. Simmer the sauce until reduced to 2 cups; return the lamb to the casserole.

4. Whisk the cream into the stew and simmer for 10 minutes, skimming occasionally. Add the lemon juice, season with salt and white pepper and serve.

—*Anick Colette*

MAKE AHEAD The recipe can be refrigerated overnight.

WINE The delicate flavors of this stew point to a less-than-intense red. Try a *cru bourgeois,* such as the 1996 Château Greysac or the 1996 Château Bel Air.

Lamb Stew with Beans and Olives

4 SERVINGS

- 1 cup dried pinto beans—soaked overnight in water to cover, drained and rinsed
- 1 bay leaf
- 2 tablespoons vegetable oil
- 2 pounds boneless lamb shoulder, cut into 2-inch pieces

Salt and freshly ground pepper

- 2½ ounces finely chopped pancetta
- 1 tablespoon unsalted butter
- 3 large shallots, minced
- 2 tablespoons all-purpose flour
- 1 tablespoon tomato paste
- ¼ cup dry red wine
- 4 cups beef stock or 1 can low-sodium beef broth diluted with 3 cups of water
- 1½ cups frozen baby lima beans
- ⅔ cup Calamata olives, pitted and halved
- ¼ cup coarsely chopped parsley

1. In a medium saucepan, cover the dried beans with water. Simmer the beans with the bay leaf over low heat until tender, about 45 minutes. Leave the beans in their cooking water.

2. In a medium enameled cast-iron casserole, heat 1 tablespoon of the oil. Add half of the lamb and season with salt and pepper. Brown the meat over moderately high heat, about 3 minutes per side; transfer to a plate. Repeat with the remaining oil and lamb.

3. Add the pancetta and butter to the casserole and cook over low heat until the pancetta is slightly crisp, about 4 minutes. Add the shallots and cook until softened but not browned, 3 to 5 minutes. Stir in the flour and cook, stirring, for 1 minute. Stir in the tomato paste and then the wine and simmer, stirring, for 3 minutes. Whisk in the stock until smooth and bring to a boil. Return the lamb to the casserole and simmer over low heat, skimming a few times, until the lamb is tender, about 1 hour. Drain the dried beans, add them

to the stew and simmer for 15 minutes longer.

4. Cook the lima beans in a small saucepan of boiling water until tender, about 4 minutes; drain well. Add the lima beans to the stew and season with salt and pepper. Stir in the olives. Spoon the stew into shallow bowls, sprinkle with the parsley and serve.

—Marcia Kiesel

MAKE AHEAD The lamb stew can be prepared through Step 3 and refrigerated for up to 2 days.

Lamb Tagine with Prunes and Carrots

4 SERVINGS

This recipe is a French adaptation of the aromatic and deeply flavored Moroccan tagine.

- 2 tablespoons pure olive oil
- 3 pounds meaty lamb neck and shoulder, cut into 1½-inch cubes

Kosher salt

- 3 large carrots, cut into 1½-inch lengths
- 2 medium onions, halved and thinly sliced
- 3 garlic cloves, finely chopped
- 1 teaspoon ground ginger
- 1 teaspoon cinnamon
- ½ teaspoon ground cumin

Pinch of saffron threads, crumbled

- 2 cups water
- 1 cup pitted prunes (6 ounces)
- 3 tablespoons fresh lemon juice

Freshly ground pepper

- ¼ cup coarsely chopped cilantro

1. Heat the olive oil in a medium enameled cast-iron casserole. Add the lamb in 2 batches, season with salt and brown lightly on all sides over moderately high heat, about 12 minutes; transfer to a plate.

2. Add the carrots, onions and garlic to the casserole and cook over moderately low heat, stirring, until the onions are softened but not browned, about 5 minutes. Add the ginger, cinnamon, cumin and saffron and cook, stirring

occasionally, until fragrant, about 3 minutes.

3. Gradually stir in the water, scraping up the browned juices from the bottom of the pan. Add the lamb, cover and bring to a boil. Reduce the heat to low and cook for 1 hour and 40 minutes. Add the prunes and continue cooking until the meat is very tender, about 20 minutes longer. Tilt the casserole and skim the fat from the sauce. Stir in the lemon juice and season with salt and pepper. Sprinkle with the cilantro and serve. —Daniel Gouret

MAKE AHEAD The tagine can be refrigerated overnight; reheat gently.

WINE Complement the tagine's sweet and spicy flavors with a refreshing, slightly chilled, sharply spicy rosé. Try a Côtes de Provence, such as the 1998 Domaine Sorin, or a Tavel, such as the 1998 Château d'Aquéria.

Spicy Lamb and Bulgur Meatballs

MAKES 12 MEATBALLS

- ½ cup medium-grade bulgur wheat (3 ounces)
- 2 tablespoons dried currants
- 1 tablespoon pure olive oil
- ½ cup minced onion
- 2 tablespoons minced red bell pepper
- 1 tablespoon plus 1 teaspoon minced garlic
- 2 teaspoons ground cumin
- 1 teaspoon ground cardamom
- 1 pound ground lamb
- ½ cup finely chopped parsley
- ½ cup minced mint
- ¼ cup minced dill
- 1 large egg white, lightly beaten
- 2½ teaspoons *harissa* (see Note) or other red chile paste
- 2 teaspoons kosher salt
- ½ teaspoon freshly ground pepper

Vegetable oil, for sautéing

1. In separate bowls, soak the bulgur and currants in water until softened, about 30 minutes for the bulgur and

Lamb Stew with Beans and olives

20 minutes for the currants. Drain, pressing on the solids to extract as much water as possible. Transfer the bulgur and currants to a large bowl.

2. Heat the olive oil in a medium skillet. Add the onion, red bell pepper and garlic and cook over moderate heat, stirring, until softened, about 4 minutes. Add the cumin and cardamom and cook until fragrant, about 1 minute. Scrape the mixture into the bulgur and let cool.

3. Add the ground lamb to the bulgur, along with the parsley, mint, dill, egg white, *harissa,* salt and pepper and mix with your hands until thoroughly combined. Divide the bulgur-lamb mixture into 12 equal portions, roll into balls and set on a large plate.

4. Heat ¼ inch of vegetable oil in a large skillet. Add the meatballs and sauté over moderate heat, turning occasionally, until evenly browned and cooked through, about 10 minutes. Drain the meatballs on paper towels, then serve. —*Roger Hayot*

SERVE WITH A refreshing salad of watercress, mint and parsley dressed with a lemon-garlic vinaigrette.

NOTE *Harissa,* a spicy condiment, is available at Middle Eastern groceries.

BEER The *harissa* adds fire to the sweet and spicy Middle Eastern flavors of these meatballs. Cool them down with an ale, such as Bass Pale Ale or Brooklyn East India Pale Ale.

Lamb Köfte with Grilled Poblanos and Yogurt Sauce

6 SERVINGS

These spicy Turkish patties can be grilled, broiled or fried on a griddle like hamburgers. The meat can also be skewered and then broiled or grilled.

- 2 slices firm-textured white bread
- 2 pounds ground lamb
- 1 cup coarsely grated onion
- 4 garlic cloves, minced
- 3 tablespoons finely chopped flat-leaf parsley
- 3 tablespoons finely chopped mint
- 1 tablespoon ground cumin
- 1 tablespoon paprika
- 2 teaspoons salt
- 1 teaspoon freshly ground black pepper
- ½ teaspoon cinnamon
- ¼ teaspoon cayenne pepper
- 4 poblano peppers
- Vegetable oil, for brushing
- 6 pita breads
- Tomato Sauce with Cumin (recipe follows)
- Yogurt Sauce (recipe follows), at room temperature

1. In a large bowl, cover the bread with water. Pour off the water and squeeze the water out of the bread. Add the lamb, onion, garlic, parsley, mint, cumin, paprika, salt, black pepper, cinnamon and cayenne to the bowl. Using your hands, knead the mixture until smooth. Divide the mixture into 12 portions and, with lightly moistened hands, form into oval patties about 1 inch thick. Refrigerate the patties until chilled or for up to 1 day.

2. Light a grill or preheat the broiler and position a rack 8 inches from the heat. Brush the poblanos lightly with oil and grill or broil, turning, until charred all over. Transfer to a bowl, cover with plastic wrap and let steam for 10 minutes. Peel, core, and seed the poblanos, then thinly slice them.

3. Brush the patties with oil and grill or broil for 6 minutes per side, or until browned and firm to the touch. Grill or broil the pitas for about 1 minute, turning once, until heated through. Tear the pitas into large pieces and arrange them in an overlapping layer on a large platter. Pour the Tomato Sauce with Cumin over the pitas and top with the lamb patties. Spoon some of the Yogurt Sauce over all and garnish with the roasted poblano strips. Serve immediately and pass the remaining Yogurt Sauce separately.

—*Joyce Goldstein*

six meatball strategies

1. Choose ground meat with some fat in it to help bind the mixture and produce juicier and tastier meatballs.

2. Blend different types of meat, such as pork and beef, for more complex flavors.

3. Mix chopped meat with bread crumbs for firm meatballs. For soft, light ones, use crustless bread cubes soaked in milk or water; be sure to mix the ingredients and shape the meatballs gently.

4. Allow cooked ingredients to cool before adding raw chopped meat.

5. If specific amounts of salt and pepper are not indicated, sauté a small amount of the meatball mixture and taste it for seasoning before cooking the rest.

6. Refrigerate the raw meatballs overnight or freeze them. —*Lily Barberio*

WINE The berry fruit in a hearty Zinfandel, such as the 1997 Haywood Los Chamizal Vineyard or the 1997 Beaulieu Vineyard Coastal, will stand up to the lamb spices as well as the tart sauces.

TOMATO SAUCE WITH CUMIN
MAKES ABOUT 2 CUPS

- ¼ cup pure olive oil
- 2 pounds large tomatoes—peeled, seeded and coarsely chopped
- 2 teaspoons ground cumin
- ½ teaspoon cayenne pepper
- Salt

1. Heat the olive oil in a medium saucepan until shimmering. Add the tomatoes, cumin and cayenne pepper and cook over moderate heat, occasionally mashing the tomatoes against the side of the pan with a wooden spoon, until the sauce thickens, about 5 minutes.

2. Season the tomato sauce with salt to taste and keep it warm until ready to use. —*J.G.*

YOGURT SAUCE

MAKES ABOUT 1½ CUPS

1½ cups plain yogurt

2 tablespoons extra-virgin olive oil

1 teaspoon minced garlic

Salt

Cayenne pepper

1. Scoop the yogurt into a paper coffee filter set in a strainer over a bowl and let drain in the refrigerator for 2 hours. Transfer the yogurt to a bowl and discard the liquid.

2. In a small skillet, heat the olive oil. Add the garlic and cook over moderate heat until fragrant and lightly golden, about 2 minutes. Let the garlic oil cool slightly, then stir into the yogurt and season with salt and cayenne.

—J.G.

Casserole-Roasted Rabbit with Herbs

8 SERVINGS

If you've never made rabbit before, this is the ideal recipe to start with. Utterly simple and delicious, it's Italian home cooking at its best.

Two 3½-pound rabbits (see Note)

4 thyme sprigs

2 marjoram sprigs

2 rosemary sprigs

2 sage sprigs

2 bay leaves

5 tablespoons unsalted butter

2 tablespoons extra-virgin olive oil

Salt and freshly ground pepper

4 garlic cloves, thinly sliced

½ cup dry white wine

2 tablespoons water

1. Remove and discard the hearts, kidneys and livers from the rabbits or save them for another use. Rinse the rabbits and pat them dry with paper towels. Divide the herbs into 2 piles and stuff them into the cavities. Close each cavity with a toothpick.

2. In a large enameled cast-iron casserole, melt 1½ tablespoons of the butter in 1 tablespoon of the olive oil. Season the rabbits all over with salt and pepper. Add 1 rabbit to the casserole, breast side down, and cook over moderately high heat until the inner legs are golden, about 4 minutes. Turn the rabbit and brown each side until golden, about 8 minutes total. Transfer the rabbit to a platter. Discard the fat and wipe out the casserole with a paper towel. Repeat with another 1½ tablespoons of butter, the remaining 1 tablespoon of olive oil and the second rabbit.

3. Using kitchen string, tie the hind legs together. Pour off all but 1 tablespoon of the fat in the casserole, add the garlic and cook, stirring from time to time, until lightly golden, about 2 minutes.

4. Return both rabbits to the casserole, add the wine and bring to a boil, scraping up any browned bits from the bottom of the pot. Add the water and the remaining 2 tablespoons of butter. Cover and cook over low heat for 40 minutes, turning the rabbits once. Baste the rabbits with the pan juices 3 or 4 times during cooking. Meanwhile, preheat the oven to 350°.

5. Transfer the casserole to the oven and roast for 1 hour and 10 minutes, or until the rabbits are meltingly tender. Turn the rabbits once and baste with the pan juices 2 or 3 times during cooking.

6. Transfer the rabbits to a cutting board and remove the strings and toothpicks. Cut off the hind legs and arrange them on a platter. Carefully remove the 2 tenderloins along the backbone and cut each piece in half; add to the platter. Remove the meaty breast flaps and cut each in half; add to the platter. Cover the rabbit loosely with foil to keep warm.

7. Boil the juices in the casserole over high heat until reduced to about ½ cup, about 10 minutes, and transfer to a bowl. Serve the rabbit and pass the reduced pan juices separately.

—Mina Vachino ➤

Casserole-Roasted Rabbit with Herbs

NOTE Rabbits can be mail-ordered from D'Artagnan (800-327-8246).

MAKE AHEAD The Casserole-Roasted Rabbit with Herbs can be prepared through Step 5 early in the day. Reheat gently before proceeding.

WINE Complement this herb-infused dish with a hearty red, such as the 1995 Alfredo Prunotto Barbaresco.

Rabbit Ali Baba

4 SERVINGS

⅓ cup extra-virgin olive oil

One 3-pound rabbit, cut into 4 leg and 2 loin pieces

Salt and freshly ground pepper

Cayenne pepper

1 small onion, coarsely chopped

2 garlic cloves, coarsely chopped

6 sage leaves

3 rosemary sprigs

1½ cups Chardonnay

1 tablespoon tomato paste

1. In a large enameled cast-iron casserole, pour the olive oil over the rabbit and turn to coat. Season with salt, pepper and cayenne. Add the onion, garlic, sage and rosemary to the casserole.

2. In a glass measuring cup, use a fork to blend the wine with the tomato paste; pour over the rabbit. Cover and bring to a simmer, then cook over low heat, turning the rabbit pieces a few times, until the loin is just cooked through, about 25 minutes. Transfer the loin pieces to a plate and cover with foil. Continue cooking the rabbit until the legs are tender, about 35 minutes longer. Add the legs to the loin pieces.

3. Boil the pan juices until thickened and flavorful, about 8 minutes. Return the rabbit to the casserole and reheat in the sauce. Season with salt, pepper and cayenne and serve.

—*Lydie Marshall*

NOTE Rabbits can be mail-ordered from D'Artagnan (800-327-8246).

MAKE AHEAD The recipe can be prepared through Step 2 and refrigerated overnight.

WINE The Rabbit Ali Baba calls for a rich, ripely fruity and earthy Rhône white that can stand up to the strong rabbit flavor and the aromatic sage and rosemary. Two good choices: the 1998 Domaine Vieux Télégraphe Châteauneuf-du-Pape Blanc and the 1998 Chapoutier Hermitage Blanc Chante-Alouette.

Kalahari Venison Medallions with Plum Sauce

4 SERVINGS

2 teaspoons grated lemon zest

1 rosemary sprig, leaves removed

2 tablespoons vegetable oil

Eight ½-inch-thick venison loin medallions (about 3 ounces each)

2 tablespoons unsalted butter

Salt and freshly ground pepper

½ cup dry red wine

1 cup beef or veal demiglace (see Note)

2 tablespoons damson plum or seedless blackberry jam

1. In a small bowl, mix the lemon zest, rosemary leaves and 1 tablespoon of the oil to form a paste. Coat the venison medallions with the paste and refrigerate for 2 hours.

2. In a large heavy skillet, melt 1 teaspoon of the butter in the remaining 1 tablespoon of oil. Scrape the lemon and rosemary paste off the venison and season the medallions with salt and pepper. Add the meat to the pan and cook over high heat, turning once, until browned, 5 to 6 minutes. Transfer the medallions to a plate, cover loosely with foil and keep warm.

3. Add the wine to the skillet and bring to a boil over high heat, scraping up the browned bits from the bottom of the pan. Boil until a thick syrup forms, 4 to 5 minutes. Add the demiglace and boil until reduced to ½ cup, 8 to 10 minutes. Stir in the jam until melted, then add any accumulated juices from the meat. Swirl in the remaining 1 tablespoon plus 2 teaspoons of butter until blended. Drizzle the sauce over the meat and serve.

—*Jacques Pépin*

NOTE Beef and veal demiglace are available at specialty food shops.

Venison with Cranberry-Chipotle Sauce

4 SERVINGS

1 cup fresh or frozen cranberries

¼ cup honey

¼ cup water

2 tablespoons unsalted butter

2 medium garlic cloves, minced

1 small canned chipotle chile in adobo sauce, seeded and minced

Salt

Freshly ground pepper

1 tablespoon vegetable oil

1½ pounds venison tenderloin, cut into 1-inch-thick medallions

¼ cup full-bodied red wine

½ cup pecans, toasted and broken into large pieces

1. In a medium saucepan, combine the cranberries with the honey and water. Simmer over moderate heat until the cranberries burst, about 5 minutes. Remove from the heat.

2. Melt 1 tablespoon of the butter in a small skillet. Add the garlic and cook over low heat until softened, about 3 minutes. Stir the garlic, butter and the chipotle into the cranberries and season with salt and pepper.

3. In a large skillet, melt the remaining 1 tablespoon of butter in the oil. Season the venison with salt and pepper. When the fat is hot but not smoking, add half of the medallions and cook over moderately high heat until browned on the bottom, about 3 minutes. Turn and cook until just rare, about 2 minutes longer. Transfer to a warmed platter. Repeat with the remaining medallions.

4. Add the wine to the skillet and boil for 30 seconds, scraping up the

browned bits on the bottom of the skillet with a spatula. Stir in the cranberry sauce, season with salt and pepper and reheat. Spoon the sauce over the venison, sprinkle with the pecans and serve. —*Marcia Kiesel*

Pimentón-Grilled Venison with Oyster Mushrooms

4 SERVINGS

This recipe originated in Moorish southern Spain. It calls for venison because of Muslim proscriptions against pork. But lamb or pork tenderloin will also work well.

- 1 pound venison tenderloin, cut into thick slices
- ¼ cup pure olive oil
- ¼ cup finely chopped flat-leaf parsley
- 1 tablespoon plus ½ teaspoon smoked *pimentón* (see Note)
- 1 tablespoon minced garlic

Salt

- ¼ cup extra-virgin olive oil
- ¾ cup finely chopped onion
- ¾ pound oyster mushrooms, thickly sliced
- ½ cup dry white wine

1. Put the venison in a large resealable plastic bag. Add the pure olive oil, 2 tablespoons of the parsley, 1 tablespoon of the *pimentón,* the garlic and ½ teaspoon of salt. Seal the bag and turn to evenly coat the meat. Let marinate for 20 minutes.

2. Heat the extra-virgin olive oil in a large skillet. Add the onion, cover and cook over moderate heat until translucent, 2 minutes. Add the mushrooms, cover and cook, stirring often, until tender, about 5 minutes. Stir in the remaining ½ teaspoon of *pimentón.* Season with salt. Add the wine; bring to a simmer. Cover partially and cook over low heat until the mushrooms are tender and almost dry, about 6 minutes. Stir in the remaining 2 tablespoons of parsley and keep warm.

3. Preheat the broiler or heat a grill pan. Thread the venison onto 4 skewers and broil or grill the meat, turning to brown all sides, 3 to 4 minutes for medium rare. Serve with the mushrooms. —*Joseph Jiménez de Jiménez*

NOTE Spanish paprika, or *pimentón,* is available in many styles, sweet being the most common. Smoky *pimentón* from La Vera, in the Cáceres region, is ground from dried red peppers smoked over oak.

WINE The hearty venison and smoky *pimentón* call for a bold red Rioja. Try the 1996 Loriñon or the 1995 or 1996 Campillo Alavesa.

Pimentón-Grilled Venison with Oyster Mushrooms

Fennel Crackers, with Chopped Salmon with Capers (p. 46).

Fennel Crackers

MAKES 4 CRACKERS

- 2 cups all-purpose flour
- ½ teaspoon baking powder
- ½ teaspoon fine salt
- 1 stick (4 ounces) unsalted butter, softened
- ½ cup whole milk
- 1 large egg, beaten

Kosher salt and fennel seeds, for sprinkling

1. In a bowl, using a fork, mix the flour with the baking powder and salt. Mash in the butter until blended. Add the milk and egg and stir until a dough begins to form. Turn the dough out onto a lightly floured work surface and lightly knead it until smooth. Flatten the dough into a disk, wrap in plastic and refrigerate until chilled, at least 1 hour.

2. Preheat the oven to 400°. Divide the chilled dough into 4 equal pieces.

On a lightly floured work surface, roll out 1 piece of dough until it is as thin as possible. Carefully transfer the dough to a large baking sheet and use a pastry brush to coat it lightly with water. Sprinkle the surface of the dough lightly with kosher salt and fennel seeds and bake for 8 to 10 minutes, or until the cracker is puffed, crisp and golden brown. Transfer it to a rack to cool. Repeat the process with the remaining dough, salt and fennel seeds. Break the crackers into irregular pieces before serving.

—*Sara Guerin*

MAKE AHEAD The crackers can be kept overnight in an airtight container.

Cornmeal Crackers with Pumpkin Seeds

MAKES ABOUT 2½ DOZEN CRACKERS

- 1 cup stone-ground yellow cornmeal
- ¾ cup all-purpose flour
- ¾ cup raw pumpkin seeds
- 2 teaspoons kosher salt
- 2 teaspoons sugar
- ¾ teaspoon crushed red pepper
- 6 tablespoons unsalted butter
- 3 tablespoons milk

1. In a large skillet, stir the cornmeal over moderate heat, shaking the pan occasionally, until lightly toasted, about 2 minutes. Transfer to a plate and let cool.

2. In a medium bowl, combine the cornmeal with the flour, ½ cup of the pumpkin seeds, the salt, sugar and crushed red pepper. Using your fingers, work the butter into the cornmeal mixture until incorporated. Mix in the milk, pressing the dough with your hands to form a ball; add a little more milk if necessary. Cover the dough and refrigerate until chilled and firm, about 1 hour.

3. Preheat the oven to 350°. Butter 2 baking sheets. Pinch off 1-inch pieces of dough and roll into balls. Arrange the balls on the baking sheet and

press into 2-inch rounds with a flat-bottomed glass. Press the remaining ¼ cup of pumpkin seeds into the rounds. Bake the crackers for about 10 minutes, or until browned around the edges. Let cool for 5 minutes, then transfer to a large plate. Serve warm or at room temperature.

—*Marcia Kiesel*

MAKE AHEAD The cracker dough can be frozen for up to 1 month. The crackers can be stored overnight in an airtight container. Recrisp them in a 300° oven for a few minutes before serving.

Roasted Garlic Flat Breads

MAKES 4 FLAT BREADS

- 20 unpeeled garlic cloves
- ½ cup extra-virgin olive oil
- 2 cups water
- 2½ teaspoons active dry yeast
- 4½ cups all-purpose flour
- 1 tablespoon kosher salt

Coarse sea salt, for sprinkling

1. Preheat the oven to 325°. In a pie plate, toss the garlic cloves with the olive oil. Cover with foil and roast for about 50 minutes, or until the cloves are soft and golden. Let cool, then peel the garlic; reserve the oil.

2. In a large bowl, combine the water with the yeast, ¼ cup of the flour and 2 tablespoons of the garlic oil. Let stand until frothy, about 30 minutes. Using a large rubber spatula, fold in the remaining 4¼ cups of flour, the roasted garlic and the kosher salt until a wet dough forms; be very careful not to smash the garlic.

3. Cover the bowl with plastic wrap and let the dough rise until doubled in bulk, about 1½ hours. Gently punch down the dough, scraping it up from the bottom of the bowl. Cover the dough and let it rise again until it is nearly doubled in bulk, about 1 hour.

4. Preheat the oven to 500° for 30 minutes with a pizza stone on the bottom shelf. Alternatively, generously oil

Cornmeal Crackers with Pumpkin Seeds

a large baking sheet. Turn the dough out onto a lightly floured surface, flatten it slightly and divide it into quarters. Roll or stretch each piece into a ½-inch-thick round and transfer the rounds to 2 floured rimless cookie sheets. Let the dough rounds rise for 30 minutes.

5. Prick the dough rounds all over with a fork. Brush with some of the garlic oil and sprinkle with sea salt. Slide 2 of the rounds directly onto the pizza stone or onto the oiled baking sheet and bake for 10 to 12 minutes, or until golden and crisp. Repeat with the 2 remaining rounds. Cut the flat breads into wedges and serve with any remaining garlic oil.

—*Bruce and Eric Bromberg*

MAKE AHEAD The Roasted Garlic Flat Breads can be frozen for up to 3 days. Reheat directly on the rack of a 350° oven until hot and crisp.

Garlic-Chive Flat Breads

MAKES ABOUT 10 FLAT BREADS

The long wide blades of garlic chives add interest to these crisp flat breads, but you can certainly use plain chives instead. Dip the breads in salsa or spread them with fish salad or goat cheese.

1½ teaspoons active dry yeast
½ cup warm water
1 cup all-purpose flour
¼ cup yellow cornmeal, preferably stone ground
Kosher salt
⅓ cup finely chopped garlic chives
3 tablespoons extra-virgin olive oil, plus more for baking sheets

1. In a small bowl, sprinkle the yeast over the warm water and let stand until foamy, 5 to 8 minutes.

2. In a medium bowl, blend the flour with the cornmeal, ½ teaspoon of salt and the chives. Add the yeast mixture and the 3 tablespoons of olive oil and stir until a firm dough forms. Cover the

bowl with plastic wrap and let the dough rise at warm room temperature until it has doubled in bulk, about 30 minutes.

3. Preheat the oven to 450°. Lightly oil 2 large baking sheets. Punch the dough down and divide it in half. On a lightly floured surface, roll out 1 piece of dough to a 12-by-10-inch rectangle. Cut the rectangle lengthwise into 2-inch-wide strips. Transfer the strips to a baking sheet. Repeat with the remaining dough. Set the strips aside until they puff and start to rise, about 8 minutes. Sprinkle lightly with kosher salt. Bake for about 8 minutes, or until browned around the edges and crisp. Transfer the breads to a rack and let them cool completely. —*Marcia Kiesel*

MAKE AHEAD The flat breads can be stored in an airtight container overnight. Recrisp them in a 350° oven for 3 to 5 minutes before serving.

Hattie's Biscuits

MAKES 1 DOZEN BISCUITS

1¾ cups all-purpose flour
1 tablespoon baking powder
1 teaspoon sugar
½ teaspoon salt
¼ cup plus 2 tablespoons vegetable shortening
½ cup plus 2 tablespoons milk

1. Preheat the oven to 375°. In a bowl, sift the flour with the baking powder, sugar and salt. Using a pastry blender or 2 knives, cut in the shortening until the mixture resembles coarse meal. Stir in the milk until just moistened.

2. Turn the dough out onto a lightly floured work surface and knead twice. Roll out the dough to ⅓ inch thick. Using a 2-inch biscuit cutter, stamp out biscuits as close together as possible; transfer to a baking sheet. Reroll the scraps and stamp out the remaining biscuits. Bake for about 20 minutes, or until lightly golden. Serve immediately.

—*Hattie's, Saratoga Springs, New York*

The Best Biscuits

MAKES 1 DOZEN BISCUITS

This delectable biscuit recipe came from legendary Southern cook Edna Lewis.

1½ cups all-purpose flour
1½ teaspoons single-acting baking powder or double-acting baking powder (see Note)
¼ teaspoon baking soda
½ teaspoon salt
¼ cup cold lard or vegetable shortening, cut into pieces
½ cup buttermilk
1 tablespoon unsalted butter, melted

1. Preheat the oven to 450°. Into a bowl, sift the flour with the baking powder, baking soda and salt. Using your fingers, work in the lard just until the mixture resembles coarse meal. Stir in the buttermilk just until the mixture is moistened.

2. Turn the dough out onto a lightly floured work surface and knead 2 or 3 times. Roll out or pat the dough ½ inch thick. Using a 2-inch round cutter, stamp out biscuits as close together as possible. Transfer the biscuits to a baking sheet. Pat the dough scraps together, reroll and cut out the remaining biscuits; do not overwork the dough.

3. Pierce the top of each biscuit 3 times with a fork and brush with the butter. Bake the biscuits for 12 to 14 minutes, or until risen and golden. Serve at once. —*Scott Peacock*

NOTE To make your own single-acting baking powder, combine 2 tablespoons of cream of tartar with 1½ tablespoons of cornstarch and 1 tablespoon of baking soda. The mix will keep in a tightly sealed jar for up to 1 month.

MAKE AHEAD The unbaked biscuits can be frozen in a single layer right on the baking sheet, then kept frozen in an airtight container for up to 1 month. Thaw before baking.

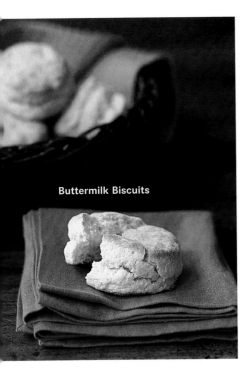

Buttermilk Biscuits

Squash and Stilton Biscuits

MAKES 8 TWO-INCH BISCUITS

The dough for these biscuits is very moist. When you pat the dough out for cutting, you'll need to use plenty of flour on the work surface and on your hands.

- 1¼ cups all-purpose flour, plus more for patting out
- 1 tablespoon plus 1 teaspoon baking powder
- 1 tablespoon sugar
- ½ teaspoon salt
- ¾ cup mashed winter squash, sweet potatoes or yams
- ⅔ cup milk, plus more for brushing
- 7 tablespoons unsalted butter, 4 melted and 3 softened
- ⅓ cup crumbled Stilton or other blue cheese (1½ ounces)

Cranberry sauce or relish, for serving

I. Preheat the oven to 450°. In a medium bowl, sift the flour with the baking powder, sugar and salt. In a small bowl, combine the squash with the ⅔ cup of milk and the 4 tablespoons melted butter. Stir the squash into the dry ingredients until a soft, wet dough forms.

2. Turn the dough out onto a generously floured surface, flour your hands and pat the dough into a 10-inch disk about ¼ inch thick. Generously dust the dough with flour. Using a 2-inch biscuit cutter, cut out 12 rounds. Gather the dough scraps into a ball, pat them out into another disk and cut out 4 more rounds, using more flour if necessary.

3. In a small bowl, blend the 3 tablespoons of softened butter with the Stilton or other blue cheese. Spoon the blue-cheese butter onto 8 of the rounds and top them with the remaining 8 rounds. Transfer the biscuits to a heavy baking sheet and brush the surface of each with milk. Bake for about 15 minutes, or until golden and firm. Serve warm, with cranberry sauce.

—Ana Sortun

Buttermilk Biscuits

MAKES ABOUT 1 DOZEN BISCUITS

This recipe has been adapted from Bill Neal's *Biscuits, Spoonbread, and Sweet Potato Pie* (Random House).

- 2 cups all-purpose flour
- 3¼ teaspoons baking powder
- 1 teaspoon sugar (optional)
- ½ teaspoon baking soda
- ½ teaspoon salt
- 5 tablespoons cold lard or butter, cut into ½-inch pieces
- ¾ cup plus 2 tablespoons buttermilk

I. Preheat the oven to 500°. In a bowl, sift the flour with the baking powder, sugar, baking soda and salt. Work the lard in until the mixture resembles coarse meal. Stir in the buttermilk.

2. Turn the dough out onto a lightly floured surface and fold it over onto itself 10 times. Pat the dough out to an 8-inch square. Using a 2½-inch round cutter, stamp out 12 biscuits; reroll the scraps and stamp out more biscuits.

3. Put the biscuits on a baking sheet and bake for 8 minutes, or until they're golden. —FOOD & WINE Test Kitchen

Southern-Style Corn Bread

MAKES ONE 9-BY-13-INCH CORN BREAD

- 2 cups yellow cornmeal, preferably stone-ground
- 2 teaspoons sugar
- 2 teaspoons baking powder
- 1 teaspoon salt
- ½ teaspoon baking soda
- ⅔ cup boiling water
- 1½ cups buttermilk
- 2 large eggs, beaten
- 1 tablespoon unsalted butter, melted

I. Preheat the oven to 450°. Oil a 9-by-13-inch baking dish and put it in the oven.

2. In a bowl, combine 1⅓ cups of cornmeal with the sugar, baking powder, salt and baking soda.

3. Put the remaining ⅔ cup of cornmeal in a medium heatproof bowl, add the boiling water and stir well. Stir in the buttermilk, eggs and melted butter, then add the dry ingredients and mix until just blended. Pour the batter into the hot baking dish and bake for 20 minutes, or until lightly browned. Turn the corn bread out onto a rack to cool completely. —Pam Anderson

MAKE AHEAD The corn bread can be stored at room temperature for up to 2 days or frozen for up to 1 month.

Buttermilk Corn Bread

MAKES ONE 8-INCH SQUARE LOAF

To create a nice crisp crust, butter the baking dish and preheat it before adding the batter.

- 1 stick (4 ounces) unsalted butter, melted, plus 2 tablespoons cold unsalted butter
- 1½ cups all-purpose flour
- 1½ cups yellow cornmeal
- ¼ cup sugar
- 1 tablespoon plus 1 teaspoon baking powder
- 1 teaspoon salt
- 2 large eggs, lightly beaten
- 1½ cups buttermilk

1. Preheat the oven to 400°. Put the 2 tablespoons of butter in an 8-inch square baking dish and put the dish in the oven to heat.

2. Meanwhile, in a medium bowl, mix the flour with the cornmeal, sugar, baking powder and salt. In a small bowl, mix the eggs and buttermilk; add to the dry ingredients along with the melted butter and stir just until combined.

3. Remove the hot baking dish from the oven and tilt to spread the butter evenly. Carefully scrape the batter into the baking dish and bake for about 25 minutes, or until a toothpick inserted in the center of the corn bread comes out clean. Let cool in the baking dish for 10 minutes, then turn the corn bread out onto a wire rack to cool completely. —*Susan Spicer*

MAKE AHEAD The Buttermilk Corn Bread can be wrapped in plastic and refrigerated for 2 days or frozen for up to 1 week.

Mrs. Harris's Crackling Corn Bread

MAKES ONE 10-INCH ROUND CORN BREAD

- 1 pound thickly sliced country-style bacon or pork rind, cut into ⅓-inch pieces
- 1½ cups yellow cornmeal
- 1 cup all-purpose flour
- 2 tablespoons sugar
- 2 teaspoons baking powder
- ½ teaspoon salt
- 1¼ cups milk
- 2 large eggs, lightly beaten
- 4 tablespoons unsalted butter, melted

1. Preheat the oven to 400°. In a 10-inch cast-iron skillet, cook the bacon over moderate heat until crisp, about 7 minutes. Drain on paper towels. Reserve 2 tablespoons of the bacon drippings.

2. Wipe out the skillet and set it over low heat. Add the 2 tablespoons of drippings and swirl them around the skillet to coat the bottom. In a medium bowl, combine the cornmeal with the flour, the sugar, the baking powder and the salt. In a glass measuring cup, stir the milk and eggs to combine and then add them to the cornmeal mixture along with the butter; stir just until the cornmeal is moistened. Fold in the bacon and pour the batter into the warm skillet.

3. Bake for about 20 minutes, or until golden and a toothpick inserted in the center comes out clean. Serve warm. —*Mary Harris*

MAKE AHEAD The corn bread can be baked 2 days before serving. Turn it out of the skillet, let cool, and then wrap it carefully in aluminum foil. To reheat, leave the bread wrapped in the foil and heat for about 20 minutes in a 350° oven.

Chive and Honey Corn Bread

MAKES ONE 9-BY-13-INCH CORN BREAD

White cornmeal has a more delicate corn flavor than yellow cornmeal. You can bake this corn bread in eight 4-inch metal or foil pie pans to reduce cooking time.

- 1⅔ cups bread flour
- 1⅓ cups stone-ground white cornmeal
- 1½ tablespoons baking powder
- 1 teaspoon salt
- 2 large eggs
- 1⅓ cups milk
- ½ cup corn oil
- ⅓ cup honey
- ½ cup finely snipped chives

1. Preheat the oven to 350°. Oil a 9-by-13-inch metal baking pan. In a bowl, sift the flour with the cornmeal, baking powder and salt. In a large

Boston Brown Bread

bowl, whisk the eggs with the milk, corn oil and honey.

2. Stir the dry ingredients and chives into the egg mixture just until blended. Pour the batter into the pan and bake for about 20 minutes, or until the corn bread springs back when gently pressed. Let cool in the pan, then cut into squares and serve. —*Daniel Bruce*

Boston Brown Bread

MAKES 3 LOAVES

Tradition dictates that this bread be baked in coffee cans to make round loaves, but you can also use 8-by-4-inch loaf pans.

2 ⅓ cups organic rye flour
1 ¼ cups organic all-purpose flour
1 ¼ cups organic whole wheat flour
½ cup organic oat flour
¾ cup coarse stone-ground cornmeal
1 tablespoon baking soda
1 ½ teaspoons baking powder
1 teaspoon salt
1 cup dried currants or blueberries (4 ounces)
1 quart milk
¾ cup unsulphured molasses

I. Preheat the oven to 300°. Generously butter three 10-ounce coffee cans. In a very large bowl, combine all the flours. Stir in the cornmeal, baking soda, baking powder, salt and dried fruit.

2. In a bowl, whisk the milk with the molasses. Slowly pour the liquid into the dry ingredients, stirring until the batter is smooth. Pour the batter into the prepared cans. Stand the cans in the center of the oven and bake for about 1 ½ hours, or until the loaves are springy to the touch. Let cool slightly, then unmold. When the loaves have cooled to room temperature, wrap them in wax paper and store in the refrigerator in a sturdy plastic bag for up to 5 days. —*René Becker*

MAKE AHEAD The loaves can be frozen for up to 1 month.

Simple Herbed Dressing

MAKES 10 TO 12 SERVINGS

Allow at least 2 hours for drying the breads before you start to make this dressing.

Southern-Style Corn Bread (p. 251), cut into ½-inch dice (see Note)
2 cups white bread, cut into ½-inch dice (4 ounces)
4 tablespoons unsalted butter
2 medium onions, finely chopped
2 medium celery ribs, finely chopped
2 cups chicken stock or canned low-sodium broth
2 large eggs, beaten
¼ cup minced flat-leaf parsley
1 tablespoon minced sage
1 tablespoon minced thyme
½ teaspoon salt
½ teaspoon freshly ground pepper

I. Spread the corn bread and white bread on large baking sheets in a single layer. Let dry for 2 to 8 hours.

2. Preheat the oven to 400°. Bake the bread for 12 minutes, stirring, until lightly browned. Transfer to a large bowl.

3. Melt the butter in a large skillet. Add the onions and celery and cook until softened, about 10 minutes. Transfer to a large bowl and stir in the stock, eggs, parsley, sage, thyme, salt and pepper.

4. Butter a 9-by-13-inch baking dish and spread the dressing in it. Cover with foil and bake for about 25 minutes, or until hot throughout. Uncover and bake about 20 minutes, or until a brown crust forms. —*Pam Anderson*

NOTE This dressing can also be made using all white bread, in place of the combination of corn bread and white bread. Substitute a 1-pound loaf of any good, fairly firm white bread—American, French or Italian.

MAKE AHEAD The unbaked dressing can be refrigerated overnight. Bring it to room temperature before baking.

Corn Bread Stuffing with Shrimp and Andouille

MAKES 10 SERVINGS

Andouille, a spicy sausage made from pork chitterlings and tripe, adds a wonderful smoky note to the sweet corn bread stuffing. *Andouille* sausage is available at most supermarkets and by mail from both Aidells Sausage (877-AIDELLS) and Nodine's Smokehouse (800-222-2059).

Buttermilk Corn Bread (p. 251), broken into 1-inch pieces
1 pound *andouille* sausage, quartered lengthwise and sliced crosswise ½ inch thick
3 tablespoons unsalted butter
2 medium onions, coarsely chopped
One 2-pound bunch of celery, coarsely chopped
8 scallions, white and tender green parts only, coarsely chopped
1 pound large shrimp—shelled, deveined and halved crosswise
1 tablespoon minced garlic
1 tablespoon chopped sage
1 tablespoon chopped thyme
3 cups Basic Chicken Stock (p. 98) or canned low-sodium broth
½ cup coarsely chopped flat-leaf parsley
Salt and freshly ground pepper
Tabasco sauce

I. Preheat the oven to 350°. Generously butter a 10-by-15-inch glass or ceramic baking dish.

2. Put the corn bread in a bowl. In a large deep skillet, cook the *andouille* over moderate heat until lightly browned and the fat is rendered, about 10 minutes. Add to the bowl.

3. Melt the butter in the skillet. Stir in the onions, celery and half of the scallions and cook over low heat until softened, about 10 minutes. Add the shrimp, garlic, sage and thyme and cook, stirring, until the shrimp are just cooked through, about 3 minutes. Add the shrimp to the corn bread and *andouille* in the bowl.

4. In the same skillet, bring the stock to a boil. Pour the stock over the corn bread, *andouille* and shrimp and stir well. Add the parsley and the remaining scallions and season the stuffing with salt, pepper and Tabasco. Spread the stuffing in the prepared baking dish and bake for 1 hour, or until crisp and browned on top. —*Susan Spicer*

MAKE AHEAD The Corn Bread Stuffing with Shrimp and Andouille can be refrigerated for 1 day before baking. Bring the stuffing to room temperature before baking.

Rye Bread Stuffing with Sausage, Apples and Bacon

MAKES ABOUT 17 CUPS

You can use store-bought breakfast sausage instead of the sage sausage called for in this recipe.

SAGE SAUSAGE

1½ **pounds ground pork**

2 **teaspoons kosher salt**

1½ **teaspoons dried crumbled sage**

1 **teaspoon coarsely ground pepper**

½ **teaspoon sugar**

STUFFING

Two 1-pound loaves of caraway rye bread, crusts removed, bread sliced ½ inch thick

1 pound thickly sliced bacon, cut crosswise into ¼-inch strips

½ cup water

1 stick (4 ounces) unsalted butter, cut into tablespoons

3 medium Granny Smith apples— peeled, cored and cut into ½-inch chunks

One 1-pound head of green cabbage, coarsely chopped

1 pound cremini mushrooms, quartered

1 tablespoon crumbled dried sage

2 teaspoons dried thyme

6 cups Rich Turkey Stock (p. 99), chicken stock or canned low-sodium broth

Salt and freshly ground pepper

1. MAKE THE SAGE SAUSAGE: Preheat the oven to 375°. In a bowl, mix all of the ingredients. Pat the sausage meat into 6 patties, about ½ inch thick. Arrange the patties on a rimmed baking sheet and bake for 10 minutes, or until cooked through but not browned. Let cool, then break into ½-inch pieces.

2. MAKE THE STUFFING: Turn the oven down to 325°. Bake the slices of bread directly on the oven racks for 8 to 10 minutes, or until crisp. Let cool, then cut the bread into ½-inch dice. Leave the oven on.

3. In a large enameled cast-iron casserole, combine the bacon with the water and cook over moderately low heat until the water has evaporated and the bacon is crisp and golden, about 12 minutes. Using a slotted spoon, transfer the bacon to a plate and pour off all but 4 tablespoons of the fat.

4. Melt the butter in the bacon fat. Add the apples, cabbage and mushrooms and cook over high heat, stirring frequently, until lightly browned, about 10 minutes. Transfer to a large bowl, then stir in the sausage, bacon, sage and thyme. Let cool. Add the bread and toss well. Stir in the Rich Turkey Stock, 2 cups at a time, allowing it to be completely absorbed before adding more. Season the stuffing with salt and pepper.

5. Butter a 9-by-13-inch baking dish. Reserve 5 cups of the stuffing for the turkey and transfer the rest to the prepared baking dish. Cover the dish with foil and bake for 45 minutes, or until the stuffing is heated through. Uncover and bake for 15 minutes longer, or until the top is crisp and golden.

—*Bruce and Eric Bromberg*

MAKE AHEAD The stuffing can be prepared ahead of time through Step 4 and refrigerated for up to 3 days. Bring it to room temperature before baking.

Prosciutto-Bread Stuffing with Sausage

MAKES 17 TO 18 CUPS

This recipe makes enough to stuff a 10-pound turkey and fill a casserole. Use five cups for the cavity and the skin flap at the top of the breast and cook the rest in a baking dish.

Two 1-pound loaves of prosciutto bread, cut into ¾-inch dice (see Note)

¼ cup extra-virgin olive oil

¾ pound sweet Italian sausages, casings removed

4 ounces sliced lean pancetta, finely chopped

1 pound leeks, white and tender green parts, sliced crosswise ¼ inch thick

1 celery rib, finely chopped, plus 1 tablespoon finely chopped celery leaves

¼ cup finely chopped flat-leaf parsley

½ cup freshly grated Parmesan cheese

3 cups Basic Chicken Stock (p. 98) or canned low-sodium broth

Salt and freshly ground pepper

2 tablespoons unsalted butter, melted

1. Preheat the oven to 325°. Lightly butter a 9-by-13-inch glass baking dish. Spread the bread on 2 large, rimmed baking sheets and bake for 30 minutes, stirring twice, until crisp and golden.

2. Meanwhile, in a large, deep skillet, heat 2 tablespoons of the olive oil until shimmering. Add the sausage meat and cook over moderately high heat, breaking it up as you stir, until cooked through, about 10 minutes. Using a slotted spoon, transfer the sausage meat to a large bowl and let cool.

3. Add the remaining 2 tablespoons of olive oil to the skillet and heat until shimmering. Add the pancetta and cook over moderately high heat, stirring occasionally, until softened, about

5 minutes. Add the leeks and chopped celery rib and cook, stirring frequently, until the leeks are softened and golden, 8 to 9 minutes. Spoon off as much fat from the pan as possible. Add the leeks to the sausage meat along with the parsley and celery leaves and let cool.

4. Add the toasted prosciutto bread and all but 2 tablespoons of the Parmesan to the bowl and toss very well. Mix in the stock, season with salt and pepper and spoon the stuffing into the baking dish. Brush with the melted butter. Sprinkle the remaining 2 tablespoons of Parmesan cheese over the top and cover with foil.

5. Preheat the oven to 375°. Bake the stuffing for 45 minutes, or until heated through and lightly browned on the bottom. Remove the foil and bake for about 20 minutes longer, until the top is golden and crisp. Serve hot.

—Grace Parisi

NOTE Prosciutto bread is sold in Italian bakeries. You can substitute two loaves of regular Italian bread and ¼ pound thinly sliced prosciutto, cut up.

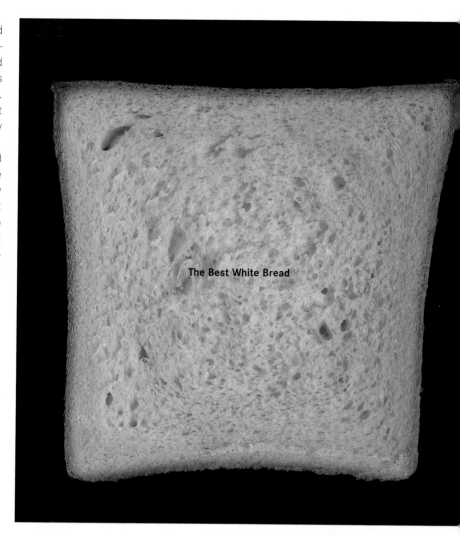

The Best White Bread

The Best White Bread

MAKES THREE 8-BY-4-INCH LOAVES
At Mrs. London's, in Saratoga Springs, New York, this rich dense white bread is baked in a pullman pan to make a perfectly rectangular, rather than balloon-topped, loaf. A pullman pan has a fitted lid that slides into place to ensure a perfectly even shape. Since most home bakers don't own a pullman pan, we call for three standard loaf pans instead.

- 4 cups all-purpose flour
- 4 cups bread flour
- 2 ¾ cups milk
- 2 envelopes active dry yeast (4 ½ teaspoons)
- 2 tablespoons plus 2 teaspoons sugar
- 2 tablespoons salt
- 3 large eggs, lightly beaten
- 1 stick plus 6 tablespoons (7 ounces) unsalted butter, softened
- 1 large egg yolk
- 2 tablespoons heavy cream

1. In a large bowl, mix the all-purpose flour and bread flour. In a small saucepan, heat ¾ cup of the milk just until lukewarm. Pour the warm milk into a medium bowl and stir in the yeast. Let stand until the yeast dissolves and the milk becomes creamy and starts to bubble, about 5 minutes. Stir in 1 ½ cups of the mixed flours. Cover with plastic wrap and let the sponge stand until slightly risen, about 20 minutes.

2. Scrape the sponge into the large bowl of a standing electric mixer fitted with a dough hook. Add the sugar, salt, eggs and the remaining 2 cups of milk and beat at medium speed until blended. Turn the machine off and carefully add the remaining 6 ½ cups of flour. Beat at low speed until the flour is just incorporated, then knead at medium speed until the dough is evenly combined, about 5 minutes, scraping down the sides of the bowl occasionally. Add the butter and continue to knead until the dough is very soft and silky, about 10 minutes longer.

3. Lightly butter a large bowl. Transfer the dough to the bowl and cover with a sheet of oiled plastic wrap. Let the dough stand in a warm, draft-free spot until doubled in bulk, about 1 hour.

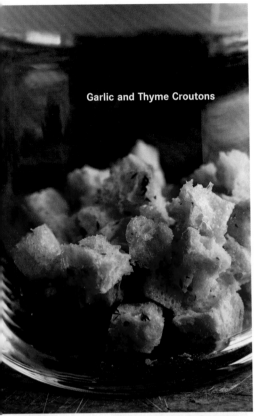

Garlic and Thyme Croutons

Toasted Bread with Olive Oil, Garlic and Herbs

Punch down the dough, then cover and let the dough rise until doubled in bulk again, about 1 hour longer.

4. Punch down the dough and turn it out onto a heavily floured work surface. Divide the dough into 3 equal pieces and let rest on a lightly floured work surface for 20 minutes.

5. Butter three 8-by-4-inch loaf pans. Using lightly floured hands, form each piece of dough into a loaf shape about the same size as the pans. Brush off any excess flour from the loaves and gently ease them into the pans. Cover the pans loosely with oiled plastic wrap and let stand in a warm, draft-free spot until the dough rises 1½ inches above the rims, about 45 minutes.

6. Preheat the oven to 350°. In a small bowl, mix the egg yolk with the cream. Brush the loaves with the egg wash and bake in the center of the oven for 1 hour, or until the tops are golden brown. Carefully turn the loaves out of the pans onto a wire rack. They should sound hollow when tapped on the bottom; if they don't, return the loaves to the pans and bake for a few minutes longer. Let the bread cool completely on wire racks before slicing.

—Michael London

MAKE AHEAD The white bread can be frozen in sturdy plastic bags for 2 weeks. Let the bread thaw completely before removing from the bags.

Garlic and Thyme Croutons

MAKES 4 CUPS

These crispy and fragrant croutons are great to use in salads or soups, or you can crush them and use them as an instant bread crumb topping for fish or vegetables.

- 1   loaf of The Best White Bread (p. 255) or one 1-pound loaf of country white bread, crusts trimmed, bread cut into ¾-inch dice (see Note)
- ¼   cup extra-virgin olive oil
- 2   teaspoons coarsely chopped thyme
- 3   garlic cloves, minced

Sea salt and freshly ground pepper

Preheat the oven to 350°. Spread the diced bread on a large rimmed baking sheet and toss with the extra-virgin olive oil, thyme and garlic. Sprinkle with salt and pepper and bake in the center of the oven for about 15 minutes, stirring occasionally, until golden and crisp.   *—Max London*

NOTE You can use any one- or two-day-old savory bread you have around the house to make the croutons.

MAKE AHEAD The Garlic and Thyme Croutons can be stored in an airtight container for 3 days. Recrisp them in a 325° oven before using.

Toasted Bread with Olive Oil, Garlic and Herbs

MAKES 6 SLICES

Bread that's grilled over an outdoor fire has a delicious, woodsy flavor and needs only the simplest of toppings.

- 6   slices of country bread, cut 1 inch thick
- ⅓   cup extra-virgin olive oil
- 2   garlic cloves, peeled
- 1   large ripe tomato, halved
- 2   tablespoons *herbes de Provence*

Light a grill. Brush both sides of the bread slices with the olive oil. Grill the bread over a moderately hot fire until lightly charred, about 1 minute per side. Rub the hot toasts with the garlic, then the tomato. Sprinkle the toasts with the *herbes de Provence* and serve at once.   *—Eric Ripert*

Chive French Toast with Lime Cream

MAKES 4 SERVINGS

This savory French toast served with Home-Cured Salmon is perfect for brunch or as an hors d'oeuvre, cut into squares.

- 2   eggs
- ⅔   cup skim milk

½ teaspoon salt

3 tablespoons snipped chives

Four ½-inch-thick slices challah, semolina, firm-textured white or whole-grain bread (1 ounce each)

¼ cup light sour cream

1 teaspoon freshly grated lime zest

4 teaspoons unsalted butter

6 ounces thinly sliced Home-Cured Salmon (p. 45)

I. In a shallow bowl, lightly beat the eggs with the milk and salt. Stir in the chives and let stand for 10 minutes. Add the bread; soak until saturated.

2. In a small bowl, mix the sour cream with the lime zest.

3. In a large nonstick skillet, melt half the butter. When it sizzles, add 2 slices of the soaked bread and cook over moderately high heat until browned on the bottom, about 3 minutes. Turn the slices and cook until browned on the other side, about 2 minutes longer. Transfer to plates. Repeat with the remaining butter and bread. Top the French toast with salmon and pass the cream on the side. —*Sally Schneider*

ONE SERVING Calories 250 kcal, Total Fat 11.1 gm, Saturated Fat 4.8 gm, Carbohydrates 18.6 gm

Pumpernickel Waffles

MAKES 20 FOUR-INCH WAFFLES
Note that the waffle batter should be made a day ahead.

3 cups whole milk

¼ cup yellow cornmeal

¼ cup unsulphured molasses

½ ounce unsweetened chocolate, coarsely chopped

2 teaspoons finely chopped caraway seeds

1 teaspoon salt

3 large egg yolks, lightly beaten

1 tablespoon active dry yeast

1½ cups all-purpose flour

¾ cup whole wheat flour

¾ cup rye flour

1 cup mashed potatoes, at room temperature

1 stick (4 ounces) unsalted butter, melted

3 large egg whites

2 tablespoons sugar

I. In a medium saucepan, warm the milk over moderately high heat until bubbles appear around the edge. Remove from the heat and stir in the cornmeal, molasses, chocolate, caraway seeds and salt. Let the mixture cool completely.

2. Add the egg yolks and yeast to the batter; stir to dissolve the yeast. Stir in the all-purpose flour. Cover loosely with plastic wrap and let stand in a warm place for 1 hour. Stir in the whole wheat and rye flours, then cover and refrigerate overnight.

3. Bring the waffle batter to room temperature. Preheat a lightly oiled 8-inch square waffle iron. Stir the mashed potatoes and melted butter into the batter. In a stainless-steel bowl, beat the egg whites with the sugar until soft glossy peaks form. With a rubber spatula, fold one-third of the beaten whites into the batter, then fold in the remaining whites.

4. Pour a scant 1½ cups of the waffle batter into the preheated iron and bake until browned and crisp, about 7 minutes. Transfer the waffles to a platter and cover loosely with foil. Bake the remaining batter; lightly brush the iron with oil between batches if necessary. —*Icebox Café, Miami Beach*

MAKE AHEAD The waffles can be wrapped in plastic and foil and frozen for up to 2 weeks; recrisp in the oven or the waffle iron.

Pumpernickel Waffles, topped with smoked salmon, poached eggs and chives.

Easy Lemon-Rosemary Focaccia

MAKES ONE 11-INCH FOCACCIA

This peppery lemon focaccia was inspired by a recipe from Kevin Taylor, the chef at Zenith Restaurant, in Denver, Colorado. It's a great partner for seafood salads as well as for soups and grilled fish, chicken or lamb. Served solo, it makes a striking hors d'oeuvre.

- 1 pound prepared pizza dough, thawed if frozen (see Note)
- 1 tablespoon extra-virgin olive oil
- 1 teaspoon finely chopped rosemary

Coarsely ground pepper

- 1 thin-skinned organic lemon, scrubbed and halved lengthwise
- ½ teaspoon coarse sea salt

1. Place a pizza stone on the bottom rack of the oven and preheat the oven to 425° for 30 minutes.

2. On a lightly floured surface, roll out or press the dough to an 11-inch round. Transfer the dough to a cookie sheet lined with parchment paper and reshape the dough with your fingers. Prick the dough all over with a fork.

3. Lightly brush the dough with some of the olive oil and sprinkle with the rosemary and a generous pinch of pepper. Slice a lemon half crosswise as thinly as possible. Discard any seeds. Reserve the other half for another use. Arrange the lemon slices on the dough and brush lightly with olive oil. Cover the dough with plastic wrap and let it rise for 15 minutes at room temperature.

4. Discard the plastic wrap and slide the parchment with the dough onto the hot stone. Bake for 25 minutes, or until the focaccia is browned and puffed. Brush with any remaining olive oil and sprinkle evenly with the salt. Cut the focaccia into wedges and serve hot. —*Sally Schneider*

NOTE Fresh and frozen pizza dough is available at many supermarkets and specialty food shops. You can also buy the dough from your favorite local pizzeria.

MAKE AHEAD The rolled-out pizza dough can be transferred to the parchment-lined cookie sheet, wrapped well in plastic and frozen for up to 1 week; thaw before proceeding.

ONE SERVING Calories 207 kcal, Total Fat 4.7 gm, Saturated Fat 0.6 gm, Carbohydrates 36.2 gm

WINE An herbal, floral and fruity white with strong notes of lemon, such as an Italian Arneis, will harmonize well with the flavor of the rosemary-lemon focaccia. Look for the 1998 Bruno Giacosa or the 1998 Carretta.

Easy Lemon-Rosemary Focaccia

Caramelized-Onion and Potato Focaccia

MAKES FOUR 8-INCH FOCACCIAS

New York City's Gramercy Tavern showcases this savory bread on their "Between Meals" menu. The secret to making focaccia that's soft and delicate with a great crust is allowing the dough to rise slowly in a cool place away from the oven.

DOUGH

- ¾ cup warm water
- 1¼ teaspoons active dry yeast

Pinch of sugar

- ¼ cup extra-virgin olive oil, plus more for sprinkling and brushing

1¾ cups all-purpose flour

½ teaspoon salt

TOPPING

2 tablespoons extra-virgin olive oil, plus more for brushing and drizzling

1 large Spanish onion, thinly sliced

1 tablespoon water

½ teaspoon chopped thyme, plus several sprigs for garnish

Salt

6 fingerling potatoes

Freshly ground pepper

14 ounces Robiola cheese

I. MAKE THE DOUGH: In a standing mixer fitted with the paddle, mix the warm water with the yeast and sugar. Let stand until foamy.

2. Add ¼ cup of the olive oil to the yeast mixture and combine. At low speed, add the flour and salt and mix for 2 minutes. Change to the bread hook and knead the dough at medium low speed for 8 minutes; the dough will be very sticky.

3. Scrape the dough into a well-oiled large bowl and brush with olive oil. Cover with plastic wrap and let the dough rise in a cool place until doubled in bulk, about 1½ hours.

4. Using floured hands, punch down the dough and turn it out onto a lightly floured surface. Cut the dough into quarters and roll it into 4 balls. Set 2 balls of dough on each of 2 oiled cookie sheets. Brush the dough with olive oil and let it stand uncovered in a cool place for 15 minutes.

5. Using oiled fingertips, press and stretch each ball of dough into an 8-inch round. Dimple the rounds slightly with your fingertips; brush with olive oil. Let the dough rise in a cool place until light, about 1 hour and 15 minutes.

6. MAKE THE TOPPING: In a large skillet, heat 2 tablespoons of the olive oil. Add the onion, water and chopped thyme and season with salt. Cook the onion over low heat, stirring occasionally, until very soft and golden brown, about 1 hour; let cool.

7. Set a pizza stone in the oven and preheat to 450°; the stone will be fully heated in about 30 minutes. Using a mandoline, thinly slice the fingerling potatoes. In a bowl, toss the potatoes with a little olive oil, salt and pepper and the thyme sprigs. Dimple the dough again and top with the caramelized onion and the potatoes.

8. Slide 2 of the focaccias onto the pizza stone and bake for 12 to 15 minutes, or until golden brown and puffed around the edges. Remove the focaccias from the oven, top them with dollops of Robiola cheese and drizzle with olive oil. Return them to the oven for 1 minute to warm the cheese. Repeat with the 2 remaining focaccias. Serve hot. —*Claudia Fleming*

WINE A light, fruity red, such as Dolcetto, accents both the sweetness and the tang of this dish. Try a 1997 Italian Dolcetto d'Alba from Renato Ratti or G.D. Vajra.

Lemon, Asparagus and Gruyère Pizza

MAKES FOUR 12-INCH PIZZAS

As an alternate take on the pizza topping below, use tangerine sections, pitted Calamata olives, sliced red onions and goat cheese.

1 envelope active dry yeast

1½ cups warm water

3½ cups bread flour, plus more for kneading and rolling

1½ tablespoons pure olive oil

1 tablespoon fine sea salt

½ pound medium asparagus, sliced ¼ inch thick on the diagonal

1 tablespoon plus 1 teaspoon extra-virgin olive oil

2 cups shredded Gruyère cheese, (½ pound)

2 small lemons, preferably Meyer, sliced paper-thin

Kosher salt

Freshly ground pepper

½ cup freshly grated Parmesan cheese (2 ounces)

I. In a large bowl, dissolve the yeast in 1 cup of the warm water and let stand until foamy, about 10 minutes. Stir in 1½ cups of the bread flour until blended, then cover with a kitchen towel and let the sponge stand at room temperature until bubbly, 1 to 1½ hours.

2. Add the remaining 2 cups of flour and ½ cup warm water to the sponge in the bowl. Add the pure olive oil and the sea salt and stir until almost combined. Scrape the dough out onto a lightly floured work surface and knead gently until smooth and silky, about 5 minutes. Transfer the dough to a lightly oiled bowl, cover with plastic wrap and refrigerate overnight.

3. Let the dough return to room temperature. Punch down and form into 4 balls. Place them on a lightly floured work surface, cover loosely with plastic wrap and let rest for 10 minutes.

4. In a pan of boiling salted water, boil the asparagus until bright green, about 20 seconds. Drain; refresh the asparagus under cold water. Pat dry.

5. Place a pizza stone in the oven and preheat to 500°. Work with 1 piece of the pizza dough at a time and keep the rest covered. On a lightly floured work surface, roll or stretch the dough out to a 12-inch round. Transfer the round to a lightly floured pizza peel or cookie sheet. Brush the dough with 1 teaspoon of the extra-virgin olive oil and top with ½ cup of the Gruyère and one-fourth of the asparagus and lemon slices. Sprinkle the pizza with kosher salt, pepper and 2 tablespoons of the Parmesan.

6. Slide the pizza onto the hot stone and bake until the crust is golden and the cheese is bubbling, about 10 minutes. Cut the pizza into wedges and serve immediately. Repeat with the remaining dough and toppings.

—*Elizabeth Falkner*

Wrede's Grilled Pizza with Grapes and Soppressata

Spinach and Olive Pizza

MAKES ONE 11-INCH PIZZA

This rustic Mediterranean-style pizza has olive oil in the pastry.

PASTRY

- 1 cup plus 2 tablespoons all-purpose flour
- ¼ cup extra-virgin olive oil
- ¼ cup warm water
- ¾ teaspoon salt

FILLING

- ¼ cup plus 1 tablespoon extra-virgin olive oil
- ¼ cup finely chopped onion
- 2 tablespoons minced garlic
- 1 pound baby spinach, rinsed
- 2 tablespoons sour cream
- 1 large egg, lightly beaten

Salt and freshly ground pepper

- ¾ cup diced eggplant (optional)
- ¼ cup Calamata olives (2 ounces), halved and pitted
- 2 plum tomatoes—peeled, halved lengthwise, seeded and thinly sliced crosswise
- ⅓ cup crumbled feta cheese (about 2 ounces)

I. MAKE THE PASTRY: In a bowl, stir the flour with the oil, water and salt until a dough forms. Transfer to a lightly floured work surface and knead just until smooth. Wrap the pastry in plastic wrap and let rest for 30 minutes at room temperature.

2. MAKE THE FILLING: In a large skillet, heat ¼ cup of the oil until shimmering. Add the onion and cook over moderately high heat until softened, about 4 minutes. Add the garlic and cook until fragrant, about 30 seconds.

3. Add the spinach to the skillet, a handful at a time, and cook just until wilted, about 2 minutes. Transfer to a colander and press out as much liquid as possible; let cool. In a bowl, combine the spinach with the sour cream and egg; season with salt and pepper.

4. Wipe out the skillet and heat the remaining 1 tablespoon of oil. Add the eggplant and cook over moderately high heat, stirring often, until golden and tender, about 5 minutes.

5. Preheat the oven to 350°. On a lightly floured surface, roll out the pastry to an 11-inch round that is a scant ¼ inch thick. Transfer the pastry to a 10-inch fluted tart pan with a removable bottom; press it into the corners and a scant ½ inch up the sides. Spread the spinach filling over the pastry and top with the eggplant, olives, tomatoes and feta. Bake the pizza for about 40 minutes, or until the crust is golden.

6. Remove the side of the pan and cut the pizza into wedges. Serve warm.

—*Thomas Gay*

MAKE AHEAD The recipe can be prepared through Step 3 and refrigerated overnight.

WINE Choose a fruity white wine to balance the tomatoes' acidity and the feta's sharpness. Try the 1997 Brancott Patutahi Gewürztraminer from New Zealand or the 1994 Zind-Humbrecht Herrenweg Turckheim Riesling from Alsace, France.

Wrede's Grilled Pizza with Grapes and Soppressata

MAKES FOUR 7-INCH PIZZAS

Grilled pizza is a great invention. Here the combination of toppings is as unusual as the cooking method. Sweet grapes balance piquant Gorgonzola and rich spicy *soppressata.*

- ⅔ cup lukewarm water
- 2 teaspoons active dry yeast
- 1⅓ cups flour, plus more for dusting
- 1 tablespoon sugar

Salt

Extra-virgin olive oil

- 4 ounces Gorgonzola dolce, diced
- 4 ounces *soppressata,* cut into ¼-inch dice (1 cup)
- ¾ cup green grapes, halved
- 2 tablespoons snipped chives

I. In a medium bowl, combine the water with the yeast and 1 teaspoon of the flour and let stand until dissolved. Add the sugar and a pinch of salt and stir in enough of the flour to form a stiff dough. Scrape the dough onto a lightly floured work surface and knead until smooth. Put the dough in a lightly oiled bowl, cover and let rise in a warm, draft-free place until doubled in bulk, 1 to 1½ hours.

2. Light a grill and lightly brush the grate with oil. Deflate the dough, divide it in quarters and shape each quarter into a ball. On a floured surface, roll each ball out to an approximate 7-inch round. Brush lightly with olive oil.

3. Transfer the rounds to the grill and cook over a moderate fire for 2 minutes, or until the bottoms are browned and crisp. Flip the rounds and sprinkle them with the diced Gorgonzola and *soppressata.* Continue to grill just until the cheese is melted and the bottoms of the pizzas are golden; move the pizzas as necessary to avoid burning. Transfer the pizzas to plates and top them with the halved grapes and the chives. Serve immediately.

—*Joseph Wrede*

Stuffed Pizza Pie with Escarole

MAKES ONE 12-INCH PIZZA

Two pounds of prepared pizza dough can be used instead of homemade.

DOUGH

- 1 cup warm water
- 3 tablespoons active dry yeast
- 4 cups all-purpose flour
- 1¼ teaspoons salt

FILLING

Two 1-pound heads of escarole, separated into leaves

Salt

- ¼ cup pine nuts
- 2 tablespoons extra-virgin olive oil
- 2 garlic cloves, minced
- ½ cup brine-cured black olives (3 ounces), halved and pitted
- 4 anchovy fillets, coarsely chopped

Freshly ground pepper

Pure olive oil, for brushing

1. MAKE THE DOUGH: In a small bowl, combine the water with the yeast and let stand until foamy, about 5 minutes.

2. In a large bowl, stir the flour with the salt. Make a well in the center and pour in the yeast mixture. Stir gently until a rough dough forms. Turn out onto a lightly floured work surface and knead gently until smooth. Transfer to an oiled bowl and cover with plastic wrap. Let rise until doubled in bulk, about 1 hour.

3. MEANWHILE, MAKE THE FILLING: Cook the escarole in a large pot of boiling salted water for 4 minutes; drain and rinse under cold water. Squeeze the escarole dry, then chop coarsely.

4. Preheat the oven to 400°. Toast the pine nuts in a pie pan for 4 minutes.

5. In a large skillet, heat the extra-virgin olive oil. Add the garlic and cook over low heat for 1 minute. Add the escarole, toasted pine nuts, olives and anchovies and cook, stirring, for 2 minutes. Season with salt and pepper, then spread the filling on a large plate to cool.

6. Lightly oil a 12-inch round pizza or tart pan. Punch down the dough and cut it in half. On a lightly floured surface, roll out 1 piece of the dough ¼ inch thick. Trim it into a 12-inch round; let rise for 10 minutes. Roll the other dough half into a 13-inch round ¼ inch thick. Transfer the larger round to the pizza pan, draping it evenly over the sides.

7. Spread the escarole filling evenly over the dough in the pan. Fold the remaining round in half and set it on the escarole filling, unfolding it to cover the top. Crimp the edges of the pie to seal. Using a fork, prick the top of the pizza all over. Brush with pure olive oil and bake in the center of the oven for about 45 minutes, or until golden brown.

8. Transfer the pizza to a rack to cool for 10 minutes. Cut into wedges and serve warm or at room temperature.

—Silvana Daniello

Tomato and Goat Cheese Panini

MAKES 10 PANINI

Feel free to experiment with different tomato varieties, but be sure to avoid overly juicy ones, which may make the panini soggy.

- 2 cups packed basil leaves (3 ounces)
- 3 tablespoons pine nuts
- 2 garlic cloves, halved
- 1½ tablespoons capers, drained

Extra-virgin olive oil

Salt and freshly ground pepper

Twenty ¼-inch-thick slices firm white sandwich bread

- ½ pound fresh goat cheese, crumbled
- 5 medium plum tomatoes, sliced crosswise ¼ inch thick

1. In a food processor, finely chop the basil leaves with the pine nuts, garlic and capers. With the machine on, slowly pour in ¼ cup of olive oil until blended. Transfer the pesto to a bowl and season with salt and pepper.

2. Brush 10 slices of the bread with olive oil and place the slices, oiled side down, on a work surface. Top each slice with 1 tablespoon of the goat cheese, 1 tablespoon of the pesto, 4 slices of tomato and 1 more tablespoon of goat cheese. Cover the 10 topped slices with the remaining slices of bread and brush the tops of the sandwiches with olive oil.

3. Set a large grill pan over low heat. Place 4 panini on the pan and weigh them down with a heavy skillet. Grill for 1 to 2 minutes on each side, until well browned and crisp. Cut the panini in half on the diagonal and serve hot while you grill the remaining panini.

—Martin Dodd

Stuffed Pizza Pie with Escarole

Four Cheese Panini

the panini until the outside is crisp and the filling is heated through, 3 minutes per side. Cut the panini in half and serve at once. —*Giuseppe Forte*

Four Cheese Panini

MAKES 4 PANINI

- ½ cup shredded fresh mozzarella cheese (3 ounces)
- ½ cup shredded Fontina cheese (4 ounces)
- ¼ cup crumbled Gorgonzola cheese (1 ounce)
- ½ cup shredded provolone cheese (3 ounces)
- 4 ciabatta rolls, halved lengthwise, or 8 slices firm white sandwich bread
- 8 arugula leaves

1. In a small bowl, combine the cheeses. Spread the cheese on the bottoms of the ciabatta rolls, top with 2 arugula leaves and close the panini.
2. Set a large cast-iron skillet or griddle over moderately high heat. Arrange the panini in the skillet and weigh them down with a smaller pan. Cook the panini until the outside is crisp and the cheese is melted, 3 minutes per side. Cut the panini in half and serve at once. —*Giuseppe Forte*

Eggplant, Fontina and Tomato Panini

MAKES 4 PANINI

Extra-virgin olive oil
- 1 medium eggplant (1 pound), cut lengthwise into eight ½-inch-thick slices

Salt and freshly ground pepper
- 6 ounces Fontina cheese, cut into 8 slices
- 4 medium tomatoes, sliced ¼ inch thick
- ½ cup packed basil leaves

Four 4-by-6-inch pieces of rosemary focaccia or 6-inch-long baguette rolls, halved lengthwise

1. Lightly coat the bottom of a large skillet with olive oil and heat until shimmering. Season the eggplant slices with salt and pepper and cook over moderately high heat until golden, 6 to 7 minutes per side. Top each eggplant slice with a slice of cheese and cook until the cheese begins to melt, 1 to 2 minutes. Transfer to paper towels to drain. Wipe out the skillet and add more oil. Repeat with the remaining eggplant and cheese.
2. Arrange the tomatoes and basil on the bottom halves of the bread; season with salt and pepper. Top with the eggplant slices and close the panini.
3. Set a large cast-iron skillet or griddle over moderately high heat. Arrange the panini in the skillet and weigh them down with a smaller pan. Cook

Wild Mushroom Panini

MAKES 10 PANINI

Mushrooms with lemon is a match made in heaven. Here lemon zest joins the juice to raise the flavor quotient.

Extra-virgin olive oil
- 4 pounds oyster mushrooms, tough stems discarded, mushrooms halved if large

Salt and freshly ground pepper
- 2 large garlic cloves, minced
- 1 tablespoon chopped thyme
- 2 tablespoons fresh lemon juice
- ½ teaspoon finely grated lemon zest

Twenty ¼-inch-thick slices firm white sandwich bread
- 10 ounces fresh mozzarella, cut into 10 slices and halved

1. Put 2 tablespoons of olive oil in each of 2 large skillets over moderate heat. When the oil is hot, add half the mushrooms to each skillet, season with salt and pepper and stir. Cover the skillets, reduce the heat to low and cook, stirring occasionally, for 10 minutes. Uncover the skillets and continue cooking the mushrooms until nicely browned, about 8 more minutes. Add half the garlic and thyme to each skillet and cook, stirring, until fragrant, about 3 minutes. Transfer the mushrooms to a bowl and stir in the lemon juice and lemon zest. Let the mushrooms cool.

2. Brush 10 slices of the bread with olive oil and place them, oiled side down, on a work surface. Top each with a slice of mozzarella, a scant ¼ cup of the mushrooms and another slice of cheese. Cover with the remaining sliced bread and brush the top of the sandwiches with olive oil.

3. Set a large grill pan over low heat. Place 4 panini on the pan and weigh them down with a heavy skillet. Grill for 1 to 2 minutes on each side, until well browned and crisp. Cut the panini in half on the diagonal and serve hot while you grill the remaining panini.

—Martin Dodd

MAKE AHEAD The cooked mushrooms can be made ahead and refrigerated for up to 2 days. Rewarm in a skillet before using.

Lobster Rolls

MAKES 6 ROLLS

Cucumber, scallions and tarragon replace the traditional celery and onions for a twist on the classic lobster salad.

Three 1½-pound lobsters

½ cup mayonnaise

2 tablespoons fresh lemon juice

1 teaspoon Dijon mustard

1 teaspoon minced tarragon

1 medium cucumber—peeled, seeded and cut into ¼-inch dice

Tabasco

Salt and freshly ground pepper

2 medium scallions, thinly sliced

6 hot dog buns

1. Bring a large pot of water to a boil. Plunge the lobsters in, head first, and cook until bright red all over, about 12 minutes. Transfer the lobsters to a bowl.

2. Crack the lobster claws and knuckles and remove the meat. Twist the tails from the bodies and slit the undersides lengthwise with scissors. Remove the meat and discard the black intestinal vein that runs along the tail. Cut the lobster into ½-inch pieces.

3. In a large bowl, mix together the mayonnaise, lemon juice, mustard and tarragon. Fold in the lobster meat and cucumber and season with Tabasco, salt and pepper. Cover and chill the lobster salad for at least 30 minutes.

Just before serving, mix in the scallions. Generously fill each hot-dog bun with lobster salad and serve.

—Jasper White

MAKE AHEAD The lobster salad can be refrigerated for up to 1 day. Stir in the scallions just before serving.

BEER Turn to a classic Northeastern beer, such as Samuel Adams Boston Lager. Lorina sparkling lemonade from France is a lovely nonalcoholic choice.

Crab and Avocado Panini

MAKES 10 PANINI

2 tablespoons fresh lemon juice

½ teaspoon finely grated lemon zest

1 tablespoon minced fresh red chile

1 garlic clove, minced

1 large avocado, cut into small dice

¾ pound lump crabmeat, picked over to remove cartilage

2 tablespoons minced parsley

Salt and freshly ground pepper

Twenty ¼-inch-thick slices firm white sandwich bread

Extra-virgin olive oil

1. In a medium bowl, combine the lemon juice, lemon zest, chile and garlic. Gently fold in the avocado, crabmeat and parsley with a rubber spatula. Season with salt and pepper.

2. Brush 10 slices of the bread with olive oil and place them, oiled side down, on a work surface. Top each with a scant ¼ cup of the crab mixture and cover with the remaining sliced

the new panino presses

All you really need to make panini are two cast-iron skillets (one to hold the sandwich, the other to weight it down). But for more convenience, consider one of the panino machines now on the market. We tested six presses; these three were the best.

Salton's Sandwich Maker (left) gets very hot very fast. The nonstick surface simplifies cleanup if any of the panino filling spills out ($25; 888-889-0899).

Black & Decker's Quick Grill seals the edges of panini so fillings don't ooze out. It also cuts the sandwiches in half ($24; 800-231-9786).

Philips' Toaster with Sandwich Maker is a regular toaster with extra-wide slots and an insert to hold panini. This is the machine to buy if you prefer using thick breads such as focaccia for panini ($70 at Target; 800-800-8800).

—Monica Forrestall

bread. Brush the tops of the sandwiches with olive oil.

3. Set a large grill pan over low heat. Place 4 panini on the pan and weigh them down with a heavy skillet. Grill for 1 to 2 minutes on each side, until well browned and crisp. Cut the panini in half on the diagonal and serve hot while you grill the remaining panini.

—*Martin Dodd*

Italian Tuna Panini
MAKES 4 PANINI ✳

Two 6-ounce cans Italian tuna packed in olive oil, drained
3 tablespoons fresh lemon juice
Salt and freshly ground pepper
¼ cup extra-virgin olive oil
8 slices firm white sandwich bread or 4 ciabatta rolls, halved lengthwise
1 medium onion, thinly sliced

1. In a small bowl, combine the tuna with the lemon juice and season with salt and pepper. Brush the olive oil on the bread or ciabatta. Spread the tuna on 4 slices of the bread and top with onion slices. Close the panini.

2. Set a large cast-iron skillet or griddle over moderately high heat. Arrange the panini in the skillet and weigh them down with a smaller pan. Cook the panini until the outside is crisp and the filling is heated through, 1 to 2 minutes per side. Cut the panini in half and serve at once.

—*Giuseppe Forte*

Artichoke and Prosciutto Panini
MAKES 4 PANINI ✳

4 ciabatta rolls or 6-inch-long baguette rolls, halved lengthwise
¼ cup extra-virgin olive oil
Salt and freshly ground pepper
½ pound sliced prosciutto
One 8-ounce jar artichoke hearts, drained and flattened slightly
8 arugula leaves

1. Brush the cut sides of the ciabatta with the olive oil and season with salt

and pepper. Layer the prosciutto, artichoke hearts and arugula on the ciabatta and close the panini.

2. Set a large cast-iron skillet or griddle over moderately high heat. Arrange the panini in the skillet and weigh them down with a smaller pan. Cook the panini until the outside is crisp and the filling is heated through, 3 minutes per side. Cut the panini in half and serve at once. —*Giuseppe Forte*

Ham, Salami and Cheese Panini
MAKES 4 PANINI ✳

2 tablespoons mayonnaise
2 tablespoons ketchup
1 teaspoon brandy
Pinch of cayenne pepper
2 ounces salami or mortadella, cut into ¼-inch dice
⅓ cup freshly grated Parmigiano-Reggiano cheese
½ pound sliced ham
Four 6-inch-long baguette rolls or one 2-foot-long baguette, halved lengthwise and cut into 4 pieces

1. In a small bowl, mix the mayonnaise, ketchup, brandy and cayenne. In another small bowl, toss the salami with the cheese. Divide the ham slices into 4 even stacks. Scatter the salami and cheese in the center of each ham stack; fold so the ham is in thirds, like folding a letter. Brush both cut sides of the baguette rolls with the mayonnaise sauce. Put a ham packet on each of the bottom halves of the rolls and close the panini with the top halves.

2. Set a large cast-iron skillet or griddle over moderately high heat. Arrange the panini in the skillet and weigh them down with a smaller pan. Cook the panini until the outside is crisp and the filling is heated through, 3 minutes per side. Cut the panini in half and serve at once.

—*Giuseppe Forte*

MAKE AHEAD The ham packets can be assembled, wrapped in plastic and refrigerated overnight.

Provençal Tuna Burgers
MAKES 10 BURGERS

The staff at The Inn at Little Washington in Washington, Virginia, uses leftover sushi-quality tuna for these burgers, but you can use very fresh regular tuna.

4 pounds 1-inch thick tuna steaks
Pure olive oil for brushing, plus more for frying
Salt and freshly ground pepper
1 cup finely chopped cornichons
½ cup finely chopped red onion
¼ cup finely chopped dill
2 tablespoons capers, drained
2 tablespoons finely chopped black olives
2 cups mayonnaise
3 tablespoons fresh lemon juice
¼ cup Dijon mustard
2 tablespoons dry mustard
All-purpose flour, for dusting
Marinated Cabbage Slaw (p. 61)

1. Preheat the broiler. Brush the tuna steaks on both sides with olive oil and season with salt and pepper. Broil half the tuna steaks for 2 minutes per side, until just rare. Repeat with the remaining tuna steaks. Let the tuna cool to room temperature, then finely chop it with a knife.

2. In a large bowl, combine the chopped tuna with the cornichons, red onion, dill, capers and olives. Fold in 1 cup of the mayonnaise and the lemon juice and season with salt and pepper. Shape the tuna mixture into 10 burgers and transfer to a baking sheet. Refrigerate the tuna burgers until they are chilled and firm, about 30 minutes.

3. In a small bowl, whisk the remaining 1 cup of mayonnaise together with the Dijon mustard and the dry mustard until well blended. Season with salt and pepper. Refrigerate the mustard mayonnaise until it is ready to use.

4. Dust the tuna burgers with flour. Heat ¼ inch of olive oil in each of 2 large skillets until shimmering. Add 3 or 4 burgers to each skillet and cook over moderately high heat until browned and crisp, about 3 minutes per side for medium. Drain the tuna burgers on paper towels and cook the remaining burgers in 1 skillet. Serve the tuna burgers with the mustard mayonnaise. Pass the Marinated Cabbage Slaw separately.

—*Patrick O'Connell*

BEER An Anchor Steam beer would have enough body to hold its own with the tuna burgers.

MAKE AHEAD The recipe can be prepared through Step 3 and refrigerated overnight.

Fried Catfish Sandwiches with Chipotle-Honey Mayo

MAKES 8 SANDWICHES

- 1 cup all-purpose flour
- ½ cup coarse yellow cornmeal
- ½ cup fine white cornmeal
- Kosher salt
- Freshly ground pepper
- 2 large eggs, beaten
- ⅔ cup milk
- 8 skinless catfish fillets (5 ounces each)
- 1 cup mayonnaise
- 3 canned chipotle chiles in adobo, halved and seeded
- 2 tablespoons honey
- 2 tablespoons fresh lemon juice
- 1½ cups vegetable oil, for frying
- 16 slices firm-textured white bread, toasted
- 1 head Boston lettuce, cut into ½-inch strips
- 2 large beefsteak tomatoes, thinly sliced

I. Line a baking sheet with wax paper. Put ¾ cup of the flour in a shallow bowl. In another shallow bowl, combine the yellow and white cornmeals with 1 teaspoon salt, ¼ teaspoon pepper and the remaining ¼ cup flour. In a third shallow bowl, beat the eggs with the milk. Dredge the catfish fillets, one at a time, in the flour; shake off any

Fried Catfish Sandwich with Chipotle-Honey Mayo

excess. Dip the fillets in the egg mixture and coat them completely with the cornmeal mixture. Set the fillets on the baking sheet and refrigerate until the coating is dry, at least 1 hour.

2. Meanwhile, in a mini food processor, combine the mayonnaise with the chipotles, honey and lemon juice; process until smooth. Transfer the mayonnaise to a bowl, cover and refrigerate.

3. Preheat the oven to 250°. Put ½ cup of the oil in a large, heavy skillet and heat until shimmering. Add 3 catfish fillets and fry over moderately high heat until golden and crisp on one side, 5 to 6 minutes. Carefully turn the fillets, reduce the heat to moderately low and fry until golden, crisp and cooked through, about 6 minutes longer. Using a slotted spatula, gently transfer the fillets to paper towels to drain; transfer the fried fish to a baking sheet and keep warm in the oven.

4. Wipe out the skillet with paper towels and add another ½ cup of oil. Fry the remaining fish in 2 batches, changing the oil between batches. Season the fried catfish with salt.

5. Spread a generous tablespoon of the mayonnaise on half the toast slices. Top with the lettuce, fried catfish and sliced tomatoes. Cover with the remaining slices of toast.

Serve the sandwiches immediately, passing any remaining mayonnaise at the table. —*Michael Lomonaco*

MAKE AHEAD The catfish sandwich recipe can be prepared through Step 2 and refrigerated overnight.

WINE This simple country fish fry will be well-balanced by a lively white wine. Consider the 1996 Chateau St. Jean Chardonnay or the Nonvintage Nino Franco Prosecco Rustico.

Next-Day Turkey Sandwiches
MAKES 4 SANDWICHES

For this sandwich, pile most of the components of the traditional Thanksgiving meal between two slices of bread. You can use any squash puree; if you only have roasted squash or sweet potatoes, just mash them up.

    1 pound leftover turkey, sliced
    ¼ cup chunky cranberry sauce
    3 cups leftover bread stuffing
       or corn bread stuffing
    8 slices white country bread
Salt and freshly ground pepper
Mayonnaise (optional)
    ½ cup winter squash puree

Stack the turkey, cranberry sauce and stuffing on half of the bread slices and season with salt and pepper. Slather the remaining bread slices with mayonnaise and the squash puree, close the sandwiches and serve.

—*Barbara Lynch*

WINE A simple, direct, fruity blush wine will stand up to the sweet and tart flavors in this sandwich. Try a chilled White Zinfandel, such as the 1999 Sutter Home or the 1999 Beringer.

Cuban Roast Pork Sandwiches with Mojo Sauce
MAKES 2 SANDWICHES

This recipe makes about 1 cup of citrusy, garlicky mojo, much more than enough for 2 sandwiches.

MOJO SAUCE

    ⅓ cup pure olive oil

Next-Day Turkey Sandwich

6 garlic cloves, minced

⅓ cup fresh orange juice

⅓ cup fresh lemon juice

1 teaspoon kosher salt

½ teaspoon freshly ground pepper

½ teaspoon ground cumin

SANDWICHES

2 soft ciabatta or Portugese rolls

About ¼ cup mojo sauce

2 tablespoons mayonnaise

6 to 8 thin slices leftover Roast Leg
of Pork with Fresh Herbs (p. 203)

2 large, very thin slices of proscuit-
to or Westphalian ham

4 slices Swiss or Italian
Fontina cheese

6 thin slices of tomato

6 thin slices of red onion

6 thin slices of sour pickle

2 tablespoons melted
unsalted butter

Coarsely chopped pickled jalapeños

I. MAKE THE MOJO SAUCE: Heat the olive oil in a small skillet. Add the garlic and cook over moderate heat, stirring, until golden, about 2 minutes. Add the orange juice, lemon juice, salt, pepper and cumin and cook, stirring, until fragrant, about 1 minute. Transfer the sauce to a bowl to cool.

2. MAKE THE SANDWICHES: Split the rolls lengthwise. Mix the mayonnaise with ¼ cup of the mojo sauce and spread over the cut sides of the rolls. On the bottom halves, layer the pork, prosciutto, cheese, tomato, onion and pickle slices. Cover the sandwiches with the tops of the rolls and press lightly.

3. Heat a medium cast-iron skillet. Brush the sandwiches with the melted butter. Put them in the skillet and top with a heavy smaller skillet. Cook over low heat until the meat is warmed through, the cheese is beginning to melt and the rolls are very crusty, about 4 minutes per side. Transfer the sandwiches to a work surface, cut them in half and serve with pickled jalapeños. *—Bruce Aidells*

MAKE AHEAD The mojo sauce can be refrigerated for up to 5 days. Bring to room temperature before using.

Ho Chi Minh City Subs with Vinegared Carrots

MAKES 6 SANDWICHES

These sandwiches are standard street fare throughout Southeast Asia. The baguettes, meats, mayonnaise and butter were introduced to the region by the French; the coriander, pickled carrots and hot chile are characteristic Southeast Asian condiments.

6 long French rolls, halved
lengthwise, or 2 long baguettes,
each split lengthwise and
cut into 3 sections

Butter, for spreading

Mayonnaise, for spreading

About 2 tablespoons minced bird chile

Vinegared Carrots (recipe follows)

¾ pound pâté de campagne or
thinly sliced mortadella, cured
ham or any other prepared meat

2 cups cilantro sprigs

I. Spread the cut sides of the rolls with butter and mayonnaise. Sprinkle some of the minced chile on the bottom half of each roll and top each with some of the Vinegared Carrots.

2. Spread the pâté or put the sliced meat on each sandwich and top with cilantro sprigs. Close the sandwiches, press them together firmly and serve.

—Jeffrey Alford and Naomi Duguid

BEER A refreshing beer with a touch of sweetness will best match the sweet-and-sour flavors in these spicy sandwiches. Look for New Amsterdam Amber, a fruity lager-ale hybrid, or Anchor Steam.

VINEGARED CARROTS

MAKES ABOUT 2 CUPS

This lightly pickled condiment can be served on its own as a refreshing side salad. Peeled daikon can be substituted for half of the carrots.

1 pound carrots

Cuban Roast Pork Sandwiches with Mojo Sauce

½ teaspoon coarse salt

1½ cups water

¼ cup rice vinegar

2 tablespoons sugar

I. Julienne the carrots on a mandoline or coarsely grate them on a box grater. In a colander, toss the carrots with the salt. Let stand in the sink for 30 minutes to drain, then rinse, squeeze dry and transfer to a bowl.

2. Meanwhile, in a small saucepan, combine the water with the vinegar and sugar and bring to a boil, stirring until the sugar dissolves. Remove from the heat and let the dressing cool to room temperature. Pour the dressing over the carrots and stir them gently. Let the carrots stand for at least 1 hour. To serve, lift the carrots from the liquid with a slotted spoon.

—J.A. and N.D.

Roast Pork and Provolone Melt

MAKES 4 SANDWICHES

Latin-style roast pork—slightly sweet and garlicky—is best for this sandwich. You can also use Chinese roast pork or baked, cured or smoked ham.

1 cup coarsely chopped parsley

½ cup green Spanish olives

2 garlic cloves, coarsely chopped

2 jalapeño chiles, seeded and coarsely chopped

1 tablespoon white wine vinegar

3 tablespoons extra-virgin olive oil

Salt and freshly ground pepper

Ketchup

4 large kaiser rolls, split

1 pound thinly sliced roast pork or ham

1 large onion, thinly sliced

Eight ¼-inch-thick slices of Italian Provolone (about 6 ounces)

1. Preheat the oven to 400°. In a food processor, combine the parsley, olives, garlic, jalapeños and vinegar. Process to a coarse paste. Add the olive oil and process briefly until thick. Scrape the olive paste into a small bowl and season with salt and pepper.

2. Spread a thin layer of ketchup on the bottom half of the rolls. Layer one-fourth of the pork, sliced onion and provolone on top. Set the sandwiches on a baking sheet; bake for about 2 minutes, or until the provolone melts. Spread 2 tablespoons of the olive paste on the top halves of the rolls. Assemble the sandwiches, cut them in half and serve.

—*Marcia Kiesel*

Italian-American Meatball Sandwiches

MAKES 4 SANDWICHES

1 tablespoon pure olive oil

½ cup minced onion

¼ cup minced fennel

1 tablespoon minced garlic

½ teaspoon fennel seeds, finely chopped

½ teaspoon crushed red pepper

½ pound ground beef

½ pound ground pork

1 large egg, lightly beaten

¼ cup finely chopped flat-leaf parsley

2 tablespoons dry bread crumbs

1½ teaspoons kosher salt

Vegetable oil, for sautéeing

½ recipe Tomato Sauce (p. 110)

4 Kaiser or other crusty rolls, split

1. Heat the olive oil in a medium skillet. Add the onion, fennel and garlic and cook over moderate heat, stirring, until softened, about 4 minutes. Add the fennel seeds and crushed red pepper and cook until fragrant, about 1 minute. Scrape the vegetable and spice mixture into a medium bowl and let cool.

2. Add the ground beef and pork to the bowl, along with the egg, parsley, bread crumbs and salt, and mix with your hands until thoroughly combined. Divide the mixture into 12 equal portions, roll into balls and set on a large plate.

3. Heat ¼ inch of vegetable oil in a large skillet. Put the meatballs in the skillet and sauté over moderate heat, turning occasionally, until evenly browned and cooked through, about 10 minutes. Drain the meatballs on paper towels.

4. Meanwhile, reheat the Tomato Sauce. Place 3 meatballs on the bottom half of each roll. Spoon tomato sauce over the meatballs and close with the top halves of the rolls.

—*Roger Hayot*

BEER The acidic flavor of the tomato sauce and the sweet flavor of the fennel seeds call for a light lager, such as Michelob.

Grilled-Fish Tacos

MAKES 36 TACOS

Set out the components of this dish separately so your guests can assemble their own tacos.

3 tablespoons extra-virgin olive oil

4 garlic cloves, minced

3 serrano chiles, seeded and minced

¾ teaspoon sweet paprika

Freshly ground pepper

Eight 6-ounce red snapper or tilapia fillets, skinned

1 pound green cabbage, shredded (3½ cups)

1 pound red cabbage, shredded (3½ cups)

¼ cup minced red onion

2 tablespoons plain yogurt

2 tablespoons mayonnaise

Salt

2 large ripe avocados—peeled, pitted and coarsely chopped

2 tablespoons fresh lime juice

½ cup sour cream

3 dozen 6-inch corn tortillas

1 cup cilantro leaves

Lime wedges and hot sauce, for serving

1. In a small bowl, combine the olive oil, garlic, serranos, paprika and 1 teaspoon of pepper. Put the snapper fillets in a large glass dish and rub with the marinade. Cover and refrigerate for at least 30 minutes or up to 4 hours.

2. In a large bowl, toss the green and red cabbage with the red onion. In a small bowl, mix the yogurt and mayonnaise. Pour over the cabbage, season with salt and pepper and toss. Cover the coleslaw and refrigerate.

3. In a food processor, puree the avocados with the lime juice. Blend in the sour cream. Scrape the avocado cream into a bowl and season with salt and pepper.

4. Light a grill. Season the snapper fillets with salt and pepper. Grill the fish over a moderately hot fire for about 3 minutes per side, or until just cooked through. Transfer the fish to a platter, break the fish into large chunks and cover loosely with foil. Wrap 3 stacks of 12 tortillas in foil and place on the grill until they are heated through, about 5 minutes.

5. To assemble each taco, spread a dollop of avocado cream on a tortilla. Top with a piece of fish, some coleslaw and cilantro leaves. Pass the lime wedges, hot sauce and remaining coleslaw.

—*Elizabeth Falkner*

MAKE AHEAD The coleslaw and the avocado cream can be refrigerated separately overnight.

WINE A crisp, floral wine complements the mild fish and avocado cream. Try the Alsatian 1998 Kuentz-Bas Pinot Blanc.

Fish Tacos

MAKES 8 TACOS 🌱

- 1 teaspoon cumin seeds
- 2 teaspoons pure olive oil
- ¾ pound herring (or Boston or Spanish mackerel or shad) fillets, skinned

Salt and freshly ground pepper

- 1 large red onion, thinly sliced
- ¼ cup Calamata olives (2 ounces), pitted and coarsely chopped
- 8 stone-ground corn tortillas
- 2 cups shredded romaine lettuce
- 1 cup coarsely chopped tomatoes
- 1 cup peeled, seeded and thinly sliced cucumber
- 2 tablespoons plus 2 teaspoons sour cream

Hot pepper sauce

I. In a large skillet, toast the cumin seeds over moderate heat until fragrant, about 1 minute. Transfer the seeds to a plate to cool, then coarsely chop them.

2. Preheat the oven to 350°. Heat the olive oil in the skillet. Season the fish with salt and lots of pepper. Add the fish to the skillet and cook over moderately high heat until browned on the bottom, about 3 minutes. Turn the fish and continue cooking over moderate heat until barely opaque throughout, about 4 minutes longer. Transfer the fish to a plate.

3. Add the onion to the skillet, cover and cook over low heat until softened but not browned, about 5 minutes. Add the cumin and olives and cook, stirring to blend the flavors. Return the fish to the skillet and gently break it up with a wooden spoon. Season with salt and pepper.

4. Warm the tortillas in the oven for 30 seconds, or just until hot but still pliable. Keep the tortillas warm in foil. To serve, toss the lettuce with the tomatoes and cucumber in a bowl. Transfer the fish mixture to another bowl. Set out the sour cream and hot sauce. Let guests build their own tacos with the fish, salad, sour cream and hot sauce. —*Marcia Kiesel*

ONE SERVING Calories 412 kcal, Total Fat 22 gm, Saturated Fat 5 gm

WINE Contrast the oily fish with a simple, cleansing Spanish white, such as the 1998 Torres Chardonnay Viña Sol or the 1997 Marqués de Cáceres Blanco.

Pork Tenderloin Fajitas

MAKES 6 SERVINGS

Fajitas have been a Texas tradition since 1973, when Mexican-born restaurateur Ninfa Laurenzo put them on the menu of her Houston restaurant, Ninfa's. Originally, fajitas were made with grilled skirt steak, but they've since been made with everything from lobster to Portobellos. This recipe calls for succulent pork tenderloin marinated in lime juice and spices and dressed with Chipotle Salsa and Pico de Gallo.

HERB AND SPICE RUB

- 1 tablespoon packed brown sugar
- 1 tablespoon paprika
- 1½ teaspoons chili powder
- 1½ teaspoons garlic powder
- 1½ teaspoons onion powder
- 1½ teaspoons coarse salt
- 1½ teaspoons ground cumin
- ¼ teaspoon freshly ground pepper
- ⅛ teaspoon ground allspice

FAJITAS

Two 1-pound pork tenderloins, halved crosswise

- 2 tablespoons herb and spice rub
- ¼ cup fresh lime juice
- ¼ cup olive oil

Vegetable oil, for the grill

- 1 red bell pepper, quartered
- 1 yellow bell pepper, quartered
- 1 poblano chile or green bell pepper, quartered
- 2 medium white onions, sliced crosswise ½ inch thick
- 2 bunches scallions, trimmed
- 18 small flour tortillas
- 2 tomatoes, seeded and finely diced
- 1 red onion, finely diced
- 1 cup coarsely chopped cilantro
- 1½ cups sour cream

Chipotle Salsa (p. 320)

Pico de Gallo (p. 319)

I. MAKE THE HERB AND SPICE RUB: Combine all of the ingredients in a ½-pint jar. Cover and shake to blend.

2. MAKE THE FAJITAS: Cut the tenderloins halfway through lengthwise; pound to ¼-inch thickness with a meat mallet. Put the meat in a baking dish; sprinkle with the rub. Drizzle on the lime juice and oil and turn to coat. Cover and set aside to marinate for 30 minutes.

3. Light a grill. Lightly brush the grate with oil. Grill the peppers, onions and scallions until they begin to char at the edges. Remove to a large platter and keep warm. Remove the meat from the marinade and pat dry. Grill the pork over high heat until browned and cooked through, about 4 minutes per side. Transfer the meat to a carving board and cut crosswise into thin slices. Transfer the meat to a platter, cover loosely with foil and keep warm.

4. Warm the tortillas on the grill until soft, 10 to 20 seconds on each side. Place them in a cloth-lined basket, cover and keep warm. Serve the fajitas and grilled vegetables with the tortillas, diced tomatoes, red onion, cilantro, sour cream, Chipotle Salsa and Pico de Gallo. —*Steven Raichlen*

vegetables
chapter 12

Sesame Spinach
(Shingumchi Namul)

4 TO 6 SERVINGS

If you like, you can replace the spinach with 1 cup of blanched bean sprouts mixed with 2 tablespoons of slivered scallions.

- 1 pound spinach, large stems removed
- 2 teaspoons Asian sesame oil
- 1 teaspoon soy sauce
- 1 teaspoon Sesame Salt (recipe follows)
- 2 teaspoons toasted sesame seeds

1. Steam half the spinach for 1 minute; chill in ice water. Repeat with the remaining spinach. Drain and squeeze dry.

2. In a bowl, toss the spinach with the sesame oil, soy sauce and Sesame Salt. Top with the sesame seeds and serve. —*Anya von Bremzen*

SESAME SALT

MAKES ½ CUP

- ½ cup sesame seeds
- 2 teaspoons coarse salt

Toast the sesame seeds in a medium skillet over moderate heat, stirring frequently, until fragrant and lightly browned, 3 to 4 minutes. Transfer the seeds to a plate to cool. In a spice grinder or mini processor, grind the seeds with the salt to a coarse powder. —*A.B.*

Creamed Spinach

6 SERVINGS

- 3 pounds fresh spinach, large stems discarded
- 1 teaspoon vegetable oil
- 1 medium shallot, minced
- 1 cup heavy cream
- 4 tablespoons unsalted butter
- ¼ cup freshly grated Parmesan cheese
- ¼ cup water

Salt and freshly ground pepper

1. Heat a large saucepan. Add the spinach by the handful and cook over moderately high heat, stirring often, until wilted, about 5 minutes. Transfer the spinach to a colander and squeeze it as dry as possible. Coarsely chop the spinach.

2. Heat the oil in the saucepan. Add the shallot and cook over moderate heat, stirring, until golden, 4 to 5 minutes. Add the cream; cook until reduced by half, 6 to 7 minutes. Add the butter and swirl to incorporate. Stir in the Parmesan and cook over low heat for 2 minutes. Add the spinach and water, season with salt and pepper and cook over low heat until the spinach is coated with the thickened sauce, about 5 minutes. Serve hot.

—*David Walzog*

MAKE AHEAD The creamed spinach can be refrigerated overnight; rewarm over moderately low heat.

Grilled Treviso-Style Radicchio

6 SERVINGS

Treviso, native to the Veneto region of Italy, is an elongated variety of radicchio that is now being cultivated in the United States.

- 6 heads of Treviso-style radicchio or Belgian endive

Extra-virgin olive oil

Herbes de Provence, for sprinkling

Salt and freshly ground pepper

Balsamic vinegar, for drizzling

1. Light a grill or heat a cast-iron grill pan. Halve the Treviso-style radicchios or Belgian endives if they are very thick. Brush lightly with oil.

2. Grill over a slow fire or over low heat until very dark and crisp on the outside and wilting and tender within, about 8 minutes for the Treviso and 10 minutes for the endives. Turn the vegetables over, sprinkle with *herbes de Provence* and salt and pepper and grill the Treviso for about 5 minutes longer, the endives about 10 minutes longer. Transfer to a platter, drizzle very lightly with balsamic vinegar and serve.

—*Paula Wolfert*

Sautéed Swiss Chard with Brandied Currants

8 SERVINGS

- ¼ cup currants
- 1 tablespoon brandy
- 2 pounds Swiss chard
- 2 tablespoons fresh lemon juice

Salt

- 3 tablespoons unsalted butter

Freshly ground pepper

1. In a small bowl, soak the currants in the brandy. Separate the Swiss chard stalks from the leaves and cut the leaves into 1-inch-wide strips. Pull the strings from the stalks and cut the stalks into 3-by-½-inch strips.

2. Bring a large saucepan of water to a boil. Add the lemon juice, salt and the Swiss chard stalks and cook until tender, about 7 minutes. Using a slotted spoon, transfer the stalks to a baking sheet to cool. Add the chard leaves to the pan and cook, stirring, just until wilted, about 1 minute. Drain the chard in a colander and let cool slightly, then gently squeeze out the excess water. Using a fork, fluff up the chard leaves to eliminate clumps.

3. Melt the butter in a large saucepan. Add the chard stems and leaves and the currants and cook over moderate heat, stirring, until warmed through, about 4 minutes. Season with salt and pepper and serve. —*Josiah Citrin*

MAKE AHEAD The cooked chard can be refrigerated overnight.

Smoky Greens

10 SERVINGS

These hearty greens develop great flavor when cooked in duck or bacon fat, but butter can be substituted. The chipotle chiles add a nice smokiness.

- 12 pounds mixed greens, such as Swiss chard, collards and turnip or beet greens, large stems discarded
- ½ cup rendered duck or bacon fat or 1 stick unsalted butter
- 4 large onions, coarsely chopped

10 large garlic cloves, minced

2 dried chipotle chiles or 2 canned chipotles in adobo

Salt and freshly ground pepper

5 tablespoons cider vinegar

Tabasco sauce

1. Wash the greens thoroughly in cold water and coarsely chop the leaves; do not dry them.

2. Heat the rendered duck or bacon fat in a large heavy stockpot. Add the chopped onions and cook over moderately high heat, stirring often, until softened, about 7 minutes. Add the minced garlic and cook, stirring, until fragrant, about 3 minutes. Stir in the chopped greens by the handful, adding more as the previous batch starts to wilt. Add the chipotle chiles and season the greens lightly with salt and pepper. Cover the stockpot and cook over low heat, stirring often, until the greens are very tender, about 1 hour.

3. Discard the chipotles if using dried. Stir in the vinegar and season the greens with salt and pepper. Transfer the greens to a bowl and pass the Tabasco at the table.   —Susan Spicer

MAKE AHEAD The Smoky Greens can be refrigerated for 2 days. Rewarm gently over low heat before serving.

Collard Greens with Fennel and Orange Butter

12 SERVINGS

1½ sticks (6 ounces) unsalted butter

4 medium fennel bulbs—halved, cored and sliced lengthwise ¼ inch thick

2 teaspoons finely grated orange zest

4 cups fresh orange juice

7 pounds collard greens, large stems discarded, leaves cut into 2-inch pieces

Salt and freshly ground pepper

1. Melt the butter in a large enameled cast-iron casserole. Add the fennel

and orange zest and cook over moderately high heat, stirring frequently, until the fennel browns at the edges, about 10 minutes. Reduce heat to moderately low and cook, stirring occasionally, until evenly browned, about 12 minutes more. Add the orange juice and boil until reduced by one-third, about 8 minutes.

2. Stir in the collards in batches, adding more as the leaves wilt. Cook the collards until just tender, about 10 minutes. Season with salt and pepper and serve.   —Bruce and Eric Bromberg

MAKE AHEAD The cooked collards and fennel can be refrigerated for up to 2 days and reheated before serving.

Cabbage Braised with Riesling and Smoky Ham

8 SERVINGS 🌸

This pared down version of a traditional French dish substitutes ham for bacon and olive oil for duck fat.

2 tablespoons extra-virgin olive oil

1 pound Spanish onions, chopped

1 bottle (750 ml) Riesling or Gewürztraminer

10 ounces lean smoked ham, sliced ⅓ inch thick

1 tablespoon thyme leaves

Pinch of crushed red pepper

Two 2-pound heads of Savoy cabbage—halved, cored and coarsely shredded

Salt and freshly ground pepper

1. In a large enameled cast-iron casserole, mix the olive oil with the chopped onions. Cover the casserole and cook over moderately low heat, stirring occasionally, until the onions are very soft, about 10 minutes. Add the Riesling or Gewürztraminer, sliced ham, thyme leaves and crushed red pepper and bring the mixture to a boil. Reduce the heat to moderately low and simmer for 10 minutes.

2. Stir in the shredded cabbage, cover the casserole and cook over moderate heat until the cabbage has softened

somewhat, about 10 minutes. Cover again and cook over moderately low heat, stirring occasionally, until tender, about 45 minutes longer. Discard the ham. Season with salt and pepper and serve.   —Sally Schneider

MAKE AHEAD The Cabbage Braised with Riesling and Smoky Ham can be refrigerated overnight.

ONE SERVING Calories 135 kcal, Total Fat 5.2 gm, Saturated Fat 1.1 gm

Baked Cabbage with Cumin and Pancetta

12 SERVINGS

½ cup extra-virgin olive oil

3 ounces pancetta, sliced ¼ inch thick and diced

2 large onions, finely chopped

4 teaspoons cumin seeds

1 cup pine nuts (5 ounces)

2 large heads of Savoy cabbage (about 2½ pounds each), cored and finely shredded

Salt and freshly ground pepper

Diced red bell pepper (optional)

1. Preheat the oven to 350°. In a large enameled cast-iron casserole, heat the olive oil until shimmering. Add the diced pancetta and chopped onions to the casserole and cook over moderately low heat until the onions are translucent, about 12 minutes. Add the cumin seeds and pine nuts and cook, stirring, until fragrant, about 5 minutes longer. Gradually stir in the cabbage a handful at a time, adding more as it wilts.

2. Cover the casserole and bake the cabbage for 20 minutes, stirring twice, until it is almost tender. Or, cover and cook on the stove for 20 minutes over moderately low heat, stirring twice. Season with salt and pepper and transfer to a platter. Sprinkle with the diced red bell pepper and serve.

—Cesare Casella

MAKE AHEAD The Baked Cabbage with Cumin and Pancetta can be cooked and refrigerated overnight.

vegetables

Stuffed Zucchini

Celery with Bacon, Brandy and Tomatoes

6 SERVINGS

¼ cup vegetable oil

One 2-pound bunch of celery, ribs
    peeled and cut into 2-inch lengths
    on the diagonal, leaves reserved

Salt

4 ounces thickly sliced bacon,
    cut into 1-inch pieces

1 cup canned peeled Italian
    tomatoes, drained and chopped

3 tablespoons brandy

Freshly ground pepper

1. In a medium skillet, heat the oil until shimmering. Add the celery leaves and fry over moderate heat until crisp, about 2 minutes. Transfer to a plate and sprinkle with salt.

2. In a large enameled cast-iron casserole, cook the bacon over low heat, stirring a few times, until the fat has rendered, about 6 minutes. Add the celery and stir to coat. Add the tomatoes and brandy, cover and cook until the celery is barely tender, about 10 minutes. Uncover and cook until the sauce thickens slightly, about 3 minutes. Season with salt and pepper and transfer to a serving bowl. Top with the leaves and serve. —*Marcia Kiesel*

Stuffed Zucchini

12 SERVINGS

¼ cup plus 1 tablespoon pure olive
    oil, plus more for drizzling

1 medium onion, coarsely chopped

6 long or round zucchini
    (6 to 8 ounces each)

4 cups coarse fresh bread crumbs

1 cup coarsely chopped parsley

5 ounces baked ham, sliced ¼ inch
    thick and cut into ¼-inch dice

Salt and freshly ground pepper

Freshly grated nutmeg

5 large eggs, beaten

¼ cup water

3 garlic cloves, halved

3 medium tomatoes, chopped

1. Preheat the oven to 350°. Heat ¼ cup of olive oil in a large skillet. Add the onion and cook over low heat, stirring occasionally, until softened, about 8 minutes. Transfer the cooked onion to a large bowl and let cool to room temperature.

2. If using long zucchini, cut them in half lengthwise; if using round zucchini cut off the top quarter of each one. Scoop out the insides, leaving ¼-inch-thick shells.

3. Add the bread crumbs, parsley and ham to the onion and season with salt, pepper and nutmeg. Mix in the eggs. Season the zucchini shells with salt and pepper and fill them with the stuffing. Cover with the lids if using round zucchini.

4. Grease a large baking pan with the remaining 1 tablespoon of olive oil. Add the water, garlic and tomatoes and arrange the stuffed zucchini in the pan; drizzle the zucchini generously with olive oil. Cover with foil and bake for 25 minutes. Uncover and bake for 25 minutes, or until browned on top. Spoon the pan juices over the zucchini and serve.
—*Sabine Busch and Bruno Tramontana*

MAKE AHEAD The stuffed zucchini can be refrigerated unbaked overnight.

Stuffed Zucchini with Pecorino Sauce

6 SERVINGS

This recipe comes from Dania Luccherini, the chef and proprietor of Italy's great Fattoria La Chiusa, in Montefollonico.

12 firm, very fresh medium zucchini
    (about 5½ pounds total)

2 tablespoons unsalted butter

2 tablespoons extra-virgin olive oil

2 large shallots, finely chopped

1 tablespoon finely chopped
    flat-leaf parsley

1 tablespoon thyme leaves

¼ cup freshly grated
    Parmigiano-Reggiano cheese

Salt and freshly ground pepper

2 eggs, lightly beaten

PECORINO SAUCE

2 hard-cooked large egg yolks

⅓ cup extra-virgin olive oil

2½ cups finely grated young
    sheep's-milk cheese, preferably
    Pecorino Toscano (¾ pound)

⅓ cup water, plus more if needed

Salt

1. Cut 8 of the zucchini crosswise into 2-inch pieces. Using a melon baller, hollow out each piece, leaving a ¼-inch cuplike shell. Set the zucchini cups aside. Mince the scooped-out flesh along with the 4 remaining zucchini.

2. In a large deep skillet, melt the butter in the oil. Add the chopped shallots and cook over moderate heat until translucent, about 3 minutes. Add the chopped zucchini and cook, stirring occasionally, until tender and lightly browned, about 25 minutes. Stir in the chopped parsley and the thyme leaves.

3. Transfer the contents of the skillet to a food processor and puree. Scrape the puree into a bowl. Then stir in the Parmigiano-Reggiano and season with salt and pepper. Allow the filling to cool to room temperature and stir in the lightly beaten eggs.

Stuffed Zucchini with Pecorino Sauce

Mashed Zucchini with Onions, Garlic and Mint

Mashed Zucchini with Onions, Garlic and Mint

6 SERVINGS

- 2 pounds zucchini, cut into 3-inch lengths
- 3 tablespoons extra-virgin olive oil
- 2 medium onions, coarsely chopped
- 4 garlic cloves, crushed
- 2 tablespoons coarsely chopped mint

Salt and freshly ground pepper

- 1 lemon, cut into wedges (optional)

I. Steam the zucchini until soft, 15 to 20 minutes. Drain well. Using a fork, mash the zucchini in the colander to press out as much liquid as possible.

2. Heat 2 tablespoons of the oil. Add the onions and cook over moderate heat, stirring, until lightly browned, about 8 minutes. Add the garlic and cook, stirring, until it just begins to color, about 30 seconds. Add the zucchini and mint, season with salt and pepper and cook, stirring, until heated through, about 5 minutes.

3. Stir in the remaining tablespoon of olive oil and serve warm or at room temperature with the lemon wedges.

—*Claudia Roden*

4. Preheat the oven to 350°. Generously butter a large baking dish. Set the zucchini cups in the baking dish, hollowed side up. Spoon the filling into the cups, mounding it slightly. Bake the stuffed zucchini for about 1 hour and 10 minutes, or until tender and lightly browned.

5. MAKE THE PECORINO SAUCE: In a food processor, pulse the egg yolks with the olive oil until a smooth paste forms. Add the Pecorino and the ⅓ cup of water and process until the sauce is smooth and has the consistency of heavy cream; add a little more water if the sauce seems too thick. Season with salt.

6. Generously spoon some of the room-temperature Pecorino sauce onto 6 serving plates and arrange about 3 warm zucchini cups on each plate. Serve the stuffed zucchini at once.

—*Sara Jenkins*

MAKE AHEAD The zucchini cups can be prepared through Step 4 and refrigerated overnight. Reheat in a 325° oven before serving with the Pecorino sauce.

WINE A fruity rosé made from Sangiovese grapes will stand up to the pungent Pecorino Toscano cheese sauce. Try the 1999 Swanson Rosato from California or the less expensive 1999 Castello di Ama from Tuscany.

Stuffed Peppers with Spicy Creamed Swiss Chard

Stuffed Peppers with Spicy Creamed Swiss Chard

10 SERVINGS

- 6 pounds red or green Swiss chard, stems removed and reserved
- 4 tablespoons unsalted butter
- 1 large onion, coarsely chopped
- 2 large jalapeños—halved, seeded and thinly sliced
- 6 garlic cloves, minced
- 2 teaspoons curry powder
- 2 cups heavy cream

Salt and freshly ground pepper

- ¾ cup long-grain white rice
- 1 cup water
- 10 medium red or yellow bell peppers

Olive oil

1. Set aside ½ pound of the nicest chard stems; reserve the rest for another use. Bring 2 inches of water to a boil in a large stockpot. Add the ½ pound of chard stems and cook until almost tender, about 4 minutes. Using tongs, transfer the stems to a plate to cool. Put the chard leaves in the boiling water in batches, adding more as each batch wilts. When all the leaves have been added, cook for 1 minute. Drain the chard leaves; let cool, then squeeze dry and coarsely chop. Cut the stems into 1-inch pieces.

2. Melt the butter in a large enameled cast-iron casserole. Add the onion and jalapeños and cook over low heat until softened, about 10 minutes. Add the minced garlic and cook, stirring, until fragrant, about 2 minutes. Add the curry powder and cook, stirring, for 2 minutes longer. Add the cream and simmer over moderately high heat until reduced to ¾ cup, about 10 minutes. Remove from the heat and let cool to room temperature. Stir in the chard leaves and stems and season with salt and pepper.

3. Meanwhile, in a small saucepan, cover the rice with the water and bring to a boil. Cover and cook over low heat until the water has been absorbed, about 12 minutes. Fluff the rice.

4. Preheat the oven to 350°. Cut the tops off the bell peppers, leaving a ½-inch ring of pepper around each stem. Scoop out the seeds and ribs. Stand the peppers in a large baking dish or roasting pan and rub the skins with olive oil. Season the insides with salt and pepper and spoon a scant ¼ cup of rice into each one. Fill the peppers with the creamed chard and replace the tops; oil the tops. Bake for about 1 hour, or until the peppers are tender and the filling is hot. —*Marcia Kiesel*

MAKE AHEAD The uncooked stuffed peppers can be refrigerated overnight. Bring to room temperature before baking.

Herbed Tomato and Zucchini Gratin

4 SERVINGS

Oven-drying tomatoes and salting zucchini before freezing helps keep them intact—a plus for recipes like this gratin.

- 6 cups frozen zucchini or 1½ pounds small fresh zucchini, sliced crosswise ½ inch thick
- 3 tablespoons extra-virgin olive oil
- 1 large garlic clove, thinly sliced
- 2 teaspoons chopped dill
- Salt and freshly ground pepper
- 6 ounces feta cheese, coarsely crumbled (1 cup)
- 12 frozen plum tomato halves or 6 fresh plum tomatoes—peeled, halved lengthwise and seeded

1. Preheat the oven to 425°. Toss the zucchini with 1 tablespoon of the olive oil and spread in a large glass or ceramic baking dish in an even layer. Sprinkle the sliced garlic and chopped dill over the zucchini and season with salt, if using fresh zucchini, and with pepper. Scatter the feta on top and cover with the tomatoes. Season with salt, if using fresh tomatoes, and with pepper and drizzle the remaining 2 tablespoons of olive oil all over the vegetables.

2. Bake the gratin for 40 minutes if using frozen vegetables; bake it for 55 minutes if using fresh vegetables. The gratin is done when all the liquid in the dish has evaporated and the zucchini is sizzling. Serve the gratin warm or at room temperature. —*Grace Parisi*

WINE A white with sharp acidity and hints of herbs will accent the tomatoes, feta and dill in this rustic gratin. The obvious choice is a lively Sancerre from France, such as the 1997 La Poussie or the 1998 Comte La Fond.

Lacquered Tofu with Green Beans

4 SERVINGS

This recipe is adapted from *This Can't Be Tofu!* (Broadway Books).

- 1 pound firm tofu, drained
- 1 red bell pepper
- ¼ cup stock
- 3 tablespoons soy sauce
- 2 tablespoons light brown sugar
- 3 garlic cloves, minced
- 1 tablespoon mushroom soy sauce
- 4 teaspoons roasted peanut oil
- ¼ pound green beans, cut into 2-inch lengths
- 5 scallions, sliced ½ inch thick
- ½ teaspoon toasted Szechwan peppercorns
- Salt
- ¼ cup roasted cashews

1. Cut the tofu and red bell pepper into 1½-inch triangles. In a bowl, mix the stock, soy sauce, light brown sugar, minced garlic and mushroom soy.

2. Heat 1 tablespoon of oil in a large nonstick skillet. Add the tofu and cook, turning once, until golden; transfer to a plate. Add the remaining teaspoon of oil to the pan; add the beans and stir-fry for 2 minutes. Add the red pepper and scallions and stir-fry until just tender. Add the tofu and Szechwan peppercorns; season with salt. Pour in the sauce and stir gently until the vegetables and tofu are evenly coated. Transfer to a platter and sprinkle with the cashews.

—*Deborah Madison*

Green Beans with Onions and Tomato

10 TO 12 SERVINGS

The beans are cut into small pieces so they fully absorb the seasonings.

- 4 pounds green beans, cut into ½-inch pieces
- ⅓ cup vegetable oil
- 1 large Spanish onion, finely chopped (2½ cups)
- One 2-inch piece of fresh ginger, peeled and finely chopped
- 4 serrano chiles, seeded and finely chopped
- 4 teaspoons cumin seeds
- 2½ tablespoons ground coriander
- 1½ teaspoons cayenne pepper
- 6 medium tomatoes—peeled, seeded and chopped
- 1½ teaspoons salt
- ¼ cup cilantro leaves

1. Bring a large pot of lightly salted water to a boil. Add the beans and cook until crisp-tender, about 6 minutes. Drain well.

2. Heat the vegetable oil in a large saucepan. Add the onion, ginger, chiles and cumin seeds and cook over high heat, stirring frequently, until the onion is softened and browned, about 8 minutes. Add the coriander and cayenne and cook, stirring, until fragrant, about 2 minutes. Add the tomatoes and cook, stirring, until most of

Green Bean and Mushroom Fricassee

1. Bring a large pot of salted water to a boil. Add the green beans and carrots and cook until crisp-tender, about 5 minutes. Drain and pat dry with paper towels.

2. In a large skillet, toast the pine nuts over moderate heat, stirring constantly, until lightly golden, about 5 minutes. Transfer the pine nuts to a plate to cool.

3. Heat the oil in the skillet until shimmering. Add the mushrooms and cook over moderately high heat, stirring, until softened and beginning to brown, about 5 minutes. Add the carrots and green beans and cook, stirring, until tender, 3 to 4 minutes. Add the tomatoes and lemon juice and season with salt and pepper. Cook until the tomatoes are just warmed through, about 1 minute. Transfer the vegetables to a platter, sprinkle with the pine nuts and serve. —*Kevin Maguire*

MAKE AHEAD The recipe can be prepared through Step 2 and refrigerated separately for up to 2 days.

ONE SERVING Calories 104 kcal, Total Fat 7.1 gm, Saturated Fat 0.8 gm

Basil Green Beans with Roasted Red Peppers

6 SERVINGS

- 3 tablespoons pine nuts
- 1½ pounds green or wax beans
- 1 cup coarsely chopped basil, plus several leaves for garnish
- ½ cup thinly sliced jarred roasted red peppers, drained
- 2 garlic cloves, minced
- ¼ cup extra-virgin olive oil
- 1 tablespoon fresh lemon juice

Salt and freshly ground pepper

1. Preheat the oven to 350°. Spread the pine nuts in a pie plate and bake for about 7 minutes, shaking the plate occasionally to prevent scorching, until the pine nuts are lightly toasted. Let cool.

2. In a pot of boiling salted water, cook the beans until just tender, about 4 minutes. Drain the beans in a colander and refresh under cold running water; drain well.

3. In a large bowl, combine the pine nuts with the chopped basil, roasted red peppers and garlic. Add the olive oil and lemon juice and season with salt and pepper. Add the green beans and toss to mix. Garnish the beans with the basil leaves and serve.

—*Liv Rockefeller*

Green and Yellow Beans with Pancetta Crisps

6 SERVINGS

- 1 pound mixed yellow wax and green beans, trimmed
- 12 thin slices pancetta (about 4 ounces)
- ¼ cup extra-virgin olive oil
- 1 small shallot, sliced paper thin
- 2 tablespoons sherry vinegar
- 1 pint mixed red and yellow pear or cherry tomatoes, halved

Salt and freshly ground pepper

1. In a large pot of boiling salted water, cook the beans over high heat until crisp-tender, 5 to 6 minutes. Drain the beans and pat dry with paper towels.

2. Arrange half the pancetta in a single layer in a large skillet and cook over moderate heat, turning once, until golden and crisp, about 6 minutes. Transfer the pancetta to a plate to cool; it will crisp as it cools. Cook the remaining pancetta; let cool. Coarsely crumble the pancetta.

3. Wipe out the skillet, add the oil and heat until shimmering. Add the shallot and cook over moderate heat until softened, about 4 minutes. Add the beans and cook until tender, about 2 minutes. Add the vinegar and cook until nearly evaporated, about 2 minutes longer. Add the tomatoes and season with salt and pepper. Transfer the vegetables to a platter and garnish with the pancetta. Serve warm or at room temperature. —*Thomas Gay*

MAKE AHEAD The recipe can be

the liquid has evaporated, about 5 minutes.

3. Add the beans and the 1½ teaspoons salt and cook, stirring, until heated through. Cover and cook over moderate heat, stirring frequently, until the beans are crisp-tender, about 10 minutes. Stir in the cilantro and transfer the beans to a large deep platter. Serve the green beans warm or at room temperature. —*Neela Paniz*

MAKE AHEAD The beans can be refrigerated for up to 2 days; add the cilantro just before serving.

Green Bean and Mushroom Fricassee

8 SERVINGS

- 1 pound thin green beans
- 24 baby carrots, halved lengthwise
- ⅓ cup pine nuts (about 2 ounces)
- 2 tablespoons canola oil
- 6 ounces shiitake mushrooms, stemmed, caps thickly sliced
- 3 plum tomatoes—peeled, seeded and thinly sliced
- 1½ tablespoons fresh lemon juice

Salt and freshly ground pepper

prepared through Step 2 and refrigerated overnight. Recrisp the pancetta in a warm oven or a skillet.

Braised Fennel with Olives and Cardamom

8 SERVINGS

¼ cup extra-virgin olive oil

8 medium fennel bulbs, quartered and cored

4 garlic cloves, thinly sliced

¼ pound oil-cured black olives (about 20), pitted

6 cardamom pods, lightly crushed

8 thyme sprigs

Salt and freshly ground pepper

2 cups Basic Chicken Stock (p. 98) or canned low-sodium broth

1. Preheat the oven to 350°. Heat the olive oil in a roasting pan set over 2 burners. Add the fennel bulbs and cook over moderately low heat, stirring occasionally, until the fennel softens slightly and is just beginning to brown, about 20 minutes. Scatter the garlic, olives, cardamom and thyme over the fennel and season generously with salt and pepper. Pour the chicken stock into the roasting pan and bring to a boil over moderately high heat. Turn off the heat.

2. Place a crumpled sheet of parchment or wax paper directly over the fennel, then tightly cover the roasting pan with foil. Bake the fennel for about 1 hour, or until tender.

3. Remove the foil and the parchment paper and roast the fennel for 25 minutes longer, or until it is very tender and the liquid in the roasting pan has reduced to a few tablespoons. Transfer the fennel and olives to a serving platter. Remove and discard the cardamom pods and thyme sprigs. Serve the braised fennel warm or at room temperature. —*Tamasin Day-Lewis*

MAKE AHEAD The fennel can be prepared in advance and refrigerated overnight. Cover loosely and reheat gently in a 325° oven.

Sautéed Asparagus with Sugar Snap Peas

8 SERVINGS

This recipe is from *Barefoot Contessa Parties!* (Clarkson N. Potter).

2 pounds large asparagus, peeled and cut on the diagonal into 1½-inch lengths

2 tablespoons extra-virgin olive oil

1½ pounds sugar snap peas

Kosher salt and freshly ground pepper

1. Bring a large pot of salted water to a boil. Add the asparagus and cook until crisp-tender, about 4 minutes. Drain the asparagus and rinse under cold water. Drain again and pat dry.

2. Heat the olive oil in a large skillet until shimmering. Add the sugar snap peas and cook over moderately high heat until crisp-tender, about 5 minutes. Add the asparagus and a generous pinch each of salt and pepper and cook until warmed through and tender, 2 to 3 minutes. Transfer the vegetables to a large platter and serve immediately. —*Ina Garten*

White Asparagus with Pistachio Polonaise

4 SIDE-DISH SERVINGS

A crunchy Polonaise topping is simply irresistible whether sprinkled over asparagus, cauliflower, fried fish or steamed rice.

⅓ cup shelled pistachio nuts

2½ pounds white asparagus, peeled, or green asparagus

2 tablespoons unsalted butter

Salt

2 hard-cooked eggs

1 tablespoon chopped chives

1 tablespoon chopped parsley

1 teaspoon minced tarragon

1. Preheat the oven to 400°. Spread the pistachios in a pie plate and toast for 8 minutes, or until lightly browned. Let cool, then coarsely chop.

2. Steam the asparagus until just tender, about 10 minutes.

3. In a large skillet, melt the butter over moderately high heat until lightly browned, about 3 minutes. Add the asparagus, season with salt and toss to coat, then transfer to a platter. Coarsely grate the eggs over the top. Sprinkle with the nuts, chives, parsley and tarragon and serve.—*Marcia Kiesel*

Falsone's Roasted Artichoke-Stuffed Artichokes

4 SERVINGS ♛

6 large, firm artichokes

2 pounds Jerusalem artichokes, peeled and halved

1 Yukon Gold potato (½ pound), peeled and quartered

1½ cups freshly grated Parmesan cheese (4½ ounces)

Coarse salt and freshly ground pepper

2 tablespoons extra-virgin olive oil, plus more for brushing

2 tablespoons balsamic vinegar

2 tablespoons chopped parsley

1 teaspoon minced rosemary

1 teaspoon minced thyme

1. Trim the stems from the artichokes and snap off the tough leaves. Cut off

White Asparagus with Pistachio Polonaise

the top third of each artichoke and snip off the leaf tips with scissors. Steam the artichokes over moderate heat until tender when pierced at the bottom, about 30 minutes; check the water level halfway through cooking. Transfer the steamed artichokes to a plate.

2. Add the Jerusalem artichokes and potato to the steamer and steam until tender, about 40 minutes; again, check the water level halfway through.

3. Pull the center leaves from the artichokes and scrape out the hairy chokes with a small spoon. Set the 4 prettiest artichokes aside. Remove the leaves from the 2 remaining artichokes and refrigerate for another use.

4. Quarter the 2 artichoke bottoms and place in a bowl. Add the Jerusalem artichokes and potato and mash the vegetables to a smooth puree with a potato masher. Stir in 1 cup of the Parmesan and season with salt and pepper.

5. Preheat the oven to 350°. Spoon the stuffing into the centers of the 4 reserved artichokes. Separate the leaves of the artichokes slightly and use a small spoon to pack the remaining stuffing in between them. Set the artichokes on an oiled baking sheet, brush with olive oil and sprinkle each with 2 tablespoons of the remaining Parmesan cheese. Bake for about 30 minutes or until very hot and browned around the edges.

6. In a bowl, whisk the 2 tablespoons of olive oil with the balsamic vinegar and season the dressing with salt and pepper. Set the stuffed artichokes on plates, drizzle the vinaigrette over them and sprinkle on the parsley, rosemary and thyme. Serve the artichokes hot. —*Loren Falsone*

Broccoli with Orange-Chile Oil

6 SERVINGS

- 2 teaspoons finely grated orange zest
- 1 teaspoon Asian sesame oil
- ⅓ cup vegetable oil
- 4 garlic cloves, thinly sliced
- 1 teaspoon minced fresh ginger
- ¾ teaspoon crushed red pepper
- ⅛ teaspoon five-spice powder (optional)
- ½ cup fresh orange juice

Salt and freshly ground pepper

Two 1½-pound heads of broccoli— stalks peeled, heads cut lengthwise into large pieces

1. In a heatproof bowl, combine the orange zest and sesame oil. In a saucepan, heat the vegetable oil over moderate heat. Add the sliced garlic and cook, stirring, until golden, about 3 minutes. Add the minced ginger, crushed red pepper and five-spice powder and cook until fragrant, about 1 minute. Stir in the orange juice and boil over moderately high heat until reduced by half, about 4 minutes. Stir the orange juice mixture into the orange zest and sesame oil; season with salt and pepper.

2. In a saucepan, steam the broccoli until just tender, about 8 minutes.

3. Transfer the steamed broccoli to a warmed platter, spoon the orange-chile oil on top and serve.

—*Marcia Kiesel*

MAKE AHEAD The orange-chile oil can be refrigerated for 3 days.

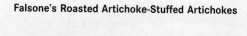

Falsone's Roasted Artichoke-Stuffed Artichokes

Cauliflower with Melted Onions and Mustard Seeds

6 SERVINGS

Cauliflower may not seem like a glamorous vegetable—at least not when you steam or boil it. But roast cauliflower and it develops an unusual, delicate sweetness that's almost exotic.

- 1 tablespoon unsalted butter
- ¼ cup vegetable oil
- Two 2½-pound heads of cauliflower, cut into 2-inch florets
- Salt and freshly ground pepper
- 2 large sweet onions, halved lengthwise and thinly sliced crosswise
- 1 teaspoon curry powder
- 1 teaspoon yellow mustard seeds
- 1 tablespoon fresh lemon juice
- ½ cup chopped cilantro

1. Preheat the oven to 450°. In a large roasting pan, melt the butter in 1 tablespoon of the vegetable oil in the oven; swirl to combine. Add the cauliflower florets, stems up, and season with salt and pepper. Cover the roasting pan with foil and bake on the bottom shelf of the oven for 30 minutes. Increase the oven temperature to 500° and bake the cauliflower for 10 minutes. Remove the foil and continue to bake for 10 minutes longer, or until the cauliflower starts to caramelize on the bottom.

2. Meanwhile, in a large skillet, heat the remaining 3 tablespoons of vegetable oil. Add the onions, cover and cook over low heat, stirring occasionally, until very tender, about 20 minutes. Stir in the curry powder and mustard seeds and cook, stirring, until fragrant, about 5 minutes. Add the lemon juice and season with salt and pepper.

3. Transfer the roasted cauliflower to a large serving bowl and spoon the onions on top. Sprinkle with the chopped cilantro and serve at once.

—*Marcia Kiesel*

Broccoli with Orange-Chile Oil

Cumin-Marinated Cauliflower and Roasted Peppers

10 SERVINGS

Jarred Spanish *piquillo* peppers add a lovely smokiness and subtle heat to this delicious side dish. They are increasingly available at specialty food stores; you can substitute jarred roasted red peppers or, better yet, roast a red bell pepper yourself.

- 1 head of cauliflower, separated into 1-inch florets
- ¼ cup minced shallots
- 3 tablespoons white wine vinegar
- 1 teaspoon ground cumin
- ⅓ cup extra-virgin olive oil

Salt and freshly ground pepper

- ⅓ cup coarsely chopped *piquillo* peppers (about 2 ounces)

1. In a large saucepan of boiling salted water, cook the cauliflower until crisp-tender, 4 to 5 minutes. Drain the cauliflower and cool under running water. Drain again and dry on paper towels.
2. In a bowl, combine the shallots, vinegar and cumin. Whisk in the oil and season with salt and pepper. Add the cauliflower and peppers and toss. Put in a shallow dish and marinate at room temperature for at least 2 hours, stirring once or twice. Season with salt and pepper and serve. —*Julian Serrano*

MAKE AHEAD The dish can be prepared and refrigerated for up to 2 days; the flavors will intensify as the cauliflower sits.

Summer Vegetable Gratin

6 SERVINGS

In this classic Provençal dish, thinly sliced vegetables are arranged in rows and drizzled with olive oil, then baked until almost caramelized.

- 1 pound eggplant, peeled and cut crosswise ½ inch thick

Salt and freshly ground pepper

- 1 pound zucchini, sliced crosswise ½ inch thick
- 1 pound tomatoes, cored and sliced crosswise ½ inch thick

Cumin-Marinated Cauliflower and Roasted Peppers

- 3 tablespoons extra-virgin olive oil
- 1 teaspoon finely chopped rosemary

1. Preheat the oven to 400°. Grease a 12-by-10-inch shallow baking dish with olive oil. Arrange one-third of the eggplant slices in an overlapping row across the dish. Season with salt and pepper. Similarly, make a row of zucchini, followed by a row of tomatoes. Repeat until all the vegetables are used.
2. Drizzle the vegetables with the olive oil and sprinkle with the rosemary. Bake for about 40 minutes, or until the vegetables are very tender and starting to brown around the edges.

—*Corinne Chapoutier*

MAKE AHEAD The gratin can be baked a few hours ahead of time and quickly reheated just before serving.

Country-Style Grilled Eggplant

4 SERVINGS

- 2 quarts water

Salt

Two ¾-pound eggplants, sliced crosswise 1 inch thick

- ⅓ cup fruity extra-virgin olive oil, plus more for brushing
- 1 tablespoon chopped parsley
- 1 tablespoon shredded basil
- 2 tablespoons shredded spearmint
- 2 garlic cloves, sliced paper thin

Freshly ground pepper

Vinegar (optional)

1. Pour the water into a bowl, add ¼ cup salt and stir to dissolve completely. Add the eggplant slices and let soak for about 30 minutes, or until the bitter brown juices are released.
2. Light a charcoal or gas grill. Rinse and drain the eggplant slices; pat dry.

Baked Eggplant with Cheese and Anchovies

When the coals are white, arrange the eggplant slices on the grill, not immediately over the coals but around them. Brush lightly with oil. Cover and grill for about 30 minutes, turning the slices occasionally, until golden brown outside and creamy-tender within.

3. Arrange the eggplant slices on a platter in a single layer and sprinkle the olive oil, parsley, basil, spearmint and garlic on top. Season the eggplant with salt and pepper and let stand for at least 4 hours, turning the slices occasionally. Drizzle on a few drops of vinegar just before serving.

—*Paula Wolfert*

Apulia-Style Stuffed Eggplant

4 SERVINGS

    4   small Italian eggplants (6 ounces
        each), halved lengthwise
Kosher salt
    4   small anchovy fillets, rinsed
        and coarsely chopped
 ¼   cup tightly packed, freshly
        grated Pecorino Romano
        cheese (1 ounce)
    1   rounded teaspoon small
        capers, rinsed
Freshly ground pepper
    3   small garlic cloves,
        thinly sliced
    2   tablespoons extra-virgin olive oil

    2   teaspoons dry white wine
    1   teaspoon red wine vinegar
Pinch of dried oregano, crumbled

1. Make 3 lengthwise slashes in the cut sides of the eggplants; be careful not to cut through the skin. Sprinkle the cut sides with salt and arrange them in a colander, cut side down. Place a heavy plate on top, weigh them down with 3 heavy cans and let stand for at least 30 minutes or up to 1 hour to drain. Rinse the eggplants thoroughly and pat dry.

2. Meanwhile, in a small bowl, mash the anchovies with the cheese, capers and pepper into a dry paste. Stuff the garlic into the eggplant slits. Using a small spoon or table knife, open the slits in the eggplants and fill them with the anchovy paste; press the filling deep into the slits. Reshape the eggplants.

3. Heat the olive oil in a large nonstick skillet. Add the eggplants, cut side down. Cover and cook over moderately low heat until softened and deeply golden, about 15 minutes. Uncover the skillet, turn the eggplants and cook until the bottoms are lightly browned and the flesh is meltingly tender throughout, about 5 minutes longer. Transfer the eggplants to a platter and sprinkle with the white wine, vinegar and oregano. Let stand at room temperature for at least 20 minutes before serving. —*Paula Wolfert*

MAKE AHEAD The eggplant can be refrigerated overnight. Bring to room temperature before serving.

Baked Eggplant with Cheese and Anchovies

4 SERVINGS ✳

These eggplants are dressed up by topping them with tomatoes and cheese, then sliding them back in the oven before serving. The recipe calls for *Idiazábal,* a Basque smoked sheep's-milk cheese, but Gouda is a good alternative.

Two 1-pound eggplants, halved
 ¼   cup extra-virgin olive oil
Salt and freshly ground pepper
    2   garlic cloves, thinly sliced
    2   cups plain tomato sauce
 ¼   cup freshly grated *Idiazábal*
        cheese (2 ounces)
 ¼   cup dry bread crumbs
 12 anchovy fillets

1. Preheat the oven to 400°. Brush the cut sides of the eggplants with 1 tablespoon of the olive oil and set them in a large baking dish, cut side up. Season with salt and pepper and bake for 40 minutes, or until tender; brush with 1 tablespoon of olive oil after about 20 minutes.

2. Heat 1 tablespoon of the olive oil in a large saucepan. Add the sliced garlic and cook over moderate heat until golden. Add the tomato sauce and cook over moderately low heat, stirring occasionally until thickened, about 20 minutes.

3. In a small bowl, toss the cheese with the bread crumbs and the remaining 1 tablespoon of olive oil. Spoon the tomato sauce over the eggplants, sprinkle with the crumb mixture and bake until the cheese melts, about 5 minutes. Transfer the eggplant halves to plates, garnish with the anchovies and serve. —*Joseph Jiménez de Jiménez*

MAKE AHEAD The recipe can be prepared through Step 2 and refrigerated overnight. Bring to room temperature and rewarm before proceeding.

WINE A red Rioja, like the 1996 CVNE Viña Real, will balance the rustic flavors in this dish.

Stewed Tomatoes with Ginger

10 SERVINGS

    3   large garlic cloves, smashed
One 2-inch piece of fresh ginger,
        peeled and smashed
    2   rosemary sprigs
    2   thyme sprigs
 ½   cup olive oil
    1   large sweet onion, thinly sliced

6 pounds ripe plum
   tomatoes—peeled, halved
   lengthwise and seeded
Salt and freshly ground pepper
1 tablespoon cornstarch
2 tablespoons water
½ teaspoon celery seeds

1. Wrap the garlic, ginger, rosemary and thyme in cheesecloth and tie in a bundle. Heat the olive oil in a large casserole. Add the sliced sweet onion and cook over moderately low heat until softened, about 10 minutes. Add the tomatoes and the herb bundle, season with salt and pepper and cook over low heat until the tomato juices have reduced by one-fourth, about 20 minutes.

2. Mix the cornstarch with the water, add to the tomatoes and simmer until slightly thickened, about 8 minutes. Add the celery seeds and season with salt and pepper. Remove the herb bundle and serve. —*Patrick O'Connell*

MAKE AHEAD The stewed tomatoes can be refrigerated for up to 2 days.

Broiled Tomatoes with Goat Cheese and Fennel Pollen

4 SERVINGS ✻

4 small round tomatoes, halved
   crosswise, or 4 medium plum
   tomatoes, halved lengthwise
¼ cup extra-virgin olive oil
Sea salt and freshly ground pepper
One 4-ounce log mild goat cheese,
   cut into 8 slices
Fennel pollen, for dusting

1. Preheat the broiler. Arrange the tomatoes, cut side up, in a broiler pan. Drizzle each tomato half with ½ teaspoon of the olive oil and season with salt and pepper.

2. Broil the tomatoes for 3 to 4 minutes, or until sizzling and browned. Remove from the oven and top each tomato half with a slice of goat cheese, 1 teaspoon of olive oil and a pinch of fennel pollen. Broil for 3 to 4 minutes, or until the goat cheese is

Stuffed Tomatoes

golden. Transfer the tomatoes to a platter with a spatula and serve warm.
—*Grace Parisi*

NOTE Fennel pollen is available from Tavolo (800-700-7336).

Stuffed Tomatoes

4 SERVINGS

3 tablespoons canola oil
8 round medium tomatoes,
   halved crosswise
1 tablespoon unsalted butter
1 small onion, finely chopped
1 garlic clove, finely chopped
¼ pound ground pork
¼ pound ground veal
1 teaspoon kosher salt
¼ teaspoon freshly ground pepper
¼ teaspoon freshly grated nutmeg
¼ cup finely chopped flat-leaf
   parsley
2 large eggs, lightly beaten
¾ cup coarse fresh bread crumbs
2 tablespoons freshly grated
   Parmesan cheese

1. Preheat the oven to 400°. Coat a rimmed baking sheet with 1 tablespoon of the oil. Using a melon baller or a grapefruit knife, hollow out the tomato halves, leaving thin yet sturdy cups; reserve the scooped out tomato flesh in a bowl. Set the tomato cups on the prepared baking sheet.

2. In a large skillet, melt the butter in 1 tablespoon of the oil. Add the onion and garlic and cook over moderate heat, stirring occasionally, until softened but not browned, about 5 minutes. Add the ground pork and veal and season with the salt, pepper and nutmeg. Cook over moderately high heat, breaking up the ground pork and veal with a wooden spoon, until the meats lose their pink color, about 4 minutes; don't let them brown. Add the reserved tomato flesh to the skillet and cook until the juices evaporate, about 5 minutes.

3. Transfer the meat mixture to a bowl and let cool slightly. Beat in the parsley, eggs, ¼ cup of bread crumbs and the Parmesan. Spoon the stuffing into the tomato cups, mounding it slightly. Sprinkle the remaining ½ cup of bread crumbs over the tomatoes and drizzle with the remaining 1 tablespoon of oil.

4. Bake the tomatoes for about 45 minutes, or until the sides are soft and the stuffing is hot throughout. Set 4 stuffed tomato halves on each plate and serve. —*Daniel Gouret*

MAKE AHEAD The baked stuffed tomatoes can be refrigerated for up to 1 day. Cover them with foil and reheat in a 350° oven for 10 minutes, then uncover and bake for about 15 minutes longer, or until heated through.

Baked Tomatoes Stuffed with Herbed Rice

12 SERVINGS

The combination of sweet tomatoes and fresh herbs in this recipe captures the essence of southern Italy.

Salt
1½ cups Arborio rice (¾ pound)
12 medium tomatoes
3 anchovy fillets, mashed
2 tablespoons unsalted
   butter, softened
½ cup freshly grated Grana Padano
   or Parmigiano-Reggiano cheese
   (1½ ounces)

1 small red bell pepper, diced

2 tablespoons chopped basil

2 tablespoons chopped
flat-leaf parsley

Freshly ground pepper

1. Preheat the oven to 350°. In a large saucepan of boiling salted water, cook the rice over high heat until al dente, about 15 minutes. Drain the rice thoroughly and transfer it to a large bowl.

2. Meanwhile, cut off the top fourth of each tomato; reserve all of the tops. Using a melon baller and working over a bowl, hollow out the tomatoes. Pass the tomato pulp, seeds and juices through a food mill that is fitted with the fine disk.

3. In a bowl, mash the anchovies with the butter. Stir the anchovy butter into the hot rice, then mix in the tomato puree, cheese, red pepper, basil and parsley. Season the rice and the hollowed-out tomatoes with salt and pepper. Stuff each tomato with ⅓ cup of the rice. Put the tops on the tomatoes and transfer to an oiled roasting pan. Bake for 30 minutes, basting with the pan juices; the tomatoes are done when they are tender and the rice is warm. Serve warm. —*Cesare Casella*

MAKE AHEAD The stuffed tomatoes can be refrigerated overnight. Bring to room temperature before baking.

Cornmeal-Fried Okra, Tomatillos and Tomatoes

6 TO 8 SERVINGS

When buying okra, look for firm, bright green, unblemished pods.

1 cup coarse yellow cornmeal, preferably stone-ground

½ cup all-purpose flour

1½ teaspoons cayenne pepper

Coarse salt

1 cup buttermilk

1 large egg, beaten

1 pound young okra, trimmed (slice off stem without cutting into pod)

½ pound cherry tomatoes, halved through the stem end

½ pound large tomatillos, husked and cut into 1-inch wedges

2 cups vegetable oil, for frying

Hot sauce, for serving

1. In a large resealable plastic bag, combine the cornmeal, flour, cayenne and 2 teaspoons of salt. In a large shallow bowl, whisk the buttermilk with the egg.

2. Dip the okra in the egg and, using a slotted spoon, transfer it to the plastic bag. Shake to coat completely; transfer the okra to a large plate. Repeat with the cherry tomatoes and then the tomatillos.

3. Heat the oil in a large cast-iron skillet until shimmering. Fry the okra over moderately high heat, turning occasionally, until golden and crisp, 2 to 3 minutes. Using a slotted spoon, transfer to paper towels to drain. Reheat the oil and fry the cherry tomatoes until golden and crisp, 2 to 3 minutes. Drain on paper towels. Reheat the oil and fry the tomatillos, then drain. Gently toss the fried vegetables, season with salt and serve hot, with hot sauce on the side. —*Michael Lomonaco*

Caramelized Carrot Mash

6 SERVINGS

Unlike standard pureed carrots, these are oven-roasted until caramelized.

¼ cup pure olive oil

3½ pounds carrots, halved lengthwise

Salt and freshly ground pepper

½ cup Basic Chicken Stock (p. 98) or canned low-sodium broth

1 tablespoon honey

1. Preheat the oven to 400°. Spread the oil on 2 large rimmed baking

Baked Tomatoes Stuffed with Herbed Rice, with Shrimp and Green Bean Salad with Marjoram (p. 39).

Cornmeal-Fried Okra, Tomatillos and Tomatoes (p. 285)

sheets. Arrange the carrots, cut side down, on the baking sheets. Rub a little of the oil over the carrots and season with salt and pepper. Bake for about 45 minutes, or until the carrots are very tender and browned on the bottom.

2. In a large saucepan, heat the chicken stock with the honey. Add the carrots and, with a potato masher, mash the carrots coarsely. Season with salt and pepper and serve hot.

—*Marcia Kiesel*

Carrot-Fennel Confit
10 SERVINGS

½ teaspoon fennel seeds (optional)
2 medium fennel bulbs (about 1½ pounds)—halved, cored and cut into 1-inch chunks, plus fronds for garnish
1½ pounds carrots, cut into 1-inch lengths
¼ cup extra-virgin olive oil
1 tablespoon fresh lemon juice
1 tablespoon finely grated lemon zest
2 teaspoons thyme leaves
2 garlic cloves, minced
Kosher salt and freshly ground pepper

I. Preheat the oven to 275°. Toast the fennel seeds in a small skillet over moderate heat until fragrant, about 2 minutes. Transfer the toasted seeds to a mortar and crush them lightly.

2. In a large glass or ceramic baking dish, toss the fennel chunks with the carrots, olive oil, lemon juice, lemon zest, thyme, garlic and fennel seeds. Season with salt and pepper. Spread the vegetables evenly in the pan and cover tightly with foil. Bake for 2 hours, or until the vegetables are very tender.

3. Warm a 10- to 12-inch heavy skillet over moderately high heat. Working in 2 batches, add the vegetables and their juices and cook, stirring gently, until slightly browned, about 8 minutes. Season with salt and pepper. Spoon the confit into a serving dish,

garnish with the fennel fronds and serve.   —*Jayne Cohen*

MAKE AHEAD The carrots and fennel can be prepared through Step 2 and refrigerated for up to 1 day.

Carrot Flan with Thyme Crumbs
6 SERVINGS

¼ cup freshly grated Parmesan cheese, plus more for sprinkling
1¼ pounds carrots, cut into 1-inch lengths
5 large garlic cloves, halved
¾ cup heavy cream
½ cup milk
4 large eggs, beaten
Salt and freshly ground pepper
⅓ cup coarse fresh bread crumbs
1 tablespoon unsalted butter, melted
1 teaspoon chopped thyme

I. Preheat the oven to 350°. Butter a 10-inch glass pie plate and sprinkle it lightly with Parmesan cheese.

2. In a large saucepan, steam the carrots and garlic until very tender, about 25 minutes. Transfer to a food processor and puree until smooth. Pour in the heavy cream and milk and process to blend. Add the eggs, 2 tablespoons of the Parmesan cheese, 1 teaspoon of salt and ¼ teaspoon of pepper and process the mixture until well blended.

3. Pour the flan mixture into the prepared pie plate. Set the pie plate in a shallow roasting pan and add enough hot water to the pan to reach halfway up the side of the pie plate. Bake for 40 minutes, or until the flan is just set.

4. Meanwhile, in a small bowl, toss the bread crumbs with the melted butter, thyme and the remaining 2 tablespoons of Parmesan cheese. Season with salt and pepper.

5. Remove the flan from the water bath. Preheat the broiler. Sprinkle the flan with the thyme crumbs and broil for 30 seconds, or until golden brown. Cut into 6 wedges and serve warm.

—*Marcia Kiesel*

MAKE AHEAD The carrot flan can be assembled and refrigerated for 4 hours. Bring to room temperature before baking.

Roasted Beets with Cheese-Stuffed Dates
8 SERVINGS

Luscious Medjool dates are preferable for this salad because they're large and easy to stuff.

8 small beets (about 1½ pounds), trimmed
2 tablespoons extra-virgin olive oil
Salt and freshly ground pepper
¼ cup unsalted pistachios
½ cup Roquefort cheese (about 3 ounces), softened
2 teaspoons heavy cream
12 large dates, preferably Medjool, halved and pitted
2 tablespoons unsalted butter
2 tablespoons sugar
1½ tablespoons fresh lemon juice
5 Belgian endives, cored and cut into thin lengthwise strips
3 tablespoons sherry vinegar
1 tablespoon canola oil
1 tablespoon walnut oil
3 tablespoons minced chives
1 large bunch watercress, large stems discarded

I. Preheat the oven to 375°. In a bowl, toss the beets with 1 tablespoon of the olive oil and season with salt and pepper. Set the beets in a baking dish and add about ½ cup of water to cover the bottom of the dish. Cover with foil and bake for about 1 hour, or until the beets are tender when pierced. If the water evaporates, add more to the dish. Let cool slightly, then peel the beets and cut each into 8 wedges. Return the beets to the baking dish. Leave the oven on.

2. In a mini processor, finely grind the pistachios. Spread out on a plate. In a bowl, blend the Roquefort with the cream. Spoon a heaping ½ teaspoon of the cheese into each date half. Roll the dates in the pistachios, pressing to coat.

3. Melt the butter in a large skillet. Add the sugar and ½ tablespoon of the lemon juice and cook over moderate heat until the sugar starts to caramelize, about 3 minutes. Add the endives, stir to coat and cook, stirring occasionally, until softened, about 5 minutes. Raise the heat to moderately high and cook until any liquid in the pan has evaporated and the endives are lightly caramelized, about 7 minutes. Add the remaining 1 tablespoon of lemon juice and season with salt and pepper. Remove from the heat.

4. In a small bowl, combine the sherry vinegar with the canola oil, walnut oil and the remaining 1 tablespoon of olive oil. Season with salt and pepper. Rewarm the beets in the oven for about 4 minutes, or until heated through. Add ¼ cup of the dressing and toss. Add the chives and season with salt and pepper. Rewarm the endives in the skillet until heated through.

5. Toss the watercress with the remaining 2 tablespoons of dressing. Arrange 8 beet wedges on each salad plate. Spoon the caramelized endives onto the plates and top each serving with 3 stuffed dates. Garnish with some of the watercress and serve.

—*Josiah Citrin*

MAKE AHEAD The beets can be prepared 1 day in advance.

Caramelized Onions with Chestnuts and Prunes

10 SERVINGS

3 pounds cipolline onions, stem and root ends trimmed

½ cup Basic Chicken Stock (p. 98) or canned low-sodium broth

½ cup water

3 tablespoons unsalted butter

1 tablespoon white wine vinegar

1 tablespoon sugar

¼ cup Cognac

1 cup pitted prunes (6 ounces)

40 cooked and peeled unsweetened chestnuts (from a vacuum-packed 16-ounce jar)

Salt and freshly ground pepper

2 tablespoons finely chopped flat-leaf parsley

1. Bring a large saucepan of water to a boil. Add the onions and blanch for 30 seconds. Drain in a colander under cold running water. Slip off the papery skins and pat the onions dry.

2. In a large deep skillet, combine the chicken stock with the water, butter, vinegar and sugar. Cover and bring to a boil. Add the onions, cover and cook over moderately low heat until crisp-tender, about 15 minutes. Uncover and cook over moderate heat, stirring occasionally, until the onions are covered with a deep-golden caramel, about 30 minutes longer; add a few tablespoons of water as the liquid evaporates.

3. Add the Cognac, prunes and chestnuts to the onions and cook just until heated through. Season with salt and pepper and transfer to a serving bowl. Add 2 tablespoons of water to the skillet and scrape up any caramel stuck to the bottom and sides. Pour the sauce over the onions, garnish with the parsley and serve. —*Grace Parisi*

MAKE AHEAD The caramelized onions, prunes and chestnuts can be refrigerated overnight in a baking dish. Rewarm in a 325° oven, adding a few tablespoons of water if needed. Garnish with parsley just before serving.

Mushroom, Leek and Parmesan Bread Pudding

8 SERVINGS

1 cup dried porcini mushrooms (1 ounce)

1½ cups hot water

4 tablespoons unsalted butter

4 medium leeks, white and tender green parts, halved lengthwise and thinly sliced crosswise

Caramelized Onions with Chestnuts and Prunes

Sea salt and freshly ground pepper

4 garlic cloves, minced

1 pound assorted mushrooms, such as oysters, chanterelles and stemmed shiitakes, thickly sliced

½ pound cremini mushrooms, thinly sliced

½ cup dry white wine

One 9-ounce baguette, cut into 1-inch dice

6 large eggs, lightly beaten

2 cups heavy cream

1½ cups freshly grated Parmesan cheese (6 ounces)

2 tablespoons finely chopped thyme leaves

2 tablespoons finely chopped flat-leaf parsley

1. In a small bowl, soak the dried porcini in the hot water until softened, about 30 minutes. Drain and finely chop the mushrooms, discarding any tough bits.

2. Melt 2 tablespoons of the butter in a large skillet. Add the leeks and a pinch each of salt and pepper and cook over moderately high heat, stirring occasionally, until softened, about 5 minutes. Add the garlic and cook for 2 minutes longer. Add the remaining 2 tablespoons of butter along with the assorted mushrooms and chopped porcini and cook over high heat, stirring frequently, until the mushrooms have released their liquid. Pour in the wine and cook, stirring frequently, until the liquid has evaporated and the mushrooms begin to brown, about 10 minutes. Season the mushrooms with salt and pepper.

3. Preheat the oven to 375°. Lightly butter a 3-quart baking dish. Spread the diced bread in the baking dish and spoon the mushrooms on top. In a large bowl, whisk the eggs with the cream, 1 cup of the Parmesan cheese, the thyme and a pinch each of salt and pepper. Pour the custard over the mushrooms. Press a sheet of plastic wrap directly on the custard and allow the bread pudding to soak for about 30 minutes.

4. Discard the plastic wrap. Sprinkle the remaining ½ cup of cheese and the parsley on top of the pudding. Bake for about 40 minutes, or until the custard is set and the top is brown. Let stand for 10 minutes before serving.

—*Max London*

MAKE AHEAD The recipe can be prepared through Step 3 and refrigerated overnight. Bring to room temperature before baking.

Tamarind-Glazed Shallots

6 SERVINGS

1½ **pounds shallots or pearl onions**
3 **tablespoons extra-virgin olive oil**
2 **cups water**
1 **tablespoon tamarind concentrate (see Note)**
1 **tablespoon sugar**

1. Cook the shallots in a medium saucepan of boiling water for about 5 minutes to loosen the skins. Let cool slightly, then peel them.

2. Heat the oil in a large skillet. Add the shallots and cook over moderately high heat for 5 minutes. Reduce the heat to moderately low and cook, shaking the skillet and turning the shallots, until lightly browned, about 5 minutes longer.

3. Bring the 2 cups of water to a boil in a saucepan. In a medium heatproof bowl, combine the tamarind with the sugar, add the boiling water and stir until the sugar dissolves. Pour the tamarind mixture over the shallots and stir well. Cover the skillet and cook over low heat until the shallots are soft, about 25 minutes. Add water as needed to keep the shallots from drying out.

4. Using a slotted spoon, transfer the shallots to a plate. Cook the sauce over high heat until reduced to a glaze, about 10 minutes. Return the shallots to the skillet and toss to coat in the glaze. Season with salt and pepper and let cool. Cover and refrigerate for at least 1 hour or overnight. Serve the shallots cold. —*Claudia Roden*

NOTE Tamarind concentrate is available at Asian markets.

Sautéed Fresh Corn

8 SERVINGS

This recipe is from *Barefoot Contessa Parties!* (Clarkson N. Potter).

3 **tablespoons unsalted butter**
7 **cups fresh corn kernels (from 10 medium ears)**
Kosher salt and freshly ground pepper

Melt the butter in a large enameled cast-iron casserole. Add the corn, season with salt and pepper and cook over moderately low heat, stirring, until tender, about 10 minutes. Serve hot.

—*Ina Garten*

Grilled Corn with Creole Butter

6 SERVINGS

The fiery Creole butter would also be delicious with grilled fish and steaks.

7 **tablespoons unsalted butter, softened**
1 **tablespoon minced red bell pepper**
2 **teaspoons finely chopped basil**
1 **teaspoon minced jalapeño**

Kosher salt and cracked pepper
6 **ears of corn, shucked**
Vegetable oil, for brushing

1. In a small bowl, blend the butter with the bell pepper, basil, jalapeño and a generous pinch each of salt and pepper. Wrap in plastic, forming a 4-inch log, and refrigerate until firm, about 3 hours or for up to 3 days.

2. Light a grill. Lightly brush the corn with oil and grill over moderately high heat, turning, until tender and charred all over, 10 to 12 minutes. Slice the butter into pats and serve with the corn. —*Alison Tolley*

Grilled Corn with Tomato Barbecue Sauce

8 SERVINGS

½ **cup tomato puree**
3 **tablespoons pure olive oil**
2 **tablespoons unsulphured molasses**
2 **tablespoons balsamic vinegar**
1 **tablespoon minced oregano**
1 **garlic clove, minced**
1 **teaspoon kosher salt**
¼ **teaspoon freshly ground white pepper**
8 **large ears corn, shucked**

1. Light a grill. In a bowl, whisk together all the ingredients except the corn.

2. Generously brush the sauce all over the ears. Grill the corn over a low fire for 8 to 10 minutes, turning and brushing with the sauce, until tender and lightly charred. Transfer the ears to a platter, brush with any remaining sauce and serve. —*Daniel Bruce*

MAKE AHEAD The barbecue sauce can be refrigerated for up to 2 days.

Pan-Fried Corn Cakes

MAKES ABOUT 12 CORN CAKES

You can substitute frozen corn for fresh here: Use 1½ cups lightly pureed kernels and 1 cup whole kernels.

8 **ears of corn, shucked**
About ½ **cup all-purpose flour**
1 **large egg, lightly beaten**

3 scallions, thinly sliced

3 tablespoons minced parsley

1¾ teaspoons salt

¼ teaspoon freshly ground pepper

Unsalted butter, for frying

1. Grate 6 ears of corn on the large holes of a box grater set in a medium bowl. Cut the kernels from the remaining 2 ears with a sharp knife and add to the bowl. Add ½ cup of the flour, the egg, scallions, parsley, salt and pepper; stir until a thick batter forms. Add more flour if the batter seems thin. It should have the consistency of a very thick cake batter.

2. Melt 1 tablespoon of butter in a large cast-iron skillet. Working in batches, spoon a scant ¼ cup of the batter into the skillet for each corn cake and cook over moderate heat until golden brown, about 4 minutes per side. Wipe out the pan and repeat with additional butter and batter. Serve the corn cakes hot.

—Liv Rockefeller

Double Corn Pudding with Leeks

10 SERVINGS

3 tablespoons unsalted butter

4 large leeks, white and tender green parts, thinly sliced crosswise

Kosher salt and freshly ground pepper

Six 6-inch organic stone-ground corn tortillas

5 large eggs

2 large egg yolks

1½ cups heavy cream

1½ cups milk

2½ cups frozen corn kernels (about 13 ounces), thawed

1. Melt the butter in a large skillet. Add the leeks and cook over moderately low heat, stirring occasionally, until softened but not browned, about 10 minutes. Season with salt and pepper and let cool to room temperature.

2. Butter an 8-by-10-inch baking dish and line it with the tortillas. In a large bowl, whisk the eggs with the egg yolks. Add the cream and milk and whisk to blend. Stir in the leeks, corn, 2 teaspoons salt and ¼ teaspoon pepper. Pour the custard over the tortillas. Cover and refrigerate overnight. Bring to room temperature before baking.

3. Preheat the oven to 325°. Put the baking dish in a roasting pan and add enough hot tap water to reach halfway up the side of the dish. Bake the corn pudding for about 1 hour, or until just set. Let stand for about 10 minutes before serving. —Marcia Kiesel

MAKE AHEAD The unbaked pudding can be refrigerated for up to 2 days.

Roasted Squash with Red Onion, Oregano and Mint

8 SERVINGS

For the best results, look for elongated rather than bulbous squash.

Two 2½-pound butternut squash, preferably organic

Salt and freshly ground pepper

½ cup extra-virgin olive oil

¼ cup red wine vinegar

1 small red onion, very thinly sliced

1 tablespoon dried oregano

1 garlic clove, very thinly sliced

½ teaspoon crushed red pepper

¼ cup mint leaves

1. Preheat the oven to 450°. Slice the squash crosswise 1 inch thick; scrape out any seeds. Lightly oil 2 baking sheets and arrange the squash slices on them. Season with salt and pepper and drizzle with ¼ cup of the olive oil. Bake for about 25 minutes, or until just tender.

2. Combine the remaining ¼ cup of olive oil with the vinegar, onion, oregano, garlic and crushed red pepper. Season with salt and pepper. Pour over the warm squash and let stand for 20 minutes.

3. Arrange the squash on plates, sprinkle with the mint leaves and serve.

—Mario Batali

MAKE AHEAD The Roasted Squash with Red Onion, Oregano and Mint can be prepared through Step 2 and kept at room temperature for up to 4 hours.

Winter Vegetable Pan-Roast

10 SERVINGS

An ideal partner for Beef Tenderloin with Roasted Garlic Crust (p. 216), this easy vegetable dish is pictured with the tenderloin on page 217.

4 pounds winter squash, such as buttercup or kabocha—halved lengthwise, seeded and cut into 2-inch-wide wedges

6 tablespoons unsalted butter, melted, plus 2 tablespoons softened

Salt and freshly ground pepper

8 thyme sprigs

4 large sweet onions, such as Walla Walla, halved lengthwise and sliced crosswise ¼ inch thick

2 pounds assorted mushrooms, such as shiitake, cremini and Portobello, stems discarded and caps quartered

½ cup dry red wine

1. Preheat the oven to 425°. Put the squash wedges on a large rimmed baking sheet and brush all over with 2 tablespoons of the melted butter. Season with salt and pepper and scatter 4 of the thyme sprigs on top. Bake in the upper third of the oven for about 25 minutes, or until just tender. When cool enough to handle, peel the squash and cut the flesh into 1-inch dice. Transfer to a large baking dish.

2. Meanwhile, in a large roasting pan, toss the onions and mushrooms with the remaining 4 tablespoons of melted butter and the red wine. Season with salt and pepper and top with the remaining 4 thyme sprigs. Cover with foil and bake in the lower third of the oven for about 30 minutes, or until the onions have softened and the mushrooms have released their liquid. Strain the liquid and save it for later

use as stock or in gravy.

3. Stir the 2 tablespoons of softened butter into the onions and mushrooms in the roasting pan. Roast uncovered for about 1 hour, or until the onions and mushrooms are very tender and deeply browned around the edges.

4. Add the vegetables to the squash in the baking dish, stir to combine and season with salt and pepper to taste. Serve the vegetables hot.

—Jamie Guerin

MAKE AHEAD The vegetables can be refrigerated for up to 2 days. Bring them to room temperature and heat, covered, in a 425° oven.

Winter Squash Flan

8 SERVINGS

This isn't so much an eggy flan as it is a rustic molded puree of squash and potatoes. It's a perfect match for homey pot- or oven-roasted meat or poultry.

- 2 pounds butternut squash, peeled and cut into 1-inch chunks
- 1 large Yukon Gold potato, peeled and cut into 1-inch chunks
- ¼ cup fine dry bread crumbs
- 2 large eggs, lightly beaten
- 2 tablespoons freshly grated Parmesan cheese
- 1 teaspoon salt
- ½ teaspoon freshly ground pepper
- ¼ teaspoon freshly grated nutmeg

1. Preheat the oven to 350°. In separate saucepans, steam the squash and the potato until tender, 10 to 12 minutes. Press the potato through a fine sieve or a ricer. Puree the squash in a food processor until smooth. Add the bread crumbs, the lightly beaten eggs, grated Parmesan, salt, pepper and nutmeg to the squash and pulse to blend. Transfer the squash to a bowl and stir in the potato.

2. Butter an 8-inch shallow round baking dish or a 4-cup ring mold and set it in a larger pan. Spoon the flan mixture into the baking dish, smoothing the top. Add enough boiling water to the pan to reach halfway up the side of the baking dish. Cover the pan with foil and bake for 30 minutes, or until set. Remove the dish from the water bath and let the flan cool slightly. Serve the squash flan directly from the baking dish or unmold it onto a platter.

—Mina Vachino

MAKE AHEAD The flan can be refrigerated overnight. Cover loosely with foil and rewarm in a 325° oven for 20 minutes.

Golden Stuffed Chayotes

8 SERVINGS

Chayotes are tropical squash. In Martinique they're known as *christophines* and traditionally baked with cheese, revealing a French influence.

- 4 medium *chayotes* (about ½ pound each)
- ½ cup milk
- 2 tablespoons all-purpose flour
- 1 tablespoon unsalted butter
- 2 strips of bacon, finely chopped
- 1 small onion, minced
- 2 garlic cloves, minced
- 1½ cups shredded Gruyère (about 6 ounces)
- 3 tablespoons finely chopped flat-leaf parsley

Salt and freshly ground pepper

1. Lay the *chayotes* on a work surface; cut them in half horizontally and pit them. Bring a large pot of lightly salted water to a boil. Add the *chayotes* and cook over high heat until just tender, about 15 minutes. Drain and let cool slightly. Using a melon baller or small spoon, scoop out the center of the *chayotes*, leaving a ¼-inch shell. Transfer the shells to a large baking dish. Finely chop the flesh.

2. Preheat the oven to 450°. In a small pitcher, whisk the milk with the flour until smooth. Melt the butter in a large skillet. Add the bacon and cook over moderate heat, stirring, until crisp, about 3 minutes. Add the onion and garlic and cook, stirring, until softened, about 4 minutes. Whisk the milk again and add it to the skillet. Cook over moderate heat, stirring, until the sauce thickens, about 1 minute. Add the chopped *chayotes* and cook over moderate heat, stirring often, until the excess liquid evaporates, 7 to 8 minutes. Add half of the cheese and the parsley and season with salt and pepper. Season the *chayotes* shells with salt and pepper. Mound the filling in the shells and sprinkle with the remaining cheese. Transfer the stuffed *chayotes* to a baking sheet.

3. Bake the stuffed *chayotes* for about 25 minutes, or until golden and bubbling. Let stand for 10 minutes before serving.

—Corinne Trang

MAKE AHEAD The stuffed *chayotes* can be refrigerated for 2 days.

Sautéed Plantains Gloria

4 SERVINGS

There is a secret to the success of this recipe: Leave the plantains at room temperature until their skins turn completely black. The long ripening process makes them sweeter, softer and tastier than yellow or brown ones.

- 2 black-skinned plantains (about 1 pound)
- 1 tablespoon unsalted butter
- ½ teaspoon canola oil

Salt

1. Cut the ends off the plantains and slit the skins lengthwise; remove the peel. Halve each plantain lengthwise.

2. In a large nonstick skillet, melt the butter in the oil. Add the plantains, cut side up, and cook over moderately high heat until golden brown, about 2½ minutes per side. Season the plantains with salt.

3. Using a meat pounder, flatten the fried plantains slightly. Reduce the heat to low, turn the plantains again and cook until they are tender and deep brown, about 2 minutes longer. Serve hot.

—Jacques Pépin

vegetables

West African Vegetable and Peanut Stew

4 SERVINGS

- 3 tablespoons vegetable oil
- 1 large onion, finely chopped
- 3 large garlic cloves, minced
- 2 jalapeños, seeded and finely chopped
- 1 tablespoon finely chopped fresh ginger
- 1½ tablespoons Madras curry powder

One 14-ounce can whole peeled tomatoes, chopped, with their liquid

- 4 cups water or canned low-sodium chicken broth
- ½ cup smooth peanut butter

Salt and freshly ground pepper

- 1 pound sweet potatoes, peeled and cut into 1-inch chunks
- 2 carrots, cut into ½-inch dice
- 2 cups frozen whole okra or 6 ounces fresh whole okra
- 1 cup frozen green beans or ¼ pound fresh green beans, cut into 2-inch lengths
- ¼ cup cilantro leaves
- ¼ cup chopped salted peanuts

Lime wedges, for serving

Steamed rice (p. 307), for serving

1. Heat the oil in a large enameled cast-iron casserole. Add the onion, garlic, jalapeños and ginger and cook over moderate heat, stirring frequently, until the onion is lightly browned, about 6 minutes. Add the curry powder and cook, stirring, until fragrant and lightly toasted, about 2 minutes. Add the tomatoes, scraping up any bits stuck to the bottom of the casserole. Whisk in the water and peanut butter, season with salt and pepper and bring to a boil. Cook over moderately high heat for 15 minutes, stirring frequently.

2. Add the sweet potatoes and carrots, cover partially and cook over moderately low heat until just tender, about 20 minutes. Add the okra and green beans, cover partially and cook until all the vegetables are tender, about 10 minutes longer. Transfer the stew to 4 deep bowls and serve hot. Pass the cilantro, peanuts, lime wedges and steamed rice at the table.

—*Grace Parisi*

MAKE AHEAD The stew can be refrigerated for up to 3 days. Reheat gently over moderately low heat.

WINE The hint of spiciness in this dish would be complemented best by an aromatic, dry-style Steen from South Africa, such as the 1999 Simonsig Stellenbosch or the 1999 Landskroon.

Fava Bean and Potato Puree with Chicory

6 SERVINGS

This traditional dish from Apulia, which combines fava beans and greens in a fluffy puree, makes a perfect partner for lamb.

- 1 cup dried, peeled, split mini fava beans (5 ounces)—picked over, rinsed and drained (see Note)
- 5⅓ cups water
- ⅓ cup extra-virgin olive oil
- 2 medium Idaho or Yukon Gold potatoes (about 14 ounces), peeled and thickly sliced
- ½ pound bitter greens, such as dandelion or chicory, thick stems discarded, leaves finely shredded

Sea salt

Freshly ground white pepper

1. In a large saucepan, combine the fava beans with 5 cups of the water and 1 tablespoon of the oil and bring to a boil. Reduce the heat to moderate, cover partially and simmer for 10 minutes. Add the potatoes and cook over moderately high heat until the favas and potatoes are tender and most of the liquid has been absorbed, about 20 minutes. Drain the favas and potatoes and put them in a medium bowl; reserve the cooking liquid.

2. Meanwhile, put the greens in a medium saucepan and add a pinch of salt. Cover and cook over low heat until the greens are almost dry, tilting the pan occasionally to drain off any bitter liquid. Add the remaining ⅓ cup of water to the greens and cook, stirring, until tender and dry, about 5 minutes. Remove from the heat and mash the greens to a coarse puree.

3. Season the fava beans and potatoes with ¾ teaspoon salt and mash them with a potato masher. Alternatively, pass the fava beans and potatoes through a food mill fitted with the fine disk. (Do not be tempted to use a food processor.) Mash in just enough of the reserved fava and potato cooking liquid to make the puree. Beat until light and smooth. Gradually beat in the remaining ¼ cup plus 1 teaspoon of olive oil, then beat in the greens. Season with salt and white pepper, spoon into a shallow dish and serve warm.

—*Paula Wolfert*

NOTE Dried, peeled and split mini fava beans are available at Middle Eastern food markets and on the Web, at www.kalustyans.com.

Lentil Salad

10 SERVINGS

- 2 quarts water
- 1 pound brown lentils

Salt and freshly ground pepper

- ¼ cup white wine
- 1 tablespoon fresh lemon juice
- 1 teaspoon Dijon mustard
- ⅛ teaspoon sugar
- ¼ cup extra-virgin olive oil
- ½ cup finely chopped celery
- ½ cup finely chopped onion
- 1 tablespoon finely chopped chives
- 1 teaspoon finely chopped thyme

1. In a large saucepan, bring the water to a boil. Add the lentils, season with salt and pepper and simmer over moderately low heat, stirring occasionally, until tender, about 25 minutes. Drain the lentils and transfer to a large bowl.

2. In a small bowl, combine the wine with the lemon juice, mustard and sugar. Slowly whisk in the olive oil until blended and season with salt and pepper. Add the vinaigrette, celery, onion, chives and thyme to the lentils, toss well and serve. —*Patrick O'Connell*
MAKE AHEAD The salad can be refrigerated overnight. Allow it to come to room temperature before serving.

Fragrant Toor Lentils with Garlic and Tomato
10 TO 12 SERVINGS
In India, lentils are often served as a side dish with rice; together the two are a rich source of protein. Orange-red *toor* lentils are not only delicious but also quick and easy to cook.

- 3 cups (1½ pounds) *toor dal* (lentils), picked over and rinsed
- 1½ teaspoons cayenne pepper
- 1 tablespoon salt
- Scant ½ teaspoon turmeric
- ¼ cup plus 2 tablespoons fresh lemon juice
- 5 tablespoons unsalted butter
- 30 fresh curry leaves
- 2½ teaspoons cumin seeds
- 1½ teaspoons mustard seeds
- ¼ cup minced garlic (9 cloves)
- 8 serrano chiles, seeded and julienned
- 6 medium tomatoes (1¾ pounds), peeled and coarsely chopped, juices reserved
- 2 tablespoons chopped cilantro

1. Soak the lentils in a large bowl of cold water for 30 minutes; drain. In a large saucepan, cover the lentils with 10 cups of water and bring to a boil. Skim off any foam that rises to the surface. Add the cayenne, salt and turmeric, cover partially and cook over moderate heat, stirring frequently, until the lentils are very tender, about 45 minutes.
2. Using a potato masher, mash the lentils until slightly smooth and thick.

Remove from the heat and stir in the lemon juice. Cover and keep warm.
3. Melt the butter in a medium saucepan. When the foam subsides, add the curry leaves, cumin seeds and mustard seeds. Cover at once and cook over moderate heat until the popping stops, about 30 seconds. Add the garlic and chiles and cook, stirring, until softened and lightly browned, 3 to 4 minutes. Add the tomatoes with their juices and cook, stirring frequently, until the sauce is thick, about 15 minutes. Stir the sauce into the lentils and simmer for 3 minutes. Serve in bowls, garnished with the cilantro.

—*Neela Paniz*
MAKE AHEAD The recipe can be made through Step 2 and refrigerated for up to 3 days. Rewarm the lentils gently, adding water if necessary.

Spiced Red Lentil Stew with Caramelized Onions
6 SERVINGS
This fragrant *dal* can be served as a side dish for roasted chicken or seafood, or as a main dish with vegetables and rice.

- 1 tablespoon vegetable oil
- 3 medium onions—1 quartered lengthwise and thinly sliced crosswise
- 2 bay leaves
- One 2-inch cinnamon stick
- 1½ teaspoons minced fresh ginger
- 1 garlic clove, minced
- ¼ teaspoon cayenne pepper
- 2 cups small red lentils (1 pound)
- 3 cups Basic Chicken Stock (p. 98) or canned low-sodium broth
- About 3½ cups hot water
- 1 lemon, halved
- Salt and freshly ground pepper
- 2 teaspoons unsalted butter
- Chopped cilantro, for serving
- Plain yogurt, for serving

1. Heat the oil in a large heavy saucepan. Add the quartered onion, the bay leaves and cinnamon stick and cook

over moderately low heat, stirring, until the onion softens, about 7 minutes. Add the ginger, garlic and cayenne and cook over moderately high heat, stirring, until fragrant, about 3 minutes. Add the lentils and stir until thoroughly coated with oil. Add 2 cups each of the chicken stock and hot water and bring to a boil. Simmer over moderate heat for 5 minutes.
2. Squeeze the lemon juice into the lentils. Add the lemon halves, 1 teaspoon salt and the remaining 1 cup of stock. Cover and cook over moderately low heat, stirring occasionally, until the lentils become a thick puree, about 25 minutes. Add more water as necessary; the lentils should be slightly soupy.
3. Meanwhile, thinly slice the remaining 2 onions lengthwise. Melt the butter in a large skillet. Add the onions, cover and cook over moderately low heat until softened, about 5 minutes. Uncover and cook over moderate heat, stirring frequently, until the onions caramelize, about 12 minutes. Remove from the heat and season with salt and pepper.
4. Discard the cinnamon stick, bay leaves and lemon from the lentils and season with salt and pepper. Serve the lentils in bowls, topped with the caramelized onions, cilantro and yogurt.

—*Sally Schneider*
ONE SERVING Calories 83 kcal, Total Fat 4.5 gm, Saturated Fat 1.5 gm

Mixed Vegetable and Lentil Curry
10 TO 12 SERVINGS
- 2 cups *toor dal* (lentils), picked over and rinsed (1 pound)
- 14 cups cool water
- 1½ teaspoons cayenne pepper
- ¾ teaspoon turmeric
- 6 ounces tamarind pulp (see The Indian Pantry, p. 171), with seeds, broken into pieces
- 1 cup boiling water

3 tablespoons vegetable oil

4 dried red chiles

1 scant teaspoon fenugreek seeds

1 scant teaspoon mustard seeds

⅛ teaspoon asafoetida (see The Indian Pantry, p. 171)

4 serrano chiles, seeded and minced

One 1-inch piece of fresh ginger, peeled and finely chopped

1 scant teaspoon cumin seeds

¾ cup lightly packed besan (see The Indian Pantry, p. 171)

1½ tablespoons ground coriander

4 small red potatoes (¾ pound), peeled and cut into 1-inch pieces

1 medium cauliflower, cut into 1½-inch florets

4 medium Japanese eggplants, halved lengthwise and cut into 1½-inch pieces

¼ pound green beans, cut into 1½-inch pieces

2 carrots, cut into 2-inch matchsticks

½ pound small okra, ends trimmed

2 medium tomatoes, each cut into 6 wedges

1½ teaspoons salt

1. In a large saucepan, combine the lentils with the cool water and bring to a boil, skimming any foam. Stir in ¾ teaspoon of the cayenne and the turmeric. Cover the pan partially and cook over low heat until the lentils are very tender, about 45 minutes.

2. Using a potato masher, lightly crush the lentils until slightly smooth and thick. Strain the lentils through a fine-mesh sieve set over a large heatproof bowl; press lightly on the solids to extract as much of the cooking liquid as possible; you should have about 10 cups. Discard the lentil pulp or save it for another use.

3. Meanwhile, soak the tamarind pulp in the boiling water, stirring occasionally, until softened. Strain the tamarind through a fine-mesh sieve set over a bowl, pressing hard on the pulp to extract as much paste as possible. Discard the seeds and pulp.

4. Heat the oil in a large enameled cast-iron casserole. Add the dried red chiles, fenugreek seeds, mustard seeds and asafoetida, cover immediately and cook over high heat just until the popping stops, about 30 seconds. Add the serrano chiles, ginger and cumin and cook, stirring, until fragrant, about 1 minute. Add the besan and cook over low heat, stirring, until lightly browned and emitting a nutty aroma, about 4 minutes. Add the coriander and the remaining ¾ teaspoon cayenne pepper and cook, stirring, for 1 minute longer.

5. Add 8 cups of the reserved lentil liquid and whisk until smooth. Stir in the potatoes and bring to a boil. Add the cauliflower, eggplants and green beans, cover and cook until crisp-tender, about 5 minutes. Add the carrots and cook, stirring occasionally, until crisp-tender, about 5 minutes.

6. Add the okra and tomatoes. Cover and cook over low heat, stirring occasionally, until all of the vegetables are tender but not falling apart, 10 to 15 minutes longer. Stir in the tamarind paste and the salt and cook over low heat just until the flavors are blended, about 3 minutes. Remove the whole chiles and serve warm. —*Neela Paniz*

MAKE AHEAD The curry can be refrigerated overnight.

Hearty Moong Dal

4 SERVINGS ✳

Protein-rich legume-based dishes called *dals*—a term that also refers to the dried legumes themselves—are prepared throughout India. In southern India, *dals* are thinner and served as soups. Northern versions, like this spicy one, are thicker and more like stews.

7 cups water

1 cup whole green *moong dal* (lentils)

3 large pitted dates

2 large garlic cloves

¼ cup shredded unsweetened coconut

1 jalapeño, seeded and coarsely chopped

One 1-inch piece of peeled fresh ginger, coarsely chopped

¼ teaspoon turmeric

3 tablespoons vegetable oil

½ teaspoon black mustard seeds

½ teaspoon cumin seeds

1 medium onion, coarsely chopped

3 plum tomatoes, coarsely chopped

1 cup (packed) baby spinach (1½ ounces)

2 teaspoons fresh lemon juice

Salt

2 tablespoons coarsely chopped cilantro

1. In a large saucepan, combine 6 cups of the water and the *moong dal* and bring to a boil. Reduce the heat to moderately low and simmer until the *dal* is soft, about 50 minutes.

2. Meanwhile, in a food processor, puree the dates, garlic, shredded coconut, jalapeño, ginger, turmeric and the remaining 1 cup of water until smooth.

3. Stir the date puree into the cooked *moong dal* and cook over low heat for 5 minutes, stirring.

4. In a medium skillet, heat the vegetable oil until smoking. Add the mustard seeds, cumin seeds and onion and cook over moderately high heat, stirring frequently, until the onion is golden brown, 6 to 8 minutes. Add the spiced onion to the simmering *dal*. Stir in the tomatoes and spinach and cook for 2 minutes. Remove from heat, stir in the lemon juice and season with salt. Sprinkle the *dal* with the cilantro and serve.

—*Gary MacGurn and Patty Gentry*

MAKE AHEAD The *moong dal* can be prepared in advance and refrigerated for up to 2 days.

Matt's Honey-Glazed Baked Field Peas

8 TO 10 SERVINGS

Red field peas, also called cow peas, are ubiquitous in the regional cuisine of the Florida panhandle.

- 1 pound dried field peas (2⅓ cups), picked over and rinsed
- 8 cups water
- ¾ cup mild aromatic honey, preferably Palmetto
- ¾ cup dry sherry
- 6 ounces country ham, cut into ½-inch dice
- 1 large onion, coarsely chopped
- 3 large garlic cloves, minced
- 1 tablespoon extra-virgin olive oil
- 1 teaspoon salt
- 1 teaspoon freshly ground white pepper

ı. In a large saucepan, combine the field peas with the water and bring to a boil. Cover and cook the peas over low heat until just tender, about 35 minutes. Drain, reserving the cooking liquid.

2. Preheat the oven to 325°. In a large heavy casserole, combine the peas, ½ cup of the honey, the sherry, ham, onion, garlic, olive oil, salt and white pepper. Stir in 2½ cups of the reserved pea–cooking liquid. Cover and bake for about 1½ hours, or until the peas are tender and some of the liquid is absorbed. Drizzle the remaining ¼ cup of honey on top and bake, uncovered, for about 45 minutes, or until the peas are glazed on top. Serve hot or warm. —*Matt Lee*

MAKE AHEAD The Honey-Glazed Baked Field Peas can be made ahead and refrigerated for up to 3 days. Rewarm over moderately low heat.

Mole-Style Baked Beans

12 SERVINGS

Similar to a Mexican mole, the sauce for these baked beans is finished with chocolate. The result is a delicious, deep dark richness that is not cloying.

- 1 pound Great Northern beans— picked over, rinsed and soaked overnight in cold water
- 10 cups cold water plus ½ cup boiling water
- 1 dried chipotle chile
- 3 tablespoons olive oil
- 1 medium onion, minced
- 4 slices of bacon, finely chopped
- ¾ cup dark brown sugar
- ⅓ cup tomato paste
- ¼ cup dry red wine
- ⅛ teaspoon freshly grated nutmeg
- ⅛ teaspoon ground cloves
- ⅛ teaspoon ground cumin
- ⅛ teaspoon sweet paprika
- ⅛ teaspoon chili powder
- 2 ounces unsweetened chocolate, chopped

Salt and freshly ground pepper

ı. Drain and rinse the beans. In a large saucepan, cover the beans with 6 cups of the water and bring to a boil. Reduce the heat to low, cover and simmer until tender, about 1 hour. Meanwhile, soak the chipotle in the ½ cup of boiling water until softened, about 20 minutes. Drain the chipotle. Discard the stem and seeds and mince the chile.

2. Heat the olive oil in a large saucepan. Add the onion and cook over moderate heat until softened, 2 to 3 minutes. Add the bacon and cook until softened, 2 to 3 minutes longer. Stir in the remaining 4 cups of water and the chipotle, brown sugar, tomato paste, wine, nutmeg, cloves, cumin, paprika and chili powder. Drain the beans and add them to the saucepan. Cover and simmer over low heat until the sauce has thickened, about 1 hour. Stir in the chocolate, season with salt and pepper and serve.

—*Elizabeth Falkner*

MAKE AHEAD The Mole-Style Baked Beans can be made up to 2 days in advance. Do not add the chocolate until after rewarming and just before serving.

Spicy Red Beans with Ham and Andouille Sausage

8 SERVINGS

- 1 pound dried red beans, picked over and soaked overnight
- 3 quarts water
- 2 meaty smoked ham hocks
- 1 large onion, coarsely chopped
- 1 green bell pepper, coarsely chopped
- 3 tablespoons minced garlic
- 2 tablespoons cider vinegar
- 2 teaspoons freshly ground black pepper
- 1 teaspoon dried thyme
- 1 bay leaf

Pinch of cayenne pepper

- ¾ pound smoked ham, cut into ½-inch dice
- 1 *andouille* sausage, thinly sliced (about 4 ounces)
- 6 scallions, white and green parts, thinly sliced

Salt

ı. Drain and rinse the beans. In a large enameled cast-iron casserole, combine the beans with the water, ham hocks, onion, bell pepper, garlic, vinegar, black pepper, thyme, bay leaf and cayenne. Bring to a simmer over moderate heat. Cover partially, reduce the heat to moderately low and cook, stirring occasionally, until the beans are tender, about 1½ hours. Add the ham, *andouille* and scallions and cook over moderate heat until the beans are just beginning to fall apart and the sauce is reduced to a thick gravy, about 30 minutes.

2. Remove the ham hocks. Pull the meat off the bones, tearing it into pieces. Return the meat to the beans and season with salt. Serve hot.

—*Bobby Holt*

MAKE AHEAD The beans can be refrigerated for up to 3 days.

Russet Potato Chips

4 SERVINGS

These divine chips are well worth the effort. They have the pure flavor of potatoes, butter and sea salt, but half the fat of commercial chips because they're baked rather than deep-fried.

- 1 tablespoon plus 2 teaspoons unsalted butter (see Note)
- 1 pound russet potatoes

Fine sea salt

I. Preheat the oven to 425°. In a small saucepan, melt the butter over low heat. Skim off the foam and pour the clear butter into a small bowl, stopping when you reach the milk solids.

2. Peel the potatoes and slice them crosswise ¹⁄₁₆ inch thick on a mandoline. Rinse the slices in several changes of cold water until the water runs clear. Put the slices in a salad spinner, spin and pat dry with paper towels.

3. Working on large rimmed baking sheets, lightly brush both sides of the potato slices with butter. Arrange the slices on the baking sheets and bake the potato chips until golden brown and crisp, 12 to 15 minutes. Sprinkle with salt and transfer to a rack to cool.
—*Sally Schneider*

NOTE Extra-virgin olive oil or goose or duck fat can be used instead of butter.

MAKE AHEAD The potato chips can be kept in an airtight container for up to 3 days. Recrisp before serving.

ONE SERVING Calories 125 kcal, Total Fat 5 gm, Saturated Fat 3 gm

Parslied Potatoes

8 SERVINGS

- 5 medium baking potatoes (about 2½ pounds), peeled and cut into 1-inch chunks
- 6 tablespoons unsalted butter

Salt and freshly ground pepper

- 3 tablespoons finely chopped flat-leaf parsley

I. Cook the potatoes in a large saucepan of boiling salted water until they are tender, about 10 minutes; drain. Return the potatoes to the saucepan and shake over moderately high heat for 1 minute to dry them out.

2. Melt the butter in a large heavy skillet. When the foam subsides, add the potatoes and cook over moderate heat, turning occasionally, until browned, about 10 minutes. Season with salt and pepper, sprinkle with the parsley and serve.   —*Emeril Lagasse*

MAKE AHEAD The potatoes can be prepared through Step 1 and refrigerated for up to 2 days.

New Potatoes with Thyme and Saffron

8 SERVINGS

- 1 cup Basic Chicken Stock (p. 98) or canned low-sodium broth

Pinch of saffron threads

- 4 tablespoons unsalted butter
- 3 pounds small new potatoes, scrubbed
- 2 medium shallots, finely chopped
- 6 thyme sprigs
- 2 bay leaves

Salt and freshly ground pepper

I. Heat the chicken stock in a small saucepan. Crumble the saffron into the stock and let stand for 15 minutes.

2. Melt the butter in a large enameled cast-iron casserole. Add the potatoes and cook over moderate heat until warm and coated with butter, about 4 minutes. Stir in the shallots, then add the thyme, bay leaves and the infused stock and season the mixture with salt and pepper.

3. Cover the casserole and cook the potatoes over low heat until tender, about 15 minutes. Uncover and cook over moderately high heat, stirring frequently, until the potatoes are tender and the stock has reduced to a few tablespoons, about 5 minutes longer. Discard the thyme and bay leaves. Transfer the potatoes and their juices to a bowl and serve.

—*Tamasin Day-Lewis*

Goat Cheese Potato Galette

Goat Cheese Potato Galette

4 TO 6 SERVINGS

- 1¼ pounds medium Yukon Gold potatoes, peeled and thinly sliced
- 3 tablespoons extra-virgin olive oil

Sea salt and freshly ground pepper

- 3 ounces mild goat cheese (6 tablespoons), crumbled
- 1 teaspoon fennel pollen

I. Preheat the oven to 425°. In a large bowl, toss the potatoes with 2 tablespoons of the oil and season with salt and pepper. In a lightly oiled 10-inch nonstick ovenproof skillet, arrange one-third of the potato slices in an overlapping circular pattern. Top with half the goat cheese and another third of the potatoes. Repeat with the remaining goat cheese and potatoes.

2. Cut out a 10-inch round of parchment or wax paper. Moisten the paper and then lay it on top of the potatoes. Cover with a lid that fits inside the skillet and cook the galette over moderate heat for 8 minutes, or until golden around the edges when the paper is peeled back. Transfer the covered skillet to the oven and bake for 15 minutes, or until the potatoes are just tender when pierced with a knife. Remove the lid and parchment and bake for 7 minutes longer, or until the top is browned. Run a spatula around the edge of the skillet and shake to loosen the galette. Invert a plate over

fennel pollen defined

Fennel pollen, the "it" ingredient of the moment, is wonderfully fragrant and versatile. It is a golden powder harvested from fennel blossoms that have been dried, put through a separator and sifted until fine. Common in Italy, it was recently popularized in the United States by chef Mario Batali of New York City's Babbo. Much of the fennel pollen sold in the United States is produced in Italy, but a new domestic producer, Sugar Ranch, in California, is hand-harvesting fennel pollen that has an extraordinary aroma and a particularly fine texture. If you're allergic to pollen, use ground, toasted fennel seed instead. Italian fennel pollen is $19.50 for a 1.65-ounce jar at Tavolo (800-700-7336); the domestic kind is $29.50 an ounce from Sugar Ranch (800-821-5989).

the skillet, flip and turn out the galette.
3. Heat the remaining 1 tablespoon of olive oil in the skillet until shimmering. Add the fennel pollen and a pinch of salt and cook over high heat until fragrant, about 30 seconds. Cut the galette into wedges and drizzle with the fennel-pollen oil. —*Grace Parisi*

Potato Gratin

4 SERVINGS
This light gratin is flavored with stock.
- 2 tablespoons unsalted butter
- 1 large onion, thinly sliced
- 1 teaspoon thyme leaves
- Salt and freshly ground pepper
- 4 russet potatoes (½ pound each), peeled and sliced ⅛ inch thick
- 2 cups Basic Chicken Stock (p. 98) or canned low-sodium broth, heated

1. Preheat the oven to 375°. Melt the butter in a medium saucepan. Add the onion and thyme, season with salt and pepper and cook until softened.
2. Generously butter a 9-by-13-inch glass baking dish. Spread half of the potatoes in the baking dish and season well with salt and pepper. Spread the onions on top and cover with the remaining potatoes. Season well with salt and pepper. Pour the hot stock over the potatoes and press gently to even them out. Bake in the top third of the oven for 1 hour, or until tender throughout and crisp on top. —*Marcia Kiesel*

Artichoke-Potato Gratin

10 SERVINGS
- 1 lemon, halved
- 8 large artichokes (about ¾ pound each)
- 1½ cups Basic Chicken Stock (p. 98) or canned low-sodium broth
- 1½ cups heavy cream or half-and-half
- 1 large thyme sprig
- Kosher salt
- 2 pounds baking potatoes, peeled and sliced ¼ inch thick
- Freshly ground pepper
- ½ cup shredded Gruyère cheese (2 ounces)
- ½ cup coarse dry bread crumbs
- 1 tablespoon unsalted butter, melted

1. Fill a large bowl with water, squeeze the lemon into it; add the lemon to the bowl. Cut off all but 1½ inches from the artichoke stems. Working with 1 artichoke at a time, pull off all the green outer leaves, leaving a cone of pale yellow leaves. With a sharp knife, cut off all but 1½ inches of the leaves. Peel the stem and trim any tough green skin from the artichoke bottom with a sturdy vegetable peeler. With a melon baller or small spoon, scoop out the hairy choke. Put the trimmed artichoke heart into the lemon water. Repeat with the remaining artichokes.
2. Bring a large saucepan of water to a boil. Cut each artichoke heart through the stem into 8 wedges. Add the wedges to the boiling water and cook until crisp-tender, about 8 minutes. Drain and rinse the wedges under cold water; pat dry.
3. In the same saucepan, mix the stock, cream, thyme sprig and 1 teaspoon of salt and bring to a boil. Add the potatoes and cook over moderately low heat until barely tender, about 8 minutes. Fold in the artichokes and season with salt and pepper.
4. Butter a 9-by-13-inch baking dish or 3-quart gratin dish. Pour the contents of the saucepan into the dish; discard the thyme sprig. Sprinkle the Gruyère over the gratin and cover with foil.
5. Preheat the oven to 375°. Bake the gratin for 30 minutes. In a small bowl, toss the bread crumbs with the butter. Remove the foil, sprinkle the crumbs over the gratin and bake for about 30 minutes longer, or until most of the liquid has been absorbed and the vegetables are tender.
6. Preheat the broiler. Broil the gratin about 6 inches from the heat for about 2 minutes, or until the crumbs are crisp and golden; turn the dish as necessary for even browning. Serve hot. —*Grace Parisi*

MAKE AHEAD The unbaked gratin can be refrigerated overnight.

Potato and Black Olive Gratin

20 SERVINGS
Slicing the potatoes thinly is essential to the success of this gratin. You can buy an inexpensive mandoline-type slicer at most kitchenware stores.
- 16 baking potatoes, peeled and thinly sliced crosswise
- ½ cup plus 2 tablespoons extra-virgin olive oil
- Salt and freshly ground pepper
- 1 cup freshly grated Parmesan cheese (3 ounces)
- ⅔ cup coarsely chopped pitted Calamata olives (6 ounces)
- 4 garlic cloves, minced
- 2 tablespoons chopped thyme
- 2 cups Basic Chicken Stock (p. 98) or canned low-sodium broth
- 2 cups dry white wine

1. Preheat the oven to 375°. Coat two

Potato and Black Olive Gratin

14-by-10-inch gratin dishes with vegetable-oil cooking spray. In a large bowl, toss the potato slices with 6 tablespoons of the olive oil. Spread one-sixth of the potatoes in an even layer in each of the gratin dishes. Season generously with salt and pepper. Top the potatoes in each dish with ¼ cup of the Parmesan cheese, 2½ tablespoons of the olives, one-fourth of the garlic and ½ tablespoon of the thyme. Repeat to form the second layer, leaving out the Parmesan cheese. Arrange the remaining sliced potatoes on top and season with salt and pepper.

2. Mix the chicken stock and wine in a large measuring cup and pour half over the potatoes in each dish. Cover the dishes with foil and bake for about 50 minutes, or until the potatoes are tender when pierced with a knife; baste twice with the liquid in the dishes during cooking.

3. Preheat the broiler. Uncover the gratins and drizzle the top of each one

with 2 tablespoons of the olive oil. Sprinkle the remaining ½ cup of Parmesan cheese evenly over the gratins and broil for about 3 minutes, rotating the dishes as necessary, until the cheese is evenly melted and lightly browned. Remove from the oven and let the gratins stand for about 15 minutes before serving. —*Martin Dodd*

MAKE AHEAD The recipe can be prepared through Step 2 up to 1 day ahead. Cool the potatoes and refrigerate. Bring to room temperature, cover with foil and bake at 375° for about 30 minutes before proceeding.

Provençal Potato Gratin

6 SERVINGS

This recipe comes from a cluster of villages in the hills of the Diois region in northern Provence, France. The potatoes are first sautéed with onions in fat (the locals use chicken fat), then moistened with pan juices and wine. Fresh thyme is scattered on top, which gives the gratin an earthy flavor. It is not an elegant dish, but it is very tasty.

- 2 **pounds Yukon Gold potatoes, peeled and sliced lengthwise ⅛ inch thick**
- 2 **medium onions, thinly sliced**
- 2 **garlic cloves, smashed**

Salt and freshly ground pepper

- ¼ **cup chicken fat, duck fat or olive oil (see Note)**
- 1 **cup dry red wine**
- ½ **cup leftover pan juices or veal, beef or chicken demiglace (see Note)**
- 1 **large thyme sprig**
- 1 **bay leaf**
- ¼ **cup water**

1. Preheat the oven to 375°. Lightly grease a shallow 3-quart baking dish. In a large bowl, toss the sliced potatoes with the onions and garlic and season with salt and pepper. Heat 2 tablespoons of the fat in each of 2 large skillets. Divide the potatoes between the skillets and cook over

moderate heat, turning the potatoes with a spatula, until browned in spots, about 10 minutes. Scrape the potatoes from 1 skillet into the other, add the wine and pan juices to the potatoes and bring to a boil.

2. Transfer the potatoes and liquid to the prepared baking dish and smooth the surface. Top with the thyme and bay leaf and bake for 30 minutes. Moisten the potatoes with the water and bake for about 25 minutes longer, or until the potatoes are tender and lightly browned. Serve the potato gratin hot. —*Lydie Marshall*

NOTE If you don't have any fat or pan juices in the refrigerator, you might try bringing a jar to a butcher who roasts chickens on a spit. He will have an abundance of fat and juices. If you're not a regular customer, you might have to buy a chicken, too, the first time. Alternatively, demiglace, which is a reduction made from thickened stock, is available at specialty food stores and by mail order from Dean & DeLuca (800-221-7714).

MAKE AHEAD The potatoes can be prepared 4 hours ahead. Cover and reheat in a 325° oven.

Potato Pancakes

MAKES 20 PANCAKES

- 1 **pound all-purpose potatoes, peeled and cut into 2-inch chunks**
- ¼ **cup self-rising flour**
- 3 **large eggs**
- ⅓ **cup heavy cream**
- ⅓ **cup milk**
- 1 **teaspoon kosher salt**

Pinch of freshly ground white pepper

- 2 **large egg whites**
- 2 **tablespoons canola oil**

1. Cook the potatoes in boiling salted water until tender, about 15 minutes. Drain, then press through a large fine strainer into a bowl. Let cool slightly, then beat in the flour and eggs.

2. In a small saucepan, bring the cream and milk to a simmer. Add to the potatoes and whisk until smooth. Season with the salt and white pepper. Beat the egg whites until firm, then fold them into the potato batter.

3. Heat ½ tablespoon of the oil in a large nonstick skillet. Spoon 3 tablespoons of the batter into the skillet for each pancake and cook over moderate heat until golden on the bottom and barely dry on top, about 2 minutes. Flip the pancakes and cook until golden, about 2 minutes longer. Add some more of the oil for each batch. Serve hot. —*Jeremy Strode*

MAKE AHEAD The pancakes can be refrigerated overnight. Rewarm, slightly overlapping, on a baking sheet in a 325° oven for about 20 minutes.

Umbrian Potato Cake with Prosciutto and Sheep's Cheese

6 SERVINGS

2½ pounds Yukon Gold potatoes, peeled and cut into 2-inch chunks

1½ tablespoons extra-virgin olive oil, plus more for frying

Salt and freshly ground pepper

1 cup coarsely grated *caciotta* or other semisoft sheep's-milk cheese (5 ounces)

2 ounces finely chopped prosciutto

1. In a large saucepan, cover the potatoes with water, bring to a boil and cook until tender, about 20 minutes; drain. Return them to the pan and shake over high heat for about 1 minute to dry. Pass the potatoes through a ricer into a large bowl. Stir in 1 tablespoon of the olive oil and season with salt and pepper.

2. Preheat the oven to 400°. Generously butter a 9-inch springform pan. Spread half the potatoes in the pan and top with the cheese and prosciutto, leaving a ½-inch border of potatoes all around. Cover the filling completely with the remaining potatoes. Smooth the top and brush with the remaining ½ tablespoon of olive oil. Bake for 25 minutes. Transfer to a rack

to cool to room temperature.

3. In a large cast-iron skillet, heat a thin film of olive oil. Unmold the potato cake and carefully transfer it to the skillet. Cook over low heat until browned on the bottom, about 15 minutes. Invert the cake onto a flat plate, add another thin film of oil to the skillet and slide the cake back in. Cook over moderately low heat until browned on the bottom, about 10 minutes. Slide the cake onto a large serving plate, cut into wedges and serve.

—*Cristina and Mauro Rastelli*

Crisp Potato Cakes with Gruyère Cheese

4 SERVINGS

1⅓ cups cold mashed potatoes

¼ pound Gruyère or Cantal cheese, cut into four ⅓-inch-thick slices

2 tablespoons unsalted butter

2 tablespoons canola oil

2 pounds Idaho or Yukon Gold potatoes, peeled and coarsely shredded (4 cups)

Salt and freshly ground pepper

2 teaspoons thyme leaves

1. Preheat the oven to 350°. Scoop up ⅓ cup of the mashed potatoes, press a slice of the cheese in the center and pat the potatoes around the cheese to enclose it. Flatten the potato cake slightly. Repeat with the remaining mashed potatoes and cheese.

2. In a medium cast-iron skillet, melt the butter in the oil over high heat. When the fat begins to brown, carefully scoop two ½-cup mounds of shredded potato into the skillet; flatten them with a spatula and season with salt and pepper. Top each with a mashed potato round and then cover with another ½ cup of the shredded potatoes. Season with salt and pepper, reduce the heat to low and cook, turning once, until the cakes are crisp and golden, about 8 minutes per side. Transfer the potato cakes to a baking sheet and keep warm in the oven.

Repeat to make the remaining 2 potato cakes. Sprinkle the cakes with the thyme and serve hot. —*Ana Sortun*

Mashed Potato-Barley Cakes

8 SERVINGS

Chewy pearl barley gives these cakes a lovely texture.

1½ pounds medium Yukon Gold potatoes, scrubbed

½ cup pearl barley

2 cups water

1 large egg, lightly beaten, plus 2 large eggs beaten with ¼ cup water

1 teaspoon salt

¼ teaspoon freshly ground pepper

½ cup all-purpose flour

2 cups Japanese *panko* bread crumbs (see Note) or coarse dry bread crumbs

Canola oil, for frying

1. Preheat the oven to 400°. Bake the potatoes for about 45 minutes, or until tender. Scoop the flesh into a large bowl and mash, then let cool.

2. Meanwhile, in a saucepan, bring the barley and water to a boil. Cover and cook over low heat until tender, about 20 minutes. Drain the barley and spread it out on a plate to cool.

3. Add the cooled barley and the 1 beaten egg to the potatoes and mix

Crisp Potato Cakes with Gruyère Cheese

Potato-Apple Latkes with Vanilla Applesauce

1 egg, lightly beaten

2 tablespoons all-purpose flour

1 tablespoon kosher salt

⅛ teaspoon freshly ground
   white pepper

4 baking potatoes (2½ pounds),
   peeled and coarsely shredded

1 medium onion, coarsely grated

1 Granny Smith apple—peeled,
   cored and coarsely shredded

Canola oil, for frying

Schmaltz, for frying (see Note)

Vanilla Applesauce (recipe follows)
   and sour cream, for serving

1. In a large bowl, mix the egg with the flour, salt and white pepper. In a colander, toss the shredded potatoes with the onion and apple and squeeze dry. Add to the bowl and stir to combine. Set aside for 10 minutes.

2. In a large skillet, heat ½ cup of canola oil with 2 tablespoons of the schmaltz until shimmering. Spoon heaping tablespoons of the latke mixture into the oil about 2 inches apart and flatten slightly with a fork. Fry the latkes over moderately high heat until golden on the bottom, 2 to 3 minutes. Lower the heat to moderate, turn the latkes and fry until golden and crisp, about 2 minutes longer. Drain the latkes on paper towels set on a rack and transfer to a platter. Repeat with the remaining latke mixture, adding more oil and schmaltz to the skillet as needed. Serve hot with Vanilla Apple-sauce and sour cream.

—Bruce and Eric Bromberg

NOTE To make schmaltz, use the large clumps of fat from the chicken's neck and body cavity and from under the skin. In a small heavy saucepan, cook the fat over low heat until completely melted. Cool, then strain the clear fat into a glass jar and refrigerate for up to 1 week or freeze.

MAKE AHEAD The Potato-Apple Latkes can be fried early in the day and recrisped on a baking sheet in a 350° oven.

well. Add the salt and pepper and shape the mixture into eight ½-inch-thick cakes. Put the flour, the 2 eggs beaten with water and the *panko* in separate bowls. Dip each cake into the flour, shaking off the excess. Dip the cakes in the eggs, then coat thoroughly with *panko* crumbs. Redip the cakes in the flour, eggs and *panko* and set them on a large plate.

4. Preheat the oven to 300°. Heat ⅛ inch of oil in a large skillet. Add 4 of the potato cakes at a time and cook over moderate heat until well browned, about 3 minutes per side. Lower the heat if necessary and add more oil to the pan as needed. Put the cakes on a plate and keep warm in the oven until serving.   —*Josiah Citrin*

MAKE AHEAD The potato cakes can be prepared through Step 3 and refrigerated for up to 2 days.

NOTE Japanese *panko* bread crumbs are unseasoned and coarse textured. They're popular with chefs because they absorb less fat than regular bread crumbs and stay crisper after frying. They're available at Asian markets.

Potato-Apple Latkes

MAKES ABOUT 40 TWO-INCH LATKES
There are many who insist that there is no flavor substitute for schmaltz (rendered chicken fat). Schmaltz is available at kosher delicatessens, or see Note, right, to make your own.

VANILLA APPLESAUCE

MAKES ABOUT 2½ CUPS

- 1 pound McIntosh apples
- 1 pound Granny Smith apples
- 1 cup water
- 1 vanilla bean, split lengthwise
- 1 tablespoon fresh lemon juice

Peel, core and quarter the apples. In a medium saucepan, combine the apples, water, vanilla and lemon juice and bring to a boil. Cover and cook over moderately high heat, stirring occasionally, until the apples are tender, about 15 minutes. Let cool, then remove the vanilla bean and whisk until a chunky sauce forms.

—*B.B. and E.B.*

MAKE AHEAD The applesauce can be refrigerated for up to 1 week.

Fingerling Potato Hash with Pancetta and Onion

2 SERVINGS

- 1 pound fingerling or small new potatoes
- 2 ounces sliced pancetta, cut into ¾-inch pieces
- 2 tablespoons unsalted butter
- ½ cup finely chopped sweet onion
- Salt and freshly ground pepper
- 1 tablespoon chopped parsley

1. In a medium saucepan, cover the potatoes with water and bring to a boil. Reduce the heat to moderately high and simmer until tender, about 20 minutes; drain. Let the potatoes cool slightly, then cut into 1-inch pieces.
2. In a medium cast-iron skillet, cook the pancetta over moderately high heat for 2 minutes. Transfer the pancetta to a plate. Melt the butter in the skillet. Add the potatoes and cook over moderate heat, turning occasionally, until golden and crisp, about 7 minutes. Add the onion and pancetta, season with salt and pepper and cook the hash until the onion is translucent, about 5 minutes. Stir in the parsley and serve the hash right away.

—*Grace Parisi*

Potato Masala

4 SERVINGS ✳

This classic southern Indian dish is also used as the filling for Indian *dosas* (lentil-flour crêpes).

- 1½ pounds red potatoes, quartered
- Salt
- ¼ cup vegetable oil
- 1½ teaspoons black mustard seeds
- 1½ teaspoons skinless split *urad dal* (lentils, see Note)
- 4 fresh curry leaves
- 1½ teaspoons cumin seeds
- 3 tablespoons minced fresh ginger
- 3 jalapeños, seeded and minced
- 2 medium onions, thinly sliced
- ½ teaspoon turmeric
- 2 tablespoons fresh lemon juice
- ¼ cup coarsely chopped cilantro

1. In a medium saucepan, cover the potatoes with cold water and bring to a boil. Add a large pinch of salt, reduce the heat to low and cook until the potatoes are tender, about 25 minutes. Drain the potatoes in a colander.
2. Meanwhile, in another saucepan, heat the oil. Add the mustard seeds and cook over moderate heat until they stop popping, about 1 minute. Add the *urad dal* and cook, stirring constantly, until they turn a light reddish brown, about 3 minutes; be sure not to let the *dal* get any darker. Stir in the curry leaves and cumin seeds and cook until fragrant, about 1 minute. Add the ginger and jalapeños and cook for 2 minutes longer. Reduce the heat to moderately low. Add the onions and turmeric and cook until the onions are very tender, about 20 minutes. Remove from the heat.
3. Stir the potatoes into the spiced onions. Add the lemon juice and cilantro, season with salt and stir well.

—*Gary MacGurn and Patty Gentry*

NOTE Skinless split *urad* lentils are available at Indian markets. The uncooked lentils are light tan. As the *dal* is fried, its color will gradually change to a light reddish brown, then to a dark brick red. If overcooked, the *dal* becomes black and bitter.

MAKE AHEAD The potato masala can be refrigerated for up to 2 days.

Potato and Onion Curry

4 SERVINGS ♚

You can add any number of ingredients to the rich curry broth, from pasta to wild greens to root vegetables. The cheese rind becomes soft enough to eat and is a great source of protein.

- 4 cups cold water
- 3 ounces thinly sliced dry-cured smoky ham
- One 3-ounce piece of Parmigiano-Reggiano rind
- 5 large shallots, quartered
- 2 bay leaves
- 2 teaspoons extra-virgin olive oil
- 1 large sweet onion, thinly sliced
- 2½ teaspoons curry powder
- 1 teaspoon fennel seeds
- Pinch of crushed red pepper
- 1 pound medium red potatoes, cut into 2-inch chunks
- Salt and freshly ground pepper

1. In a medium saucepan, combine the water, ham, Parmigiano-Reggiano rind, shallots and bay leaves and bring to a simmer. Cook over low heat until the broth is fragrant and has reduced to 2 cups, about 20 minutes.
2. Heat the oil in a medium skillet. Add the onion, cover and cook over low heat, stirring occasionally, until softened and golden brown, about 10 minutes. Stir in the curry powder, fennel seeds and crushed red pepper and cook, stirring, until fragrant, about 3 minutes. Add the potatoes and cook, stirring, for 2 minutes. Pour the broth into the skillet, leaving all of the solids behind. Cover and simmer the stew over low heat until the potatoes are very tender, about 20 minutes. Season with salt and pepper and serve.

—*Sally Schneider*

ONE SERVING Calories 189 kcal, Total Fat 5 gm, Saturated Fat 2 gm ➤

Golden Potato Tart

MAKES ONE 10-INCH TART

Creamy potato wedges piled in a rich, crisp puff-pastry crust make a simple and utterly delicious tart.

- 14 ounces all-butter puff pastry, chilled
- 3 medium Yukon Gold potatoes (¾ pound total), peeled and cut into ½-inch wedges

Extra-virgin olive oil, for brushing

- 1 large egg beaten with
  1 tablespoon milk

Coarse sea salt

1. Preheat the oven to 400°. On a lightly floured work surface, roll out the puff pastry ⅛ inch thick. Using a sharp knife, cut out an 11-inch round. Fold the round in half and transfer it to a 10-inch springform pan 2 inches high. Unfold and gently pat the pastry up the sides of the pan so that it reaches the rim. Refrigerate the pastry until it is firm and well chilled, about 10 minutes.

2. In the chilled pastry shell, arrange the potato wedges in overlapping circles. If you wind up with extra potato wedges, tuck them into the center of the arrangement. Lightly brush the wedges with olive oil. Fold over the pastry rim around the edge of the potatoes. Brush the egg wash over the surface of the pastry rim.

3. Bake the tart for approximately 1 hour, or until the pastry is deeply browned and the potato wedges are tender. Sprinkle the potatoes generously with the coarse salt and let the tart cool slightly on a rack for about 5 minutes. Then unmold the tart, cut it into wedges and serve it warm.

—*Ibu Poilâne*

Two-Potato Stuffed Potatoes with Celery Root

10 SERVINGS

Five ½-pound baking potatoes, scrubbed

One ½-pound sweet potato, scrubbed

- 2 cups half-and-half or whole milk
- ¾ pound celery root, peeled and cut into 1-inch chunks
- 3 large garlic cloves
- 4 tablespoons unsalted butter plus 1 tablespoon melted butter

Salt and freshly ground pepper

1. Preheat the oven to 375°. Pierce the baking potatoes and the sweet potato in 2 or 3 places and bake for 1 hour, or until tender. Let cool slightly.

2. Meanwhile, in a saucepan, bring the half-and-half to a simmer. Add the celery root and garlic and cook over moderately low heat until the celery root is tender and the half-and-half has reduced to ½ cup, about 30 minutes.

3. Transfer the contents of the saucepan to a food processor. Peel the sweet potato, add it to the processor and puree until smooth. Scrape the potato puree into a bowl.

4. Halve the baking potatoes lengthwise and scoop out the flesh, leaving ¼-inch-thick shells. Arrange the shells in a baking dish. Lightly brush them inside and out with the melted butter. Pass the potato flesh through a ricer into the bowl with the potato puree. Stir in the remaining 4 tablespoons of butter and beat with an electric mixer until light and fluffy. Season with salt and pepper. Using a spoon or a pastry bag fitted with a large star tip, fill the potato shells with the puree.

5. Preheat the oven to 375°. Bake the potatoes for about 1 hour, or until the filling is heated through and browned on top and the shells are crisp.

—*Grace Parisi*

MAKE AHEAD The recipe can be prepared through Step 4 and refrigerated overnight. Bring the potatoes to room temperature before baking.

Sweet Potato Soufflé with Molasses Sauce

12 SERVINGS

This dish is a French take on an American classic. You can serve it without the molasses sauce for a lighter and less sweet version.

SOUFFLE

- 5 pounds sweet potatoes or yams, preferably organic
- 1 cup heavy cream
- 5 whole cloves
- 5 whole star anise pods
- ½ teaspoon freshly grated nutmeg
- 1 stick (4 ounces) unsalted butter, softened
- 8 large egg yolks

Kosher salt and freshly ground pepper

- 4 large egg whites

SAUCE

- 1½ cups unsweetened pineapple juice
- 1 cup unsulphured molasses
- ½ cup honey
- ½ cup packed light brown sugar

1. MAKE THE SOUFFLE: Preheat the oven to 375°. Butter a 3-quart baking dish. In a large saucepan, cover the sweet potatoes with water and boil over high heat until tender, about 35 minutes. Let the sweet potatoes cool, then peel and slice them thickly.

2. Meanwhile, in a small saucepan, combine the cream with the cloves, star anise and nutmeg and simmer over low heat for 20 minutes. Remove from the heat and let stand for 10 minutes. Strain the cream, discarding the whole spices.

3. In a food processor, puree the sweet potatoes with the spiced cream, butter and egg yolks. Scrape the soufflé base into a large bowl and season with 1½ teaspoons of salt and ¼ teaspoon of pepper.

4. In a clean stainless-steel bowl, beat the egg whites with a pinch of salt until firm peaks form. With a rubber spatula, fold one-third of the beaten whites into the soufflé base; fold in the

Golden Potato Tart

remaining whites. Pour the soufflé mixture into the prepared dish and bake for about 1 hour, or until risen and firm. Let the soufflé rest for about 10 minutes.

5. MAKE THE SAUCE: Combine all of the ingredients in a medium saucepan and bring to a boil. Simmer over low heat, stirring occasionally, until very thick, about 20 minutes. Serve the molasses sauce warm alongside the sweet potato soufflé.

—*Bruce and Eric Bromberg*

MAKE AHEAD The soufflé can be prepared through Step 3 and refrigerated overnight. Bring the soufflé base to room temperature before proceeding. The molasses sauce can be refrigerated for up to 2 days. Gently rewarm the molasses sauce before serving alongside the soufflé.

Sweet Potatoes with Honey, Lemon and Toasted Spices

6 SERVINGS

   3 pounds sweet potatoes, peeled and sliced crosswise ¼ inch thick
⅓ cup hot water
   2 tablespoons honey
   1 tablespoon unsalted butter
   1 teaspoon cumin seeds
   1 teaspoon coriander seeds
¼ cup fresh lemon juice
   2 tablespoons vegetable oil
   2 garlic cloves, minced
   2 teaspoons finely grated ginger
Salt and freshly ground pepper

1. Preheat the oven to 350°. Butter a baking dish. Arrange the sweet potato slices in concentric circles in the dish.
2. In a bowl, combine the hot water with 1 tablespoon of the honey and the butter; swirl to melt the butter. Pour the liquid over the potatoes. Cover with foil and bake for 40 minutes, or until the potatoes are tender.
3. Meanwhile, in a small skillet, toast the cumin and coriander seeds over moderate heat until fragrant, about 40 seconds; let cool. Transfer the seeds

to a spice grinder and grind to a powder. Transfer the powder to a small bowl. Stir in the lemon juice, oil, garlic, ginger and the remaining 1 tablespoon of honey; season with salt and pepper. Pour the dressing over the potatoes and serve.
—*Marcia Kiesel*

Sweet Potatoes and Snow Peas with Crème Fraîche

6 SERVINGS

   2 pounds sweet potatoes, peeled and cut into ¾-inch rounds
   2 tablespoons olive oil
Kosher salt and freshly ground pepper
¼ cup crème fraîche or sour cream
   2 teaspoons sherry vinegar
½ pound snow peas
   1 tablespoon snipped chives

1. Preheat the oven to 400°. In a large baking dish, toss the sweet potatoes with 1 tablespoon of the olive oil and season with salt and pepper. Roast for about 50 minutes, or until tender and browned, turning halfway through.
2. In a small bowl, whisk the crème fraîche with the vinegar.
3. Heat the remaining 1 tablespoon of olive oil in a large skillet. Add the snow peas and cook over high heat until crisp-tender, 6 to 8 minutes. Season with salt and pepper and transfer to a large platter. Add the sweet potatoes and top with dollops of the crème fraîche. Sprinkle with the chives and serve right away.
—*Alison Tolley*

Vegetable Bibimbop

4 TO 6 SERVINGS

It is said that *bibimbop* was originally served in Korea after ceremonies to honor one's ancestors, when bits and pieces from ritual offerings would be mixed with freshly cooked hot rice. This vegetarian version comes from the city of Chonju in southwest Korea, and it can be prepared with or without the eggs. Have all the ingredients prepared and assembled by the time the rice finishes cooking. If the rice does

cool down, cover it with plastic wrap and reheat it in a microwave oven for 3 to 4 minutes.

½ pound spinach, large stems removed
   1 cup mung bean sprouts
   1 medium carrot, cut into 2-by-½-inch strips
   1 medium zucchini, cut into 2-by-½-inch strips
   2 ounces shiitake mushrooms, stems discarded, caps thinly sliced (1 cup)
   1 tablespoon plus ½ teaspoon Asian sesame oil
2½ teaspoons minced garlic
   1 cup shredded red-leaf lettuce
   2 scallions, cut into thin matchsticks
One 8-inch-square nori (dried seaweed), cut into thin strips with scissors
   2 large eggs (optional)
Steamed Rice (recipe follows)
   2 tablespoons toasted sesame seeds
Korean Chili Sauce (p. 318)
Salt

1. Steam the spinach until just wilted, about 2 minutes. Transfer the spinach to a bowl of ice water to stop the cooking. Drain, squeeze dry and chop coarsely.
2. In a small saucepan of boiling water, blanch the bean sprouts for 30 seconds. Drain and refresh the bean sprouts under cold running water; pat them dry.
3. Put the bean sprouts, spinach, carrot, zucchini and shiitakes in separate small bowls; toss each vegetable with ½ teaspoon of sesame oil and ½ teaspoon of minced garlic.
4. In a small skillet, stir-fry each vegetable (except the spinach) separately over moderate heat; the carrot, zucchini and bean sprouts should stay crisp and the shiitakes should be tender. Decoratively arrange the cooked vegetables, lettuce, scallions and nori

in small bowls or in piles on a platter.

5. In a medium skillet, heat the remaining 1 teaspoon of sesame oil. Crack in the eggs and fry them, sunny side up. Meanwhile, reheat the rice if necessary.

6. Bring the rice to the table with the vegetables and the fried eggs. Toss the rice with the eggs first, to break them up, then add all of the vegetables and the toasted sesame seeds. Stir in about 2 tablespoons of Korean Chili Sauce and mix lightly but thoroughly. Season with salt and serve at once.

—*Anya von Bremzen*

STEAMED RICE

MAKES ABOUT 4 CUPS

1½ cups medium-grain rice,
   well washed

2 cups water

In a heavy saucepan, combine the rice and water and bring to a boil over high heat. Reduce the heat to low, cover and cook for 20 minutes. Remove from the heat and let steam, covered, for 10 minutes before serving. —*A.B.*

Risi e Bisi

4 MAIN-COURSE OR
6 FIRST-COURSE SERVINGS

This recipe is a twist on the Venetian classic that was supposedly served to the doges at the Feast of Saint Mark.

1½ pounds ham hocks

6½ cups water

1 bay leaf

1 tablespoon extra-virgin olive oil

2 large shallots, minced

1 large jalapeño, seeded
   and minced

1 cup medium-grain rice (7 ounces)

½ teaspoon chopped fresh thyme

1½ cups frozen petite peas

½ pound Maine crabmeat

1 scallion, thinly sliced

1 teaspoon fresh lemon juice

Salt and freshly ground pepper

1. In a medium saucepan, cover the ham hocks with the water, add the bay

leaf and bring to a boil. Simmer over low heat until the hock meat is tender, about 1 hour. Remove the hocks from the saucepan and skim any fat from the surface of the stock; keep the stock warm.

2. Remove the meat from the ham hocks; discard the skin, fat, tendons and bones. Cut the meat into small dice; you should have about ¾ cup.

3. Heat the olive oil in a medium saucepan. Add the shallots and jalapeño and cook over low heat until softened, about 5 minutes. Add the rice and thyme and stir to coat the rice with the flavorings. Pour in the ham stock and bring to a boil. Reduce the heat to low and simmer, stirring occasionally, until the rice is just tender and the stew is somewhat soupy, about 15 minutes. Add the peas, crabmeat, scallion, lemon juice and the

reserved ham and simmer for 1 minute to heat through. Season with salt and pepper and serve at once.

—*Marcia Kiesel*

Basmati Rice and Peas

10 TO 12 SERVINGS

1 teaspoon cumin seeds

2½ cups basmati rice (15 ounces)

Salt

4½ cups water

One 10-ounce package frozen
   peas (2 cups)

1. In a large saucepan, toast the cumin seeds over moderate heat until fragrant, about 1 minute. Add the rice, a large pinch of salt and the water. Bring to a boil over high heat and boil for 1 minute. Cover, reduce the heat to low and cook for 12 minutes.

2. Add the peas to the rice, cover and cook for 3 minutes longer, until the

Risi e Bisi

peas are hot. Fluff the rice with a fork and serve immediately. —*Neela Paniz*

Cardamom Rice Pilaf

4 SERVINGS ✳

¼ cup whole unsalted
    cashews (optional)
1¾ cups water
5 whole cardamom pods
1 cinnamon stick
1 tablespoon unsalted butter
¼ teaspoon salt
1 cup basmati rice
½ cup frozen peas
¼ cup coarsely chopped cilantro,
    for garnish

1. Preheat the oven to 350°. Spread the cashews in a pie plate and bake for about 5 minutes, shaking the plate for even browning, until the cashews are fragrant and lightly toasted. Transfer the cashews to a plate to cool.

2. In a medium saucepan, bring the water to a boil with the cardamom pods, cinnamon stick, butter and salt. Add the rice, toasted cashews and peas and stir continuously for 1 minute. Reduce the heat to moderately low and simmer the rice for 8 minutes. Remove the rice from the heat, cover and let stand for about 15 minutes, or until all the water has been absorbed. Fluff the rice with a fork, sprinkle with the cilantro and serve.

—*Gary MacGurn and Patty Gentry*

Carmellini's Tomato Risotto

4 SERVINGS ♛

2 ripe yellow tomatoes (½ pound
    each), peeled and cut into eighths
2 ripe red tomatoes (½ pound
    each), peeled and cut into eighths
1 tablespoon crème fraîche
2½ cups extra-virgin olive oil
1 small rosemary sprig
2 garlic cloves, minced
Coarse salt
About 4½ cups Basic Chicken
    Stock (p. 98) or canned
    low-sodium broth

Carmellini's Tomato Risotto

1 tablespoon unsalted butter
1 large onion, finely chopped
1 cup Arborio rice
½ cup dry white wine
2 tablespoons mascarpone cheese
1 tablespoon freshly grated
    Parmesan cheese
Freshly ground white pepper

1. Working over a fine-mesh stainless-steel strainer set over a bowl, scoop the seeds from the tomato wedges. Press the seeds to extract all the tomato juice. Stir the crème fraîche into the tomato juice and set aside.

2. In a medium saucepan, combine the tomatoes with the olive oil, rosemary, garlic and a pinch of salt. Cook over moderately low heat, without stirring, until the tomatoes are tender but still intact, about 10 minutes. Give the tomatoes a gentle push, if necessary, to keep them submerged. Using a slotted spoon and allowing as much of the oil to drain back into the saucepan as possible, transfer the tomatoes to a plate. Reserve 3 tablespoons of the oil; strain and refrigerate the rest for later use.

3. Heat the chicken stock in a medium saucepan. In another medium saucepan, melt the butter in 1 tablespoon of the reserved tomato oil. Add the onion and cook over moderate heat, stirring occasionally, until softened but not browned, about 5 minutes. Add the rice and stir until coated with fat.

4. Add the wine and cook, stirring, until it is absorbed. Add the hot stock, 1 cup at a time, and cook, stirring constantly, until the rice is tender and most of the liquid is absorbed. Stir in the mascarpone, Parmesan and the remaining 2 tablespoons of the reserved tomato oil. Season with salt and pepper. Gently fold the olive oil–poached tomatoes into the risotto.

5. Put the tomato juice–crème fraîche mixture in a blender; blend at high speed until frothy. Spoon the risotto into 4 shallow soup plates, pour the tomato froth around it and serve right away. —*Andrew Carmellini*

Risotto Primavera

8 SERVINGS

- 2 large artichokes (½ pound each)
- ½ lemon
- About 7 cups beef stock or canned low-sodium broth
- 3 tablespoons extra-virgin olive oil
- 2 carrots, cut into ¼-inch dice
- 1 onion, finely chopped
- 1 celery rib, cut into ¼-inch dice
- 1 medium leek, white part only, quartered lengthwise and thinly sliced crosswise
- 1 medium zucchini, cut into ½-inch dice
- 2 cups Arborio rice
- ½ cup dry white wine
- ½ cup freshly grated Parmesan cheese, plus more for serving
- 3 tablespoons unsalted butter
- 1 tablespoon chopped parsley
- 1 tablespoon chopped chives
- 1 tablespoon chopped basil

Salt and freshly ground pepper

1. Pull off the dark green outer leaves of the artichokes until you reach the pale green leaves. Cut off the top two-thirds of the leaves. Using a melon baller or spoon, scoop out the hairy chokes. Using a vegetable peeler or a paring knife, peel the stems and trim away any dark green portions from the bottoms. Rub the artichokes with the lemon half. Cut the artichokes in half lengthwise, then thinly slice them crosswise. Squeeze the lemon all over the artichokes.

2. In a saucepan, bring the stock to a boil; keep warm over low heat. Heat the olive oil in a large heavy saucepan. Add the artichokes, carrots, onion, celery and leek and cook over moderate heat for 5 minutes. Add the zucchini and cook, stirring occasionally, until the vegetables are crisp-tender, about 5 minutes longer. Add the rice and stir over moderate heat until translucent, 2 to 3 minutes. Add the wine and cook over moderately high heat, stirring, until absorbed. Add 1 cup of the stock and cook, stirring, until absorbed. Continue adding the stock, 1 cup at a time, stirring constantly until it is absorbed before adding more. The rice is done when it's tender and creamy but still firm to the bite, 20 to 25 minutes.

3. Stir the ½ cup of Parmesan and the butter, parsley, chives and basil into the risotto and season with salt and pepper. Spoon the risotto into shallow bowls and serve as soon as possible. Pass additional Parmesan at the table.

—*Mina Vachino*

WINE This light vegetable risotto demands a crisp, fruity white wine, such as the 1998 Michele Chiarlo Rovereto Gavi di Gavi.

Pan-Roasted Corn Risotto

6 SERVINGS

This recipe was developed at Todd English's restaurant, Figs, in Charlestown, Massachusetts.

- 5 cups light chicken stock or canned low-sodium broth
- 5 tablespoons unsalted butter
- 2 tablespoons extra-virgin olive oil
- 3 shallots, minced
- 3 cups fresh corn kernels (from 5 to 6 ears)
- 1½ cups Italian medium-grain rice, preferably Carnaroli (10 ounces)
- ¼ cup dry white wine
- ¼ cup freshly grated Parmigiano-Reggiano cheese
- 2 tablespoons finely chopped flat-leaf parsley

Salt and freshly ground pepper

1. In a medium saucepan, bring the chicken stock to a boil over moderately high heat. Lower the heat to keep the stock at a bare simmer.

2. Meanwhile, in a large heavy saucepan, melt 4 tablespoons of the butter in the olive oil. Add the shallots and cook over moderate heat until they

Pan-Roasted Corn Risotto

have softened, about 4 minutes. Raise the heat to high, add the corn and cook, stirring frequently, until lightly browned, about 12 minutes. Add the rice and stir until the grains are thoroughly coated with fat, 1 to 2 minutes. Pour in the wine and continue stirring until most of the wine has evaporated.

3. Add 1 cup of the simmering stock to the rice and cook over moderate heat, stirring constantly, until the stock has been absorbed. Continue adding stock, 1 cup at a time, stirring the risotto until the stock is absorbed before adding more; the risotto is done when the rice is just tender and the sauce is creamy, about 22 minutes. Stir in the Parmigiano-Reggiano, parsley and the remaining 1 tablespoon of butter. Season with salt and pepper and serve at once.

—Sara Jenkins

WINE The sweet corn flavor and creamy texture of this classic risotto find echoes in a softly fruity, balanced Chardonnay. Try one from Friuli, such as the 1995 Ronco del Gnemiz, or the 1998 Pier Paolo Pecorari, from the Isonzo area.

Winter Squash Risotto

12 SERVINGS

- 10 cups vegetable stock or water
- ⅓ cup pure olive oil
- 1 large onion, finely chopped
- 1 pound Arborio rice (2 cups)
- ½ cup dry white wine
- 2 pounds winter squash—peeled, seeded and cut into ¼-inch dice
- ¾ cup freshly grated Parmigiano-Reggiano cheese (2½ ounces)

Salt and freshly ground pepper

1. Bring the stock to a simmer in a medium saucepan and keep it warm over low heat. Heat the olive oil in a large, wide casserole. Add the onion and cook over moderately low heat, stirring often, until it softens, about 8 minutes. Add the rice and cook over moderate heat, stirring, until the grains are coated with the oil. Add the wine and boil until almost evaporated. Stir in the squash.

2. Add about 3 cups of the hot stock to the casserole and cook, stirring constantly with a wooden spoon, until the rice has absorbed most of the stock. Continue to cook the risotto, adding the stock 1 cup at a time and stirring constantly between additions until it is absorbed. The risotto is done when it is creamy and the rice is just tender, about 30 minutes total.

3. Remove the casserole from the heat. Stir in the Parmigiano-Reggiano and season with salt and pepper. Spoon the risotto into 12 warmed bowls or soup plates and serve.

—Sabine Busch and Bruno Tramontana

WINE A fruity red wine pairs well with this slightly sweet risotto. Choose the 1998 Le Cinciole Chianti Classico, a wine with an intense perfume of cherry and red currant, or the 1997 Dei Vino Nobile di Montepulciano.

Vegetable Fried Rice

4 SERVINGS

While Wesley Snipes was recently shooting a movie in Montreal, his partner at China One restaurant, Donna Wong, came to visit from Los Angeles. "The first thing he said to me was, 'Didn't you bring me some Chinese food?' I had to go marching around Montreal, looking for vegetable fried rice for him," Wong recalls. This recipe adds a little hot mustard to the China One version.

- 1 tablespoon dry mustard
- 2 tablespoons water
- 2 tablespoons soy sauce
- ¼ teaspoon kosher salt
- ¼ teaspoon sugar
- ¼ teaspoon sesame oil
- 1 cup small broccoli florets
- 1 carrot, cut into ⅓-inch dice
- 3½ tablespoons vegetable oil
- 3 large eggs, lightly beaten

- 4 ounces shiitake mushrooms, stemmed, caps thinly sliced
- ¾ cup snow peas
- 3 cups cooked jasmine rice, preferably leftover
- 2 scallions, thinly sliced
- ¼ cup sliced water chestnuts

1. In a small bowl, mix the mustard and water; let stand for at least 10 minutes. In another small bowl, combine the soy sauce, salt, sugar and sesame oil.

2. Bring a small saucepan of water to a boil. Add the broccoli and carrot and cook until crisp-tender, about 5 minutes. Drain well.

3. Heat a wok or large skillet over high heat. Add ½ tablespoon of the oil, swirling to coat the pan. Stir the eggs and add them to the wok. Let the eggs cook without stirring until the bottom is set, about 20 seconds. Stir until very loose, large curds form, 10 to 20 seconds longer. Scrape the eggs onto a plate.

4. Add 1 tablespoon of the oil to the wok and heat until shimmering. Add the mushrooms and cook over high heat, stirring occasionally, until tender and beginning to brown, 5 to 6 minutes. Transfer the mushrooms to a plate. Add the remaining 2 tablespoons of the oil to the wok and heat until shimmering. Add the snow peas and stir-fry until crisp-tender, about 4 minutes.

5. Add the broccoli, carrot, mushrooms, rice, scallions and water chestnuts to the wok and stir-fry until heated through, about 4 minutes. Stir the soy mixture and drizzle it over the rice mixture. Add the scrambled eggs and toss gently but thoroughly. Transfer the fried rice to a bowl and pass the mustard separately.

—China One, West Hollywood

WINE An Oregon Pinot Gris, such as the 1998 King Estate or the 1998 Ponzi Willamette Valley, won't overwhelm the delicate flavors in this dish.

Brown Lentils and Rice with Caramelized Onions

6 SERVINGS

This dish, called *megadarra,* is enormously popular in Egypt and throughout the Arab world.

　5　tablespoons extra-virgin olive oil
　2　large Spanish onions (about 1½ pounds), halved and thinly sliced
1¼　cups large brown or green lentils, rinsed (9 ounces)
　5　cups water
1¼　cups long-grain rice (8½ ounces)
Salt and freshly ground pepper
　1　cup plain yogurt
　1　small garlic clove, finely chopped
　1　teaspoon fresh lemon juice
　¼　teaspoon ground cumin

1. Heat 3 tablespoons of the olive oil in a large skillet. Add the onions, cover and cook over low heat, stirring occasionally, until softened, about 10 minutes. Uncover and cook, stirring from time to time, until the onions are golden brown, about 10 minutes longer.

2. In a medium saucepan, combine the lentils and water. Bring to a boil, then simmer over low heat until the lentils are partially cooked, about 15 minutes. Stir in half the onions, the rice and 1 tablespoon of olive oil and season with salt and pepper. Cover and cook over low heat until the rice and lentils are tender, about 20 minutes. Add more water if needed to prevent sticking.

3. Meanwhile, cook the remaining onions over high heat until dark brown and caramelized, about 5 minutes. Stir frequently so they don't stick to the bottom of the skillet and burn.

4. In a small bowl, mix the yogurt, garlic, lemon juice and cumin. Transfer the lentils and rice to a shallow bowl and drizzle with the remaining 1 tablespoon of olive oil. Sprinkle with the caramelized onions and serve. Pass the yogurt separately. —*Claudia Roden*
MAKE AHEAD This dish can be refrigerated overnight. Let it come to room temperature before serving.

Wild and Dirty Rice

10 SERVINGS

This Cajun rice dish is called dirty because the chopped poultry livers turn the grains a brownish gray. Wild rice gives this classic a twist.

1½　cups wild rice (11 ounces)
　½　pound ground pork
　2　tablespoons unsalted butter or bacon fat
　1　large onion, coarsely chopped
　1　cup finely chopped celery
　½　cup finely chopped red bell pepper
　½　cup finely chopped green bell pepper
　1　tablespoon minced garlic
　1　pound chicken or duck livers, trimmed and coarsely chopped
　2　cups long-grain white rice (14 ounces)
　4　cups Basic Chicken Stock (p. 98) or canned low-sodium broth
　2　teaspoons chopped thyme
　2　bay leaves
Salt and freshly ground pepper
Tabasco sauce
　½　cup finely chopped scallions

1. In a medium saucepan of boiling salted water, cook the wild rice over moderate heat until the grains are tender, 30 to 45 minutes. Drain the wild rice in a colander.

2. In a medium skillet, cook the ground pork over moderately high heat, stirring well to break up any clumps, until no longer pink, about 10 minutes.

3. Melt the butter in a large deep skillet. Add the onion, celery, red and green bell peppers and garlic and cook over moderately high heat, stirring, until softened, about 5 minutes. Add the livers and ground pork and cook, stirring, until the livers are browned on the outside, about 5 minutes. Stir in the wild and long-grain rice, chicken stock, thyme, bay leaves and 1 teaspoon of salt and bring to a boil. Cover and cook over low heat until the long-grain rice is tender, about 20 minutes.

Discard the bay leaves. Season the dirty rice with salt, pepper and Tabasco and stir in the chopped scallions. Transfer the rice to a bowl, fluff with a fork and serve. —*Susan Spicer*
MAKE AHEAD The cooked pork and wild rice can be refrigerated overnight.

Wild Rice with Hazelnuts and Bacon

10 SERVINGS

2½　quarts water
2½　cups wild rice (1 pound)
1½　cups hazelnuts (6 ounces)
　½　pound sliced bacon
　3　tablespoons unsalted butter
　2　pounds leeks, white and tender green parts, halved lengthwise and sliced ¼ inch thick
　1　celery rib, finely chopped
1½　teaspoons finely chopped thyme
Salt and freshly ground pepper
　2　tablespoons finely chopped flat-leaf parsley

1. Bring the water to a boil in a large saucepan. Add the wild rice, cover and cook over moderate heat until tender, about 1 hour. Drain well.

2. Meanwhile, preheat the oven to 350°. Spread the hazelnuts on a baking sheet and toast for 15 minutes, or until fragrant. Transfer the nuts to a kitchen towel and let cool, then rub off the skins. Coarsely chop the nuts.

3. In a large deep skillet, cook the bacon over moderate heat until crisp, about 8 minutes. Drain the bacon on paper towels. Pour off all but 2 tablespoons of the bacon fat from the skillet. Add 2 tablespoons of the butter and the leeks, celery and thyme. Season with salt and pepper and cook over moderate heat until the leeks are tender, 7 to 8 minutes. Add the wild rice, season with salt and pepper and cook just until warmed through.

4. Stir the toasted hazelnuts, the remaining 1 tablespoon of butter and the parsley into the wild rice and serve. —*Grace Parisi* ▶

MAKE AHEAD The Wild Rice with Hazelnuts and Bacon can be prepared through Step 3 and refrigerated for 3 days. Reheat the rice and add the hazelnuts and parsley before serving.

Desert Polenta with Cheddar

4 TO 6 SERVINGS

Craig Higgins, the chef at Tongabezi Camp in Zambia, has been instrumental in devising menus and training chefs at many safari camps. This polenta has become a menu standby.

  1 tablespoon unsalted butter
  1 teaspoon minced garlic
Pinch of nutmeg
Pinch of ground cloves
2½ cups milk
2½ cups water
  2 teaspoons kosher salt
  1 cup coarse cornmeal or polenta
  4 ounces Cheddar cheese, grated (1 cup)
Pinch of paprika

I. Melt the butter in a large heavy saucepan. Add the garlic, nutmeg and cloves and cook over moderately high heat, stirring, until fragrant, about 1 minute.

2. Add the milk, water and salt and bring to a boil. Whisking constantly, add the cornmeal in a thin stream. Cook over moderately low heat, stirring frequently, until the polenta is thick and creamy, about 30 minutes. Stir in the cheese and paprika and serve. —*Jacques Pépin*

Polenta with Fontina and Croutons

6 TO 8 SERVINGS

Polenta di Taragna is a blend of ground corn and buckwheat. The buckwheat adds its characteristic earthy flavor to the polenta, which is studded with melted cheese and crisp croutons.

  ¼ cup extra-virgin olive oil
1½ cups diced (½ inch) crustless, day-old bread
  5 cups water

1½ cups *polenta di Taragna* or coarse cornmeal (10 ounces)
  1 cup milk, at room temperature
Salt and freshly ground pepper
  6 ounces Italian Fontina cheese, cut into ½-inch dice (1 cup)
  2 tablespoons unsalted butter, melted (optional)

I. In a large skillet, heat the oil until shimmering. Add the diced bread and cook over moderately high heat, stirring, until golden brown, about 4 minutes. Drain the croutons on paper towels.

2. In a large saucepan, bring the water to a boil. Gradually add the polenta, whisking until smooth. Cook over low heat for 10 minutes, stirring frequently with a wooden spoon. Add the milk and continue cooking, stirring often, until the polenta is tender, about 20 minutes longer. Season with salt and pepper and fold in the croutons and cheese. Spoon the polenta onto plates, drizzle with the melted butter and serve. —*Nancy Harmon Jenkins*

Polenta with Porcini Stew

4 SERVINGS

  ½ cup dried porcini mushrooms
  ¾ cup boiling water
  ¼ cup diced dry-cured smoky ham, such as Westphalian (1 ounce), plus 2 teaspoons minced ham fat
  1 medium sweet onion, minced
  ½ teaspoon minced fresh rosemary
  ½ teaspoon minced fresh thyme
  2 small dried figs, finely diced
Salt and freshly ground pepper
4½ cups cold water
1½ cups instant polenta (8 ounces)
  3 tablespoons freshly grated Parmigiano-Reggiano cheese, plus ¼ cup of thin shavings
  1 teaspoon extra-virgin olive oil

I. Put the porcini in a heatproof bowl and cover with the boiling water. Let stand until the porcini soften, about 20 minutes. Rub the porcini to remove any grit, then lift them out of the

soaking liquid and finely chop. Reserve the soaking liquid.

2. In a medium skillet, cook the 2 teaspoons of ham fat over low heat until rendered and any cracklings are golden, about 4 minutes. Add the onion, rosemary and thyme, and cook, stirring, until the onion is softened and golden, about 10 minutes. Add the porcini, figs and diced ham. Carefully pour the reserved porcini soaking liquid into the skillet, leaving behind any grit. Bring the stew to a simmer over low heat and cook for 3 minutes. Season the stew with salt and pepper, cover and set aside.

3. In a saucepan, combine the water and polenta and bring to a boil over moderately high heat. Cook, stirring constantly, until thick, about 2 minutes. Remove from the heat and stir in the grated Parmigiano-Reggiano and olive oil and season with salt and pepper. Spoon the polenta onto plates and top with the stew. Garnish with the Parmigiano-Reggiano shavings and serve at once. —*Sally Schneider*

ONE SERVING Calories 307 kcal, Total Fat 5 gm, Saturated Fat 2 gm

WINE Pair this dish with a big, fruity Chardonnay. Two inexpensive choices are the 1998 Columbia Crest Columbia Valley and the 1998 Tessera.

Borlotti Bean Polenta

8 SERVINGS

  ⅓ cup dried *borlotti* or cranberry beans (2½ ounces)—picked over, rinsed and soaked overnight
  6 garlic cloves, lightly smashed
  5 large sage leaves
Salt
1½ cups coarse cornmeal or non-instant polenta
4½ cups cold water
  ⅓ cup grated Pecorino Toscano (1 ounce)
Freshly ground pepper
  4 teaspoons extra-virgin olive oil

I. Drain and rinse the beans. In a medium saucepan, cover the beans with 3 inches of water, add the garlic cloves and sage leaves and bring to a boil. Reduce the heat and simmer until the beans are tender, about 1 hour; season the beans with salt after 40 minutes. Drain the beans and discard the garlic and sage.

2. In a large heavy saucepan, combine the cornmeal with the water and 1½ teaspoons of salt and bring to a boil, stirring constantly. Cook over moderate heat, stirring frequently, until the polenta is very thick and pulls away from the side and bottom of the pan, about 25 minutes. Stir in the cheese and season with pepper. Gently fold in the beans with a spatula, being careful not to break them up.

3. Scrape the polenta into one 8-by-3-inch glass loaf pan or two mini loaf pans, pressing to remove air pockets. Let the polenta cool to room temperature, then cover and refrigerate until completely firm.

4. Turn the polenta loaf out onto a work surface. Using a thin sharp knife, slice the polenta ½ inch thick. Heat 2 teaspoons of the olive oil in each of 2 large nonstick skillets. Arrange the polenta slices in the skillets and cook over moderate heat, turning once, until golden and crisp, about 6 minutes. Serve hot.   —*Sally Schneider*

ONE SERVING Calories 148 kcal, Total Fat 4.4 gm, Saturated Fat 1.2 gm, Carbohydrates 22.6 gm

Tabbouleh with Roasted Chicken

8 SERVINGS

Serve this versatile tabbouleh as part of a picnic or buffet, stuffed into pita bread for lunch or as a first course at dinner.

- 1   cup medium-grade bulgur (6 ounces)
- 1½ cups boiling water
- ⅓   cup fresh lemon juice

Kosher salt

- 2   chicken breast halves on the bone (about ½ pound each)
- ¼   cup plus 1 tablespoon extra-virgin olive oil

Freshly ground pepper

- 1   cup finely chopped scallions
- ⅔   cup finely chopped flat-leaf parsley (1 bunch)
- ⅔   cup finely chopped mint
- 1   European seedless cucumber, halved lengthwise and cut into ⅓-inch dice
- 1   pint cherry tomatoes, halved

I. In a large heatproof bowl, combine the bulgur with the boiling water, lemon juice and 1½ teaspoons of salt and let stand until the water has been absorbed and the grains are tender, about 1 hour.

2. Meanwhile, preheat the oven to 350°. Set the chicken breasts on a baking sheet. Rub with 1 tablespoon of the oil and season with salt and pepper. Roast for about 40 minutes, or until just cooked through. Let the chicken cool slightly, then discard the skin and remove the meat from the bones. Cut the chicken into ¾-inch chunks.

3. Add the scallions, parsley, mint and the remaining ¼ cup of olive oil to the bulgur and let stand for 15 minutes. Add the chicken, cucumber and tomatoes, season with salt and pepper and toss well. Transfer the tabbouleh to a bowl or platter and serve at room temperature or chilled.

—*Ina Garten, Barefoot Contessa*

MAKE AHEAD The recipe can be refrigerated for up to 1 day.

Polenta with Porcini Stew

sauces condiments
chapter 14

Simple Balsamic Vinaigrette

MAKES ABOUT ¼ CUP

- 1 tablespoon balsamic vinegar
- ½ teaspoon Dijon mustard
- 3 tablespoons extra-virgin olive oil

Sea salt and freshly ground
   black pepper

In a bowl, whisk together the vinegar and the mustard. Whisk in the extra-virgin olive oil in a thin stream until emulsified. Season with sea salt and pepper. —*Grace Parisi*

Creamy Lemon Vinaigrette

MAKES ABOUT ⅔ CUP

Serve with lettuces, any shellfish or crudités.

- ½ large egg yolk
- 2 tablespoons fresh lemon juice
- ⅓ cup extra-virgin olive oil
- 2 tablespoons heavy cream

Salt and freshly ground pepper

In a small bowl, whisk the egg yolk and the lemon juice until combined. Whisk in the olive oil and cream. Season with salt and pepper. —*Bill Telepan*

A range of flavor-packed dressings.

Cabernet and Fresh Herb Vinaigrette

MAKES ABOUT 1¼ CUPS

- ¼ cup plus 2 tablespoons
   Cabernet Sauvignon
- ¼ cup rice vinegar
- ⅔ cup olive oil
- 1 teaspoon sugar
- 2 tablespoons finely chopped basil
- 1 teaspoon finely chopped thyme
- 1 teaspoon finely chopped oregano

Salt and freshly ground pepper

In a bowl, whisk the Cabernet, vinegar and oil until combined. Whisk in the sugar, basil, thyme and oregano. Season with salt and pepper. —*Kevin Maguire*

MAKE AHEAD The vinaigrette can be refrigerated for up to 2 days.

ONE TABLESPOON Calories 68 kcal, Total Fat 7.2 gm, Saturated Fat 1 gm

Red Chile–Cumin Vinaigrette

MAKES ABOUT 1 CUP

Use this vinaigrette as a marinade for white-fleshed fish, chicken, beef or pork, or to dress potato salad.

- 1 teaspoon cumin seeds
- 2 dried New Mexican chiles
- ½ cup cilantro leaves
- ½ jalapeño, preferably red, chopped
- ½ teaspoon finely chopped shallot
- ¼ teaspoon chopped garlic
- 6 tablespoons rice vinegar
- ¼ cup plus 2 tablespoons canola oil

Salt and freshly ground pepper

1. In a small skillet, toast the cumin seeds over moderately low heat, stirring, until fragrant, about 2 minutes. Transfer to a plate to cool, then grind to a powder in a mortar or spice grinder.

2. In a mini processor, blend the cumin, chiles, cilantro, jalapeño, shallot, garlic and rice vinegar. With the machine on, add the oil until the vinaigrette is emulsified. Season with salt and pepper. —*Kevin Maguire*

ONE TABLESPOON Calories 48 kcal, Total Fat 5.2 gm, Saturated Fat 0 gm

Garlic Vinaigrette

MAKES ABOUT ⅔ CUP

This vinaigrette is great as a dressing for salad greens, as a sauce for roasted or grilled meats and as a dip for raw vegetables.

- 1 large garlic clove, minced
- 2 tablespoons fresh lemon juice
- 1 teaspoon Worcestershire sauce
- ½ teaspoon hot sauce
- ½ cup extra-virgin olive oil

Salt and freshly ground pepper

Mash the garlic to a paste, and then transfer it to a small bowl. Whisk in the lemon juice, Worcestershire sauce and hot sauce. Whisk in the olive oil and season with salt and pepper. —*Bill Telepan*

Bacon-Balsamic Vinaigrette

MAKES ABOUT ½ CUP

Serve this hot or warm as a sauce over chicken or full-flavored fish, such as bluefish, or as a dressing for spinach or curly endive salad.

- ¼ cup pine nuts
- 6 ounces thickly sliced
   double-smoked bacon,
   cut into ½-inch dice

Salt

- ¼ cup extra-virgin olive oil
- ¼ cup balsamic vinegar

Freshly ground pepper

1. In a medium skillet, toast the pine nuts over moderate heat until lightly browned, about 3 minutes. Transfer to a plate to cool.

2. Add the diced bacon to the skillet, cover with cold water and add 1 teaspoon of salt. Bring to a boil; drain and pat dry.

3. Heat the olive oil in the skillet. Add the bacon and cook until crisp. Transfer the bacon to a plate.

4. Whisk the vinegar into the bacon fat in the skillet and season it with salt and pepper. Add the toasted pine nuts and crisp bacon just before serving the vinaigrette hot or warm.

—*Bill Telepan*

Rich Pan Gravy

MAKES ABOUT 1 QUART

2 teaspoons vegetable oil

Turkey neck, wing tips and giblets, cut
into 1-inch pieces

1 medium onion, coarsely chopped

4½ cups water

Reserved pan juices from Perfect
Roast Turkey (p. 190)

1 cup dry white wine

3 tablespoons cornstarch

Freshly ground pepper

1. Heat the oil in an enameled cast-iron casserole. Add the turkey parts and onion and cook over moderately high heat until lightly browned, about 5 minutes. Cover and cook over low heat for 20 minutes. Add 4 cups of water and bring to a boil. Cover partially and simmer until reduced to 3 cups, about 1 hour. Strain into a medium saucepan and skim off the fat.

2. Pour the reserved turkey pan juices into a glass measuring cup and skim off the fat. Set the roasting pan over 2 burners on moderately high heat. Add the wine and boil for 2 minutes, scraping up the browned bits from the bottom of the pan. Scrape the contents of the pan into a strainer set over the turkey broth and press on the vegetables. Bring the broth to a boil. Mix the cornstarch with the remaining ½ cup of water until smooth, then whisk this slurry into the boiling broth. Reduce the heat to low and simmer until lightly thickened, about 2 minutes. Season with pepper, pour into a gravy boat and serve. *—Pam Anderson*

MAKE AHEAD Prepare through Step 1 and refrigerate for up to 3 days.

Pumpkin Seed and Tomatillo Sauce

MAKES 2 CUPS

Serve this creamy Mexican sauce as a dip, with grilled shrimp, poultry, pork or mild fish, or with steamed vegetables. You can also cook shelled raw shrimp in the sauce, or warm the

Pumpkin Seed and Tomatillo Sauce, with grilled shrimp and warm tortillas.

sauce with shredded chicken to use as a tortilla filling.

½ pound tomatillos, husks removed

¼ cup shelled raw pumpkin seeds

1 teaspoon vegetable oil

3 jalapeños, seeded and minced

1 small onion, minced

1 garlic clove, minced

2½ tablespoons minced cilantro

⅔ to 1 cup Basic Chicken Stock
(p. 98) or canned low-sodium
broth

½ teaspoon salt

Pinch of sugar

1 tablespoon sour cream

1. Preheat the broiler. Broil the tomatillos as close to the heat as possible for 8 to 10 minutes, until softened and charred in spots. Transfer to a plate.

2. In a medium skillet, toast the pumpkin seeds over moderate heat, stirring, until most of them pop, 2 to 3 minutes. Transfer to a plate to cool.

3. In the same skillet, combine the oil, jalapeños, onion and garlic. Cover and cook over low heat until softened, about 3 minutes. Uncover and cook, stirring, until golden, about 3 minutes. Stir in the cilantro and cook for 1 minute, then add the tomatillos and ⅔ cup of the stock and simmer for 4 minutes.

4. Transfer the mixture to a blender, add the pumpkin seeds and puree until smooth. Season with the salt and sugar. Transfer to a bowl and stir in the sour cream. If the sauce seems thick, thin it with some of the remaining ⅓ cup stock. *—Sally Schneider*

ONE-QUARTER CUP Calories 49 kcal, Total Fat 3.2 gm, Saturated Fat 0.8 gm

Hot Sauce

MAKES ABOUT 1¾ CUPS

This spicy condiment is wonderful with all kinds of fried seafood as well as with grilled beef, chicken and pork.

1 cup coarsely chopped seeded tomatoes
⅓ cup minced onion
1 teaspoon minced garlic
1½ teaspoons minced jalapeño
½ teaspoon salt
2 tablespoons ketchup
¼ cup cold water
¼ cup canola oil

Stir together all of the ingredients in a medium bowl and cover the bowl with plastic wrap. Refrigerate the sauce until it's thoroughly chilled.

—*Jacques Pépin*

MAKE AHEAD The sauce can be made ahead and refrigerated for up to 2 days.

---

health nuts

Cholesterol free, rich in protein and high in the "good" fats that have been found to decrease the risk of heart disease, nuts—in moderation—are a healthy pleasure.

almonds High in oleic acid, which has been shown to reduce cholesterol and heart disease, as well as in fiber, which aids digestion.

cashews Rich in oleic acid, copper, magnesium and calcium, which protects bones and reduces the risk of heart disease.

hazelnuts Full of oleic acid and vitamin E, which has cancer- and cholesterol-fighting properties.

walnuts Packed with omega-3 fatty acids, which have been shown to lower cholesterol and ameliorate conditions such as asthma, arthritis, allergies and skin inflammation.

pistachios A good source of oleic acid, calcium, magnesium, iron and folic acid, a compound that lessens the risk of heart disease.

Korean Chili Sauce

MAKES A SCANT ½ CUP

3 tablespoons Korean sweet-spicy chili paste *(kochujang)*
2½ tablespoons water
1 tablespoon Asian sesame oil
1 teaspoon sugar

Whisk all of the ingredients together in a small bowl. —*Anya von Bremzen*

Walnut Pesto

MAKES ABOUT 1¼ CUPS

Toss this pesto with pasta or roasted vegetables, spread it on thick tomato slices and broil, or stuff it under the skin of a chicken before roasting. If you don't have a mortar, make the pesto in a food processor by quickly pulsing the ingredients.

1½ cups walnut halves (6 ounces)
2 garlic cloves, finely chopped
Crushed red pepper
Kosher salt
¼ cup minced flat-leaf parsley
½ cup extra-virgin olive oil
½ cup freshly grated Parmesan cheese

1. Preheat the oven to 350°. Spread the walnuts on a rimmed baking sheet and toast for 12 minutes, or until golden. Cool the walnuts and finely chop.
2. In a mortar, mash the garlic to a paste with a pinch each of crushed red pepper and salt. Add the walnuts and parsley and pound to a coarse paste. Slowly add the olive oil, pounding and stirring until blended. Add the Parmesan and salt to taste. —*Grace Parisi*

Peanut Dipping Sauce

MAKES 2 CUPS

1 tomato—peeled, seeded and coarsely chopped
¼ cup cilantro leaves
2 garlic cloves, minced
2 scallions, finely chopped
1 Thai chile, seeded and minced
1 stalk of fresh lemongrass, tender inner bulb only, minced
¾ cup chunky peanut butter

½ cup Basic Chicken Stock (p. 98) or canned low-sodium broth
3 tablespoons Asian fish sauce *(nuoc mam)*
3 tablespoons fresh lime juice
2½ tablespoons light brown sugar
½ teaspoon freshly ground pepper

In a processor, combine the tomato, cilantro, garlic, scallions, chile and lemongrass; pulse until they are finely chopped. Add the peanut butter, stock, fish sauce, lime juice, sugar and pepper and process until smooth. Transfer to a bowl and serve.

—*Steven Raichlen*

Ecuadoran Peanut Sauce

6 SERVINGS ☀

Spoon this sauce over steamed or boiled new potatoes. It's also good with grilled or poached chicken and shrimp.

¼ cup vegetable oil
1½ teaspoons ground achiote or sweet paprika
1 medium onion, coarsely chopped
½ teaspoon freshly ground pepper
¼ teaspoon ground cumin
⅔ cup roasted unsalted peanuts, coarsely chopped
½ cup whole milk
¼ cup finely chopped cilantro leaves
Salt

1. In a small saucepan, combine the oil with the achiote and bring to a simmer. Transfer to a bowl and let stand until the achiote settles to the bottom.
2. Carefully pour the oil into a medium skillet, leaving the achiote behind. Add the onion and cook over moderate heat until softened and lightly browned. Add the pepper and cumin and stir for 30 seconds until fragrant. Add the peanuts, milk and cilantro and bring to a boil. Transfer the peanut sauce to a food processor and pulse until chunky. Season with salt and serve warm. —*Maricel Presilla*

MAKE AHEAD The sauce can be refrigerated for up to 3 days.

Pico de Gallo

MAKES ABOUT 4 CUPS

- 2 large vine-ripened tomatoes, finely diced
- ½ large onion, finely diced
- ⅓ cup finely chopped cilantro
- 4 large radishes, finely diced
- 2 jalapeños, seeded and finely diced
- 2 tablespoons fresh lime juice
- 1 garlic clove, minced
- ¾ teaspoon coarse salt

Combine all of the ingredients in a bowl and serve. —*Steven Raichlen*

MAKE AHEAD The Pico de Gallo can be made ahead and kept refrigerated overnight.

RIGHT: **Fourth-of-July Firecracker Salsa, with Garlic-Chive Flat Breads (p. 250).**
BELOW (CLOCKWISE FROM BOTTOM): **Hot Chilean Salsa (p. 220), Ecuadoran Peanut Sauce (p. 318), Passion Fruit and Ginger Sauce (p. 199), Zafra's Salsa Verde (p. 320) and Cuban Mojo (p. 59).**

Fourth-of-July Firecracker Salsa

MAKES 4 CUPS

The Fourth-of-July tomato plant produces smallish fruit (about 3 inches) with a nice tartness—perfect for salsa. And, yes, they really do ripen early: in time for Independence Day. That holiday is also a good time to have incendiary firecracker chiles, which are ornamental as well as delicious and grow well in pots.

- 2 pounds tomatoes, coarsely chopped
- 1 medium onion, minced
- ½ cup coarsely chopped cilantro
- 3 or 4 small red chiles, minced and seeded
- 3 garlic cloves, minced
- 2 tablespoons fresh lime juice

Salt and freshly ground pepper

In a bowl, combine the coarsely chopped tomatoes with the onion, cilantro, red chiles, garlic and lime juice. Season the mixture with salt and pepper to taste and stir. Let stand at room temperature for 20 minutes before serving. —*Marcia Kiesel*

BEER The lime accents and the spiciness of this tomato salsa both point to a relatively simple, bright, cooling lager from Mexico. Good choices would be Tecate or Corona.

Cucumber and Herb Blossom Salsa over grilled halibut.

Zafra's Salsa Verde

MAKES ABOUT 2 CUPS ❋

In Chile, salsa verde, or green sauce—which gets its vibrant color from cilantro and fresh chiles—is a traditional accompaniment to sea urchins. It also works well with vegetables and chicken and is particularly good with steamed or grilled shrimp.

- ½ cup fresh lemon juice
- 1 medium white onion, finely chopped
- ⅓ cup finely chopped cilantro leaves
- 1 jalapeño, seeded and very finely chopped
- ½ cup extra-virgin olive oil

Salt and freshly ground pepper

In a medium bowl, combine the lemon juice with the onion, cilantro and jalapeño and stir to blend gradually. Slowly whisk in the olive oil until thoroughly combined. Season the salsa verde with salt and pepper and serve.

—*Maricel Presilla*

MAKE AHEAD The salsa can be refrigerated for up to 3 days.

Cucumber and Herb Blossom Salsa

MAKES ABOUT 4 CUPS

It's important to use either Kirby or small Japanese cucumbers that aren't waxed (of course, homegrown cucumbers don't have any wax to remove). You can substitute any flowering herbs for those listed below. Serve the salsa with grilled fish, chicken or thick slices of peasant bread.

- 1½ pounds cucumbers, cut into ½-inch dice
- 1 teaspoon minced and seeded red chile

Kosher salt

- 1 cup chive flowers, pulled apart
- 1 cup torn nasturtium flowers
- ¼ cup small basil leaves and flowers
- 2 tablespoons small spearmint leaves and flowers
- 1 tablespoon fresh lemon juice
- 1 tablespoon extra-virgin olive oil
- ¾ teaspoon finely grated lemon zest

In a bowl, toss the cucumbers with the chile and ¼ teaspoon of salt and let stand for 15 minutes. Stir in the chive flowers, nasturtiums, basil, spearmint, lemon juice, olive oil and lemon zest. Season with salt and serve.

—*Marcia Kiesel*

Chipotle Salsa

MAKES ABOUT 2 CUPS

- 6 small tomatillos, husked
- 5 large garlic cloves
- 4 plum tomatoes
- ¼ large onion
- 3 canned chipotle chiles in adobo, seeded and finely chopped, with 2 teaspoons of the adobo sauce
- 3 tablespoons finely chopped fresh cilantro
- ½ teaspoon sugar

Coarse salt

I. Heat a large cast-iron skillet. When it is very hot, add the tomatillos, garlic cloves, tomatoes and onion and cook over low heat, turning frequently, until blackened in spots and softened, 8 to 10 minutes. Transfer the vegetables to a plate and let cool.

2. Put the tomatillos, garlic, tomatoes and onion in a food processor and pulse until coarsely chopped. Add the chipotles and the adobo sauce, the cilantro and the sugar; salt to taste and pulse just until combined.

—*Steven Raichlen*

MAKE AHEAD The Chipotle Salsa can be made ahead of time and refrigerated in an airtight container for up to 2 days.

Roasted Poblano Salsa

MAKES ABOUT 4 CUPS

- 6 poblano chiles
- 1 pound tomatoes, coarsely chopped (2 cups)
- ½ cup finely chopped sweet onion
- ¼ cup chopped pitted green olives
- 3 tablespoons coarsely chopped cilantro
- 2 tablespoons extra-virgin olive oil
- 1 tablespoon fresh lime juice

Salt and freshly ground pepper

1. Preheat the broiler. Roast the chiles under the broiler until charred all over. Transfer to a bowl, cover with plastic wrap and let steam for 5 minutes. Skin, stem and seed the chiles, then cut them into ⅓-inch dice.

2. In a serving bowl, combine the chiles with the tomatoes, onion, olives, cilantro, olive oil and lime juice. Season with salt and pepper, toss to mix and serve. —*Marcia Kiesel*

MAKE AHEAD The salsa can be refrigerated overnight. For a fresh taste, wait to add the cilantro until just before serving.

Avocado and Pumpkin Seed Salsa

MAKES ABOUT 4 CUPS

The toasted pumpkin seeds give this salsa a great crunchy texture.

- 1 cup raw pumpkin seeds (4 ounces)
- 1 red bell pepper
- ¼ cup fresh lemon juice
- 2 garlic cloves, minced
- 1 red chile, minced
- 3 large ripe firm Hass avocados, cut into ½-inch dice

Salt and freshly ground pepper

1. Preheat the oven to 400°. Spread the pumpkin seeds on a rimmed baking sheet and bake for 4 minutes, or until lightly browned. Transfer to a plate to cool.

2. Roast the bell pepper over a gas flame until it is charred all over. Transfer to a bowl, cover with plastic wrap and let steam for 5 minutes. Peel, stem and seed the pepper; cut it into ½-inch dice.

3. In a bowl, mix the lemon juice with the garlic and chile. Stir in the pumpkin seeds, bell pepper and avocados. Season with salt and pepper and serve. —*Marcia Kiesel*

Grilled Tomatillo and Purple Basil Salsa

MAKES ABOUT 3 CUPS

Use opal basil here: It's deep purple, very flavorful, sturdy and—unlike most other basil—it dries beautifully.

- 1 pound tomatillos, husked
- 1 large ear of corn, shucked
- 1 small red onion, sliced ⅓ inch thick
- 4 slices of bacon
- 1 garlic clove, minced
- ½ chipotle chile in adobo, minced
- ¼ cup torn purple basil leaves

Salt and freshly ground pepper

1. Light a grill or preheat a grill pan. Grill the tomatillos and corn over a moderately hot fire or moderate heat until lightly charred all over, about 4 minutes per side. Transfer to a plate. Grill the onion slices until lightly charred, about 3 minutes per side. Remove the charred skins from the tomatillos and quarter them. Slice the corn kernels off the cob. Cut the onion into ¼-inch dice.

2. In a skillet, fry the bacon until crisp. Drain on paper towels and coarsely chop. In a bowl, combine the garlic with the chipotle, then stir in the tomatillos, corn, onion and bacon. Fold in the purple basil, season with salt and pepper and serve.

—*Marcia Kiesel*

Habanero and Fruit Salsa

MAKES 1 CUP 🌸

- ⅓ dried ancho chile, seeded
- ½ dried habanero chile, seeded
- 1 cup boiling water
- ½ cup finely diced mango
- ½ cup finely diced papaya
- 1 tablespoon minced onion
- 1 tablespoon finely diced tomato
- 1 teaspoon finely chopped cilantro
- 1 teaspoon finely chopped mint
- ½ teaspoon minced garlic
- 1 tablespoon sherry vinegar
- ½ teaspoon fine sea salt

In a bowl, soak the ancho and habanero in the hot water until softened, about 20 minutes. Drain the chiles; pat dry. Mince the chiles and transfer to a bowl. Stir in the mango, papaya, onion, tomato, cilantro, mint, garlic, vinegar and salt.

—*Kevin Maguire*

ONE TABLESPOON Calories 6 kcal, Total Fat 0 gm, Saturated Fat 0 gm

Mango-Jicama Salsa

MAKES 5 CUPS

- 1 pound jicama, peeled and cut into ¼-inch dice (about 2 cups)
- 1 medium red onion, finely chopped
- 1 cup coarsely chopped cilantro
- 6 garlic cloves, minced
- ¼ cup plus 2 tablespoons fresh lime juice
- 1 chipotle chile in adobo sauce, seeded and minced
- 1 jalapeño, seeded and minced
- 2 teaspoons kosher salt
- 4 large mangoes (14 ounces each), peeled and cut into ¼-inch dice

Freshly ground pepper

Tortilla chips, for serving

In a large bowl, combine the jicama, red onion, cilantro, garlic, lime juice, chipotle, jalapeño and salt. With a rubber spatula, fold in the mangoes. Season the salsa with pepper and refrigerate. Serve with tortilla chips.

—*Elizabeth Falkner*

MAKE AHEAD The salsa can be made ahead of time and refrigerated for up to 4 hours.

Warm Olivada with Thyme

MAKES ABOUT 1½ CUPS

Use this full-flavored olive spread as a topping for bread, pizza, and grilled meat, poultry or fish. It's great stirred into mashed potatoes or tossed with pasta.

- 1 large garlic clove, smashed
- 4 teaspoons thyme leaves
- ½ teaspoon grated orange zest
- 2 cups mixed green and black olives (¾ pound), pitted and coarsely chopped, juices reserved

Freshly ground pepper

Crusty bread, for serving

I. In a mortar, pound the garlic until pureed. Add the thyme leaves and orange zest and pound until pureed.

Add the pitted olives, ½ cup at a time, and pound until a coarse paste forms. Season with pepper.

2. Just before serving, transfer the olive mixture to a medium skillet and add a tablespoon or two of the reserved olive juices to moisten it. Cook over moderate heat, stirring frequently, until the olive mixture is warmed through. Transfer the olivada to a bowl and serve with crusty bread.

—*Sally Schneider*

MAKE AHEAD Make the olivada through Step 1 well ahead of time, if you like, and keep it refrigerated for up to 1 week.

ONE TABLESPOON Calories 14 kcal, Total Fat 1.4 gm, Saturated Fat 0.2 gm

Warm Olivada with Thyme

Spinach Raita

10 TO 12 SERVINGS

This cooling version of *raita,* a creamy salad-like combination of yogurt and chopped vegetables, features spinach and tomatoes.

- 1 large bunch spinach (¾ pound), large stems discarded
- 3 cups plain whole-milk yogurt
- 2 medium tomatoes—peeled, seeded and finely chopped

One 1-inch piece of fresh ginger, peeled and minced

- 1 teaspoon salt
- 1 teaspoon cayenne pepper

I. Wash the spinach leaves in several changes of cold water and dry thoroughly in a salad spinner. Stack the leaves and slice them crosswise into thin julienne strips.

2. In a large bowl, mix the yogurt with the chopped tomatoes, fresh ginger, salt and cayenne. Fold in the spinach. Refrigerate for at least 1 hour before serving. —*Neela Paniz*

Ginger-Scallion Butter

4 SERVINGS

Fresh ginger is sweeter than the ground dried kind. This whipped butter carries the essence of ginger beautifully. Use dollops of it on roasted sweet potatoes, winter squash, fresh green beans and spring peas as well as on grilled fish and pork.

- 4 tablespoons unsalted butter, at room temperature
- 2 scallions, thinly sliced or minced
- 1 heaping teaspoon finely grated peeled fresh ginger

Salt and freshly ground pepper

In a small bowl, beat the butter with the scallions, grated ginger, salt and pepper. —*Marcia Kiesel*

Pili Pili Ha Ha

MAKES ABOUT 4½ CUPS

This fiery homemade condiment is simple to make but it does require patience—it needs to stand for more

ginger

Ginger's palate-cleansing bite comes from zingerone, a substance chemically similar to piperine, which gives black pepper its kick. This pungency brightens ingredients that have unassertive flavors, such as chicken and pork. Ginger also complements the rich, sweet, spicy tastes of tropical foods like citrus fruits, curry pastes, pickles and chutneys. Young ginger has delicate, silvery skin with occasional pink shoots and a mildness that allows it to be used unpeeled, almost as a vegetable, in stir-fries. As ginger ages, its flavor grows more intense and its texture becomes fibrous. That's why mature peeled ginger is often grated, minced or juiced. Look for ginger that is smooth-skinned, heavy and firm, since ginger that feels light or has soft spots may be dried out or less than fresh.

than 6 months before it's ready to use. The hot sauce is a staple at the dinner table of Ralph Bausfield, an owner of a camp in Botswana. His family sprinkles it on everything from soups and salads to main dishes. *Pili pili* is a generic term for hot sauce. The *ha ha* refers to the sauce's hot kick, which sneaks up on you.

- ¼ cup halved and seeded bird chiles
- ½ cup gin
- 4 cups sherry

Put the bird chiles in a bottle and cover with the gin. Shake once a day for 2 weeks, then store in a dark place for 6 months. Pour half of the gin and chiles into another bottle. Fill both bottles with sherry and serve. —*Jacques Pépin*

Green Chile Chutney

MAKES ABOUT 1 CUP

Chutney, a sweet, spicy condiment, can be served with rice dishes as well as with curries and *dals*. It also makes a great dip for Indian-style breads.

- ½ pound serrano chiles, seeded and coarsely chopped
- 1 bunch fresh cilantro (about 2 ounces), stems removed and leaves finely chopped
- ½ bunch fresh mint (about 1 ounce), stems removed and leaves finely chopped

About ¼ cup fresh lemon juice

- 2 tablespoons *dalia* (see The Indian Pantry, p. 171)
- 2 teaspoons salt, or more to taste

In a food processor, combine the chiles, cilantro, mint, ¼ cup lemon juice, the *dalia* and 2 teaspoons of salt. Process until smooth. Season with additional lemon juice and salt, and serve. —*Neela Paniz*

Mint Chutney

MAKES 3 CUPS

Not only is this fresh herb chutney easy to make, but it enhances so many foods that it appears regularly on Indian tables. To keep the mint from darkening, process it with the rest of the ingredients.

- 1½ tablespoons cumin seeds
- 1 medium onion, coarsely chopped
- 4 lightly packed cups mint
- 2 lightly packed cups cilantro
- ½ cup fresh lemon juice
- 4 serrano chiles, seeded and chopped
- 4 garlic cloves, coarsely chopped
- 1½ teaspoons salt

Pinch of sugar

- ½ cup plus 2 tablespoons water
- 2 tablespoons plain whole-milk yogurt

1. In a small skillet, toast the cumin seeds over moderately high heat until fragrant, about 3 minutes. Transfer the seeds to a plate and let cool. Grind the cumin to a coarse powder in a mortar or spice mill.

2. In a blender, combine the onion, mint, cilantro, lemon juice, chiles, garlic, salt, sugar and ground cumin. Blend well, scraping the sides of the bowl as necessary. Add the water and yogurt and blend until smooth.
—*Neela Paniz*

MAKE AHEAD The Mint Chutney can be refrigerated in an airtight container for up to 1 day.

Apricot Chutney with Nigella Seeds

MAKES 2½ CUPS

The apricots for this sweet and tangy chutney need to soak until softened, so plan accordingly. Traditionally, the whole spices remain in the chutney, but they can be removed before serving if you prefer. This aromatic condiment goes well with grilled meat and poultry.

- ½ pound dried apricots
- 1¼ cups boiling water
- ⅓ cup plus 1 tablespoon white vinegar
- ¼ cup granulated sugar
- 1½ ounces jaggery (see The Indian Pantry, p. 171) or 3 tablespoons brown sugar
- 1 teaspoon cayenne pepper
- 1 teaspoon nigella seeds (see The Indian Pantry, p. 171)

One 1-inch piece cinnamon stick

- ½ teaspoon ground cinnamon
- 4 whole cloves
- 5 whole peppercorns
- 1½ cups water

1. In a medium bowl, cover the dried apricots with the boiling water. Let stand for 6 hours at room temperature or overnight in the refrigerator.

2. In a food processor, puree the apricots with their liquid. Put in a medium saucepan and add the vinegar, granulated sugar, jaggery, cayenne, nigella seeds, cinnamon stick, ground cinnamon, cloves, peppercorns and water. Bring to a simmer over moderately high heat, stirring frequently until the sugar melts. Reduce the heat to moderate and cook, stirring frequently, until thick, about 45 minutes. Let cool completely.
—*Neela Paniz*

buffet menu

mini potato pancakes with lemon and cilantro (p. 24) | chicken masala (p. 171)

basmati rice and peas (p. 307) | fragrant toor lentils with garlic and tomato (p. 293)

green beans with onions and tomato (p. 277) | mixed vegetable and lentil curry (p. 293)

cucumber and peanut salad (p. 62) | spinach raita (p. 322) | green chile chutney (p. 323)

apricot chutney with nigella seeds (p. 323) | tamarind and date chutney | mint chutney (p. 323)

fennel seed cookies (p. 359) | coconut pistachio meringues (p. 357)

LARGE BOWLS, CLOCKWISE FROM LEFT: Apricot Chutney with Nigella Seeds, Green Chile Chutney, and Tamarind and Date Chutney. SMALL BOWLS: Mint Chutney and two bowls of Spinach Raita.

Tamarind and Date Chutney

MAKES 3¾ CUPS

The tamarind and the dates need to soak overnight until softened before making this chutney; plan ahead.

½ pound seedless tamarind pulp

Boiling water

½ pound pitted dates

2 tablespoons cumin seeds

6 ounces jaggery (see
    The Indian Pantry, p. 171)
    or ¾ cup brown sugar

¾ cup granulated sugar

2 teaspoons freshly ground pepper

2 teaspoons black salt

1 teaspoon cayenne pepper

Pinch of asafoetida (see
    The Indian Pantry, p. 171)

I. Put the tamarind in a heatproof bowl and pour 3 cups of boiling water over it. Put the dates in another bowl and pour 1 cup of boiling water over them. Cover and soak the tamarind and dates overnight at room temperature.

2. Break up the tamarind with a fork. Strain it through a fine sieve, pressing hard on the pulp to extract as much of the paste as possible. Set the paste aside. Scoop the pulp in the sieve back into the bowl. Add another ½ cup of boiling water to the pulp and repeat the process to extract as much paste as possible from the tamarind. You should have about 2½ cups of paste. Follow the same procedure with the dates, using ¼ cup of boiling water for the second soaking and straining. You should have about 1¼ cups of date paste.

3. In a small skillet, toast the cumin seeds over moderately high heat just until they're fragrant, about 3 minutes. Transfer to a plate to cool. Grind the cumin to a coarse powder in a mortar or a spice mill.

4. In a large saucepan, combine the tamarind and date pastes with the toasted cumin, jaggery, granulated sugar, pepper, black salt, cayenne and asafoetida. Cook over moderately high heat, stirring frequently, until the jaggery has melted. Reduce the heat to moderately low and cook, stirring frequently, until the chutney is thick, about 10 minutes. Transfer the chutney to a heatproof bowl and let cool before serving. —*Neela Paniz*

MAKE AHEAD The chutney can be refrigerated for several months.

Peanut Chutney

MAKES ABOUT 3 CUPS ※

This is a thick chutney that can be thinned slightly with water, if desired.

2 cups roasted unsalted peanuts

1 cup pitted dates (5 ounces)

2 jalapeños, seeded

2 garlic cloves

1 teaspoon finely grated
    fresh ginger

3 tablespoons apple cider vinegar

3 teaspoons fresh lime juice

1 tablespoon vegetable oil

½ teaspoon black mustard seeds

½ teaspoon cumin seeds

1 cup water

2 tablespoons coarsely
    chopped cilantro

Salt

I. In a food processor, combine the peanuts with the dates, jalapeños, garlic, ginger, vinegar and lime juice. Process until smooth.

2. In a small skillet, heat the oil until smoking. Add the mustard seeds and cook over moderately high heat until the mustard seeds stop popping, about 1 minute. Stir in the cumin seeds and cook until fragrant, about 1 minute. Remove from the heat; let cool slightly, then scrape the seasonings into the chutney and pulse to blend. Add the water and cilantro and process until incorporated. Season with salt and serve.

—*Gary MacGurn and Patty Gentry*

MAKE AHEAD The chutney can be refrigerated for 1 week. Bring to room temperature before serving.

Pumpkin Chutney

MAKES ABOUT 1¾ CUPS ※

Aside from traditional uses, this seasonal chutney is a great dip for vegetables and a fine sandwich spread.

One 10-ounce can unsweetened
    pumpkin puree

1 jalapeño, seeded

1 tablespoon minced fresh ginger

2 tablespoons fresh lemon juice

¼ cup light brown sugar

⅓ cup water

2 tablespoons vegetable oil

1 tablespoon minced garlic

1 teaspoon cumin seeds

2 tablespoons coarsely
    chopped cilantro

Salt

I. In a food processor, combine the pumpkin, jalapeño, ginger, lemon juice and sugar. With the machine on, slowly add the water until smooth.

2. Heat the oil in a small skillet. Add the garlic and cumin and cook over moderate heat until fragrant, about 2 minutes. Remove from the heat and let cool slightly; then add to the pumpkin. Add the cilantro and puree until incorporated. Season with salt and serve.

—*Gary MacGurn and Patty Gentry*

MAKE AHEAD The chutney can be refrigerated for 1 week.

A trio of chutneys.

Cucumber Relish

MAKES ABOUT 1½ CUPS

- 3 tablespoons rice vinegar
- 1 tablespoon sugar
- ½ teaspoon salt
- ¼ teaspoon freshly ground pepper
- 2 Kirby cucumbers, peeled and sliced paper thin
- 1 large shallot, sliced paper thin and separated into rings
- 1 hot red chile, thinly sliced into rings

In a bowl, combine the vinegar with the sugar, salt and pepper. Add the cucumbers, shallot and chile.

—*Steven Raichlen*

MAKE AHEAD The relish can be made a little bit ahead of time and refrigerated for up to 1 hour.

Clove and Red Onion Relish

MAKES ABOUT 1 CUP

This relish is delicious with roast pork, chicken and duck, and it's great on sandwiches, especially slathered on a crusty baguette layered with baked Virginia ham and sharp Cheddar cheese.

- 1 large red onion, cut into ½-inch dice
- 2 tablespoons extra-virgin olive oil
- 6 whole cloves
- ¼ cup Ruby Port
- ½ teaspoon pure maple syrup

Salt and freshly ground pepper

In a medium saucepan, cook the onion in the olive oil over moderate heat, stirring, until softened, about 4 minutes. Add the cloves, cover and cook over low heat until the onion is deeply caramelized on the bottom, about 12 minutes. Add the port and cook, stirring, for 1 minute. Add the maple syrup and remove from the heat. Remove and discard the cloves. Season the relish with salt and pepper and let cool. —*Marcia Kiesel*

MAKE AHEAD The relish can be made ahead of time and refrigerated for up to 1 week.

Red and Green Bell Pepper Relish

MAKES ABOUT 4 CUPS

This relish needs a week in the refrigerator; plan accordingly.

- 1½ cups finely shredded green cabbage
- 3 large red bell peppers, cut into ½-inch dice
- 1 large green bell pepper, cut into ½-inch dice
- 1 small onion, finely chopped
- 1 celery rib, finely chopped
- 1 tablespoon minced jalapeño
- 1 cup white vinegar
- 1½ teaspoons kosher salt
- 1½ teaspoons yellow mustard seeds
- ¾ teaspoon turmeric
- ½ teaspoon celery seeds
- ¼ cup sugar

I. In a large stainless-steel saucepan, toss the shredded cabbage with the bell peppers, onion, celery and minced jalapeño. Add the vinegar, salt, mustard seeds, turmeric, celery seeds and sugar; bring to a boil. Cover, reduce the heat to low and simmer, stirring occasionally, until the vegetables just soften, about 20 minutes.

2. Transfer the relish to glass jars and let cool, then cover and refrigerate for 1 week before serving.

—*Kristie Trabant Scott*

MAKE AHEAD The relish can be refrigerated for up to 1 month.

Crisp Asparagus-Lemon Relish

MAKES ABOUT 1½ CUPS

This is a refreshing, lemony topping for oysters on the half shell as well as for grilled fish and smoked salmon.

- 1 pound white asparagus, peeled, or green asparagus
- 3 tablespoons minced red onion
- 2 tablespoons mascarpone
- 1 tablespoon fresh lemon juice
- ½ teaspoon finely grated lemon zest

Salt and freshly ground pepper

I. Steam the asparagus until crisptender, about 4 minutes. Rinse under cold running water and drain. Cut into ¼-inch dice.

2. In a bowl, combine the onion with the mascarpone, lemon juice and zest. Fold in the asparagus and season with salt and pepper. Cover and refrigerate until chilled, at least 30 minutes and up to 3 hours. —*Marcia Kiesel*

Spiced Pear Relish

MAKES 4 CUPS

- 6 firm, ripe Bartlett or Anjou pears—peeled, cored and finely chopped
- 1 medium onion, finely chopped
- ¼ cup kosher salt
- 2 large jalapeños, seeded and minced
- 1 cup sugar
- 1 cup white vinegar
- 1½ cups golden raisins
- 1 tablespoon minced peeled fresh ginger
- 1 teaspoon turmeric
- 1 teaspoon yellow mustard seeds

I. In a large bowl, toss the pears with the onion, salt and jalapeños. Cover and refrigerate overnight.

2. Drain the pears in a colander and rinse them. In a large saucepan, combine the pears with the remaining ingredients and bring to a boil. Simmer over low heat for 25 minutes, or until thickened. Let the pear relish cool. Serve cold or at room temperature.

—*Susan Spicer*

MAKE AHEAD The pear relish can be refrigerated for up to 2 weeks.

Tangerine Cranberry Sauce

MAKES 4 CUPS

The sugared tangerines need to stand overnight, so plan accordingly.

- 4 small tangerines or clementines, preferably organic, well-washed
- 1 cup sugar
- 2 cups fresh orange juice
- 12 ounces fresh cranberries

Clove and Red Onion Relish spices up a ham and Cheddar cheese sandwich.

1. Cut the tangerines crosswise through the skins into ½-inch slices, then quarter the slices. In a small bowl, toss the tangerines with ½ cup of the sugar. Cover and refrigerate overnight.

2. In a heavy medium saucepan, combine the candied tangerines and their liquid with the remaining ½ cup of sugar and the orange juice. Bring to a boil and then simmer over moderately low heat until the tangerine skins are soft and the liquid is syrupy, about 50 minutes. Add the cranberries and cook over moderately low heat until their skins just begin to split, about 15 minutes.

3. Drain the cranberries and tangerines in a colander set over a bowl and return the liquid to the saucepan. Boil the liquid over moderately high heat until syrupy, about 15 minutes. Pour

the syrup over the fruit and let cool completely. —*Bruce and Eric Bromberg*
MAKE AHEAD The sauce can be refrigerated for up to 1 week. Bring to room temperature before serving.

Quince and Cranberry Compote

MAKES ABOUT 3 CUPS
Crisp Bosc pears make a fine alternative to quinces here, and they need to cook for only 20 minutes.

- 2 cups apple juice
- ½ cup sugar
- 1 cinnamon stick
- 1 pound quinces—peeled, cored and cut into ¾-inch pieces

One 12-ounce bag of cranberries
In a heavy medium saucepan, combine the apple juice with the sugar and cinnamon stick and bring to a boil, stirring to dissolve the sugar. Add the quinces

and cook over moderate heat, stirring occasionally, until tender, about 30 minutes. Add the cranberries and bring to a simmer. Cook until the compote is thick, about 20 minutes. Discard the cinnamon stick before serving. —*Grace Parisi*
MAKE AHEAD Refrigerate in an airtight container for up to 2 weeks.

Brown Sugar Syrup

MAKES ¾ CUP ✳
Use this sweet Latin sauce to top vanilla, chocolate or coffee ice cream.

- ½ pound dark brown sugar or *piloncillo* (see Note)
- 1 cup water

One 4-inch cinnamon stick
Finely grated zest of 1 lime
Pinch of salt
Combine all the ingredients in a small saucepan and bring to a boil over high heat. Boil until thick and syrupy, about 15 minutes. Strain and cool.
—*Maricel Presilla*
NOTE *Piloncillo,* unrefined brown sugar that is typically used in Latin desserts, is also known as brown loaf sugar because it is sold in cone-shaped pieces. It is available at Latin markets.
MAKE AHEAD The syrup can be refrigerated for up to 1 week.

cakes tarts cookies
chapter 15

Cinnamon Butter Cake

8 SERVINGS

2 ¼ cups cake flour
  1 teaspoon cinnamon
  1 teaspoon baking powder
  ¾ teaspoon baking soda
  ½ teaspoon salt
  2 sticks (½ pound) plus 2
     tablespoons unsalted
     butter, softened
  1 cup plus 2 tablespoons sugar
  4 large eggs
  2 teaspoons pure vanilla extract
  2 teaspoons brandy
  ¼ cup plus 2 tablespoons
     sour cream

I. Preheat the oven to 350°. Butter and flour an 8-cup kugelhopf pan. In a medium bowl, sift the flour with ½ teaspoon of the cinnamon, the baking powder, baking soda and the salt.

2. In a large bowl, using an electric mixer, beat the butter at medium speed until creamy. Beat in 1 cup of the sugar. Add the eggs, 1 at a time, beating well after each addition. Add the vanilla and brandy. Alternately beat in the sour cream and the dry ingredients in 3 batches at low speed. Scrape the batter into the prepared pan and bake for about 50 minutes, or until a tester inserted in the center of the cake comes out clean. Transfer the cake to a rack set over a sheet of wax paper and let cool in the pan for 10 minutes.

3. In a small bowl, combine the remaining 2 tablespoons of sugar and ½ teaspoon cinnamon. Invert the cake onto the rack and sprinkle with the cinnamon sugar. Let cool completely before serving.

—*Icebox Café, Miami Beach, Florida*

MAKE AHEAD The cake can be made ahead and stored in an airtight container overnight.

Almond and Carrot Cake

MAKES ONE 10-INCH CAKE

Because it's not overly sweet or rich, this dessert—a cross between a coarse-textured flourless nut cake and a carrot cake—would be perfect with a glass of sweet wine.

  2 cups whole blanched almonds
     (10 ounces)
  ¾ cup all-purpose flour
2 ½ teaspoons baking powder
  ½ teaspoon finely grated
     lemon zest
Salt
1 ½ cups granulated sugar
  3 large carrots (10 ounces),
     coarsely chopped
  4 large eggs, separated
Confectioners' sugar, for dusting

I. Preheat the oven to 400°. Generously butter and flour a 10-inch springform or fluted cake pan. Toast the almonds on a rimmed baking sheet for about 8 minutes, or until lightly browned. Transfer the almonds to a large plate to cool to room temperature. Reduce the oven temperature to 350°.

2. In a large mixing bowl, using a fork, blend the flour with the baking powder, lemon zest and a pinch of salt. In a food processor, grind the toasted almonds with the sugar to a fine powder; do not let the nuts turn into a paste. Add the almond powder to the flour mixture in the bowl. Add the carrots to the processor and whir until very finely chopped; add them to the bowl. Add the egg yolks to the bowl and stir until blended.

3. In a large stainless steel bowl, beat

Almond and Carrot Cake

Cinnamon Butter Cake

the egg whites with a pinch of salt until they hold firm peaks. Using a rubber spatula, stir one-third of the egg whites into the carrot mixture to loosen it, then gently fold in the remaining whites until the batter is just blended.

4. Scrape the batter into the prepared pan and bake for 30 minutes, or until the cake is just set. Transfer the cake to a rack and let it cool slightly in the pan. Unmold the cake onto a serving dish. Just before serving, sift confectioners' sugar over the top. Serve warm or at room temperature.

—*Silvana Daniello*

MAKE AHEAD The cake can be wrapped in foil and refrigerated for up to 1 week. Do not sift the confectioners' sugar over the top of the cake before refrigerating it.

Almond-and-Polenta Cake
MAKES TWO 9-INCH CAKES
You can bake the batter for this cake in two 9-inch pans or one 12-by-3-inch round pan. Either way, make certain that the cake is fully baked before removing it from the oven; otherwise it may sink in the center while cooling.

1½ cups instant polenta or fine cornmeal (½ pound)
½ cup all-purpose flour
1½ teaspoons baking powder
¼ teaspoon salt
3 sticks (¾ pound) unsalted butter, softened
2 cups sugar
4 cups (1 pound) finely ground blanched almonds (see Note)
2 teaspoons pure vanilla extract
6 large eggs, at room temperature
3 tablespoons fresh lemon juice
2 tablespoons grated lemon zest
Crème fraîche and assorted fresh fruits and berries, for serving

1. Preheat the oven to 325°. Butter and flour two 9-inch springform pans. In a medium bowl, sift together the polenta, flour, baking powder and salt.
2. In a large bowl, using an electric mixer, beat the butter and sugar at moderate speed until light and fluffy, about 5 minutes. Beat in the ground almonds and vanilla. Increase the speed to moderately high and add the eggs, 1 at a time, beating well after each addition. Add the lemon juice and lemon zest.
3. Reduce the speed to low and add

the sifted dry ingredients. Stir gently until thoroughly blended. Divide the batter between the 2 prepared cake pans. Bake for about 50 minutes, or until the cakes are golden brown and a cake tester inserted in the center comes out clean. Transfer the cakes to a rack and let cool completely.
4. Unmold the cakes onto serving platters. Cut into thin wedges. Serve with crème fraîche and fruit, if desired.

—*Martin Dodd*

NOTE To grind the almonds, pulse them in a food processor with 2 tablespoons of the sugar until finely ground; do not overprocess.

MAKE AHEAD The cakes can be made up to 1 day ahead. Cover them tightly and store at room temperature.

Semolina Soufflé Cake
MAKES ONE 10-INCH CAKE
This cake has a surprisingly delicate, soufflé-like texture. It needs to be refrigerated overnight, so take care to plan accordingly.

4½ cups milk
1½ cups sugar
1 cup semolina flour
1 stick (4 ounces) unsalted butter, softened
3 large eggs, lightly beaten
9 large eggs, separated
1 tablespoon pure vanilla extract
Pistachio Crème Anglaise and Tart Cherry—Pinot Noir Syrup (recipes follow)

1. Butter and flour a 10-inch springform pan. Wrap the outside of the pan with foil.
2. In a large heavy saucepan, combine the milk with ¾ cup of the sugar and bring to a boil. Whisk in the semolina and cook over low heat, whisking often, until thickened, about 2 minutes. Stir in half of the butter and the remaining ¾ cup of sugar and transfer to a large bowl. Let the semolina cool completely, stirring occasionally. Stir in the remaining butter, then

Almond-and-Polenta Cake

Semolina Soufflé Cake, with Pistachio Crème Anglaise and Tart Cherry–Pinot Noir Sauce.

stir in the 3 whole eggs, 9 egg yolks and the vanilla extract.

3. Preheat the oven to 350°. In a large bowl, beat the egg whites until stiff peaks form. Stir one-third of the beaten egg whites into the semolina to lighten it, then fold in the remaining whites. Pour the batter into the prepared pan.

4. Set the cake pan in a roasting pan and add enough hot water to reach halfway up the side of the cake pan. Bake in the center of the oven for 1 hour and 15 minutes, or until the cake is puffed and the center is still slightly jiggly. Transfer the cake to a wire rack to cool completely, then cover with plastic wrap and refrigerate overnight.

5. Run a knife around the edge of the cake and remove the side of the springform pan. Cut the cake into wedges and serve with the Pistachio Crème Anglaise and Tart Cherry–Pinot Noir Syrup.   —*Susan Spicer*

WINE Try a smooth, medium-sweet Vouvray. The subtle flavors of nuts and pears in the 1996 Domaine du Clos Naudin Foreau Demi Sec will nicely match the pistachios and complement the tart cherry flavor in this dessert.

PISTACHIO CREME ANGLAISE
MAKES 2 CUPS

The almond extract, although optional, adds more rich, nutty flavor to the silky crème anglaise.

- 1 **cup shelled unsalted pistachios (4 ounces)**
- 2 **cups milk**
- ½ **cup sugar**

Salt

- 8 **large egg yolks**
- ½ **teaspoon pure almond extract (optional)**

1. Preheat the oven to 350°. Spread the shelled pistachios on a rimmed baking sheet and bake for 5 minutes, or until lightly toasted. Let cool completely, then rub the pistachios in a kitchen towel to remove the skins. Transfer the pistachios to a food processor and grind to a fine powder.

2. In a medium saucepan, combine the milk with the pistachios and bring to a boil. Cover, remove from the heat and let stand for 30 minutes.

3. Strain the pistachio milk through a fine sieve into another medium saucepan. Add the sugar and a pinch of salt. Whisk in the egg yolks and cook over low heat, whisking constantly, until the custard sauce is thick enough to coat the back of a spoon, about 8 minutes. Do not let the custard boil.

4. Strain the sauce through a fine

sieve into a bowl. Stir in the almond extract and let cool, stirring often. Cover and refrigerate until ready to serve. —S.S.

MAKE AHEAD The crème anglaise can be refrigerated for 2 days.

TART CHERRY—PINOT NOIR SYRUP

MAKES 2 CUPS

- 2 **cups dried tart cherries (¾ pound)**
- 2 **cups Pinot Noir**
- ½ **cup sugar**

Combine all of the ingredients in a saucepan and bring to a boil. Simmer over low heat for 5 minutes. Using a slotted spoon, transfer the cherries to a medium bowl. Simmer the wine over moderate heat until syrupy and reduced to ¾ cup, about 8 minutes. Transfer the Pinot Noir syrup to a small bowl to cool, then stir in the cherries. Serve at room temperature. —S.S.

MAKE AHEAD The syrup can be made before the rest of the dessert and refrigerated for 1 week. Bring to room temperature before serving.

Cinnamon Financiers

MAKES 8 INDIVIDUAL CAKES

Financiers are small, buttery French almond cakes. They're often served at teatime, but with poached figs they make a great ending to a meal.

- ½ **cup whole blanched almonds**
- 1½ **cups confectioners' sugar**
- ⅓ **cup all-purpose flour**
- 1 **teaspoon cinnamon**

Salt

- 4 **large egg whites**
- ½ **tablespoon Calvados**
- 6 **tablespoons unsalted butter, melted and kept warm**

Figs Poached in Port (recipe follows)

I. Preheat the oven to 350°. Butter 8 cups of a 12-cup muffin pan. In a food processor, grind the almonds to a fine powder, taking care not to over-process them to a paste. Transfer to a

Cinnamon Financiers, with Figs Poached in Port.

medium bowl and whisk in the confectioners' sugar, flour, cinnamon and a pinch of salt.

2. In a large stainless-steel bowl, beat the egg whites with a pinch of salt until soft peaks form. Using a rubber spatula, gradually fold in the almond mixture and then the Calvados. Gently fold in the melted butter and spoon the batter into the prepared muffin cups. Bake for about 25 minutes, or until the *financiers* spring back when lightly pressed. Transfer to a rack and let cool for 15 minutes. Run a paring knife around the *financiers* and lift them out of the pan.

3. Set a warm *financier* on each plate. Arrange 2 poached fig halves beside each *financier,* spoon a little of the port syrup over the figs and serve.

—*Victor Scargle*

WINE The black Mission figs and port reduction call out for a wine with the flavor of blackberry preserves. The 1995 Case Pinot Noir provides this as well as the flavors of dark cherry, blueberry, black currants and spice.

FIGS POACHED IN PORT

8 SERVINGS

These poached figs make a delicious accompaniment to cakes and ice creams. Double the recipe to use the figs as a dessert on their own or served with butter cookies.

- ½ **cup water**
- ¼ **cup sugar**
- 1 **cup Ruby Port**
- 4 **thin slices of lemon**
- ½ **cinnamon stick**
- ½ **vanilla bean, spilt lengthwise**
- 8 **dried plump black Mission figs, halved lengthwise**

In a medium saucepan, combine the water and sugar and bring to a boil. Add the port, lemon slices, cinnamon stick and vanilla bean. Cover and simmer over low heat for 15 minutes. Add the figs, cover and simmer until tender, about 15 minutes. Let cool slightly and remove the lemon slices, cinnamon stick and vanilla bean. —*V.S.*

MAKE AHEAD The poached figs can be refrigerated in the port syrup for up to 3 days. Serve at room temperature.

Hazelnut Tea Cake with Moscato Pears

MAKES ONE 8-INCH CAKE

- 2 Bartlett pears—peeled, cut into 8 wedges and cored
- ¾ cup Moscato d'Asti
- 1 cup hazelnuts (4 ounces)
- 7 tablespoons unsalted butter, softened
- ¼ cup plus 2 tablespoons sugar
- 4 large egg yolks
- ½ teaspoon pure vanilla extract
- ¼ cup all-purpose flour
- 3 large egg whites
- ½ cup heavy cream

I. In a bowl, combine the pears with the Moscato d'Asti and let stand at room temperature for 2 to 4 hours.

2. Preheat the oven to 350°. Butter and flour an 8-by-1-inch round cake pan. Put the hazelnuts on a rimmed baking sheet and bake for 12 minutes, or until richly browned. Transfer the hazelnuts to a kitchen towel and let cool completely. Rub the hazelnuts in the towel to remove the skins. In a food processor, pulse the nuts until they're finely ground; be careful not to overprocess to a paste.

3. In a large bowl, using a handheld mixer, beat 6 tablespoons of the butter with ¼ cup of the sugar until light and fluffy. Beat in the egg yolks, 1 at a time, until thoroughly incorporated. Add the vanilla, then fold in the hazelnuts and flour.

4. In a stainless-steel bowl, beat the egg whites until soft peaks form. Add the remaining 2 tablespoons of sugar and beat until almost-firm shiny peaks

form. Stir one-third of the egg whites into the cake batter to lighten it, then fold in the remaining whites. Scrape the batter into the prepared pan and bake for about 20 minutes, or until a cake tester inserted in the center comes out clean. Transfer the cake to a rack and let it cool slightly in the pan. Run a thin knife around the cake and unmold it. Cover loosely with a kitchen towel.

5. Drain the Moscato d'Asti into a small saucepan. Simmer over low heat until reduced to 3 tablespoons, about 10 minutes. Let the syrup cool, then refrigerate.

6. In a large skillet, melt the remaining 1 tablespoon of butter. Add the pear wedges and cook over moderately high heat until browned, about 4 minutes per side. Arrange the pear wedges on top of the cake in a radiating pattern.

7. In a stainless-steel bowl, beat the cream until it starts to thicken. Add the reduced Moscato d'Asti and beat until soft peaks form. Serve the hazelnut cake with the whipped cream.

—*Marcia Kiesel*

WINE The low-alcohol (5.5 percent), off-dry 1999 La Spinetta Moscato d'Asti Bricco Quaglia from Giorgio Rivetti is sweet without being cloying, and its fruit aromas and nutty overtones point up similar flavors in this subtly sweet dessert. The wine's elegant, crisp bubbles also provide a delicious contrast to the whipped cream accompaniment.

Gingerbread

MAKES THREE 9-BY-4-INCH LOAVES

- 4 cups all-purpose flour
- 2 teaspoons baking soda
- 1 teaspoon baking powder
- 1 tablespoon plus 2 teaspoons ground ginger
- 1 tablespoon freshly grated nutmeg
- 1½ teaspoons ground cloves
- ¼ teaspoon freshly ground pepper

- 1 stick (4 ounces) unsalted butter, at room temperature
- 1 box (1 pound) dark brown sugar
- 4 large eggs
- 1 cup sour cream
- ⅓ cup finely grated peeled fresh ginger (from a 2-ounce piece)
- ¾ cup plus 2 tablespoons unsulphured molasses dissolved in 1 cup hot water
- ¼ cup finely chopped candied ginger

Lightly sweetened whipped cream, for serving

I. Preheat the oven to 350°. Grease and flour three 9-by-4-inch loaf pans. In a large bowl, sift together the flour, baking soda, baking powder, ground ginger, nutmeg, cloves and pepper.

2. In another large bowl, using a handheld electric mixer, beat the butter until creamy. Add the brown sugar and beat until blended. Add the eggs, 1 at a time, and beat until smooth, then beat in the sour cream and grated ginger. At medium speed, beat in the dry ingredients in 3 batches, alternating with the molasses.

3. Pour the batter into the prepared pans and sprinkle with the candied ginger. Bake in the center of the oven for about 50 minutes, or until a toothpick inserted in the loaves comes out clean. Let cool in the pans for 15 minutes, then turn the loaves out onto a rack to cool completely. Cut the gingerbread in thick slices and serve with whipped cream. —*René Becker*

MAKE AHEAD The loaves can be wrapped in wax paper and then in foil and frozen for up to 1 month.

Country Cake with Strawberries and Whipped Cream

MAKES ONE 8-INCH CAKE

This recipe comes from *Barefoot Contessa Parties!* (Clarkson N. Potter). You can double it and prepare two cakes at a time: one to serve right away and a second to freeze for later.

Country Cake with Strawberries and Whipped Cream

1 cup all-purpose flour

2 tablespoons cornstarch

¼ teaspoon baking soda

¼ teaspoon salt

6 tablespoons unsalted butter, softened

¾ cup plus 3 tablespoons sugar

2 large eggs

¼ cup plus 2 tablespoons sour cream

1½ teaspoons finely grated orange zest

½ teaspoon finely grated lemon zest

1 teaspoon pure vanilla extract

1 cup heavy cream

1 pint strawberries, hulled and sliced

1. Preheat the oven to 350°. Butter and flour an 8-inch round cake pan. In a medium bowl, sift the flour with the cornstarch, baking soda and salt.

2. In a large bowl, using a handheld mixer, beat the butter until creamy. Add the ¾ cup of sugar and beat at medium speed until light and fluffy. Add the eggs, 1 at a time, beating until incorporated. Add the sour cream, the orange and lemon zests and ½ teaspoon of the vanilla and beat until blended. Add the dry ingredients and beat at low speed until smooth.

3. Scrape the batter into the prepared pan and bake for about 40 minutes, or until golden and a skewer inserted in the center comes out clean. Transfer the pan to a wire rack and let the cake cool for 15 minutes before turning it out onto the rack to cool completely.

4. Beat the cream with the remaining 3 tablespoons of sugar and ½ teaspoon of vanilla until soft peaks form.

5. Slice the cake in half horizontally. Spread most of the whipped cream over the cut side of the bottom cake half. Layer most of the sliced strawberries on top. Replace the top half of the cake and garnish with the remaining whipped cream and strawberries.

—*Ina Garten*

MAKE AHEAD The Country Cake can be frozen for up to 1 month. Let it cool completely before wrapping in plastic and then foil. The fully assembled cake can be prepared up to 2 hours before serving.

WINE The delicate and elegant 1996 Wölffer Brut Sparkling Wine, made by the traditional *méthode champenoise,* is wonderful with this citrus-spiked, light and not-too-sweet cake.

Orange and Cardamom Upside-Down Cake

MAKES ONE 10-INCH CAKE

The cardamom in this cake is an exotic accent for a very traditional recipe.

TOPPING

4 navel oranges

2 tablespoons unsalted butter

¾ cup light brown sugar

½ teaspoon ground cardamom

CAKE

1½ cups all-purpose flour

1½ teaspoons ground cardamom

1½ teaspoons baking powder

½ teaspoon salt

6 tablespoons unsalted butter, softened

⅔ cup granulated sugar

2 large eggs, at room temperature

½ cup whole milk

1 teaspoon pure vanilla extract

Finely grated zest of 1 orange

Lightly sweetened whipped cream, for serving

1. MAKE THE TOPPING: Preheat the oven to 350°. Using a knife, peel the oranges; be sure to remove all of the bitter white pith. Working over a bowl, cut in between the membranes to release the sections into the bowl; pour off and reserve the juice for another use.

2. In a 10-inch cast-iron skillet, melt the butter with the brown sugar and the ½ teaspoon of cardamom until moistened. Remove from the heat and let stand for 10 minutes.

3. Arrange the orange sections in the skillet in 2 concentric circles with all of the oranges facing the same direction. Pack the oranges tightly together and place 1 orange section in the center to fill the empty space.

4. MAKE THE CAKE: In a small bowl, mix the flour with the 1½ teaspoons of cardamom, baking powder and salt. In a large bowl, using an electric mixer, beat the butter with the sugar until fluffy. Add the eggs 1 at a time, beating well after each addition. Stir in half of the dry ingredients, then stir in the milk, vanilla and orange zest. Stir in the remaining dry ingredients until just combined.

5. Spoon the batter over the orange sections. Bake for about 40 minutes, or until the cake springs back when pressed. Let the cake cool for at least 15 minutes, then turn it out onto a platter. Serve with whipped cream.

—*David Lebovitz*

MAKE AHEAD The cake can be kept at room temperature for up to 1 day. Serve at room temperature or rewarm in a 325° oven for 10 minutes.

Giraffe-Spot Cake

MAKES ONE 6-INCH LAYER CAKE

1⅔ cups cake flour

2 teaspoons baking powder

Pinch of salt

1 stick plus 2 tablespoons (5 ounces) unsalted butter, at room temperature

1 cup sugar

3 large eggs

1 teaspoon pure vanilla extract

Finely grated zest of 1 lemon

1 cup milk

1 cup apricot preserves—melted, strained and cooled

Cream Cheese Frosting (recipe follows)

Red and green food coloring

2 tablespoons water

¼ teaspoon unflavored gelatin

1. Preheat the oven to 350°. Butter an 11-by-17-inch jelly-roll pan and line the bottom with wax paper. Butter the paper and flour the pan, tapping out the excess flour.

2. In a medium bowl, whisk the flour with the baking powder and salt. In a large bowl, using a handheld electric mixer, cream the butter. Add the sugar and beat until fluffy. Add the eggs, 1 at a time, beating well between additions. Beat in the vanilla and lemon zest. Beat in the dry ingredients in 3 additions, alternating with the milk; beat at medium speed until smooth.

3. Pour the batter into the prepared pan and smooth the surface. Bake for 20 minutes, or until the cake is golden and beginning to brown around the edges. Transfer the cake to a wire rack and let it cool.

4. Turn the cake out onto a work surface and peel off the wax paper. Using a 6-inch plate or pot lid as a guide, cut out 3 rounds from the cake. Save the cake scraps for a snack.

5. Beat 1 tablespoon of the apricot preserves into ½ cup of the Cream Cheese Frosting. Place 1 cake round on a plate. Spread it with half the apricot frosting and top with a second cake layer. Spread with the remaining apricot frosting and top with the last cake layer. Brush the remaining melted apricot preserves all over the top and sides of the cake. Refrigerate the cake for at least 10 minutes.

6. Spread all the remaining Cream Cheese Frosting over the top and sides of the cake. Refrigerate until chilled.

7. In a heatproof bowl, mix 3 drops each of red and green food coloring with the water. Sprinkle the unflavored gelatin over the dyed water and let stand until softened. Place the bowl in a small skillet of boiling water and stir the mixture just until the gelatin melts.

Using a small paintbrush, paint rounded squares all over the cake to create a giraffe-spot pattern. —*Grace Parisi*

CREAM CHEESE FROSTING
MAKES 1⅓ CUPS

- 8 ounces cream cheese, softened
- 4 tablespoons unsalted butter, at room temperature
- ¼ cup sifted confectioners' sugar
- ½ teaspoon fresh lemon juice
- 1 tablespoon water
- ¾ teaspoon unflavored gelatin

1. In a medium bowl, beat the softened cream cheese with the butter at medium speed until smooth. Beat in the sifted confectioners' sugar and fresh lemon juice.

2. Put the water in a small heatproof bowl. Add the unflavored gelatin and let stand until softened, approximately 5 minutes. Place the bowl in a small saucepan of boiling water and stir just until the gelatin melts. Beat the gelatin mixture into the frosting and use immediately. —*G.P.*

Almond Layer Cake with Lemon Frosting
MAKES ONE 9-INCH CAKE

CAKE

- 1¾ cups all-purpose flour
- 1½ teaspoons baking powder
- ¼ teaspoon salt
- 1⅓ cups granulated sugar
- 7 ounces almond paste
- 2 sticks (½ pound) unsalted butter, softened
- 4 large eggs, at room temperature
- 2 large egg yolks
- ½ cup whole milk

FROSTING AND FILLING

- 4 tablespoons unsalted butter, softened
- 3½ cups sifted confectioners' sugar
- Finely grated zest of 2 lemons
- 3 tablespoons whole milk
- ½ cup seedless raspberry jam
- ½ cup sliced almonds, lightly toasted

Giraffe-Spot Cake

1. MAKE THE CAKE: Preheat the oven to 350°. Butter two 9-inch cake pans and line the bottoms with parchment paper. Butter the paper.

2. In a bowl, combine the flour with the baking powder and salt. In another bowl, using an electric mixer, beat the granulated sugar with the almond paste until it forms fine crumbs. Add the butter and beat until light and fluffy. Add the eggs and yolks 1 at a time; beat well after each addition. Stir in half of the dry ingredients and then the milk. Stir in the remaining dry ingredients until the batter is smooth.

3. Pour the batter into the prepared cake pans. Bake for about 40 minutes, or until a tester inserted in the center of each cake comes out clean. Transfer the cakes to a wire rack and cool them completely in their pans.

4. MAKE THE FROSTING: In a bowl, using an electric mixer, beat the butter with 1½ cups of the confectioners' sugar and the lemon zest until smooth. Beat in the milk. Stir in the remaining 2 cups of confectioners' sugar and beat until smooth.

5. Invert the cakes onto a work surface; peel off and discard the paper. Set 1 cake on a plate and spread the jam on top. Set the other cake on top and spread the frosting all over the top and sides. Sprinkle the almonds on top and refrigerate for 30 minutes before serving.   —*David Lebovitz*

MAKE AHEAD The cake can be refrigerated for up to 2 days. Bring to room temperature before serving.

Coconut Custard Cake

MAKES ONE 9-INCH CAKE

San Francisco's Boulevard restaurant reinterprets a traditional Hawaiian *haupia,* a coconut custard–like dessert, as a creamy frosting sandwiched between layers of simple yellow cake. The cake is topped with shredded coconut and served chilled with fresh pineapple or a tropical fruit salad.

CAKE

1½ **cups cake flour**
1½ **teaspoons baking powder**
1 **teaspoon baking soda**
Pinch of salt
½ **cup buttermilk**
¼ **cup unsweetened coconut milk**
½ **teaspoon pure vanilla extract**
6 **tablespoons unsalted butter, softened**
1 **cup sugar**
2 **eggs, at room temperature**

TOPPING AND FROSTING

1½ **cups shredded sweetened coconut (3 ounces)**
1½ **cups unsweetened coconut milk**
¼ **cup sugar**
3 **tablespoons cornstarch**
4 **ounces cream cheese, at room temperature**
2 **ounces white chocolate, finely chopped**
½ **teaspoon pure vanilla extract**
Pinch of salt
½ **cup heavy cream**

1. MAKE THE CAKE: Preheat the oven to 350°. Butter and flour a 9-by-2-inch round cake pan. In a medium bowl, sift the cake flour with the baking powder, baking soda and salt. In another bowl, combine the buttermilk with the coconut milk and the vanilla extract.

2. In a large bowl, using an electric mixer, beat the butter until creamy. Add the sugar and beat at medium speed until light and fluffy. Add the eggs, 1 at a time, beating well after each addition. At low speed, beat in the dry ingredients in 3 batches, alternating with the buttermilk mixture.

3. Scrape the batter into the prepared pan and lightly smooth the surface. Bake for about 40 minutes, or until the cake is golden and a tester inserted in the center comes out clean. Let the cake cool in the pan for 15 minutes, then invert it onto a wire rack and let cool completely. Wrap the cake in plastic and refrigerate until chilled.

4. MAKE THE TOPPING AND THE FROSTING: If toasting the coconut, spread it on a rimmed baking sheet and bake for about 7 minutes, stirring frequently, until golden and crisp. Transfer the toasted coconut to a plate and let cool completely.

5. In a small saucepan, combine 1 cup of the coconut milk with the sugar and bring the mixture to a boil over moderate heat, stirring until the sugar dissolves. Meanwhile, in a small bowl, mix the remaining ½ cup of coconut milk with the cornstarch until smooth, and then whisk the mixture into the boiling coconut milk. Cook this custard over moderate heat, stirring constantly with a wooden spoon, until it is very thick, about 2 minutes.

6. Remove the coconut custard from the heat and whisk in the cream cheese, white chocolate, vanilla and salt; stir until completely smooth. Scrape the coconut custard into a large bowl and press a sheet of plastic wrap directly on the surface. Refrigerate the custard until chilled, at least 2 hours.

7. In a medium bowl, beat the heavy cream until stiff. Whisk one-fourth of the whipped cream into the coconut custard until blended, then fold in the remaining whipped cream.

8. Using a long serrated knife, cut the cake in half horizontally. Center the top cake layer on a plate, cut side up. Using a long metal spatula, thinly spread 1 scant cup of the frosting over the cake. Center the bottom layer of the cake, cut side down, on top of the frosting.

9. Spread the top and sides of the cake with the remaining coconut custard frosting. Sprinkle the shredded coconut evenly over the top and sides of the cake, pressing it lightly to adhere. Refrigerate until chilled, at least 2 hours. Cut the cake with a hot knife, wiping the blade between slices.
—*Heather Ho*

Coconut Cake

MAKES ONE 8-INCH LAYER CAKE

2½ cups cake flour

2½ teaspoons baking powder

¼ teaspoon salt

½ cup milk

½ cup unsweetened coconut milk

1 stick plus 2 tablespoons (5 ounces) unsalted butter, softened

1½ cups granulated sugar

3 large egg yolks

1 teaspoon pure vanilla extract

5 large egg whites

½ cup seedless raspberry jam

Seven-Minute Frosting (recipe follows)

Confectioners' sugar, for dusting

2½ cups (7 ounces) freshly grated coconut (see Note) or shredded sweetened coconut

1. Preheat the oven to 350°. Butter two 8-inch round cake pans and line the bottoms with parchment paper. Butter and flour the pans, tapping out excess flour.

2. In a small bowl, sift the cake flour with the baking powder and salt. In a small pitcher, combine the milk with the coconut milk. In a medium bowl, beat the butter at medium speed until creamy. Slowly add the granulated sugar and beat until light and fluffy, scraping down the sides of the bowl. Add the egg yolks and vanilla and beat until smooth. At low speed, add the dry ingredients in 3 batches, alternating with the milk mixture; beat until smooth.

3. In another bowl, using clean beaters, beat the egg whites at high speed until firm but not dry. Stir one-third of the beaten whites into the batter until smooth, then fold in the remaining whites until no white streaks remain.

4. Divide the batter evenly between the prepared cake pans and smooth the surfaces. Bake for 35 minutes, or until the tops spring back when lightly pressed and a toothpick inserted into the centers comes out with just a few moist crumbs attached. Let the cakes cool in the pans for 10 minutes, then turn them out onto a wire rack to cool completely. Peel off the parchment.

5. Using a sharp serrated knife, cut each cake into 2 even layers. Spread the raspberry jam between the cut layers of each cake and then reassemble. Place 1 cake on a serving plate, right side up. Tuck 4 wide strips of wax paper under the cake to cover the plate. Spread 1½ cups of the Seven-Minute Frosting on the top and then center the second cake over the first. Spread the frosting liberally over and around the cake. Dust your hands lightly with confectioners' sugar and press the coconut onto the side of the cake. Sprinkle the rest of the coconut on the top. Let the cake stand at room temperature for at least 30 minutes before slicing. —*Grace Parisi*

NOTE To grate fresh coconut, crack open a whole coconut; discard the liquid. Place the coconut pieces on a baking sheet and bake at 350° for 5 minutes to loosen the flesh from the shell; let cool. Peel the brown skin from the coconut meat, then shred the pieces in a food processor using the fine grating disk.

MAKE AHEAD The cake can be kept at room temperature in an airtight container for up to 3 days. The layers can be frozen separately for 1 month.

WINE Sparkling wine is an elegant partner for this classic cake. Opt for a sweet, round-textured bottling, such as Veuve Clicquot's Demi-Sec Champagne or a Schramsberg Demi-Sec Crémant from California.

SEVEN-MINUTE FROSTING

MAKES ABOUT 4 CUPS

4 large egg whites, at room temperature

2 cups sugar

⅓ cup water

Pinch of salt

½ teaspoon pure vanilla extract

In a large stainless-steel bowl, mix the egg whites with the sugar, water and salt. Set the bowl over a saucepan filled with 2 inches of boiling water and beat the egg whites at high speed until stiff and glossy, about 7 minutes. Remove the bowl from the heat, add the vanilla and continue to beat at high speed until the frosting is cool to the touch, about 8 minutes longer. Use immediately. —*G.P.*

Double-Baked Chocolate Cake

MAKES ONE 9-INCH CAKE

This rich and luscious chocolate cake is great for entertaining because it can be prepared through the first baking, kept in the refrigerator and then popped in the oven for the second baking just before serving.

½ pound bittersweet or semisweet chocolate, coarsely chopped

2 sticks (½ pound) unsalted butter

¾ cup unsweetened cocoa powder

7 large eggs, separated

1⅓ cups sugar

Hazelnut Ice Cream (p. 385) or vanilla ice cream, for serving

1. Preheat the oven to 350°. Butter a 9-inch springform pan and line the bottom with wax paper. Butter the paper, then dust the pan with flour, tapping out any excess.

2. In a large saucepan, melt the chopped chocolate with the butter over moderately low heat. Add the cocoa powder and stir until smooth.

3. In a medium bowl, using an electric mixer, beat the egg yolks with ⅔ cup of the sugar until pale and light, about 3 minutes. In a large bowl, using clean beaters, beat the egg whites until soft peaks form. Gradually add the remaining ⅔ cup of sugar and beat until the whites are firm and glossy.

4. Fold the chocolate into the egg yolk mixture until barely combined. Fold in the egg whites just until no white streaks remain. Spoon 2 cups of the batter into a medium bowl and refrigerate. Scrape the remaining batter into

the prepared pan and smooth the top with a spatula. Bake for 45 minutes, or until the cake is puffed and a toothpick inserted in the center comes out clean. Cool completely on a wire rack.

5. Remove the side from the springform pan and spread the reserved cake batter over the top of the cake, leaving a 1-inch border around the edge. Chill the cake for at least 1 hour.

6. Preheat the oven to 425°. Bake the cake for 10 minutes, or until a thin crust forms on top and the batter is soft and creamy beneath the crust. Let the cake cool for 10 minutes, then cut into wedges and serve warm with the Hazelnut Ice Cream. —*Sara Guerin*

N O T E Bake all of the chocolate cake batter in Step 4 if you have any concerns about eating egg yolks that are less than fully cooked.

M A K E   A H E A D The cake can be prepared through Step 4 and refrigerated, covered, for up to 2 days.

W I N E The dense chocolate pairs well with an aromatic, spicy wine, like the 1997 Pepper Bridge Vineyard Apogee.

Soft Chocolate Cakes

MAKES 6 INDIVIDUAL CAKES

When they're both in Paris, Johnny Depp and John Malkovich often drop in together at Man Ray. They have a ritual: First they go into the kitchen and say hello. Then the chefs make a menu for them that often includes sushi, the restaurant's specialty. They almost always finish with this chocolate cake.

- 1 stick (4 ounces) unsalted butter, cut into pieces
- 4 ounces bittersweet chocolate, coarsely chopped
- 3 large eggs
- ½ cup sugar
- ⅓ cup all-purpose flour

Whipped cream, for serving

I. Preheat the oven to 450°. Butter and lightly flour six 6-ounce ramekins; tap out the excess flour. Set the ramekins on a baking sheet.

2. Melt the butter in a small saucepan. Put the chocolate in a small bowl, pour the butter on top and stir until smooth.

3. In a bowl, using an electric mixer, beat the eggs with the sugar at medium speed until thick and pale. Beat in the flour; add the chocolate. Spoon the batter into the prepared ramekins. Bake in the center of the oven for about 12 minutes, or until the tops of the cakes begin to crack.

4. Let the cakes cool in the ramekins for 1 minute. Run a thin knife around the sides of the cakes to loosen them, then cover each ramekin with an inverted dessert plate. Turn them over, let stand for a few seconds and then remove the ramekins. Serve the cakes immediately with a dollop of whipped cream. Alternatively, serve the cakes in the ramekins and pass the whipped cream at the table. —*Man Ray, Paris*

Grandma Martha's Chocolate Roll

12 SERVINGS

- 6 ounces semisweet chocolate, finely chopped
- 3 tablespoons strong brewed coffee
- 6 large eggs, separated
- ¾ cup sugar

Unsweetened cocoa, for sifting

- 1 cup heavy cream
- 1 tablespoon dark rum

Candied flowers, such as violets, for garnish (optional)

I. Preheat the oven to 350°. Lightly butter a 10-by-15-inch jelly-roll pan and line it with wax paper. Butter the paper. In a medium saucepan, melt the chocolate in the coffee over low heat, stirring constantly. Let cool slightly.

2. In a large bowl, using an electric

Soft Chocolate Cake

Chocolate Cake with Cashews, Berries and Whipped Cream

whipped cream evenly over the cake. Beginning at a long edge and using the kitchen towel to help guide you, carefully roll up the cake. Transfer the cake to a platter and sift additional cocoa on top. Garnish with candied flowers, if using, and serve.

—*Bruce and Eric Bromberg*

MAKE AHEAD The chocolate roll can be made a day before serving and refrigerated overnight.

Chocolate Cake with Cashews, Berries and Whipped Cream

MAKES ONE 9-BY-13-INCH CAKE
For a moist and dense brownie-like effect, reduce the cake's baking time by about 5 minutes.

- 2 cups all-purpose flour
- 1½ cups unsweetened cocoa powder, plus more for dusting
- 1 teaspoon baking powder
- ½ teaspoon salt
- 2 sticks (½ pound) unsalted butter, softened
- 2 cups sugar
- 6 large eggs, at room temperature
- 2 tablespoons light corn syrup
- 2 teaspoons pure vanilla extract
- ½ cup chopped roasted cashews

Whipped cream and raspberries, for serving

1. Preheat the oven to 350°. Butter a 9-by-13-inch metal baking pan. In a medium bowl, sift the flour with 1½ cups of cocoa, the baking powder and the salt. In a large bowl, beat the butter with the sugar until light and fluffy. Beat in the eggs, 1 at a time, then the corn syrup and vanilla. Using a rubber spatula, fold in the dry ingredients and the cashews.

2. Scrape the batter into the prepared pan and bake for about 25 minutes, or until just set. Let the cake cool to room temperature in the pan. Sift cocoa over the cake and cut it into squares. Serve the cake with freshly whipped cream and raspberries.

—*Daniel Bruce*

mixer, beat the egg yolks with the sugar until pale and thick. Add the melted chocolate and beat at low speed until blended.

3. In a large stainless-steel bowl, using clean beaters, beat the egg whites until firm peaks form. Stir one-fourth of the beaten egg whites into the chocolate mixture to lighten it, then gently fold in the remaining whites.

4. Spread the batter evenly in the prepared pan and bake for about 15 minutes, or until a toothpick inserted in the center comes out clean. Move

the pan to a rack. Cover the cake with a kitchen towel and let it cool completely. Refrigerate for 30 minutes.

5. Remove the towel and generously sift cocoa over the entire surface of the cake. Run a knife along the edge of the pan to loosen the cake. Cover the cake with a clean kitchen towel. Place a large flat baking sheet over the towel; invert the cake onto the baking sheet and remove the jelly-roll pan. Gently peel the paper off the cake.

6. Beat the cream until stiff peaks form, then stir in the rum. Spread the

Flourless Chocolate-Almond Cakes

MAKES EIGHT 3-INCH CAKES

Mélisse, in Santa Monica, California, adds a twist to traditional molten chocolate cakes by stirring in sliced toasted almonds.

3 cups sliced almonds (about 10 ounces)

1½ sticks (6 ounces) unsalted butter, softened

⅔ cup plus 2 tablespoons sugar

4 large eggs, separated

½ pound bittersweet chocolate, finely chopped

2 large egg whites

Confectioners' sugar, for dusting

Lightly sweetened whipped cream, for serving

1. Preheat the oven to 350°. Lightly butter eight 3-inch-wide, 2-inch-deep metal rings or cleaned 6-ounce tuna cans, bottoms removed; coat with flour. Butter a large rimmed baking sheet and arrange the molds on the sheet.

2. Spread the sliced almonds on another rimmed baking sheet and toast in the oven for about 6 minutes, stirring a few times, until golden brown. Transfer the almonds to a plate and let cool completely. Set aside ½ cup for garnish; pulse the remaining almonds in a food processor until finely ground, taking care not to overprocess to a paste. Leave the oven on.

3. In a large bowl, using an electric mixer, beat the butter with ⅔ cup of the sugar on moderately high speed until light and fluffy, about 5 minutes. Beat in the egg yolks, 1 at a time, until thoroughly incorporated. Fold in the ground almonds and the chocolate.

4. In a large bowl, beat all 6 egg whites until soft peaks form. Add the remaining 2 tablespoons of sugar and beat until firm, glossy peaks form. Fold one-third of the beaten whites into the chocolate mixture to loosen it, then fold in the remaining whites just until

blended. Spoon the batter into the prepared molds, filling them three-quarters full. Bake the chocolate-almond cakes for about 25 minutes, or until risen and just set in the center. Let the cakes cool slightly in the molds.

5. Run a thin knife around the sides of the molds, then lift them off the cakes. Transfer the cakes to individual plates. Garnish the tops of the cakes with the reserved toasted almonds and dust them with confectioners' sugar. Spoon a dollop of whipped cream alongside and serve.

—Josiah Citrin

WINE For this rich but not overly sweet cake, try the 1990 Château d'Yquem Sauternes or the much more affordable Bonny Doon Nonvintage Muscat Vin de Glacière.

Elizabeth David's Chocolate Cake

MAKES ONE 8-INCH CAKE

Based on a recipe in *Elizabeth David's French Provincial Cooking,* this cake has been popular since the early 1960s.

5 ounces bittersweet chocolate, chopped

6 tablespoons unsalted butter

1 tablespoon brewed espresso

1 tablespoon dark rum

½ cup sugar

½ cup almonds, blanched whole, then finely ground (see Note)

3 large eggs, separated

1. Preheat the oven to 300°. Butter and flour an 8-inch round cake pan.

2. In a large heatproof bowl set over a pan of simmering water, combine the chocolate with the butter, espresso and rum and stir until melted and smooth. Remove the bowl from the heat and stir in the sugar and ground almonds. Let the chocolate mixture cool slightly, then beat in the egg yolks, 1 at a time.

3. In a clean stainless-steel bowl, beat

the egg whites to stiff peaks. Stir one-third of the beaten whites into the chocolate mixture, then fold in the remaining whites until fully incorporated. Pour the batter into the prepared pan and bake for 45 minutes, or until a toothpick inserted in the center of the cake comes out clean. Let the cake cool completely on a rack before inverting it onto a platter.

—Sara Jenkins

MAKE AHEAD The cooled cake can be wrapped in plastic and stored overnight at room temperature.

NOTE When grinding almonds in a food processor, pulse only until they turn to a fine powder; overprocessing will create a paste.

WINE This intense cake calls for a beautifully balanced red Amarone Recioto from the Veneto. The 1994 Quintarelli, with its rich, dark notes of dried raisins, is perfect. Less expensive options are the 1994 Santi, the 1993 Tedeschi and the 1993 Allegrini.

Elizabeth David's Chocolate Cake

Mango Cheesecakes with Macadamia Shortbread Crust

MAKES 6 INDIVIDUAL CAKES

CHEESECAKES

- 3 large ripe mangoes
- 1/3 cup plus 1 teaspoon sugar, plus more for dusting
- 12 ounces cream cheese, softened
- 2 eggs, at room temperature
- 1 tablespoon fresh lemon juice
- 1/2 teaspoon pure vanilla extract

SHORTBREAD

- 1/2 cup unsalted macadamia nuts, toasted and finely chopped
- 1/2 cup all-purpose flour
- 2 tablespoons rice flour
- 2 tablespoons granulated sugar
- 2 tablespoons dark brown sugar
- 1/4 teaspoon salt
- 4 tablespoons cold unsalted butter, cut into small pieces
- 1 tablespoon cold milk
- 1/4 teaspoon pure vanilla extract

Coconut-Tapioca Sauce, for serving (recipe follows)

I. MAKE THE CHEESECAKES: Preheat the oven to 325°. Spray six 6-ounce ramekins with cooking spray. Lightly dust the ramekins with granulated sugar, tapping out the excess.

2. Peel the mangoes. Cut 1 of the mangoes off the central pit in neat slices and set aside. Coarsely chop the 2 remaining mangoes. In a food processor, combine the chopped mangoes with 1 teaspoon of the sugar and puree until smooth. Strain the puree through a fine sieve set over a small bowl.

3. In a large bowl, beat the cream cheese with the remaining 1/3 cup sugar until creamy. Add the eggs, 1 at a time, and beat until smooth. Stir in the mango puree, lemon juice and vanilla. Pour the mixture into the prepared ramekins and set them in a roasting pan. Pour enough water into the pan to reach halfway up the sides of the ramekins.

4. Bake the cheesecakes for about 30 minutes, or until firm around the edges and slightly soft in the middle. Remove the ramekins from the water bath and let cool. Cover the cheesecakes with plastic wrap and refrigerate for at least 6 hours or for up to 2 days.

5. MAKE THE SHORTBREAD: In a food processor, combine the macadamias with the all-purpose flour, rice flour, granulated sugar, brown sugar and salt; pulse until the nuts are finely chopped. Add the butter and pulse until the dough resembles coarse meal. With the machine on, add the milk and vanilla, and process until the dough just comes together.

6. Roll out the dough between 2 sheets of wax paper to form a 1/4-inch-thick rectangle. Refrigerate until firm, at least 1 hour or overnight.

7. Preheat the oven to 325°. Peel off the top layer of wax paper and use a 2 3/4-inch round biscuit cutter to stamp out 6 rounds. Set the rounds on a baking sheet lined with parchment paper and bake for 12 to 15 minutes, or until the edges are light brown and the centers are firm. Transfer the rounds to wire racks to cool completely.

8. Just before serving, tilt the ramekins over the sink to drain off any liquid. Top each cheesecake with a shortbread round and invert them onto dessert plates. Garnish with the mango slices. Serve with the Coconut-Tapioca Sauce. —Heather Ho

COCONUT-TAPIOCA SAUCE

MAKES ABOUT 1 1/2 CUPS

- 1/3 cup small pearl tapioca
- 1 1/4 cups unsweetened coconut milk
- 1/2 cup sugar
- 1/2 vanilla bean, split and scraped

Tiny pinch of salt

I. In a small bowl, cover the tapioca with cold water and let soak for 1 hour. Drain the tapioca in a fine sieve.

2. Bring a medium saucepan of water to a boil. Add the tapioca and cook until it turns clear, about 4 minutes.

Drain immediately and return the tapioca to the saucepan. Add the remaining ingredients and bring to a simmer over moderate heat. Transfer the sauce to a bowl and let cool to room temperature, then refrigerate until chilled. Serve cold. —H.H.

Whole-Milk Ricotta Tart

MAKES ONE 11-INCH TART

PASTRY

- 1 1/2 cups all-purpose flour
- 3 tablespoons sugar

Pinch of salt

- 6 tablespoons unsalted butter, cut into small pieces and chilled
- 1 large egg beaten with
- 1 tablespoon water

FILLING

- 2 cups whole-milk ricotta cheese
- 3/4 cup sugar
- 1 tablespoon cornstarch
- 1 teaspoon finely grated lemon zest
- 1 teaspoon pure vanilla extract
- 3 large eggs, beaten

I. MAKE THE PASTRY: In a food processor, combine the flour, sugar and salt and pulse to blend. Add the butter and pulse until the mixture resembles coarse meal. Transfer the mixture to a bowl. Add the egg and stir with a fork until the pastry just comes together. Transfer the pastry to a lightly floured work surface and knead a few times. Pat the pastry into a disk, wrap in plastic and refrigerate for at least 1 hour.

2. On a lightly floured surface, roll out the pastry to a 13-inch round. Ease the pastry into an 11-inch tart pan with a removable bottom, pressing it into the corners and up the sides without stretching it. Trim any overhanging pastry and prick the bottom every inch or so with a fork. Refrigerate the tart shell until it's chilled and firm, at least 20 minutes.

3. Preheat the oven to 350°. Line the pastry with foil and fill with pie weights or dried beans. Bake the tart shell on the bottom shelf of the oven for 10 minutes, or until it starts to dry out. Remove the foil and weights and return the shell to the oven to bake for another 10 minutes, or until it begins to brown around the edge. Transfer the cooked pastry shell to a wire rack to cool; do not turn the oven off.

4. MAKE THE FILLING: In a large bowl, mix the ricotta with the sugar and cornstarch. Stir in the lemon zest, vanilla and eggs. Scrape the filling into the pastry shell and smooth the top. Bake on the bottom shelf of the oven for about 20 minutes, or until the filling is just set. Cool the ricotta tart on a wire rack before unmolding. Serve warm or at room temperature.

—*Cesare Casella*

MAKE AHEAD The pastry dough can be wrapped in plastic and refrigerated overnight or frozen for up to 1 month.

LIQUEUR *Limoncello,* an intensely lemony liqueur from Naples, will echo the lemon in the tart. Try Caravella Limoncello or Villa Massa Liquore di Limoni.

Jam Crostata

MAKES ONE 9-INCH TART

For extra flavor and visual appeal, try making this tart with two jams of different flavors and contrasting colors—perhaps apricot and strawberry, or blueberry and peach—one on each side of the tart.

- 1   cup all-purpose flour
- ½   cup cake flour
- ¼   cup sugar
- ½   teaspoon finely grated lemon zest

Pinch of salt

- 6   tablespoons unsalted butter at room temperature, cut into 6 pieces
- 1   large egg, beaten
- 1½ cups jam or preserves (14 ounces)
- 1   large egg yolk, beaten with 1 or more teaspoons water

I. In a large bowl, using a fork, stir together the all-purpose flour, cake flour, sugar, lemon zest and salt. Using your fingertips, work in the butter until the dough resembles coarse meal. Make a well in the center and add the whole egg. Gently blend the ingredients with a fork to form a soft dough. Gather the dough into a ball and flatten it into a disk. Wrap the disk in plastic and refrigerate until firm, at least 1 hour or overnight.

2. Preheat the oven to 350°. Using a knife, cut two-thirds of the dough from the disk; wrap the rest in plastic and return it to the refrigerator. Roll out the dough between 2 large sheets of wax paper to a 10-inch round about ⅛ inch thick; refrigerate the dough until chilled but pliable, about 5 minutes. Peel off the wax paper and fit the dough into a 9-inch tart pan with a removable bottom. Patch any weak spots and refrigerate the shell. Roll out the remaining dough between sheets of wax paper into a 9-by-6-inch rectangle about ⅛ inch thick. Refrigerate until chilled.

3. Spoon the jam into the tart shell and spread it evenly. Cut the dough rectangle lengthwise into 12 strips. Arrange half of the strips across the tart; for a decorative look, twist the strips first. (Discard the wax paper.) Working in the opposite direction, repeat with the remaining strips to form a lattice. Brush the lattice with the egg yolk wash. Bake the tart on the bottom rack of the oven for 30 minutes, or until the crust is golden brown and crisp. Serve at room temperature.

—*Nancy Harmon Jenkins*

MAKE AHEAD The dough can be made ahead, wrapped well and refrigerated for 2 days or frozen for up to 1 month.

Jam Crostata

Peach and Walnut Tart

a wooden spoon, until the custard comes to a boil and has the consistency of thick pancake batter, about 7 minutes. Transfer the custard to a bowl and press a piece of plastic wrap directly on the surface. Let the custard cool completely.

3. Preheat the oven to 375°. On a lightly floured surface, roll the larger disk of dough out to a 13-inch round. Ease the dough into a 10-inch tart or cake pan with a removable bottom, pressing it into the corners. Fold the overhanging dough into the pan and press it against the side. Spread the custard in the pan and sprinkle the amaretti crumbs evenly over the top.

4. Roll the remaining dough out to an 11-inch round and set it over the custard. Pinch the edges together to seal the dough. Trim any overhang with a sharp knife. Prick the top crust with a fork and bake for 35 to 40 minutes, or until the pastry is golden and the custard is steaming through the top crust. Let the crostata cool completely before unmolding and serving.

—*Mina Vachino*

MAKE AHEAD The crostata can be stored at room temperature for up to 8 hours before serving.

Peach and Walnut Tart

MAKES ONE 8-INCH TART

In this tart, pastry scraps are used as the base for a streusel-like mixture that is spread in the tart shell to absorb juices and sprinkled over the fruit for crunch. The peach skins are left on for color, but you can peel them if you prefer.

PASTRY

⅔ cup all-purpose flour

½ teaspoon sugar

⅛ teaspoon salt

2 tablespoons unsalted butter

1 tablespoon vegetable oil

1 tablespoon cold water

FILLING

¼ cup walnut pieces

Custard-Filled Crostata with Amaretti

MAKES ONE 10-INCH CROSTATA

DOUGH

1¾ cups all-purpose flour

Pinch of salt

1 stick plus 1 tablespoon cold unsalted butter, cut into small pieces

1 large egg, lightly beaten

1 large egg yolk

FILLING

2 cups milk

3 large egg yolks

¼ cup sugar

2 tablespoons all-purpose flour

½ cup finely crushed amaretti cookies (about 3 ounces)

I. MAKE THE DOUGH: Combine the flour and salt in a food processor. Add the butter and pulse until the mixture resembles coarse meal. In a small bowl, combine the beaten egg with the egg yolk. Add it to the flour mixture and pulse just until a smooth dough forms. Gather the dough into a ball and divide it into 2 pieces, 1 slightly bigger than the other; pat each piece into a disk. Wrap the disks of dough well in plastic or wax paper and refrigerate for at least 1 hour or overnight.

2. MAKE THE FILLING: In a heavy medium saucepan, heat the milk just until steaming. In a large heatproof bowl, whisk the egg yolks with the sugar until pale. Whisk in the flour. Whisk in ½ cup of the hot milk, then whisk the egg mixture into the milk in the saucepan until blended. Cook over moderate heat, stirring constantly with

1 tablespoon all-purpose flour

1 tablespoon sugar

5 small ripe white or yellow peaches (1¼ pounds), cut into quarters

¼ cup apricot preserves, melted and strained

1. MAKE THE PASTRY: In a food processor, mix the flour with the sugar and salt and pulse several times to blend. Add the butter and vegetable oil and process until the mixture resembles coarse meal. Add the water and process just until the dough begins to come together, about 5 seconds.

2. Transfer the dough to a work surface, gather the pieces together and press them into a smooth, flat disk. Roll out the pastry between 2 sheets of wax paper to a 9-inch round. Remove the top sheet of wax paper and invert the pastry into an 8-inch fluted tart pan with a removable bottom. Remove the wax paper and gently press the pastry into the corners of the tart pan. Patch any tears or holes in the pastry if necessary, then run the rolling pin across the rim of the pan to cut off any overhanging dough.

3. MAKE THE FILLING: Preheat the oven to 400°. Gather any leftover pastry dough (there won't be much) and put it in the food processor. Add the walnuts, flour and sugar and pulse until fairly fine crumbs form.

4. Scatter half the walnut crumbs over the bottom of the tart shell. Arrange 16 of the peach quarters, skin side down, in the tart shell in a slightly overlapping circle, with the ends pointing toward the center. Place the remaining 4 peach quarters in the center, skin side up. Sprinkle the remaining walnut crumbs over the peaches and bake the tart for 1 hour and 10 minutes, or until the crust is golden and the peaches are soft and beginning to brown.

5. Transfer the tart to a rack. While the tart is still warm, drizzle the apricot preserves over the peaches. Let the tart cool completely, then remove the pan ring. Cut the tart into wedges and serve at room temperature.

—*Jacques Pépin*

WINE Showcase a sweet wine with good acidity and notes of ripe peaches and apricots: a Late Harvest Riesling from Germany, such as the 1998 Robert Weil Auslese, or a lighter Muscat wine from Italy, such as the 1998 Michele Chiarlo Nivole Moscato d'Asti.

Blueberry-Pecan Crunch Pie

MAKES ONE 10-INCH PIE

PIE SHELL

1 cup all-purpose flour

⅛ teaspoon salt

5 tablespoons cold unsalted butter, cut into small pieces

2 to 3 tablespoons ice water

TOPPING

¾ cup sugar

½ cup all-purpose flour

1 teaspoon cinnamon

6 tablespoons cold unsalted butter, cut into small pieces

½ cup chopped pecans (2 ounces)

FILLING

½ cup fine pound-cake crumbs

2 pints blueberries

1 cup sugar

3 tablespoons cornstarch

3 tablespoons fresh lemon juice

1 teaspoon finely grated lemon zest

1 teaspoon cinnamon

Pinch of freshly grated nutmeg

Scant ½ teaspoon finely grated fresh ginger

1. MAKE THE PIE SHELL: In a food processor, pulse the flour with the salt. Add the butter and pulse until the mixture resembles coarse meal. With the machine on, add the ice water, 1 tablespoon at a time, and process until the dough just comes together. On a lightly floured surface, gently knead the dough 3 times. Pat the dough into a 6-inch disk, wrap in plastic and refrigerate for at least 30 minutes or overnight.

2. On a lightly floured surface, roll out the dough to a 12-inch round about ⅛ inch thick. Fit the dough into a 10-inch glass pie plate. Trim the overhang to 1 inch. Fold it under and crimp. Prick the bottom of the pie shell all over with a fork and refrigerate until chilled.

3. Preheat the oven to 375°. Line the pie shell with foil and fill with dried beans or pie weights. Bake in the center of the oven for 10 minutes, or until the rim is slightly dry. Remove the foil and beans and bake for 3 minutes longer, or until the shell is dry but not colored. Gently deflate any bubbles in the pie shell and let cool on a rack. Leave the oven on.

4. MAKE THE TOPPING: In a medium bowl, whisk the sugar with the flour and cinnamon. Using a pastry blender, 2 table knives or your fingers, blend the butter into the dry ingredients. Pinch the topping into small crumbs and stir in the pecans.

5. MAKE THE FILLING: Spread the pound-cake crumbs in a pie plate and bake for 3 to 4 minutes. Transfer to a plate to cool. Sprinkle the crumbs over the bottom of the pie shell.

6. In a large bowl, toss the blueberries with the sugar, cornstarch, lemon juice, lemon zest, cinnamon, nutmeg and ginger. Spoon the fruit into the pie shell and bake for about 15 minutes, or until the blueberries swell. Scatter the topping over the filling, covering it completely.

7. Set a baking sheet on the bottom rack of the oven to catch any drips. Bake the pie on the middle rack for about 45 minutes, or until the topping is crisp and golden and the filling is bubbling; cover the rim with strips of foil if it browns too quickly. Let the pie cool completely on a rack. Cut into wedges and serve.—*Michael Lomonaco*

MAKE AHEAD The pie can be stored at room temperature for several hours.

Orange and Lemon Tart (p. 350), with Frozen Custard with Herbs (p. 385).

Lemon—Passion Fruit Meringue Pie (p. 350)

Orange and Lemon Tart

MAKES ONE 10½-INCH TART

PASTRY

1⅔ cups all-purpose flour

½ cup sugar

1½ teaspoons active dry yeast

1 stick (4 ounces) cold unsalted butter, cut into small pieces

2 large eggs, beaten

FILLING

3 juice oranges, thinly sliced, seeds discarded

1 thin-skinned lemon, thinly sliced, seeds discarded

1¼ cups sugar

6 tablespoons unsalted butter, cut into small pieces

2 tablespoons orange liqueur

4 large eggs, beaten

1. MAKE THE PASTRY: In a food processor, combine the flour with the sugar and yeast and pulse to mix. Add the butter and 2 tablespoons of the beaten eggs and process just until a dough forms. Scrape the dough out onto a work surface and pat into a flat disk. Wrap in plastic and refrigerate for at least 1 hour.

2. Preheat the oven to 350°. Let the dough soften slightly, then transfer it to a 10½-inch tart pan with a removable bottom. Press the dough over the bottom and up the side, about ½ inch beyond the rim of the pan. Line the dough with foil and fill with pie weights or dried beans. Bake for 10 minutes. Remove the foil and weights, brush the bottom with some of the remaining beaten eggs and bake for 10 minutes longer, or until golden brown.

3. MAKE THE FILLING: In a food processor, combine the fruit slices with the sugar, butter and liqueur and process to a chunky puree. Add the eggs and process to blend. Pour the filling into the tart shell and bake for about 1 hour, or until just set. Let the tart cool. Cut into wedges and serve warm or at room temperature.

—Sabine Busch and Bruno Tramontana

WINE A semisweet dessert wine would contrast nicely with the bitter tones of the Orange and Lemon Tart. Choose the 1991 Piazzano Vin Santo, which has a dried-fig and honey bouquet and a spicy maple flavor.

Lemon–Passion Fruit Meringue Pie

MAKES ONE 9-INCH PIE

FILLING

¼ cup plus 2 tablespoons fresh lemon juice

¼ cup passion fruit puree or melted passion fruit sorbet

2 large egg yolks

1 large egg, lightly beaten

1 cup plus 2 tablespoons sugar

¼ cup plus 1 tablespoon cornstarch

1 cup water

1 tablespoon unsalted butter

1 tablespoon grated lemon zest

Buttery Baked Pie Shell (recipe follows)

TOPPING

5 large egg whites

¾ cup sugar

2 tablespoons water

Pinch of salt

1. MAKE THE FILLING: In a bowl, mix the lemon juice with the passion fruit puree, egg yolks and beaten whole egg. In a saucepan, whisk the sugar with the cornstarch. Add the water, whisking until smooth. Cook over moderately high heat, whisking constantly, until thick, translucent and bubbling, about 5 minutes. Remove from the heat.

2. Whisk a few tablespoons of the cornstarch mixture into the egg mixture, then gradually whisk the egg mixture back into the saucepan. Bring it to a boil over moderately high heat, whisking it constantly for about 1 minute, until the filling is thick; then remove from the heat.

3. Stir in the butter and lemon zest and scrape the filling into the Buttery Baked Pie Shell. Let cool completely.

4. MAKE THE TOPPING: Preheat the oven to 425°. In a large stainless-steel bowl, using an electric mixer, beat the egg whites with the sugar, water and salt until well blended. Set the bowl over a saucepan filled with 2 inches of boiling water and beat the egg whites until the sugar is dissolved and the mixture is warm. Remove from the heat and beat until the meringue is stiff, glossy and cool, about 5 minutes.

5. Spread the meringue evenly over the filling, swirling it decoratively. Bake the pie on the top rack of the oven until the meringue is deep golden and set, about 7 minutes. Transfer the pie to a wire rack in a draft-free place and let cool completely. Serve at room temperature or chilled. *—Grace Parisi*

MAKE AHEAD The pie can be refrigerated for up to 1 day.

BUTTERY BAKED PIE SHELL

MAKES ONE 9-INCH PIE SHELL

1 cup all-purpose flour

Pinch of salt

5 tablespoons unsalted butter, cut into ½-inch pieces and chilled

3 tablespoons ice water

1. In a food processor, combine the flour and salt and pulse to blend. Add the butter and pulse just until the mixture resembles coarse meal. Add the ice water and pulse until the dough just begins to come together. Turn the dough out onto a lightly floured work surface and pat it into a 6-inch disk. Wrap in plastic and refrigerate for at least 30 minutes or overnight.

2. Preheat the oven to 350°. On a lightly floured work surface, roll out the dough to an 11-inch round. Fit the dough into a 9-inch glass pie plate and trim the overhang to 1 inch. Fold in the overhang and crimp the edges. Prick the bottom in several places with a fork. Refrigerate until firm, about 10 minutes.

3. Line the pie shell with a sheet of foil that extends 2 inches beyond the pie

Lionel Poilâne's Apple Tartlets

plate. Fill the shell with pie weights or dried beans. Bake for 30 minutes, or until the edges are lightly golden. Remove the foil and weights and bake the shell for about 10 minutes longer, or until golden and cooked through. Let cool on a wire rack. —*G.P.*

Lionel Poilâne's Apple Tartlets

MAKES 6 TARTLETS

1½ pounds Golden Delicious apples—peeled, quartered and cored

21 ounces all-butter puff pastry, chilled

1 small egg, beaten with 1 tablespoon milk

Light brown sugar, for sprinkling

I. Preheat the oven to 375°. Line a large rimmed baking sheet with parchment paper. Cut each apple quarter into 5 lengthwise slices.

2. On a lightly floured work surface, roll out the puff pastry ⅛ inch thick, working in batches if necessary. Using a bowl or plate as a template, cut out six 6½-inch rounds. Put the rounds, slightly overlapping, on a cookie sheet and chill until firm, about 10 minutes.

3. Arrange about 6 of the apple pieces in the center of each round in a loosely packed pile, leaving a 1½-inch border. Tuck 2 small apple pieces in the center. Fold the pastry up and over the apples to partially cover them. Transfer the tartlets to the lined baking sheet and brush the pastry with the egg wash. Bake for about 45 minutes, or until the apples are tender and the pastry is puffy and browned. Sprinkle the tartlets with the brown sugar and let cool on the sheet for 5 to 10 minutes. Serve hot or warm.

—*Lionel Poilâne*

MAKE AHEAD The dough rounds can be refrigerated overnight.

Rustic Apple Tarts with Brown Sugar Topping

MAKES 6 TARTS

PASTRY

1¾ cups all-purpose flour

1 teaspoon salt

½ teaspoon baking powder

1 stick cold unsalted butter, cut into ½-inch pieces

¼ cup solid vegetable shortening, chilled and cut into small pieces

4 to 5 tablespoons ice water

FILLING

7 large Granny Smith apples— peeled, cored and cut into ¼-inch dice

1 tablespoon fresh lemon juice

1 tablespoon dark rum

4 tablespoons unsalted butter

½ cup sugar

TOPPING

¼ cup packed light brown sugar

½ cup all-purpose flour

4 tablespoons cold unsalted butter, cut into ½-inch pieces

½ cup chopped pecans or almonds

I. MAKE THE PASTRY: In a food processor, combine the flour, salt and baking powder and pulse to mix. Add the butter and shortening and process just until the mixture resembles coarse meal. With the machine on, slowly add

4 tablespoons of the ice water and pulse just until the dough is evenly moistened and comes together; add more water if necessary. Transfer the dough to a work surface, then gather it into a ball. Pat the dough into a disk, wrap it in plastic and refrigerate for at least 1 hour.

2. MAKE THE FILLING: In a large heatproof bowl, toss the apples with the lemon juice and rum. Melt the butter in a large skillet. Add the sugar and cook over moderate heat, stirring occasionally, until golden brown, 5 to 7 minutes. Add the apples and cook until tender, about 15 minutes. Return the apples to the bowl and let cool completely.

3. MAKE THE TOPPING: In a bowl, mix the brown sugar and flour. Using a pastry blender or 2 knives, cut in the butter until crumbly. Stir in the nuts.

4. Preheat the oven to 375°. On a lightly floured surface, roll out the dough ⅛ inch thick. Using a 6-inch pan lid as a guide, cut out 6 rounds. Transfer them to a baking sheet. Spread the apple filling evenly over each round to within 1 inch of the edge. Fold up or pinch the edges to hold the filling. Sprinkle the topping over the tarts and bake for 30 to 40 minutes, or until the crust is golden, the filling is bubbling and the tops are lightly browned. Let the tarts cool slightly on racks before serving. —*Kristie Trabant Scott*

Apple Tart with Bananas and Cranberries

MAKES ONE 12-INCH TART

Cream Cheese Pastry, made without the optional spices (p. 355)

1 large egg yolk, lightly beaten

8 medium Granny Smith apples (about 3½ pounds)—peeled, halved and cored

4 tablespoons unsalted butter

1 vanilla bean, split

¼ cup dark brown sugar

½ cup aged rum

Apple Tart with Bananas and Cranberries

3. Meanwhile, cut 4 of the apples into ¾-inch dice. Melt the butter in a large deep skillet. Stir in the vanilla bean and brown sugar. Add the diced apples and cook over high heat, stirring frequently, until the sugar melts, about 2 minutes. Carefully add the rum and continue to cook until the apples are just tender and the rum is almost evaporated, about 6 minutes. Stir in the banana and dried cranberries; remove the vanilla bean.

4. Pour the filling into the cooled tart shell and spread in an even layer. Set the 8 remaining apple halves, rounded side up, on a work surface and thinly slice them, keeping the halves intact. Starting at the edge of the tart, arrange the apples over the filling in overlapping concentric circles. Sprinkle with the granulated sugar.

5. Bake the tart for 1 hour and 10 minutes, or until the apples are golden and tender. Remove from the oven and brush the top of the tart with the apricot preserves. Let cool on a rack. Unmold the tart and serve with dollops of whipped cream or vanilla ice cream.

—*Bruce and Eric Bromberg*

MAKE AHEAD The baked apple tart can be refrigerated overnight and rewarmed in a 325° oven.

BEVERAGE Point up the rum in the tart by serving an aged dark rum with mellow toffee-molasses notes, such as Mount Gay Extra Old from Barbados.

Tarte Tatin

8 SERVINGS

PASTRY

1½ cups all-purpose flour

1½ tablespoons sugar

¾ teaspoon salt

1 stick (4 ounces) unsalted butter, cut into tablespoons and chilled

3 tablespoons cold water

APPLES

10 Golden Delicious apples (about 4 pounds), peeled and halved lengthwise

---

1 banana, halved lengthwise and cut into ½-inch pieces

⅓ cup dried cranberries

2 tablespoons granulated sugar

¼ cup apricot preserves, melted and strained

Whipped cream or vanilla ice cream, for serving

1. Preheat the oven to 375°. On a lightly floured surface, roll out the Cream Cheese Pastry to a round about ⅛ inch thick. Fit the pastry into a 12-inch fluted tart pan with a removable bottom. Use a rolling pin to trim off any overhang. Prick the bottom of the pastry several times with a fork.

2. Line the shell with foil and fill with pie weights or dried beans. Bake for 25 minutes, or until lightly colored around the edge. Remove the foil and weights. Bake the shell for about 7 minutes longer, or until it is dry and golden. Let cool slightly, then brush with the egg yolk.

1½ sticks (6 ounces) unsalted butter

1½ cups sugar

Crème fraîche or vanilla ice cream,
for serving

I. MAKE THE PASTRY: In a food processor, pulse the flour with the sugar and salt. Add the butter and pulse until it is in pea-size pieces. Add the water and process just until a dough forms. Transfer to a lightly floured work surface and knead 3 times. Pat the pastry into a disk, wrap in plastic and refrigerate until firm.

2. PREPARE THE APPLES: Using a melon baller, scoop out the cores from the apples. In a 9½-inch cast-iron skillet, melt the butter with the sugar over high heat, stirring often. Remove from the heat. Arrange the apple halves on their sides in the skillet in very tight concentric circles; stand them upright in the center if necessary, packing them in as tightly as possible.

3. Bring the apples to a boil. Reduce the heat to moderate and cook for 25 minutes, keeping the apples at a steady simmer.

4. Using a fork, carefully turn the apples over on their other side. Cook until the liquid in the pan becomes a deep-brown caramel, about 30 minutes; turn the skillet occasionally to even the heat.

5. Meanwhile, preheat the oven to 400°. On a lightly floured surface, roll out the pastry to an 11-inch round. Trim the pastry to a 10-inch round, using a dinner plate as a guide; transfer the pastry to a cookie sheet and refrigerate.

6. Remove the skillet from the heat and let the steam subside, about 5 minutes. Cover the apples with the pastry, carefully tucking it in at the edge. Set the skillet on the cookie sheet. Bake for 25 minutes, or until the pastry is golden brown. Let the tart cool for 10 minutes.

7. Run a knife around the edge of the tart. Set a large heavy plate over the skillet. Using good kitchen mitts, turn the skillet over to unmold the tart onto the plate; remove the skillet. Use a spatula to replace any apples that stick to the pan. Let cool slightly and serve with crème fraîche.

—*Charles Pierce*

Apple-Coconut Macaroon Tarte Tatin

MAKES ONE 9-INCH TART

2 cups unsweetened apple juice

½ vanilla bean, split lengthwise

Salt

5 large Granny Smith apples (7 to 8 ounces each)—peeled, cored and each cut into eighths

1 cup plus 1 tablespoon granulated sugar

1 teaspoon fresh lemon juice

¼ teaspoon cinnamon

¼ cup avocado oil (see Note) or canola oil

⅓ cup packed light brown sugar

1½ cups pecan halves (6 ounces)

⅔ cup unsweetened shredded coconut (2 ounces)

4 large egg whites, at room temperature

I. In a medium saucepan, combine the apple juice with the vanilla bean and a pinch of salt and boil over high heat until reduced to ½ cup, 10 to 15 minutes. Remove the vanilla bean. In a large bowl, carefully toss the apples with the reduced apple juice, 1 tablespoon of the granulated sugar, the lemon juice and the cinnamon. Let stand for 20 minutes.

2. In a deep 9-inch cast-iron skillet, combine the oil with the brown sugar and ⅓ cup of the granulated sugar and cook over moderately low heat for 4 minutes. Add the apples and stir just until the sugar melts. Carefully turn the apples rounded side up and cook over

Apple-Coconut Macaroon Tarte Tatin

moderately high heat for 10 minutes. Remove the skillet from the heat, carefully turn the apples cored side up and cook over moderately high heat for 5 more minutes. Let cool for 20 minutes.

3. Meanwhile, preheat the oven to 350°. Spread the pecans on a baking sheet and toast for 7 minutes, or until fragrant and lightly browned. Let cool completely. In a food processor, combine the nuts and 1/3 cup of the granulated sugar and pulse until finely ground. Transfer the mixture to a bowl and stir in the coconut.

4. In another large bowl, using a handheld electric mixer, beat the egg whites with a pinch of salt until soft peaks form. Add the remaining 1/3 cup of granulated sugar, 1 tablespoon at a time, and beat at high speed until the whites are glossy and stiff. Fold the egg whites into the pecan-coconut mixture.

5. Using tongs, arrange the apples, rounded side down, in concentric rings in the skillet. Spoon the pecan-coconut mixture over the apples, spreading it smoothly to the edge of the skillet. Bake for 30 minutes, or until the macaroon crust is golden and the juices bubble up the side. Let the tart cool in the skillet on a wire rack for 20 minutes.

6. Invert a large plate over the skillet and, using 2 oven mitts, grab the plate and skillet together and flip. Still wearing the oven mitts, lift off the skillet. Remove any apples that stick to the skillet and replace them in the tart. Let the tart cool slightly. Cut into wedges with a moist knife, wiping the blade after each slice. Serve the tart warm or at room temperature. —*Jayne Cohen*

NOTE Avocado oil has a lovely buttery taste. It is available at health-food stores and specialty shops.

MAKE AHEAD The tart can be made up to 1 day ahead. Unmold it and wrap in foil. Store the tart at room temperature or in the refrigerator.

Fresh Fruit Tart

MAKES ONE 12-INCH TART

TART SHELL

- 2 cups all-purpose flour
- ¼ cup confectioners' sugar
- ¾ teaspoon salt
- 1¼ sticks (5 ounces) cold unsalted butter, cut into tablespoons
- 1 large egg yolk
- ¼ cup ice water

ALMOND CREAM

- 1½ cups confectioners' sugar
- 1 stick (4 ounces) unsalted butter, softened
- 3 large eggs
- 1½ cups finely ground almonds (see Note)
- 3 tablespoons all-purpose flour
- 1½ tablespoons rum

Pinch of salt

FRUIT

- 6 cups seasonal fresh fruit and berries—peeled, pitted and sliced or cut up
- 2 tablespoons sugar
- 1 tablespoon fresh lemon juice

I. MAKE THE TART SHELL: In a food processor, pulse the flour with the confectioners' sugar and salt. Add the butter and pulse until the mixture resembles coarse crumbs. In a small bowl, whisk the egg yolk with the water. With the machine on, slowly add the egg yolk mixture and process just until the dough comes together. Turn the dough out onto a work surface and gently knead it 3 times. Pat the dough into a large disk. Wrap the disk in plastic and refrigerate for at least 1 hour or overnight.

2. On a lightly floured surface, roll the dough out to a large round about ⅛ inch thick. Fit the dough into a 12-inch fluted tart pan with a removable bottom. Prick the bottom with a fork. Wrap the tart shell in plastic and refrigerate until chilled, at least 1 hour.

3. Preheat the oven to 375°. Line the tart shell with foil and fill it with pie weights or dried beans. Bake for 20 minutes, or until lightly browned around the edges. Remove the foil and weights and bake the shell for about 20 minutes longer, or until the bottom is dry and the sides are browned.

4. MAKE THE ALMOND CREAM: In a large bowl, using a handheld electric mixer, beat the confectioners' sugar with the butter until creamy. Add the eggs, 1 at a time, beating thoroughly after each addition. Add the ground almonds, flour, rum and salt and beat at low speed until well blended. Cover and refrigerate the almond cream. Remove it from the refrigerator 15 minutes before using.

5. Using a spatula, spread the almond cream in the baked tart shell in an even layer. Bake for 20 to 25 minutes, until pale golden and firm in the center. Transfer the shell to a rack and let cool completely before filling with fruit.

6. PREPARE THE FRUIT: In a large bowl, gently toss the fruit with the sugar and lemon juice. Arrange the fruit on the tart just before serving.

—*Jean-Christophe Royer*

NOTE When grinding almonds in a food processor, pulse only until they turn to a fine powder; overprocessing will create a paste.

Pumpkin Meringue Pie

MAKES TWO 10-INCH PIES

Cream Cheese Pastry, made with the optional spices (recipe follows)

FILLING

- 1 quart heavy cream
- 2 cinnamon sticks
- 6 whole cloves
- 1 whole nutmeg
- 1 cup light brown sugar
- 4 large eggs, separated

One 29-ounce can unsweetened pumpkin puree (3½ cups)

- ¼ cup granulated sugar

MERINGUE TOPPING

- 1 cup sugar
- ½ cup water
- 4 large egg whites

I. PREPARE THE PIE SHELLS: Preheat the oven to 350°. On a lightly floured surface, roll out each disk of pastry to ⅛ inch thick. Fit the rounds into two 10-inch glass pie plates and trim the overhang to 1-inch. Fold the overhang under the rim and crimp. Line the pie shells with foil and fill with pie weights or dried beans.

2. Bake the pie shells for 30 minutes, or until lightly colored around the edges. Remove the foil and weights and bake the shells for about 5 minutes longer, or until lightly browned and dry. Let the shells cool slightly.

3. MAKE THE FILLING: In a saucepan, simmer the cream with the cinnamon sticks, cloves and nutmeg over moderately low heat until reduced to 2½ cups, 25 to 30 minutes. Let cool, then strain; discard the spices.

4. In a large bowl, using an electric mixer, beat the brown sugar with the egg yolks until thick and pale, about 3 minutes. At low speed, beat in the pumpkin puree. Gradually add the cream and beat until blended.

5. In a stainless-steel bowl, using clean beaters, beat the egg whites until soft peaks form. Slowly beat in the granulated sugar and continue beating until the whites are stiff and glossy. Stir one-fourth of the beaten egg whites into the pumpkin filling to lighten it, then fold in the remaining whites. Pour the filling into the pie shells and smooth the surfaces. Bake the pies for about 1 hour, or until the custard is lightly golden and just beginning to crack all over. Let the pies cool completely on racks.

6. MAKE THE MERINGUE TOPPING: In a small heavy saucepan, mix the sugar and water and bring to a boil; stir just until the sugar dissolves. Boil, without stirring, until the temperature registers 220° on a candy thermometer, about 10 minutes.

7. In a large stainless-steel bowl, using an electric mixer, beat the egg whites

Pumpkin Meringue Pie

at medium speed until firm. Beating constantly, carefully add the hot sugar syrup to the whites in a thin steady stream; be careful not to splatter against the beaters or the side of the bowl. Increase the speed to high and beat the meringue until stiff, glossy and slightly cool.

8. Preheat the broiler and position a rack 8 inches from the heat. Starting from the edge of the crust, spoon the meringue all over the pies and spread with a spatula, making decorative dips and swirls. Broil the meringue for about 30 seconds, shifting the pies as necessary for even browning.

—*Bruce and Eric Bromberg*

MAKE AHEAD The pies can be prepared through Step 5 and refrigerated overnight.

CREAM CHEESE PASTRY
MAKES ENOUGH FOR ONE 12-INCH TART OR TWO 10-INCH PIES
Use this tender cream cheese pastry plain or seasoned with cinnamon, nutmeg and ginger to complement traditional holiday pie and tart fillings.

- 2½ **cups all-purpose flour**
- 1 **tablespoon light brown sugar**
- ¼ **teaspoon cinnamon (optional)**
- ⅛ **teaspoon freshly grated nutmeg (optional)**
- ⅛ **teaspoon ground ginger (optional)**

¼ cup cream cheese
   (2 ounces), softened
1 stick (4 ounces) cold unsalted
   butter, cut into tablespoons
3 tablespoons ice water
1 large egg, lightly beaten
1 teaspoon vegetable oil
½ teaspoon pure vanilla extract

I. In a food processor, combine the flour, brown sugar and spices, if using, and pulse to mix. Add the cream cheese and pulse until the mixture is sandy. Add the butter and pulse until the mixture resembles coarse meal.

2. In a small pitcher, combine the ice water with the egg, oil and vanilla and pour into the food processor; pulse until the dough just forms a ball. Turn the dough out onto a lightly floured surface and pat it into 1 large disk for a tart or 2 small disks for pies. Wrap the dough in plastic and refrigerate for at least 30 minutes or overnight.

—B.B. and E.B.

MAKE AHEAD The dough can be frozen for up to 2 weeks.

Sweet-Potato Pie

MAKES ONE 9-INCH PIE
Sweet-potato pie has become an all-American dish, but this version is topped with bourbon-spiked Praline Sauce to accent its Southern roots.

DOUGH

1½ cups all-purpose flour
2 teaspoons sugar
½ teaspoon salt
6 tablespoons cold unsalted butter,
   cut into small pieces
2 tablespoons vegetable shortening
5 tablespoons ice water

FILLING

3 pounds sweet potatoes
½ cup heavy cream
½ cup packed light brown sugar
3 large eggs, lightly beaten
2 tablespoons unsalted
   butter, melted
1 tablespoon pure vanilla extract
½ teaspoon salt

½ teaspoon cinnamon
½ teaspoon ground allspice
¼ teaspoon freshly grated nutmeg
Vanilla ice cream, for serving
Praline Sauce (recipe follows)

I. MAKE THE DOUGH: In a food processor, pulse the flour with the sugar and salt. Add the butter and shortening and pulse just until the mixture resembles coarse meal. Add the ice water and process until a dough just starts to form. Transfer the dough to a floured work surface and knead gently. Pat the dough into a disk, wrap in plastic and chill for at least 1 hour.

2. Preheat the oven to 375°. On a lightly floured work surface, roll out the dough to an 11-inch round about ⅛ inch thick. Transfer the dough to a 9-inch pie dish and trim the overhang to ¾ inch; fold the overhang under itself and crimp decoratively. Prick the bottom of the pie shell all over and refrigerate until firm.

3. Line the shell with foil and fill with pie weights or dried beans. Bake for about 20 minutes, or until lightly golden around the edge. Remove the foil and the weights and bake for about 12 minutes longer, or until the pie shell is golden brown and cooked on the bottom. Cover the rim of the pie shell with foil when it starts to brown. Leave the oven on.

4. MAKE THE FILLING: Pierce the sweet potatoes and bake them for 1 hour, or until tender; cool slightly. Slit the skins and scoop the potatoes into a bowl. Mash until smooth. Whisk in the cream, brown sugar, eggs, butter, vanilla, salt, cinnamon, allspice and nutmeg and scrape into the pie shell.

5. Bake the sweet-potato pie for 15 minutes. Turn the oven down to 350° and continue to bake for about 40 minutes longer, or until the filling is set. Transfer the pie to a wire rack to cool. Serve warm or at room temperature with vanilla ice cream and Praline Sauce.

—Susan Spicer

MAKE AHEAD The unbaked pie shell can be frozen for up to 1 week. The sweet potatoes can be baked and refrigerated overnight.

WINE A smooth, medium-sweet Vouvray, such as the 1996 Domaine du Clos Naudin Foreau Demi Sec, is an ideal partner to the creamy pie.

PRALINE SAUCE

MAKES 2 CUPS
2 cups pecans (7 ounces)
1½ cups sugar
1 cup water
1 cup heavy cream
¼ cup bourbon

I. Preheat the oven to 350°. Spread the pecans on a rimmed baking sheet and bake for 12 minutes, or until browned and fragrant. Let cool, then coarsely chop the pecans.

2. In a medium saucepan, combine the sugar and water and cook over moderate heat without stirring, until a deep amber caramel forms, about 20 minutes. Gradually stir in the heavy cream and continue stirring to dissolve any lumps of caramel, about 2 minutes. Remove from the heat and stir in the bourbon and the pecans. Serve the sauce warm or at room temperature.

—S.S.

MAKE AHEAD The sauce can be refrigerated for up to 3 days. Bring to room temperature or rewarm gently before serving.

Chocolate Pecan Pie with Bourbon

MAKES ONE 9-INCH PIE
Coarsely chopping the pecans makes the pie easy to slice, but you may want to leave some whole for visual effect.

CRUST

1¼ cups all-purpose flour
2 teaspoons sugar
¼ teaspoon salt
1 stick (4 ounces) cold unsalted
   butter, cut into pieces
¼ cup ice water

FILLING

- 2 cups (about 7 ounces) pecans
- 3 large eggs
- ¾ cup dark brown sugar
- ⅔ cup light corn syrup
- 1 teaspoon pure vanilla extract
- 2 tablespoons unsalted butter, melted
- 3 tablespoons bourbon
- ½ teaspoon salt
- ¾ cup semisweet or bittersweet chocolate chips

I. MAKE THE CRUST: In a food processor, pulse the flour with the sugar and salt. Add the butter and pulse until the mixture resembles coarse meal. Transfer to a bowl and stir in the ice water. Knead the dough 2 or 3 times on a lightly floured surface and pat into a disk. Wrap in plastic and refrigerate for at least 30 minutes.

2. On a lightly floured surface, roll out the dough to a 12-inch round. Fit the dough into a 9-inch glass pie plate. Trim the overhang to ½ inch, fold the edge under itself and crimp decoratively. Refrigerate until firm.

3. MAKE THE FILLING: Preheat the oven to 375°. On a rimmed baking sheet, toast the pecans for about 8 minutes, or until fragrant; coarsely chop. In a large bowl, whisk the eggs with the brown sugar, corn syrup, vanilla, melted butter, bourbon and salt until blended. Stir in the toasted pecans and chocolate chips until they are evenly distributed.

4. Pour the pecan filling into the chilled pie shell. Bake the pie on the bottom shelf of the oven for about 55 minutes, or until the center of the pie is set. Tent the crust with foil halfway through the baking time if the edge seems to be browning too quickly. Transfer the pie to a rack and let it cool for at least 1 hour before serving.

—David Lebovitz

MAKE AHEAD The pie can be stored at room temperature for up to 1 day. Rewarm at 325° for 15 minutes.

Coconut Pistachio Meringues

MAKES ABOUT 3 DOZEN MERINGUES

- 4 large egg whites
- ½ teaspoon cream of tartar
- 1¼ cups sugar
- ½ pound shredded unsweetened coconut (2¾ cups)
- ¼ cup coarsely ground unsalted pistachios, plus ½ cup whole unsalted pistachios

I. Preheat the oven to 300°. Line 2 large baking sheets with parchment paper. In the bowl of a standing electric mixer, beat the egg whites with the cream of tartar at high speed until firm peaks form. Add the sugar, 2 tablespoons at a time, beating for 2 seconds between additions; beat until glossy and stiff. At low speed, beat in the coconut and ground pistachios.

2. Transfer the meringue to a pastry bag fitted with a ½-inch round tip. Pipe 1½-inch mounds of meringue onto the baking sheets about 1 inch apart. Decorate each meringue with a whole pistachio. Bake on the upper and middle racks of the oven for 30 minutes, or until pale brown and dry; shift the pans from top to bottom and back to front halfway through baking. Let the meringues cool completely on the sheets before serving or storing.

—Jill Pettijohn

MAKE AHEAD The meringues can be stored for up to 1 week.

Cornmeal Cats' Tongues

MAKES ABOUT 10 DOZEN COOKIES
These slender little cookies are based on an old Italian recipe called *crumari*. The cornmeal gives the cookies a distinctive crunch and flavor.

- 1 stick plus 6 tablespoons (7 ounces) unsalted butter, at room temperature
- ¾ cup sugar
- 1 teaspoon pure vanilla extract
- ½ teaspoon salt
- 2 large eggs

- 1¾ cups triple-sifted all-purpose flour
- ⅔ cup finely ground cornmeal

I. Preheat the oven to 350°. Line 2 cookie sheets with parchment paper. Using a pencil and ruler and leaving 1 inch between the sets, draw 3 lengthwise sets of 2 parallel lines 3 inches apart on the parchment. Invert the parchment onto the cookie sheets.

2. In a large bowl, beat the butter with the sugar, vanilla and salt. Add the eggs 1 at a time and beat well after each addition. Add the flour and cornmeal and beat at low speed just until blended.

3. Spoon one-third of the batter into a pastry bag fitted with a ⅓-inch round (#3) tip. Between and perpendicular to the parallel lines, pipe pencil-thin lines of batter 1 inch apart to look like railroad tracks. Bake the cookies on the middle and lower racks of the oven for 17 minutes, or until golden around the edges and on the bottom; shift the sheets halfway through baking. Cool the cookies on the sheets for 5 minutes, then transfer them to a wire rack to cool completely. Let the cookie sheets cool slightly between batches.

—Maida Heatter

MAKE AHEAD The cookies can be stored in an airtight container for 3 days or frozen for up to 1 month.

Crisp Cinnamon Sugar Cookies

MAKES ABOUT 5½ DOZEN COOKIES
This simple recipe is a great base for infinite flavoring and spice combinations. Try replacing the cinnamon and vanilla with ginger, nutmeg and lemon oil, or with orange oil, orange zest and a few drops of espresso.

- 2¼ cups plus 2 tablespoons all-purpose flour
- ¾ teaspoon cinnamon
- ⅛ teaspoon salt
- 1½ sticks (6 ounces) unsalted butter, softened
- 1 cup sugar, plus more for sprinkling

1 large egg, lightly beaten

½ teaspoon pure vanilla extract

I. In a medium bowl, whisk the flour with the cinnamon and salt and set aside. In a large bowl, using an electric mixer, beat the butter until creamy. Add 1 cup of the sugar and beat until light and fluffy. At low speed, beat in the egg and vanilla. Add the dry ingredients and mix at low speed until a soft dough forms. Divide the dough in half and pat it into 2 disks. Wrap each disk in plastic and refrigerate until firm, at least 1 hour or overnight. Let stand at room temperature for 10 minutes before rolling out.

2. Preheat the oven to 325°. Line several baking sheets with parchment paper. On a lightly floured surface, roll out each disk of dough ⅛ inch thick. Using 2-inch cookie cutters, stamp out shapes as close together as possible and arrange them on the prepared baking sheets. Lightly sprinkle the cookies with the additional sugar and bake for 17 to 20 minutes, or until crisp and light brown around the edges and on top; rotate the baking sheets once for even baking. Slide the parchment paper with the cookies onto a rack to cool.

—Suzanne Lombardi

MAKE AHEAD These Crisp Cinnamon Sugar Cookies will keep well for up to 1 week. Put them in an airtight container with a sheet of wax paper between each layer.

Ginger and Citrus Wafers

MAKES ABOUT 7 DOZEN
WAFERS

⅓ cup plus 1 tablespoon unsalted butter, at room temperature

⅔ cup sugar

1¼ teaspoons finely grated lemon zest

1¼ teaspoons finely grated tangerine or clementine zest

1 teaspoon finely grated fresh ginger

Ginger and Citrus Wafers

1 egg

1½ tablespoons fresh tangerine or clementine juice

1½ tablespoons fresh lemon juice

¼ teaspoon pure vanilla extract

¼ teaspoon salt

¾ cup unbleached all-purpose flour

I. Preheat the oven to 350°. In a medium bowl, beat ⅓ cup of the butter with the sugar, the lemon and tangerine zest and the ginger at high speed until pale and fluffy. Beat in the egg, citrus juices, vanilla and salt, then beat in the flour.

2. Lightly grease a large heavy cookie sheet with some of the remaining butter. Drop ½-teaspoon-size mounds of batter onto the prepared sheet, spacing them 2 inches apart. Using your index finger or the back of a spoon and a swirling motion, spread each mound of batter into a 2-inch round.

3. Bake the wafers for 6 to 7 minutes, or until their edges begin to turn golden brown. While the wafers are still hot, use a thin, flexible metal spatula to transfer them to wire racks to cool completely. Regrease the cookie sheet and repeat Step 2 with the rest of the batter. Pack the cooled wafers in tins.

—*Sally Schneider*

MAKE AHEAD You can store the Ginger and Citrus Wafers in airtight tins at room temperature for 3 weeks.
ONE WAFER Calories 19.2 kcal, Total Fat 1.0 gm, Saturated Fat 0.6 gm, Protein 0.2 gm, Carbohydrates 2.5 gm

Fennel Seed Cookies

MAKES ABOUT 3 DOZEN COOKIES

- 1½ sticks (6 ounces) unsalted butter, softened
- 1 cup sugar
- 2 large egg yolks
- 1 large egg
- 2 teaspoons anise liqueur, such as anisette or ouzo
- 2 cups all-purpose flour
- 2 tablespoons coarsely ground fennel seeds, plus 1 tablespoon whole fennel seeds
- 1 teaspoon ground coriander
- ½ teaspoon baking powder
- ½ teaspoon salt

I. Preheat the oven to 300°. In a large bowl, using a handheld electric mixer, beat the butter with the sugar until the mixture is light and fluffy. Add the egg yolks, whole egg and anise liqueur and beat until smooth. By hand, stir in the flour, ground fennel seeds, coriander, baking powder and salt.

2. Drop slightly rounded tablespoons of the dough onto large baking sheets, 2 inches apart. Decorate each with 2 or 3 fennel seeds. Bake the cookies on the upper and middle racks of the oven for 30 minutes, or until golden on the bottoms and around the edges; shift the pans from top to bottom and front to back halfway through baking. Let the cookies cool completely on wire racks before storing in an airtight container. —*Jill Pettijohn*

MAKE AHEAD The cookies can be made ahead and stored for up to 2 weeks.

Peppermint Shortbreads

MAKES ABOUT 3 DOZEN COOKIES

- 2 cups unbleached all-purpose flour
- ¾ teaspoon baking powder
- ¼ teaspoon salt
- 2 sticks (½ pound) unsalted butter, softened
- ⅔ cup confectioners' sugar
- ½ teaspoon pure peppermint oil
- 4 ounces peppermint candies, crushed into ¼-inch pieces (about ⅔ cup)

I. In a medium bowl, whisk the flour with the baking powder and salt. In a large bowl, using an electric mixer, beat the butter until it's creamy. Add the confectioners' sugar and beat until the mixture is light and fluffy. At low speed, beat in the peppermint oil and the dry ingredients until a soft crumbly dough forms.

2. Scrape the dough out onto a lightly floured surface and gently knead about 3 times. Pat the dough into a 6-inch disk, wrap in plastic and refrigerate until chilled, at least 1 hour or overnight. Let the dough stand at room temperature for about 10 minutes before rolling out.

3. Preheat the oven to 350°. Line 3 baking sheets with parchment paper. On a lightly floured surface, roll out the dough ⅛ inch thick. Using 3-inch cookie cutters, stamp out shapes as close together as possible and arrange them on the prepared baking sheets. Lightly sprinkle the cookies with the crushed peppermints and bake for about 15 minutes, or until golden brown around the edges.

4. Slide the parchment paper with the cookies onto racks to cool completely. Briefly chill the remaining dough, then reroll and repeat.

—*Suzanne Lombardi*

MAKE AHEAD The cookies can be made ahead and stored between sheets of wax paper in an airtight container for up to 4 days.

Skinny Peanut Wafers

MAKES ABOUT 2 DOZEN WAFERS

If you can imagine a cookie version of peanut brittle, this would be it. These thin wafers are crisp yet chewy and are loaded with a whole pound of honey-roasted peanuts.

- 1 pound honey-roasted peanuts (about 3 cups)
- 1 cup sugar
- 1 cup sifted all-purpose flour
- ½ teaspoon baking soda
- 1 large egg
- 2 tablespoons milk
- 2 tablespoons unsalted butter, melted and cooled

I. Preheat the oven to 400°. Line several cookie sheets with aluminum foil, shiny side up.

2. In a food processor, pulse 1 cup of the honey-roasted peanuts with ¼ cup of the sugar several times, until some of the nuts are finely chopped and some are coarsely chopped. In a small bowl, whisk together the flour with the baking soda.

3. In a large bowl, beat the egg with the milk, butter and the remaining ¾ cup of sugar until blended. Beat in the flour and the chopped peanuts. Spoon slightly rounded tablespoons of the dough about 3 inches apart on the prepared baking sheets. Press 1 tablespoon of the remaining peanuts onto each cookie, flattening the cookies slightly.

4. Bake the cookies in the middle of the oven, 1 sheet at a time, for about 15 minutes, or until golden brown; turn the sheet front to back halfway through baking. Slide the foil onto a wire rack and let the cookies cool completely. Bake the remaining cookies. When they are cool, invert the cookies and peel off the foil.

—*Maida Heatter*

MAKE AHEAD The cookies can be made ahead and stored in an airtight container for 3 days or frozen for up to 1 month.

TOP: **Triple Chocolate Peanut Butter Sandwich Cookies.**

BOTTOM: **Chocolate Whoppers.**

Coconut-Walnut Haystacks

MAKES ABOUT 2½ DOZEN COOKIES
These sweet, nutty and chewy cookies are like a cross between a macaroon and a meringue.

- ⅔ cup walnut halves (about 2½ ounces)
- 2 cups sweetened shredded coconut (about 6 ounces)
- ½ teaspoon cinnamon
- 3 large egg whites
- ¼ cup sugar

1. Preheat the oven to 350°. Line 2 large baking sheets with parchment paper. Spread the walnuts in a pie plate and bake for about 7 minutes, until lightly toasted. Transfer the nuts to a plate to cool, then finely chop. Leave the oven on.

2. In a medium bowl, toss the chopped walnuts with the coconut and cinnamon. In a medium stainless-steel bowl, beat the egg whites until frothy. Gradually add the sugar and continue beating until stiff peaks form. Using a rubber spatula, fold in the coconut mixture.

3. Mound rounded tablespoons of the batter 1 inch apart on the baking sheets and gently mold each cookie into a haystack shape. Bake for 20 to 25 minutes, or until dry to the touch and lightly browned. Set the sheets with the cookies on wire racks and let cool before removing.

—*Suzanne Lombardi*

MAKE AHEAD The cookies can be kept in an airtight container for 4 days.

Almond-Grappa Cookies

MAKES ABOUT 3½ DOZEN COOKIES
These crunchy cookies are meant for dunking in espresso or *vin santo.*

- 1½ cups almonds (7 ounces), blanched whole, then coarsely chopped
- 1 cup sugar
- 1½ cups all-purpose flour
- ¼ teaspoon cinnamon
- ½ cup grappa

1. Preheat the oven to 350°. Line a baking sheet with parchment paper. Put the almonds and sugar in a food processor and grind the nuts to a fine powder; do not let the nuts turn into a paste. Transfer to a large bowl and whisk in the flour and cinnamon. Add the grappa and stir until the dough resembles wet sand but holds together when pressed.

2. Form 1 tablespoon of dough into a bean or crescent shape and place it on the prepared baking sheet. Alternatively, form the dough into a ball, flatten it slightly and press down the center with your thumb. Repeat until the sheet is filled, spacing the cookies about ½ inch apart. Bake for 20 minutes, or until the cookies are pale brown and firm. Transfer the cookies to a wire rack to cool and repeat with the remaining dough. —*Cesare Casella*

MAKE AHEAD The cookies can be stored for up to 3 days.

Triple Chocolate Peanut Butter Sandwich Cookies

MAKES ABOUT 3½ DOZEN SANDWICH COOKIES
Chocolate peanut butter cups were the inspiration for these soft and fudgy sandwich cookies.

- 1 cup unbleached all-purpose flour
- ½ cup unsweetened cocoa powder, preferably Dutch process
- ½ teaspoon baking soda
- ¼ teaspoon salt
- 4 ounces unsweetened chocolate, coarsely chopped
- 1 stick (4 ounces) unsalted butter, cut into tablespoons
- 1½ cups granulated sugar
- 1 teaspoon pure vanilla extract
- 2 large eggs, lightly beaten
- 4 ounces milk chocolate, chopped into ¼-inch chunks
- ½ cup chunky or smooth all-natural peanut butter
- ½ cup confectioners' sugar

1. Preheat the oven to 325°. Line several baking sheets with parchment paper. In a medium bowl, whisk the flour with the cocoa powder, baking soda and salt.

2. In a medium saucepan, melt the unsweetened chocolate with the butter over low heat. Transfer to a medium bowl and let cool. Stir in the granulated sugar and vanilla until blended, then mix in the eggs. Stir in the dry ingredients until a soft dough forms, then fold in the milk chocolate.

3. Roll slightly rounded teaspoons of the dough into ¾-inch balls. Arrange the balls 2 inches apart on the prepared baking sheets and flatten them slightly. Bake the cookies for about 13 minutes, or until firm outside but still soft in the center; rotate the baking sheets halfway through. Slide the parchment paper with the cookies onto wire racks to cool.

4. In a small bowl, blend the peanut butter with the confectioners' sugar. Spread the flat side of half the cookies with the peanut butter filling, top with the remaining cookies and serve.

—*Suzanne Lombardi*

MAKE AHEAD The cookies can be prepared through Step 3 and stored, between sheets of wax paper in an airtight container, for up to 1 week.

Chocolate Whoppers

MAKES ABOUT 15 LARGE COOKIES

- 1 cup pecan halves (4 ounces)
- 6 ounces semisweet chocolate, coarsely chopped
- 2 ounces unsweetened chocolate, coarsely chopped
- 6 tablespoons unsalted butter, cut into tablespoons
- ¼ cup sifted all-purpose flour
- ½ teaspoon salt
- ¼ teaspoon baking powder
- 2 large eggs
- ¾ cup sugar
- 2 teaspoons instant espresso
- 2 teaspoons pure vanilla extract
- 6 ounces chocolate chips
- 1¼ cups walnut halves, broken into large pieces (4 ounces)

I. Preheat the oven to 350°. Line 3 large baking sheets with parchment paper. Spread the pecans in a pie plate and bake for about 8 minutes, stirring once or twice, until the nuts are lightly browned and fragrant. Transfer to a plate to cool completely, then break them into large pieces.

2. In a saucepan, combine the semisweet and unsweetened chocolate

with the butter and stir over low heat until melted. Remove from the heat.

3. In a small bowl, whisk the flour with the salt and baking powder. In a large bowl, combine the eggs with the sugar, instant espresso and vanilla and beat at high speed until light and fluffy. Add the chocolate mixture and beat at medium speed just until blended. Add the flour mixture and beat at low speed just until incorporated. Using a wooden spoon, stir in the chocolate chips, walnuts and toasted pecans.

4. Scoop up the cookie dough with a ⅓-cup measure and drop 5 mounds of dough on each baking sheet; space the mounds as far from each other as possible. Bake the cookies on the upper and middle racks of the oven for about 17 minutes, or until the tops are dry and shiny; shift the sheets halfway through baking. Slide the cookies on the parchment onto wire racks and let cool completely. Remove the cookies from the paper and invert them onto the racks to allow the bottoms to dry slightly. —*Maida Heatter*

MAKE AHEAD The Chocolate Whoppers can be stored in an airtight container for 3 days or frozen for up to 1 month.

Heavenly Chocolate Sandwich Cookies

MAKES 32 SANDWICH COOKIES

COOKIES

- 1⅔ cups all-purpose flour
- ¾ cup unsweetened cocoa powder
- ½ teaspoon salt
- 2 sticks (½ pound) unsalted butter, at room temperature
- ½ cup sugar

FILLING

- 1 stick (4 ounces) unsalted butter, at room temperature
- 2½ cups confectioners' sugar

I. MAKE THE COOKIES: In a medium bowl, sift together the flour, cocoa and salt. In a standing electric mixer fitted with a paddle, cream the butter

Heavenly Chocolate Sandwich Cookies

with the sugar until fluffy. Gradually mix in the dry ingredients at low speed. Turn the dough out onto a lightly floured work surface and knead lightly. Pat the dough into an 8-inch square. Wrap in plastic and refrigerate until very firm, at least 4 hours or overnight.

2. Preheat the oven to 350°. Cut the dough into quarters; work with 1 piece at a time and keep the rest chilled. On a lightly floured surface, roll out the dough to an 8-inch square about ⅓ inch thick. Using a sharp knife, cut the dough in quarters. Cut each square in quarters again. Transfer the 16 square cookies to an ungreased cookie sheet and bake for about 15 minutes, or until firm. Let the cookies cool on the sheet for a few minutes, then transfer them to a rack to cool completely. Repeat with the remaining 3 pieces of dough.

3. MAKE THE FILLING: In a large bowl, using a wooden spoon, beat the butter with the confectioners' sugar until thick and creamy. Spread the underside of each of 32 cookies with 2 teaspoons of the filling. Top each to make a sandwich. —*René Becker*

MAKE AHEAD The cookie dough can be refrigerated for up to 5 days or frozen for up to 1 month.

fruit desserts
chapter 16

Summer Fruit Salad

10 SERVINGS

- 2 cups water
- ¾ cup sugar
- 1 teaspoon pure vanilla extract
- 1 cantaloupe, cut into ½-inch dice
- ½ pound fresh apricots, quartered
- ½ pound sweet cherries, pitted and halved
- ½ pound red seedless grapes
- 6 fresh figs, quartered
- 2 apples, cut into ½-inch dice
- 2 pears, cut into ½-inch dice
- 2 peaches, cut into ½-inch dice
- 1 banana, sliced

Purple basil leaves, for garnish

1. In a small saucepan, bring the water to a boil over moderate heat. Add the sugar and vanilla and simmer until a light syrup forms, about 15 minutes. Let cool for 10 minutes.

2. Pour the warm syrup into a large bowl. Gently stir in the fruit and let macerate at room temperature for several hours, stirring occasionally. Refrigerate the fruit salad until chilled. Garnish with purple basil leaves just before serving. —Jean-Christophe Royer

Raspberry Gelatin with Nectarines

6 SERVINGS

This silky, sophisticated fruit gelatin is an ideal dessert for a late-summer day.

- 4 half-pints raspberries
- 1 cup water
- ½ cup sugar
- 1 envelope unflavored gelatin
- ½ cup finely diced peeled nectarines or mangoes

Lightly sweetened whipped cream

1. In a medium saucepan, combine the raspberries with the water and cook over moderately high heat, crushing the berries with a potato masher or a fork, until very juicy, 5 to 6 minutes. Pour the hot berries into a fine-mesh stainless-steel sieve set over a medium bowl and let drain.

2. Gently stir the berries, scraping them up from the bottom of the sieve with a spatula; don't press on the solids or the gelatin will be cloudy. You should have 2 cups of juice. Stir in the sugar until dissolved and let cool.

3. Transfer ¼ cup of the raspberry juice to a small bowl. Sprinkle the gelatin over the juice and let stand until the gelatin is evenly moistened.

4. In a small skillet, warm the gelatin mixture over moderate heat just until the gelatin melts. Stir the mixture into the remaining raspberry juice in the medium bowl and pour it into 6 wineglasses. Refrigerate until barely set, about 1 hour. Gently stir in the fruit and refrigerate until firm, about 1 hour longer. Garnish with whipped cream.

—Grace Parisi

Cranberry Champagne Gelée with Oranges

8 SERVINGS

- 4½ teaspoons unflavored gelatin
- ½ cup cold water
- One 11½-ounce can frozen cranberry juice cocktail concentrate, thawed
- 1 cup sugar
- 2¾ cups dry Champagne
- 6 navel oranges

1. In a large heatproof bowl, sprinkle the gelatin over the water. Let stand for 5 minutes, or until the gelatin softens.

2. In a saucepan, mix the cranberry juice with the sugar and bring to a boil. Reduce the heat and simmer until the sugar dissolves. Pour the hot juice over the gelatin and stir until smooth. Stir in the Champagne. Cover and refrigerate until set, at least 4 hours or overnight.

3. Using a sharp knife, peel the oranges; be sure to remove all of the bitter white pith. Working over a bowl, cut in between the membranes to release the orange sections into the bowl. Pour off and reserve the juice for another use.

Cranberry Champagne Gelée with Oranges

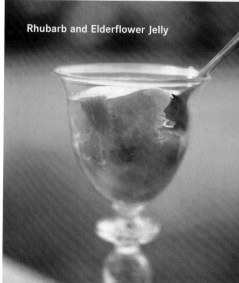

Rhubarb and Elderflower Jelly

4. Spoon the gelée into glasses, alternating with layers of orange segments. Refrigerate until cold. —David Lebovitz

MAKE AHEAD The assembled gelées can be refrigerated for up to 6 hours.

Rhubarb and Elderflower Jelly

8 SERVINGS

Elderflower concentrate is made from elderflowers and lemons. It can be ordered from Mushrooms & More (914-682-7288).

3 pounds rhubarb, stalks only, cut into 1-inch lengths (12 cups)

¼ cup fresh orange juice

3 tablespoons elderflower concentrate

1½ cups sugar

1 teaspoon pure vanilla extract

1¼ cups cold water

2 envelopes unflavored gelatin

1. Preheat the oven to 300°. In a large roasting pan, toss all but 1 cup of the rhubarb with the orange juice, elderflower concentrate, sugar, vanilla extract and 1 cup of the water. Place a crumpled sheet of parchment or wax paper directly on the rhubarb, then cover the roasting pan tightly with foil. Bake the rhubarb for 1½ hours, or until tender.

2. Strain the cooked rhubarb through a fine-meshed sieve set over a bowl, pressing lightly on the solids to extract as much juice as possible; there should be 4 cups of juice. Reserve the mashed rhubarb for another use.

3. Meanwhile, blanch the remaining 1 cup of rhubarb in boiling water until just tender, about 5 minutes. Transfer the rhubarb to a plate to cool.

4. Pour the remaining ¼ cup of cold water into a small bowl. Sprinkle the gelatin over the water and let stand for 10 minutes, or until the gelatin is completely softened.

5. Heat ½ cup of the rhubarb juice in a small saucepan. Add the gelatin mixture and cook over low heat, stirring until the gelatin is completely dissolved. Stir the mixture into the remaining 3½ cups of rhubarb juice and let cool slightly. Pour the jelly into 8 glasses and refrigerate until slightly set but still very jiggly. Stir the blanched rhubarb into each glass, being careful not to create too many bubbles, and refrigerate until firm, at least 2 hours. —*Tamasin Day-Lewis*

MAKE AHEAD The jelly can be covered with plastic wrap and refrigerated for up to 2 days.

Apricots in Vanilla-Cardamom Syrup

MAKES ABOUT 5 PINTS

Note that California apricots have a more intense flavor and a denser texture than Turkish ones. Also, the apricots should steep in the syrup for at least 1 week before serving.

2 quarts water

1½ cups sugar

2½ tablespoons fresh lemon juice

20 cardamom pods, preferably green

2 small vanilla beans

1½ pounds moist and plump dried apricots

1. In a medium saucepan, mix the water with the sugar, lemon juice and 10 of the cardamom pods. Crush the remaining 10 cardamom pods and remove the black seeds; add the seeds to the pan. Split the vanilla beans lengthwise and scrape out the seeds with the back of a table knife; add the seeds and the beans to the saucepan. Bring the liquid to a simmer over moderate heat and cook until fragrant and slightly syrupy, about 30 minutes. Let cool.

2. Put the apricots in a large glass or ceramic bowl. Pour the syrup over them, cover and set aside to steep at room temperature for 24 hours; the apricots will plump and soften and the syrup will thicken. Pack the apricots and their syrup into jars and refrigerate for at least 1 week before serving.

—*Sally Schneider*

MAKE AHEAD The apricots can be refrigerated for up to 4 months.

ONE-QUARTER CUP Calories 83 kcal, Total Fat 0.1 gm, Saturated Fat 0 gm, Protein 0.8 gm, Carbohydrates 21.4 gm

Gingered Berry Crumble

8 SERVINGS

1 cup unbleached all-purpose flour

⅓ cup plus 1 tablespoon granulated sugar

1 cup rolled oats

⅓ cup packed light brown sugar

½ teaspoon cinnamon

¼ teaspoon freshly grated nutmeg

Pinch of salt

1 stick (4 ounces) cold unsalted butter, cut into small pieces

2 pints fresh blackberries or other berries

2 peaches, nectarines, pears or apples, or 4 apricots, thinly sliced

¼ cup finely diced candied ginger

1 tablespoon fresh lemon juice

Blackberry Gelato (p. 373) or vanilla ice cream, for serving

1. Preheat the oven to 350°. In a large bowl, combine the flour with the ⅓ cup of granulated sugar and the rolled oats, brown sugar, cinnamon, nutmeg and salt. Using a pastry blender or 2 knives, cut in the butter until the mixture resembles coarse meal.

2. In a 9-by-13-inch glass or ceramic baking dish, toss all the fruit with the ginger, lemon juice and the remaining 1 tablespoon of granulated sugar. Press the topping to form large crumbs and sprinkle them evenly over the fruit.

Gingered Berry Crumble, with Blackberry Gelato (p. 373).

3. Transfer the crumble to the oven and bake for about 30 minutes, or until the topping is browned and the fruit is bubbling around the edges. Let the crumble cool slightly, then serve with a scoop of Blackberry Gelato.

—*Darryl Joannides*

Plum-Raspberry Crisp with Almond Crumb Topping

6 SERVINGS

Crisps and their next of kin, crumbles, offer many of the satisfactions you get from pie, but they require much less work. In this recipe, dried lavender flowers add a delicate nuance to the warm, rich summer fruit.

¼ cup plus 2 tablespoons sliced unblanched almonds (1½ ounces)

½ cup all-purpose flour

¼ cup plus 2 tablespoons dark brown sugar

Pinch of salt

3 tablespoons cold unsalted butter, cut into ¼-inch pieces

1½ pounds red or purple plums—halved, pitted and cut into ½-inch wedges

1½ pints raspberries (2 cups)

⅓ cup granulated sugar

1½ teaspoons fresh lemon juice

1 teaspoon pure vanilla extract

Scant ¼ teaspoon dried lavender flowers (optional)

Vanilla or toasted-almond frozen yogurt, for serving

1. Preheat the oven to 350°. Spread the sliced almonds in a pie plate and toast in the oven for about 6 minutes, or until the nuts are fragrant and lightly browned. Transfer the almonds to a plate and let them cool completely.

2. In a food processor, combine the almonds with 6 tablespoons of the flour, the brown sugar and the salt and pulse until the nuts are fairly finely chopped, with some larger pieces remaining. Transfer the almond mixture to a bowl and work in the butter with your fingers until the topping is

Plum-Raspberry Crisp with Almond Crumb Topping

crumbly. Refrigerate until chilled, at least 15 minutes.

3. In a large bowl, gently toss the plums and raspberries with the granulated sugar, lemon juice, vanilla, lavender flowers and the remaining 2 tablespoons of flour. Gently spread the fruit in a 10-inch round glass or ceramic baking dish and sprinkle with the almond crumb topping. Bake the crisp for about 40 minutes, or until the topping is browned and the fruit is bubbling. Serve warm, with vanilla frozen yogurt.

—*Sally Schneider*

MAKE AHEAD The almond crumb topping can be prepared in advance and refrigerated in a sturdy plastic bag for up to 1 week.

ONE SERVING Calories 306.3 kcal, Total Fat 10.7 gm, Saturated Fat 4.1 gm, Carbohydrates 52.1 gm

WINE This tangy dessert calls for a sweet wine that has high acidity, intense fruit and hints of almonds. Consider a bright, low-alcohol Late Harvest Riesling, such as the 1998 Mount Horrocks Clare Valley Cordon Cut from Australia or the 1999 Cairnbrae Riesling Marlborough Noble from New Zealand.

Pear Crisp with Polenta-Pecan Topping

8 SERVINGS

8 ripe Bartlett or Anjou pears (about 4 pounds)—peeled, halved, cored and sliced ½ inch thick

1 cup plus 1 tablespoon all-purpose flour

¼ cup granulated sugar

½ teaspoon pure vanilla extract

½ cup pecans, finely chopped

½ cup light brown sugar

⅓ cup coarse non-instant polenta

1 teaspoon cinnamon

Salt

1 stick (4 ounces) cold unsalted butter, cut into tablespoons

Vanilla ice cream, for serving

1. Preheat the oven to 375°. In a bowl, toss the pears with 1 tablespoon of the flour, the sugar and the vanilla. Spread the pears in a 9-by-13-inch baking dish.

2. In a food processor, pulse the cup of flour with the chopped pecans, the brown sugar, coarse polenta, cinnamon and a pinch of salt. Add the cold butter and pulse just until clumps start to form.

3. Sprinkle the topping over the pears and bake the crisp in the center of the oven for 45 to 50 minutes, or until the topping is browned and the pears are tender when pierced with a knife. Serve warm with vanilla ice cream.

—*David Lebovitz*

MAKE AHEAD The crisp can be covered and kept at room temperature for up to 1 day. Reheat the crisp in a 300° oven, loosely covered with foil, for about 10 minutes, or until heated through.

Warm Apple and Dried Cherry Crisp

6 SERVINGS

- 1½ cups rolled oats
- ¾ cup light brown sugar
- ½ cup all-purpose flour
- 2 teaspoons cinnamon
- ¾ teaspoon salt
- 1 stick (4 ounces) unsalted butter, melted
- 4 Granny Smith apples—peeled, cored and cut into 1-inch chunks
- ½ cup dried tart cherries (2 ounces)
- ½ cup granulated sugar
- 2 tablespoons honey
- 1 tablespoon fresh lemon juice

Pinch of freshly grated nutmeg

Unsweetened whipped cream

1. Preheat the oven to 400°. Set a baking sheet on the bottom of the oven to catch any spills. In a medium bowl, combine the rolled oats with the brown sugar, flour, 1½ teaspoons of the cinnamon and the salt. Add the melted butter and toss until evenly moistened, then pinch the topping into large crumbs.

2. In a bowl, toss the apples with the cherries, granulated sugar, honey, lemon juice, nutmeg and remaining ½ teaspoon cinnamon. Spread the apples in a 9-inch deep-dish pie plate. Scatter the crumbs over the apples all the way to the edge. Bake for about 45 minutes, or until the apples are tender, the filling is bubbling and the topping is golden. Let rest for 20 to 30 minutes. Serve warm or at room temperature with whipped cream.—*Thomas Gay*

MAKE AHEAD The baked crisp can be made 1 day ahead, refrigerated overnight and rewarmed.

Inside-Out Apple Charlottes

2 SERVINGS

- ½ cup diced (¼ inch) brioche
- 1½ tablespoons unsalted butter, melted
- 1 teaspoon sugar

Pinch of cinnamon

- 2 Granny Smith apples
- 1 teaspoon Calvados

1. Preheat the oven to 350°. In a pie plate, toss the brioche pieces with half the butter and bake for 5 minutes, or until golden. Transfer to a bowl, add the sugar and cinnamon and toss well.

2. Cut ½ inch from the tops of the apples. Using a melon baller, scoop out the seeds and cores. Spoon the bread filling into the apples and drizzle with the remaining butter and the Calvados. Bake the apples for about 40 minutes, or until tender; cover them with foil if the brioche browns too quickly.

—*Grace Parisi*

Warm Apple Charlottes

10 SERVINGS

You will need ten 4-inch ramekins to make this dessert. Decorate the dessert plates with caramel sauce if you like.

- 4 sticks (1 pound) unsalted butter
- 2 cups sugar
- 6 pounds Granny Smith apples— peeled, cored and cut into 1-inch pieces
- ½ teaspoon cinnamon
- 2 pounds packaged thin-sliced white sandwich bread

Cinnamon or vanilla ice cream, for serving

1. Melt 1 stick of the butter in a large casserole. Add the sugar and cook over moderately high heat, stirring until pale gold but grainy, about 5 minutes. Add the apples and stir until the mixture is bubbling.

2. Add the cinnamon and cook over moderately low heat, stirring occasionally, until the apples are broken down, about 40 minutes. Begin gently

Pear Crisp with Polenta-Pecan Topping

stirring from the bottom of the casserole and cook until the mixture is lightly caramelized, about 10 minutes longer. Transfer to a platter to cool.

3. Preheat the oven to 350°. Melt the remaining 3 sticks of butter in a medium saucepan; skim off the foam. Pour the melted butter into a small bowl, leaving any milk solids behind. Brush ten 4-inch ramekins with the melted butter.

4. Using a 4-inch round biscuit cutter, stamp out 10 disks from 10 of the bread slices; discard the trimmings. Brush the disks on both sides with melted butter and set them in the ramekins. Remove the crusts from the remaining slices of bread. Brush the slices on both sides with the melted butter and cut each slice into 3 equal rectangles.

5. Stand 10 of the bread rectangles inside the rim of each ramekin, overlapping them slightly. Spoon ⅔ cup of the apple mixture into each ramekin and smooth the surface. Carefully fold the bread over the filling, pressing lightly to enclose the filling. Cover the ramekins with foil and bake for 1 hour, or until the bread is slightly browned and the filling is bubbling. Remove the foil and bake for 10 minutes longer, or until the bread is browned and crisp.

6. Slip on an oven mitt and unmold the charlottes 1 at a time by turning them onto the mitt and then setting them right side up on dessert plates. Let cool for 15 minutes. Set a scoop of ice cream on top and serve right away.

—*Jeremy Strode*

MAKE AHEAD The Warm Apple Charlottes can be completed and then refrigerated overnight. Reheat them in their ramekins in a 350° oven for about 30 minutes.

WINE This dessert would be well matched by a fresh, fruity Late Harvest Riesling that echoes the dish's fine balance of sweetness and acidity. The 1998 Mount Horrocks Cordon Cut is perfect.

Silky Apple Confit

8 SERVINGS

Four hours of slow baking reduces four pounds of apples to a dense, sliceable loaf with a concentrated apple flavor.

- 2 tablespoons unsalted butter
- 3 cups dry white wine
- ¾ cup light brown sugar
- ½ vanilla bean, split
- 4 pounds Granny Smith apples— peeled, cored and sliced ½ inch thick
- 1 tablespoon fresh lemon juice
- Whipped cream or vanilla frozen yogurt, for serving (optional)

1. Preheat the oven to 300°. Melt the butter in a very large deep-sided skillet and cook over low heat until golden brown. Add the wine, sugar and vanilla bean and simmer for 5 minutes. Add the apples and lemon juice and cook over moderately low heat, turning the apples occasionally, until tender, about 30 minutes.

Warm Apple Charlotte

Coconut-Fried Mango with Cinnamon Rum Sauce

2. Transfer the apples to a bowl with a slotted spoon, letting the juices drain back into the skillet. Remove the vanilla bean. Boil the juices over high heat until reduced to ¼ cup and syrupy, about 6 minutes. Pour the syrup over the apples and toss gently to coat.

3. Lightly butter an 8-by-4-inch loaf pan. Cut an 8-by-16-inch rectangle of parchment or wax paper. Lightly butter the paper. Fit the paper into the loaf pan, buttered side up, leaving a 4-inch overhang on both long sides. Layer the apples in the pan, filling in any gaps or holes. Press the apples down, packing them in the pan as tightly as possible; the apples will be mounded slightly on top. Fold the overhanging parchment over the apples and cover with foil, sealing it tightly around the rim of the loaf pan.

4. Set the loaf pan in a baking dish and add enough hot water to reach two-thirds of the way up the side of the pan. Bake for 2 hours. Transfer the pan to a baking sheet and bake for 2 hours longer. Remove the foil and let the confit cool to room temperature on a wire rack. Refrigerate for at least 2 hours.

5. Open the parchment. Set a plate over the pan, invert and unmold the confit. Remove and discard the parchment paper. Using a moistened knife, cut the confit into 1-inch slices and serve with whipped cream or frozen yogurt. —*Sally Schneider*

MAKE AHEAD The apple confit keeps well. It can be refrigerated for up to 3 days.

ONE SERVING Calories 236 kcal, Total Fat 3.6 gm, Saturated Fat 2 gm

Coconut-Fried Mango with Cinnamon Rum Sauce

6 SERVINGS

- 2 cups fresh orange juice
- 2 cups water, plus 1½ cups ice water
- 1 cup granulated sugar

Golden Strawberry Gratin (p. 370)

- 3 tablespoons amber rum, such as Mount Gay
- ½ teaspoon cinnamon
- 3 firm ripe mangoes—pitted, peeled and quartered lengthwise
- 1 cup all-purpose flour
- ½ cup confectioners' sugar, plus more for dusting
- ¼ cup cornstarch
- 1 cup packed sweetened shredded coconut (2½ ounces)

Vegetable oil, for frying

Crème fraîche (optional)

1. In a large saucepan, combine the orange juice with the 2 cups of water, the granulated sugar and the amber rum and bring the mixture to a boil. Simmer it over moderate heat until it's reduced to 1½ cups, approximately 30 minutes. Add the cinnamon and continue simmering for 5 minutes longer.

Pour the sauce into a heatproof bowl or pitcher.

2. Pat the mango quarters dry with paper towels. In a large bowl, whisk together the flour, the ½ cup of confectioners' sugar, the cornstarch and the 1½ cups of ice water until they're smooth. Then whisk in the coconut until evenly distributed.

3. In a large saucepan, heat 1 inch of vegetable oil to 375°. Dip 4 pieces of mango in the batter and add them to the hot oil. Fry, turning once, until golden, about 2 minutes per side. Drain the mango fritters on paper towels and repeat with the remaining mangoes. Transfer the fritters to a warmed platter and dust with confectioners' sugar. Serve with the sauce and crème fraîche alongside.

—*Alison Tolley*

Golden Strawberry Gratins

8 SERVINGS

- 3 pints strawberries, hulled and sliced ¼ inch thick
- 3 large eggs
- 2 large egg yolks
- ½ cup sugar
- ¼ cup Grand Marnier

1. Preheat the broiler. Arrange the berries attractively in 8 shallow heat-proof dishes.

2. Bring several inches of water to a simmer in a medium saucepan. In a medium stainless-steel bowl, whisk the eggs with the yolks and sugar for 2 minutes. Add the Grand Marnier and whisk for 1 minute. Set the bowl over the simmering water and whisk continuously until the sabayon is thick and fluffy, 4 to 5 minutes; be sure to whisk in the sabayon from the side of the bowl. Remove the bowl from the heat.

3. Spoon ¼ cup of the sabayon on each dish of strawberries. Set 4 of the dishes on a baking sheet and broil for 1 minute, or until the sabayon is lightly browned. Repeat with the remaining dishes. —*Dominique Macquet*

Honey-Caramelized Pears with Orange-Vanilla Flan

Lemon Mousse with Candied Lemon Slices

6 SERVINGS

Sweetened condensed milk adds a rich and creamy consistency to this lovely mousse, which has been adapted from *Sweet Simplicity: Jacques Pépin's Fruit Desserts* (Bay Books).

LEMON MOUSSE

- ⅓ cup sugar
- 5 tablespoons cold water
- 3 large egg yolks
- 1½ tablespoons lemon zest
- 2 teaspoons unflavored powdered gelatin
- ⅔ cup sweetened condensed milk
- ¼ cup plus 2 tablespoons fresh lemon juice
- 1 cup heavy cream

CANDIED LEMON

- 1 large lemon, thinly sliced crosswise and seeded
- 1 cup water
- ⅓ cup sugar
- 1 tablespoon rum (optional)

1. MAKE THE LEMON MOUSSE: In a medium saucepan, combine the sugar with 3 tablespoons of cold water and boil until a light syrup forms.

2. In a standing mixer fitted with a whisk, beat the egg yolks with the lemon zest. Gradually beat in the hot sugar syrup, then beat at high speed until thick and fluffy, about 10 minutes.

3. Meanwhile, in a small glass bowl set in a small skillet, sprinkle the gelatin over the remaining 2 tablespoons of cold water. Add enough water to the skillet to reach halfway up the side of the bowl. Warm the water bath over moderately high heat, stirring the gelatin until it melts. Whisk the gelatin, condensed milk and lemon juice into the egg yolk mixture.

4. In another bowl, beat the cream until it holds soft peaks, then quickly fold it into the egg yolk mixture. Spoon the lemon mousse into bowls or tulip glasses. Cover and refrigerate until chilled, at least 2 hours or overnight.

5. MAKE THE CANDIED LEMON: Blanch the lemon slices in a medium saucepan of boiling water for 5 seconds. Drain and rinse under cold water. Repeat the blanching process once.

6. In the same saucepan, combine the water and sugar with the lemon slices and bring to a boil, stirring to dissolve the sugar. Simmer over low heat until syrupy, about 30 minutes. Let cool slightly, then stir in the rum, if using. Let cool completely. Garnish each mousse with candied lemon slices and serve. —*Jacques Pépin*

Honey-Caramelized Pears with Orange-Vanilla Flan

10 SERVINGS

The custard for the flan needs to stand overnight so that it becomes infused with the flavors of the orange zest and the vanilla bean. Start the recipe a day in advance. You'll need ten 3- to 4-ounce ramekins.

- 2½ cups milk
- 1½ cups heavy cream
- 2 oranges, zest removed with a vegetable peeler
- 1 vanilla bean, split lengthwise
- 2⅔ cups sugar
- 8 large egg yolks
- 2 large eggs, lightly beaten
- Vegetable oil, for coating
- 2 quarts water
- 1 lemon, zest removed with a vegetable peeler
- 10 firm Bartlett pears (about ½ pound each)—peeled, quartered and cored
- 1 stick (4 ounces) unsalted butter
- ¾ cup honey

1. In a medium saucepan, combine the milk with the cream, half of the orange zest, half of the vanilla bean and ⅔ cup of the sugar and bring just to a simmer. Let the custard cool to room temperature, then whisk in the egg yolks and whole eggs. Transfer the custard to a bowl, cover with plastic wrap and refrigerate overnight.

2. Preheat the oven to 250°. Lightly coat ten 3- to 4-ounce ramekins with vegetable oil and arrange them in a roasting pan. Strain the custard into a large glass measuring cup and pour it into the ramekins, filling them about three-quarters full. Add enough hot water to the roasting pan to reach halfway up the sides of the ramekins. Transfer the roasting pan to the oven and bake for about 1 hour or until the flans are set. Carefully remove the ramekins from the water bath and let them cool to room temperature. Refrigerate the flans until well chilled, about 4 hours.

3. Meanwhile, in a large saucepan, combine the water with the lemon zest and the remaining 2 cups of sugar, orange zest and vanilla bean. Bring to a boil, stirring to dissolve the sugar. Add the pears and cover with a heat-proof plate or pot lid that's slightly smaller than the saucepan, to keep the pears submerged. Simmer over moderately low heat until the pears are just tender and a knife inserted in the thickest part comes out easily, about 15 minutes. Using a slotted spoon, transfer the pears to a platter. Let the pears and poaching liquid cool separately.

4. Divide the butter and the honey between 2 large skillets and bring them both to a boil. Cook over high heat, stirring occasionally, until the honey and butter mixture turns light gold, about 4 minutes. Add half of the pears to each skillet, cut side down, and cook, turning occasionally, until they're golden and beginning to caramelize, about 12 minutes.

5. Add ¾ cup of the reserved pear poaching liquid to each skillet and cook over moderate heat, turning and basting the pears, until the liquid reduces to a thick syrup, about 8 minutes. Using a slotted spoon, transfer the pears to a platter. Stir into each skillet 2 tablespoons of the poaching liquid to thin the syrup. Pour the sauce over the pears.

6. Run a thin-bladed knife around the flans to loosen them and dip the bottom of each ramekin in hot water. Top each flan with a dessert plate and invert; holding the ramekin and plate together, give the dish a good shake to unmold the flan. Arrange 2 pear halves alongside each flan. Drizzle the flans and pears with the syrup and serve.

—Julian Serrano

MAKE AHEAD The dessert can be prepared through Step 3 up to 3 days in advance; refrigerate the poached pears and flans separately.

Summer Berry Clafoutis
12 SERVINGS
This flourless dessert is more like a delicate custard with fruit than like the traditional sturdy country clafoutis from France.

- 8 large egg yolks
- 4 large eggs
- ½ cup sugar
- One 2-inch piece of vanilla bean, split
- 1½ cups whole milk
- 1½ cups heavy cream
- 2 tablespoons kirsch
- 2 pints blueberries
- 1 pint raspberries
- Confectioners' sugar, for dusting (optional)

1. Preheat the oven to 350°. Butter two 9-by-13-inch baking dishes. In a medium bowl, whisk the egg yolks with the eggs and sugar. Holding the vanilla bean over the bowl, scrape the seeds into the egg mixture; save the pod for another use. Whisk in the milk, heavy cream and kirsch.

2. Put half the berries in each baking dish and pour the custard over the top. Bake for 20 minutes, or until just set. Remove from the oven and let cool slightly. Dust the tops with confectioners' sugar and serve warm.

—Jean-Louis Palladin

Fresh Fruit with Tea-Infused Custard
4 TO 6 SERVINGS
The *rooibos* tea called for below is the tea of choice in southern Africa.

- 2 cups milk
- 1 *rooibos* or Earl Grey tea bag
- 3 large egg yolks
- ½ cup superfine sugar
- 2 tablespoons cornstarch
- 2 tablespoons unsalted butter
- ½ cup damson plum jam
- 2 tablespoons Cognac
- 3 cups sliced fresh fruit

1. Bring the milk to a simmer in a medium saucepan. Add the tea bag, remove from the heat and let steep for 15 minutes. Discard the tea bag.

2. In a medium bowl, whisk the egg yolks with the sugar and cornstarch. Whisk in half of the warm milk. Pour the mixture into the milk in the saucepan and cook over moderate heat, whisking constantly, until the custard is thick, 6 to 7 minutes. Stir in the butter and transfer the custard to a bowl.

3. In a small saucepan, melt the jam with the Cognac. In a bowl, toss the fruit with the melted jam, then transfer to plates or bowls. Spoon the warm custard over or around the fruit and serve.

—Jacques Pépin

MAKE AHEAD The custard can be refrigerated overnight.

Banana-Bread-and-Butter Pudding
8 SERVINGS
You will need eight 4½-inch ramekins to make this dessert.

- One ½-pound brioche, crust removed, cut into ¼-inch dice (about 6 cups)
- 7 tablespoons unsalted butter, 4 tablespoons melted
- 1¼ cups sugar
- 3 tablespoons light corn syrup
- 3 tablespoons water
- 1⅓ cups heavy cream

Pinch of salt

    4 large ripe bananas,
       2 of them sliced
    ½ cup milk
    5 large egg yolks
    1 teaspoon pure vanilla extract
Vanilla ice cream or whipped cream,
    for serving

1. Preheat the oven to 350°. Lightly butter eight 4½-by-2-inch ramekins. In a large bowl, toss the brioche with the melted butter. Spread the brioche on a large baking sheet and bake for about 15 minutes, stirring occasionally, until golden and crisp.

2. Meanwhile, in a small heavy saucepan, combine ¾ cup of the sugar with the corn syrup and water; cook over moderate heat, stirring until the sugar dissolves. Boil the syrup without stirring until a deep amber caramel forms, about 7 minutes. Remove the caramel from the heat and carefully stir in ⅓ cup of the cream, the remaining 3 tablespoons of butter and the salt. Immediately pour 2 tablespoons of the caramel into each of the prepared ramekins and set them in a large roasting pan. Arrange the sliced bananas decoratively in the caramel.

3. In a large bowl, mash the remaining 2 bananas until smooth. Whisk in the milk, yolks, remaining ½ cup of sugar, vanilla and remaining 1 cup of heavy cream until smooth. Fold in the toasted brioche and let stand, stirring occasionally, until the liquid is completely absorbed, about 20 minutes.

4. Spoon the bread mixture into the ramekins and smooth the surfaces. Pour enough hot water into the roasting pan to reach halfway up the sides of the ramekins. Bake the puddings in the water bath for 35 minutes, or until they are firm and a knife inserted in the center comes out clean. Remove the ramekins from the water bath and let cool slightly.

5. To unmold, run a knife around the puddings. Top each with a plate. Invert the plates and lift off the ramekins. Pour any remaining caramel around the puddings. Serve warm with ice cream or whipped cream.—*Heather Ho*

MAKE AHEAD The baked puddings can be wrapped tightly with foil and refrigerated overnight. Rewarm, covered, in a 325° oven for about 15 minutes before unmolding.

Banana-Split Strudel

6 SERVINGS

    1⅓ cups finely chopped walnuts
         (4½ ounces)
     ½ pound cream cheese, softened
      1 large egg yolk
     ¾ cup granulated sugar, plus more
         for sprinkling
      1 teaspoon pure vanilla extract
     ¼ teaspoon cinnamon
      2 ounces bittersweet or semisweet
         chocolate, finely chopped
      4 sheets phyllo dough
      1 stick (4 ounces) unsalted
         butter, melted
      4 medium bananas, peeled
Confectioners' sugar, for dusting
      1 pint vanilla ice cream

1. Preheat the oven to 375°. Spread the walnuts on a rimmed baking sheet and toast for 6 minutes, or until browned. Transfer the walnuts to a plate to cool.

2. In a bowl, using a handheld mixer, beat the cream cheese until smooth. Beat in the egg yolk. Add ¼ cup of granulated sugar, the vanilla and cinnamon and beat until blended. Stir the chocolate into the cream cheese mixture and chill for at least 10 minutes.

3. Line a large rimmed baking sheet with parchment paper. Lay 1 sheet of phyllo on the parchment paper. Brush the phyllo with melted butter and sprinkle with ⅓ cup of the walnuts and 2 tablespoons of the granulated sugar. Cover with another phyllo sheet, butter it and sprinkle with walnuts and granulated sugar as before; repeat 2 more times to make 4 layers.

4. Turn the baking sheet so that a long side is facing you. Spoon half the cream cheese mixture in a long strip along the length of the phyllo, leaving a 2-inch border of phyllo below and on each side. Lay 2 bananas end to end on the cream cheese. Set the 2 remaining bananas next to them, so you have a double row. Trim the bananas if needed. Spoon the remaining cream cheese mixture in a strip on the bananas.

5. Starting with the long edge closest to you and using the parchment paper as a guide, lift the phyllo over the bananas and roll into a compact log; fold in the sides to enclose the filling. Discard the parchment paper. Slide the strudel to the center of the baking sheet, making sure the seam is down. Brush the strudel with melted butter and sprinkle with granulated sugar.

6. Bake the strudel for 40 minutes, or until crisp and brown. Let it stand for about 25 minutes, then transfer to a cutting board. Dust with confectioners' sugar. Using a serrated knife, thickly slice the strudel crosswise and serve warm with vanilla ice cream.

—*Gale Gand*

Banana-Bread-and-Butter Pudding

Orange Soufflé Surprise

6 SERVINGS

- 6 large navel oranges
- 1 pint orange sorbet
- 4 large egg whites
- ½ cup granulated sugar

Confectioners' sugar, for dusting

1. Cut off the top third of each orange. Finely grate the zest from the orange tops and reserve 2 tablespoons. Using a spoon, scrape out the insides of the oranges to make neat shells. (Reserve the orange flesh for making juice or smoothies.) Cut a thin slice from the bottom of each orange shell, without making a hole, so that the shell stands upright.

2. Fill each orange shell to within ½ inch of the rim with about ⅓ cup of the sorbet. Cover with plastic wrap and freeze until solid, at least 1 hour or overnight.

3. Preheat the oven to 400°. Arrange 6 ramekins or 3-inch ring molds in a small roasting pan. Set the frozen orange shells in the ramekins, cut side up. Pack ice in the pan around the orange shells and add a little water to the pan.

4. In a large stainless-steel bowl, beat the egg whites until very soft peaks form. Add the granulated sugar and the reserved 2 tablespoons of orange zest and beat the whites until stiff and glossy. Transfer the meringue to a pastry bag fitted with a star tip and pipe it on top of the oranges. (Alternatively, use a spoon to top the oranges with the meringue.) Bake for about 7 minutes, or until the tops are nicely puffed and browned. Sift confectioners' sugar over the oranges and serve at once.

—*Jacques Pépin*

WINE Partner this citrusy dessert with an Orange Muscat. Quady Winery, in California, offers two delicious ones, either of which would work beautifully here, depending on your taste: the low-alcohol Electra and the heavier, more intense Essensia.

Frozen Lime Soufflé

6 TO 8 SERVINGS

The top of this dessert stands above the rim of the dish with the help of a foil collar, which should be removed once the mixture sets.

Vegetable oil, for brushing

- 1 envelope unflavored gelatin (2 teaspoons)
- ¼ cup cold water
- 4 large eggs, separated
- ½ cup fresh lime juice
- 1 cup sugar

Pinch of salt

Finely grated zest of 1 lime

- 1 cup heavy cream

Fresh berries and diced mango, for garnish

1. Lightly brush a 4-cup soufflé dish with oil. Fold a 2-foot-long piece of foil in half lengthwise and wrap it around the outside of the soufflé dish to form a collar. Secure the collar with tape and lightly brush the inside with oil.

2. In a small bowl, sprinkle the gelatin over the water and let stand about 5 minutes. In a heavy medium saucepan, whisk the egg yolks with the lime juice, ½ cup of the sugar and the salt. Cook over moderately low heat, whisking constantly, until boiling and thickened, about 5 minutes. Remove from the heat, add the gelatin and whisk until dissolved. Add the lime zest and transfer to a large bowl to cool.

3. Using a handheld electric mixer at medium speed, beat the egg whites to soft peaks. Gradually beat in the remaining ½ cup of sugar until stiff.

4. In a large bowl, whip the cream until stiff peaks form. Fold the beaten whites into the whipped cream. Stir one-third of this mixture into the lime custard, then fold in the rest. Spoon the soufflé mixture into the prepared dish and smooth the top.

5. Freeze until firm, at least 4 hours. Serve the soufflé garnished with fresh berries and diced mango.

—*Joyce Goldstein*

Blackberry Gelato

MAKES ABOUT 2 QUARTS

- 2 pints blackberries
- 1¼ cups half-and-half
- 1 cup sugar
- ¼ cup nonfat dry milk
- 6 large egg yolks
- 2 cups heavy cream
- 2 teaspoons pure vanilla extract

1. Puree the blackberries in a food processor or blender. Strain the puree through a fine sieve, pressing hard on the solids to extract as much puree as possible; discard the seeds.

2. In a large heavy saucepan, combine the half-and-half with the sugar and cook over moderate heat, stirring, until warm to the touch and the sugar has dissolved. Remove from the heat and stir in the dry milk.

3. In a medium bowl, lightly whisk the egg yolks. Slowly whisk in ½ cup of the warm half-and-half mixture to temper the eggs, then gradually whisk in the rest. Return the mixture to the saucepan and cook over moderate heat, stirring constantly until it thickens to a runny custard and registers 180° on an instant-read thermometer, about 6 minutes. Remove the saucepan from the heat and stir in the heavy cream, blackberry puree and vanilla. Strain the custard through a fine sieve into a medium bowl set over ice water. Stir occasionally until the custard is completely chilled.

4. Freeze the custard in an ice cream maker, in 2 batches if necessary, according to the manufacturer's instructions. Transfer to an airtight container and press a layer of plastic wrap directly on the surface, then seal with a tight-fitting lid and freeze for at least 2 hours before serving.

—*Darryl Joannides*

MAKE AHEAD The gelato can be prepared, well wrapped and frozen for up to 2 days. Let it soften for 15 minutes in the refrigerator before serving so it's not rock hard.

chapter 17

Chocolate Fondue with Fresh Fruit

1. In a medium stainless-steel bowl, whisk the eggs with the sugar and amaretto liqueur. Set the bowl over a large saucepan of simmering water and whisk constantly until the mixture turns bright yellow and thickens, about 10 minutes. Do not let the eggs get too hot or they will scramble. Remove the bowl from the heat and continue whisking for a few minutes to cool the mixture slightly. Set aside and let cool to room temperature, then fold in the amaretti.

2. In a large stainless-steel bowl, beat the cream to soft peaks. Fold the cream into the egg mixture. Spoon the *semifreddo* into an airtight container, cover with plastic wrap and freeze until firm, at least 6 hours or up to 5 days.

3. Remove the *semifreddo* from the freezer and let stand at room temperature for 5 to 10 minutes so that it softens slightly. Meanwhile, in a small saucepan, melt the chocolate over low heat, stirring occasionally. Scoop the *semifreddo* into flutes or parfait glasses, drizzle with the melted chocolate and serve. —*Cristina and Mauro Rastelli*

WINE The rich, honeyed 1997 Barberani Calcaia would be an ideal match for this frozen-custard dessert.

Chocolate Fondue with Fresh Fruit

6 SERVINGS

For an intense fondue, use a bittersweet chocolate with a minimum of 56 percent cocoa, such as Valrhona or Lindt.

- ½ **cup milk**
- ¼ **cup heavy cream**
- 1 **tablespoon sugar**
- 6 **ounces bittersweet chocolate, coarsely chopped**
- 2 **tablespoons unsalted butter, at room temperature**
- 12 **strawberries, hulled**
- 2 **bananas, sliced ½ inch thick**
- 1 **small pineapple—peeled, quartered, cored and cut into 2-inch chunks**
- 1 **apple, sliced ½ inch thick**

In a saucepan, mix the milk, cream and sugar and bring to a boil. Add the chocolate and remove the pan from the heat. Let stand until the chocolate melts, about 5 minutes; stir until smooth. Stir in the butter. Serve the fondue in the pan, letting everyone dip their own fruit. —*Eric Ripert*

Amaretto Semifreddo with Chocolate Sauce

6 SERVINGS

- 4 **large eggs**
- ½ **cup sugar**
- 2 **tablespoons amaretto liqueur**
- 6 **ounces amaretti cookies, crushed (about 2½ cups)**
- 1 **cup heavy cream**
- 3 **ounces bittersweet chocolate, chopped**

Hungarian Palacsinta

6 SERVINGS

Palascinta are thin pancakes that are often stacked with a savory or sweet filling; here they enfold melted apricot jam and ground walnuts.

- 4 **large eggs**
- About 1½ **cups milk**
- Pinch of salt
- 1 **cup all-purpose flour**
- 1 **tablespoon melted unsalted butter, plus more for cooking the crêpes**
- ½ **cup apricot jam**
- 1 **teaspoon fresh lemon juice**
- ½ **cup coarsely ground walnuts**
- Confectioners' sugar, for dusting
- Chocolate sauce, for serving (optional)

I. In a bowl, whisk the eggs with ½ cup of the milk and the salt. Whisk in the flour until smooth, then whisk in the remaining milk and the butter; the batter should have the consistency of cream. Let the batter rest for 1 hour.

2. Heat a 7-inch crêpe pan and brush with butter. Pour ¼ cup of batter into the pan and rotate it immediately to coat the bottom evenly; pour any excess batter back into the bowl. Cook the crêpe over moderate heat until lightly browned on the bottom, about 30 seconds. Flip the crêpe and cook the second side until brown dots appear, about 10 seconds longer. Transfer to a large plate. Repeat with the melted butter and remaining batter to make 18 crêpes.

3. In a saucepan, melt the apricot jam with the lemon juice; stir until smooth.

4. Preheat the oven to 400°. Butter a 9-by-13-inch baking dish. Spread each crêpe with 1 teaspoon of jam and 1 tablespoon of walnuts. Fold it into quarters and transfer to the baking

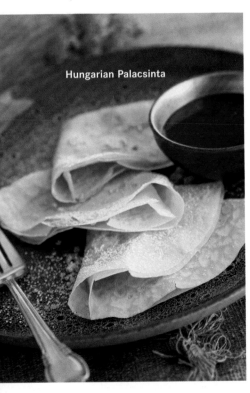

Hungarian Palacsinta

dish. Repeat with the remaining crêpes. Cover the dish with foil and bake for 10 minutes, or until hot. Sprinkle with the remaining walnuts and sift confectioners' sugar on top. Serve the crêpes warm, with chocolate sauce if you like. *—Tina Ujlaki*

Moshier's Chocolate-Filled Bomboloncini

8 SERVINGS 👑

- ½ cup heavy cream
- 4 ounces semisweet chocolate, coarsely chopped
- 2 tablespoons lukewarm water
- 2 teaspoons active dry yeast
- 1½ cups all-purpose flour, plus more for kneading
- ½ cup milk, scalded and cooled
- 2 tablespoons granulated sugar
- ½ teaspoon salt
- 2 tablespoons plus 8 teaspoons unsalted butter, softened
- ½ cup confectioners' sugar

I. In a small saucepan, heat the cream until steaming. Remove from the heat, add the chocolate and stir until melted. Transfer the mixture to a shallow bowl and refrigerate until firm, about 2 hours.

2. In a standing electric mixer fitted with a paddle, combine the warm water with the yeast and let stand until frothy, about 5 minutes. Add the flour, milk, granulated sugar and salt and mix at low speed until the dough just comes together, about 1 minute. Add 2 tablespoons of the butter and mix, scraping down the sides occasionally, until a smooth dough forms, about 5 minutes.

3. Turn the dough out onto a lightly floured surface and knead until smooth. Transfer the dough to a lightly oiled bowl, cover and let rise in a warm place until doubled in bulk, 1 to 1½ hours.

4. With the remaining 8 teaspoons of butter, make 8 buttered rounds on 2 heavy baking sheets: Using a whole

Moshier's Chocolate-Filled Bomboloncino

teaspoon for each round, smear the butter to make four 5-inch circular areas on each baking sheet. Neatly sprinkle 1 tablespoon of the confectioners' sugar on each buttered round.

5. Punch down the dough and divide it into 8 pieces; work with 1 piece at a time and keep the rest covered with plastic wrap. Divide the first piece of dough in half. On a lightly floured surface, press each half into a 3-inch round, slightly thicker in the center and thinner around the edges. Lightly brush the edges with water and spoon 1 tablespoon of the cold chocolate filling into the center of 1 piece. Top with the other piece and press the edges together to seal. Pinch and smooth the seam as you form the dough into a smooth ball. Set the ball on 1 of the sugared rounds on the baking sheet. Repeat with the remaining dough and filling. Loosely cover the *bomboloncini* with plastic wrap and let rise in a warm, draft-free place for 45 minutes.

6. Preheat the oven to 400°. Bake the *bomboloncini* in the middle of the oven, 1 sheet at a time, for about 10

Chocolate Sweethearts

minutes, or until puffed and golden and the confectioners' sugar on the baking sheet is lightly caramelized. Using metal tongs, carefully swirl the *bomboloncini* in the caramel and invert them onto a wire rack to cool for 5 minutes. Transfer the *bomboloncini* to plates and serve warm. —*Eric Moshier*

Chocolate Sweethearts

MAKES 12 SWEETHEARTS

- 4 ounces bittersweet, milk or white chocolate, coarsely chopped
- 1 tablespoon sliced almonds
- 1 tablespoon pecans
- 1 tablespoon unsalted pumpkin seeds
- 1 tablespoon golden raisins
- 1 tablespoon dark raisins
- 3 small strawberries, quartered
- 12 tiny mint leaves

Melt the chocolate in a double boiler or microwave oven. Spoon the chocolate into 12 miniature foil cups and let cool slightly. Lightly press the nuts, seeds, raisins, strawberries and mint into the chocolate and refrigerate for at least 1 hour, or until set. Discard the foil, set the chocolates on a plate and serve. —*Jacques Pépin*

Valrhona Chocolate Mousse

6 SERVINGS

This ultra-rich, dense mousse shows off the unique smoky character of Valrhona chocolate.

- 4 large egg yolks
- ¼ cup plus 1 teaspoon sugar
- 1 tablespoon Cognac
- ½ pound bittersweet chocolate, preferably Valrhona, coarsely chopped, plus more for shaving (see Note)
- 6 tablespoons unsalted butter, cut into small pieces

Pinch of salt

- ½ cup heavy cream
- 6 apricots, halved, or 3 peaches, quartered lengthwise, for serving

I. In a medium stainless-steel bowl, combine the egg yolks with ¼ cup of the sugar and the Cognac. Set the bowl over a medium saucepan of simmering water. Using a handheld electric mixer, whisk the mixture constantly at medium speed until pale yellow and thick, about 4 minutes. Remove the bowl from the pan once in a while, whisking all the time, so the mixture doesn't get too hot.

2. Remove the bowl from the saucepan, still whisking, and add the chopped chocolate, butter and salt. Set the bowl over the water and stir, using a wooden spoon or a heatproof spatula, over low heat until the chocolate and butter are melted. Remove the bowl from the heat and let the mixture cool to room temperature, stirring often. Refrigerate until slightly chilled, about 20 minutes.

3. In a medium stainless-steel bowl, whip the cream with the remaining 1 teaspoon of sugar until the cream holds soft peaks. Using a rubber spatula, blend one-third of the cream into the chocolate mixture to lighten it, then carefully fold in the remaining cream until blended. Cover and refrigerate the mousse until firm, at least 2 hours.

4. Spoon ⅓ cup of the mousse onto each plate. Set 2 apricot halves next to the mousse and shave some chocolate over each serving.

—*Corinne Chapoutier*

NOTE If Valrhona is not available, choose another brand that contains a minimum of 50 percent cocoa, such as Lindt's extra-bitter chocolate. The additional cocoa makes desserts taste as chocolaty as they look.

MAKE AHEAD The chocolate mousse can be made through Step 3 and refrigerated for up to 1 day.

WINE Practically unknown outside of France, Banyuls, which is fortified with alcohol, is one of the few wines that are strong and sweet enough to stand up to chocolate. The 1996

Valrhona Chocolate Mousse

Banyuls, with its roasted aromas, is a perfect match for the smoky flavor of Valrhona chocolate.

Bruschetta with Honey Ricotta and Strawberries

4 SERVINGS

Serve this sweet and simple bruschetta for breakfast with coffee or for dessert with port. Since this bruschetta is so simple, all the ingredients must be absolutely topnotch.

- ¾ cup fresh ricotta (6 ½ ounces)
- 1 tablespoon honey, plus more for drizzling
- 4 slices raisin or currant bread
- 1 tablespoon unsalted butter, melted
- ½ pint strawberries, sliced

I. Beat the fresh ricotta with the 1 tablespoon of honey. Toast the raisin or currant bread. Brush the toast with the melted butter and top with the ricotta.

2. Garnish the bruschetta with the sliced strawberries and drizzle honey over all. Serve immediately.

—*Donna Hay*

Glazed Ricotta with Vanilla Bean

4 SERVINGS

This recipe demonstrates one of the best ways to appreciate the complex aroma of vanilla: Steep the seeds in a soft, mild fresh cheese like ricotta, then serve the cheese as a dessert.

- ¼ **cup pure maple syrup**
- 1 **vanilla bean, split**
- 1 **pound fresh ricotta cheese**
- 2 **egg yolks**

Fresh fruit, for serving

1. Preheat the broiler. In a small saucepan, put the maple syrup and the seeds scraped from the vanilla bean. Warm and then let cool slightly.

2. In a bowl, mix the ricotta with the syrup. Whisk in the egg yolks until blended. Spread the ricotta in 4 shallow 5-inch gratin dishes and broil 6 inches from the heat, rotating the dishes as needed to glaze the ricotta evenly. Serve with fresh fruit.—*Marcia Kiesel*

WINE Go for a light, fruity, not-too-sweet Muscat-based wine, such as the 1998 Vietti Moscato Cascinetta or the 1997 Robert Mondavi Moscato d'Oro.

Fried Sweet Cheese Ravioli with Bitter Honey

6 SERVINGS

This typical Sardinian dessert, called *sebadas,* is traditionally made with tangy fresh sheep's-milk cheese, but a creamy fresh goat cheese can be used instead. Look for Sardinian bitter honey at specialty food shops, or order it by mail from Singerman's (888-636-8162) or Formaggio Kitchen (888-212-3224).

PASTA DOUGH

- 1½ **cups semolina**
- ½ **cup unbleached all-purpose flour**
- ¼ **teaspoon salt**
- 3½ **tablespoons pure lard or vegetable shortening**
- 1 **large egg, lightly beaten**

About ½ cup very warm water

FILLING

- ¾ **pound fresh sheep's-milk cheese**
- ⅓ **cup hot water**
- 1½ **tablespoons semolina**

About 1 teaspoon sugar

- 1½ **teaspoons finely grated orange zest**
- ½ **teaspoon finely grated lemon zest**

Olive oil, for frying

- ¾ **cup Sardinian bitter honey, for serving**

1. MAKE THE PASTA DOUGH: In a food processor, combine the semolina, flour and salt and pulse to blend. Add the shortening and pulse until evenly distributed. Add the egg and pulse. With the machine on, add about ⅓ cup of the water and process just until the dough comes together; if it is crumbly, add a little more water, 1 tablespoon at a time. Shape the dough into a ball, cover with plastic wrap and let rest for 1 hour.

2. MAKE THE FILLING: In a small saucepan, combine the cheese with the hot water and stir over moderately low heat. As soon as the mixture starts to bubble around the edges, stir in the semolina and cook over low heat, stirring, until thickened to the consistency of sour cream. Remove from the heat and stir in the sugar and citrus zests. If the mixture tastes very tangy, add a little more sugar, but keep in mind that it should not be noticeably sweet. Let cool.

3. Cut the pasta dough in quarters. Working with 1 piece at a time and keeping the rest covered, roll the dough through a pasta machine set on successively narrower settings until you reach the second-to-the-thinnest. Set the pasta sheet on a work surface and, using a 3-inch round biscuit cutter, stamp out 12 rounds. Mound 2 teaspoons of the cheese filling into the center of half of the rounds. Moisten the edges and cover with the remaining rounds. Seal the edges with the tines of a fork and set the ravioli on a rack. Repeat with the remaining dough and filling.

4. In a large deep skillet, using a deep-fry thermometer, heat 1½ inches of olive oil to 360°. Slip 4 ravioli into the hot oil and fry until they are lightly golden, turning after they have risen to

Glazed Ricotta with Vanilla Bean

Coconut Flan with Rum

milk, rum, vanilla and cinnamon. Pour the custard into the ramekins. Pour boiling water into the roasting pan to reach two-thirds of the way up the sides of the ramekins. Bake the custards for about 50 minutes, or until set. Let cool in the water bath. Using paper towels, blot any coconut oil that has risen to the surface.

3. Run a thin knife around each flan. Invert each ramekin onto a dessert plate; let the caramel drizzle onto the plate. Garnish with mint and serve.

—*Corinne Trang*

MAKE AHEAD The flans can be prepared through Step 2. Wrap with plastic and refrigerate for up to 2 days.

Claudia Fleming's Panna Cotta

6 SERVINGS

1½ teaspoons unflavored gelatin

1½ tablespoons cold water

1¼ cups heavy cream

¼ cup plus 3 tablespoons sugar

1¾ cups buttermilk

Macerated fresh berries, for serving

1. In a small bowl, combine the gelatin and cold water. In a small saucepan, stir the cream and sugar over moderate heat until the sugar dissolves. Add the gelatin mixture and stir until melted. Remove from the heat.

2. Stir the buttermilk into the gelatin mixture, then strain the *panna cotta* through a fine sieve. Pour into six 4-ounce ramekins and chill for at least 2 hours. Unmold the *panna cotta* onto dessert plates and serve, with berries on the side. —*Claudia Fleming*

Rice Pudding

8 SERVINGS

This classic dessert is served at almost every Portuguese celebration. It's very sweet—as are most desserts in Portugal—but this recipe has been modified to suit American tastes.

1 quart whole milk

1½ cups Arborio rice (10 ounces)

1½ tablespoons unsalted butter

the surface, about 30 seconds per side. Using a slotted spoon, transfer the ravioli to a rack set over paper towels to drain while you fry the rest.

5. In a small saucepan, warm the honey with a few tablespoons of water until it is liquid and quite warm. Serve the *sebadas* on warmed plates with the bitter honey drizzled on top.

—*Nancy Harmon Jenkins*

Coconut Flans with Rum

8 SERVINGS

This flan is a Martinique-inspired variation on the French crème caramel.

1 cup sugar

3 tablespoons water

4 large eggs

One 13-ounce can unsweetened coconut milk

1 cup whole milk

½ cup sweetened condensed milk

1½ tablespoons aged rum

1 tablespoon pure vanilla extract

¼ teaspoon cinnamon

Boiling water

Mint sprigs, for garnish

1. Preheat the oven to 300°. Set eight ½-cup ramekins in a roasting pan. In a small heavy saucepan, bring the sugar and water to a boil over moderately high heat; stir occasionally until the sugar dissolves. Boil the mixture without stirring until an amber caramel forms, 6 to 8 minutes. Immediately pour the caramel into the ramekins, swirling them to coat.

2. In a large bowl, whisk the eggs until frothy. Whisk in the coconut milk, whole milk, sweetened condensed

Rice Pudding

Finely grated zest of 1 lemon
Pinch of salt
2 cups heavy cream or
half-and-half
1 cup plus 2 tablespoons sugar
4 large egg yolks
1 teaspoon cinnamon

1. In a large nonstick saucepan, combine the milk with the rice, butter, lemon zest and salt and bring to a boil, stirring constantly. Cover and cook over low heat, stirring occasionally, until the rice is tender and the milk is absorbed, about 20 minutes. Remove from the heat and let stand, covered, for 10 minutes.

2. Add the cream and sugar and bring to a simmer. In a small bowl, whisk the egg yolks with ½ cup of the hot rice. Pour the egg mixture into the saucepan in a thin stream, whisking constantly to prevent scrambling. Bring to a boil and cook over moderate heat, stirring constantly, until creamy and slightly thickened, about 4 minutes. Pour the rice pudding into a large heatproof dish and let cool to room temperature. Cover with plastic and refrigerate until chilled, about 4 hours. Serve the rice pudding in bowls, dusted with cinnamon.   —*Emeril Lagasse*
MAKE AHEAD The rice pudding can be refrigerated for up to 4 days.
WINE A rich, medium-sweet Bual Madeira will add flavors of almonds, walnuts, orange and raisins to this sweet rice pudding. Look for one from Leacocks or Cossart-Gordon.

Panettone Bread Pudding
8 SERVINGS
4 large eggs
2 cups whole milk
1 cup heavy cream
1 teaspoon pure vanilla extract
¼ teaspoon cinnamon
¼ teaspoon freshly grated nutmeg
One 2-pound loaf panettone, crust
removed, bread cut
into 2-inch cubes
Confectioners' sugar, for dusting
Pure maple syrup, for serving

1. In a large bowl, whisk the eggs with the milk, cream, vanilla, cinnamon and nutmeg. Add the panettone cubes, stir to coat and let soak until the liquid is completely absorbed, about 1 hour.
2. Preheat the oven to 350°. Butter a 9-by-13-inch glass baking dish. Spread the panettone in the dish and bake for 40 minutes, or until golden brown.
3. Remove the baking dish from the oven and preheat the broiler. Dust the panettone with confectioners' sugar and broil for 30 seconds, shifting the pan for even browning. Sprinkle again with confectioners' sugar, cut into squares and serve with maple syrup.

—*Icebox Café, Miami Beach, Florida*
MAKE AHEAD The panettone mixture can be refrigerated in the prepared baking dish overnight. Bring it to room temperature before baking.

Molasses-Cinnamon Cake Doughnuts
MAKES ABOUT TWENTY 3-INCH
DOUGHNUTS
The secret to nongreasy homemade doughnuts is to keep the temperature of the cooking oil at 360°. If the temperature is lower, the doughnuts will be soggy; if it's higher, they will be scorched.

4 cups unbleached all-purpose flour
2 teaspoons baking powder
1½ teaspoons freshly grated nutmeg
1 teaspoon salt
½ teaspoon baking soda
¼ teaspoon ground mace
2 large eggs
1 large egg yolk
1 cup sugar
4 tablespoons unsalted
butter, melted
½ cup buttermilk
¼ cup unsulphured molasses
1½ quarts peanut oil, for deep-frying
¼ cup cinnamon mixed with 1 cup
sugar, for dipping
Chocolate Glaze (recipe follows),
for dipping (optional)

1. In a large bowl, sift the flour with the baking powder, nutmeg, salt, baking soda and mace. In a small bowl, whisk the eggs and egg yolk with the sugar and the melted butter. Stir in the buttermilk and molasses. Add the liquid mixture to the dry ingredients and mix vigorously with a wooden spoon, until a soft and slightly sticky dough forms.
2. Turn the dough out onto a heavily floured surface and gently knead 3 times. Roll out the dough to a 10-by-14-inch rectangle ¼ inch thick. Stamp out the doughnuts with a floured 3-inch doughnut cutter (see Note), dipping the cutter in flour between each cut. Let the doughnuts rise for 5 minutes before frying. Meanwhile, gently knead and reroll any remaining dough and repeat.
3. In a large heavy saucepan or deep cast-iron skillet, heat the peanut oil until it registers 375° on a deep-frying thermometer. Working in small batches of 3 or 4, carefully slide 1 doughnut at a time into the hot oil; the temperature of the oil should drop to 360° as soon as you have a full batch. As soon as the doughnuts float to the surface, turn them with a slotted spoon and fry for 45 seconds. Turn them again and fry for 45 seconds longer. Carefully

transfer the doughnuts to paper towel–lined racks and drain on both sides. Dip the warm doughnuts in the cinnamon sugar or Chocolate Glaze and serve at once. —*Suzanne Lombardi*

NOTE A round biscuit cutter is a fine substitute for a doughnut cutter. Use an apple corer with a round edge to stamp out the doughnut hole.

CHOCOLATE GLAZE
MAKES ABOUT 1 CUP

- 2 ounces bittersweet chocolate, coarsely chopped (about ⅓ cup)
- 4 tablespoons unsalted butter, cut into tablespoons
- 1½ cups confectioners' sugar
- ¼ cup boiling water

In a small saucepan, melt the chocolate with the butter over moderately low heat. Whisk in the sugar, then stir in the boiling water until smooth. Remove from the heat. Place a piece of plastic directly on the surface of the glaze and keep warm until ready to use. —*S.L.*

Raspberry Brioche Diplomates
8 SERVINGS

The precise origin of the name *diplomate* is unclear, but this pudding, which is classically made with brioche or sponge cake, dried fruit and custard and served cold, is also referred to as cabinet pudding and *chancelière*.

- 1 quart whole milk
- 1 vanilla bean, split
- 8 large egg yolks
- 5 large eggs, lightly beaten
- 1¾ cups sugar, plus more for sprinkling
- One 17- to 18-ounce brioche, crusts trimmed, bread cut into ½-inch dice (about 9 cups)
- 2 cups fresh or individually quick-frozen raspberries
- Boiling water

I. Preheat the oven to 325°. Butter eight 1½-cup ramekins and coat with sugar, tapping out the excess.

Raspberry Brioche Diplomates

2. In a medium saucepan, heat the milk with the vanilla bean until it just begins to simmer. In a large bowl, gently whisk the egg yolks with the whole eggs just until combined. Whisk in the 1¾ cups sugar just until blended. Gradually whisk the warm milk into the eggs, whisking constantly. Remove the vanilla bean and, using a sharp knife, scrape the seeds from the vanilla bean into the custard; discard the bean. Strain the custard, then skim off any foam.

3. Spread one-third of the brioche in the ramekins and top with half of the raspberries. Repeat with another third of the brioche, the remaining raspberries and a final layer of brioche. Move the ramekins to a large roasting pan. Pour the custard into the ramekins; press down to submerge the brioche. Let the ramekins stand for about 10 minutes.

4. Sprinkle each *diplomate* with ½ teaspoon of sugar. Put the roasting pan in the oven and carefully add enough boiling water to the pan to reach halfway up the sides of the ramekins. Bake the *diplomates* for about 1½ hours, or until the custard is set and the *diplomates* are puffed and golden.

5. Preheat the broiler. Carefully transfer the ramekins to a rimmed baking sheet and broil 8 inches from the heat for about 30 seconds, or until lightly browned. Serve warm or cold.

—*Michael London*

MAKE AHEAD The *diplomates* can be prepared through Step 3 and refrigerated overnight. Serve cold or reheat in a 325° oven.

Coffee Granita with Lemon Cream

6 SERVINGS

- 4 cups brewed espresso
- 1½ cups granulated sugar
- 1½ cups heavy cream
- 2½ tablespoons confectioners' sugar

- ¾ teaspoon pure vanilla extract
- 3 tablespoons fresh lemon juice
- 1 tablespoon grated lemon zest

1. Combine the espresso with the granulated sugar and stir until the sugar is dissolved. Pour the espresso into a 9-by-13-inch glass or metal baking dish. Freeze until ice crystals begin to form around the edges, about 2 hours. Using a fork, stir the mixture well and return to the freezer. Continue freezing, stirring and scraping every 30 minutes, until the mixture is thoroughly frozen and the crystals are fluffy, about 2 hours.

2. In a large bowl, whip the cream with the confectioners' sugar and vanilla until firm but not stiff. Fold in the lemon juice and lemon zest. Spoon 2 tablespoons of the lemon cream into each of 6 large chilled wineglasses and top with a layer of coffee granita. Continue alternating the layers, ending with a dollop of lemon cream, and serve right away. —*Joyce Goldstein*

MAKE AHEAD The granita can be frozen for up to 2 days. If it solidifies, thaw it slightly in the refrigerator and break it up with a fork or quickly pulse it in a food processor. The lemon cream can be refrigerated for up to 1 hour.

Goat's Milk and Brown Sugar Ice Cream

MAKES ABOUT 1½ QUARTS

- 2 cups goat's milk
- 2 cups heavy cream
- 8 large egg yolks
- 1⅓ cups dark brown sugar

Pinch of salt

Splash of rum

1. In a medium saucepan, bring the goat's milk and cream just to a boil; remove from the heat.

2. Meanwhile, in a medium stainless-steel bowl, whisk the egg yolks with the brown sugar. Very gradually whisk in ½ cup of the hot milk and cream, then gradually whisk in the rest.

Return the mixture to the saucepan and cook over low heat, stirring constantly, until the custard thickens, about 10 minutes. Remove from the heat and stir in the salt and rum.

3. Strain the custard into a stainless-steel bowl set in an ice-water bath and stir occasionally until thoroughly chilled. Working in 2 batches, freeze the custard in an ice cream maker according to the manufacturer's instructions. Freeze the ice cream in airtight containers for up to 1 day.

—*Elizabeth Falkner*

Hazelnut Meringue Ice Cream Sandwiches

MAKES 24 SANDWICHES

- ½ cup hazelnuts
- ¼ cup confectioners' sugar, plus more for dusting
- 3 large egg whites
- ½ teaspoon cream of tartar

Pinch of coarse salt

- ½ cup superfine sugar

Goat's Milk and Brown Sugar Ice Cream or store-bought ice cream

Hazelnut Meringue Ice Cream Sandwich

1. Preheat the oven to 400°. Put the hazelnuts in a pie plate and toast in the oven for about 8 minutes, or until fragrant. Turn the oven down to 200°. Transfer the hot hazelnuts to a kitchen towel and rub them together to remove the skins. Let the nuts cool.

2. In a food processor, pulse the hazelnuts with the ¼ cup of confectioners' sugar just until finely ground.

3. In a large bowl, using an electric mixer, beat the egg whites with the cream of tartar and salt at low speed until frothy. Add 2 tablespoons of the superfine sugar and increase the speed to medium. Add another 2 tablespoons of sugar and beat for 30 seconds. Increase the speed to high and slowly beat in the remaining ¼ cup of sugar. Beat for about 5 minutes, until the meringue is stiff and glossy. Fold in the nuts.

4. Place a heaping tablespoon of the meringue on a baking sheet lined with parchment paper and spread it into a 2½-inch round; repeat to form 48 rounds. Bake for 20 minutes. Turn off the oven and leave the meringues in to dry for at least 3 hours or overnight.

5. For each ice cream sandwich, scoop ¼ cup of the ice cream onto the underside of a meringue and top with another meringue. Serve at once or wrap individually in plastic and freeze.

—Elizabeth Falkner

MAKE AHEAD The ice cream sandwiches can be frozen for up to 2 days.

Hazelnut Ice Cream

MAKES 2 QUARTS

1 cup hazelnuts (½ pound)
1½ quarts half-and-half
1¼ cups sugar
16 large egg yolks

1. Preheat the oven to 350°. Spread the hazelnuts on a rimmed baking sheet and bake for about 12 minutes, or until fragrant and browned; cool. Transfer the nuts to a kitchen towel and rub them together to remove the skins. Coarsely chop the hazelnuts.

2. In a large heavy saucepan, combine the half-and-half and sugar and bring to a simmer over moderate heat, stirring to dissolve the sugar. Add the hazelnuts, cover and let steep off the heat for 30 minutes.

3. In a large stainless-steel bowl, whisk the egg yolks. Very gradually whisk in ½ cup of the hot half-and-half, then gradually whisk in the rest. Pour the mixture into the saucepan and cook over very low heat, stirring constantly, until the custard thickens, about 10 minutes. The custard should be thick enough to coat the back of a spoon.

4. Strain the custard into a large stainless-steel bowl set in an ice-water bath and discard the hazelnuts. Stir occasionally until the custard is thoroughly chilled. Freeze the custard in an ice cream maker, in batches, according to the manufacturer's instructions. Store the ice cream in airtight containers in the freezer for up to 3 days.

—Sara Guerin

Frozen Custard with Herbs

12 SERVINGS

Try this custard alongside the Orange and Lemon Tart (p. 350).

9 large egg yolks
¾ cup sugar
3 tablespoons milk
2¼ cups heavy cream
¼ cup mixed finely chopped fresh herbs, such as basil, mint, lemon verbena and tarragon

1. Lightly oil twelve ½-cup ramekins or have ready a 6-cup airtight container. In a large stainless-steel bowl, whisk the egg yolks with the sugar and milk. Set the bowl over a large saucepan with 1 inch of simmering water and whisk the mixture constantly over low heat until the yolks are fluffy and hot, about 10 minutes. Remove the bowl from the heat and continue whisking to cool the mixture slightly. Set aside and let cool to room temperature, whisking often.

2. In a large stainless-steel bowl, whip the cream to soft peaks. Using a rubber spatula, fold the cream into the egg yolk mixture, then fold in the herbs. Spoon the custard into the ramekins or the container. Cover with plastic wrap and freeze until firm, at least 3 hours and up to 1 week.

3. To unmold ramekins, prepare a bowl of boiling hot water. Quickly dip each ramekin into the hot water and run a small, sharp knife around the frozen custard. Dry the ramekins. Invert the custards onto plates. Or scoop the custard from the container onto plates.

—Sabine Busch and Bruno Tramontana

Caramel Ice Cream Sundaes

MAKES 8 SUNDAES

1 cup light brown sugar
¼ cup light corn syrup
¼ cup heavy cream
2 tablespoons water
1 tablespoon unsalted butter
1 teaspoon pure vanilla extract
2 pints vanilla ice cream

In a medium saucepan, combine the sugar, syrup and cream and bring to a boil over moderate heat. Cook, stirring constantly, until slightly darkened and thickened, about 4 minutes. Add the water, butter and vanilla and stir until smooth. Serve warm over the ice cream.

—Christine Dimmick

MAKE AHEAD The caramel sauce can be refrigerated for up to 1 week. Reheat before serving.

beverages
chapter 18

Citrus Coolers

Lemonade

1. In a saucepan, combine 4 cups of the water with the sugar, star anise, ginger and mint. Bring to a boil. Remove from the heat and let stand for 30 minutes. Strain the syrup and refrigerate.

2. In a very large pitcher or bowl, stir together the citrus juices, the syrup and the remaining 4 cups of water. Serve over ice and garnish with lime wedges. —*Elizabeth Falkner*

MAKE AHEAD The syrup can be refrigerated for up to 1 week.

Lemonade

MAKES ABOUT 2 QUARTS

Sugar syrup is key to making lemonade that is evenly sweetened, with no undissolved sugar at the bottom.

  2 quarts plus ¾ cup cold water
  ¾ cup sugar
  1 cup fresh lemon juice
  1 lemon, thinly sliced

1. In a small saucepan, combine the ¾ cup of water with the sugar. Bring to a boil, then simmer until the sugar is dissolved. Remove from the heat and let the syrup cool to room temperature.

2. In a large pitcher, combine the remaining 2 quarts of water with the fresh lemon juice and sugar syrup. Add the lemon slices and refrigerate until chilled. Serve the lemonade over ice. —*Patrick O'Connell*

Citrus Cooler

MAKES 12 DRINKS

To turn this cooler into a cocktail, stir in 5 cups of tequila in place of the water in Step 2 and serve over ice, in salt-rimmed glasses.

  8 cups cold water
  2 cups sugar
  4 star anise pods, crushed
Two 4-inch pieces of fresh ginger, peeled and sliced into thin coins
  2 cups loosely packed mint leaves
  2 quarts fresh grapefruit juice
  1 quart fresh orange juice
  1 quart fresh lime juice
Lime wedges, for garnish

Ginger Mint Lemonade

MAKES 8 DRINKS

  2 cups water
  1 cup sugar
One 2-inch piece of fresh ginger, thinly sliced
  1 cup fresh mint leaves
  2 cups fresh lemon juice
  6 cups cold water

1. In a medium saucepan, mix the 2 cups of water with the sugar and the ginger. Bring to a simmer and add the mint leaves. Remove the syrup from the heat and let stand for 1 to 12 hours; strain and cool.

2. Mix the syrup with the fresh lemon juice and the 6 cups of cold water. Stir to combine. Serve over crushed ice.

—*Elizabeth Falkner*

Rock Shandy

MAKES 1 DRINK

2 tablespoons Rose's lime juice

3 dashes Angostura bitters

Cold sparkling water

Half fill a tall glass with ice. Add the Rose's lime juice and Angostura bitters. Fill the glass with sparkling water.

—*Jacques Pépin*

Masala Chai

MAKES 4 DRINKS ✳

Chai is tea leaves steeped in water, milk and sugar. The addition of spices makes it *masala chai*. Overbrewing causes *chai* to become bitter. Taste it halfway through the brewing time, as different teas vary in strength.

3 cups water

1 cup milk

¼ cup sugar, or to taste

½ teaspoon ground cardamom

One ½-inch piece of peeled
   fresh ginger

½ cinnamon stick

3 tablespoons loose black tea,
   preferably Darjeeling

In a saucepan, combine the water, milk, sugar, cardamom, ginger and cinnamon stick and bring to a boil. Remove from the heat and add the tea. Let brew until the *chai* turns a light caramel color, about 4 minutes. Strain through a fine-mesh sieve and serve hot.   —*Gary MacGurn and Patty Gentry*

Vanilla Steamed Milk with Caramel Swirls

MAKES 4 DRINKS

It is important to use whole or two-percent milk in this recipe for a rich and creamy froth.

1¾ cups sugar

½ cup water

⅔ cup heavy cream

1 quart whole or 2% milk

1 vanilla bean, split lengthwise

⅓ cup coffee liqueur (optional)

1. In a heavy medium saucepan, bring the sugar and water to a boil. Cook over moderate heat, without stirring, until a deep amber caramel forms, about 12 minutes. Remove the pan from the heat. Slowly and carefully add a little of the cream to stop the cooking and then whisk in the remaining cream until the sauce is smooth. Let cool to room temperature.

2. In a large saucepan, simmer the milk with the vanilla bean over moderately low heat for 5 minutes. Remove from the heat and stir in the coffee liqueur. Remove the vanilla bean and scrape the seeds into the milk. Using an immersion blender, beat the milk until a layer of froth forms. Pour the frothy milk into warm mugs, then spoon the froth on top and drizzle with the caramel sauce. Serve at once.

—*Suzanne Lombardi*

MAKE AHEAD The caramel sauce can be refrigerated for up to 1 week; reheat before using.

Hot Chocolate with Whipped Cream

MAKES 4 TO 6 DRINKS

The intense chocolate flavor in this recipe comes from using top-quality chocolate rather than cocoa powder.

2 ounces bittersweet chocolate,
   finely chopped

½ cup boiling water

3½ cups whole milk

1 vanilla bean, split lengthwise

⅓ cup sugar

½ teaspoon cinnamon

⅛ teaspoon salt

⅓ cup Frangelico liqueur (optional)

Sweetened whipped cream,
   for serving

1. In a medium saucepan, melt the chocolate in the boiling water. Remove from the heat.

2. In another medium saucepan, heat the milk with the vanilla bean; cook it over moderately high heat until bubbles appear around the edge. Remove the pan from the heat. Scrape the seeds from the vanilla bean into the hot milk and then carefully whisk in the sugar, cinnamon and salt. Save the seeded vanilla bean for another use.

3. Pour the hot milk into the melted chocolate, add the Frangelico and whisk until smooth. Pour the hot chocolate into warm mugs and garnish with a dollop of whipped cream.

—*Suzanne Lombardi*

Peanut-Butter Banana Smoothie

MAKES 2 DRINKS

1 banana

2 spoonfuls smooth peanut butter

2 cups apple or orange juice

½ cup plain nonfat yogurt

½ cup ice

Put all the ingredients in a blender and blend until smooth. Serve at once.

—*Elizabeth Falkner*

Tropical Mimosa

MAKES 2 DRINKS

⅔ cup pineapple juice

3 tablespoons ginger liqueur

Champagne or sparkling wine, chilled

Divide the pineapple juice and ginger liqueur between 2 Champagne flutes. Fill with Champagne.   —*Grace Parisi*

Champagne Cobbler

MAKES 1 DRINK

One ½-inch-thick orange slice

One ¼-inch-thick lemon slice

2 tablespoons maraschino
   liqueur or Cointreau

½ cup cold Champagne

1 lemon-peel twist

Partially fill a Champagne flute with ice. In a separate glass, muddle the orange and lemon slices with the liqueur. Strain into the Champagne flute. Add the Champagne and garnish with the lemon-peel twist.

—*Laura Moorhead*

beverages

Champagne Cobblers

Rosemopolitan

MAKES 1 DRINK

Rose syrup is available at many Indian and Pakistani groceries.

- ¼ **cup vodka**
- 1 **tablespoon cranberry juice**
- 2 **teaspoons rose syrup**

Juice of ½ lemon

Fill a cocktail shaker with ice. Add the ingredients and shake vigorously. Strain into a chilled martini glass and float an organic rose petal on top of the drink. —*First, New York City*

Tom Collins

MAKES 1 DRINK

- ¼ **cup gin**
- 1½ **tablespoons fresh lemon juice**
- 2 **tablespoons Simple Syrup (recipe follows)**
- ½ **cup cold soda water**
- 1 **maraschino cherry**
- 1 **orange slice**

Shake the gin, lemon juice and syrup with cracked ice. Strain into a chilled collins glass over ice. Top with the soda water; garnish with the cherry and the orange slice. —*Paul Harrington*

SIMPLE SYRUP

MAKES ½ CUP

- ½ **cup water**
- ½ **cup granulated sugar**

In a small saucepan, simmer the water with the sugar, stirring, until the sugar dissolves completely.—*Laura Moorhead*
MAKE AHEAD The syrup can be refrigerated for up to 1 week.

Le Petit Rum Punch

MAKES 1 DRINK

This cocktail is known colloquially in the French Caribbean as *'ti* punch (short for *petit punch*).

- 1 **lime wedge**
- 1 **tablespoon sugar**
- 3 **tablespoons white rum**

Squeeze the lime wedge into an old-fashioned glass; add the lime wedge to the glass. Stir in the sugar and rum, mixing until the sugar has completely dissolved. Add ice cubes and serve.

—*Jacques Pépin*

Sixth Avenue Rum Runner

MAKES 1 DRINK

The name "rum runner" can be affixed to any number of rum drinks. This one was invented in the FOOD & WINE test kitchen one day when we happened to have on hand some fresh pineapple juice, which is less sweet than canned.

- ¼ **cup plus 2 tablespoons fresh pineapple juice**
- ¼ **cup fresh orange juice**
- 1½ **tablespoons fresh lime juice (from about ½ lime)**
- ¼ **cup white rum**
- 1 **teaspoon sugar**
- 1 **orange slice**

Fill a shaker with ice. Add the pineapple juice, orange juice, lime juice, rum and sugar. Shake well and strain into a large cocktail glass. Garnish with the orange slice. —*Pete Wells*
NOTE This cocktail has a lower alcohol content than most, so feel free to increase the rum by as much as 2 tablespoons.

Agua Fresca

MAKES 1 DRINK

In Mexico, an Agua Fresca is a combination of fresh fruit juice, sugar, water and ice, sometimes fortified with tequila. Here's a delicious rum-based version. The fruit purees can be made in a blender or a juicer.

- 3 **tablespoons white rum**
- 3 **tablespoons mango puree**
- 3 **tablespoons passion fruit puree**
- 2 **tablespoons kiwi puree**
- 1 **pineapple wedge**

Fill a shaker with ice. Add the rum, mango puree, passion fruit puree and kiwi puree. Shake well and strain into a cocktail glass. Garnish with the pineapple wedge. —*Isla, New York City*

Hemingway Daiquiri

MAKES 1 DRINK

Ernest Hemingway once wrote that daiquiris "felt, as you drank them, the way downhill glacier-skiing feels running through powder snow." The daiquiri that made Hemingway feel best of all included grapefruit juice and maraschino liqueur. It was invented at La Floridita bar in Havana, and it was called The Papa in Hemingway's honor. If you ordered a double, that was a Papa Doble. Papa always had a *doble*.

- ¼ **cup white rum**
- 2 **teaspoons maraschino liqueur**
- 1 **teaspoon fresh grapefruit juice**
- 1½ **tablespoons fresh lime juice (from about ½ lime)**
- 1 **teaspoon sugar**

Fill a shaker with ice. Add all the ingredients. Shake well and strain into a cocktail glass. —*Paul Harrington*

Milk Punch

MAKES 1 DRINK

In *Guys and Dolls,* Jean Simmons and Marlon Brando drank their milk punch by Havana moonlight. Off the silver screen, this drink is more commonly served at brunch or as a morning-after

Tom Collins

Simmer over moderately low heat, stirring frequently, until the sugar dissolves. Stir in the rum. Pour the lemonade into warm mugs and garnish with lemon slices and candy swizzle sticks. *—Suzanne Lombardi*

Zombie

MAKES 1 DRINK

This is the cocktail that made Hollywood's Don the Beachcomber famous. Much of the drink's renown was due to a brilliant marketing gimmick: The menu sternly decreed "Only two to a customer." This, of course, practically guaranteed that everybody would have two and that almost everybody would try to secure a third, if not a fourth and fifth.

- 1 teaspoon sugar
- 1 tablespoon fresh lime juice,
- 2 tablespoons fresh orange juice
- 2 tablespoons pineapple juice
- ¼ cup gold rum
- 2 tablespoons white rum
- 2 tablespoons dark Jamaican rum
- 2 teaspoons apricot liqueur
- 1 pineapple wedge

Fill a cocktail shaker with ice. Add the sugar, the lime juice and the orange juice, the white rum and the dark rum and the apricot liqueur. Shake well and strain the cocktail into a tall glass. Garnish with the pineapple wedge.
—Don Beach

Planter's Punch

MAKES 1 DRINK

- ¼ cup dark rum
- 1 tablespoon fresh lemon juice
- ½ tablespoon Simple Syrup (p. 390)
- 3 dashes Angostura bitters
- 1 orange-peel twist

Partially fill a wine goblet with ice. Fill a shaker with cracked ice and add the rum, lemon juice, Simple Syrup and Angostura. Shake and strain into the wine goblet and garnish with the orange-peel twist. *—Paul Harrington*

pick-me-up. Feel free to vary the amount of sugar to taste, but do keep in mind that unlike daiquiris or Mai Tais, milk punch should be relatively sweet.

- ½ cup milk
- ¼ cup white rum
- 2 tablespoons dark Jamaican rum
- 1 tablespoon sugar
- 2 or 3 drops pure vanilla extract

Fill a cocktail shaker with ice. Add the milk, the white and dark rums, the sugar and the vanilla and shake well. Strain the punch into an old-fashioned glass or, for exotic effect, an empty coconut shell. *—Pete Wells*

Hot Lemonade with Rum

MAKES 4 TO 6 DRINKS

Many grandmothers consider hot lemonade to be good for whatever ails you. It is especially soothing when spiked with high-quality dark rum. This version is also great served chilled and poured over ice.

- 2 cups water
- 1½ cups fresh lemon juice
- 1 cup sugar
- ¾ cup dark rum

Lemon slices and cinnamon candy swizzle sticks, for garnish

In a medium saucepan, combine the water with the lemon juice and sugar.

Caribbean Rum Zing

MAKES 6 DRINKS

1½ cups fresh orange juice
1½ cups guava nectar
1 cup amber rum
2 cups ice cubes
1½ cups cold ginger ale
Grenadine
Freshly grated nutmeg
Fresh fruit, for garnish (optional)

In a large pitcher, combine the orange juice, guava nectar and rum. Add the ice and stir until cold; add the ginger ale. Pour into cocktail glasses, adding a splash of grenadine and a sprinkling of nutmeg to each glass. Garnish with fresh fruit.

—Alison Tolley

Mai Tai

MAKES 1 DRINK

If the only Mai Tais you've ever had were pink, you've never had a Mai Tai. The drink is not supposed to look like Hawaiian Punch: When made according to the original recipe, it is a darker, almond-flavored variation on the daiquiri.

¼ cup dark Jamaican rum
1 tablespoon orange Curaçao
½ tablespoon orgeat (almond syrup)
½ tablespoon sugar
1 lime, halved
1 mint sprig

Fill a large old-fashioned glass with cracked ice. Fill a shaker with ice and add the rum, orange Curaçao, orgeat and sugar. Squeeze the lime halves and add the juice. Shake well and strain into the glass. Add 1 of the squeezed lime halves and garnish the drink with the mint sprig.

—Trader Vic's, Emeryville, California

Dark & Stormy

MAKES 1 DRINK

This classic cooler is always made with Gosling's, a black rum from Bermuda, and ginger beer, a spicy soft drink from Jamaica. In this version, it gets an added kick from fresh ginger.

¼ lime, cut into small pieces, plus 1 wedge
1 quarter-size slice of fresh ginger
½ teaspoon sugar
¼ cup Gosling's Black Seal rum
¾ cup ginger beer

In a collins glass, muddle the lime pieces with the ginger and sugar until the lime is juicy and the ginger is bruised. Stir in the rum. Add ice and the ginger beer. Garnish with the lime wedge.

—Pete Wells

Buena Vista

MAKES 1 DRINK

Frosting the rim of the glass with green sugar is optional but does make things more festive.

4 mint sprigs
½ lime, cut into pieces, plus 1 slice
1 teaspoon sugar
1½ tablespoons Captain Morgan Spiced Rum
1½ tablespoons Peachtree Schnapps
¼ cup Bacardi Limón
Crystalline green sugar (optional)

In the bottom of a shaker, muddle 3 of the mint sprigs with the lime pieces and the sugar. Fill the shaker with ice and add the spiced rum, Peachtree Schnapps and Bacardi Limón. Shake vigorously and strain into a martini glass rimmed with crystalline green sugar. Garnish with the remaining mint sprig and the lime slice.

—Chicama, New York City

Blackberry Shrub

MAKES ABOUT 3 CUPS

2½ pints blackberries or blueberries
¼ cup water
1½ cinnamon sticks
¾ cup sugar
1 pint brandy
Lemon slices, for garnish

1. Simmer the berries with the water, cinnamon sticks and sugar until the berry juices are released and the sugar is dissolved. Let cool. Strain the berry syrup into a glass jar and add the brandy. Cover and set the shrub aside for at least 1 month.

2. Fill a tumbler with ice and pour in the shrub until the glass is about three-quarters full. Top with still or sparkling water and garnish with a slice of lemon.

—Laura Moorhead

Caribbean Rum Zings

guide to special recipes

The recipes marked with symbols throughout the book are listed here so that
you can quickly locate all the dishes of a particular type.

✳ Quick

59

87

index

Page numbers in **boldface** indicate photographs.

index

index

index

index

index

index

index

index

index

index

index

index

index

contributors

Bruce Aidells owns the Aidells Sausage Company. He is co-author of *The Complete Meat Cookbook* (Houghton Mifflin), voted one of FOOD & WINE's Best Cookbooks of 1998, and, most recently, of *Bruce Aidells' Complete Sausage Book: Recipes from America's Premier Sausage Maker* (Ten Speed Press).

Pam Anderson is the author of *The Perfect Recipe: Getting It Right Every Time* (Houghton Mifflin), which was named one of FOOD & WINE's Best Cookbooks of 1998. Her latest book is *How to Cook Without a Book* (Broadway Books).

Stephen Attoe is the co-owner and the executive chef at Swifty's in New York City.

Lily Barberio is an assistant editor at FOOD & WINE Magazine.

Judith Barrett is the author of several cookbooks, including *Pasta Verde* (IDG Books Worldwide) and, most recently, *Saved by Soup* (William Morrow).

Mario Batali is the co-owner of the New York City restaurants Babbo, Lupa and Esca. His forthcoming TV Food Network show is called *Mario Eats Italy,* and his newest cookbook, *Mario Batali: Holiday Food* (Clarkson N. Potter).

Josette Batteault owns a charcuterie with her husband, Roger, in Beaune, France.

Don Beach was the owner of Don the Beachcomber, a legendary 1930s Hollywood watering hole.

René Becker is the baker and owner of Hi-Rise Bread Company in Cambridge, Massachusetts.

Rob Boone is the executive chef at Bambú in Miami Beach, Florida.

Jimmy Bradley is the chef at the Red Cat in New York City.

Anya von Bremzen is the author, with John Welchman, of *Please to the Table: The Russian Cookbook* (1990) and *Terrific Pacific Cookbook* (1995), both published by Workman.

Bruce and **Eric Bromberg** are the force behind New York City's Blue Ribbon restaurants —Blue Ribbon Sushi, Blue Ribbon Bakery and the original Blue Ribbon. They plan to open Blue Ribbon Brooklyn in the spring of 2000.

Daniel Bruce is the executive chef at the Boston Harbor Hotel, home to both the Rowes Wharf Restaurant and Intrigue Café, in Boston.

Sabine Busch and **Bruno Tramontana** are a husband-and-wife catering team based in Florence, Italy.

Andrew Carmellini was named one of FOOD & WINE's Best New Chefs in 2000. He is the chef at Café Boulud in New York City.

Cesare Casella is the chef-owner of Beppe, a restaurant specializing in Tuscan cuisine, in New York City.

Joanne Chang, formerly of New York City's Payard Pâtisserie & Bistro and Boston's Rialto and Mistral, now owns Flour, a bakery and café in Boston.

Corinne Chapoutier is married to Michel Chapoutier, who owns and runs the Maison M. Chapoutier, the Rhône Valley wine empire that has been in his family since 1808.

Michael Chiarello is the chef and owner of the Napa Valley restaurant Tra Vigne. He is co-author of *The Tra Vigne Cookbook: Seasons in the California Wine Country* (Chronicle Books), named one of FOOD & WINE's Best Cookbooks of 1999.

Josiah Citrin is executive chef at Mélisse in Santa Monica, California.

Ted Cizma was named one of FOOD & WINE's Best New Chefs in 2000. He is the executive chef and owner of the restaurant Grace in Chicago.

Melissa Clark, a freelance writer and *New York Times* contributor, lives in New York City.

Jayne Cohen is a cookbook author and freelance food writer. Her most recent book is *The Gefilte Variations: 200 Inspired Re-Creations of Classics from the Jewish Kitchen* (Scribner).

Anick Colette, a skilled home cook, is a butcher's wife in the seaside town of Courseulles-sur-Mer in Normandy, France.

Helen Cribbs is a fine home cook in Wellborn, Florida.

Andrea Curto was named one of FOOD & WINE's Best New Chefs in 2000. She is the chef at Wish in Miami Beach, Florida.

Charles Dale was named one of FOOD & WINE's Best New Chefs in 1995. He is the chef and owner of Renaissance Restaurant and Rustique Bistro in Aspen, Colorado.

Silvana Daniello is the cook at the Villa Matilde wine estate in Campania, Italy.

Tamasin Day-Lewis is the food writer for the *London Daily Telegraph.* She is the author of *West of Ireland Summers: A Cookbook* (Roberts Rinehart) and, most recently, *The Art of the Tart* (Random House).

Christian Delouvrier is the executive chef at Lespinasse in New York City.

Christine Dimmick, founder of The Good Home Company, is the author of *Home File: A Realistic Decorating Guide for Real Life* (Andrews McMeel).

Martin Dodd is the executive chef of London-based Urban Productions Ltd.

Naomi Duguid and **Jeffrey Alford** are cookbook authors. *Seductions of Rice* (Artisan) was voted one of FOOD & WINE's Best Cookbooks of 1998. Their latest book is *Hot Sour Salty Sweet: A Culinary Journey Through Southeast Asia* (Artisan).

Mildred Hart Duvall was the mother of actor Robert Duvall. Her crab cakes are featured on the menu of his restaurant, The Rail Stop, in The Plains, Virginia.

Elizabeth Falkner is a pastry chef who has worked in the kitchens of San Francisco's Masa's and Rubicon. She is the owner of Citizen Cake, a bakery-café also in San Francisco.

Loren Falsone was named one of FOOD & WINE's Best New Chefs in 2000. She is co-owner and co-chef, with her husband, Eric Moshier, at the restaurant Empire in Providence, Rhode Island.

Claudia Fleming is the pastry chef at New York City's Gramercy Tavern.

Monica F. Forrestall is market editor at FOOD & WINE Magazine.

Giuseppe Forte, a native of Sicily, is co-owner of the restaurant La Vita E Bella in Seattle, Washington.

contributors

Trey Foshee, chef and partner at George's at the Cove in La Jolla, California, was named one of FOOD & WINE's Best New Chefs in 1998.

Gale Gand is the executive pastry chef and co-owner of the restaurants Tru and Brasserie T, both in Chicago. She is the author of *American Brasserie* (MacMillan) and of *Butter Sugar Flour Eggs* and *Just a Bite* (both published by Clarkson N. Potter).

Ina Garten, co-owner of Barefoot Contessa, a specialty food store in East Hampton, New York, is the author of *The Barefoot Contessa Cookbook* and *Barefoot Contessa Parties!* (both published by Clarkson N. Potter).

Susan and **Cassie Gary** are a mother-and-daughter chef team at the Owl Cafe in Apalachicola, Florida.

Thomas Gay is the executive chef at the Wildflower restaurant at The Lodge at Vail in Colorado.

Paul Gervais is an author whose most recent book is *A Garden in Lucca* (Hyperion).

Joyce Goldstein is a consulting chef, author and Mediterranean food authority. Her latest cookbook is *Sephardic Flavors: Jewish Cooking of the Mediterranean* (Chronicle).

Tim Goodell was named one of FOOD & WINE's Best New Chefs in 2000. He is the chef and owner of Aubergine & Troquet in Newport Beach, California.

Daniel Gouret is a butcher in Paris, France.

Jamie Guerin is the chef at Whitehouse-Crawford in Walla Walla, Washington.

Sara Guerin is both sous chef and pastry chef at Whitehouse-Crawford in Walla Walla, Washington.

Paul Harrington is co-author of *Cocktail: The Drinks Bible for the 21st Century* (Viking).

Mary Harris is a fine home cook in White Springs, Florida.

Donna Hay lives and cooks in Sydney, Australia. Her new cookbook, *Flavours,* was published by Whitecap.

Roger Hayot owns Authentic Café in Los Angeles.

Reed Hearon is the chef-owner of three San Francisco restaurants: Rose Pistola, Black Cat and Rose's Café. He is co-author of *The Rose Pistola Cookbook* (Broadway Books), which was named one of FOOD & WINE's Best Cookbooks of 1999.

Maida Heatter is the author of seven cookbooks, including *Maida Heatter's Cookies* (Cader Books), *Maida Heatter's Brand New Book of Great Cookies* (Random House) and *Maida Heatter's Book of Great Desserts* (Andrews McMeel).

Heather Ho is the pastry chef at Boulevard in San Francisco.

Bobby Holt is the chef at Hattie's in Saratoga Springs, New York.

Nancy Harmon Jenkins lives much of the year in Cortona, Italy. Her latest cookbook, *Flavors of Tuscany* (Broadway Books), was named one of FOOD & WINE's Best Cookbooks of 1998. She is working on a book about key Mediterranean ingredients.

Sara Jenkins is the chef at I Coppi, a Tuscan restaurant in New York City's East Village.

Joseph Jiménez de Jiménez is the chef and co-owner of The Harvest Vine Restaurant in Seattle. He is currently at work on a cookbook about the cuisine of both his restaurant and his homeland, the Basque region of Spain.

Darryl Joannides is the chef and co-owner of Assaggio in Portland, Oregon.

Marcia Kiesel is the test kitchen supervisor at FOOD & WINE and co-author of *Simple Art of Vietnamese Cooking* (Simon & Schuster).

Anna Kovel has worked both at Chez Panisse in Berkeley, California, and at Nicole's in New York City.

Gray Kunz, former executive chef at New York City's Lespinasse, will soon open his own restaurant, also in New York City.

Emeril Lagasse is the chef and proprietor of Emeril's Restaurant, NOLA and Emeril's Delmonico Restaurant and Bar, all in New Orleans, and has restaurants in Las Vegas and Orlando as well. He hosts two TV Food Network shows and has written several cookbooks. His books *Emeril's Creole Christmas* and *Every Day's a Party* (both published by Morrow) were named by FOOD & WINE among the Best Cookbooks of the Year for 1998 and 1999, respectively.

Sarah Lambert is the owner of Patisserie Lambert in Mill Valley, California. She worked previously at Manhattan's Le Cirque and San Francisco's La Folie.

David Lebovitz, formerly of Berkeley's Chez Panisse, is the author of *Room for Dessert* (HarperCollins), honored by FOOD & WINE as one of the Best Cookbooks of 1999.

Matt and **Ted Lee** write about food, travel and local color. They are frequent contributors to FOOD & WINE Magazine and the *New York Times* and are working on their first cookbook.

Michael Leviton was named one of FOOD & WINE's Best New Chefs in 2000. He is the chef at Lumière in West Newton, Massachusetts.

Suzanne Lombardi is one of three founding owners of Boston's Dancing Deer Baking Company.

Michael Lomonaco is the chef at Windows on the World and Wild Blue, both in New York City. He is co-host of the Discovery Channel television show *Epicurious*.

Max London works under the tutelage of executive chef Eberhard Müller at Bayard's in New York City.

Michael London is co-owner —with his wife, Wendy—of Mrs. London's, the renowned bakery-café in Saratoga Springs, New York.

Mitchel London owns Mitchel London Foods in New York City.

Amanda Lydon was named one of FOOD & WINE's Best New Chefs in 2000. She is the chef at the Boston restaurant Truc.

Barbara Lynch is the chef and owner of No. 9 Park in Boston.

Gary MacGurn and **Patty Gentry,** with Gary's wife, Isabel, are the owners of the Hampton Chutney Company, a south Indian restaurant in New York City.

Jean Mackenzie owns the Clamman Seafood Market in Southampton, New York.

Leslie Mackie, owner of the Macrina Bakery & Café in Seattle, has been featured as a regional baker in the *Baking with Julia* series and companion book.

Dominique Macquet is the chef and owner of Dominique's in New Orleans. Her latest cookbook is *Dominique's Fresh Flavors: Cooking with Latitude in New Orleans* (Ten Speed Press).

Deborah Madison is the author of five cookbooks, including *Vegetarian Cooking for Everyone* and *This Can't Be Tofu!* (both published by Broadway Books).

contributors

Kevin Maguire is the former executive chef at Enchantment Resort's Yavapai Restaurant, located at the bottom of Boynton Canyon in Sedona, Arizona.

Lydie Marshall is the author of several cookbooks, including *A Passion for My Provence* (HarperPerennial Library) and the forthcoming *Soup of the Day* (HarperCollins). She lives in Nyons, France.

Laura Moorhead is co-author of *Cocktail: The Drinks Bible for the 21st Century* (Viking).

Eric Moshier was named one of FOOD & WINE's Best New Chefs in 2000. He is co-owner and co-chef, with his wife, Loren Falsone, at the restaurant Empire in Providence, Rhode Island.

Patrick O'Connell is the executive chef and co-owner of The Inn at Little Washington in Washington, Virginia. He is the author of *The Inn at Little Washington Cookbook: A Consuming Passion* (Random House).

Jean-Louis Palladin is the executive chef and proprietor of the restaurant Palladin in New York City's Time Hotel.

Neela Paniz is the author of *The Bombay Café* (Ten Speed Press), a cookbook named after her Los Angeles restaurant.

Grace Parisi, test kitchen associate at FOOD & WINE, is also the author of *Summer/Winter Pasta* (William Morrow).

François Payard, a third-generation pâtissier, is the owner of Payard Patisserie & Bistro in New York City.

Scott Peacock is the executive chef at Watershed restaurant in Decatur, Georgia.

Jacques Pépin, master chef, TV personality, food columnist, cooking teacher and contributing editor to FOOD & WINE, is the author of numerous books and is co-host, with Julia Child, of the television show *Julia and Jacques: Cooking at Home* on PBS. His books *Jacques Pépin's Kitchen: Encore with Claudine* (Bay Books and Tapes, Inc.) and, written with Julia Child, *Julia and Jacques Cooking at Home* (Alfred A. Knopf) were honored by FOOD & WINE among the Best Cookbooks of the Year in 1999 and 2000, respectively.

Jill Pettijohn is a private chef, caterer and food stylist. She co-owns a Malibu, California–based catering company called Picholine.

Charles Pierce is a New York–based food writer and cookbook author and editor.

Gayle Pirie and **John Clark,** former chefs at San Francisco's Zuni Café, are husband-and-wife restaurant consultants now at work on a cookbook for "families on the go." Their most recent cookbook, *Country Egg, City Egg*, was published by Artisan.

Ibu Poilâne, artist and wife of baker Lionel Poilâne, lives in Paris and runs her own design studio.

Lionel Poilâne is the baker-owner of the famous Poilâne bakeries on Paris's rue du Cherche-Midi and boulevard de Grenelle.

Maricel Presilla is the chef and co-owner of the restaurant Zafra in Hoboken, New Jersey.

Steven Raichlen is the author of 22 books, including the IACP/Julia Child Award–winning *Barbecue! Bible,* also honored by FOOD & WINE as one of the Best Cookbooks of 1999; and, most recently, *How to Grill* (both published by Workman). He is currently working on a book on regional American barbecue called *America on Fire.*

Cristina and **Mauro Rastelli** own the restaurant Il Capanno in Spoleto, Italy.

Eric Ripert is co-owner and executive chef of Le Bernardin in New York City. He is co-author of *Le Bernardin Cookbook: Four Star Simplicity* (Doubleday), one of FOOD & WINE's Best Cookbooks of 1998.

Liv Rockefeller is a former caterer and an enthusiastic home cook.

Claudia Roden is the author of numerous cookbooks, including *The New Book of Middle Eastern Food* (Alfred A. Knopf).

Janet Rosener, caterer-turned-entrepreneur, is the founder and owner of Dahlias™ Exotic Flavor Pastes.

Jean-Christophe Royer is the chef and owner of the restaurant Christophe in Amsterdam.

Victor Scargle is the executive chef at Grand Café in San Francisco.

Sally Schneider is a contributing editor to FOOD & WINE Magazine. Her new book, *A New Way to Cook,* will be published by Artisan in the fall of 2001.

Agostino Sciandri is the executive chef and co-owner of the Los Angeles restaurant Ago.

Kristie Trabant Scott is a home cook who lives in Lincolnville, Maine.

Julian Serrano is the executive chef at Picasso in Las Vegas.

Jane Sigal is a senior editor at FOOD & WINE and the author of *Backroad Bistros, Farmhouse Fare* (Doubleday) and *Normandy Gastronomique* (Abbeville).

Ana Sortun is the chef and owner of Oleana in Cambridge, Massachusetts.

Katy Sparks was named one of FOOD & WINE's Best New Chefs in 1998. She is the executive chef at Quilty's in New York City.

Susan Spicer is the executive chef at Bayona in New Orleans' French Quarter. She recently opened Herbsaint, a 100-seat bistro in the city's Warehouse District. In 1989 she was named one of FOOD & WINE's Best New Chefs.

Jeremy Strode is the chef and co-owner of Pomme in Melbourne, Australia.

Bill Telepan is the chef at JUdson Grill in New York City.

Alison Tolley is the chef aboard the *Ocean Kestrel,* a charter boat that sails throughout the Caribbean.

Corinne Trang is the author of *Authentic Vietnamese Cooking: Food from a Family Table,* honored by FOOD & WINE as one of 1999's Best Cookbooks, and of the forthcoming *Essentials of Asian Cuisine* (both published by Simon & Schuster).

Barbara Tropp is a cookbook author and Asian-restaurant and food consultant based in San Francisco. Her books include *The Modern Art of Chinese Cooking* (Morrow) and *China Moon Cookbook* (Workman).

Jeff Tunks is co-owner and executive chef of the seafood restaurant DC Coast and the Asian restaurant TenPenh, both in Washington, D.C.

Tina Ujlaki is the executive food editor at FOOD & WINE Magazine.

Mina Vachino is co-author, with Anna Zegna, of a book on the cuisine of the Piedmont region of Italy.

contributors

James Villas is the author of several cookbooks, including *My Mother's Southern Desserts,* honored by FOOD & WINE as one of the Best Cookbooks of 1998, and, more recently, *My Mother's Southern Entertaining* (both published by Morrow).

Jean-Georges Vongerichten is chef and co-owner of the New York City restaurants Jo Jo, Mercer Kitchen, Jean Georges and Vong (which also has locations in Chicago, London and Hong Kong), as well as Prime Steakhouse in Las Vegas and Dune in the Bahamas. He is co-author of *Jean-Georges: Cooking at Home with a Four-Star Chef* (Broadway Books), named one of FOOD & WINE's Best Cookbooks of 1998. His new cookbooks are *Simple to Spectacular* (Broadway Books) and *Simple Cuisine* (Macmillan).

David Waltuck is the chef and owner of Chanterelle in New York City. He is the author of *David Waltuck's Staff Meals from Chanterelle,* published by Workman.

David Walzog is executive chef at Michael Jordan's The Steak House N.Y.C. in Manhattan's Grand Central Station.

Annie Wayte is executive chef at Nicole's in New York City.

Joanne Weir, a San Francisco cooking teacher, hosts the television show *Weir Cooking in the Wine Country.* Her book *Joanne Weir's More Cooking in Wine Country* (Simon & Schuster) will be published in early 2001.

Pete Wells is a senior editor at FOOD & WINE Magazine.

Jasper White is the author of *Lobster at Home* (Scribner), which was named one of FOOD & WINE's Best Cookbooks of 1998. His latest book is called *50 Chowders* (also published by Scribner). He is chef and partner at the Summer Shack restaurant in Cambridge, Massachusetts.

Paula Wolfert is the author of six cookbooks, most recently *Mediterranean Grains and Greens* (HarperCollins), honored by FOOD & WINE as the Best Cookbook of 1998. She is currently at work on *Mediterranean Cooking— Slow and Easy.*

Joseph Wrede was named one of FOOD & WINE's Best New Chefs in 2000. He is the chef at Joseph's Table in Taos, New Mexico.

Takashi Yagihashi was named one of FOOD & WINE's Best New Chefs in 2000. He is the chef at the restaurant Tribute in Farmington Hills, Michigan.

Special thanks to the following restaurants for their contributions to this book:

Chicama, New York City
China One, West Hollywood
First, New York City
Hattie's, Saratoga Springs, New York
Icebox Café, Miami Beach, Florida
Isla, New York City
La Boca del Conga Room, West Hollywood
Man Ray, Paris
RL, Chicago
Trader Vic's, Emeryville, California

photo credits

Sang An: 60 (bottom), 275 (right), 360 (bottom); **Quentin Bacon:** front and back covers, 5 (right), 15, 19, 22 (right), 51, 57, 60 (top), 61, 62, 67, 68 (bottom), 70, 114, 115, 117, 119, 129, 130, 136, 145, 146, 162 (top), 166, 176 (top), 179, 185, 186, 202, 220, 221, 229, 247 (Emeril Lagasse with Celina Oliveira, left, and Elza Botelho at Carreiros Barcelos Bakery in Fall River, Massachusetts), 274, 275 (left), 298, 309, 319 (bottom), 341, 343, 346, 348, 365, 372, 381, 382, 388 (bottom); **Edmund Barr:** 6 (kitchen at the Victorian Gardens, a Mendocino, California, inn), 28 (top), 37, 54, 101 (Pauline Zamboni, co-owner of the Victorian Gardens Inn in Mendocino, California), 217, 248, 375 (boy eating an ice-cream sandwich), 384, 388 (top); **Fernando Bengoechea:** 338; **Bill Bettencourt:** 43; **Mirjam Bleeker:** 215 (Parisian butchers); **Earl Carter:** 11 (Virginia Dowzer, wife of chef Jeremy Strode, serving hors d'oeuvres), 75 (Melbourne chef Jeremy Strode serving soup), 126, 173, 178, 368 (left); **Beatriz Da Costa:** 18 (bottom), 23 (right), 44 (top), 55, 58 (top and bottom), 85, 87, 88, 91, 96, 97 (top), 99, 106, 113, 118, 138, 177, 187, 188, 193, 199, 213, 251, 266, 267, 281, 301, 307, 345; **Reed Davis:** 14, 17, 22 (left), 28 (bottom), 42, 80, 81, 84, 141, 151, 160 (top), 164, 170, 205, 237, 278, 316, 324, 333, 334; **Miki Duisterhof:** 13, 44 (bottom), 125 (fishermen in Portoscuso, on the southwest coast of Italy), 235, 271 (Sardinian boy carrying eggplants), 297 (Sardinian woman mixing couscous); **Hotze Eisma:** 39, 63, 69; **Dana Gallagher:** 41 (bottom), 249, 276, 288, 364 (top), 367; **Gentl & Hyers:** 38, 83, 157 (Bruce Bromberg, co-owner of New York City's Blue Ribbon restaurants, carving a turkey), 191, 302, 352, 355; **John Gruen:** 154; **Matthew Hranek:** 133, 336; **John Huba:** 104, 256 (bottom), 376; **Richard Jung:** 224 (top and bottom), 315 (Janet Rosener, owner of Dahlias™ Exotic Flavor Pastes); **Keller & Keller:** 360 (top); **John Kernick:** 206, 257, 265, 286, 331; **David Loftus:** 65, 135, 364 (bottom); **Maura McEvoy:** 5 (top left), 26, 29, 71, 73, 82, 131, 139, 197 (right), 211, 243, 260, 261, 280, 308, 330, 377 (right), 378; **Amy Neunsinger:** 20, 30, 41 (top), 137 (left), 150, 180, 183, 236, 282, 369, 370; **David Prince:** 40; **Maria Robledo:** 12 (top and bottom), 18 (top), 53, 68 (top), 86, 127, 184, 197 (left), 234, 255, 256 (top), 258, 313, 317, 322, 327, 358, 366, 380, 383; **Tara Sgroi:** 363 (girl with popsicle); **Evan Sklar:** 23 (left), 31, 56, 78, 102, 132, 161, 227, 262, 263, 353, 368 (right), 377 (left), 393; **Brooke Slezak:** 387 (Colin MacLean at Hattie's in Saratoga Springs, New York); **Karen Stead:** 195 (Frank Ottomanelli, co-owner of O. Ottomanelli & Sons Meat Market in New York City); **Ann Stratton:** 149, 279; **Petrina Tinslay:** 2 (Corinne and Michel Chapoutier with friends at the Maison M. Chapoutier in France's Rhône Valley), 35, 50, 76, 140, 176 (bottom), 216, 305, 351, 379; **Luca Trovato:** 66, 109 (cook making pasta in Spoleto, in the Umbria region of Italy), 110; **David Tsay:** 8 (Elaine Krankl at Sine Qua Non winery in Ventura, California); **Simon Watson:** 112, 160 (bottom), 209, 285, 300, 332; **Stuart Watson:** 245, 283; **Jonelle Weaver:** 5 (bottom), 95, 97 (bottom), 174, 319 (top), 320; **John Welchman:** 33 (cook in Seoul, Korea), 49 (street vendor at Kyonguju Market, Seoul, Korea); **Michael Weschler:** 252, 361; **Anna Williams:** 34, 90, 120, 128, 137 (right) 143, 147, 159, 162 (bottom), 169, 189, 196, 207, 223, 231, 241, 284, 325, 342, 349, 390, 391; **Roy Zipstein:** 329 (boy with a tray of cookies in Marrakech, Morocco).